FREEDOMS OF SPEECH

Anthropological Perspectives on L Ethics, and Power

Edited by Matei Candea, Taras Fedirko, Paolo Heywood, and Fiona Wright

Bringing together leading anthropologists, this collection sheds light on the vast topic of freedoms of speech from a comparatively human perspective. *Freedoms of Speech* provides a sustained, empirical exploration of the variety of ways freedom of speech is lived, valued, and contested in practice; envisioned as an ideal; and mediated by various linguistic, ethical, and material forms.

From Ireland to India, from Palestine to West Papua, from contemporary Java to early twentieth-century Britain, and from colonial Vietnam to the contemporary United States, the book broadly interrogates the classic vision of a singular "Western liberal tradition" of freedom of speech, exploring its internal complexities and highlighting alternative perspectives on the relationship between speech, freedom, and constraint in various times and places. Chapters analyse subjects commonly linked to freedom-of-speech debates, shedding new light on familiar topics that include campus speech codes, defamation, and press freedom, while also exploring unexpected ones such as therapy, gift-giving, and martyrdom. These analyses not only provide unexpected perspectives and unique insights but also address a myriad of questions, contributing to a rich, interdisciplinary, and human understanding of the nature of freedom of speech.

(Studies in the Anthropology of Language, Sign, and Social Life)

MATEI CANDEA is a professor of social anthropology at the University of Cambridge.

TARAS FEDIRKO is a lecturer in the School of Social and Political Sciences at the University of Glasgow.

PAOLO HEYWOOD is an associate professor of social anthropology at Durham University.

FIONA WRIGHT is a research fellow at the Advanced Care Research Centre at the University of Edinburgh.

Studies in the Anthropology of Language, Sign, and Social Life focuses on cutting-edge developments in the analysis of linguistic and semiotic processes within a comparative, ethnographic, and socio-historical context. The series provides a home for innovative, boundary-pushing scholarship in linguistic anthropology, as well as work in sociolinguistics, the sociology of interaction, and semiotics. Including both ethnographic monographs and theoretical explorations, books in this series present new ways of understanding the centrality of language and other sign systems to social and cultural life.

Editor: Jack Sidnell, University of Toronto

Freedoms of Speech

Anthropological Perspectives on Language, Ethics, and Power

EDITED BY MATEI CANDEA, TARAS FEDIRKO, PAOLO HEYWOOD, AND FIONA WRIGHT

UNIVERSITY OF TORONTO PRESS
Toronto Buffalo London

© University of Toronto Press 2025
Toronto Buffalo London
utorontopress.com
Printed in the USA

ISBN 978-1-4875-4884-1 (paper)   ISBN 978-1-4875-5087-5 (EPUB)
                                   ISBN 978-1-4875-5022-6 (PDF)

Studies in the Anthropology of Language, Sign, and Social Life

___

Library and Archives Canada Cataloguing in Publication

Title: Freedoms of speech : anthropological perspectives on language, ethics, and
    power / edited by Matei Candea, Taras Fedirko, Paolo Heywood, and Fiona Wright.
Names: Candea, Matei, editor | Fedirko, Taras, editor. | Heywood, Paolo, editor |
    Wright, Fiona, 1985– editor
Description: Series statement: Studies in the anthropology of language, sign, and
    social life | Includes bibliographical references and index.
Identifiers: Canadiana (print) 20240478371 | Canadiana (ebook) 20240478398 |
    ISBN 9781487548841 (paper) | ISBN 9781487550226 (PDF) |
    ISBN 9781487550875 (EPUB)
Subjects: LCSH: Freedom of speech – Cross-cultural studies. | LCSH: Freedom of
    speech – Political aspects – Cross-cultural studies. | LCSH: Freedom of speech –
    History – Cross-cultural studies. | LCSH: Freedom of speech – Moral and ethical
    aspects – Cross-cultural studies.
Classification: LCC JC591 .F74 2025 | DDC 323.44/3 – dc23

___

Cover image and design: Heng Wee Tan

We wish to acknowledge the land on which the University of Toronto Press
operates. This land is the traditional territory of the Wendat, the Anishnaabeg, the
Haudenosaunee, the Métis, and the Mississaugas of the Credit First Nation.

University of Toronto Press acknowledges the financial support of the Government of
Canada, the Canada Council for the Arts, and the Ontario Arts Council, an agency of
the Government of Ontario, for its publishing activities.

 Canada Council **Conseil des Arts**
for the Arts **du Canada**

 ONTARIO ARTS COUNCIL
CONSEIL DES ARTS DE L'ONTARIO
an Ontario government agency
un organisme du gouvernement de l'Ontario

Funded by the   Financé par le
Government   gouvernement
of Canada   du Canada

Contents

Figures

FREEDOMS OF SPEECH

Introduction: Anthropologies of Free Speech

MATEI CANDEA, TARAS FEDIRKO, PAOLO HEYWOOD, AND
FIONA WRIGHT

Introduction

A core tenet of liberal political philosophy, and a criterion frequently invoked to distinguish liberal democracies from their political "Others," freedom of speech has in recent years become a focus of extensive and embittered debates within the US and Europe. Critics fear the rise of a "cancel culture" and accuse proponents of "safe spaces," "trigger warnings," and "no-platforming" of challenging freedom of speech. The latter in turn accuse their critics of invoking freedom of speech disingenuously in order to protect established interests. Yet the notion of free speech tends to operate more as an idiom of accusation in these debates than as a focus of sustained analysis in its own right. However much they might disagree about the rights and wrongs of specific cases, participants in these debates tend to assume that, for better or worse, an unlimited aspiration to individual freedom of speech is a distinctive feature of "modern Western liberalism." For some this makes freedom of speech an avatar of a cherished way of life perceived as being under threat. For others this makes appeals to such freedom potentially suspect, insufficiently socially conscious, and culturally parochial – if not an outright ally of neo-liberalism or a reactionary Eurocentrism.

This is where anthropologists can make a distinctive contribution by putting these Euro-American debates about freedom of speech into a broader and richer comparative frame. As Webb Keane (2007, 6) has shown, free speech debates are one instance of a much more widespread phenomenon – that of struggles entailing "moral questions about semiotic form" (see also Keane in this volume). From that perspective, as we shall see below, liberal concerns with freedom of speech emerge as distinctive, but not unique. As philosopher Richard Sorabji (2021) has recently demonstrated, it is possible to construct a much richer and more diverse genealogy for freedom of speech that goes beyond the usual reference points of contemporary Euro-American legal and philosophical discussion – classical Athens, Milton, John Stuart Mill, the First Amendment of the US Constitution, and resistance to official censorship under twentieth-century state socialism. Sorabji's account revisits these standard references, but in light of precursor and parallel visions of the benefits of freedom of speech, religious dialogue, and philosophical critique, including the edicts of Indian ruler Ashoka in 300 BCE, defences of religious and philosophical freedom in sixth-century Persia and tenth-century Baghdad, the Levellers in seventeenth-century England, Shakespeare's struggles with censorship, and the thought of twentieth-century anti-colonial political figures such as Gandhi.

Crucially, the imaginaries of freedom of speech in this broader landscape are not hermetically sealed from each other but rather intersect and recombine in multiple ways, as Sorabji makes clear. Historian Christopher Bayly (2011, 73) has also shown how, for nineteenth-century Indian liberals arguing for a free press, "Mughal exemplars of free access to authority were invoked to root ideas which were appropriated from European and American debates." The chapters in this volume can be seen as an exploration of the contemporary echoes and traces of this much broader and richly entangled genealogy. As such, they also trouble the idea that concerns about free speech across the world are necessarily a "derivative discourse" (Chatterjee 1986) of Euro-American political thought and ideology, liberal or otherwise. Chapters in part one explore a range of different yet often recombinant traditions: Islamic notions of advice and reasoned criticism, early twentieth-century Vietnamese rethinking of Confucian language norms, Mormon truth-speaking in the contemporary American right, and subversive plays with grammar and vocabulary in contemporary Russia. At the same time, this comparative outlook reminds us that visions of freedom of speech, in Western liberal settings as elsewhere, are not mere philosophical abstractions but rather thickly rooted in understandings of the person and ideologies of language, grounded and contested in daily practices, institutions, and ongoing historical power struggles (Fedirko 2021; Fedirko, Samanani, and Williamson 2021). This in turn means that celebrations of freedom of speech can and often do entail, enable, or accompany forms of silencing and oppression.

If anthropology can help us reframe the topic of freedom of speech, the converse is also true. Reflecting on freedom of speech poses a productive challenge for anthropology itself as currently constituted. It is striking, for instance, that the single most prominent anthropological text with free speech in its title, Asad et al.'s *Is Critique Secular? Blasphemy, Injury and Free Speech* (2013), in practice ends up focusing on the multiple ways in which speech is limited and curtailed, even in "liberal" settings. This is an important point, of course, echoed in a number of contributions to this volume, and we explore its ramifications at some length below. Yet by itself, the conclusion that free speech is far from unlimited even in putatively liberal settings falls short of that book's stated goal of exploring "the shape that free speech takes at different times and in different places" (19).

The authors in fact provide us with a comparative anthropology of silencing rather than with a comparative anthropology of free speech.

This failure, we argue, is not idiosyncratic – it reflects something structural about anthropology. Indeed the discipline has a much stronger record and toolkit for thinking of the impossibility of free speech than for thinking about freedom of speech itself (cf. Laidlaw 2002). Anthropologists have demonstrated the extensive determinations, from grammar through sociolinguistics and into language ideologies, that are entailed in any speech act; they have pointed to the pervasive and sometimes productive nature of silencing in social life; and they have shown the multiple ways in which authoritative speech is entangled in and produced by controls and limitations of other kinds of expression. Anthropology has given us many reasons, in other words, for challenging the idea that speech can ever be "free." This also reflects many anthropologists' opposition to the perceived hegemony of liberalism in their home societies, and the Romantic and republican sources of much anthropological thought. It thus requires a particular effort of the anthropological imagination and ethnographic sensibility to attend to the persistent fact that many of the people anthropologists work with value, desire, or imagine something like freedom of speech as a particular goal and mourn, fear, or protest its absence. This is the challenge taken up by this volume: to consider freedom of speech, in its many forms, as something more than a mere ideology or a mirage, while remaining critically attuned to the distinctive assumptions it entails about the nature of language, and about speaking subjects and the polities they inhabit.

This is another way of saying that an anthropology of freedom of speech remains to be built. As the title of this volume suggests, this would in our view need to be an anthropology of *freedoms* of speech – plural. In this, we are following the lead of James Laidlaw's (2002, 2014) efforts to pluralize anthropological understandings of freedom. Taking the counterpoint of reductive critiques of "Western liberal freedom," Laidlaw begins by laying out the variety of kinds and types of freedom in Western philosophical sources: some scholars understand freedom as a negative absence of constraint, or, quite differently, as a positive characterization of the capacities of a fully free human subject (Berlin 1969); others link it to a vision of collective political independence and non-domination (Q. Skinner 2016); others still cast freedom in terms of a reflective attitude towards the self (Foucault 1984). There are further multiplicities within these multiplicities: where freedom is characterized as autonomy, this in turn can take many forms, both in the degree of autonomy that is required (from total autarchy to merely partial detachment) and in the way the limits to autonomy are understood – are they linked to external conditions or to the incomplete integration of the self? (Laidlaw 2014, 165–6). Through his exploration, Laidlaw reminds us that not all kinds of freedom are, strictly speaking, liberal; nor is liberalism tantamount to "the Western ideology," as is often implied (Fedirko, Samanani, and Williamson 2021). As Taras Fedirko (2021, 471) has argued, liberalism has been too often assumed to be a shared "background of 'Western culture' against which ethnographers examine the world of ethnographic difference." This has stood as an obstacle to ethnographic exploration of the multiplicity of liberalisms, and to ethnographic appreciation of the relation between liberal and non-liberal political ideologies and social formations in and beyond Euro-America.

Keeping this multiplicity in view matters for comparative purposes. Having multiplied "freedom" internally, Laidlaw begins to suggest how this might enable us in turn to expand our comparative imaginary in relation to non–Euro-American understandings of freedom. Russian visions of freedom as collective unity (Humphrey 2007), the hierarchical and gendered autonomy of the honourable Bedouin self (Abu-Lughod 1986), sensitivity about ascribing thoughts to others among the Korowai (Stasch 2008a), material independence achieved through "deliberate dependencies" in Malawi (Englund 2006), the complex symbolic and material strategies Hungarian Rom deploy to produce a collective space of disengagement from wider society (M. Stewart 1997) – these and other ethnographic instances can all be considered alongside each other in an expansive lateral comparative exploration of freedom.

If we cast each of the cases above as the Other of a putatively unitary liberal or "Western freedom," they will eventually collapse into one another as instances of the same. But if we begin, as Laidlaw does, by highlighting the multiplicities internal to such visions of freedom, this also allows non-Western instances to be more than a mere counterprojection of some single Western form. Consequently, this also allows us to comprehend the varieties of liberal freedom in their parochial particularity. It is true that some of the anthropologists cited in the previous paragraph do deploy a frontal comparative device (cf. Candea in this volume) to cast their ethnography as some kind of alternative to "the" liberal vision of freedom. But Laidlaw observes that in each case the key elements identified as characteristic of liberal freedom are slightly different. As a result, the emphasis in the counterpoint ethnographic accounts is slightly different too. We begin to envisage the possibility of multiple kinds of freedom, beyond a liberal/non-liberal, Western/non-Western contrast. In particular, the various Western visions of freedom surveyed by Laidlaw do not all hinge on the familiar contrast between individual freedom and its social constraints. In certain versions of positive liberty, of freedom as non-domination, or indeed as a reflective relation to the self, freedom is achieved through, not against, relations and limits. The same is true beyond nominally "Western" settings. Some of the examples Laidlaw evokes could be described as dissolving the individual/society binary, while others rely on it substantively. Venkatesan (2023), in her useful recent review of the anthropology of freedom, exemplifies Laidlaw's point by showing how differently invocations of freedom can animate political and ethical projects in three contemporary Euro-American settings: among right-wing free-market libertarians, "freegan" dumpster divers, and adepts of Free/Open Source Software. As Candea discusses at greater length in chapter 1 (see also Candea, forthcoming), such lateral expansions of our comparative imaginary take us beyond the us/them contrasts and the tired polarities between individual and society, abstraction and concreteness, freedom and its limits.

In this spirit, the present volume brings together leading anthropologists and fresh new voices in the discipline to consider freedom of speech in a wide comparative lens. From Ireland to India, from Palestine to West Papua, from contemporary Java to early twentieth-century Britain, and from colonial Vietnam to the contemporary United States, the volume's broad comparative frame interrogates the classic vision of a singular "Western liberal tradition" of freedom of speech, exploring both its internal multiplicities and paying attention to alternative understandings of the relationship between speech, freedom, and constraint in other times and places. The chapters engage with but also radically expand the register of topics that are habitually associated with discussions of freedom of speech. Familiar topics, such as campus speech codes, defamation, and press freedom, emerge in a strikingly new light, while unexpected ones, such as therapy, gift-giving, and martyrdom, provide surprising insights into what freedom of speech might be.

The volume is divided into four parts. Part one frames the discussion through a comparative consideration of the very idea of "traditions" of freedom of speech. Chapters in this section provide a number of concrete ethnographic and historical cases that highlight the internal diversity of the so-called liberal tradition of free speech and consider its historical interweaving with and differentiation from a range of other religious and secular visions: ancient Greek *parrhesia* and its various historical reinventions, Islamic piety, Confucian and anti-Confucian visions of the self, and Mormon spirituality. Parts two, three, and four each then take on a key theme in relation to which visions and practices of freedom of speech are deployed. Part two explores the diverse ways in which publics and counter-publics are constituted, challenged, and unmade in and around discussions of freedom of speech. Chapters in part three examine the intersection of concerns with freedom of speech and questions of history, haunting, and memorialization. Finally, part four pinpoints the unexpected ways in which theories and practices of freedom of speech intersect with therapeutic imaginaries, aimed both at suffering persons and at somehow misaligned collectives. This introduction follows the structure of these four parts, bringing the contributions into dialogue before drawing some broader conclusions about the anthropology of freedom of speech. As a preliminary to this discussion, however, the next section provides a synthetic guide to some of the main genres of existing literature on freedom of speech and explores the existing conceptual and empirical resources anthropologists have in order to examine the varied ways in which free speech is imagined, valued, and practised as a lived ideal in necessarily compromised and imperfect conditions.

The Story So Far ...

While anthropologists may not have had a great deal to say about freedom of speech, much has been written on the topic in adjacent fields. Popular and academic writing on freedom of speech has proliferated exponentially over the past decades, such that even the task of giving a broad-brush overview of the shape of this literature is daunting. Nevertheless – braving the dangers of simplification in order to help orient the reader – one might suggest that there are two broad yet overlapping genres in contemporary academic writing on freedom of speech: the first sits at the intersection of history, the humanities, and cultural studies and examines specific practices of free speaking and censorship in particular contexts; the second spans legal theory, philosophy, and political science and engages free speech as a political, moral, or judicial principle, often in dialogue, critical or otherwise, with the liberal philosophical canon. They are distinct yet not mutually exclusive. For instance, Stanley Fish's famous book, *There's No Such Thing as Free Speech, and It's a Good Thing, Too* (1994), belongs squarely to both genres, while another foundational work, Robert Post's (2006) collection on *Censorship and Silencing*, self-consciously brings them into conversation with each other. These two overlapping academic genres in turn shade into and provide the more systematic underpinnings for a range of more self-consciously polemical public arguments for and against restrictions on speech, often commenting on specific cases or "scandals" and seeking to document and address a broader perceived crisis. These have come from various points on the political spectrum and range from tweets, to op-eds, to full-length books.

One Path through the Literature: History and Cultural Studies of Free Speech and Censorship in Context

In the first academic genre, historical studies of censorship, publication, and freedom of speech (Colclough 2005; Darnton 2015; Gilbert 2013) rub shoulders with the body of critique Matthew Bunn (2015) has dubbed "new censorship theory" (see Candea 2019b; Fedirko 2020; Heywood 2019). Associated with a range of scholars at the intersection of philosophy and the social sciences, such as Michel Foucault (1976), Pierre Bourdieu (1991), and Judith Butler (1997),

New Censorship Theory has overturned a paradigmatic model in which censorship constitutes an extraordinary, repressive intervention into the default norm of "free speech," a violation of a natural freedom usually, if not exclusively, undertaken by agents of the state. In place of the dichotomy of free speech and censorship, New Censorship Theory offers a conception of censorship as a ubiquitous, even necessary part of communication. (Bunn 2015, 27)

Rooted in post-structuralism, new censorship theory nevertheless builds, as Bunn perceptively notes, on a much older tradition within Western political theory, namely Marxist critiques of the liberal public sphere. Marx and his followers, such as Antonio Gramsci and Louis Althusser, have long critiqued the liberal claim that the lifting of state censorship opens up a zone of free and unimpeded communication. Many, they noted, are still de facto excluded from this public sphere mainly, but not only, along lines of class, education, and wealth; nor is this supposedly free "marketplace of ideas" without its own subtler determinations, silences, and exclusions. The formal equality of the bourgeois civil society, Marxists argued, conceals exploitation; state censorship is exercised "not at the *expense* of civil society but rather at its *behest*" (Bunn 2015, 34; original emphasis). New censorship theory builds on these insights to articulate a more general sense that censorship is pervasive and indeed (like power more generally in the Foucauldian view) inherently productive and fundamentally necessary to any act of meaning-making. Bunn makes the interesting observation that what unites these authors is less a specific vision of censorship (the hyperextension of the term in this literature is precisely the point) than a shared scepticism over free speech. "From this perspective," Bunn (2015, 28) notes, "the intellectual development from Marxism to the post-structuralism of New Censorship Theory appears much more gradual, even linear, than has hitherto been fully appreciated."

These arguments are broadly familiar to anthropologists, and we will find elements of them deployed throughout these pages. Indeed, while some of these arguments – such as Fish's (1994) claim that there is "no such thing as free speech," because all speech is made possible by silencing, which is itself a matter of power and politics – may still seem counterintuitive or perhaps even shocking to an uninitiated readership, they have become, as we argued above, broadly part of the anthropological subconscious. Convincing contemporary anthropologists that "free speech" is not a simple reality out there is hardly difficult. The real challenge for the discipline at this point is to figure out what, given that speech is clearly never "free" in any simple sense, people might mean by that term in the first place.

In addressing this challenge, some of the contributors to our volume draw on one author in particular: Michel Foucault. Though a prime mover of new censorship theory, Foucault also explicitly sought to explore the genealogy of "free speech" as a virtue. Foucault's late work on classical self-cultivation investigates how people work to make themselves into particular kinds of virtuous subjects. Despite its individualist overtones, self-cultivation does not occur in isolation. It is something done in a particular cultural and historical context, and in relation to others. In his final two lecture series at the Collège de France, Foucault (2010, 2011) sought to clarify this relationship between subject and context by turning to a very specific aspect of self-cultivation in the ancient world. He believed that then – as now – there was a "necessary other person" involved in work on the self. These are types of people whose role it is to help us decipher and establish the "truth" of our selves (e.g., teachers, doctors, psychoanalysts, jurists, policemen). In the classical world, unlike ours, however, Foucault thought that this "necessary other" was not an institutionally defined position. Rather, it was predicated on the possession of a particular virtue, namely *parrhesia*, translated in the title of one of the lecture series as "the courage of truth." To be the right sort of person to help others work on themselves, one had to possess the ability to speak freely and frankly, regardless of risk or consequence.

The history of this particular virtue in the ancient world is varied. For instance, there is what we might think of as "political" *parrhesia*, characteristic of pre-Socratic Athens. This is "free speech" in which what is at stake are questions of the government of others. Later, and exemplified most obviously in Socrates, we find a virtuous "free speech" that is much more concerned with "ethics" and with the government of the self. Socrates eschews the political field to focus instead on the conduct of individuals and to measure the gap between the way they think they ought to live and the way they actually do. Later still we find these modalities combined in the philosophy of the Cynics, who sought both to live their own lives as bare truth (naked and in the open) and to missionize this life to those around them, to make their lives speak as examples to others (Foucault 2011).

Like any concept, *parrhesia* is situated in a particular context. While Foucault's own account ends, broadly speaking, in the classical period, tracing the later history of *parrhesia* gives us some insights into the ways in which later liberal visions of freedom of speech have cannibalized and reinvented their supposed "classical roots." As Candea discusses in chapter 1, historian David Colclough (2005) argues, for instance, that classical *parrhesia* served as one of the sources for imagining freedom of speech in seventeenth-century England – the period that also gave us some of the classic sources of liberal defences of freedom of speech, such as Milton's *Areopagitica*, or the works of John Locke. Somewhat ironically, however, Colclough notes that *parrhesia* by this point was primarily a figure of rhetoric. Rhetorical manuals drew on examples from speeches by classical Greek and Roman orators that consisted of prefacing one's speech by warning that one's position was controversial, daring, and likely to offend. For seventeenth-century English commentators, "*parrhesia*" as a rhetorical figure therefore posed an inherent problem of sincerity. It could be a genuine warning and apology for speech that was necessary but might offend. Equally, it could be merely a cynical way to flatter an audience by delivering, as if they were surprising or extreme, views that the speaker knew were perfectly conventional and likely to gain broad assent in any case.

Colclough notes that the debates around *parrhesia* were only one among the cultural sources of seventeenth-century English discussions of the value of free speech. Others included stories from the lives of Christian martyrs who had continued to speak the truth of their faith in the face of torture and death, and the legal prerogatives of unrestricted speech that applied (in principle at least) to parliamentary discussions. Colclough's and Foucault's accounts point to the complex, diverse, and contested genealogy of liberal visions of freedom of speech – a point further developed in part one of this volume.

Anthropologists have used Foucault's discussion of *parrhesia* to ask comparative questions about the ways in which freedom of speech is understood and valued in various contexts today. Dominic Boyer (2013), for instance, has suggested that some contemporary political movements based on satire, such as Iceland's iconoclastic "Best Party" – a joke political party that eventually achieved electoral success – may resemble aspects of ancient *parrhesia*. On the other hand, Harri Englund (2018) has pointed to the dangers of assuming that *parrhesia* is portable beyond its own specific context. In Finnish talk radio, he argues, what might look like "parrhesiastic" speech on the part of individual callers is in fact a process carefully cultivated by the show's hosts, an arrangement of multiple voices, rather than any individual "speaking truth to power" (see also Englund in this volume). As with many concepts, there is probably little to be gained by arguing over exactly how transposable the precise details of classical *parrhesia* are or are not. The point is rather that one can ask of any context questions similar to those Foucault was asking about ancient Greece, or Colclough about early Stuart England: What is it about "free" or "direct" speech that people value when they value it? To what ends is it directed? What role does it play in relation to the broader system of ethics in which it exists? How is speaking freely supposed to affect one's relationship to oneself and to others? Who is assumed to have the right or duty to do so? And what does it take to be heard (cf. Lempert in this volume)?[1] As we shall see below, these questions are at the heart of many of the chapters in this volume.

---

1 From this perspective, if *parrhesia* serves as a useful concept for exploring the ways in which people value free speech in relation to themselves and to others, it may be worth returning to another classical Greek term to highlight the setting, context, and audience that make it possible to be heard. In the works of Herodotus, Demosthenes, and Xenophon, *isegoria* signified "freedom of speech" in the sense of the possibility opened up by Athenian democracy for any citizen to come forward and be heard (Foucault 2010; Bejan 2020; Rathnam 2023). By contrast to the tyrant's reduction of other speakers to silence, *isegoria* established what one might think of as an equality of opportunity to speak, albeit an equality that was of course radically limited since Athenian citizens were exclusively free men (but not women or slaves).

Another Path through the Literature: Freedom of Speech as a Principle in Legal and Philosophical Scholarship

The second academic genre may be less familiar to many readers of this book. Situated at the intersection of legal scholarship, philosophy, and political science, this genre seeks to elucidate core justifications (and establish proper limits) for freedom of speech. In this literature, much of which remains primarily focused on the US context and the First Amendment, arguments for free speech stemming from a particular Euro-American canon (Milton, Mill, Oliver Wendell Holmes Jr., etc.) are confronted with critiques by feminist and antiracist scholars against the background of a consideration of concrete legal cases and hypothetical "trolley problems." It is beyond the scope of this introduction to map out all of the arguments and controversies in this extensive literature (MacKinnon and Dworkin 1997; Passavant 2002; interested readers might also begin to pull the threads of these debates in Stone and Schauer 2021b; Waldron 2014). From the perspective of an anthropology of freedom of speech, however, one of the most interesting aspects of this literature can be cast as an ethnographic observation: it highlights the diversity of normative arguments for freedom of speech already present in the Euro-American, "liberal" canon. This literature distinguishes at least three canonical ways of arguing for freedom of speech in the liberal tradition (Barendt 2005; see also Schauer 1982; Stone and Schauer 2021b).

The argument from truth – popularly associated with John Stuart Mill – turns on the idea that protections from the imposition of orthodoxy by the state or other social pressures are the most effective means of ensuring that truth can be collectively discovered through debate and error eliminated. This much-caricatured vision of a "marketplace of ideas" is often imagined as the main or only argument in the liberal tradition, but there are two equally if not more influential arguments that have also been made for freedom of speech in the same tradition. Arguments from democracy link freedom of speech – including the right to critique and protest one's government – to the possibility for and legitimacy of democratic self-government, and arguments from autonomy see in freedom of speech a crucial means of self-development for individual persons and collectives and a fundamental aspect of their (individual and collective) dignity. These different justifications of freedom of speech rely on different versions or visions of what persons, polities, and language are, what matters about them, and the proper relation between them. Furthermore, each of these justifications has been substantively countered and debated, leading to a host of countervisions and counterproposals (Hornsby et al. 2011; Langton 1993; MacKinnon 1985; Waldron 2014).

This diversity is a useful reminder for anthropologists, who as we noted above have too often tended to treat "liberal freedom" as a singular form, a convenient foil for accounts of "other" forms of freedom (e.g., Mahmood 2005; cf. Fedirko, Samanani, and Williamson 2021). The failure to register the range and variety of visions and versions of freedom within liberal traditions is also an impediment to proper comparative consideration of alternatives elsewhere. This point is explored at greater length by Matei Candea in chapter 1. For the sake of this introduction, however, one key distinction is worth outlining: namely, Isaiah Berlin's contrast between negative freedom – a "freedom from" – characterized as an absence of external constraint, and positive freedom – a "freedom to" – characterized as an actual capacity to undertake certain actions (Berlin 1969; and see Humphrey in this volume). Much of the legal and philosophical scholarship above focuses on negative freedom from legal or other constraints. Some of it, however, particularly arguments centring on the importance of autonomy, dignity, and human flourishing, open up onto the question of a positive freedom to speak. The latter is a rather more ambitious, expansive, and perhaps problematic notion – it does, however, open up a range of fascinating comparative questions by linking freedom of speech to a potentially unlimited variety of visions of human flourishing, as we shall see particularly in the discussion of part three of this volume.

Another important axis of diversity highlighted by this body of legal-philosophical literature concerns the nature and meaning of speech. This literature shows that while representationalist ideology (see Keane 2007, 2009, and in this volume) is indeed an important resource in liberal defences of freedom of speech, it is not the only one. Debates over hate speech and pornography in particular attest to the extent to which the performative and social aspects of language, far from being invisible in these liberal discussions, are front and centre in them. The thought that liberal defences of freedom of speech rely on the strange idea that words are not really actions (Fish 1994) is a crude oversimplification (see Candea, forthcoming). In fact, as Frederick Schauer (1982) perceptively notes, it is precisely *because* speech is understood to have real and harmful effects that a distinctive argument can or needs to be made about its protection under law. More broadly, Schauer has noted how far the word "speech" in discussions of freedom of speech differs from ordinary uses of the word, such that participants in the above discussions often implicitly accept that some instances of verbal behaviour (such as promises, advertisements, or witness statements) do not count as "speech" for the purposes of these discussions, while some instances of non-verbal behaviour (writing, obviously, but also drawing, hand gestures, or flag burning) do. The "speech" in free speech thus sometimes seems to evoke communication, at other times expression, or even something as broad as semiosis – yet, in each case with some quite specific exceptions. Philosophers such as Schauer feel the need to resolve such definitional questions from the outset. From an anthropological perspective, however, this variety and uncertainty is an ethnographic datum: the diversity of visions and versions covered by the word "speech" (and indeed "freedom") is, for us, not a definitional issue to be resolved but the starting point of further investigation.

In sum, even within the limited frame of liberal legal and philosophical discourse around freedom of speech, an anthropologically informed exploration can identify a variety of implicit and explicit understandings of how persons, knowledge, and politics are made and unmade through speech. This diversity highlights all the more clearly what this literature does share, however, including most obviously perhaps a primary focus on individuals as the main units of analysis and ethical concern – an area in which anthropologists are likely to be able to make some productive comparative disruptions. Nevertheless, the internal variety of this literature reminds us that an anthropology of freedom of speech can already be a comparative project even before it leaves the "familiar" spectrum of liberal Euro-American imaginaries.

Language, Traditions, and Comparisons

Anthropologists have already begun to make some contributions to the discussions above, and part one of this book picks up and draws together existing threads of anthropological discussions on freedom of speech to map new perspectives and directions.

The main sustained anthropological explorations of the question of freedom of speech to date have all focused on recent debates around religious and secular representation and, more specifically, the case of the "Danish cartoon controversy" (Asad et al. 2013; Favret-Saada 2016; Keane 2009; Candea, forthcoming). This controversy, in which satirical representations of the Prophet Muhammad sparked outrage and violence, was a natural entry point into the subject of freedom of speech for anthropologists because of the wealth of material in the anthropology of religion focusing on comparable disputes about the morality and politics of speaking, silencing others, or staying silent oneself, or of representing and stopping others from representing. Such disputes arose, for instance, in the struggles of seventeenth-century Quakers in England to separate out the word of God from everyday language as a "thing of the flesh" (Bauman 1983). The Quakers' project included a wholesale repudiation of accepted forms of politeness and honorific titles as insincere words that glorify the earthly person – a practice that exposed Quakers to violence from offended interlocutors (see also Sidnell in this volume). The moral and political stakes of speech were similarly high in missionary encounters in non-Western contexts. For instance, Webb Keane (2007, 176–9) details the struggles between Calvinist missionaries and followers of *marapu* (Sumbanese ancestral ritual) in the Dutch East Indies (modern Indonesia) about how to address spiritual entities. The Calvinists condemned the *marapu* followers' uses of traditional ritual formulae as a violation of the "proper" norm of speaking sincerely to God in one's own words. Conversely, *marapu* followers decried a form of hubris in Calvinist prayer aimed directly from the individual to the godhead without the mediation of ancestral formulae.

Considering liberal debates and concerns over freedom of speech alongside these cases points to the deep cultural assumptions about the nature and effects of language and representation that inform all of these moral struggles over semiotic form – "language ideologies" (Silverstein 1976), or more broadly, "semiotic ideologies" (Keane 2007). This in turn allowed anthropologists to gain a distinctive vantage point on what was at stake in debates such as the Danish cartoon controversy. Keane, for instance, argued that

> the classic [liberal] defence of freedom of expression draws, in part, on a semiotic ideology that takes words and pictures to be vehicles for the transmission of opinion or information among otherwise autonomous and unengaged parties and the information they bear to be itself so much inert content more or less independent of the activity of representation. (2009, 58)

While we have argued above that anthropologists may wish to nuance this characterization (see also Candea in this volume; Candea, forthcoming), it remains a powerful way of framing liberal contextualizations. The semiotic ideology identified by Keane is what enables liberal commentators to dismiss Muslims offended by cartoons of the Prophet as committing a category error, and one that designates them, furthermore, as insufficiently "modern" in their continued attachment to the transcendent power of "mere" images (Brown, Butler, and Mahmood 2013, xiii). But as anthropologists such as Talal Asad (2013) have been at pains to point out, liberal freedom of speech also has well-defined limits, for instance in respect of patents, copyright, or pornography. These "liberal" limits point to the extent to which liberal freedom of speech is premised on and limited by notions of property and ownership – ownership of one's texts, ideas, or body. One might add that hate speech laws show that modern liberals do seem quite concerned with the capacity of words to do harm, at least in some contexts (Butler 1997; Heywood 2019). And that contemporary laws of libel or insult in places like France and Germany have a genealogy that links them to honour codes, which many sociologists imagined to be extinct in "modernity" (Candea 2019a; Whitman 2000). While such comparisons may occasionally sound as if they are trying to score points by showing that liberals are not as liberal as they think, at its best this work provides a more subtle understanding, rather than a mere deconstruction, of aspirations to freedom of speech, liberal or otherwise. The point, as Asad (2013, 29) puts it, is that "the shape that free speech takes at different times and in different places [reflects] different structures of power and subjectivity."

That being said stark contrasts between "Western/liberal" and "Muslim" language ideologies, while providing a useful critical intervention on the Danish cartoon controversy, downplay the diversity of understandings within each of these ensembles and the connections across them (see, in this volume, Bhojani and Clarke; Candea). While this diversity is explicitly acknowledged by the anthropologists who draw these contrasts (Brown, Butler, and Mahmood 2013, viii; Keane 2009, 57), there is nevertheless a tendency for characterizations cast in binary form to run away with themselves, despite the best efforts of their authors to prevent this (see Candea in this volume). As we noted above, a distinctive aspect of the present collection, in this regard, is the way its contributions collectively unpick the purported singularity of liberal ideas of freedom of speech and their implied difference from what lies elsewhere.

Matei Candea's opening contribution in this volume sets the tone for this endeavour by calling on anthropologists to go beyond this binary or "frontal" form of contrast. Pointing to the fractal and iterative nature of such distinctions between "us" and "them," Candea shows how easy it is for even the most complex varieties of such arguments to fall back on some variant of the simple and unpersuasive idea that "the West" is dominated by an impoverished linguistic ideology of abstract individualism, while "the rest" understand the reality of the relational, affective, and contextual ties that bind people together in communities (an understanding, happily, that anthropologists share; see Heywood in this volume). Taking the notion of "liberal free speech" as his foil, Candea shows that far from being a monolithic and homogenous "ideology," appeals to freedom of speech in European and American settings are in fact enormously heterogenous and internally diverse, both historically and ethnographically. Ancient Athenian notions of *parrhesia* were different in crucial and fundamental ways from those of early Stuart England (Colclough 2005), just as they are different from imaginaries of free speech at work in a contemporary Finnish radio show (Englund 2018a). These "lateral" comparisons, which are not built on an underlying opposition between "liberal" and "non-liberal" freedom, not only allow for a more realistic and fine-grained account of what passes as the former but also allow what passes as the latter to become more than just a counterposition to whatever are taken to be "our" ideas about free speech.

Webb Keane's contribution in chapter 2 is similarly wide-ranging in scale and focus, examining instances of semiotic transgression from name taboos to blasphemy and pornography. Keane shows how attention to the pragmatics and metapragmatics of such cases reveals them to be far more complex than any simple struggle over "freedom" or "censorship," often involving clashing linguistic or semiotic ideologies, yet in a far more nuanced and subtle sense than any simple contrast between "us" and "them." Keane shows how debates about what can or cannot be said are usually not simply reducible to the dichotomy of "society" or "context" versus "the individual," but are very often precisely about what is and is not the context at issue, and who does or does not get to decide that question.

Jack Sidnell's contribution (chapter 3) zooms in on the very particular context of early twentieth-century Vietnamese arguments over language reform. Yet out of this very particular context Sidnell manages to accomplish the feat of bringing to ethnographic life what many might see as the "abstract" or "context-free" liberal ideology of free speech. He achieves this by showing how a specific understanding of "freedom," as articulated by poet and journalist Phan Khôi, among others, relied on the idea that the Confucian language norms then dominant – such as, for example, name taboos – inhibited the moral development of the autonomous person. What we see here, in other words, is not a "liberal freedom of speech" that *assumes* the existence of autonomous individuals using signs simply to express and represent their ideas, but a variant of one that seeks precisely to *create* such individuals by modifying the ways in which language works. Like Keane's chapter, in other words, Sidnell's shows how the acceptance or rejection of linguistic forms has real and ontological effects; and like Candea's, it takes us beyond debates over whether or not freedom of speech "exists" by showing how people sought to produce it in one particular linguistic context, and sought to do so precisely by transforming that context itself.

In chapter 6, Paolo Heywood takes us to a different setting in which actors seek a measure of freedom from a certain sort of linguistic context. The inhabitants of the Italian town of Predappio have to contend with the fact that their town is known and reviled across Italy as Mussolini's birthplace, that it became and remains a showcase of fascist architecture under the rule of the Duce, and that it more recently has become a centre of annual pilgrimage for neo-fascists from across Italy and beyond. Navigating past the obvious – the ways in which neo-fascists claim to be expressing their "freedom of speech" when they congregate in Predappio – Heywood focuses on the more subtle and ambivalent ways in which Predappio's full-time residents seek to negotiate some freedom from the oppressive burden of living in *that* town. Whereas the association between Predappio and Fascism seems blindingly obvious to outsiders, Heywood traces the ways in which Predappiesi insert a measure of scepticism into their everyday talk about Fascism. Many historical Fascists in Predappio – even unto the originator of Fascism, Mussolini himself – can be recast as self-serving opportunists, as can the shopkeepers selling fascist souvenirs today. Others are seen to have been motivated by family loyalty rather than ideology. As for the visitors, they are described in Predappio as "nostalgics," their Fascism thereby recast as somewhat risible, or reduced and scaled down to mere paraphernalia and costume. In describing such "everyday scepticism," Heywood returns to Ludwig Wittgenstein's influential critiques of sceptical speech as "language on holiday" – "language that is 'free' … in the sense of being somehow unmoored or divorced from its proper context, not doing the job it usually does" (Heywood, this volume, p. 133). Language on holiday, for Wittgenstein, is the polar opposite of "ordinary language," and this contrast casts a long shadow also on anthropological commitments to the everyday. These are the very commitments that, as we argued at the outset of this introduction, make talk of "freedom of speech" seem like an abstract and uninteresting fiction to so many anthropologists, whose gaze is fixed on the many ways in which "real, everyday" speech is structured, framed, and determined. By showing how Predappiesi work to make scepticism ordinary, to insert a measure of freedom into their everyday speech by "untether[ing] Fascism from any real world referent" (p. 146), Heywood self-consciously seeks to unsettle these Wittgensteinian and anthropological distinctions, and to make a space for another kind of "freedom of speech" within the everyday.

If in Sidnell's and Heywood's chapters we find instances of the heterogeneity of liberal ideas of free speech (and one in a non-Western context), in Ali-Reza Bhojani and Morgan Clarke's contribution (chapter 4) we find a very similar point made about Islamic ideas of orthodoxy, speech, and critique. Drawing on a more comparative essay of Asad's (1993) than that cited in Candea's chapter, they point to the crucial role "advice" or "reasoned criticism" plays in some version of Islamic theology, and they note that while Asad does emphasize the differences between this and a "Western," Kantian version of critique, there are in fact many classical assumptions shared between them, particularly with regard to notions of speech as a tool of moral instruction (as in the idea of *parrhesia*). Echoing Keane's chapter, Bhojani and Clarke suggest that it is increasingly untenable to imagine linguistic ideologies as mapping on to distinct forms of public space, whether "liberal" or "Islamic."

Extending these reflections on secular versus religious forms of free speech, chapter 5 sketches out the possibility that a faith-based commitment to the importance of speaking the truth has inflected the responses of some Mormon American politicians to the presidency of Donald Trump. Noting that several of Trump's staunchest critics in Congress are Mormon, Fenella Cannell emphasizes the importance that individual choice has to Mormon understandings of responsibility and salvation and therefore suggests that in the Mormon case, far from constituting an authoritarian or censorious obstacle to expression, organized religion can generate a commitment to forms of what we might see as parrhesiastic speech.

Concluding this first part of the book, Caroline Humphrey's contribution (chapter 7) returns us to the theme of language, focussing, like Sidnell's chapter, on a particular linguistic context, this time Russia. Humphrey argues that while "freedom of speech" in the straightforward sense of the term is virtually at the point of extinction in contemporary Russia, Russians, like Phan Khôi in Sidnell's account, are nevertheless able to exert some agency within the sphere of language itself. Following Ingunn Lunde (2009; but see also Keane in this volume), Humphrey refers to a "performative metalanguage" – oblique and indirect speech that plays with the meanings of signs and the rules of grammar and writing, breaking certain linguistic taboos and so on – through which Russians are able to express controversial ideas, or simply to signal their opposition to conformism. Here, the "freedom" of "freedom of speech" is not the "negative freedom" of absence of censorship, but a certain delimited "positive freedom" of the ability to express thoughts and ideas from an independent subject position.

Taken together, the contributions to this first part of the book open up some of the most fundamental questions about freedom of speech in relation to language, context, and the individual, and they show how fruitful an anthropological approach to such questions can be by exploring them in relation to particular religious and national contexts. Once we move beyond the idea that our task is to situate any given instance on a scale in which individually autonomous free speech forms one pole and collective or contextual censoriousness forms the other, we see just how widely varied are people's own reflections on that very distinction.

Rethinking the Political Economy of Free Speech

Chapters in part two continue to "provincialize" and multiply freedom of speech (Chakrabarty 2008; Fedirko, Samanani, and Williamson 2021, 382) by focusing in particular on the relationship between the value of speech and its imagined freedom across a range of polities, liberal-democratic and otherwise. Collectively, these chapters demonstrate that what people take "expression" to mean, how they understand what "expression" is, does, and is worth – morally, politically, or economically – has consequences for their understandings and practices of expressive freedom. The five contributors to this section examine how people – from West Papua to Ireland, from Zambia to Hungary – seek to render their speech effective in eliciting a desired transactional response from economically powerful others (Rupert Stasch); deal with their social critique of neo-liberal urban development being incorporated into the very forces of value creation it seeks to challenge (Natalie Morningstar); find value in "bullshit" radio testimonies (Harri Englund); and challenge the Israeli state's attempts to devalue or otherwise incapacitate their critical expression on Palestine (Amahl Bishara). Each chapter highlights a different aspect of speech's valuation to suggest that the meaning of freedom in relation to speech, even in societies that have hitherto had little encounter with liberal models of communicative freedom, often depends on what speech can achieve socially.

The section begins, however, with a consideration of how such struggles over the meaning and value of freedom of speech take place within broader institutional contexts that are both a frame and crucial stake of such struggles. In chapter 8, Susan Gal focuses on three different cases in which freedom of speech has recently been at issue in Viktor Orbán's Hungary: a controversy over a comment made by Orbán himself in a public speech, a court case against a satirist, and the systemic shift towards unification of the press landscape. The difference in scale between these cases is precisely the point: building on the comparative explorations of part one (Candea, Keane) and on her own previous work on comparison and scale (Gal 2016), Gal highlights how the political stakes of freedom of speech weave in and out of the personal and the systemic in ways that are often both elusive and powerful. Her three cases take readers through the ways in which supposedly impersonal market forces, legal formalisms, and personal networks of influence can be made to shape and constrain what is and is not sayable, without any explicit challenge to formal commitments to freedom of speech. In so doing, Gal extends Keane's call (in this volume) for anthropologists to attend to broader metapragmatic struggles that go beyond and frame single face-to-face events of communication. This outlook enables her to unpick and highlight what she terms "design": planned intentional intervention in the institutional arrangements for regulating public speech that evoke what Andrew Graan (2022) calls "discursive engineering." Beyond the Hungarian case, Gal's chapter provides a powerful guide for re-thinking the political stakes and mechanisms surrounding freedom of speech by attending to the subtle yet powerful ways in which institutional arrange-ments can be inflected and set up, in plain view yet often just out of sight.

Institutional arrangements come in many forms. In chapter 9, Rupert Stasch puts forth a bold and richly detailed analysis of the changing understandings and practices of freedom among the Korowai of Indonesian-controlled Papua. Fiercely egalitarian, until the late twentieth century the Korowai "were not involved with any state and had no tradition of conflict or conviction around 'free speech'" (Stasch, this volume, p. 188). Nevertheless, their politics was defined through "configuration of speech roles" (p. 207), and central to their complex understandings of freedom were "images of speaking" and listening (p. 188). Noting that the old Korowai name for family feud was "big talk," Stasch describes three main modalities of freedom: freedom from subordina-tion (from "being told what to do"), freedom as aggressive impingement on others (understood as "anger" or "asking"), and freedom as solicitous self-low-ering (encapsulated in the image of "hearing" or "fulfilling the talk"). Over the last thirty years, the balance between these different modalities of commu-nicative freedom has shifted. Stasch argues that this happened for a number of reasons.

Most Korowai went from living in small familial groups in forests at large distances from their neighbours to living in villages, coming into contact with state and market-based social arrangements from which they now understand themselves as excluded. Yearning to be more like the city dwellers whose domination they resent, many Korowai have embraced new forms of state-based domination and hierarchy rather than rejecting them as they might have done before. Stasch argues that this process follows the basic pattern of Korowai's self-lowering mode of freedom, in which wilful subordination inherent in "fulfilling the talk" of others is meant to elevate the "hearer." He demonstrates that the Korowai accept one relation of subordination – to new village heads and regents – "in order to ease the larger, more painful one of collective exclusion from urban consumer prosperity" (p. 207). These changes have in turn reorganized old and complex Korowai understandings of freedom and introduced a new, non–speech-based form of political relation based on access to material wealth. Overall, Stasch paints a troubling picture of Korowai's freedoms profoundly transformed through their gradual incorporation into the Indonesian state and capitalism.

Developing the theme of the relation between speech's social consequences and speech's freedom, Natalie Morningstar turns to young artists in postrecession Ireland in chapter 10. Morningstar asks: "How should we make sense of the fact that in liberal democracies, public criticism, even when it appears risky or provocative, can function to consolidate the critic's prestige, cement social hierarchies, and energize the elites nominally targeted with criticism?" (p. 212). Against the backdrop of a crisis of social reproduction in Ireland, Morningstar's artists are painfully aware that their work is frequently made possible by policies that seek to "revitalize" marginalized communities and neighbourhoods abandoned by their erstwhile industrial residents. These policies commission artistic works and provide artists with space for studios and gatherings. They promote the very kind of economic growth that also socially displaces the artists to as yet not redeveloped neighbourhoods and towns. Morningstar argues that artistic critique's unwilling complicity with capitalist value creation makes it not only ineffective in challenging power but also an instrument in the expansion of the ruling elite. Her ethnography's focus on the social production of unfreedom among a generation of Irish youth dependent on, but resentful of how their expression – their creative labour – is valued by, the powers-that-be hints at a broader problematization of the plight of the global middle-class and explains why her subjects have the bitter experience of expressive freedom that they do.

One of the lessons of Morningstar's chapter for the comparative enterprise of this volume is that in liberal democracies artistic expression can become morally devalued by the inconsistency between its intent and its effects, especially when expressive acts are co-opted into the circuits of economic value. In chapter 11, which takes off from Harry Frankfurt's famous exploration of "bullshit" as a sideways-on attitude to truth and lying, Harri Englund examines the problem from the opposite direction. Englund compares how *vox populi* program hosts on Finnish and Zambian public radio deal with callers whose testimonies are neither true nor false and indeed disregard truth altogether. The radio hosts nevertheless engage the callers to incorporate their accounts into the broader moral community of "the people," whose voice the programs are meant to construct and project. Why is "bullshit" compatible with the pursuit of *vox populi* on the airways? England asks. The chapter suggests several answers, yet finds all of them of limited use. Enumerating the similarities and differences between the two contrasting examples, in particular with regard to the different ways that the Finnish and Zambian hosts construct their moral authority and project a vocal polyphony by skilfully editing their vox pops, the chapter resists calls to embrace "critical anthropology's own preferred genre of exposé" (Englund, this volume, pp. 237–8). Instead, Englund's "modest comparison" brings forth the different ways that, in contrast to rather narrow understandings of populism in political anthropology, the radio genre of *vox populi* elicits an idea of the people and imbues it with sonic and social qualities.

One might read Englund's account as describing the work of determining and assigning value to public speech on the airwaves. As the Finnish Kansanradio's hosts subscribed to a professional ethos that refrained from giving anyone advice and avoided interfering in the broadcast, they sought to project through the broadcasts' vocal polyphony a sense of a public of individuals united by mutual recognition and respect. From this perspective, a "bullshit" caller's performance of a particular social type, even if inauthentic with regard to the caller's identity, nevertheless added to the overall value of the program – indeed could be re-evaluated and included as part of a communicative public. In the case of Gogo Breeze, the Zambian Breeze FM's host who cultivated a media persona of a wise grandfather dispensing moral guidance to his listeners, the community of the people was brought together exactly through the host's criticism of such callers. In both cases, this happened through a dynamic alignment of communicative roles that brought out a larger, collective truth from the callers' free-form "bullshit."

Morningstar's and Englund's chapters decentre the question of *freedom* of speech, demonstrating how practices typically associated with free speaking might in fact acquire other kinds of value and worth that make the questions of freedom per se fade into the background. In contrast, Amahl Bishara's contribution (chapter 12) brings us back to a familiar liberal frame of freedom of speech as understood through individual rights, restrictions, and censorship. It does so through an analysis of global environments of expression. Bishara proposes this concept to capture how "states can influence what is sayable beyond their boundaries ... because of the ways in which people move and because of the interdependence writers and speakers have with one another" (Bishara, this volume, p. 239). Bishara seeks to explain why what can be said about Palestinians, and the Israeli state's violence towards them, differs so significantly across locations. Building on Pierre Bourdieu's field theory, she draws on numerous examples from Israel, the European Union, and North America to analyze how the Israeli state seeks to influence critical discourse by designating speakers as "terrorists," making arrests, hindering cross-border movement, and collaborating with organizations that undermine credentials of foreign critics of Israel. Her crucial example is Israel's reliance on global anti-terror legislation, passed in the aftermath of 9/11, for silencing and discrediting Palestinian activists or anyone who seeks to collaborate with them. Beyond immediate damage to the activists, this has far-reaching repercussions across multiple contexts of knowledge production and administration where activists' findings are used – from European funding bodies to US and Canadian universities who fear losing funding or being confronted with legal challenges for sponsoring critical research. Translocal actors, infrastructures, and discourses that make expression relevant and valuable in one place and worthless in another stitch together disparate social spaces into uneven environments of expression. On the one hand, these amplify critical speech beyond its immediate publics, but on the other, magnify the state's attempts to silence such critics.

In sum, the chapters in part two offer various routes for rethinking the political economies of free speech, at some remove from the rather repetitive debates between the right and left over "cancel culture" and the role of political and economic power in enabling acts of expression and censorship. Here we find more challenging comparative explorations (Stasch, Englund), insights into the self-defeating dynamics of critique under "late liberalism" (Morningstar), the multifarious ways in which public speech can be managed by design (Gal), and the materiality of the transnational politics of silencing (Bishara). Each of these chapters suggests new positions from which the sense in which freedom of speech is political might be expanded and rethought.

Free Speech and Historical Narration: On Witnessing and Troubling

This introduction began with the entangled historical trajectories of concerns with freedom of speech. Part three, by contrast, examines the converse question: How are understandings and practices of free speech entailed in the writing and rewriting of history, and more broadly in the production of historical experience? One of the persistent modes in which freedom of speech is invoked in contemporary debates relates to what Adam Reed in his chapter describes as "the right to speak frankly and freely about what *really* happened" (Reed, this volume, p. 270). This is often envisaged as a "negative freedom" in Isaiah Berlin's terms, a freedom *from*, asserted through a struggle against official censorship or the pervasive power of dominant narratives. Decolonial critiques of racist bias in memorializations of the First and Second World Wars (Reed in this volume) are often cast in this oppositional vein, as are, on the other end of the political spectrum, neo-fascist "nostalgics" attempts to rewrite the stakes of Italian history (Heywood in this volume). While touching on this way of articulating free speech and history, the chapters in this section seek to open up different ways of imagining this relationship.

One strand, most evident in chapter 13 by Heonik Kwon and chapter 14 by Adam Reed, enquires into the "positive" – again in Berlin's sense – valence of freedom of speech in relation to history. Both chapters explore a freedom *to* speak the truth of history, not as an abstract right or entitlement but as the effect of particular forms of witnessing, genealogical continuities, and forms of transmission. Kwon's contribution focuses on one such instance of speaking out about the past. In 1989, after the end of four decades of military rule, a group of islanders of Jeju in South Korea published a collection of eyewitness accounts of an episode of state violence in 1947–9. Echoing other contributors (cf. Candea and Humphrey in this volume), Kwon's account highlights the tensions between different visions of freedom entailed in such instances of speaking out. Such struggles over the meaning of freedom are perhaps to be expected when memorializing the complex intersection of postcoloniality and the Cold War, but Kwon's story starts from a more surprising point: the first account in the collection published by the islanders is actually by a Jeju shaman, recalling and invoking the testimony of the dead on both sides in the uprising. This initial invocation opens up a broader question of the freedom of spirits to speak in the public sphere – a cosmopolitical question that exceeds yet at the same time colours the geopolitical struggles over the freedom to give witness to historical events.

Reed's chapter evokes another haunting. It traces the ways in which contemporary English – mostly white, middle-class – members of the Henry Williamson Society seek to experience the truth of war through forms of "uncritical reading" of their favourite author's First World War novels. Immersing themselves in Williamson's vivid descriptions of the battlefield, these readers seek to live aspects of the experience of war, channelling – the reader, fresh from Kwon's chapter, might almost say shamanically – those who experienced the war first hand. In the process, some of these readers arrive at what they feel are profound realizations not only about the historical experience of the First World War but also about the nature of courage and fear, measuring themselves up to those they think of as their forebears in ways that can be challenging and uncomfortable. These readers, Reed points out, are also in a small way contributing to the collective production of a broader national narrative and memory. Reed deploys this material as a way to inform contemporary debates about modes of public remembrance in the UK that have been marked by parrhesiastic critiques of the exclusive, racist, and classist aspects of the national narrative. Williamson readers' "uncritical" experience of the truth of war might form a rather more formidable counterpoint than some revisionist historians imagine when they set out to critique traditional modes of memorialization. At the same time, revisionist Marxist and decolonial accounts that seek to render vivid the bravery of soldiers in the face of discrimination, and to re-weave ties of community and kinship across time, may actually share some key features with the types of truth-telling experienced by Williamson's readers. In sum, Kwon's and Reed's chapters give a sense of the richness and thickness of witnessing as it travels through people and back and forth across the boundaries of life and death, memory, and imagination. Here are instances in which the abstract contours of a negative freedom from dominant narratives are filled in by substantive kinds of positive freedom to speak an experiential truth of history.

Andreas Bandak's contribution (chapter 15) provides a pivot point between these themes and a second set of concerns that animate this section. On the one hand, Bandak's chapter continues the theme of witnessing, focusing on the work of exiled Syrian documentarists producing narratives of the 2011 uprising and its tragic aftermath. He shows, echoing the previous two contributors, how the historical and the personal, event and memory, the collective and the singular are interwoven through "the narrative efforts placed in keeping particular pasts alive in order to make way for the future" (Bandak, this volume, p. 287). Yet, at the same time, Bandak's chapter opens up onto another kind of freedom of speech in relation to historical truth – a freedom to "take liberties" with the very idea of a singular, starkly factual, and morally clear-cut narrative. In Bandak's chapter, this freedom is indexed by the locution "as it were," which Bandak counterposes both to the "as if" of out-and-out fiction and the "as it was" of unchallengeable factuality. As Syrian documentarists keep reweaving their narratives to keep track of a changing set of stakes and shifting forms of remembrance, "the 'as it were' operates as a particular form of freedom of speech that opens up the personal and private registers and continuously attempts engaging what happened, without the fixity of an official form of narrative, and perhaps even allows for a certain playfulness" (p. 299).

Bandak thus introduces us to a different kind of freedom of speech in relation to history. This is not simply the freedom – be it negative or positive – to speak the truth of the past, but rather a freedom from certain kinds of fixities of discourse, which is also, simultaneously, a freedom to articulate and rearticulate memory otherwise. Lotte Hoek's contribution (chapter 16) extends and expands this insight. Hoek focuses on an exhibition entitled *Age of Saturn* by Bangladeshi "trickster artist-historian" Omar A. Chowdhury. In a context of increasingly violent policing of official narratives of Bengali history, *Age of Saturn* presented a meticulously documented account of the life and times of a Dr. Shahidul Zaman as he and his family traversed the history of twentieth-century Bengal. Photographs, published papers, maps, and documents alternated with visceral images and live installations. Except that, confusingly, Dr. Shahidul Zaman himself seems to be a fictional composite – his photo at the entrance of the exhibition was actually that of contemporary Bangladeshi artist Dhali Al Mamun. Rather than a simple parafictional critique of historical realism, however, *Age of Saturn*, Hoek argues, produced a more subtly disorienting feeling of the simultaneous elusiveness and visceral presence of the past. Just days after opening, the exhibition was shut down, the curator resigned, and Chowdhury himself fled to the countryside before moving to Europe. Yet the nature, source, and cause of the pressures that led to this silencing remain unclear and nebulous, matching the disconcertingly nebulous factuality of the exhibition itself. In its evocative and precise writing, Hoek's chapter shares with the reader these overlapping disorientations.

In sum, the chapters in part three seek to enrich and complicate the standard vision of freedom of speech as a right to puncture established historical narratives – "the right to speak frankly and freely about what *really* happened" (Reed, this volume, p. 270). They point, on the one hand, to the substantive engagements with historical experience, transmission, and creativity that are required in order to exercise such a freedom to speak the truth of what was. On the other hand, they open up the question of the freedom of speech in relation to a particular vision of history as settled and determined factual narrative. The two points are in productive tension. If speaking freely about history is imagined purely as an "as if" storytelling unmoored from any realist constraints, it would lose the ability to make a difference to settled historical narratives. But conversely, there would be little hope of ever unsettling history "as it was" without the minute ordinary freedoms of scepticism, elusiveness, and evocation.

Therapies, Individual and Collective

If the chapters in part three spotlighted the often complex and ambivalent ways in which collective historical narration is rooted in personal forms of experience, those in part four approach this relationship from the opposite end, by asking about the ways in which personal, therapeutic imaginaries and practices of free speaking can be situated within broader socio-historical assemblages.

Since Freud's systematization of the "talking cure," and his "free association" method in particular, therapeutic approaches to psychological distress have placed the speaking subject at the centre of ideas about pathology and healing. Within and outside of therapeutic spaces, the idea that traumatic experiences are buried within the mind and body, and that they must be excavated through encounters based on speaking and response, has shaped and challenged cultural notions of the self and its relation to others. Whether by pivoting around cathartic practices of verbally working through what is censored by the unconscious, or by pointedly positioning themselves against psychoanalytic notions, trajectories of psychological and psychiatric practices have been profoundly influenced by such ideas since the early twentieth century. Yet in this section, therapeutic speech provides a pivot around which the chapters' authors explore and unsettle Freudian ideas and the ways they dovetail with broader cultural assumptions about the kinds of freedom associated with speaking and listening, and concealment of supposed inner states and their disclosure. In different ways, each of the chapters here suggests that speech that is intended to facilitate psychological healing, however that is construed, at the very least points to, if not actively calls forth, ideologies of communication and the (individual and collective) subjects upon which they are premised.

In chapter 17, Michael Lempert helpfully places what he describes as the therapeutically inflected speech practices of American feminist consciousness-raising circles of the 1960s and 1970s within a broader trajectory of ways in which Americans have aspired to or contested democratic and liberal ideals in the Cold War era and beyond. His chapter outlines an "ecological" approach to ideals and practices of speaking freely, which, crucially, reminds us of the importance of the reception of speech as well as its voicing. Taking three flashpoints in post-war America's political history, Lempert considers the centrality of listening practices in ideologies of free speech and suggests this oft-neglected aspect of semiotic ideology is an important element in ideals and struggles around liberal democratic ideals. As becomes clear in his consideration of the examples of Kurt Lewin's "small group science," feminist consciousness-raising circles, and post-2016 student debates about speech on campus, it is not only what is said or how it is said that matters in assessments of free speech, but also what kind of listening is at play: who, when, and how people listen are all part of various notions of what liberal and democratic communication should look like. Providing an initial typology of "deliberative," "validational," and "interventionist" listening, Lempert draws our attention to the role played by those who listen and the listening they choose to enact on whether communication is understood as harmful or healing, authoritarian or liberatory. Lempert takes care, however, not to suggest that these are ideal types that are practised with rigid separation or purity, demonstrating how contestation within and among differently identified and politicized groups can play out when, for example, one or more of these styles of listening is in play, or when people disagree about the extent to which others are listening, and thus communicating, in the correct way. A useful corrective to the focus in public debates around campus politics, free speech, and, in particular, modes of expression (who speaks, with whom, how, and when), the chapter brings linguistic anthropology's tools to bear on the semiotic ideologies of reception that are a key part in how a politics of free speech has unfolded and continues to do so.

E. Summerson Carr's contribution (chapter 18) to the section focuses in on one particular part of the story Lempert has outlined in broader strokes, examining the debate between Carl Rogers's person-centred therapy and B.F. Skinner's behaviourism that, as Carr shows, reveal how American therapies are one key site where ideals of free speech, and their underlying semiotic ideologies, have been thrashed out. For it is not only the health of individual persons that psychotherapies have aspired to promote but also that of communities and collectives. Nowhere was this more the case than in Cold War America, where the perceived enemy threat to practices of freedom of thought and expression was at the forefront of the concerns of both therapists and politicians. Carr's insightful reading of a public debate between Rogers and Skinner demonstrates, though, that notions of freedom, and how they relate to the intervention of the professionals, the therapists, are as varied and contested in the therapy room as they have been outside of it. The reflective listening of Rogers's person-centred therapy, intended to be non-interventionist, leaving the client free to express their inner thoughts and feelings, was subject to Skinner's critique, as the latter suggested that the words of reinforcement and affirmation, as well as the silences, of the therapist in fact direct the client's speech as much as any other form of talking therapy would. For Skinner, "freedom" of therapeutic speech was only a result of the conditions of its production, as with other forms of speech or behaviour. Carr shows how an alternative ideal of freedom – that of reflective self-control within socially conditioned environments – was held up by Skinner in his proposal of ethical speech, whether in therapeutic or political contexts. In doing so, she traces a struggle around the dominance of a semiotic ideology of inner reference in American free speech ideals, showing how contemporary debates around the conditions that enable or limit free speech, as well as what kinds of freedom are valued or disavowed in them, were prefigured in this earlier instance of political questions being worked though in psychological terms.

Lempert and Carr, in sum, show how American therapeutic practices have both been spaces where political struggles have played out, and have come to inform assumptions about speaking and listening subjects in political spaces. This is echoed and extended in Fiona Wright's contribution (chapter 19) on dialogical therapy and its evocations of a global reparative politics. Based on her ethnographic work with practitioners of a dialogical therapy in the UK, Wright demonstrates the similarities between this therapy's performative ritualization of group dialogues with practices of testimony and witnessing common to attempts at facilitating reparative politics in post-conflict settings, such as with truth and reconciliation commissions. What both share is an embodied mode of public speech considered to enable a reckoning with harms considered past, as well as an invitation to speakers to identify as victims of, or complicit with the doing of, those harms. Ideals of collective repair through these modes of affective, public truth-telling and listening run through this dialogical therapy, which Wright shows to have political as well as interpersonal aspirations. Some of the democratic ideals of American therapeutic speech, highlighted in Carr's and Lempert's chapters, can be seen here to have been very effectively globalized, as attention to, for example, how one listens to a speaker, the proper forms of response, and how people should place and move their bodies in the therapeutic space are also understood in this ethnographic context to be key in this therapy's capacity to manifest a desired form of political community. As in Carr's reading of Skinner's behaviourism, or Lempert's of Lewin's small group science, here speaking freely involves cultivating the right conditions for certain truths to be spoken, heard, and taken on board as the basis of the transformation of polity as well as person.

Perhaps unsurprisingly, the majority of attention in this section, in the chapters by Carr, Lempert, and Wright, is paid to therapeutic ways of speaking freely in Euro-American contexts. As Sarah Pinto's contribution (chapter 20) also makes clear, however, psychotherapeutic imaginaries are embedded in global and post-colonial knowledge economies, which have never been one-way, as reductive analyses of Western therapies being "imported" into contexts depicted as radically different would suggest. Rather, in juxtaposing and reading together an array of different kinds of texts (academic, literary, filmic, legal) that variously locate representations of homosexuality and non-binary gender definitions vis-a-vis a hermeneutics of secrecy and revelation, and whose authors and readers are variously located in both time and place, Pinto raises the notion of a subject speaking freely against repressed desires as one that has travelled back and forth among authors, editors, and readers, all variously emplaced within imperial contexts. Resisting a culturalist analysis that would map Freudian psychologies onto a (geo)politics of liberal ideals of freedom (in speech, as in sexuality), Pinto traces a hermeneutic of concealment and exposure in her readings of films, literature, and academic work in and about India that addresses questions of gender and sexuality as issues assumed to be subject to diagnosis and revelation as well as secrecy and censorship. Freedom of speech, here, is complicated as a liberal ideal. Pinto demonstrates how notions of the expression of inner truths, or their repression, are straightforward neither in the nineteenth- and twentieth-century psychoanalytic thinking that seemed to align repressed speech with repressed desire, nor in the Indian texts that have recursively reframed such repressions. In this reframing, repressions evade the psychiatrists whose repeated appearances in their dramas somehow undercut a formulation of the talking cure as something as straightforward as recovery through the speaking of truths that reveal what has been hidden.

Importantly, Pinto invites us to interrogate how particular texts in queer theory have been framed as Euro-American, or Western, placing Eve K. Sedgwick's *Epistemology of the Closet* (1990) as one of those works that cannot be extricated from what Pinto describes as a "history of entangled texts." What would it mean, Pinto asks, to think about the closet as an imperial assemblage, reconsidering the sexual politics of freedom as one that has travelled back and forth, writing and rewriting notions of authenticity and inner truths, secrets and curses, in therapeutic languages that unsettle as well as underpin liberal conceptualizations of freedom and selfhood? In this sense, Pinto's chapter complements, but also challenges, one of the recurrent conclusions of this section, in which freedom in therapeutic speech involves the transfiguration of individual but also collective selves – polities and communities whose wellbeing is thought to depend in some way on the possibility of healing transformation through particular speech practices. As Pinto concludes, sometimes the therapeutic appears as that which does not reveal, but which rather resists the compulsion to transform, or be transformed, through speaking freely. Irreconcilable difference and ambiguity may be what remains in the wake of such freedom, a possibility yet ill accounted for in the kinds of therapeutic speech practices otherwise considered in part four, limited as they are by very particular transpositions of ideologies of interpersonal communication onto collective and political encounters.

Parting Thoughts

Taken together, the chapters in this volume pose and answer a range of questions destined to expand understandings of freedom of speech: What notions of the self and selflessness, what forms and understandings of will, intention, and action underlie different imaginaries and practices of free speech? How do failure, inconsistency and the inability to live up to ideals feature? How are imaginaries of freedom of speech scaffolded, enabled, and constrained by different techniques and technologies, be they material, legal, linguistic, social, or spiritual? What bodily techniques, what skills and educated feelings underpin such practices? What epistemologies are embedded or contested in different visions of freedom of speech? How, if at all, are these premised on a commitment to truth, a concern with the substance in relation to the effect of language? What is the role of critique, revelation, indirection, irony, humour, evasiveness, and partiality? What pedagogical assumptions are built into ways of enabling, and also ways of blocking or silencing, speech across these various contexts? What geographies, collectives, and temporalities are imagined, hoped for, or disavowed in the name of freedom of speech? How do particular physical spaces (the classroom, the town hall, the courtroom, the street, the museum) enable, require, or prohibit particular forms of speech? Which histories are revealed, occluded, or made in the process?

These questions are not meant to be exhaustive – no such collection could be. Taken together, however, they map a set of openings, a problem space for an anthropology of freedoms of speech, and a preliminary conversation that is set to grow and expand. Internally diverse and multivocal, this conversation, at the intersection of ethnography, comparison, and contextualization, emerges nevertheless as a distinctively anthropological contribution to a broad and urgent set of contemporary debates.

PART ONE

Traditions and Comparisons

1 Comparing Freedoms: "Liberal Freedom of Speech" in Frontal and Lateral Perspective

MATEI CANDEA

What might a comparative anthropology of freedom of speech look like? The question is slightly disconcerting in part because "freedom of speech" is a concern that is already laden with its own comparative thrust. Before anthropologists have had a chance to place them "in comparative perspective," liberal[1] invocations of and debates over freedom of speech are themselves multiply, pointedly, and normatively comparative. These comparisons, often cast in national or civilizational terms, echo anthropological modes of contextualization, yet deploy them in ways that many anthropologists would find unsatisfactory and uncomfortable.

One classic comparative vision arranges contexts (typically, nation states) in terms of the greater or lesser presence of freedom of speech within them. Here, freedom of speech operates as a single universal scale that makes social and cultural differences commensurable. Anthropologists are inured to this type of comparative device. This laying out of global cases side by side, along a linear scale indexed on a core "Euro-American" value, recalls the kinds of positivist ambitions of functionalist and evolutionist anthropologies we have forcefully left behind. That form holds little appeal, and I suspect many contemporary anthropologists are likely to agree with Foucault that

> comparing the quantity of freedom between one system and another does not in fact [make] much sense ... We should not think of freedom as a universal which is

---

1 I use liberal here, initially, in the sense outlined by Talal Asad (2013, 26–7) when he writes: "Its theorists seek to present liberalism as consistent and unified, but it is precisely the contradictions and ambiguities in the language of liberalism that make the public debates among self-styled liberals and with their 'illiberal' opponents possible ... I call the society in which political and moral arguments using this vocabulary are sited 'liberal.'" I will give a more precise account of this setting below. For an overview of the anthropology of liberalism, see Fedirko, Samanani, and Williamson (2021).

gradually realized over time, or which undergoes quantitative variations, greater or lesser drastic reductions, or more or less important periods of eclipse. It is not a universal which is particularized in time and geography. Freedom is not a white surface with more or less numerous black spaces here and there and from time to time. (2008, 46–7)

In lieu of this comparative vision of freedom as a single quantitative variable, Foucault proposes another comparative view. This view examines multiple kinds and types of freedom, each sustained by and sustaining different material, political, and discursive formations. Throughout his later work, Foucault (2011) gave multiple instances of this vision of heterogeneous kinds of freedom that clash and overlap, sometimes intermingling and sometimes succeeding each other in time. This is a promising precedent for those of us seeking to develop a comparative anthropology of freedoms of speech. In doing so, anthropologists can combine relatively new forays into a comparative anthropology of freedom(s) (Humphrey 2007; Laidlaw 2014; Englund 2006; Heywood 2015; Zigon 2007; Venkatesan 2023), with the well-established comparative tradition on speech and expression developed by linguistic anthropologists and others. From considerations of language ideologies and semiotic ideologies, through to literature on voice, rhetoric, and oratory, we have extensive resources at hand to add something substantial to the often rather thin portrayal of "speech" entailed in popular discussions of freedom of speech (for an overview, see Candea et al. 2021).

In order to do so, however, we should distinguish this vision of multiple and overlapping freedoms of speech from another comparative imaginary. This imaginary is distinct from the two sketched out above, even though it echoes aspects of each. This is a comparative vision in which freedom of speech is mapped onto a contrast between two contexts: a familiar "us" (the anthropologist and their imagined readership), and an unfamiliar "other." This is a form I have elsewhere characterized as a "frontal comparison" (a comparison of "us" and "them"), in opposition to the "lateral comparison" of cases (this and that), which is evidenced in both the quantitative display of a global map of free speech and in the multiple formations of freedom envisioned by Foucault (Candea 2018). Unlike the quantitative vision of degrees of freedom, this frontal comparative mode retains significant appeal for anthropologists. Indeed, it is in this mode that some of the most influential anthropological engagements with freedom of speech (Keane 2009; Asad et al. 2013) have been articulated – as contrasts between (implicitly "our") liberal freedom of speech and other visions and versions elsewhere. While such frontal comparisons might seem to promise a radical critique or "provincialization" (cf. Chakrabarty 2008) of liberal preconceptions, I will argue in this chapter that this is not always or straightforwardly the case. Anthropologists engaging in a frontal comparison of freedom(s) of speech are likely to be hampered by the fact that this is also one of the key comparative modes in which debates over freedom of speech occur in the liberal discursive fora they are seeking to provincialize. By contrast, a more lateral imaginary holds unsuspected radical potential.

A Maelstrom of Comparisons

On 7 January 2015, two men entered the offices of the satirical journal *Charlie Hebdo* in Paris, France, and opened fire, killing twelve people. These murders were ostensibly committed in retaliation against the journal's publication of satirical drawings of the Prophet Muhammad. Across French media and social media, the event was met with a wave of public support for the victims of the shooting, for the journal, and for freedom of speech, which was cast as a universal and yet (somehow) also distinctly French value. A black sign stating "Je suis Charlie" became a ubiquitous fixture on social media, appearing on the front pages of newspapers and on public buildings across France. A public demonstration was organized by the president of the republic, the socialist François Hollande, at which over a million people walked side by side in support of *Charlie Hebdo* and freedom of speech. A number of French newspapers republished some of the cartoons as a statement of their support. These reactions were echoed internationally in many quarters, and indeed a raft of foreign heads of state came to walk alongside Hollande at the front of the march. The *Charlie Hebdo* killings thus reactivated a theme that has agitated public discourse in Europe and America periodically since the famous "Rushdie Affair" of 1989, namely, that of an incompatibility between "liberal freedom of speech" and certain kinds of "radical Islam." In this framing, freedom of speech is typically aligned with "the West," modernity, secularism, democracy, reason, and abstract principles, and contrasted with tradition, religion, community, affect, and particularist commitments. As Saba Mahmood (2013, 67) argued of the earlier instantiation of this debate around the publication of some of the same cartoons by the Danish newspaper *Jyllands Posten*, "even the calmer commentators seemed to concur that this was an impasse between the liberal value of freedom of speech and a religious taboo"; and as Webb Keane (2009, 48) argued in his own comparative exploration of the Danish cartoons debate, "by linking purportedly secular language to concepts of freedom and of voice, some familiar ideologies of the press can manifest a certain moral narrative of modernity, a story of human agency emancipated from its captivation with fetishes and other unrealities."

Concomitantly, however, another comparative framing came to the fore, turning on national rather than civilizational differences in approaches to freedom of speech. This centred on the observation that whereas a certain uniformity of public discourse reigned in France in the aftermath of the killings, initial reactions elsewhere were rather more varied – not only in Niger, Pakistan, Afghanistan, Iran, and Chechnya, where large public demonstrations took place against *Charlie Hebdo*, but also in other liberal democracies such as the United States and the UK, where public figures, cultural critics, and journalists questioned the cultural and racial politics of *Charlie Hebdo*'s publication of the "Muhammad cartoons" and worried about the stigmatization of Muslims in France, about French approaches to state secularism, and about the enforced univocality of the "Je suis Charlie" message (CM 2015; Fisher 2015; Karpiak 2015; Trudeau 2015). Instantly, many voices in France and elsewhere rushed to situate, explain, and defend *Charlie Hebdo* – and France's purportedly "Voltairean" tradition of free speech more generally – against "foreign misreadings." Some French commentators were dismayed by the refusal of American and British publications to reprint the cartoons, which they cast as a marker of the comparatively degraded state of freedom of speech in those "multiculturalist" countries.

Thus, alongside and seemingly at odds with the grand civilizational claims about "Western" liberal freedom of speech, another, equally recurrent debate bears on the comparative state of freedom of speech in different Western liberal democracies. In this particular case, a "distinctly French" approach to robust anti-religious polemics was contrasted (by detractors as well as by supporters) with the more cautious approach to religious controversy stemming from American or British "multicultural tolerance." In that vision, France was cast as a setting in which, for better or worse, speech was "freer" and less encumbered by civility and concerns for giving offence to religious sensibilities. Just as often, however, the shoe is on the other foot: discussions of freedom of speech in liberal democracies frequently pivot on a contrast between the American First Amendment's "exceptional" and "uniquely far-reaching" protection of freedom of speech and European legal regimes in which constitutional guarantees of freedom of speech are limited by legal provisions against hate speech, libel, or Holocaust denial. For a number of authors, this is a contrast that reaches beyond the realm of law, narrowly understood, into different sociological and historical imaginaries: a core commitment to "liberty" in the United States versus a tempering of free speech in reference to "dignity" in European (legal) cultures (Whitman 2000; Carmi 2008).

This nationalized framing of the debate was not unchallenged, of course. Just as *Charlie Hebdo* found supporters abroad (Chait 2015; Douthat 2015), there were also dissenting voices within France (Chemin 2015; Fassin 2015; Nunès 2015). These dissenting voices were rather muted in the immediate aftermath of the killings, when public support for *Charlie Hebdo* took on huge normative weight. Yet dissenting opinions did emerge, cautiously at first, then more fulsomely over the subsequent months and years, to the stated horror of other French commentators – including survivors of the *Charlie Hebdo* killings – who saw this as a betrayal of an erstwhile national consensus and an encroachment of "Anglo-Saxon" thinking into France (Devecchio and de Nouël 2018; Gernelle 2020; Malka 2020). To others, such tensions speak to a generational struggle between an older republicanist left, which recognized its own 1968-style ethos in the indiscriminate and anti-systemic irreverence of *Charlie Hebdo*, and a newer progressive left more in tune with decolonial critiques and perspectives. What had briefly seemed to be an international debate was coming to look like a domestic one – or rather the question of the proper comparative framing of the debate (is there such a thing as a "French model"?) became itself a hotly disputed issue (Bacqué and Chemin 2016; Hazareesingh and Clarini 2017; Mahler 2017).

Indeed, outside of moments of self-consciously international discourse, like those following the *Charlie Hebdo* killings, contrasts between national or civilizational approaches to freedom of speech usually play second fiddle to a – once again comparative – contrast between differently situated political, generational, or philosophical positions within specific national contexts. In France, the US, or the UK, recurrent arguments rage over the proper relationship between freedom of speech and social responsibility in both legal and more broadly social contexts. Looked at carefully, comparative claims about different national or civilizational traditions of free speech often seem like they are primarily interventions into these domestic debates, in which the stakes are stated and restated, over and over again, in terms of a tension between freedom and its proper limits. International or civilizational comparisons emerge here as geographical mappings of these two "poles": the American First Amendment, French combative secularism, or quite simply "the Western liberal approach to free speech" epitomize the possibilities or the pitfalls of going further (going too far?) with freedom; conversely, "US campus culture," French Holocaust denial laws, or "Islamic tradition" are invoked to highlight the dangers, the necessity, or the promise of placing socialized limits on speech. These international framings are simultaneously comparative claims about the different ways in which freedom of speech is valued, "at home," by one's consociates and intimate others: people of different political persuasions and/or generations.

Given the pervasive essentialisms, the slippery scale-shifting, and the intense normative commitments discussed above, it is perhaps not so surprising that anthropologists have, so far, only dipped their toe into the comparative maelstrom surrounding freedom of speech. In the above debates, some of our best comparative moves seem to have been made for us – to a rather unsettling effect. Relativism? Here, freedom of speech is already contextualized as "cultural." It is already relativized and "provincialized" – which is not to say necessarily diminished, since one can, after all, be combatively and chauvinistically proud of one's province. Anti-essentialism? While essentialisms fly around pretty freely, the fact that they recur on multiple scales challenges the coherence of various entities that seem to sit at cross-purposes (civilizational, national, political, and generational). This liberal debate seems to deconstruct its own certainties precisely as it articulates them.

The debate above may seem dizzying – yet it is far from unstructured. The confusing effect comes not purely from the diversity of objects, scales, and opinions but also from the way this diversity is traversed by the repetition of one single form, over and over again, like a backbeat. The contrast may be civilizational, national, generational, political, or some combination of the above; its amplitude and stakes may vary; yet its basic outline is fundamentally stable. In all its various iterations, this is a contrast between individual liberty and social responsibilities, between freedom of speech and its limits. Out of a maelstrom of controversy, a stable and limited vocabulary of argument emerges (Asad 2013, 27). The form is stable in another way also: over and over again, the contrast is cast in terms of a frontal comparison between "them" and "us." The positions are interchangeable: "they" may be obsessed by social control while "we" defend freedom, or on the contrary, "they" may be foolishly touting an irresponsible right to insult and demean, while "we" defend respect and care. But the form of the contrast, and the shape of its two poles, remains.

Where anthropologists have entered the fray, they have tended to miss the self-perpetuating nature of this formal dynamic, and thus been captured by it. Talal Asad's (2013) and Saba Mahmood's (2013) attempt to interrogate liberal freedom of speech in the wake of an earlier iteration of the "Danish cartoons" controversy is a case in point. Both deploy a familiar anthropological move, setting up a comparison between what they characterize as liberal notions of freedom of speech and certain selected aspects of Islamic tradition, a comparison intended to defuse triumphalist contrasts between liberal freedom and religious taboos. Asad's (2013) contribution insists on the fact that freedom of speech is nowhere unlimited. Liberal limits on free speech (in respect of copyright for instance), he argues, paint the contours of a self-owning individual; by contrast in some aspects of Islamic tradition – a point developed in greater depth in Mahmood's essay – the objection to insulting images of the prophet hints at an economy of relational entanglements. The "cartoons" are not, as liberal commentators assume, to be read as mere discursive challenges to propositional belief, but rather as attacks on a lived relationship between the faithful and the prophet.

Asad's (2013) and Mahmood's (2013) essays are sophisticated, complex, and carefully structured. And yet the comparative dynamic of free speech debates that I have sketched above exerts such a strong gravitational pull that their claims are constantly in danger of collapsing back into precisely the kind of civilizational contrast that they are seeking to work against. Even Judith

Butler – who is hardly an unsympathetic or unsophisticated reader – restates
Asad's and Mahmood's case in a way that comes to sound worryingly familiar:

> So the critical question that emerges is whether ways of life that are based on
> dispossession in transcendence (and implicit critique of self-ownership) are legi-
> ble and worthy of respect. It is then less a legal question than a broader question
> of the conditions of cohabitation for peoples whose fundamental conceptions of
> subjective life divide between those that accept established secular grounds and
> those at odds with secular presumptions of self-coincidence and property. (Butler
> 2013, 120)

Put like this, the question does little to unsettle the pervasive narrative of a
clash between secular and religious "peoples" as a problem of cohabitation for
liberal democracies.[2] More subtly, while Asad's and Mahmood's comparative
moves go some way towards tempering visions of liberalism as committed
to "unlimited" freedom of speech, they remain somewhat ambivalent about
the place of freedom of speech in the Islamic tradition(s) they counterpose to
this liberal model. As James Laidlaw (2014) argues in relation to Mahmood's
portrayal of freedom more generally in her earlier work *The Politics of Piety*
(2005), it is not clear whether Asad and Mahmood are suggesting that Islamic
tradition as they characterize it offers an alternative vision of free speech or an
alternative *to* free speech. What Asad and Mahmood propose, in fact, is not a
comparison of freedoms of speech, but a comparison of ways in which speech
is unfree, in the liberal West as much as elsewhere (see also the introduction
and Bhojani and Clarke in this volume).

Frontal Comparison and Liberalism

The key issue I wish to surface here is that attempts to set up an anthropological
comparatism along the lines suggested by Asad (2013) and Mahmood (2013)
are overshadowed by their isomorphism with the particular kind of comparatism built into liberal debates about freedom of speech. Both kinds of comparison – all of the comparisons evoked in the previous section, in fact – share a
distinctive structure. They are what I have described elsewhere, in relation to

---

2 By contrast, Keane's (2009) comparative framing of the Danish cartoon debates in light of
Indonesian press bans is much less amenable to such reductive polarizing, even though his
account of liberal semiotic ideology informs Asad's (2013) and Mahmood's (2013) later
characterization – a point I return to below. This is due in part to Keane's attention here and
elsewhere (see also Keane 2007) both to the multiplicity of language ideologies within any
given setting and to what is shared, as well as what is not, across different semiotic ideologies.

anthropology's own comparative devices, as "frontal comparisons" (Candea 2018). To briefly reprise that argument, one can distinguish two modalities or valences within anthropological comparisons. One, which I term "lateral," involves setting up cases side by side, comparing this (and this, and this ...) and that. The other, which I term frontal, compares an "other" context with one marked as the context of a collective "self," which includes the anthropologist and their intended readership. From this simple formal distinction – including or not including "us" as one term of the comparison – flow a number of other differences that give each mode its own quite distinct epistemological and political affordances. The two forms of comparison are interwoven in most anthropological arguments (Asad's and Mahmood's included). I hold them apart heuristically before considering their interplay.

By situating the position of the anthropologist as one term of the comparison, frontal comparisons lend themselves extremely well to the classic anthropological move of self-critique. Frontal comparison has long been the go-to device for relativizing, provincializing, and parochializing Western concepts and assumptions. From that perspective, frontal comparison has often been seen and valued as more radical, philosophically and politically, than the merely lateral consideration of cases side by side. On the other hand, lateral comparisons keep a multiplicity of cases in play, whereas introducing "us" as one term of the comparison tends to draw attention inexorably back towards a single overarching binary. Frontal comparisons as a result are regularly charged with overstating the coherence of the "us" and the difference of the "other," while essentializing both terms. More generously, one might allow that frontal comparisons rely on bracketing the question of where exactly one might draw the line, empirically, between "them" and "us," in order to draw an essentially theoretical or conceptual contrast between the two. Frontal comparisons are in this sense "not-quite-fictions" – one might think of them as empirically grounded thought experiments. The key device through which frontal comparisons achieve this is through a distinctive play on scale: "us" and "them" are scalar shifters, which allow anthropologists to move back and forth between the frontal moment of ethnographic encounters ("Whereas I assumed...") to grander contrasts ("Whereas Euro-American concepts of the person..."). This is not so much a sleight of hand as a performative effect. An anthropologist can succeed in this scaling up if they have correctly identified and can convincingly portray a difference that their readership will also recognize. The "us" of frontal comparison is thus a relational achievement.

This contrast between frontal and lateral modes of comparison was crafted in reference to the heuristics of anthropology, but it can help us recognize some patterns in liberal debates about freedom of speech such as those following the *Charlie Hebdo* killings. To begin with, one can note that, beyond the question of freedom of speech specifically, frontal comparison is deeply entwined with the history of liberalism. As Duncan Bell (2014, 685) has persuasively argued, the currently popular vision of a single broad liberal tradition that can stand as "the constitutive ideology of the West" is surprisingly recent. Bell notes that "while claims about the intellectual coherence, historical continuity, and ethicopolitical superiority of 'the West' stretched back at least as far as the eighteenth century, it was only in the mid-twentieth century that this potent civilizational narrative came to be routinely classified as liberal" (705). Thus while the term "liberal" began to be used as a label for political ideology in the nineteenth century, its extension was significantly narrower than at present and the term was "barely visible in surveys of political thought written [before] the 1930s" (693). Locke himself was not characterized as a "liberal" before that period. The construction by political scientists of a broad liberal canon with Locke as its pivotal figure coincided with the emergence and spread of the term "liberal democracy" as a designator for the American and Western European states. Both moves were deeply entangled with the ideological war against totalitarianisms on the left and the right. The idea of an unbroken and coherent intellectual tradition of liberalism reaching back to the eighteenth century (or possibly to classical Athens) was, according to Bell, a late retroprojection. It was an instance of canon-building in which disparate intellectual and political positions and resources were grouped together and rendered as a characteristic cultural matrix that distinguishes "Western liberal democracies" from their fascist, socialist, or (one might add) theocratic alternatives. As a result, liberalism "came to denote virtually all non-totalitarian forms of politics as well as a partisan political perspective within societies" (705). It became "the metacategory of Western political discourse" (683), which somehow persists despite the often mutually contradictory positions taken up by self-styled liberals.

Returning to the terms I articulated above, we might say that, on D. Bell's (2014) account, liberalism as we currently know it emerged historically in the twentieth century as one term in a frontal comparison – it appeared as an "us" position, dialectically defined by contrast to a "them" position. Freedom of speech sits squarely within that history. Recruited as one central or even foundational feature of the emergent liberal "canon," freedom of speech was polemically defined against state socialist censorship throughout the second half of the twentieth century (Boyer 2003). It survived the demise of its totalitarian "other" by finding another "other" in radical Islam. As Paul Passavant (2002) observes, 1989 was a pivotal year in this respect, marking both the fall of the Berlin Wall and the "Rushdie Affair." The polemical contrast between liberalism and its "other(s)" papers over complexities and contradictions within. Similarly, in their frontal comparisons, anthropologists allow themselves the latitude to generalize about "Euro-America" in order to pick out heuristically some crucial differences that will unsettle their readers' assumptions. Of course, when anthropologists like Asad (2013) and Mahmood (2013) take up "Western liberalism" as one term of their comparisons, they take it up with a critical intent, whereas the canon-builders D. Bell (2014) describes were articulating a triumphalist metanarrative. But the analogy of form – the frontal comparison device – has distinctive effects that are not always easily turned to one's intended purposes.

One of these effects is scalar: frontal comparison is a self-replicating, fractal form. Thus D. Bell's (2014) genealogy allows us to articulate a more precise account of the dynamic Asad (2013, 26) points to when he writes that while "its theorists seek to present liberalism as consistent and unified, ... it is precisely the contradictions and ambiguities in the language of liberalism that make the public debates among self-styled liberals and with their 'illiberal' opponents possible." The double meaning of liberal as a term, which points simultaneously to a civilizational metacategory (all political debate in a liberal democracy is thus – definitionally – liberal) and to a partisan political position within any given liberal political debate, gives it a peculiar scalar dynamic (cf. Latour 2005; Carr and Lempert 2016). Beyond mere "contradictions and ambiguities," there is a fractal, recursive pattern here, of the kind Susan Gal (2002) has identified in relation to distinctions between the private and the public. The fact that critiques of liberalism in Western public debate are themselves, on another scale, an instance of liberal discourse, is one effect of the way a distinction between liberal and illiberal replicates fractally within itself – just like private conversations can take place within a public space, or public figures can allow themselves private moments.

This recursive pattern allows critics to place themselves in a powerfully dual position, both inside and outside "us." Frontal comparison has long enabled anthropologists to speak simultaneously with two kinds of authority – the authority of one of "us," engaging in a self-critique of misconceptions rife in a conceptual world they share with their readers, and the authority of one who sees this world ("us") as merely one context among others.[3] In her comment on Asad's and Mahmood's texts, Butler (2013) (again not unsympathetically) makes explicit the exhortative charge of their comparisons, the appeals they implicitly make to shared moral intuitions. The pattern holds in popular critiques of the excesses of the American First Amendment, or French combative secularism, or quite simply of "the Western liberal approach to free speech." It is because "we" are assumed to share certain moral assumptions (which in the broadest sense could still, as D. Bell [2014] points out, end up being characterized as liberal), that "we" ought to be outraged by the hypocrisy of certain liberal double standards.

---

3 On the mutations of this double authority, from *The Chrysanthemum and the Sword* through to *Provincialising Europe*, see Candea (2018, 279–304).

Yet this double authority also comes at a cost. However radical one's critique of liberalism, it must still, on another scale, remain within liberal proprieties in order to be heard as a frontal self-critique – as a critique of "our" familiar liberalism. Even as they seek to provincialize "liberal freedom of speech," Asad (2013) and Mahmood (2013) are still, after all, exemplifying it. Their work stays within the eminently "liberal" mode of academic disquisition on political matters, in commenting on others they observe proprieties of liberal debate, as well as, of course, the liberal expectations of intellectual ownership in their practices of citation and in the copyright they retain on their own words. The same is true of even the most radical critical positions taken up in the swirling public debates over *Charlie Hebdo*. Insofar as they are cast as critiques of "our" liberalism, they necessarily find themselves exemplifying, on a higher scale, the very principles they critique.

These paradoxes are familiar (cf. Barbara Smith 1993). A more interesting effect of the recursive structure of frontal comparison is that it tends towards a certain kind of repetition in terms of content. This point has been made a number of times of the most frontally oriented anthropological approaches. Critics charge that frontal comparatisms map onto "us" and "them" contrasts and concerns that are actually internal to Euro-American intellectual and political debates – such as contrasts between individualism versus holism, dualism versus monism, or Descartes versus Deleuze (see, for instance, T. Turner 2009; Murray 1993). As a result, anthropology's frontal contrasts tend towards a certain kind of repetitiveness. Not to put too fine a point on it, once one has decided – reductively – that "we" are essentially Cartesian or individualist, one always keeps discovering that "they" happen to be fundamentally Deleuzian or relational (see Holbraad 2017 for an attempt to rebut this critique).

A similar dynamic emerges in the public debates around freedom of speech. Under the dizzying variety of concrete contexts evoked in the *Charlie Hebdo* debates above (the West/Islam, America/Europe, France/America, multiculturalism/republicanism, older progressives/younger progressives, etc.), the same conceptual form in the end keeps replicating. Despite the diversity of situations, characters, and scales, all of these contrasts are polarized around a tension between something like a decontextualized individual freedom and a contextualized social or relational responsibility. Battle is engaged around the respective value of each of these poles and around the nature of the contrast: Are they necessarily interwoven or mutually exclusive? Do they stand to each other as ideal to pragmatic accommodation or as ideology to reality? But the general polarity of the debate is preserved as scales shift up and down. This is how "American campuses" and "Western civilization" can be smoothly deployed in domestic arguments between French republicanist and decolonial leftists. This is how, despite the diversity and multiplicity of issues and framings, the pervasive sense that these multiple debates are after all just "one" debate, in which the only real choice, in the end, seems to be about what balance to strike between two given poles: individual freedom and social limits. Anthropologists building on Louis Dumont's theories of value encompassment have shown in other contexts how a binary between seemingly incompatible values can be shuffled and reshuffled to produce such patterns (Robbins 2015; Iteanu 2015; Moya 2015). In the case of freedom of speech, in end, this binary framing circles back to the quantitative comparative form with which we began, in which different contexts can in principle be *ranked* along a sliding scale between the two bogeys of "First Amendment fundamentalism" (absolute, irresponsible freedom) and "totalitarianism" (total social control).

Of course, Asad and Mahmood are seeking to unsettle this binary between freedom and social context. Following Foucault, they urge that freedom is an effect of social and cultural context, not its opposite. And yet, the form of Asad's and Mahmood's comparison, in which "Western liberalism" is opposed to "Islamic tradition," undermines this worthwhile goal. For once it is recast in these binary terms, the Foucauldian glimpse of multiple social formations of freedom collapses back into a contrast between abstract freedom as a foil (the false story "we" liberals tell ourselves about ourselves) and socialized freedom as an empirical reality (the real truth of liberal freedom as merely possessive individualism). Furthermore, what we find contrasted to liberal visions of freedom as self-ownership and self-sufficiency is once again a more relational reality – a world of persons entangled in affective links that belies the abstractness and detachment of liberal language ideologies. This is a contrastive vision in which, as I noted above, the question of an alternative version of freedom of speech (rather than an alternative to it) fades out of view.

The dynamic is perhaps clearest in Mahmood's (2013) critique of Stanley Fish's response to the Danish cartoons controversy, which begins in terms almost exactly analogous to my own arguments about frontal comparison above, yet ends up restating that comparison in a different mode. The passage deserves quoting at length.

> For [Fish], the entire controversy is best understood in terms of a contrast between "their" strongly held religious beliefs and "our" anemic liberal morality, one that requires no strong allegiance beyond the assertion of abstract principles (such as free speech). I want to argue that framing the issue in this manner must be rethought both for its blindness to the strong moral claims enfolded within the principle of free speech (and its concomitant indifference to blasphemy) as well as the normative model of religion it encodes. To understand the affront the cartoons caused within terms of racism alone, or for that matter in terms of Western irreligiosity, is to circumscribe our vocabulary to the limited conceptions of blasphemy and freedom of speech – the two poles that dominated the debate. Both these notions – grounded in juridical notions of rights and state sanction – presuppose

a semiotic ideology in which signifiers are arbitrarily linked to concepts, their meaning open to people's reading in accord with a particular code shared between them. What might appear to be a symbol of mirth and merrymaking to some may well be interpreted as blasphemous by others. In what follows, I will suggest that this rather impoverished understanding of images, icons, and signs not only naturalizes a certain concept of a religious subject ensconced in a world of encoded meanings but also fails to attend to the affective and embodied practices through which a subject comes to relate to a particular sign – a relation founded not only on representation but also on what I will call attachment and cohabitation. (2013, 69–70)

I couldn't agree more with Mahmood's initial characterization here of the limits of Fish's frontal contrast, which she reiterates in an endnote to this passage: "It is because of this rather impoverished view of liberal ideology that Fish does not appreciate the strong and visceral reactions among secular liberal Europeans against Muslim protests" (95n10). However, Mahmood challenges Fish through a reiteration of a frontal contrast. She recodes the poverty of Fish's view as an instance of what she later characterizes, drawing on Keane (2007, 2009), as a Protestant-inflected, modern semiotic ideology, which she contrasts with "Islamic" relational semiotic ideologies of attachment and cohabitation. Keane's (2009, 58, 60) own account stresses the internal multiplicity of liberal language ideologies. In its rendering in Mahmood's (2013, 72) argument, however, the "dismay that Protestant Christian missionaries felt at the moral consequences that followed from native epistemological assumptions" (in Keane's work on the colonial Dutch East Indies) echoes fairly directly "the bafflement many liberals and progressives express at the scope and depth of Muslim reaction over the cartoons today." Where Fish characterizes liberal ideology as anaemic (by contrast to Muslim strength of belief), Mahmood in the end characterizes liberal semiotic ideology as impoverished (by contrast to a more relational and embodied Muslim alternative). These contrasts are not the same, but the structure of the recursion is clear. Like a phoenix from the flame, polarization between individual abstract liberal free speech and the relational, concrete sociocultural contexts that challenge it seems impervious to deconstruction.

Going Lateral

Impervious to deconstruction, that is, as long as our comparisons remain primarily frontal. What might a more lateral comparative anthropology of freedom of speech look like? So far, I have left lateral comparison in the shadow of its putatively more radical counterpart, frontal comparison. The former has been defined negatively, by the fact that it is not mapped across an "us/them" contrast. But this absence opens up a number of radical possibilities.

As I have noted above, frontal and lateral comparisons are complementary and indeed interwoven within most anthropological arguments. Yet the precision and multiplicity of lateral comparison, its refusal to toe the line of any simple us/them contrast, can also temper, or in a critical mode, challenge and debunk some of the wilder claims of frontal comparison. In particular, lateral comparisons of multiple settings within contexts routinely characterized as Western or Euro-American, can be used to unpick the mechanism through which frontal comparisons project outwards, as a contrast between "us" and "them," binaries and alternatives internal to Euro-American debates.

A striking recent instance is James Laidlaw's (2014) exploration of the multiplicity of notions and forms of freedom in both "liberal" philosophical literature and the ethnographic record, which we discuss at length in the introduction to this volume (see also Venkatesan 2023).[4] Following Laidlaw's example, we might begin by acknowledging the multiplicity of philosophical arguments for (and against) freedom of speech even within the restricted and recondite space of academic liberal legal and philosophical discourse. As outlined in the introduction, canonical liberal philosophical discussions of freedom of speech have come to parse a complex and entangled literature into three fundamentally different justifications for freedom of speech (Stone and Schauer 2021a): the argument from truth turns on the thought that protections from the imposition of orthodoxy by the state or other social pressures are the most effective means of collectively discovering truth and eliminating error; the argument from autonomy sees in freedom of speech a crucial means of self-development for individual persons and a fundamental aspect of their dignity; the argument from democracy links freedom of speech to the possibility for and legitimacy of democratic self-government. These different justifications of freedom of speech rely on different versions or visions of what persons, polities and language are, what matters about them, and the proper relation between them. Furthermore, each of these justifications has been substantively countered and debated, leading to a host of counter-visions and counter-proposals. Thus, even within the limited frame of liberal legal and philosophical discourse around freedom of speech, an anthropologically informed exploration can identify a variety of implicit understandings of how persons, knowledge, and politics are made and unmade through speech.

But this is only a starting point. In seeking to expand and multiply our lateral apprehension of "liberal visions of freedom of speech," we can also reach beyond the legal and philosophical scholarship to historical accounts that are beginning to diversify and reconstitute histories of freedom of expression. Some

---

4 The move also parallels Robbins's (2013) call to multiply the contrast between monism and pluralism.

of these studies highlight the ways in which various distinctly non-canonical visions and versions of liberalism emerged in colonial settings (Hunter 2017; Bayly 2011). Others focus on revising and recasting the canonical settings and periods to which contemporary liberal visions of free speech are indexed, such as ancient Athens (Saxonhouse 2006), the French Revolution (Walton 2011), seventeenth-century Britain (Colclough 2009), or rereading canonical texts against the grain (Peters 2005). All of these studies can radically expand our sense of what has been and, in many cases, continues to be at stake in liberal understandings of and struggles around freedom of speech.

For instance, David Colclough (2009), in his study of freedom of speech in early Stuart England, scans a variety of cultural and philosophical resources and reference points at play in seventeenth-century debates about freedom of speech. In conceptualizing free speech, Colclough argues, classically trained seventeenth-century British subjects engaged with a tradition in which the figure of *parrhesia* – frank counsel to princes – was an established and formalized trope, explicitly laid out in manuals of rhetoric and illustrated through famous classical examples of oratory. Colclough traces the fascinating problems that arose once *parrhesia*, initially seen as the epitome of a risky and unpopular type of sincerity, was characterized as a rhetorical form. Frank and fearless speech, once it is characterized as a formal style, is immediately open to the suspicion of being exactly the opposite: a flattering and calculated appeal to the sympathy of one's audience, as a preface to telling them precisely what they want to hear. As Marcel Proust (1982) wrote in a different context, "The courage of one's opinions is always a form of calculating cowardice in the eyes of the other side."

But *parrhesia*, even thus complicated, was not the only cultural resource available to contemporaries. Preachers and pamphleteers, Colclough notes, drew on a different Christian tradition in which freedom of speech was the attribute of the true believer when facing persecution. Parliamentary procedure and precedent was another setting in which the possibility of and need for freedom of speech was forcefully debated. Finally, Colclough explores a vibrant culture of manuscript miscellanies and "libels" that evaded the system of licensing laws applied to print, and enabled individuals who collected and circulated them among neighbours and acquaintances to experience and shape themselves as participants in the political life of the realm. These various visions overlap and recombine in some key respects, yet they each elicit different types of concern around the nature of the free speaker, the social relations and types of power within which they are constituted, and the nature and effects of speech. In this one single setting, freedom of speech emerges as fundamentally different in its implications, whether one is speaking freely because compelled by faith; or whether under the protection of a formal precedent one is seeking to curate and sustain; whether self-consciously demonstrating one's courage through public frankness; or whether one is privately circulating challenging material to like-minded acquaintances. Some of these modes map neatly onto the semiotic ideology of subject/object separation, abstraction and arbitrariness (Keane 2007), others call up other understandings of language as an affective and embodied vector of attachment and cohabitation. Some of these seem to evoke an egalitarianism familiar to contemporary liberal sensibilities. Others embed freedom of speech within existing hierarchies, in ways that recall alternative versions of freedom articulated in and through community in mid-twentieth-century Africa (Hunter 2017).

Arlene Saxonhouse (2006) shows that classical visions of *parrhesia* that loomed so large in Colclough's (2009) seventeenth-century Britain had a different valence in their original formulation. The key opposite of *parrhesia* in Classical Athens was not state control so much as *shame* – a pervasive sense of deference and keeping one's place in the social order. Cast in opposition, not to external coercion but to senses of propriety, *parrhesia* as "shameless" speech takes on a more complex ethical shading than simply as "speaking truth to power." On the one hand, as shown in Saxonhouse's (2006) account, *parrhesia* was praised and valued as essentially democratic in its irreverence for (some aspects of) sedimented social order, and its concern with the present and future; on the other hand, some measure of decorum and concern with the past continued to be understood as an important feature of any balanced polity. In adapting *parrhesia* to the parliamentary politics of seventeenth-century Britain, and in worrying over the calculations embedded in its rhetorical frankness, Colclough's (2009) subjects were thus moving in a distinctly different direction from the classical sources they were emulating. And yet a concern with decorum and "propriety" as a counterbalancing form to frankness was still woven into the debates that Colclough tracks. It emerges also in the long-standing concern with libel and honour, which fundamentally shaped, for instance, French revolutionary reticences around unbounded freedom of speech (Walton 2011) and continues to inhabit legal cultures of freedom of speech to this day (Candea 2019a; Candea, forthcoming; Post 1986; Whitman 2000). In a different way, this tension between *parrhesia* and decorum, having one's say and retaining a polite consensus, speaks to the different imaginaries of free speech described by Harri Englund (2018a) in his study of a Finnish radio talk show.

As for the religious strand of freedom of speech in the face of persecution, John Durham Peters (2005) offers a fascinating genealogy of its transformations through his rereading of some of the liberal classics such as Milton, Locke, and Mill. Peters tracks the emergence of a liberal vision of freedom of speech that is deeply rooted in an ambivalent and profoundly non-secular concern with evil, not as something that needs to be eradicated, but indeed as a positive test and challenge through which the goodness of the self can be strengthened and shaped. "There is something satanic," Peters (2005, 15) argues, "about many liberal arguments in favour of free expression-satanic not in the sense of gratuitous evil but in the Miltonic sense of confronting or even sponsoring an adversary whose opposition provides material for redemptive struggle." Tracing a line from these Miltonic sensibilities through to contemporary debates over the First Amendment, Peters provides a distinctly unfamiliar yet highly convincing vision of liberal arguments over freedom of speech as fundamentally "enchanted" in their concerns with questions of evil, sin, catharsis, courage, compassion, and pity.

Back to the Present

One might think of the above as "counter-histories" of liberal freedom of speech, which cut against the classic modernization narrative, and this is often how their authors themselves portray them. But it would be a shame to allow this to collapse once again into a (now temporal) frontal comparison. The key value of these backwards glances lies rather in the multiplicity and heterogeneity they uncover. There are many distinct and often mutually contradictory visions of the person, of the polity, and of the nature and effects of language entwined in the history of liberal freedom of speech and these versions and visions continue to shape current debates. Attending to this recombinant multiplicity expands our comparative imaginary. Asad's (2013) observations about possessive individualism can be productively added to this sense of a teeming multiplicity of types and forms of personhood entailed in the imaginaries of liberal freedom of speech. The interweaving of authorship and ownership adds another context – but it is no longer the only context – for understanding and situating liberal freedom(s) of speech.

Tracing echoes and analogues of these different modes of imagining, valuing, and experiencing freedom of speech might help us expand the comparative imaginary of what is at stake in liberal debates around cases such as *Charlie Hebdo* (see Candea, forthcoming). Alongside the "moral narrative of modernity," with its image of "words and pictures [as] vehicles for the transmission of opinion or information among otherwise autonomous and unengaged parties" (Keane 2009, 57)[5] and its vision of subjects as self-owning authors (Asad 2013), lie a number of other aesthetics and semiotic ideologies of free speech. Some of them are at cross-purposes with these familiar delineations of the modern self. For instance, the repeated references to courage and bravery in justifications for publishing the cartoons draw their conviction from a well-established, yet very different vision of free speakers to that of disengaged,

---

5 Keane (2009, 58–60) himself acknowledges the multiplicity of language ideologies in liberal settings.

abstracted transactors of meanings. Conversely, the move through which critics of *Charlie Hebdo* (or earlier, *Jyllands Posten*), dismiss such appeals to courage as empty rhetoric, recall the concerns over the parrhesiastic style as a route to flattering one's audience, while safely reaffirming its prejudices. Similarly, the frequent discussions of taste and aesthetics that gravitate towards *Charlie Hebdo*'s "ugly, ugly" drawings (CM 2015), feed off of concerns with decorum, moderation, and shame that have never left the ambit of liberal discussions.

In 2007, a Parisian court cleared *Charlie Hebdo* of having broken the French freedom of the press law for (re)publishing cartoons depicting the prophet Muhammad (see Candea, forthcoming). This same court is also the setting in which French intellectuals and public figures come to settle their affairs of "honour and consideration" in a legal tradition that harks back self-consciously to the late-nineteenth-century culture of duelling (Candea 2019a; cf. Whitman 2000). As part of their decision in the *Charlie Hebdo* case, the judges noted that some of the drawings could be taken to damage the "honour and consideration" of Muslims, yet that *Charlie Hebdo* was not seeking to "wound" (*blesser*) Muslims but to take part in "a public debate which was in the general interest" (Pasamonik 2007). Thus when Mahmood's (2013, 76) Muslim interlocutor says that the *Jyllands Posten* drawing of the prophet "felt like it was a personal insult," they were speaking in a language that French law recognizes perfectly well. Something important is lost in the argument that such claims are inaudible because of a liberal semiotic ideology that "fails to attend to the affective and embodied practices through which a subject comes to relate to a particular sign – a relation founded not only on representation but also on what I will call attachment and cohabitation" (71). There are extensive resources within the broad cacophony of liberal semiotic ideologies for acknowledging attachment, cohabitation, and the relational injuries made through speech. In a detailed analysis of the court case (Candea, forthcoming), I have suggested that one might distinguish at least three modes in which freedom of speech was envisioned and enacted. At the risk of caricaturing them, one might briefly describe these as, respectively, a Habermasian concern with reasonable public discourse; a Bakhtinian passion for untrammeled excess; and a Foucauldian commitment to daring relational honesty. These modes entail very different semiotic ideologies, visions of personhood, and understandings of freedom, even though they coexist, ally, and clash within the discourses of liberal defenders of the cartoons and echo also among some of the cartoons' most vehement critics. While I do not have space to pursue this argument in detail here, the broader point is that, in asking why this particular relational claim to injury was so difficult to hear and could so easily be trumped by other concerns, we need to reach beyond stark contrasts between "our" representationalism and "their" relationalism, if only because contrasts cast in those terms are still, after all, "our" contrasts (cf. Strathern 1988, 19).

Freedom, Freedom Everywhere?

I have mainly focused in this chapter on one restricted problem: how to multiply our comparative account of the variety of liberal freedoms of speech. Important as this question is to anthropologists of Europe and America, this may seem a parochial concern for anthropologists more broadly. Worse, expending so much effort on elucidating and taking seriously "our own" complexity may seem like precisely the kind of navel-gazing that anthropology was built to unmake and move beyond. Critics will object that "we want anthropology to reach and remain in the far territory, out in the open, away from the ironical recesses of the liberal intellect and thus faithful to the project of exteriorizing reason – the project that, nolens volens, insistently takes our discipline out of the suffocation of the self" (Viveiros de Castro 2011, 132). Yet this parochial concern has the critical potential of unmaking certainties about the "us" and the "self." In doing justice to the complexity of liberal understandings of freedom of speech, we also allow ourselves to encounter – as something other than a counterprojection of "our own" concerns, other visions of freedom of speech, and alternatives to it, beyond that liberal conversation.

In closing, I should reiterate that I have here overdrawn, for the purposes of argument, the contrast between frontal and lateral comparisons. The two forms are deeply imbricated within anthropological arguments: grand frontal contrasts build on more modest lateral collections of instances; lateral comparisons work from and across cases each of which is often grounded in a frontal comparison on a smaller scale. Indeed, the forms themselves are variations of each other – as I have outlined elsewhere, one might think of frontal comparison as a special case of lateral comparison, a "mutation" that nonetheless retains many of its original features (Candea 2018).

The distinction is rather a matter of emphasis, a matter of where the account and the narrative are made to come to rest. Thus, one could easily draw together the various historical and philosophical strands outlined in the previous section into a singular account of liberal freedom of speech, particularly if we hedge this account with plentiful acknowledgments that there are exceptions, and order it internally by adding a direction of travel (away from enchantment, or honour, or shame, and towards the detached, self-possessed individual, for instance), or a contrast between "dominant" and "minor" strands. Or one could, as I have tried to do here, hold these various strands apart, bracket questions of priority or historical direction, while of course acknowledging that there are family resemblances and recombinant connections across these different liberal imaginaries of freedom of speech. The difference between these two comparative sensibilities is not likely to be amenable to empirical resolution – how do we finally settle the amount of real difference within and between conceptual traditions? Rather, which comparative device we choose to emphasize is a matter of purpose. I have argued in this chapter that lateral comparison provides a more effective way of challenging the self-similarities of liberal debates over freedom of speech than a frontal comparative challenge, which in the end risks repeating the logic it seeks to undo.

This matters because, as I have noted above, there is a surprising kinship between frontal comparisons that reiterate a sharp contrast between "us" and them," and the quantitative visions of a world of contexts arranged along a single scale of degrees of freedom. The kinship is less surprising perhaps if we recall the way in which, in anthropology, critical visions of frontal comparison emerged out of, even as they sought to challenge, the gradualist visions of nineteenth-century evolutionism in which "we" played the role of an endpoint in a trajectory through multiple "thems." If there is fundamentally just one kind of difference (Heywood 2018), then it is an easy step to imagine it as a matter not of absolute or heuristic contrasts but of a scale of more or less.

By contrast, the lateral sensibility I have tried to evoke here challenges – in a more stable and reliable way than a frontal critique – the quantitative mapping of freedom from which this chapter began. These multiple versions and imaginaries of freedom of speech are not mutually fungible, either in putatively liberal contexts or anywhere else. There is no single scale along which the above cases can be ranked, as in a global index of freedoms. There is no single scale, not because evaluation is somehow abandoned and politics forgotten, but precisely because evaluation and politics are multiplied. There is no single scale because there are many scales.

2 When Speech Isn't Free: Varieties of Metapragmatic Struggle

WEBB KEANE

Introduction

Free Expression or Semiotic Transgression?

The words "freedom of expression," I suspect, are most often taken to refer to a political and aesthetic good. They invoke an emancipatory narrative of struggle against the unenlightened or anti-Enlightenment forces of suppression over centuries. It is a tale with a clear directionality to it, in which the forces of church, state, conformism, and bourgeois morality slowly give way to those of reason, progress, individual autonomy, artistic creativity, and, above all, democracy (Rosenberg 2021). And yet for roughly the last half century, that progressive storyline has become increasingly less straightforward. When feminist-inspired speech codes were first introduced in the 1970s, progressives often found themselves defending constraints on speech, and "freedom" became a rallying cry for the right (Cameron 1995). More recently, incidents of book banning in American libraries and charges of "cancel culture" and so forth have further tangled the narrative thread.

Nor are the parties to these arguments easily parsed into straightforward divisions between left and right. For example, anti-pornography feminists have battled pro-pornography ones, and secular leftists may side with traditionalist complaints about religious defamation. Recent years have seen a flurry of cases in which avowedly progressive academics have been attacked by other progressives for mentioning the so-called N-word in the classroom, even when they do so to condemn the very racism the word expresses (Flaherty 2018; Parikh 2018). Euphemisms have a way of absorbing the toxicity they were meant to avoid, so let's call this "racist lexicon."

Vehement reactions to the academic citation of racist lexicon seem to break down the purported "use/mention" distinction. This refers, for example, to the difference between the speaker's own intentions and those they attribute to someone else whom they are quoting. Those who object even to quoting or mentioning certain words invoke various reasons for their reactions. These include the assertion that the very utterance of the word, no matter how much the speaker disclaims it, is an act of violence and/or can trigger trauma in the hearer. Objections like these tend to scandalize liberal thought (McWhorter 2021). How, they may ask, can the mere citation of a word be an act of violence in and of itself? And hasn't the word been detoxified when taken up by the appropriate speakers, as in rap music (Crenshaw 1993), much as the word "queer" was resignified by LGBTQ+ activists?

It goes without saying that current responses to uttering racist lexicon, at least in the United States, must be understood in the context of a larger struggle against racism and the rise of increasingly unrestrained expressions of white ethnonationalism (Hodges 2020b). And a growing body of research finds that hate speech can exact a psychological and somatic toll on those at whom it is directed (Delgado 1993; Silva 2017). But racist lexicon is not unique in confounding the supposed use/mention distinction. After all, there are still certain scatological and obscene words, like the "F-word," that the *New York Times* will not report, even when quoting the speech relevant to the story.

This chapter is not about racist lexicon as such. My purpose is both narrower and broader. It is narrower because I cannot possibly attempt to address all the issues that racist lexicon involves. It is broader because it points us towards a host of problems in the power and politics of language – ones that extend well beyond the anglophone context. To understand conflicts over free speech we must examine the modalities of semiotic *un*freedom and the risks, transgressions, and harms that can be imputed to verbal expression. Defenders of freedom of expression and those who oppose them often presume different *semiotic ideologies* (Keane 2009, 2018b). As a result, they may fail to grasp or take seriously just what the problem between them is. If the defence of free expression is not to become mere shadowboxing, it should grapple with this problem.

Semiotic transgression refers to any of the acts that can be attributed directly to signs themselves. The field includes libel, slander, defamation, blasphemy, obscenity, incitement, hate speech, threats, and pornography, but it can be extended as well to the revealing of secrets, sedition, idolatry, plagiarism, copyright infringement, perjury, and other sorts of dissimulation, even lying (Bok 1989; Denery 2015). These are the kinds of acts that may prompt censorship, taboo, euphemism, or legal sanctions – and sometimes physical violence. As we will see, such semiotic actions and reactions often involve a *metapragmatic struggle*.

In many of these cases, for the action to be transgressive, it must be taken to be intentional. This is, for instance, the distinction between a lie and an error, and a defining feature of American libel law. When speakers defend their mention of racist lexicon, for example, they may invoke their benign intentions. But stressing speaker intentionality can depoliticize the act by turning the action and its effects into private matters of interior subjectivities and hurt feelings. As I will suggest, this often misses the point. And some semiotic transgressions, like blasphemy and obscenity, need not depend on anyone's intentions at all.

Semiotic transgression, therefore, is not confined to purposeful acts, discrete events, or particular kinds of addressee. Some acts centre on immediate interpersonal relations, others are more diffused in their social range. This chapter is an attempt to sketch out some of the contours of this field by looking at name taboos, blasphemy, pornography, linguistic sovereignty, and truth-telling. Disparate though these topics are, a pragmatist approach to verbal expression reveals some of the features that semiotic transgressions share. It may shed light on why the supposed use/mention distinction can fail to insulate purportedly innocent occurrences of prohibited words.

Representational Economy

Semiotic transgression takes place within a *representational economy*. This refers to how different media, their infrastructures, and the larger social context can have unintended effects on one another that go beyond those of logic, meaning, or interpretation: they can also be matters of brute causality. For example, the advent of photography changed what it was possible for painting to achieve. In effect, it pulled the rug out from under the function of providing mimetic representation. At the same time, the ability to reproduce paintings mechanically had consequences for the uniqueness of the individual work of art. One might then argue, contrary to Walter Benjamin's (1935) celebrated thesis, that the European work of art in the age of mechanical reproduction acquired *more* aura rather than less, because only after there are reproductions can there be an "original" as understood today. (It may be that AI chatbots will soon do something similar to writing!)

Two special aspects of representational economy concern us here. The first is intertextuality, of which the use/mention distinction is a species. The variety of ways that texts can circulate, and ways in which one instance of a sign can be taken as identical to another, make it extraordinarily difficult to define an incontestable context within which words should be understood or responsibility attributed (see Hill and Irvine 1993).

The second aspect is the relationship between visual and linguistic media, including such things as gesture (e.g., the *digitus impudicus*, or giving someone the middle finger; see I. Robbins 2008) and dance (e.g., twerking; see Onishi 2010; Sarahtika 2018). As we will see, the sign's transgressive character may or may not be preserved under transduction, the move from one medium to another (Silverstein 2003b; Keane 2013). In the United States, for instance, where state control of media is often viewed with suspicion, restrictions on television have been more acceptable than those over print, on the grounds that print functions to inform more than does television, which regulators considered at the time to be primarily a medium of entertainment (Bollinger 1991). (Think of the one-time Fox News political commentator Tucker Carlson's legal defence against charges of lying on air, to the effect that no one would take him seriously: he's just an entertainer.)

Both aspects involve identifications, seeing one way of using a sign (e.g., "citing") as tantamount to another ("using"), or taking one semiotic medium (e.g., "burning a cross") to be equivalent to another (e.g., "issuing a verbal threat"; see *Virginia v. Black* [2003]). Arguments about freedom of expression often turn on disputes about these equivalences – that is, they are metapragmatic struggles.

Metapragmatic Struggle

The founder of philosophical pragmatism, Charles Sanders Peirce (1955, 99), defines a *sign* as "something which stands to somebody for something in some respect or capacity." This broad definition indicates that the same "something" (technically, the "sign vehicle") can stand to someone else in some different capacity. If a full-fledged sign includes not just that "something" or vehicle but also what it stands for and how it does so, then it follows that there is no such thing as a sign *as such*, independent of those *for whom* it serves as a sign. This introduces an irreducibly social component to signification, the consequences of which are crucial to arguments over freedom of expression.

The pragmatist definition has another important implication. To stand "in some respect or capacity" refers to the famous distinction among icon, index, and symbol. These denote the different ways someone might take a sign to be connected to the object it signifies. A sign is iconic if it is taken to be connected to its object by virtue of resemblance (e.g., a portrait to its subject; or, more to the point here, a quotation to the speech it quotes). It is indexical if it is taken to be connected to its object either causally (e.g., as smoke to fire) or by juxtaposition (e.g., an exit sign over a door). It is symbolic when the connection is established by a rule or convention (e.g., the so-called arbitrary signs of language).

Icons, indexes, and symbols do not simply exist as facts of the matter – they are possible ways someone can *take* the sign to signify. How one takes sign and object to be connected is a function of semiotic ideology (Keane 2018b). For example, many Muslims hold the language of the Qur'an to be an indexical icon of divine speech. It is iconic because its very sound resembles divine speech, because it was originally uttered by, and thus indexically linked to, a divine being. By contrast, for a Saussurean linguist, that same language is symbolic – a set of arbitrary signs established by convention. When an expression becomes so toxic that even its mention is disturbing, the iconicity of form comes to the foreground. Even near homophones may have to be euphemized.

Of particular importance for understanding semiotic transgression is indexicality. Luke Fleming (2011, 144) notes that the most common linguistic forms subject to verbal taboos are those that are inherently indexical. As Peirce ([1885] 1933, 211) writes, the indexical sign "takes hold of our eyes … and forcibly directs them to a particular object." An index can impose itself on us like a blow or a shock (one of Peirce's more vivid examples of indexicality is a bullet hole in a wall). Systems of deference like Javanese speech levels function in part by elaborately muting the directness of reference to the person being deferred to, as if to blunt the blows of indexicality (Errington 1988).

For these reasons, indexicality plays a central role in the social actions that signs can carry out. Indexical signs can "point" in two directions (Silverstein 1976, 2003b; Nakassis 2018). *Presupposing* indexicals indicate something that is given in advance: smoke points to the prior existence of fire, a Brooklyn accent to the speaker's origins in that borough of New York. But indexicals can also be *creative* or *entailing*. Creative indexicals bring something new into the context through the very act of using them. To point towards a chair brings that chair into play as the object of reference, just as to utter the word "I" constitutes the speaker as the person being referred to.

The two sides of indexicality work in a dialectical relation to one another to configure manifest social identities and relations (Gal and Irvine 2019). Students being taught elementary French are commonly told that certain rules determine whom you address as *tu* and whom as *vous*. This treats these deference indexicals as presupposing fixed social identities – say "tu" to your sister, "vous" to your teacher, and so forth. But in practice a shift in pronouns can redefine a relationship, for instance from one of hierarchy to equality, or intimacy to distance (Friedrich 1979). Moreover, indexicals are commonly multiplex: my skill at displaying respect *to you* (a deference indexical) also reflexively signals *my own* character or sensitivity (a demeanour indexical).

Inferences of indexicality depend on what Peirce calls abduction – a best guess for now, subject to revision. The intuitions that guide abduction are directed, in part, by semiotic ideology. By their very nature, indexical signs are vulnerable to contestation. They are potentially subject to metapragmatic struggle. By this I mean the struggle over how to define a situation in a given context: what is going on here, who is doing what to whom, and who are they to one another. Whatever else is going on when people argue, whether the utterance of a certain word is "use" or "mention," it is always a metapragmatic struggle over the definition of the situation.

To gather the full import of this struggle, consider this pragmatist definition: "a *conception* ... lies exclusively in its conceivable bearing upon the conduct of life" (Peirce 1966, 183). It follows that signs are not just vehicles for transmitting meanings, ideas, or information in any conventional sense. "The conduct of life" is precisely what metapragmatic struggle is often about. In the process, that struggle determines what aspects of the larger context (what histories, ontologies, identities, projects, solidarities, etc.) *count*. And it is only through the mediation of signs that anyone has access to the conceptions in play in any situation. If it can seem that arguments about semiotic transgression pay too much attention to signs rather than to something more substantial, this is because it is only through signs that people engage with one another. This is crucial to how politics and power shape and are shaped by the flow of everyday experience.

Domains of Transgression and Unfreedom

Self

Like racist lexicon, many systems of name taboo do not observe a use/mention distinction and focus on specific lexical items in discrete interactions between one individual and another, as members of certain classes of person. Across a wide range of languages, the pre-eminent object of avoidance is the personal name. The name is commonly linked to its bearer by virtue of an original indexical act, some version of a "baptismal event" (Kripke 1980) that establishes a direct and singular connection between name and person. Like the second person singular pronoun, the use of the name in address has the marked effect of picking out an individual and pointing at them. Name avoidance is often motivated by the effort to mute or blunt this very pointedness and the intimacy it can imply. The courtier who addresses the queen as "Her Majesty" is replacing direct address with third person reference to something other than the addressee. In some systems of verbal deference, such as Javanese speech levels, entire registers are shaped by the blunting of indexical force (Errington 1988). And one may reject one's own name, like members of the Nation of Islam, who took new ones (e.g., Muhammad Ali) or place markers (e.g., Malcolm X) in order to repudiate the indexical links to the enslavers who had un-named and re-named their ancestors (Benson 2006).

The figurative violence of indexicality can become literal. One of the first riots after the fall of Indonesia's President Suharto's authoritarian regime in 1998 was triggered by the violation of a name taboo. It occurred on Sumba, during a local election in a newly competitive political landscape. Tensions between supporters of the regent and his opponent came to a head when demonstrators openly called out the tabooed name of the regent. In the resulting battle, at least twenty-six people were killed and an entire village burned to the ground (Mitchell 1999; Vel 2008, 136–7).

Obviously uttering the name was merely the match that lit the kindling, but the sense of outrage it provoked was real. To make sense of this, I draw here on my earlier analysis of central Sumbanese name avoidance (Keane 1997, 129–33). Everyone has an "original name" given at birth. It is bestowed through a divination process implying spiritual sanction. Only those family members intimate enough to witness this event are authorized to know it. At least it remains a public secret, in place of which people use a substitute "name that is uttered." Over a lifetime, additional layers of protective naming such as nicknames, teknonyms, titles of office, or the name of a favourite horse shroud the dignity of the person. The name you utter thus indexically presupposes the degree of your intimacy with its holder.

Name taboos often elaborate on the fact that you only know the original name through a chain linking you to that first baptismal act (Fleming 2011, 145; Stasch 2011). To utter the original name is as intrusive as the brute act of pointing. Since my name is most often spoken by others, it is in *their* use of my name that *my* identity is publicly recognized: delicacy around the uttering of my name displays my reputational dependence on others, the vulnerability of my self-possession. To demonstrably avoid that name indexically presupposes that which is not said, reproducing the power of its suppression. The violent reaction to the public utterance of the regent's name on Sumba was a response to an assault by outsiders on that potent zone of intimacy.

God

In some cases, there is only one name taboo, the ultimate one, that of a divinity. The way divine names and other sacred words are handled indexically presupposes an overarching ontological system with potentially far-reaching implications well beyond face-to-face interaction.

In 2008, the Vatican announced that the use of the name "Yahweh" should be avoided in Catholic liturgical settings out of respect for Jewish teaching (*The Compass* 2009). Protestant churches, by contrast, play down the name's power. This reflects the Reformation's moral narrative of a historical emancipation from erroneous attachments to the materiality of signs (Keane 2007). The semiotic ideology underlying this remains evident in secular form in the linguistic doctrine of the arbitrariness of the sign: the sounds and shapes of language are merely vehicles that contribute nothing to the immaterial meanings they convey.

In Islam, the Qur'an consists of divine words that were transmitted orally by the angel Gabriel to the Prophet Muhammad. The nature of this transmission places an enormous premium on the very sounds of the text. Seen in this light, the Arabic language is not merely a set of arbitrary signs that serve to transmit the real message but an embodiment of that message. Divine content is inseparable from semiotic form, its sound part of its moral power (Gade 2004; Haeri 2003; Sells 2007). It is for this reason that it is commonly held that the scripture cannot be translated, only paraphrased.

Although renderings of the Qur'an in other languages are common, they normally take this background into consideration in one way or another. So when a prominent Indonesian literary critic, H.B. Jassin, ignored this scruple when translating the Qur'an into Indonesian in the 1990s, he received strenuous pushback from clerics (Keane 2018a). Among their objections was his attempt to reproduce the beauty of the original in what he described as "poetic" language. It is widely accepted that the Qur'an's verses are indeed beautiful, but Jassin, schooled in a self-consciously cosmopolitan appreciation of European high literary culture, was presenting the scripture as a text on a par with other great literature. His critics saw this as a dangerous category error, conflating two ontologically distinct *kinds* of signs. In their view, to treat the scriptural words as arbitrary signs even implicitly, as Jassin did by equating them with other literary texts, is to threaten the security of the connection to Allah established by that original vocal transmission. They argued that it threatens the community of the faithful who are constituted as a "we" by virtue of being the addressees of divine speech (Alatas 2021).

For this reason, one of the primary accusations against Jassin was that his translation posed an existential threat to the community itself. The Qur'anic linguistic sign here is treated as indexically creative, a constitutive form of address. To put it on a plane with other literary texts risks taking as indexically presupposing that its words have only an arbitrary relation to their meanings, grounded in the intentions of a human author. In the European literary tradition, this relative arbitrariness is one precondition for authorial agency, the freedom to wield signs as one will – to be a creator. To some of Jassin's critics, this comes too close to competing with the Creator.

Yasmin Moll discusses a related set of problems in her work on a religious television station in Cairo in the 2010s. The station grappled with an emerging representational economy that included print media, oral sermons, TV, radio, and the internet. One challenge was how to handle the translation of Arabic sermons for English-speaking viewers. Translators sometimes worked with sermons they considered to be doctrinally incorrect. As Moll (2017, 351) notes, "the task of the translator was not to 'literally' translate but rather to attempt to understand the meaning behind the speaker's words and to rephrase it in a manner appropriate for the target audience. This meaning was fixed not by the intentions of the speaker but rather by the intentions of God and the Prophet." For instance, one interpreter left untranslated a preacher's dubious assertion, lest she "be complicit in the serious sin of slander through further circulating this potentially false assertion through subtitles" (355). As with racist lexicon, the use/mention distinction fails to hold.

Transgressions, like blasphemy, turn on ontological predicates whose practical consequences are mediated by semiotic ideologies. Seen in this light, constraints on freedom of expression do not arise from censorious agents like church or state, but from the very nature of things. If God demands the respect of name avoidance, we are not free to utter His name with impunity. If divine truth and its moral meanings have been transmitted in a sacred language, we are not free to manipulate its semiotic form, since that form is an indexical icon of its own divinity. If the ultimate source of our expression is itself divine, we should avoid participating in error. On the other hand, if divine truths are fundamentally immaterial, as maintained by certain strains of Islamic and Christian purism, too much attention to semiotic form is itself potentially idolatrous, a fetishistic distraction (Keane 2007).

Sex

According to one moral narrative of modernity, immaterial meanings are detachable from their materialization in semiotic form. This favours the view that signs function above all as vehicles of reference and denotation. It makes it hard to account for *other* effects that signs and their forms might have on the world. Underlying one of the prominent liberal defences of free expression (as this volume's introduction points out, there are others) is the semiotic ideology that signs convey meanings but are *in themselves* merely empty vehicles, created and wielded by human agents.[1] In this view, signs do not cause things to happen apart from the cognitive effects of the meanings they transmit, nor does their material form have any significance in its own right. One of the most obvious counters to this claim is pornography, whose function is physical arousal. But there is no agreement on just what is the nature of the semiotic transgression in question. Here I consider two alternatives in the American context: the scriptural hermeneutics of evangelical Protestants, and the secular rationality of anti-pornography feminists.

By the first decades of the twenty-first century, evangelical Protestants remained a strong exception to the ongoing decline in Americans' support for the banning of pornography. According to the sociologist Samuel Perry, however, the reasons they opposed pornography had changed since the 1980s. Whereas earlier pornography had been seen as a threat to moral purity, increasingly it

---

1 Arguably even US Supreme Court Justice Oliver Wendell Holmes's (1918) "clear-and-present-danger" test for suppressing speech, which acknowledges that speech can be a harmful action, focuses more on speakers' intentions than on the sign vehicle.

was being portrayed in psychological terms, as a source of harmful addiction. The idea of pornography addiction is based on the claim that its habitual use harms the brain by rewiring neural circuitry (Perry 2019, 714). In effect, there is a materially causal relationship between the sign and its effects.

But pornography still remains a moral problem as well. Curiously, Perry reports that over the same period masturbation mostly lost its moral disapproval among religious authorities. He attributes this divergence to two features of evangelical thought, biblicism and pietistic idealism. Biblicism refers to the familiar semiotic ideology that (among other things) "the Bible is God-inspired and inerrant" (701). The current consensus among evangelical pastors is that the Bible contains no reference to masturbation (the story of Onan having been misinterpreted in the past), and therefore offers no guidance to its morality (708). On the other hand, lusting after partners other than one's spouse is clearly proscribed by scripture. The distinction is reinforced by pietistic idealism, the claim that "ideas or beliefs rather than actions are what truly matter to God (701). In this light, if masturbation is carried out without fantasies about illicit partners, as some evangelicals say is possible, then the material act itself is morally neutral. By contrast, consuming pornography – even without any physical actions other than reading or viewing it – presents the consumer's mind with partners who, being other than their spouse, are illicit.

Unsurprisingly, many feminists arrive at their opposition to pornography by way of quite different semiotic ideologies. Although feminist discussions of this topic are diverse, complex, and highly contested, for the purposes of this chapter I will consider just one important intervention. The philosopher Rae Langton refines Catherine MacKinnon's (1993) arguments for banning pornography. Defining pornography as the "sexually explicit subordination of women in pictures or words" (quoted in Langton 1993, 294), MacKinnon attacks it not just for its sexual content, but for taking women as its object. Subordination is something that pornography *does* even without *depicting* it. Put in semiotic terms (not Langton's or MacKinnon's), pornography *indexically entails* a relation of subordination between an indexically presupposed male consumer and (any) female.

Moreover, both MacKinnon and Langton claim, the effects are found well beyond the scene of immediate consumption: if evangelicals worry about pornography's causal effects on the individual viewer, MacKinnon and Langton are interested in its consequences for women who may never directly encounter it. In short, they seek to explain pornography's effects on the entire representational economy in which it operates.

Langton aims to show how pornography defines certain actions, establishes their possibilities, and distributes them among possible social actors. Drawing on J.L. Austin's (1962) speech act theory, she argues that pornography silences women by making certain illocutionary acts impossible for them. The argument turns on an essentially metapragmatic contrast between speech and act. Under the American Constitution's First Amendment, courts have ruled that pornography is protected *speech*. The classic liberal defence of freedom of speech by thinkers such as John Stuart Mill ([1859] 1989) equates speech with ideas. It privileges the semantico-referential "content" of expression over pragmatics.

Langton (1993, 328) reverses this priority. The harms effected by pornography are not about ideas, she says, "but about people and what they do ... because it constrains people's actions." This claim rests on two presuppositions. One is that a key felicity condition for any illocutionary act is uptake. If a woman says "no" to a man and he does not recognize that she means it (that "No means no," as the slogan goes), then her speech act of refusal is infelicitous – a metapragmatic consequence. This is different from a situation in which a man understands what she means but chooses to ignore it. The former, I suggest, is a social effect on a representational economy, the latter the personal result of an individual choice.

Langton mentions in passing the memoir of the actress known as Linda Lovelace, who starred in the notorious 1972 movie *Deep Throat*. She wrote the book in order to expose the abuse to which she was subjected in her work in the pornography industry, but she was unable to control the context in which the book was taken. As a result, the book was sometimes marketed as pornography, her very objections being taken – like the rape victim's "no!" – to be further incitement to sexual fantasy.

This metapragmatic failure has to be understood within the representational economy in which texts and images circulate across an anonymous public and an indeterminate number of markets – some of which, according to Langton, are more authoritative than others. We might see here an analogy to the objection to mentioning racist lexicon. It may be that the aftermath of Donald Trump's presidency in the United States, in which expressions of overt racism receive authorization from high sources, is so powerful that it overwhelms any attempt at local metapragmatic control of the word's uptake.

But how exactly does pornography determine felicity conditions and bring about the "illocutionary disablement" of women's intentions to speak in certain ways? This turns on a second presupposition, that pornography holds a certain authority (within what I am calling a representational economy) to define "which moves in the sexual game are legitimate" (Langton 1993, 312). But does pornography hold such a systemic authority? This is an empirical question. At this point, the logic of speech act theory and its focus on face-to-face interaction reach their limits, and we need an analysis of the social and political struggle to establish and stabilize metapragmatic frames.

Sovereignty

So far our focus has been on actions – uttering a tabooed name, manipulating divine speech, producing and consuming pornography – that test the limits of freedom of expression by putting different semiotic ideologies about agency into contention. Some problems of freedom, however, concern entire semiotic systems in which questions of agency are diffused. The model of direct assault or affront is less helpful for understanding these. What is at stake in some kinds of prohibition may be not so much individual acts as collective identities and their claims to sovereignty over, or on the basis of, certain semiotic systems.

How far to go in accepting the ethical limits to knowledge and its legitimate circulation is a long-standing conundrum for anthropologists. As a discipline developed in the scholarly episteme of the Global North, anthropology is predicated on certain largely tacit assumptions about the inherent value of knowledge and its unhindered dissemination within a marketplace of ideas. But the slow process of decolonization has made it increasingly difficult to ignore or override the objections of communities that try to control others' knowledge about them.

Erin Debenport (2015) writes of her work on the language revitalization project of one of the casino-wealthy Rio Grande pueblos, which she calls San Ramón, where the language she pseudonymously dubs Keiwa has a dwindling number of fluent speakers. However, despite the work of the language revivalists, the pueblo governors decided to keep the written materials they had produced from circulating freely even within the pueblo itself. Debenport ultimately chose not to include any linguistic tokens of Keiwa in her monograph about the project. She goes beyond leaving things out: she displays excerpts from texts in the language that have been blacked out, as if by a censor. In this way, the reader cannot avoid seeing that there is something there to which they do not have rights of access.

Debenport's strategy is consistent with the larger pedagogical goal of the project leaders, in effect teaching the reader the appropriate stance towards local knowledge. The leaders were treating texts not just as linguistic samples, but as ethical instructions to the reader about how to behave and to live in a proper, traditional way. Given that much of this way of life is presently unavailable to the addressee of the texts, this resulted in an aspirational act of creative indexicality seeking to bring about that to which it points. In effect the leaders were treating what to the linguist looks like mere citation or mention as real uses of language. These uses of language are inseparable from the social and cosmological relations they entail.

Discussing a similar case, in which the Hopi sought legal control of a dictionary of their language, Jane Anderson, Hannah McElgunn, and Justin

Richland (2017, 197–8) conclude that labelling some items as sacred and se-cret positions the reader as a non-initiate and thereby "restores something of the social relations that underlie tribal distinctions about access to knowledge." Through stringent restrictions on rights to textual artefacts bearing tokens of the language, Hopi seek to establish a metapragmatic frame in accord with "specific cultural rules of obligation, responsibility and circulation" (194). In their view, for an individual to use the language "freely" is to deny the respon-sibilities entailed by the community membership its use presupposes. This in-volves a strong form of iconic indexicality in which semiotic form and practice are tightly bound to social identity.

Protecting some of the specialized knowledge of ritual even from those other Hopi who are non-initiates helps sustain the efficacy of the practices. Each kiva in a Hopi village, for instance, controls certain rites that must be kept from the others. This representational economy facilitates the "radically decentralized Hopi theocratic order, giving the different clans and ceremonial societies that make up Hopi society an important, but different, role to play in the welfare of the community as a whole" (Anderson, McElgunn, and Richland 2017, 190). If in the Islamic examples noted above semiotic action is constrained by the need to bind a community through address by a singular voice, here the constraints arise from the need to construct community by assuring the conditions for mu-tual interdependence by diversified address.

The effort to control the circulation of the Keiwa and Hopi languages is a direct confrontation of a community with the representational economy that ar-ticulates them with the larger, vastly more powerful society surrounding them. In the final examples, I turn to another set of contestations over representa-tional economy. Here we should consider the marketplace of ideas model of freedom as itself a particular understanding of the representational economy, in which neither media nor agents, nor their effects on one another, are given much specificity.

Truth

One classic argument for freedom of speech envisions a marketplace of ideas. In a seemingly egalitarian refusal to grant anyone the authority to determine the truth, the market puts ideas in competition with one another. Against this view I have tried to establish two things. First, a semiotic ideology that takes the primary function of expression to be the conveying of information through reference and denotation often fails to grasp the nature of semiotic action (even though referring and denoting are themselves actions). As Susan Seizer (2011, 218) points out, when stand-up comics exclaim "fuck!" they are rarely referring to copulation. Contrary to Supreme Court Justice Antonin Scalia's assertion that this supposedly normal denotational content is invariably their meaning, the pragmatics of words like "fuck" and "shit" as used by Seizer's comics virtually never depend on their purported referents but rather on the pragmatics of expressive transgression.

At stake in arguments over freedom of expression is often a struggle over metapragmatics. The very denial or downplaying of the pragmatic dimension of speech, like Scalia's, is itself a metapragmatic claim. To reiterate, metapragmatic struggle is about defining what kind of action is going on in any given instance, on whose authority, including what participants, and with what possible consequences. These actions often take their power from the dialectics of indexical presupposition and creativity as they play out within a representational economy. At stake is the determination of social identities and relations among them.

But do these get at what most worries many people about constraints on freedom of expression? The forces of repression are not just phantoms: the press, for example, is under siege in many countries, where journalists often work in mortal danger (Blanchard 2019). So let me be clear: in raising questions about freedom of expression, I am certainly not calling for its suppression but for a clearer self-understanding of what underlies arguments around it. The examples given so far do not concern the circulation of ideas or truth claims pure and simple but are primarily speech insofar as it is recognized as action. But of course, truth-telling is itself a kind of action. Here I turn to the idea that truth emerges from the marketplace of ideas. One alternative to the marketplace model is the ancient Greek idea of *parrhesia*. In Michel Foucault's (2019) version, this refers to the obligation of one person to speak the truth to another. *Parrhesia* is speech addressed to someone more powerful by someone who is less so. The freedom to speak this way is something that is granted from above, by the speaker's master, prince, or spiritual councillor. This is a crucial difference from the marketplace model, which tends to portray ideas as contending on a level field. By contrast, *parrhesia* presumes inequality as a given.

Whereas the marketplace is agnostic regarding truth, the parrhesiast has no doubts: he (and Foucault's examples are typically male) says what is true because he thinks that it is true, and he thinks that it is true *because it is really true* (Foucault 2019, 41–2). He has no need to produce evidence for his truth claims. You might say here is a pre-modern standpoint epistemology. Certain people know the truth *simply by virtue of who they are*. By contrast, a virtue of the marketplace model is precisely that, at least in principle, it grants no one a privileged grasp of the truth.

Perhaps the most prominent modern candidate for the role of parrhesiast is the journalist in struggle against an oppressive regime. Consider one clear case of the state suppressing truth-tellers (see Keane 2009). In 1994, Indonesia's Ministry of Information shut down the newsweekly *Tempo* after it had reported on internal disputes within Suharto's authoritarian regime. Although *Tempo* was considered one of the most influential periodicals in Southeast Asia, its elite readership was miniscule compared to the tabloids (Steele 2005). Yet unlike the regime's far more violent actions, including several massacres, this suppression provoked an unprecedented wave of public protests. We can make sense of the public response in light of the observation by the social scientists Ariel Heryanto and Stanley Yoseph Adi (2002, 51) that "all dominant narratives of the rise of the nation in Indonesia are inseparable from the history of the press" (see also Anderson 1991). Tirto Adhi Soerjo, founder of the Dutch East Indies' first Indigenous paper in 1903, referred to himself as the "defender of the common people" (*pembela rakyat*), anticipating what came to be the dominant image of the press in Indonesia a half century later, the "press of struggle" (*pers perjuangan*) (Pramoedya 1985), propelled by "crusading journalists" (*wartawan jihad*) (Atmakusumah 1992).

The idea that the press speaks for the nation turns on its role as a teller of truth. Moreover, it does so against an identifiable opponent who tries to suppress that truth. It is the existence of this opposition that defines what will count as freedom (Boyer 2003; Candea 2019b). Indeed, one might argue that it is precisely the experience of repression that has made the metonymic idea that the press is, or should be, the voice of the people so persuasive.

In Indonesia, all this changed when press controls were rapidly removed after Suharto's fall. The representational economy was dramatically transfigured as free-wheeling, and newly commercialized media sprang up. Many of the same journalists who had fought bravely for freedom of expression found themselves worried that things had gone too far. One editor who had previously risked prison in order to expose the regime's violence wrote: "The hundreds of newspapers sold on the streets are full of slander and abuse ... with a rhetoric that knows no bounds" (Ajidarma 1999, 170–1; cf. Cody 2015). With gossip, accusation, and salaciousness on the rise, newspapers and magazines became more profitable, making it harder to overlook the fact that they were selling a commodity. In the absence of a clear, powerful opponent, the courageous truth-telling of journalists became harder to square with their role in the actual political economy of the media. Real though the constraints of the market are, they are diffuse and hard to portray in the same agonistic light as those posed by the clearly defined censor. Truth-telling journalists who had previously faced suppression found themselves instead to be unconfined by anything other than the demand they produce saleable goods. Lacking an identifiable censorious agent, journalists found themselves engaged in metapragmatic struggle, the stakes no longer a truth suppressed but whether "truth" was even at stake in the first place. This is the world that helps lay the groundwork for the accusation of "fake news."

Conclusion

As I've argued here and elsewhere (Keane 2009), a tacit premise of some of the most prominent defences of free speech is a certain semiotic ideology. In this view, words and pictures are (at least normatively) vehicles for the transmission of opinion or information among otherwise autonomous and unengaged parties. This ideology treats the information they bear to be content largely independent of the activity of representation or the semiotic forms it takes. Speech, in this view, is only action by virtue of the intentions of the person wielding it. Certainly, in any given moment, other semiotic ideologies are in play even in the Euro-American context, for instance in Marxism, psychoanalysis, Burkean conservatism, satirical and subversive performance, Black Twitter, queer counter-discourses, numerous religious traditions, all sorts of literary styles, to say nothing of post-colonial and subaltern thought and the so-called new censorship theory (Bunn 2015). And, as the introduction to this volume makes clear, there are other grounds for conceiving of and defending free speech. But the view I sketch here dominates much of contemporary public debate in the West.

In contrast to this semiotic ideology, one argument against accepting even "mentions" of racist lexicon is that the word as such evokes the entire history of previous, explicitly racist "uses" of it (Lawrence 1993). This argument foregrounds the iconicity that links the sonic or graphic form of one utterance to previous utterances. To focus on those links (as advocated, for instance, by critical race theory) resituates the immediacy of face-to-face interaction within the deeper histories that focusing on the intentions of individual speakers obscures. "Mere form" in this way can – under certain metapragmatic construals – help forge links across different scales of social time and place (see Benson 2006; Carr and Lempert 2016).

The speaker, of course, may object to how those links are taken by the offended listener, to say "that's not what I meant." But just as we should not reduce meaning to conscious intentions, so too it is a mistake to reduce the taking of offence to magical thinking or individual psychology. What's often at stake is a question of authority, a metapragmatic struggle over who gets to define "what is going on here" and "what is the context" and "for whom." Outside special cases, the individual speaker's intentions cannot do this alone.

The detachment of social relations from their semiotic modalities is one reason why it is often so difficult to deal with verbal or visual expressions of hatred or sexual violation. To the extent that signs are "mere" words or pictures, it can be hard to see clearly how they are also modes of action in any serious way, beyond, say, making misleading truth claims or hurting someone's feelings. Even accepting that they are actions, they are actions often understood as taking place between otherwise independent agents. But, as the examples of pueblo language and pornography show, metapragmatic struggle can engage entire semiotic systems, the communities that sustain or try to claim them, and the relations of power they entail.

Pragmatism emphasizes the creative, socially consequential, dialogic, and potentially conflictual processes of semiosis. For the object of a sign – what it is a sign *of* – is never simply a static anchor for signification. Semiosis, mediated by semiotic ideology, summons new contexts and new objects into existence, just as others change or disappear.

Just *how* a sign is taken is shaped by – though not reducible to – the projects and needs of people who take them to *be* signs of a certain sort (Gal and Irvine 2019, 100–1). "Who" those people are, who they are to one another, what they are engaged in doing together, and with what consequences are, if not wholly open-ended, also not entirely fixed in advance. They are defined and redefined through metapragmatic processes. Semiosis indexically presupposes the identities that it creatively brings into play and whose relevance it establishes or denies – this race, that gender, this tribe, that faith, this social status, that character flaw (Fleming and Lempert 2011). This is the field of metapragmatic struggle.

At stake in the unfreedom of speech is often the defining of social relations. The resignification of racial and ethnic slurs, like the defence of private or secret vocabularies, takes place at the shifting boundary between insider and outsider: the rapper or gay activist, Sumbanese kin or pueblo elders, may be authorized to use certain words that others should not. In using them, they are indexically *presupposing* their identification with a community that they are engaged in the indexically *creative* act of defining.

Whatever else may be going on, those who object when someone they define as an outsider utters the very same words they themselves might use are often denying that that person has the metapragmatic authority to presuppose the context in which their words will be taken. When someone objects to the "citation" of, say, racist lexicon or sacred names, they do not necessarily have to claim psychological harm, memories of historical racism, or personal affront. Their objection might just amount to this: "I do not accept *your* assertion of the right to tell me, unilaterally, how *I* should take your choice of words." And thus, perhaps, "I doubt that we share the reality your semiotic actions presuppose."

Only through the mediation of signs do people have access to, establish, affirm, and contest one another's thoughts, feelings, intentions, moral character, values, affiliations, political motives, and social identities. This is why arguments about semiotic transgression can be far more than just quibbles over "mere" words, gestures, or images. Obviously constraining or suppressing signs does not magically change power relations just like that. And of course, no one can fully control semiosis. But signs articulate the immediate field of experience – you talking to me, for instance – with social realities and their histories. It is by establishing the indexicality of signs that different scales of politics and power are brought, palpably, into the here and now. You might say that those who object to even the "mention" of racial slurs, the "quoting" of sacred texts, the "citation" of secret names, are demanding that we not forget this.

Acknowledgments

I am grateful for input from Sarah Buss, Matei Candea, Don Herzog, Paolo Heywood, an insightful anonymous reader for Toronto University Press, and the participants in the Cambridge Freedom of Speech: Anthropological Perspectives 2021 conference and in the Michicagoan Linguistic Anthropology faculty workshop, especially the extensive input of Summerson Carr, Susan Gal, and Michael Lempert.

3 Speaking for Oneself: Language Reform and the Confucian Legacy in Late Colonial Vietnam

JACK SIDNELL

Introduction

In the winter of 1906, Phan Châu Trinh, a former mandarin who had resigned his post in the colonial bureaucracy the year before to pursue reformist politics, arrived at the home of nineteen-year-old Phan Khôi, accompanied by a mutual friend, Nguyễn Bá Trác, and sporting a new haircut: "shaggy short hair, wrapped in a headscarf."[1] Recently returned from a trip to Japan, Phan Châu Trinh stayed with Phan Khôi for several days before inviting him and Nguyễn Bá Trác to accompany him first to the village of Diên Phong, where they collected another young man named Mai Dị, and eventually to the village of An Chánh where they stayed with a friend of Phan Châu Trinh who was a farmer of tea and cinnamon. Phan Khôi reports that when he entered the farmer's house, he noticed the "most amazing thing": everyone there, from worker to owner, had the same short haircut. Phan Khôi and his two friends, with their long hair tied in a bun on the top of the head in the usual Confucianist style, seemed markedly out of place.

When the group sat down for their first breakfast together, Phan Châu Trinh, renowned for his persuasive speeches, remarked:

> People everywhere, but especially we Confucians, are timid and are often afraid to act. Whenever there is something to be done, they find an excuse, saying: "Small things, are not worth doing." In their minds, they think, I'll wait for the big one. But if they already have the intention of not wanting to do something, everything will be small to them, so they will do nothing for the rest of their lives! (quoted in Phan Khôi 1939)

---

1 The most detailed account of these events is in Phan Khôi (1939). I also draw here on discussions in Sinh Vinh (2009), Marr (1971), and Jamieson (1993).

This, according to Phan Khôi, was a typical beginning for Phan Châu Trinh, who revelled in telling moral anecdotes, but then he continued: "If we judge by appearances as to whether a person is old-fashioned, only three of us sitting here … are out of date, because these three brothers still have a bun on top of the head" (quoted in Phan Khôi 1939).

Everyone smiled while the three young men sat in bashful silence. Phan Châu Trinh continued using the French rather than the Vietnamese verb to convey his exhortation, "Will any of you *cúp*? Don't say it's a small thing. If you can't do this, I wonder what you can do!" After the meal was over, the group went to the threshing house and, there, the host's younger brother cut the top knots off the heads of the three young Confucians: "the hair from the three heads filled a basket." Although the cut was clumsy, Phan Châu Trinh, sitting in a chair like a monk, complimented each one of the young men, saying: "Good cut! It's beautiful!"

On their way home, the group stopped off at the village of Diên Phong again and there encouraged others to cut their long hair as well. About sixty men did so. Soon, others, having heard of the hair cutting trend, came to visit and were persuaded to join in. This included eminent, reformist former mandarins such as Huỳnh Thúc Kháng and even Phan Khôi's old teacher Trần Quý Cáp. By 1907, many more had joined the hair-cutting movement. Wherever there was a school, someone set up a shop to offer haircuts (this having become a lucrative business). The superintendent of the school at Diên Phong started barbering in his spare time and Phan Khôi composed a little folk song (*ca dao*) for him to sing as he worked:

Tay trái cầm lược,	The left hand holds the comb,
Tay mặt cầm kéo,	The right, the scissors,
Cúp hè! Cúp hè!	Clip! Clip!
Thẳng thẳng cho khéo!	Straight, straight, be careful!
Bỏ cái hèn mầy,	No more with cowardliness,
Bỏ cái dại mầy,	No more with cowardliness,
Cho khôn, cho mạnh,	Get wise, get strong,
Ở với ông Tây!"	You are living with the French![2]

The chant served to contextualize the haircut, specifying the meaning of an otherwise indeterminate symbol by associating it with courage, wisdom, strength, and a new modern, Western outlook (all central principles of Phan Châu Trinh's

---

2 The translation is from Vinh Sinh's edition, *Phan Châu Trinh and His Political Writings* (2009, 21–2). Sinh, somewhat surprisingly given the issues I point to below, complains that this song has often been mistranslated by previous scholars. A more literal translation reveals some details that are relevant to the present discussion. First, the expressions *Bỏ cái hèn* and

political stance). The movement gathered momentum and during the uprisings of 1908, demonstrations included the cutting of hair. Gradually, the short hair-cut came to be seen as a sign of defiance – not only a rejection of Confucian tradition but of the status quo more generally, including the French colonial government. The French began to refer to these activities as the "Révolte des cheveux tondus." Meanwhile, Phan Khôi's "haircutting chant" spread through-out the country, spawning more elaborate versions, with additional verses. The song had been composed of four syllable lines, a common metre of folk poetry and also of proverbs. As such, it could easily accommodate additions of this sort. One of the added lines was a proverb *ăn ngay, nói thẳng*, which translates as "eat immediately, speak straight" and, used in context, means "speak freely" or "speak without fear." This addition further specified, or, better, metasemiot-ically elaborated, the symbol of the short haircut by linking it to a new inter-actional freedom and a self-consciously modern approach to communication in which relatively autonomous individuals, "abstracted from the constraints of former social entanglements" (Keane 2002, 67), might debate matters of common interest and concern.

Freedom and Unfreedom

In "A Plea for Excuses," J.L. Austin (1957) advocates an approach to the study of action, and philosophy, that focuses on occasions of failure and misfire and more specifically on the particular ways we talk about such occasions, that is, the way such failures are defended, justified, excused, explained away, and so on. Such a method, he suggests, would allow us to describe a "model of the machinery of acting" (6). In the course of his discussion, almost as an aside, Austin makes the remarkable assertion that, "in this sort of way ... a number of traditional cruces or mistakes in this field can be resolved or removed. First among these comes the problem of Freedom" (6). He goes on:

> While it has been the tradition to present this as the "positive" term requiring elucidation, there is little doubt that to say we acted "freely" ... is to say only that

---

Bỏ cái dại are more precisely rendered as "Let go of cowardice" and "Let go of foolishness," and thus clearly suggest a reluctance to change. Second, both of these exhortations end with a dialect variant of the non-honorific second person, singular pronoun *mày*. Given that the song is addressed to Confucianists being encouraged to cut their hair (learned men in other words), the use of this pronoun embodies a rejection of traditional practices of address that force speakers to position themselves and their interlocutors within social space. Finally, although often taken to mean "the French" or "France," *tây* actually means "West," and this is surely closer to what is intended here – that is, not the French colonial administration but the "the West" conceived of as all that is new and modern.

we acted not un-freely, in one or another of the many heterogeneous ways of so acting (under duress, or what not). Like "real," "free" is only used to rule out the suggestion of some or all of its recognised antitheses. As "truth" is not a name for a characteristic of assertions, so "freedom" is not a name for a characteristic of actions, but the name of a dimension in which actions are assessed. In examining all the ways in which each action may not be "free", i.e., the cases in which it will not do to say simply "X did A," we may hope to dispose of the problem of Freedom. (6)

For Austin, then, the philosophical attempt to identify "freedom" as a universal value or a decontextualized quality rests upon certain underlying and wrong-headed assumptions about the relation of language to reality; it is yet another manifestation of a widespread "'descriptive' fallacy" (Austin 1962, 3).

As anthropologists and ethnographers we, like Austin, are committed to the study of "freedom" and other such notions not as metaphysical qualities or ontic bedrock but as historically situated concepts that people use to think and talk about the particular circumstances in which they find themselves. Words such as "freedom" demand an analysis as much in terms of their performative effects as their purported referential extension. At the same time, even if we enrich the analysis with ethnography, an anthropological account demands more. After all, the people we study are not limited to the kind of unselfconscious usage that Austin's (1957) analysis seems often to presuppose (though note that excuses are inherently reflective acts). Indeed, it's doubtful that such a thing could exist (see Lempert 2013). Like the philosophers Austin (1957, 9) criticizes, the people we write about are concerned as much with "the beautiful" as with "the dainty and the dumpy," and, in some contexts at least, as much with freedom as with what is permitted and what is prohibited. If it is true that ordinary speech contains the "wisdom of the ages" – "a battery of distinctions that men have found useful through the centuries, and which have stood the test of time" (Williams 2014, 43) – it is also true that such usage, and the ways of thinking which it provides for, are subject to more or less continuous reflective consideration, critique, and reanalysis. What Peirce (1998, 270) called "hypostatic abstraction" plays an essential role here. This is the process by which "goodness" is derived from "good," which converts the proposition "Opium puts people to sleep" into "Opium has a dormitive virtue" (Peirce 1976, 49), which, in other words, "furnishes us with the means of turning predicates from being signs that we think or think *through,* into being subjects thought of" (Peirce [1906] 1933, 549).

Thus, while it may be true that saying one acted freely is to say only that one "acted not unfreely," it also seems to be the case that people often talk and think about these matters through the lens of quite abstract concepts such as, for instance, "freedom" and "liberty" and so on and that this allows them to consider the problem in other than purely negative terms (i.e., "not unfreely"). In this way, freedom can indeed come, contra Austin, to serve as the "name for a characteristic of action." Specifically, through these processes of reflexive reanalysis, particular ways of speaking (along with other aspects of conduct) may combine to form a cultural model of positively free action. In the case I discuss here, hairstyles, dress codes, and other aspects of embodied conduct, social life, and artistic production were linked to a wide range of lexical and grammatical alternates so as to constitute a recognizable way of speaking and acting "freely" (see Agha 2004).[3]

My remarks in what follows focus, then, on the way questions of freedom and free speech, or at least their nearest analogues (*sự tự do,* "freedom"; *tự do ngôn luận,* "free speech"), were posed in the writings of some Vietnamese intellectuals in the 1930s, and in the work of the journalist, essayist, and poet Phan Khôi in particular. Phan Khôi and his contemporaries identified two obvious yet very different obstacles to be overcome in their struggle for freedom. On the one hand, there was the often brutally repressive French colonial state and the persistent threat of censorship by the government and, more immediately, the "Sûreté Générale Indochinoise" established by Governor Albert Sarraut in 1917 with the expressed aim of preventing the development of Vietnamese nationalism. On the other hand, there were the lingering effects of a Confucian past, imagined as an enduring legacy of stultifying, esoteric, and rigid moral behavioural codes reaching back well into the precolonial period.

My focus is on this second obstacle and my main contention is that we cannot hope to understand how freedom was conceptualized in this (or any other) context without first attempting to understand the forms of unfreedom from which people sought to liberate themselves. To this end, I consider a number of arguments put forth by Phan Khôi, beginning with those in which he described Confucian tradition as a sickness that limits and constrains thinking, prevents self-realization and inhibits the cultivation of moral integrity, before then turning to those in which he suggested that the widespread practice of referring to the participants in a communicative encounter using kin terms forces the speaker to make explicit his or her relation to those being addressed and so anchors all communication to its context of occurrence. Comparing Vietnamese with French and Chinese, Phan Khôi suggested that this requirement emerges as particularly inconvenient and troublesome with the rise of text-mediated public discourse in the twentieth century precisely because it frustrates any

---

3 An added complication for the Austinian account is to be found in the fact that such reflective activities not uncommonly involve the conjunction, if not confrontation, of two or more languages (e.g., in this case, French and Vietnamese), each embodying a quite distinct point of view.

attempt to transcend local particularities so as achieve the "utopian universality" (Warner 2005) of a truly modern, public sphere.[4]

Within a few months of publishing his essays on language reform, Phan Khôi (1932b) introduced what he described as a new approach to poetry, one that abandoned the strict conventions of the Tang-style "regulated poem," as well as the looser requirements of Vietnamese *lục bát* (six-eight) metre which, by general agreement, had achieved its most refined expression in Nguyễn Du's epic *Tale of Kiều* composed in the second decade of the nineteenth century. In the short essay, which accompanied his poem "Old Love" (*Tình Già*), Phan Khôi proposed that the old forms had been exhausted and that a new style of verse was required to express adequately the intentions of the modern poet. In this way, he advanced an argument for the reform of poetry that paralleled almost exactly his arguments for language reform in general – here too he found old Confucian traditions to be an impediment to the exercise of a universal human freedom.

The Vietnamese case suggests two conclusions of broad significance for an anthropological approach to the problem of free speech – both quite obvious but important nonetheless. First, the modernist, liberal conception of free speech is intimately tied to the imagining of, and the infrastructural conditions for, a particular kind of public discourse in which persons are able to participate as self-abstracted individuals. As Nancy Fraser (1990, 59) puts it, in this context, "discussion was to be open and accessible to all, merely private interests were to be inadmissible, inequalities of status were to be bracketed, and discussants were to deliberate as peers." Because, in reality, what someone says and how they say it is always shaped to a large extent by the context in which it is produced (e.g., by whom it is said, to whom it is addressed, to what it responds), the very notion of "free speech" presupposes just the kind of disembedding and decontextualization that the liberal public sphere promises to provide. Second, and relatedly, the notion of free speech, or at least some familiar rendering thereof, assumes a near total and radical disassociation of language and "communication" from all other aspects of social conduct and social life more generally. That is, language and communication have to be conceptualized in a particular way for the idea of free speech – as a *specific kind* of freedom – to gain traction. In the period of Vietnamese history I am concerned with here, we can see one way these interdependencies – between language, speech, and social life – can manifest. In relation to his contemporaries, it was

---

4 Phan Khôi also wrote several essays addressing questions of free speech explicitly (see, for example, Phan Khôi 1936). In this he argued that (1) the freedom to speak is not something one can "ask for," and (2) even if the Vietnamese people had the right to free speech, many at least would not be able to exercise such rights.

Phan Khôi who most clearly articulated a vision of public life within which a person might freely express their views as a self-abstracted individual, and it was he who suggested that in order for this to be realized some degree of language reform would be required. Not surprisingly, about twenty years after he made these arguments, he was arrested for his participation in what was perhaps the first "free speech" movement in Vietnam.

Colonial Censorship: Confucian Invisible Strings

The early decades of the twentieth century were a time of quickened change and profound social transformation in Vietnam, especially within intellectual circles. Before the 1900s, both education and advanced literacy were elite pursuits available only to a small number of Vietnamese people. Mandarins, trained in the classics of Chinese civilization, monopolized intellectual life and wielded considerable influence as high-ranking civil servants in the colonial administration. Then, in an effort to undermine the power and prestige of the mandarins along with the practices of literacy upon which it was largely predicated, the French colonial government introduced local schools and actively promoted the romanized orthography that came to be known as *quốc ngữ*, the "national script." Within twenty years, *quốc ngữ* had all but completely replaced Chinese as the language of higher learning as well as the old system for writing Vietnamese, which involved the use of Chinese characters in somewhat idiosyncratic and often cryptic ways to represent Vietnamese words. The emergence of *quốc ngữ* (which had been invented some 250 years earlier by Jesuit missionaries Alexandre de Rhodes and Francisco de Pina) coincided with the availability of modern printing technology and the result was an explosion of literacy. In 1918, Emperor Khải Định issued a declaration abolishing the traditional writing system based on Chinese characters. And, in 1919, the colonial government suppressed the Confucian examination system, thereby forcing Vietnamese elites to educate their children either in French, Vietnamese, or some combination of the two (see DeFrancis 1977; Zinoman 2002).

As Shawn McHale (2004, 5) puts it, these changes, resulted in a "dramatic expansion in the use of the printed word." McHale surmises that "by the mid-1930s, 10 to 20 percent of the population was literate and that this figure was increasing" (27). A lively public discourse emerged in the pages of *quốc ngữ* periodicals ranging from the generally conservative *Southern Wind* (*Nam Phong*), the more progressive *Women's News* (*Phụ Nữ Tân Văn*), to the self-consciously modernist *Mores* (*Phong Hóa*) and *These Days* (*Ngày Nay*). Although committed in principle to a relatively free press, the French were nevertheless concerned that this would provide a forum for nationalist and anti-colonial sentiment and perhaps an instrument of revolution. Not surprisingly, colonial authorities in Indochina attempted to tamp down protest and unrest through censorship of radical political views in periodicals. Newspapers and weeklies were, intermittently at least, subject to pre-publication review and censorship. Books were less controlled and, by all accounts, the more radical and politically volatile volumes tended to sell out before the authorities were able to ban them. Despite such limits of effective enforcement in practice and the ambivalent stance on press freedom in principle, the sense that speech was constrained and, in many ways, unfree was widespread. However, many journalists and writers of the day saw another threat to their freedom as a far greater concern: like Marx, they imagined the traditions of "dead generations" weighing "like a nightmare on the brains of the living." More specifically, they characterized the Vietnamese people as trapped within a Confucian social order, which, through its capacity to ritualize and thus regulate the most mundane aspects of everyday life, had produced persons incapable of self-realization and autonomous action (see Marr 1981).

This view was articulated most clearly and explicitly in the writings of members of the avant-garde "Self-Reliant Literary Group" (Tự Lực Văn Đoàn, sometimes translated as "Self-Strengthening Literary Group") formed in 1932 by Nhất Linh and Khái Hưng. For instance, in his Đoạn tuyệt (Severance of ties, or Breaking away) published in 1935, Nhất Linh used the image of invisible strings to describe the way in which women were tied to the oppressive gender roles and normative expectations of the traditional Vietnamese family. The novel tells the story of Nguyễn Thị Loan, a modern-oriented woman who is forced to marry a man in exchange for money that her parents need to pay off a debt. Loan moves into her new husband Thân's home but finds that his primary loyalty remains focused on her mother-in-law. Loan eventually becomes pregnant and gives birth to a son, thereby fulfilling a key duty as a wife and daughter-in-law. However, the child becomes sick and dies after the mother-in-law insists on treating him only with traditional medicine. Thân marries a second wife and when tensions arise due to this polygamous arrangement, Loan accidentally kills Thân with a letter opener. She is tried and exonerated in the colonial court but, as Tran (2017, 76) writes, she "is only truly free after her father, husband, and son die, enabling her break with the social bonds of Confucianism. This trinity represented a woman's 'three obediences' throughout her life: obedience to her father as daughter, to her husband as wife, and to her son as widow."[5]

---

5 In Vietnamese, tam tòng, tứ đức, "three obediences, four virtues." As Tran notes, the three obediences demanded that a woman recognize the authority of the father, the husband, and the son. The virtues specified appropriate modes of feminine comportment in the domains of công, "work" (skillful in women's work), dung, "appearance" (neat and attentive to one's own appearance), ngôn, "speech" (graceful and compliant), and hạnh, "behaviour" (well-mannered and respectful).

The group shared this understanding of Confucian tradition as an oppressive, totalitarian regime of largely unconscious custom and habit reinforced through the ritualization of everyday behaviour with many other intellectuals of the day, including Phan Khôi whose writings on language extended these ideas in important ways.[6] For, if these conceptions so permeated everyday life, making it nearly impossible to escape from them, what was the mechanism by which that hegemony was achieved?

Phan Khôi's Critique of Confucianism and His Proposals for Modernizing Language Reform

Compared to the authors of the Self-Reliant Literary Group, Phan Khôi was older and had received a much more traditional education. Born in 1887 to a family of Confucian scholars, he earned a *tú tài* degree in the regional examinations of 1905. This was, however, insufficient to secure a position in the colonial bureaucracy, and Phan Khôi began to explore other options. He first worked as a teacher of Vietnamese *quốc ngữ* and of Chinese characters at a school associated with the Duy Tân movement (a campaign for reform led by Phan Châu Trinh). Sometime in early 1908, he travelled to Nam Định to study French with the writer Nguyễn Bá Học but after only a month was arrested for his participation in nationalist activities and was imprisoned at Hội An until 1911 (Jamieson 1993, 109–10, offers a slightly different chronology). After writing for many different newspapers in the 1920s, in 1929 Phan Khôi settled in as the star editorialist for the weekly periodical *Women's News*. This was an innovative publication explicitly addressed to women but not to them exclusively – it featured articles on a broad range of topics. Moreover, it responded to the widely held contention that women would figure centrally in the process of modernization.

Like members of the Self-Reliant Literary Group, Phan Khôi identified the legacy of Confucianism as a particularly significant obstacle to modernization in the Vietnamese context. In part, this was a result of the way in which

---

6 "For the Self-Strengthening Literary Group, Confucianism permeated all aspects of social life, from ritualized events to personal habits and behavior. Self-Strengthening authors viewed it as an institution of doctrines and principles enforced by the familial collective: Confucian beliefs condition, saturate, and organize social life, in particular, through the reinforcement of gender differences. From their perspective, Confucianism is limited neither to the erudite traditions of the civil service examination and its mandarin candidates nor to the realm of religious doctrines to which followers adhere for moral or spiritual guidance. They did not understand Confucianism as a repertoire of ideas and principles that individuals referred to for specific situations but instead as a ubiquitous and accepted social force that compelled individuals to act and behave accordingly, unaware of the imposed rules, roles, and norms" (Tran 2017, 72).

Confucianism had penetrated the consciousness of everyday life and so exerted lingering effects even when it was explicitly rejected. Thus, in an essay titled "Confucianism and Democracy," he wrote: "Up until now we have never had a bold and powerful program of reform to overturn the corrupt thinking of Confucianian scholars. This kind of thinking takes root and grows in the minds of people and so runs very deep and is naturally very stable even though Confucianism is falling into decay" (Phan Khôi 1937).

Along similar lines, Phan Khôi (1930a) described Confucianism as a sickness that manifests as a willingness to discuss matters without first researching them, and as a refusal to base one's arguments on historical fact. Confucianism, rather, encourages the summary of all things in a single sentence, or even a single word.[7]

Like the members of the Self-Reliant Literary Group, Phan Khôi located the source of the sickness in the traditional family. As he bluntly put it in another essay also published in 1931, "I write this article, intending only to report … that Vietnamese society is sick, the family system is no longer suitable for it; … the family in this country has become a problem." Phan Khôi was quite explicit about the connection between family organization and politics, suggesting later in the same essay that, in reviewing human history, one finds that, "never has a people suffered oppression in the family and yet managed to achieve freedom within society" (Phan Khôi 1931a).

And again, with his contemporaries in the Self-Reliant Literary Group, Phan Khôi focused much of his attention on women and particularly on the dire consequences of the traditional family system for in-marrying wives. He suggested, for instance, that laws surrounding marriage treat women as "things" that are owned by their husbands. Moreover, even if the husband dies, the widow is not permitted to remarry – thus the relationship of bondage is maintained in perpetuity. According to Phan Khôi (1932a) these laws treat women as things not as persons, though, "in reality, a person has freewill (ý chí tự do) and is therefore different from a thing!" Elsewhere, perhaps meaning to invoke Rousseau, Phan Khôi (1929a) writes, "A person born into this world is a free person … Woman and girls are also people (so why say) one is inferior to another?"

---

7   Some aspects of Confucian language ideology in Vietnam are discussed by Luong (1990). In a book that argued for the continuing relevance of Confucianism in the twentieth century, Trần Trọng Kim ([1930–2] 2012) wrote of differences between Eastern and Western practices of reading and the use of language more generally, suggesting, for instance, that "the Chinese usually think intuitively and sum up their ideas in a few short sentences," whereas Western learning "uses reason and makes deductions and inferences, proceeding continuously from one point to another." Phan Khôi reviewed the book in *Women's News*, and this led to an extended exchange with Trần Trọng Kim over several subsequent issues.

It is clear, however, that Phan Khôi sees the traditional family as just one element in a larger totalitarian social order. In the traditional Confucian system, a person is caught in a series of nested social relations, and within each of these the person is conceptualized as belonging to others, as a possession, or as an instrument – in this way, there's no room for freedom or autonomy.

> One is not only subordinate to the king alone. Anyone who has parents, must say that the body belongs to the parents as long as they live. And not the body only, if one has property, has a wife and children, one must say that all this also belongs to the parents. According to the *Book of Rites*: if a son loves his wife but the parents hate her, then he must leave his wife. And if a son hates his wife but his parents love her, then he must get along with her ... This is much too strict. Most important is the king and the parents. Then comes the mandarin, the village, the extended family, all of whom also have rights over a person ... [A person like this] cannot be his own master; he is always subordinate to king, parents, mandarin, village, clan, and, if it is a woman, then she is also subordinate to her husband as well. Because of that, our society is like a ladder with many steps. (Phan Khôi 1928)

Against this conception of dependence on hierarchically arranged others, Phan Khôi insists on the fundamental autonomy of the individual, which he glosses as "belonging to oneself" (the word is *tự chủ*). This, he says, is the root of individualism (*cá nhân chủ nghĩa*).[8] And while Phan Khôi (1928) emphasizes the oppressive effects of institutional structures, he nevertheless maintains that, because a person is innately endowed with a capacity for critical judgment, freedom is within reach of everyone. He concludes: "And so, whomsoever takes ownership of himself (*tự chủ lấy người ấy*) is subordinate to no one. That's why there is freedom."

In conjunction with this critique of the Confucian social order, Phan Khôi develops a parallel psychological argument that opposes the blind adherence

---

8 Although Phan Khôi (1928) indicates that this idea of individual autonomy has been most fully realized in the West, he also suggests some Eastern precedents. For instance, he cites a line from the *Tale of Kiều*: "Between heaven and earth he lived free" (*Đội trời đạp đất ở đời*, line 2171),

Đội	trời	đạp	đất	ở	đời
Carry on one's head	heaven	kick	earth	LOC	life

Huỳnh Sanh Thông (1987, 199) writes: "Carrying heaven on [his] head and trampling the earth, [he] lived in the world.' To 'carry heaven overhead and trample the earth underfoot' (*đội trời đạp đất*) is to lead a proudly independent life, acknowledging nobody's authority."

to tradition with, on the one hand, the exercise of critical judgment, and, on the other, the universal standard of truth. Truth is a universal measure that can be applied to any religion, any way of thought.

> In my opinion, those people who are considered educated in this life, really should not close their eyes like in the old days, but must have their own critical judgment. This critical judgment is independent and free, it does not depend upon anyone, it does not owe allegiance to anyone. The only master of such a mind is universal truth. It takes truth as a ruler to measure all saints and sages, from ancient times until now, Eastern or Western, any person, anywhere. It also uses the ruler of truth to measure religious doctrines, then it criticizes all and decides what to reject and what to keep. (Phan Khôi 1929b)

Phan Khôi concludes this passage on a biographical note saying that he has been reading the books of Confucianism from the time that he was six years old, and then shifting footing to address the imagined Confucian master using the respectful term *ngài*, he asserts that "I was born into your house, and so today I have the right to criticize you and to judge everything about your religion." He ends on a defiant note with "in the past I was your subordinate; but now I, in relation to you, am an independent and free person."

In these respects, Phan Khôi agreed with his contemporaries in the Self-Reliant Literary Group that Confucianism had penetrated the everyday, habitual ways of thinking both of ordinary people and of the highly educated. But Phan Khôi went beyond Nhất Linh and others in his attempt to identify more precisely the semiotic mechanism by which the pernicious unfreedom of Confucian ideology had become ingrained in the Vietnamese mentality. Yes, ritual and custom were important but more fundamental was language – language, operating below the level of conscious awareness, was capable of reproducing the traditional, Confucian order and ideology even when this was explicitly rejected. Indeed, Phan Khôi often seems on the verge of articulating a fundamental insight: conventionalized ways of speaking carry with them a picture of the world that people repeat to themselves (and others) every time they speak.

Consider, for instance, the collection of practices Phan Khôi refers to as the custom of name taboo (*tục kiêng tên*), one of his favourite examples of the communicative problems wrought by Confucian ideas (see Phan Khôi 1930b, 1931b). These practices embodied much of what Phan Khôi objected to in "traditional" ways of speaking: they were irrational in prohibiting not just the saying of a name but also the saying of words homophonous with that name; they involved the performance of elaborate and unwarranted deference; they caused speakers to talk in a manner that was confusing and often inaccurate. In sum, the name taboo impeded the rational and effective use of language as an instrument of reference and predication, and, as Phan Khôi pointed out on several occasions, it actually provided much fodder, or at least occasion, for mockery.

But it was in the practices of interlocutor reference that Phan Khôi identified the most serious obstacle both to modernizing public discourse and individual autonomy. For instance, in an essay on the topic of *khí tiết* (moral integrity), Phan Khôi (1933) casts a series of arguments for individual autonomy and freedom in a linguistic idiom as, specifically, a matter of claiming the right to say *ta*, a markedly informal and non-deferential first person pronoun.[9] Here, Phan Khôi suggests that in former times, *khí tiết* was cultivated through Confucian ritual and was an exclusive preserve of the mandarins along with other members of the educated elite. But, Phan Khôi suggests, *khí tiết* is a good thing for everyone, not just a particular type of person. After all, although everyone lives in the world and thus their actions depend upon their social position – some are high (*sang trọng*, "opulent") while others are low (*hèn*, "base, vile") – everyone is, at the same time, human, "and everyone has a way of being human, no one is inferior to anyone else."[10] It is at this point that Phan Khôi introduces the linguistic argument to illustrate, writing, "The word 'ta' can be used by anyone to refer to him or herself, everyone has the right to proudly proclaim that 'ta.' But they also have the obligation to protect that voice of 'ta,' from dishonor."

Phan Khôi continues by introducing the figure of the humble beggar and proposing that possession of *khí tiết*, and the associated right to refer to oneself as *ta*, is not distributed according to social class: "Even the beggar can assert his own autonomy (i.e., what is conveyed by "ta", J.S.). And so that group is divided between those who have *khí tiết* and those that do not."[11] He develops the argument with the example of a particular person in Hanoi:

Here in Hanoi, in the botanical garden, there is often a person sitting on the grassy bank: shabbily dressed, sometimes playing a flute, sometimes plucking away, with an upturned hat placed in front (of him) to ask for money from visitors. To

---

9 The form *ta* takes its significance in large part as an alternative to other possibilities, most prominently, within the set of pronouns, *tôi*. Thus, as a pragmatic alternative to *tôi*, which is derived from a word meaning "subject of the king" and was thought until recently to have a self-humbling connotation, *ta* is vulnerable to being heard as arrogant or, as Thompson (1987, 248) puts it, "superior." Indeed, elsewhere, Phan Khôi characterized the proposal to use *ta* as a universal pronoun as "bold" and suggested that most people would not accept this.

10 The expression used here is *làm người*, literally, "make a person," but widely used to mean the cultivation of virtue or the teaching of virtue by parents to their children.

11 Phan Khôi's point is, of course, that moral integrity does not depend on social position. His focus on the figure of the beggar, however, is suggestive of an unarticulated sense that the cultivation of virtue, in this case at least, may involve some degree of alienation from kith and kin, and separation from the ordinary pulls of domestic life. This would certainly align with his arguments about the oppressive character of traditional Vietnamese family.

whomever gives, he nods his head in thanks, but to those who don't give he does not bow: That is to say, the beggar has *khí tiết*. (Phan Khôi 2018, 38)

Phan Khôi goes on to explain that such moral integrity cannot be equated with simple pride or vanity. Thus, even though the beggar asks for money (in his way) he does not feel the need to commit suicide, that is, he does not feel ashamed by this. Rather, he comports himself in a noble way (*cách cao thượng*). No one can deny the beggar his own moral integrity – this is an inalienable, constitutive aspect of the person. Voicing the beggar, Phan Khôi writes:

> I (*ta*) ask for money, I (*ta*) have self-respect, and yet cannot commit suicide. I (*ta*) respect the honor of I (*ta*), I cannot beg and beseech, rather I (*ta*) must ask in a noble way: who can forbid me? Who can deprive me of my character? … putting it this way is meant to show that all classes of people can have self-respect, can preserve their position. (2018, 38–9)

Phan Khôi's discussion here must be understood against the normative background of everyday linguistic usage. In Vietnamese, in almost all situations, speakers avoid using pronouns altogether, preferring instead various common nouns, most prominently kin terms. So, rather than, "*I* see *you* are already quite old," a Vietnamese speaker might say, "Younger sibling (*em*) sees elder brother (*anh*) is already quite old." Kinterms such as *em*, "younger sibling," and *anh*, "elder brother" (along with those which denote "elder sister," "mother's brother," "father's sister," and so on), are used across a wide range of contexts and with persons who are not genealogically related to the speaker (see Luong 1990 for the definitive account). Against this, Phan Khôi suggests that everyone has the right to proclaim their own individuality and autonomy which is grounded in a potential for moral integrity. Everyone, he suggests, even the beggar, can cultivate this moral integrity and so proudly proclaim their status as an "I."

Phan Khôi's argument here resonates with that made by the linguist Emile Benveniste in his famous essay on subjectivity in language. There, Benveniste ([1956] 1966, 224) proposes that "it is in and through language that man [*sic*] constitutes himself as a subject, because language alone establishes the concept of 'ego' in reality … 'Ego' is he who says 'ego.' That is where we see the foundation of 'subjectivity,' which is determined by the linguistic status of 'person.'" Soon after introducing the idea that the universal source of subjectivity is pure deictic self-reference, Benveniste adds the following caveat:

> A language without the expression of person cannot be imagined. It can only happen that in certain languages, under certain circumstances, these "pronouns" are deliberately omitted; this is the case in most of the Far Eastern societies, in which

a convention of politeness imposes the use of periphrases or of special forms between certain groups of individuals in order to replace the direct personal references. But these usages only serve to underline the value of the avoided forms; it is the implicit existence of these pronouns that gives social and cultural value to the substitutes imposed by class relationships. (225–6)

Like Phan Khôi, then, Benveniste identifies the use of lexical nouns ("periphrases or ... special forms") such as kin terms or titles to refer to the speaker and addressee as involving a *substitution* of the *original* (or, underlying) pronominal forms. Both writers seem to agree that pronominal forms that do no more than point to the speaker constitute an authentic subjectivity, one that is obscured by the use of substitutes. In other words, an orientation to the social as conveyed by a "polite" formula threatens to overwhelm, or undermine, the expression of a more authentic subjectivity and individual autonomy.[12]

Elsewhere, Phan Khôi (1930c) adopted a more technical approach, comparing Vietnamese with Chinese and with French and suggesting that the latter languages included neutral pronouns, that is, pronouns that conveyed neither respect nor disdain. The Vietnamese language on the other hand was "troublesome" and "inconvenient," obliging speakers to constantly signal their relative social position in ways that were not only cumbersome and confusing but also opened up the possibility of error and of giving offence. He proposed that reform of the practices of referring to speaker and addressee would be necessary for the establishment of a public discourse, one in which distinctions of status and social position were bracketed so that persons might speak as self-abstracted individuals (see Sidnell 2023).

The specific solution for which Phan Khôi consistently advocated involved the promotion of the first-person singular pronoun *tôi*. While acknowledging that this form is etymologically derived from a word meaning "servant" or "subject of the king," Phan Khôi suggests that it could be readily adapted to a new function as a simple, neutral form that conveys neither deference to the addressee not derogation of the speaker. Again, there is a parallel to the work of Emile Benveniste ([1956] 1966, 218) who, in his essay "The Nature

---

12 Costas Nakassis (2013) suggests "zero-degree individual" – a phrase from Sudipta Kaviraj (1997, 90) that means "zero-degree individuals, reduced to the hypothetical points of their being, stripped of the attributes they carry in actual life" – would better capture what Benveniste and Phan Khôi are describing here. My sense is that while such a notion fits the technical facts at issue, the larger question being raised is fundamentally about "authentic" and individual subjectivity (ego) as opposed to something like the mere performance of an institutionalized social role.

of Pronouns," argued that whereas each use of a "noun" refers to a "a fixed and 'objective' notion, ... always identical with the mental image it awakens," each use of the word "I" has its "own reference and corresponds each time to a unique being who is set up as such." Or, as he goes on to put it, the reality to which "I" refers is a "reality of discourse."

While Benveniste's analysis of pronouns in terms of token-reflexivity is more sophisticated than that of Phan Khôi in terms of neutrality, they point in the same general direction. Both notice an important characteristic of such deictic forms, one often obscured by the emphasis, within linguistic anthropology, on what is somewhat unfortunately described as "social indexicality." Namely, deictic forms offer a minimal characterization of their referents. The English "I" and the Vietnamese *tôi* come close to merely pointing to their referents, that is, the speaker of the utterance that contains the token (or the writer of the written passage). In contrast, when used to refer to the participants in a communicative event, terms meaning the equivalent of "elder brother," "younger sibling," "father's elder brother," and so on, invoke the literal or metaphorical relevance of such institutionalized social relationships (Fleming and Sidnell 2020). These social relations, in Vietnamese at least, are inherently asymmetrical, and so the use of kin terms points also to the hierarchical character of those relations. This, however, was not what Phan Khôi found objectionable. Rather, his concern was with the way such practices of reference tethered the universal roles of speaker and addressee (sender and receiver) to the particular social and institutional context within which an exchange takes place. His proposed reforms can be seen, then, as an attempt to lift the communicative encounter out of its social context, and so elevate it to a higher level of rationality. Phan Khôi imagined a radical disarticulation of discourse from its contexts of occurrence made possible by linguistic reform.

"Old Love": The New Poetry and Freedom from Form

The only son of Phan Trân (1826–1935), a minor mandarin and the prefect (*tri phủ*) of a rural district in Khánh Hòa province, Phan Khôi began studying Chinese characters at the age of five. By his early twenties, he was steeped in the Confucian classics and so expert in brushwork that he was recruited by the warden of the prison where he was held from 1908 to 1911 to paint decorative banners for the warden's home. He also composed his own poetry in the tradition of the "regulated poem" in which each line consists of exactly five or seven syllables, and specifically in the genre of *trúc chi từ*, a pastoral style that draws on imagery of mountains, rivers, willow trees, and such to convey the emotions of the poet. However, in the early 1920s Phan Khôi stopped writing poetry. He became a social critic and a prolific essayist. It was not until 1932 that he returned to poetry with a short essay titled "A Style of 'New Poetry' Presented to the Poetic Community," accompanied by the original composition, "Old Love" (*Tình Già*).[13]

The essay begins with Phan Khôi recounting a conversation with Phạm Quỳnh (1892–1945) in which the latter encouraged him to return to the pastoral poems of his youth, several of which Phạm Quỳnh had translated into French. Phan Khôi writes that, though Phạm Quỳnh may have been teasing him, this nevertheless prompted him to make another try at composing his own poetry. But, then, when he sat down to write, he found he could not. He was confused. Should he write in Chinese? In Nôm?[14] He felt as though the great poets of the past – Nguyễn Du (1765–1820), Bà Huyện Thanh Quan (1805–48) – were pressing down against his chest, making it impossible to breathe. Whatever he wrote appeared merely to repeat what they had already said. And those things that he wanted to say, that the great poets of the past had not said, were impossible to articulate within the constraints established by the rules of *luật* (governing the distribution of even and uneven tones within each line), *niêm* (specifying certain lines that must have the same distribution of tones and are thus "sealed" to one another), *vần* (specifying the possible patterns of rhyme), and *bố cục* (governing the arrangement or structure of the poem as a whole).

So, Phan Khôi writes, the old poetic style, with all its rules and regulations, seemed to him too restrictive, but, more than that, he found something repugnant in it and every poem seemed to him the same. He decided to write in a "new poetic style," the aim of which would be to "reveal the true meaning in the soul with verse not bound by poetic rules." Phan Khôi then presents the

---

13 Hoài Thanh and Hoài Chân ([1942] 1999, 24) describe the appearance of Phan Khoi's essay and poem as a "fire-starting revolution" (*cuộc cách mệnh về thi ca đã nhóm dậy*) that "breached the stronghold of old poetry" (*trong thành trì thơ cũ hiện ra một lỗ thủng*). And while they go on to suggest that it served as an inspiration to "a large number of young people" (*một số đông thanh niên*), they also contemptuously suggest that "it is not clear if anyone liked it" (*không rõ có được ai thích không*). Phan Thị Mỹ Khanh (2017, 90) reports on a conversation between Phan Khôi, Lưu Trọng Lư, and Nguyễn Vỹ in which Phan Khôi denied that he had played this role, saying that he wrote poetry for fun (i.e., did not consider himself a poet) and then in the tradition of the Song Dynasty (i.e., was not doing anything "new"). Both the essay and poem in question were actually first published in a special issue of *Đông Tây* (East–West) magazine (see Lại Nguyên Ân 2013a, 2013b).

14 *Chữ nôm* (literally, "southern script") is a writing system invented in the thirteenth century. It uses Chinese characters to represent Sino-Vietnamese vocabulary and some non-Sinitic Vietnamese words represented by characters created through phono-semantic compounding (i.e., one character to represent the sound, one to represent the meaning).

poem titled *Tình Già*, which was widely seen as having initiated the new poetry movement by later commentators.[15]

One of the first people to respond to the essay and poem was a young poet and journalist named Lưu Trọng Lư. He wrote a letter to Phan Khôi "commending his effort but complaining that since its publication neither Phan Khoi nor anyone else had written any additional works in the new style." Later, in 1934, he gave a speech in which he attempted to convey the significance of the new poetry when it was first presented:

> As external conditions are altered, the human soul changes as well. Our pain and sadness, happiness and pleasure, love and hatred are no longer the same as the pain and sadness, happiness and pleasure, love and hatred of our forefathers. Our ancestors led lives that were simple and tranquil: life was easy, there was little contact with the outside, so their souls were simple, impoverished, torpid, atrophied, just like their lives. And in addition to that, Chinese culture engulfed them, bringing to them the stern and narrow discipline of Confucianism. The totalitarian political rule also had a great impact on poetry and writing, because our ancient poets were all devoted Confucians who had buried their noses in books for ten years only out of eagerness to embark upon a public career at some future date. Their poetry was an aristocratic, majestic, public type of poetry, with well-established forms, used to make toasts to each other or to sing the praises of contemporary power figures, the honors and exploits of both others and themselves. And if these Confucians were so unfortunate as to lose out on their opportunities ... they were capable of no more than chanting a cliche: "The flowers wilt, the clouds pass, life is a sea of misery." In fact, their disillusionment was as commonplace and as meager as their love of life. With such common place and paltry sentiments, what need did they have for a broader, more flexible framework? (quoted in Jamieson 1993, 110–11)

Like Phan Khôi, then, Lưu Trọng Lư suggested that the traditional styles were no longer capable of conveying "the actual thoughts that are in the bottom of our hearts."

---

15 It is often suggested that the poem is meant as a critique of the custom of arranged marriage (see Jamieson 1993, 109). However, in a later autobiographical essay, Phan Khôi seems to imply that the poem is actually about a romantic encounter with the wife of the warden of the prison where he was held from 1908 to 1911 (see Phan Thị Mỹ Khanh 2017). Somewhat later, Phan Khôi became involved in some exchanges about the new poetry and the ways in which this had been taken up by a new younger generation. He recoiled from what he saw as poetry that didn't make sense and that lacked rhyme.

Conclusion

With his emphasis on the conditions of possibility of public discourse and by distinguishing technical linguistic problems of communication from the context of social relations, Phan Khôi laid the foundations of an argument for free speech – an argument which, in other words, presupposes both the existence of some public forum within which such a freedom might be exercised and a rigid demarcation of communication as distinct from all other forms of human conduct. In the period I have considered here, Phan Khôi was primarily concerned with what he saw as the fundamental autonomy of the individual evidenced in the capacity for critical judgment and what he referred to as *khí tiết*, "moral integrity." I have suggested that these arguments were consistent with his more technical elaboration of specifically linguistic issues and the kinds of reform for which he advocated. Specifically, Phan Khôi insisted that a modern public discourse could only be realized if certain technical, infrastructual, linguistic, *and* cultural or psychological conditions were met.

Phan Khôi's arguments of the 1930s focused then on the freedom to speak rather than the freedom to say something (in particular). That is to say, he was concerned primarily with the right of each individual to speak *as an individual*, and to speak without being required to position himself or herself in relation to others. This was a vision of freedom that grew directly out of the perceived unfreedom wrought by the Confucian social order – a social order which was imagined, in the 1930s, to rigidly assign to each person a place and a set of rights and duties associated with that place. Phan Khôi's vision for the future involved transcending this social order by tapping into a universal truth and an inalienable "moral integrity," expressed most unequivocally in self-reference with the plain, neutral pronoun *ta*. In sum, Phan Khôi's arguments of the 1930s are about the freedom to speak, and to speak as oneself, as an individual abstracted from social relational ties. He arrives at this view through a consideration of the kinds of unfreedom experienced while living under a Confucian regime in which each action and each utterance most reflect, and do no more than reflect, the pre-established relations which link participants in a social encounter.

In later life, Phan Khôi along with a number of high-profile contemporaries, established the journals *Nhân Văn* (Humanity) and *Giai Phẩm* (Works of art), both of which routinely featured articles criticizing the party-state for imposing limits on what could be said. Contributors called for free discussion, "greater respect for views "from below," and an end to highhandedness on the part of party officials" (Zinoman 2011, 93). These journals included essays with titles such as "An Honest Struggle for Democratic Freedoms," "Interview on the Problem of Expanding Freedom and Democracy," and "Efforts to Develop Democracy and Freedom." Along with other reformers in Eastern Bloc countries, and like them emboldened by Khrushchev's "Secret Speech" delivered at the Twentieth Congress of the Soviet Communist Party, members of the Nhân Văn Giai Phẩm group criticized the cult of personality that had developed around Stalin and pressed for a more open debate within the party. Trần Đức Thảo, for instance, wrote that the Twentieth Congress had "sternly denounced the cult of personality, proposed guidelines for ideological liberalization, shored up the enforcement of socialist legality and initiated reforms designed to democratize all organizations." And, he went on to say, these "historic resolutions of the congress have deeply marked fraternal people's democracies and working class movements, the world over. Our country cannot remain alone on the sidelines" (quoted in Zinoman 2011, 86).

In this context, Phan Khôi's anti-Confucianism was reignited, and he likened the party's cultural commissars to authoritarian mandarins under a feudal regime:

> They make me recall the old dynastic Vietnam of the Emperors Thiệu Trị and Tự Đức[16] when the source of all authority lay in the Chinese classics. Vietnam today is still a dynasty with the main difference being that the source of authority is Marxism. But the fidelity to authority is unchanged. (Phan Khôi 1956)

In this period, then, the issue became one of freedom to express opinion, freedom to criticize authorities (including the state), and freedom not just to speak but to say certain things in speaking. In the face of an increasingly authoritarian political context, Phan Khôi's focus shifted from an emphasis on the cultivation of positive freedom through the use of a neutral pronoun expressing universal speakership, self-abstraction, and social autonomy to more familiar concerns about censorship and constraint and the right to criticize those who occupy positions of power. And note that, in comparing the party-state to the imperial dynasties of the past, Phan Khôi was both exercising free speech and thematizing it, indeed he was exercising free speech *in* thematizing it. With this, the kind of heightened self-awareness and reflexivity that characterizes discussions of free speech in contemporary discourse had emerged in Vietnam.[17]

---

16 Thiệu Trị (1807–47) was the third emperor of the Nguyễn Dynasty. He was the eldest son of Emperor Minh Mạng and reigned from 14 February 1841 until his death on 4 November 1847. Tự Đức (1829–83) was the fourth emperor of the Nguyễn Dynasty of Vietnam; he ruled from 1847 to 1883.

17 This presented the party-state with a conundrum, for to censor such speech is, necessarily, to validate the claims it makes. Perhaps for this reason the party-state attempted to silence members of the Nhân Văn Giai Phẩm group not by directly controlling what they could say in print but through a campaign of character assassination.

Acknowledgments

I am much indebted to the other workshop participants for helpful comments and suggestions on the presented version of this chapter. For insightful comments on an earlier written draft, I thank Paolo Heywood, Sumayya Kassamali, Michael Lambek, Michael Lempert, David Marr, Costas Nakassis, and Ginger Sidnell-Greene.

4 Risking Speech in Islam

ALI-REZA BHOJANI AND MORGAN CLARKE

Introduction

Free speech and its ethics with relation to Islam are topics of intense
concern – in Europe, but also in the Islamic world. The controversies and
violence associated with *The Satanic Verses*, the Danish cartoons, and
Charlie Hebdo – now including the near-fatal stabbing of Salman Rushdie in
2022 – have lent this issue a singularly intense charge, almost overwhelming
the possibility of clear-headed analysis. But in Muslim-majority contexts we
can also think, for example, of the debates over blasphemy charges and their
political uses from Egypt to Pakistan, or the brutal repression of Muslim
activists across the authoritarian world. Are Muslims uniquely sensitive
to criticism? Does this constitute a challenge to free speech? Do Islamic
traditions have different ideas about free speech, or no free speech at all? Or
do these controversies throw into relief problems with Western liberal ideas
of free speech? Are unrealistic demands being made of Muslims? How can
the right to free speech for Muslims be preserved in Europe and elsewhere?
Are there in fact alliances to be made between Islamic traditions and liberal
ones rather than ruptures?

These are issues of pressing importance, although the high temperature
around the arguments means that the right questions are not always being
asked, let alone the right answers being found. We come to them obliquely,
from the perspective of our own, less heated ethnographic material. This concerns the everyday life of the sharia (Islamic law, i.e., the religious rules of
Islam) among a Twelver Shi'i Muslim community in the UK. Although our
research focuses on attitudes towards and practice of Islamic norms, freedom
of speech was immediately striking as a topic of concern. Within the community, as among Muslim communities almost everywhere, questions of theology
and religious law are the subject of keen interest, and their suitable form in
our contemporary world – especially in a Muslim minority context such as the

UK – a matter of keen debate. Some "traditionalist" parties find some of the more progressive or critical responses troubling, to such an extent that they attempt to police what can and cannot be said within the community. Banning preachers whose speech is deemed too challenging or divisive has become a frequent practice and is socially violent enough to have caused considerable internal controversy. How, then, to find the right balance between preserving the unity and traditions of the community on the one hand, and progressive critique on the other?

Anthropologists of Islam have considered such questions before, although they have been more inspired by events of public concern like the Danish cartoon controversy (and before that the *Satanic Verses* affair) than their own ethnographic considerations. Two of the most prominent scholars in the field, Talal Asad and Saba Mahmood, contributed to a volume (Asad et al. 2013) that sought "to challenge the presumption that critique is necessarily secular and, conversely, that secularism is by definition the condition of critique and self-criticism, distinguished from religious orthodoxy, which is regularly considered to be dogmatic" (Brown, Butler, and Mahmood 2013, vii). While Mahmood (2013) argued that Muslims were so upset by the Danish cartoons because they relate to the Prophet Muhammad in ways unfamiliar to modern Westerners – an exotic difference in "semiotic ideology" (cf. Keane 2009) – Asad's (2013) contribution characteristically focused on a genealogical critique of liberal secular presumptions, through the lens of the notion of blasphemy in particular.[1] Neither attempted an account of what "free speech" or critique might (or might not) look like in the Islamic traditions.

Asad had, however, previously written a paper in a more comparative vein that we thus prefer as our theoretical foil here, where he explicitly contrasted the liberal/Enlightenment tradition of public critical speech with an Islamic one. This is his chapter titled "The Limits of Religious Criticism in the Middle East" (Asad 1993, 200–36), which we discuss in more detail below. In brief, Asad presents an Islamic tradition that stresses the duty to provide not criticism but advice for the moral education of others in good faith, despite the possible risks, linking this to a wider interest in the cultivation of virtue, a theme which Mahmood (2005) and Charles Hirschkind (2006) have developed in ways highly influential for the anthropologies of Islam and ethics more generally. In presenting the "Western" half of his comparison, Asad follows Foucault's genealogical approach, although he does not make much of the Foucauldian theme of *parrhesia*, discussed elsewhere in this volume, despite its obvious resonances (but cf. Asad 2013, 42). Asad traces his genealogy of

---

1 This could equally be said of his earlier comments on the furore over the publication of Salman Rushdie's *Satanic Verses* (collected in Asad 1993).

liberal modern approaches to public criticism only as far as Kant. With regard to the cultivation of virtue more generally, however, both he and Mahmood note that Islam and the Christian West share genealogical roots in classical Greek ideas, not least those of Aristotle (Asad 2003, 250–1; 2015, 173–4, 181n33; Mahmood 2005, 137–8). And yet, Asad and Mahmood are clear that they see this virtue ethical tradition as distinct from liberal modernity, echoing the position of Alasdair MacIntyre ([1981] 2006). Islamic and liberal traditions are portrayed as fundamentally "other" to each other, just as they have been in the discussions of blasphemy and intolerance around the Danish cartoons and *The Satanic Verses* (see also Candea in this volume). No doubt there are many differences. But shared genealogical roots also mean that they have things in common. Drawing on our own ethnography, we end by suggesting some such commonalities, which may – we hope – offer possibilities for more positive forms of engagement.

Ethical and Critical Speech in Islam

For Asad (1993, 200), "the limits of public criticism in the Middle East," while undoubtedly present, are to be understood in the light of the norms of the Is-lamic traditions rather than the prejudices of liberal modernity.[2] The latter are, however, hegemonic in the world today. As a result, "non-Westerners who seek to understand their local histories must also inquire into Europe's past, because it is through the latter that universal history has been constructed" (200). Cri-tique must take the form of genealogy. Asad assumes (perhaps tendentiously) that contemporary Westerners take the Enlightenment as their yardstick, and he takes Kant as a paradigmatic reference point, in particular his famous essay of 1784, "What Is Enlightenment?" Westerners see the modern Middle East as largely made up of autocratic regimes, and public criticism as alien to an Islamic state. "But how did Europeans in that era of early modernity connect public critical discourse with religion while living under an absolute ruler?" Asad asks, as Kant did in Prussia under Frederick the Great. Kant thought the enlightened ruler should have the confidence to allow free public debate while insisting on obedience as regards the enacting of his commands. Such free ra-tional discourse would be to the improvement of the ruler's policy. Religion – a fraught topic in the wake of the Reformation's antagonisms, persecutions, and wars of religion – should not be exempt.

---

2   There is a tendency, which Asad does not comment on here, to identify Islam with the Middle East and vice versa. Against this, see, for example, Shahab Ahmed's (2016) attempt to shift the centre of gravity of Islamic studies towards the "Balkans-to-Bengal complex."

Asad (1993, 207–8) then turns to the modern Middle East, and Saudi Arabia in particular, and argues that although Middle Eastern societies do not practise public critique in a Kantian sense, they do have their own institutionalized forms of "reasoned criticism." In Saudi Arabia, where Islamic professional scholars (*ulama*) play a crucial role in securing the legitimacy and authority of the state, such scholars can air reasoned criticism, albeit in certain forms: again, not as criticism (*naqd*), but as "advice" (*nasiha*), most appropriately in sermons (especially those given at Friday prayers) and lessons in the new Islamic universities. Asad's examples come from the tumultuous period of the First Gulf War (1990–1), when, with the blessing of King Fahd and the Grand Mufti, American troops massed in Saudi Arabia's eastern province for the repulsion of Iraq's invasion of Kuwait. Not only was there much concern as to the propriety of the presence of so many non-Muslims, but there were also calls for more general political reform.

Nasiha constitutes a distinct form of critique. First, it should be well-intentioned. But it also "carries the sense of offering moral advice to an erring fellow Muslim," a sort of "morally corrective criticism" (Asad 1993, 214). Such pedagogical speech (or "ethical" speech, in the sense of virtuous cultivation foregrounded in the recent anthropology of ethics) can be seen as a duty in itself.[3] "This," Asad claims, "stands in sharp contrast to the Enlightenment view of criticism as a *right*, whose exercise is therefore optional" (215; emphasis in original).[4] Following one of the lectures that he takes as an example, Asad links this duty of ethical speech to wider aspects of Islamic tradition: the cultivation of virtue more generally, but also the much discussed obligation to "command the right and forbid the wrong" (*al-Amr bi al-Maruf wa'l-Nahy min al-Munkar*, an institutionalized form of which is known as *hisba*, or "accountability").[5] This latter duty is explicitly commanded in the Qur'an, which gives it particular weight:

Let there be one community [*umma*] of you, calling to good, and commanding right and forbidding wrong; those are the prosperers. (3:104)

And the believers, the men and the women, are protectors one of the other; they command right, and forbid wrong. (9:71)

---

3 The ethics of speech more generally is a key concern in Islamic thought, with pernicious talk behind someone's back, the sin of *ghiba*, seen as especially condemnable (Asad 1993, 224).

4 Cf. Asad's (2013, 48–9) later observation that "the practice of secular criticism is now a sign of the modern, of the modern subject's relentless pursuit of truth and freedom … It has almost become a *duty*."

5 For references for the points that follow, and on "commanding right" more generally, see Michael Cook's (2000) monumental study.

Such moral interventions might take different forms, including speech, but also more direct action, as a famous saying (Hadith) attributed to the Prophet explains:

> Whoever sees a wrong and is able to put it right with his hand, let him do so; if he cannot, then with his tongue; if he cannot, then in his heart, and that is the bare minimum of faith.

In theory, "commanding right and forbidding wrong" is something that all Muslims should be doing. But in practice, as the Hadith suggests, there may be limits as to who can, or should, best do what. Here another famous saying, often attributed to the well-known early legal scholar Abu Hanifa (d. 767 CE), suggests a conventional – and hierarchical – division of labour:

> Putting things right with the hand is for the political authorities [umara'], with the tongue for the scholars [ulama], and in the heart for the common people ['amma].

Speaking truth to power has its dangers.[6] Islamic history is replete with examples of scholars who have suffered as a consequence, the parrhesiasts of the Islamic traditions (including Abu Hanifa himself, who died in prison). There are also, it is worth noting, less politically compromising strands of thought than that Asad describes, less shy of direct criticism, even urging open revolt against oppression where necessary. Given our own case study, we could cite the traditions of the Shi'a, who have long seen themselves as marginalized and oppressed, and where the intellectual and practical ramifications of this duty to command right and resist wrong have thus been exhaustively debated (Cook 2000, 252–301, 530–60). One recent instance of the fiercest of public criticism, a cause célèbre, casts a starker light than Asad's on politics in Saudi Arabia, whose Shi'i citizens have been harshly repressed. Sheikh Nimr al-Nimr (d. 2016) was a leading Shi'i clerical activist and advocate of political freedoms and greater rights (see Matthiesen 2013). A famously fiery speech on the death of the crown prince and interior minister Nayef in 2012 was the last straw in his long-running battle with the Saudi authorities. Hardly an attempt at kind-hearted "advice," it would cost Nimr his life: he was executed in 2016 in circumstances that brought about diplomatic and other protests worldwide.

---

6 Seeing "commanding right" as entailing speaking truth to political power, as in Asad's account, has not, however, been the norm across all schools of Islamic legal thought or throughout history. In many ways it could be seen as a modern phenomenon. The Saudi context privileges one variety of approach to these themes (Cook 2000, 165–92).

Where is Nayef's army now? ... Where are his intelligence agencies? Where are his officers? Can they protect him from the Angel of Death? He will be eaten by worms and suffer the torments of Hell in his grave ... Some say: "Don't talk ill of Nayef because he's dead." Are you stupid? ... Don't you see that the Quran says: "On that day shall the believers rejoice"? Why shouldn't we be happy at the death of the man who imprisoned and killed our children? (Al-Nimr 2012)

If we are looking for a body of Islamic thought that could bear comparison with the liberal tradition of thought on the ethics of speech, then the rich and varied juristic literature on the duty to "command right" might indeed be a good place to start. In so doing, Asad (1993) emphasizes the differences between the Islamic traditions and Western liberal modernity. Regarding the Islamic emphasis on the general duty to make such pedagogical interventions, he observes that, to liberal eyes, such "advice" might "be regarded as a repressive technique for securing social conformity to divinely ordained norms" (233). Viewed positively, however,

it reflects the principle that a well-regulated polity depends on its members being virtuous individuals who are partly responsible for one another's moral condition – and therefore in part on continuous moral criticism. Modern liberalism rejects this principle. The well-regulated modern polity – so it argues – depends on the provision of optimum amounts of social welfare and individual liberty, not on moral criticism. The primary critical task, according to political liberalism, is not the moral disciplining of individuals but the rational administration and care of entire populations. Morality, together with religious belief, has become essentially a personal matter for the self-determining individual – or so the liberal likes to claim. (233)

The Islamic emphasis on "calling" (da'wa) people to virtue thus "stand[s] in a conceptual world quite unlike that of the Enlightenment" (219; see also Mahmood 2005; Hirschkind 2006). In the Enlightenment world, or in Asad's Kantian version of it at least, reason is the foundation of morality rather than disciplined virtue. The liberal right to freedom of speech for the rational improvement of the polity contrasts with the Islamic duty to offer ethical speech for the moral improvement of one's consociates.

This contrast is important to Asad because he is a critic of the pretensions of liberal modernity and wishes to defend Muslims from the undoubted aggression and sense of diminishment they have suffered under Western hegemony. Indeed, Asad (2015) later goes so far as to suggest that al-Amr bi al-Maruf, in what could be seen as its "positive" dimensions at least – friendship, advice, and so on – could form part of a political alternative to the violence of the secular liberal nation state (see also Asad 2018, 158–9). That might surprise, not just because the more "negative" aspect of "commanding right" – telling people off – seems less obviously attractive, but also because *al-Amr bi al-Maruf* has been institutionalized in much more clearly repressive ways by "Islamic states" such as Saudi Arabia and Iran in the form of "religious police."[7] Asad's comments have thus been criticized by some liberals from the region (e.g., Fahmy 2018, 182ff).

As Asad himself concedes, the contrast he draws between a liberal modern privileging of nominally universal reason and a non-liberal/non-modern emphasis on virtue is too stark. Leaving aside (for now) the intensely moralizing nature of contemporary Western public discourse, early modern European "virtue politics" have also been the subject of recent attention (Hankins 2019); Kant himself was no stranger to the significance of virtue (Louden 1986). Further, in the Islamic traditions virtue and moral discipline were never viewed in isolation from public reason; law and statecraft are deep wells of Islamic thought.[8] The pursuit of virtue comes together with, rather than instead of, that of reason. Differences with Asad aside, however, we have arrived at some key points of orientation: the relative importance of ethical speech – speech designed to shape the moral conduct of others; its relationship to reason; and its obligations, limits, and risks.

Ethical Speech in a British Muslim Community

With that in mind, we now turn to our ethnography, based on fieldwork in the UK in 2018–19 with the Twelver Shi'i Khoja, a global Muslim diaspora with roots in South Asia (Sind and Gujerat) that expanded through trade across the Indian Ocean and retains important and enduring ties to East Africa (see, for example, Akhtar 2016). The majority of the Khoja worldwide are Isma'ili, but a significant number (more than 100,000) are Twelver Shi'i, the result of a historical split in the nineteenth century driven by the newly assertive authority of the Isma'ili Agha Khan.[9] Among this diaspora, the UK Twelver Shi'i community is important, in both size and influence, and comprised of a number of autonomous local associations (*jamaats*) in various towns and cities.[10]

---

7 And, in different forms, in Egypt (see Agrama 2012). The role of Iran's "morality police" has been especially highlighted by the protest movement subsequent to the death of Mahsa Amini in police custody in 2022, having been arrested for allegedly not correctly covering her hair.

8 Ibn Miskawayh (d. 1030), for instance, whose rendition of Christian Arabic works of virtue ethics were formative for the subsequent development of virtue ethics in the Islamic traditions, discusses the role of sharia in society as akin to the role of the rational faculties over the lower faculties within the self (Miskawayh 1968).

9 From here on, where we refer simply to "Khoja," we mean the Twelver Shi'i Khoja.

10 Our fieldwork was conducted in the Midlands and Greater London. We prefer not to name the individual associations where we worked to preserve the anonymity of our participants.

English is the dominant vernacular, although Gujarati is widely spoken and Urdu still current as a devotional language. The Twelver Khoja are, generally speaking, relatively prosperous and highly educated, and they have become a well-respected and influential element of the global Twelver Shi'i *ecumene* (as well as within the British Muslim landscape) – not only because of their wealth but also because of their impressive level of organization and unity. In contrast with Asad's case, then, we are thinking in terms of the local politics of a small-scale and relatively homogenous minority religious community, rather than those of a nation state.

We have spent many days at local associations, attending religious services, and speaking with people. Again, our research has focused on people's understanding and practice of sharia, the religious rules of Islam, but our conversations and observations have ranged more widely. With reference to the theoretical discussion above, the sheer volume of ethical speech with which the community is presented is striking in terms of sermons and religious instruction. There is a veritable flood of talks, lessons, and discussions for youth, seniors, men, and women. Not all is within the relatively specialized field of Islamic virtue ethics (*akhlaq*) that Mahmood and Hirschkind privilege – but all could be counted as ethical in so far as it aims to make better Muslims of the audience.

This speech has its own risks and controversies. Contrary to the stereotype of religious, not least Islamic, discourse as "dogmatic" (Brown, Butler, and Mahmood 2013, vii), the many diverse traditions of thought within Islam, including the Twelver Shi'i, have always been and still are intensely debated. The upheavals of modernity, migration, and life as minorities in non-Muslim majority countries have led to intense concern – in this community as in others – as to whether and how the obligations of the sharia, or attitudes towards theology, should change in light of contemporary circumstances. Reason is central to such debates. People worry that some traditional teachings "don't make sense." There are many whose ideas in response could rightly be described as progressive.

We spoke at length with one such person, a woman whose wisdom and learning, as well as her energy and leadership, are made much use of in the community, and whose reputation and achievements as an educator are global in scope. She confessed herself impatient at best with the attitudes and teachings of some religious scholars. "I was brought up, for example, to say that even whilst you had your periods you would pray." (In contrast with the normative view, dominant among Muslims across the world, that during their periods women are in a state of ritual impurity and thus not obliged to offer the normal daily prayers, performance of which would not be accepted by God.) "My father said there's nobody, anywhere, written anywhere, that says you wouldn't." By contrast, when she had "come to the greater community ... my God, it's written in light you know, you can't sit on the prayer mat." So had she then ignored the consensus?

> Ignored it completely. That's my lifelong practice and I tell my children that. Show me a place where it's written and tell me that it's authentic and I will consider it, and nobody yet has come up with ... somewhere. I mean, how can I not connect to my God for whatever times in the month and say, "Excuse me, I can't pray to you because ..." Anyway, that's just an example of the way I think.

However, this view, which is controversial, is not something that she can communicate freely in her role as a religious teacher.

> I cannot, I would not, express [it]. I speak from the pulpit. I wouldn't because I would not want to break the fabric of the society or tear it. But I will gradually introduce it for my students, with my friends, with whoever it is, I will tell them this is the way I feel.

Here she spoke of limiting herself out of concern for social harmony. It became clear that she had also come under a great deal of pressure from others to do so. The potential intensity of such pressure should not be understated.

We were discussing attitudes towards sharia with the leader of one local association when he told us of an incident that had occurred the previous year, before he became the association's president. A speaker came for a discussion circle held by a religious youth group. It was "an amazing discussion." The speaker questioned the audience's beliefs, arguing that culture had become mixed up with religion. He said that he sometimes does not cry on the day of Ashura – the peak of the mourning period for the martyrs of the Battle of Karbala, when the third Imam, Husayn, refused to give allegiance to the oppressive rule of the time, and a central pillar of the Shi'i imaginary and religious calendar. This, which speaks presumably to a sort of modernist rationalism, was seen as very controversial by some within the community. One child told his father about it, and the father, who happened to be a member of the management committee of the local association, brought it up the next day. "How dare he?" he said. This sort of discussion should be held in a seminary research-level class (*dars al-kharij*), not with children. Some members of the committee said, "Let's ban him," and, to the discomfort of others, they dug into the speaker's online social media content trying to find further justification for doing so. (It turned out that the speaker had also been performing stand-up comedy, although the issue was not so much the nature of this other form of speech, as that it had apparently been performed in the morally dubious setting of bars and clubs.)

This ready recourse to banning people from speaking is not just part of the low-level frictions of everyday community life. There are higher profile incidents as well. One, dating back to the 1990s, involved a distinguished member of the academic Islamic studies community, now based in the United States, Abdulaziz Sachedina. Professor Sachedina is a Khoja, born in East Africa, and a vibrant progressive voice. While his academic career in North America burgeoned, his sharing of his progressive views at Khoja community religious meetings became perceived as worryingly unorthodox by some within the community. A dossier of his teachings was sent to the scholarly authority whom the Khoja Twelvers take to be the most authoritative in the world, Ayatollah Ali al-Sistani, currently the leading figure in the prestigious Shi'i seminaries of Najaf, Iraq. After some deliberations and a meeting between Sachedina and Sistani, Sachedina was effectively banned from speaking within community institutions and has not done so since.[11]

A more recent affair is still very much alive and an acutely sensitive point of tension (and so citing specific names seems unwarranted). For many years now, members of the community have supported the development of local institutions of scholarly instruction, a sort of British grass-roots Shi'i seminary, independent from similar projects funded and directed by transnational networks, such as those of the Islamic Republic of Iran. This stemmed not so much from a desire for independence as from the sheer distance a non-Iranian, non-Arab, British Shi'i Muslim might need to travel – linguistically, intellectually, and socially – to gain access to the famous seminaries of Iran or Iraq, let alone their highest echelons. But, given the particular challenges of Muslim life in the UK, these local sites of scholarly instruction and research have also become a focus for progressive thought and jurisprudence. A leading and notably radical voice has become the subject of a campaign to silence him, again including an open letter to Sistani in 2019.

The letter, which is framed in general rather than particular terms, starts by stating: "We would like to submit to your Eminence that in the recent years there have appeared some people who claim to be learned, and who spread amongst our youths issues especially about the fundamental beliefs of the faith (Usool-e-Deen) and the practical branches of faith" (i.e., the rules of right conduct). After a series of examples (concerning salvation for non-Muslims, the need to change the rules of inheritance for women, etc.), they end by asking

---

11 For Sachedina's account of the affair (which we refer to below), see Sachedina ([1998] 2011); for that of the other side, those bringing the case to Sistani, see Rizvi (1998). Very recently (as we were finalizing this chapter), Sachedina, suffering ill health, felt the need to publish a recantation of his prior position that has revived the debate over the rights and wrongs of the affair (see Sachedina 2023).

the Ayatollah's office "to guide our youths … on how to deal with such people" (World Federation of KSIMC 2019). Unsurprisingly, the Ayatollah's reply (as translated from Arabic by the petitioners) takes a dim view of such teaching as presented, stressing precisely its role in proper ethical formation:

> The duty of the Muslim preacher (muballigh) is to invite people towards Usool-e-Deen and to spread its well established teachings as represented in the clear verses of the holy Book and the beautiful sayings of the Holy Prophet Mustafa (SA) and the Holy Guides (AS)[12] ; and to enjoin people and to guide them so they can grow in faith in God and in preparation for the day of judgement, and to strive to spiritually develop their souls and to purge them from evil traits and moral vices, and to adorn them with moral virtues and noble traits; and to better their relations and interactions with others even with those who differ with them in faith and belief.
>
> It is inappropriate for the religious preacher (muballigh) to use the mimbar [pulpit] to spread his personal opinions which create divisions and differences among the religious people. So, whoever adopts this style of teaching and lecturing, it does not behoove [sic] the believers (may Allah increase their honour) to be inclined towards them and to entrust them with the religious training of their children; rather it is their duty to refer to others who are reliable from among the people of knowledge, piety and righteousness. (Sistani 2019b)

With this reply, the opponents of the scholar and teacher in question (who, anecdotally, saw their intervention as an instance of "commanding right and forbidding wrong") felt that they had gotten their way, and he was prevented from speaking at religious events within community institutions. His sermons and teachings are still available on YouTube, and he still receives invitations to teach and preach around the world, albeit not within Khoja institutions. But it was nevertheless a considerable blow that has left hard feelings.

Ethical, pedagogical speech is thus a ubiquitous element of religious community life. Its importance can be attested by the readiness of some to employ socially violent forms of exclusion to police it. "Traditional" discourse is, however, under considerable pressure from the realities of life in the contemporary West – and thus from reasoned critique. What is at stake is how, where, and when such reasoned critique can be expressed. Preaching from the pulpit, the paradigmatic location of ethical speech and authority, is seen as especially sensitive.[13] (Which is, conversely, what made it a relatively secure point from

---

12 Mustafa, "the chosen one," is one of the names of the Prophet Muhammad. "SA" stands for *salawat Allahi 'alay-hi*, "the blessings of God be upon him," and "AS" for *'alay-him al-salam*, "upon them be peace."

13 According to the female preacher quoted above, "When you sit on the pulpit they think you know everything, which you don't."

which to issue public critique in Asad's Saudi case.) The preaching of controversial views, however sincerely delivered, might cause division as well as mislead, and some thus make a principled decision to censor themselves. Other locations, such as the learned seminary, the *hawza*, may be more suitable for the airing of radical thought.[14] Critical debate is a deeply embedded element of *hawza* culture and Islamic learning more generally (see, for example, Mottahedeh 1985), and the Twelver Shi'i legal tradition maintains a central place for the role of human reason (Bhojani 2015). But how, where, and when critical reason impinges on the life of ordinary Muslims is a distinct and somewhat fraught issue.

Comparisons

This gives us a fresh point of engagement with the somewhat awkward comparison that Asad sets up between the Islamic traditions and Western liberal modernity, as represented by Kant. The question that our ethnographic case poses as to the proper location of public critical reason is one to which Kant has an interesting and famous answer, which bears re-examination. In his essay on "What Is Enlightenment?," Kant makes a distinction between the sorts of speech appropriate in public and in private, although he has a rather unfamiliar (to liberal moderns) way of making this distinction:

> The *public* use of man's reason must always be free ...; the *private use* of reason may quite often be very narrowly restricted ... By the public use of one's own reason I mean that use which anyone may make of it *as a man of learning* addressing the entire *reading public*.[15] What I term the private use of reason is that which a person may make in a particular *civic* post or office with which he is entrusted. (1991, 55; emphasis in original)

His most fully fleshed out example – which Asad (1993, 203) cites at length – is, significantly for our purposes, that of the religious teacher:

> A clergyman is bound to instruct his[16] pupils and his congregation in accordance with the doctrines of the church he serves, for he is employed by it on that condition. But as a scholar, he is completely free as well as obliged to impart to the public all his carefully considered, well intentioned thoughts on the mistaken

---

14 Although we should not forget the repression of scholarly voices within the seminary too.

15 A then highly restricted portion of society. Kant's model has of course been seen more widely as crucial to genealogies of the liberal public sphere (Habermas [1962] 1989).

16 Kant's gendered assumptions are relevant to our Khoja context, even if there are a good number of women preachers and teachers.

aspects of those doctrines, and to offer suggestions for a better arrangement of religious and ecclesiastical affairs. And there is nothing in this which need trouble his conscience. For what he teaches in pursuit of his duties as an active servant of the church is presented by him as something which he is not empowered to teach at his own discretion, but which he is employed to expound in a prescribed manner and in someone else's name. (1991, 56)

And then Kant continues:

Thus the use which someone employed as a teacher makes of his reason in the presence of his congregation is purely *private*, since a congregation, however large it is, is never any more than a domestic gathering. In view of this, he is not and cannot be free as a priest, since he is acting on a commission imposed from outside. Conversely, as a scholar addressing the real public (i.e., the world at large) through his writings, the clergyman making *public use* of his reason enjoys unlimited freedom to use his own reason and to speak in his own person. (1991, 57; emphasis in original)

This has been called a "two hats" doctrine, where an individual might play more than one role in society (Laursen 1996). Kant's particular usage looks odd in the contemporary context in so far as one might expect the opposite wording: that the clergyman speaks to their congregation in their public (or professional) capacity and shares their personal thoughts in their writing in a private one. It was unusual in Kant's time too, arguably a (subversive) recapturing of what had become a restricted, lawyer's use of "public" to refer to the state. Also subversively, Kant was effectively extending the traditional liberty of men of learning to wider circles: civil servants, soldiers, and clergymen.

The "two hats" view of the cleric's role makes more sense in a Christian context than in an Islamic one, where there is no "church" to be an "active servant" of, and where the difference between the religious specialist and the non-specialist is a matter of greater knowledge rather than ordination.[17] Admittedly, not least in Shi'i society, we can think of a distinct "turbaned" (*mu'ammam*) class of trained religious specialists, of whom a form of professionalism might certainly be expected. The various local associations of the Khoja community do indeed employ some to serve their local needs: leading prayers, providing

---

17 In Kant's Prussia, clergymen were also civil servants, paid by the state, just as professors like Kant were (Laursen 1996). Historically, the Imam al-Jum'a, the Muslim preacher of the Friday sermon, has itself been seen as a state appointment, as would be the case in Asad's Saudi Arabia. For this reason, the Shi'i tradition has often maintained the impermissibility of participating in Friday prayers under illegitimate rule (Newman 2001).

edifying sermons and lessons, helping people with their dilemmas. And we know of some highly talented scholars whose teachings have proved not to the taste of their community (or influential sections of it) and whose contracts have not been renewed. And yet, provision of ethical speech to the community – and the sense of a calling to do so – is not restricted to such paid employees. The voice of a non-turbaned intellectual, a "lay preacher," or simply an engaged community member, is as often heard. As we have noted, the duty to correct and improve the morality of others and of society at large is incumbent upon all Muslims. And in doing so, there is no higher (human) authority to which they are formally answerable. As Professor Sachedina said in 1998 of the attempts to bar him from speaking within the Khoja community, "there was absolutely no ground ... to silence me ... Islam is not Catholicism where there is no room for another interpretation or dissension in the authoritative system of the 'church.'" The Ayatollah's preferred solution was thus to ask Sachedina to bind himself, through a vow not to teach (or if he taught – as he was employed to do in the American academy – not to express his own opinion in so doing), which Sachedina felt he could not in good conscience do. "However fallibly, I have served my fellow believers in all sincerity and devotion," he wrote. While the dangers must be weighed in the balance, a scholar has a duty to share their knowledge – indeed, they are forbidden to withhold it.[18]

That said, the notion that the religious teacher's speech before the community is in some way private, or domestic, in that it is oriented towards and governed by their particular needs and institutions, and thus not wholly free, has meaning in our ethnographic setting where the sense of a bounded community within a larger multi-cultural polity is strong – and its means of social exclusion effective. And Kant's notion that there is then a distinct "learned" or "scholarly" domain, where critical reason may be exercised more freely, also resonates, although Kant's framing of this domain as "public" might be less comfortable. It proved uncomfortable for Kant too, as he famously later had to withdraw his own writings on religion at the behest of the new king, Frederick William II, and retreat on his attempted extension of the privilege of free debate beyond the academy. The Prussian Edict on Religion in 1788 guaranteed freedom of conscience "so long as [the citizen] keeps any peculiar opinion to himself and carefully guards himself from spreading it or persuading others" (quoted in Laursen 1996, 259). Kant's 1793 *Religion within the Limits of Reason Alone* was, he was forced to concede, "not at all suitable for the public" here meaning precisely not "scholars of the faculty" (quoted in Laursen 1996, 259).

---

18 Several Hadiths speak of someone who conceals their knowledge having to wear "a bridle of fire" on the day of resurrection. We should mention again that Sachedina has recently renounced his earlier position (see Sachedina 2023).

For Ayatollah Sistani (2019b) too, "it is not right for the one who addresses the general public to present to them specialist issues wherein the audience has no grasp of the prerequisites of the issue as per the required academic standards."[19] Here, what has been translated as "the general public" (*'ammat al-nass*), but could equally be rendered "commoners" or "the masses," refers to a (Shi'i) Muslim public made up of non-specialists rather than the predominantly non-Muslim national and global public spheres, where other sensitivities may be more salient. (Ironically, before these latter publics, it is the progressive, "reasonable" voices that are more likely to be pushed to the fore.) It is thus not necessarily the difference between a teacher's pedagogical speech and a scholar's theoretical writings that is at stake here (the two hats), or that the pulpit is in some sense sacred (still less restricted to paid appointees). Rather, the latter is the paradigmatic point of dissemination of religious knowledge to the non-learned, who are – for Sistani – not equipped to discriminate between right and wrong teaching for themselves.[20] Every audience demands an appropriate level of discourse.

Here, the Ayatollah maintains a classical but enduring view of intellectual hierarchy from his perspective as the pre-eminent figure in one of the greatest religious colleges of the Middle East – a gulf only widened for "traditionalist" Khoja by their geographic, ethnic, and linguistic distance from the scholarly centre. But, as we have seen, far from all of today's community members are content to suspend religious reason. Laursen (1996, 258) says of Kant's distinctive notion of the public, "'Everyman a part-time man of learning' would have been a radically levelling slogan in Kant's day." It is a reality for Muslim modernity. The contemporary burghers of the British Khoja community – accountants, doctors, lawyers, businesspeople – take a keen interest in religious debate. And the seminary is no longer an exclusive domain: lectures, debates, and scholarly treatises are widely available on the internet and in translation. More than that, given the ubiquity of social media, a compartmentalization of different discursive domains – as Kant also hoped for – has become all but unsustainable. A British Muslim preacher or academic cannot realistically hope to preserve the boundary between their more scholarly interventions and their sermons to their flock, not even between what is intended for a Muslim audience and what might be scrutinized by a potentially hostile secular

---

19 Professional courtesy might also enjoin keeping scholarly disagreements within the seminary rather than airing them in public. Sachedina ([1998] 2011) reports that Sistani admitted he had not always agreed with his great teacher, Ayatollah Khu'i, but had refrained from saying so publicly.

20 In a separate message of advice to preachers, Sistani (2019a) likens the approach required to that of talking to "family members and children."

one. Speech itself has become radically freed – with potentially explosive consequences, as we are all now aware.

Conclusion

The bitter debates about the Danish cartoons and parallel cases have been framed by many as highlighting the difference between liberal modernity and Islam. Modern liberal ideas of "free speech" and Muslim ones may well be different, although the Danish cartoon controversy – rooted in discussions of fear, blasphemy, and insult – is not necessarily the most productive place to start in thinking about those differences. Inspired both by Asad (1993, 200–36) and our own ethnographic material, we have looked instead to the ethics of public critical reason within Muslim communities themselves. Asad, discussing politics in Saudi Arabia, stresses the moral pedagogical role of speech, as seen paradigmatically in sermons and religious lessons, and invokes the duty incumbent on all Muslims to "command right and forbid wrong." "Commanding right" is potentially risky, as in the modern idea of "speaking truth to power," with its genealogical roots in classical *parrhesia*, although Asad focuses on Kantian notions of critical public reason as his focal point of comparison. In our British Shi'i Muslim community, such ethical speech directed towards the community is also important, and thus debated. Some speakers censor themselves for fear of causing division; on occasion, some are censored by others. An earlier presumption, reflected in both Kant's discussion and Asad's Saudi case, that such tensions might be, if not resolved, at least handled through careful consideration of the register appropriate to different settings and audiences, seems radically challenged by the impossibility of compartmentalizing speech in today's digital media environment.

While whether one can say what one must is crucial – and contested – in these Muslim contexts, it is not so much that "freedom" (to speak) is the central value around which all else turns. Rather, as a member of the moral community one has a duty to share one's knowledge and to contribute morally efficacious speech. And yet, one must balance that against the dangers of doing so – to oneself, but also to others: the danger that others might be misled or corrupted, or the community divided, the polity undermined. These are ethical concerns whose understanding will not be exhausted by a comparative study of different notions of freedom (or offence for that matter). Rather, contemporary liberal "free speech" is one approach to the ethics of speech – one that shares genealogical roots with these contemporary Muslim notions of ethical speech and its dilemmas. The Muslim interest in public morality and pedagogical speech is surely not as alien to contemporary liberal society as Asad suggests. One can hardly imagine today's public sphere as one where virtue is not debated, or didacticism not attempted (not least in the university, whose "safe spaces" have been another focus for the current burning debates). Was there not an explicit sense even that the Danish cartoonists and *Charlie Hebdo* were trying to teach Muslims a lesson? (If so, hardly a well-judged one.) Or perhaps the lesson was more one for the majority non-Muslim audience. But then it would be naive at best to imagine such an audience as neatly bounded.

It is not just that these are shared questions and themes. It is our public space that is shared. The cultural intimacy of speech has become almost impossible to maintain, just as has the distinction between different "hats" one might wear and the different audiences and registers they entail. Perhaps the moral calculus required to finesse such distinctions has become simply too complicated. The absolutism of liberal notions of the right to speak freely, and the modern imperative to be above all authentic to one's convictions, would then be one kind of response – one mirrored in, if not born of, the moral/religious impulse to say and do what one must, come what may. "Here I stand, I can do no other, so help me God," as Luther is said to have put it (cf. Asad 2013, 40n42). But another sort of response to these complexities would be to grasp that, if we are to form a moral community, we will need to get to know each other a little better.

Acknowledgments

We gratefully acknowledge the assistance of the Khoja associations and institutions that made our fieldwork possible, as well as all those who spoke with us. We also thank James Laidlaw for his comments on an earlier version of the chapter and the editors of this volume for their careful scrutiny.

5 Ten-and-a-Half Seconds of God's Silence: Mormon *Parrhesia* in the Time of Donald Trump

FENELLA CANNELL

In the Senate

I begin with a statement that Utah Republican Senator Mitt Romney made in Congress in February 2020.

Saturday, February 13, 2020

WASHINGTON – U.S. Senator Mitt Romney (R-UT) today released the following statement regarding his vote on the article of impeachment:

After careful consideration of the respective counsels' arguments, I have concluded that President Trump is guilty of the charge made by the House of Representatives. President Trump attempted to corrupt the election by pressuring the Secretary of State of Georgia to falsify the election results in his state. President Trump incited the insurrection against Congress by using the power of his office to summon his supporters to Washington on January 6th and urging them to march on the Capitol during the counting of electoral votes. He did this despite the obvious and well known threats of violence that day. President Trump also violated his oath of office by failing to protect the Capitol, the Vice President, and others in the Capitol. Each and every one of these conclusions compels me to support conviction. (Romney 2020)

Romney was one of only seven Republicans in the Senate to vote to convict Donald Trump following the attack on the Capitol Building by Trump's supporters on 6 January 2021 (Broadwater 2021; Leibovich 2020); earlier, Romney was the *only* Republican senator to vote to convict Trump during his first impeachment. Romney stated that he considered the evidence showed that Trump had abused his power as president. Mitt Romney is, of course, a member of the Church of Jesus Christ of Latter-day Saints (often known as Mormons or

LDS), and was the first LDS candidate to run for the presidency of the United States in 2012. This, at least, is how his candidacy was often reported in the media, but it should be qualified: Romney was the first LDS presidential candidate to run *since* the first prophet of the LDS Church, Joseph Smith Jr., did so in 1844. So great was the animus against Latter-day Saints in mainstream Christian America in the nineteenth century, that Smith's candidacy ended in his assassination in the same year. Into the 1900s, America's Mormons were persecuted by the evolving federal government and wider Protestant public as unchristian, "barbarous," and unreliable citizens (Givens 2013). Their religious organization and kinship institutions were cast by their critics as theocratic and nepotistic, and were said to be in tension with the Constitution (Gordon 2002; McKinnon and Cannell 2013). In the 2020s, key LDS figures have, however, been found among those most committed to protect American constitutionalism. This is not really a novelty, or a result of simple assimilation, but expresses continuities in distinctive LDS religious understandings, as I will explain further below.

I have been interested for some time in the Mormon response to Trump and, in particular, the tendency of several LDS Republican public figures to speak out in bold criticism of Trump, against the rightwards trend of their party in both the US Congress and the US Senate during and after Trump's term of office from 2016 to 2020.[1] This is despite these politicians' unswerving Republican positions on issues that include the Second Amendment (the right to bear arms) and their conservative small-government preferences that include the demand for more local say in the use of public lands. Historically, the church of Latter-day Saints has not always been a majority-Republican church, but the Utah LDS have been the majority Republicans for the last twelve presidential voting cycles. Utah Republican senators have a generally highly reliable record on voting with their party and president and this loyalty did not just collapse under Trump; as Romney says, he voted with Trump "80% of the time" (Romney 2020).

Trump himself has been a divisive figure in Utah Mormonism. The vote for Trump in 2016 was the lowest majority won there by any Republican president (World Atlas 2019). Many Utah Mormons greatly disliked Trump's personal behaviour, and his often misogynistic, crude, or cruel ways of speaking. In an unprecedented move, the church-owned newspaper the *Deseret News* (2016), in an editorial, called on Donald Trump to resign his candidacy ahead of the presidential election. As the paper said then, "For eighty years, the *Deseret News* has not entered the troubled waters of presidential endorsement. We are

---

1 This chapter was written in 2022; events around Trump are, of course, still unfolding.

neutral in matters of partisan politics ... [but] ... character matters ... [and] 'where the wicked beareth rule, the people mourn' (Proverbs, 29:2).'" Still, Utah's saints are mostly political conservatives and find it difficult not to vote for the Republican candidate; 45.5 per cent of the vote went to Trump and only 27.5 per cent to Democrats, with some Utah protest voters turning to independent candidates. Since 2016, Trump has gained a Republican right-wing following among some, mostly male, Utah Mormons, while continuing to provoke opposition among others in the church. Mitt Romney is one of those Mormon Republicans for whom that opposition came to a head around the 2020 election and around Trump's attempts to hold on to power despite having lost the vote to Joseph Biden.

For what reasons did Mitt Romney refuse to accommodate Donald Trump, rigorously condemn Trump's actions, and even vote to convict him? I suggest that we can consider the statements of Romney and other Mormon senators and public officers contradicting Trump as instances of *parrhesia*, in some of the key senses that concern the contributors to this volume, including as they relate to the last two lecture series of Michel Foucault in 1983 at the University of California, Berkeley and in 1984 at the Collège de France. One of the more condensed definitions of *parrhesia* Foucault offered was "verbal activity in which a speaker expresses his personal relationship to truth and risks his life because he recognizes truth telling as a duty to improve or help other people" (Foucault 2001, 19–20; see also Warren 2009, 8). This formulation perhaps at first seems exaggerated. Not every incidence of frank speech carries an *immediate* risk of death. In the American case with which we are concerned, though, the definition is sadly apt. Five people were killed and 138 injured during the assault on the Capitol on 6 January 2021. Other deaths have been said to be indirectly associated with these events, and very many more only avoided becoming casualties by a thin margin. Trump's statements targeting his critics and opponents have resulted in his followers sending multiple death threats, and visiting people's homes and places of work to bully and harass them publicly for their supposed misdeeds. Many people so targeted by Trump live in fear for their physical safely and that of their families. As well, Republican critics of Trump (whether or not LDS) often risk their careers, the approval of their peers, their reputation, and their incomes.

In this chapter, my first aim is to describe what I will call a "Mormon *parrhesia*." I understand Mormonism to be a constitutive, not an accidental, feature of opposition to Trump from LDS conservatives. More Republican Latter-day Saint voters than Republican Protestant Evangelicals are questioning Trump's actions (e.g., Burge 2020). Several Republican Latter-day Saint individuals, including Mitt Romney, also played a key part in resisting Trump's political trajectory and thwarting his attempt to hold on to power despite losing the 2020 election.[2] I will describe some of the specifically Mormon logics, resources, and dynamics that Mitt Romney and others have drawn on in opposing Trump. Since Mormon Republicans are, as noted, nevertheless split between critics and supporters of Trump – and some Mormons were among the crowds who breached the Capitol – I will trace some of the Mormon expressions on each side, including some widely divergent interpretations of the Book of Mormon hero of "liberty," Captain Moroni. By contrast, I will also sketch the consortium of Protestant Evangelical, Catholic, and other ultra-conservative religious constituencies prominently backing Trump,[3] which Katherine Stewart (2022) refers to as a new development in the America of "religious nationalism." I revisit Laidlaw's (2014) account of religious actors in his landmark argument for the criterion of "freedom" in the anthropology of ethics and suggest that Laidlaw's perspective on traditions of Christians "speaking freely" should be expanded. Our understanding of the religious dimensions of current US politics also needs to avoid oversimplifications. Drawing on the testimony of LDS Republican Speaker from Arizona Rusty Bowers at the January 6th Committee hearings, as well as on Mitt Romney's addresses in the Capitol, I describe particularly the importance of *free will* in Mormon understandings of duty and responsibilities to others.

The Context of Mormon *Parrhesia*: Religion and Politics in the Time of Donald Trump

Most people thinking about the points of convergence between American religion and the politics of Trump, his allies, and emulators would be likely to think first (or perhaps only) about conservative Christian politics, especially among white Protestant Evangelicals. It is to this powerful constituency that Trump apparently wanted to address himself when he posed to be photographed holding up a Bible, after the widely criticized forcible clearing of Black Lives Matter protesters from Lafayette Square in Washington, DC, on 1 June 2020.[4]

---

2 Among Democrats there are many principled bases for resistance to Trump's populist authoritarianism, including for members of Black Lives Matter and the NAACP, as reflected in Senator Bennie Thompson's role as chair of the January 6th Committee. The minority of Republican lawmakers who did not co-operate with Trump are not all LDS; others include Liz Cheney, Adam Kitzinger, and Mike Pence.

3 As K. Stewart (2022) notes, these are not always limited to Christian conservatives but sometimes also include conservative actors of other faiths.

4 For more about this widely reported event, see Mangan (2021). As many people pointed out, the church in the photograph is Episcopalian, and its clergy were outraged by the annexation of their buildings as a background by Trump (e.g., see Kuruvilla 2020).

Trump himself is not personally a typical conservative Evangelical; he was apparently brought up in churches influenced by Norman Vincent Peale and theologies of "positive thinking" (e.g., Brody and Lamb 2018). These churches are part of the broad range of complex prosperity theologies that have been importantly described by Kate Bowler (2014) and that also have many secularized derivatives, often emphasizing the power of prayer to manifest wealth or success as blessings from God. Trump, however, has keenly sought the support of Evangelicals and has seemed happy to accept their spiritual assistance. Televangelist Paula White-Cain, Trump's "spiritual advisor" during the 2020 election, seems to combine elements of both prosperity and Evangelical idioms. White-Cain was seen on widely shared video summoning "angels from Africa" to Trump's aid as the ballot was counted, speaking in tongues and chanting repeatedly, "I hear the sound of victory!" (Idowu 2020; see also Graeber 2020).

One of the most helpful accounts of the alliance between Trumpism and Evangelical churches has been given by Ben Howe who came to the conclusion that his own religious tradition was losing its way. In *The Immoral Majority: Why Evangelical Christians Chose Political Power over Christian Values* (2019), Howe explains that he himself was formerly attracted to the expression of right-wing outrage against liberal Americans, who he and others experienced as dehumanizing and belittling them. He gives an account of how, in his view, Evangelicals convinced themselves that the ends justified the means and began to pursue political power at the expense of their own guiding principles. Abandoning the standards to which their churches were centrally committed, Howe says – that is, standards of integrity in Christian character, charity (Christ-like loving kindness) towards others and the obligation of leading by example – they began to reason that Trump, though unworthy, was God's instrument in bringing about policy changes that would conform with Evangelical ideas of the good. Specifically, stories began to circulate that two people at least (a fireman and a businessman) had received direct prophetic messages that Donald Trump would play a part God intended for him. Trump himself apparently found the idea of divine prophesies of his victory both palatable and believable.

Howe (2019) rejects what he ironically calls "the new Good News," arguing that it will only alienate others, cause damage to the Evangelical churches, and increase the polarization of American politics. Howe, himself a parrhesiast, has received considerable opprobrium from Trump-supporting Christians as a consequence of his writing and remains in the minority of Evangelical opinion. Many influential Evangelical preachers have continued to argue that Trump is the instrument of God and that he is therefore destined for a second presidential victory in 2024. The appointment to the Supreme Court by Trump of enough ultra-conservative judges to overturn *Roe v. Wade* in 2022 is understood by many as sufficient proof of their interpretation and the rightness of their approach.

Josh Hawley, a Republican Senator from Missouri, is another figure who came into the wider public eye after 6 January; a photograph of him holding up a clenched fist in a salute to the gathering crowd of Trump supporters outside Congress on that day was widely circulated in the press. The same image was used for publicity (without copyright permission) by Hawley himself, who printed it onto mugs he sells from his campaign website.[5] Hawley, a Yale Law School graduate, said to have his own presidential ambitions, has a profile that combines right-wing conservatism with claims to be an authoritative interpreter of the meaning of Christianity *in toto*. Hawley bases his arguments on the view that most Americans are "heretics" of the kind identified in the fifth century BCE as Pelagianists. Pelagius (a British monk) argued that God had made human beings perfectible, doubted the doctrine of Original Sin (as defined by Augustine above all), and argued that human duty was to work towards self-perfection. The debates around Pelagianism are serious and complex for many Christians and I do not pretend to summarize them here; for the purposes of this chapter, the key point is that Hawley characterizes his opponents as overclaiming their entitlements of free choice, and of being both antinomian and heretical. Hawley's view of the matter is that he, Hawley, understands the reality of Christian teaching and God's will, and is able to point unambiguously to what this is; interestingly, God's will then turns out to coincide closely with Hawley's ultra-conservative political views.[6]

Hawley's position appears to have things in common with the tendency noted as "originalism," for example with respect to conservative judges' attitudes towards the Constitution. The conservative Catholic Supreme Court Judge Amy Coney Barrett, for example, is often seen as an originalist, in that she claims that only the text of the Constitution itself, dating from 1787, is binding, and that all subsequent legal interpretations and agreements with respect to the Constitution are not (Chemerinsky 2020).

Originalists tend to argue also that the meaning of the Constitution itself is self-evident, and that their own understanding of it is unarguable rather than interpretative. These forms of argument clearly extend the tendency described early on by Vincent Crapanzano (2000) as "literalism" in Evangelical religious and judicial contexts in America. For many commentators from different kinds of Christian traditions, having any such claim to *monopolize* the interpretation of God and to *enforce* this interpretation on others is fundamentally unchristian because in doing so they are failing in humility, indulging in inappropriate judgment, and abandoning the primary duty of love for others.

---

5 See "Shop the Team Hawley Store" at https://secure.winred.com/josh-hawley-committee/storefront/.

6 For a profile of Josh Hawley, see K. Stewart (2021). For Hawley's explanation of Pelagianism in the modern world, see Hawley (2019).

An important commentary on this situation has been offered by Katherine Stewart in her recent book *The Power Worshippers*: *Inside the Dangerous Rise of Religious Nationalism*:

> The religious right has become more focused and powerful even as it is arguably less representative. It is not a social or cultural movement. It is a political movement, and its ultimate goal is power. It does not seek to add another voice to America's pluralistic democracy but to replace our foundational democratic principles and institutions with a state grounded on a particular version of Christianity, answering to what some adherents call a "biblical worldview" that also happens to serve the interests of its plutocratic funders and allied political leaders. (2022, 3)

Stewart describes the ways in which the movement is directed by coalitions of elite political and *financial* or lobbying interests. These are not, therefore, representative politics for any given constituency (including particular conservative churches),[7] but are likely to advance a kind of minority rule by a small in-group. As Stewart argues, it is these alliances in what she calls "religious nationalism" that have generated some of the crucial support for Donald Trump to date. The objections on grounds of character that at one time would have created difficulties for a politician such as Trump have been circumvented, especially by Evangelical arguments that Trump is God's (flawed) instrument.

Who Is Captain Moroni?

So far, I've suggested both that there is an important, and importantly, *Mormon* aspect to the Republican critique of Donald Trump and the authoritarian/populist politics in America. I've also noted that even so, the split in Republican and conservative politics between Trumpism and more traditional Republicanism has divided opinion within churches and denominations, as it has within minority-Evangelical critiques and also within Black-Evangelical critiques. Despite considerable scepticism from established Mormon leaders, Donald Trump has gained a substantial group of (mostly male) Mormon followers in Utah and other LDS homeland states since 2016.

We can trace some of these differences by comparing three interpretations of the Book of Mormon scriptural figure known as Captain Moroni in relation to Donald Trump that emerged among LDS actors. Specifically, former Republican Senator Jeff Flake of Arizona, a critic of Trump, identified himself with Moroni in one way; Republican Senator Mike Lee of Utah, a Trumpist, identified Donald Trump as Captain Moroni in another way; and Nathan Wayne

---

7 K. Stewart (2022) specifies that she is not speaking only of Evangelical Christians and that not all Evangelicals share these politics.

Entrekin, a Latter-day Saint from Arizona, attended the assault on the Capitol Building dressed *as* Captain Moroni; he was later charged, pleaded down, took a guilty plea and was sentenced on two counts: for knowingly entering a restricted building and for violent entry and disorderly conduct on the Capitol grounds.[8]

Captain Moroni is a figure described in the Book of Mormon (Book of Alma, 46), as a leader of the Nephites, who Mormons understand to be an ancient people of the Americas. Captain Moroni is understood in Mormon culture as a righteous defender of democracy and religious freedom against tyranny, who, in LDS commentary, is always noted as *not having sought power for himself.* He is one of the LDS gospel characters who can be "good to think about" but who can also be viewed in different ways. The story is often debated in Mormon popular sources and blogs,[9] and sometimes creates confusion, in part because it has several episodes. In one story, Captain Moroni rallies the Nephites and defeats the would-be tyrant Amalickiah, raising a Title of Liberty (a flag he made himself from cloth torn from his coat) on which is written, "In memory of our God, our religion, and freedom, and our peace, our wives, and our children." As one can observe, Captain Moroni is himself therefore a figure of Mormon *parrhesia.* Later, Captain Moroni battles against another group of "king-men" and calls for help from the judge and leader Pahoran; Pahoran seems to be a traitor as he first fails to answer the call; it later transpires he was loyal, but had been held captive by the same king-men.

Senator Mike Lee's use of this story can be most briefly explained, as Lee saw fit to urge audiences to vote for Trump in the run up to the 2020 election by painting Trump in Mormon heroic colours: "'To my Mormon friends – think of him as Captain Moroni,' Lee said to the crowd at one event, pointing to Trump at his right. 'He seeks not power but to pull it down; he seeks not the praise of the world or of the fake news'" (Bigelow 2021). Senator Jeff Flake's thoughts about Captain Moroni were along other lines. Flake made repeated criticisms of Trump during Trump's presidency. In a speech delivered on 17 January 2018, for example, Flake rebuked Trump for inviting the American public to view the press as "enemies of the people," frankly reminding the House of Representatives that the originator of that phrase was Joseph Stalin

8 For more details, see "Entrekin, Nathan Wayne," United States Attorney's Office, https://www.justice.gov/usao-dc/defendants/entrekin-nathan-wayne. Additional documents – Statement of Offense, Entrekin Plea Agreement, and Criminal Complaint and Statement of Facts – can be accessed on this website. For additional commentary, see Kalmbacher (2021).

9 For a discussion that includes popular illustrations of Captain Moroni of the kind that presumably inspired Entrekin's Roman-style costume, see "Why Did Mormon See Captain Moroni as a Hero?" (2016).

of the Soviet Union. Flake's speech turned on making explicit the idea that all American liberty and civility rests on a mutually constraining sharing of truth between the president and the people:

> Mr. President, near the beginning of the document that made us free, our Declaration of Independence, Thomas Jefferson wrote: "We hold these truths to be self-evident ..." So, from our very beginnings, our freedom has been predicated on truth. The founders were visionary in this regard, understanding well that good faith and shared facts between the governed and the government would be the very basis of this ongoing idea of America.
>
> As the distinguished former member of this body, Daniel Patrick Moynihan of New York, famously said: "Everyone is entitled to his own opinion, but not to his own facts." During the past year, I am alarmed to say that Senator Moynihan's proposition has likely been tested more severely than at any time in our history.
>
> It is for that reason that I rise today, to talk about the truth, and its relationship to democracy. For without truth, and a principled fidelity to truth and to shared facts, Mr. President, our democracy will not last. (CNN 2018)

The reporter Zoe Chace (2018) shadowed Flake for four months for the National Public Radio program *This American Life*. Her original intention was to follow a Republican senator critical of Trump during a re-election campaign, but Flake decided not to stand again. This decision, however, gave him some unexpected leverage within his party, which became less confident about influencing his vote. Flake used this leverage to try to help take a step towards a bipartisan agreement on the so-called Dreamers' bill (the Development, Relief, and Education for Alien Minors Act, or DACA) to secure the path to citizenship of people who had been brought to America as children but who were lacking complete documentation for legal status.

The *This American Life* story mostly did not turn on Flake's Mormonism, but did provide one interesting insight. Chace remarks that Flake seems unusually positive, even after numerous discouraging events, possibly even a touch naive; he responds to her questions about his can-do persistence by referring to the character Captain Moroni in the Book of Mormon, whom Flake calls "a really good guy." What Flake takes from the story is this: Captain Moroni asks for support from the leader of the government, Pahoran, and gets no reply, so he sends him a letter of criticism, calling him to account. But it turns out Pahoran was really a good leader, who himself had been under siege and prevented from responding. Eventually, the two men reconcile. So, the message Flake takes away, which he says was a family motto, is that "Something like that tells you to bridle your passions, not assume the worst. Assume the best. Look for the good. Things usually work out." Chace comments, "'Look for the good'... It's his attitude towards everyone, even Trump, who Flake can't stand" (Chace 2018).

So Flake kept trying for DACA. Unfortunately, he was unsuccessful in working around Trump, and left office without the Dreamers' bill moving forward. Jana Riess (2021) wrote in the *Salt Lake Tribune* (the main non-church-owned paper in Utah) that the January 6th crisis made visible "the best and the worst of Mormonism." Among the best examples of Mormonism, she counted Mitt Romney, to whom we will return below; among the worst examples of Mormonism, she referred to several members of the church who had been won round to Trump's version of Republicanism and who were found to have taken part in the assault on the Capitol Building. A former missionary for the church was among those present inside the debating chamber on that day.

As noted above, it later emerged that another LDS attendee at the Capitol on 6 January was there dressed as Captain Moroni himself. Nathan Wayne Entrekin, a forty-eight-year-old Republican from Cottonwood, Arizona, was a conspicuous although not a violent figure, dressed in what seemed to be a Roman centurion's outfit from a commercial costume supplier. He carried a home-made flag tied to a pole, which he referred to as the Title of Liberty. The statement of facts supplied at Entrekin's trial included video footage he was apparently sending back to his mother. Several people in the crowd addressed him during the riot as "Caesar" or "Hail, Caesar!" Each time, Entrekin corrected them, explaining that he was not Caesar, but Captain Moroni, something he also told press reporters outside the Capitol. Entrekin told an interviewer, "I am Captain Moroni. I am the William Wallace of the Book of Mormon. In the Book of Alma … a freedom fighter named Captain Moroni fought for his freedom against kingmen. He was a freeman, the freemen movement" (Grossarth 2022).

Latter-day Saints are well-known for their historical pageants,[10] which display the church's vision of its prophetic mission in restoring lost teachings from the time of Christ through the mediation of ancestral peoples of the ancient Americas. Those who take part in these pageants connect with these sacred figures from the Mormon past, and sometimes also with deceased members of their own families who have participated in the same pageants before them (see also Jones 2018). Entrekin's costume may therefore have been more than just a publicity stunt.[11] His comments suggest that he identified Washington, DC, with the ancient site of Captain Moroni's defense of freedom, and that his thoughts had turned to a connection with the Nephites across the centuries. He is noted as exclaiming: "Captain Moroni! Same Fight, Same Place, different

---

10 I discuss the Hill Cumorah Pageant (and its recent discontinuation) in my unpublished manuscript "Book of Life."

11 As noted above, he also referenced William Wallace, who led the Scottish resistance against the medieval king Edward I, perhaps (based on his surname) because he has Scottish ancestry and thinks of this as part of his heritage.

time! 76BC. I'm here for Trump. Four more years, Donald Trump! Our rightful president!" (Kalmbacher 2021). Elsewhere, the accounts of Entrekin's comments also include some seemingly bitter statements on homelessness, and rather inchoate references to those who take people's money while leaving them without housing in a "free" nation (Kalmbacher 2021). Money is also mentioned in the Criminal Complaint.[12]

Possibly, Entrekin was referring to the default Republican accusation against Democrats that they raise taxes. In any case, the hinterland of economic anxiety this suggests would be typical of many of those who went to the Capitol. The social, economic, and health vulnerabilities among some of the rioters, as well as the terrible scale of the damage and pain they caused to others, have started to emerge in the stories of the now 840 or more people charged and convicted in relation to the January 6th crisis (see, e.g., Popli and Zorthian 2023); some of which are being been documented by journalists, including Andrea Bernstein and Ilya Marritz (2022) in their podcast series *Will Be Wild* (produced by Wondery). What has also become very clear from these accounts is the importance they have placed on the idea that it was the president of the United States who had called them to the Capitol and who had told them they were righting a historic wrong. The deposition interview of one convicted rioter, Danny Rodriguez, who used a Taser that injured Capitol policeman Michael Fanone during the attack, has been made public domain by the courts and has been reported widely. In a tearful statement that strikes most listeners as genuine, Rodriguez can be heard apparently struggling with disorientation about his own actions, saying at one point, "I thought I was a good guy" (see, for example, Keller 2021). Like so many of those who attended, he repeatedly said he understood the president of the United States had called him to be there, that it was his obligation to be there, to protect the Constitution.

FBI interviews reminded those deposed that even if the election results had been falsified, nobody was entitled to use violence as a means of redress, unless they were certain that someone had called them to arms who was authorized to do so. But as many people have pointed out, the American system is not designed to cope well with rogue presidents who lie, send their supporters into harm's way, and claim authorization where they have none. From the perspective of 2022, Captain Moroni in the Book of Mormon looks fortunate; he was able to tell the difference between tyranny and truth most of the time. When he erred, his mistake was to see treachery where there was in fact loyalty, not vice versa. As Chace (2018) noted, there is a marked strand of optimism in Mormon doctrine. Captain Moroni probably stands for most Mormons as a figure of

---

12 See United States District Court, Criminal Complaint, 3, https://www.justice.gov/usao-dc /case-multi-defendant/file/1413181/download.

good judgment under difficulties, and Latter-day Saints believe that all faithful members of the church should look for the promptings of the Holy Spirit to guide them. But there are risks to thinking one is called to heroic acts.[13] It's obviously difficult to know who Captain Moroni is or whether you are standing in his shoes if you cannot identify the true or false leaders to whom he must relate.

Later in the chapter, I return to other crucial Mormon framings for *parrhesia* in relation to Mitt Romney and Rusty Bowers, but first I want to argue for a widening of our default theorizations of Christian ethical action.

"Freedom" and Free Will

One of the most widely read and productive anthropological texts on ethics is James Laidlaw's *On the Subject of Virtue* (2014). As is well-known, Laidlaw argues for a focus on "freedom," while others in the field, including Michael Lambek (2010), have taken a different approach via "ordinary ethics." Discussion by these and other authors has been extensive and wide-ranging. For the purposes of this chapter, I want to consider just one strand of Laidlaw's argument, which is the placement of Christianity in relation to the core value of freedom he selects.

Laidlaw's (1995) own studies of Jainism, on ritual and on other topics in the anthropology of religion, are of course well known. I find it interesting, therefore, that Laidlaw's (2014) landmark study of ethics seems to set up a certain tension around the relationship of "religion" and "freedom," such that the two implicitly pull away from each other. This tension resides partly in the selection of Laidlaw's leading examples. In the culminative arguments of the book, Laidlaw's key virtue of "freedom" is illustrated by reference to Foucault's essays (1997, 2011) on fifth-century Athenian (pre-Christian) male elite ethics and the care of the self; exploring " the way individuals might take themselves as the object of [voluntary] reflective action" (Laidlaw 2014, 111). One of his most important case studies for the discussion of the history and theology of Christianity, on the other hand, is Alasdair MacIntyre ([1981] 2006), for whom as Laidlaw (2014, 68) puts it, "modernity is a calamity for which a viable (indeed the only) remedy is to undo the Enlightenment, by returning to religious authority." By "religious authority" I assume both Laidlaw and MacIntyre mean hierarchical, clerically mediated interpretations of religious

---

13 The FBI noted in their case against Entrekin that Captain Moroni executed those Nephites who continued to follow Amalickiah the tyrant. This is in the text, although it is not what Mormons take from the story in any mainstream commentary to my knowledge, and apparently Entrekin did not mention this.

teachings. Laidlaw is not a great admirer of MacIntyre's approach to "tradi-tion" in this sense, and prefers liberalism in which he locates the freedom of reflexive subjectivity.

The tension also emerges as a side-effect of Laidlaw's (2014) debates with Saba Mahmood and Charles Hirschkind. Without entering into these, what in-terests me here is one of the resting-points of Laidlaw's critique, where rightly or wrongly he claims that Mahmood has accidentally borrowed (or perhaps "caught"?) an implausible fiction of the "traditional," obedient self from Mac-Intyre ([1981] 2006), and misdescribed Egyptian women's piety movements with it such that the reader cannot know whether or not they actually experi-ence conflicts between different ethical goals in daily life. It is not wholly clear, on my reading, whether Laidlaw (2014, 166ff) thinks that, like Macintyre, the leaders of Egyptian pietism believe the problems of modernity need to be fixed by obedience, clerical hierarchy, and "tradition," but that remains possible.

A little earlier in the text, Laidlaw (2014) has already introduced the idea of how this is supposed to play out in daily life according to (his reading of) Mahmood, as a religious practice that aims at "bypass[ing] thinking" and that "inculcates habit" (borrowing the phrase from MacIntyre [1981] 2006) such that fear of Allah's judgment eventually induces or permits a cultivated automaticity in obedience to divine commands. According to Laidlaw (2014, 154), the ideal here is that "freedom is exercised towards its own future curtailment," and he remarks that the ideas "of a self-extinguishing moral will are not uniquely a feature of reformist Islam, but are common in ethicized 'world religions,' espe-cially those traditions in which life in this world is negatively valued in relation to either an afterlife or a state of enlightened liberation from human existence." He lists a number of additional examples, including Rebecca Lester's (2005) eth-nography of contemporary Mexican nuns, *Jesus in Our Wombs*. Laidlaw (2014) then goes on to explore a range of ethnographies that illustrate aspects of the con-flict of values between religious ideals and lived practices of the good, including his own account of the contradiction between Jain asceticism (which ultimately leads towards the good of self-extinction) and the navigation of a good life for lay Jains for whom family and prosperity are also important.

What is missing is any substantive discussion of the kinds of religious ideal in salvational religion that *differ* from the MacIntyre model of the self in reme-dial obedience to "tradition." Laidlaw (2014) does not say these do not exist, but he also does not show us what they might be, and the effect is to make it seem as though "obedience" and asceticism were the most typical forms, standing in contrast to the reflective Athenian (or liberal) self. Yet the reality is much more varied, even in Christianity alone (see also Cannell 2017). Lester's (2005) ethnography, on my reading, centres *not* on a telos of fear and obedi-ence but on the pursuit of a healing realization of a self that is dialogically constituted and sustained by the dynamic love of God.

Foucault himself, although stressing Christianity as the historical entry-point of self-mistrust and modes of confessional self-hood, also recognizes that obedience and fear have never been the totality of available modes of thought within Christian traditions. He acknowledges a parallel mode of trust in God not discussed by Laidlaw (2014). In this mode, Christians could speak freely of the goodness of God, confident in the ability of God to sustain them in his sight, despite any human displeasure or punishment visited on them by earthly power-holders.[14] For Foucault (1983, 337), "the parrhesiastic pole of confidence in God … not without difficulty, has subsisted in the margins against the great enterprise of anti-parrhesiastic suspicion that man is called upon to manifest and practice with regard to himself and others, through obedience to God, and in fear and trembling before this same God." Foucault situates this tradition primarily within what he calls "mysticism," but as Warren (2009) and other historians have pointed out, it is closely applicable to sociality, understanding of sacred presence, and language of nonconformist groups such as the Seekers and Quakers in seventeenth-century England. For Warren (2009, 9), Quaker reproofs to the established religion and monarchy for persecuting nonconformists exemplified "a parrhesiastic tradition of confident public speech emerging from the tradition of mysticism."[15]

Although with a different doctrine and institutional history than either Quakers or Catholics, Mormons also have a parrhesiastic modality of confidence and trust in God that enables the public challenge of overmighty power for the good of others. As I will show in the final section of this chapter, that tradition particularly expresses a version of Christian theologies of free will (of which there are many different traditions). This kind of Christian freedom converges with the parrhesiast rebuke to political oppression and demonstrates a reflective process of conscious choice for courage, and not automaticity.

Speaking Freely to Donald Trump

Let's go back to Senator Mitt Romney, with whom we began this chapter. As noted above, Romney was the *only* Republican senator who voted to convict Trump on Trump's *first* impeachment. The charges then concerned abuse of power relating to the pressure Trump had placed on Ukrainian President Volodymyr Zelenskiy in an extempore phone call. In a speech to Congress on

---

14 This is originally the radical trust in God exemplified by Christian martyrs, who were willing to die for their faith (but did not kill or coerce others for it).

15 Matei Candea notes the importance of the Quakers in his introduction to this volume.

5 February 2020, explaining why he had voted to convict, Romney spoke extremely frankly:

> The grave question the Constitution tasks senators to answer is whether the President committed an act so extreme and egregious that it rises to the level of a "high crime and misdemeanor."
>
> Yes, he did.
>
> The President asked a foreign government to investigate his political rival.
>
> The President withheld vital military funds from that government to press it to do so.
>
> The President delayed funds for an American ally at war with Russian invaders.
>
> The President's purpose was personal and political.
>
> Accordingly, the President is guilty of an appalling abuse of the public trust.
>
> What he did was not "perfect" – No, it was a flagrant assault on our electoral rights, our national security interests, and our fundamental values. Corrupting an election to keep oneself in office is perhaps the most abusive and destructive violation of one's oath of office that I can imagine.

Romney rightly anticipated that many Republicans would vehemently condemn his speaking out:

> … and in some quarters, I will be vehemently denounced. I am sure to hear abuse from the President and his supporters. Does anyone seriously believe I would consent to these consequences other than from an inescapable conviction that my oath before God demanded it of me?

He emphasized that he understood it to be the inescapable duty of the Senate to provide an objective judgment on impeachment trials:

> The allegations made in the articles of impeachment are very serious. As a Senator-juror, I swore an oath, before God, to exercise "impartial justice." I am a profoundly religious person. I take an oath before God as enormously consequential. I knew from the outset that being tasked with judging the President, the leader of my own party, would be the most difficult decision I have ever faced. I was not wrong. (Romney 2020)

Indeed, there was considerable backlash against Romney, as he anticipated. He was censured by the Republican Party and divided Utah voters.[16] Those

---

16 One 2021 poll showed 50 per cent of Utah Republicans approving Romney's conduct and 46 per cent disapproving; his stand was approved of by most Democrats and Independents. See Romboy (2021).

who were supportive, recalled that Romney's father had been a critic of Richard Nixon, and they also compared Romney to Captain Moroni (Christensen 2021).

Mitt Romney is a wealthy and powerful man, who is well placed to survive these experiences, but clearly opposing Trump was not easy for him, nor for any Mormon Republican who did so. In the video of this speech, Romney appears as usual, somewhat wooden (to my eye) in delivery, conservatively suited, temperate in demeanour, with a habit of slightly clicking his teeth at intervals, which can make it more difficult to listen to him talking. His delivery in the recording differs slightly from the transcript in one important way when he says: "I am profoundly ... religious. My faith is at the heart of who I am." And then follows a pause of complete silence, Romney looking down, without a word, at his notes for almost eleven seconds – which on a video recording feels like a long period of time. Despite his stiff and formal approach, it gradually dawns on the observers that Romney is fighting back tears. He succeeds and resumes his speech in exactly the same tone of voice as before. It is only the pause, and the shorter pause between "profoundly" and "religious" together with a bit of an uneven pitch on the phrase "who I am" that makes it clear one is not mistaken.

Some reporters noted that his speech had been "emotional," which is clearly true. For anyone familiar with LDS church services, though, I suggest there is a clear message here. It derives from the ways in which Latter-day Saints commonly register and acknowledge the work of the Holy Spirit when they testify to their faith – a frequent practice during weekly Sunday services, especially on Fast and Testament Sundays, which occur on the first Sunday of each month. Tears are understood as a sign of the possible presence of the guidance of the Holy Spirit in both oneself and others; at the same time, LDS congregations acknowledge that one might just be emotionally overwhelmed or tired (see also Cannell 2005). Establishing whether or not one is receiving sacred guidance is therefore a matter for discernment; private reflection, prayer, and perhaps counsel with others, especially when making a consequential decision. Although Mormons not uncommonly receive visions, they usually expect the promptings of the Holy Spirit may come quietly and subtly; therefore, one should be thoughtful as well as receptive to occasions when, as they say, "the veil is thin" between this and other worlds.

This attitude to the sacred is connected with a crucial principle of Mormon doctrine, which is the centrality of human free will. In Mormon doctrine, for reasons I will not fully reprise here, humans can only ever attain earthly or post-mortal happiness by exercising responsibility. "Choose the right" is a Mormon catchphrase, and although Mormons can sometimes be socially conformist within a powerful church hierarchy, they are not always or necessarily so. In the end, *choosing* what is right to do as best one can, even when this is confusing and hard, is crucial to Mormon understandings of humanity and God's purposes in the world. In strong contrast to the idea of automaticity, or unthinking obedience, as a mode of virtuous action necessitated by salvational religions, Mormons (and other Christians also) therefore emphasize the processual, risky, and unpredictable nature of acting according to one's conscience. The right decision is valuable – virtuous – only because it requires effort each and every time. It is always possible that one might fail in any number of ways; become confused and make an error, be overwhelmed by fear; or – worse – give way to pride, rage, greed, or ambition. Even when one is confident about what the right decision is, carrying it through still requires a form of emotional and ethical labour that is never done in advance.

What we see in the almost eleven seconds of silence on the Romney video is, in my understanding, not just Romney being troubled, but Romney connecting with the sources of sacred guidance in the light of which he has laboured to make a decision of conscience.

The emphasis on the sacredness of the oath of public office that Romney mentioned was common among all those (whether or not LDS) who did not defer to Trump on 6 January 2021. Still, this too has a special resonance for Mormons. First, an oath in LDS understandings is given great cultural weight, as something that the Heavenly Father (God) would literally see and hear one doing, as if one stood before him at that moment. Second, as the historian Matthew Bowman has argued, despite the earlier federal repression and sometimes stigmatization of Latter-day Saints, Mormon doctrine and history supports the notion that the first prophet, Joseph Smith Jr., understood the Constitution of America as divinely inspired (see Noyce and Stack 2022). Smith perhaps hoped throughout his life that eventually the federal government would, like Pahoran, reveal itself as a loyal friend despite appearances, and extend to Latter-day Saints a constitutional protection for freedom of religion, as their leaders thought they deserved. Given also that Latter-day Saints readily conceive of moving through time to speak with the holy dead and those unborn, the oath of public office, for Latter-day Saints, likely has resonances of being witnessed by many persons seen and unseen, including perhaps the church's first prophet and others of personal importance to the oath-taker, such as deceased parents and grandparents.

I describe this possibility (although we have no direct statements in the news coverage to date) to convey how important the social aspects of Mormon salvationalism are. For Latter-day Saints, the dead, especially dead relatives and members of the church, are always nearby and people think a great deal about how present, past, and future family and friends will be united and how they will socialize in the life to come. Equally, a person's obligations to and conduct towards others is the central terrain on which Latter-day Saints learn and practise to "choose the right." Like Mitt Romney, Speaker Rusty Bowers placed great emphasis on his oath to serve the Constitution when giving testimony to the January 6th Committee hearings. Bowers spoke at the Day 8 Session on 21 July 2022. "It is a tenet of my faith," Bowers said at one point, "that the constitution is ... divinely inspired." Bowers, a strong conservative Republican, stated repeatedly that he was not willing to pretend to win an election by cheating. Recounting several phone calls from Donald Trump and his acting lawyer Rudy Giuliani, in which Bowers was pressured to appoint false electors and to say that Trump had won Arizona, Bowers also made careful reference to others around him to whom his actions mattered. He repeated more than once that he would not put his people or his district through a process of false election claims, in the absence of evidence or qualified legal counsel, because his oath was taken to serve his state and to uphold the law. He also mentioned his wife, "a very strong woman," who suggested they take one of Trump's calls jointly, presumably so that they could witness for each other what was being said. Giuliani reportedly urged Bowers repeatedly to accept that there had been hundreds or thousands of fake votes for Biden cast by illegal immigrants, and thousands cast in the names of dead people. Bowers's response was to ask Giuliani to send him the list of *names* involved. Giuliani promised to do so, but no name of any supposed fake voter was ever sent to Bowers (Associated Press 2022).

In this exchange, Bowers's language in referring to the supposed fake voters is notably less careless and harsh than that used by Rudy Giuliani. Giuliani jokes about "dead people" while Bowers refers to "deceased individuals" and asks for the names of each person. Giuliani may likely not have realized that neither immigrants nor the dead are throwaway categories of people for Latter-day Saints. Mormons identify themselves as a church of immigrants and a church with a global mission, and are less negative in their views of immigration than other Republican voters. The dead are a primary relational category for Mormons, since Mormon doctrine teaches that vicarious rituals and genealogy for the dead of the entire world must be completed before the end of the world. In order to pursue their religious obligations, the LDS church collects, organizes and makes available millions of genealogical records, as well as putting immense energy into the researching of Mormon history. Latter-day Saints are therefore unlikely to find it a matter of indifference to lie about or falsify important documents relating to the lives of either of those from across a national boundary or from across the boundary between life and death.

As part of his testimony to the committee, Speaker Bowers described the physical threats, intimidation and slanders to which he and his family and neighbours had been already subjected to for many months as a result of Trump's assertion that he had acted improperly, including the distress suffered by his severely sick daughter when mobs gathered around their house every Saturday with loudspeakers and, sometimes, with firearms. Following the delivery of his powerful testimony to the January 6th Committee, Bowers (like Romney earlier) was formally censured by the Republican Party. Bowers reported that the environment manufactured around him was "so hostile" that it would be a miracle if he were to win the primary. Trump referred to him as a "terrible" person, and urged voters in Bowers's tenth district to vote for an alternative candidate in the GOP primary for a state Senate seat. Trump's candidate, David Farnsworth, won by a large margin following the ballot on 2 August, despite Bowers's seventeen years of service to his state (A. Smith 2022).

Conclusion

In advocating for the "American Renewal Project," Josh Hawley explained the political consequences of what (he claimed) as his view that Americans generally are guilty of Pelagian heresy: "'We are called to take that message into every sphere of life that we touch, including the political realm,' Mr. Hawley said. 'That is our charge. To take the lordship of Christ, that message, into the public realm, and to seek the obedience of the nations. Of our nation!'" (K. Stewart 2021). The American Renewal Project that Hawley pursues in part through alliance-making, profit-raising, and networks of influence is what K. Stewart (2021) describes as "religious nationalism." It is interesting to place Hawley's announcement alongside the Mormon scholar Hugh Nibley's commentary on Captain Moroni and his people, known in the Book of Mormon as the free-men: "Eschewing ambition, they were not desirous or envious of power and authority; they recognized that they were 'despised' by the more success-oriented King-men" (quoted in Welch 1985).

Religious parrhesiasts, as Warren (1985, 8) has argued for the Quakers, fulfil Foucault's description that they "recognise truth telling as a duty to improve or help other people" as well as themselves, and they also "remind ... the church ... of its duty to bring its members into a deeper, living union with God rather than simply provide a salvation machine which promises heavenly bliss if members follow the requisite steps" (6). I have argued here that Mormon Republicans are acting as parrhesiasts in a similar way, and also that although they may express "confidence" in God as Foucault and Warren both predict, they also must act as fallible human beings under the privilege and burden of free will, for whom *parrhesia* requires a constant labour of courage.

Nibley, like a number of his co-religionists, was familiar both with the teaching of the first prophet, Joseph Smith Jr., that warned against coercion of others as "unrighteous dominion" and also with the New Testament in which to my knowledge there is nothing that suggests that the Jesus of the gospels justified, countenanced, or sanctioned power-seeking, bullying, lying, fraud, the exploitation of the poor, or inciting or committing violence, even against those who mistreat you. It would seem that Josh Hawley has not recently read the Sermon on the Mount; he is too busy claiming to be an authority on what fifth-century church fathers mean for our times. As Robert Orsi (2004, 1) has said, religion is not automatically either harmful or helpful to human thriving in its effects, but depends on the social relationships through which it flows. Egregious harm and violence has been committed and still is committed by religious hierarchies and institutions, and also, justified with respect to religious teachings. The LDS church itself has had numerous internal conflicts with its own members over the proper balance of power between a heteronormative male lay priesthood and other members, including Mormon women and LGBTQO members, and these are by no means resolved. This chapter has aimed to demonstrate, however, that in the currently bleak American scene, and among conservative political constituencies, a committed religious stance can and does generate multiple kinds of responses to political authoritarianism, not reducible to the Evangelical-Trump alliance, nor sufficiently described as religious "obedience."

6 Fascism, Real or Stuffed: Ordinary Scepticism at Mussolini's Grave

PAOLO HEYWOOD

Introduction: Dear Fascist Dickhead

Many politicians are habituated to receiving hate mail or abuse, perhaps due to their gender, ethnicity, sexual orientation, or because of some particular policy they espouse. Giorgio Frassineti, mayor of Predappio during most of the period of my fieldwork, received regular postcards from different holiday destinations while he was in office, all from the same anonymous individual, and all beginning, "Dear Fascist Dickhead." Another regular writer would address all of his correspondence to Giorgio as the "Podestà" of Predappio, the official designation for a mayor under the fascist regime.

"Predappio" and "Fascism" are indissolubly linked in the minds of most outsiders who have heard of the town. This is because Benito Mussolini was born in the tiny hamlet of Predappio (as it was), because he reconstructed it in its entirety as a monument to fascist urban engineering and as a sort of open-air museum to his early life, because his regime bussed thousands and thousands of tourists there to visit the house in which he was born, and because his remains were buried there in 1957, making it Italy's most famous place of neo-fascist pilgrimage (see Heywood 2019, 2021, 2023b, 2024a).

So, it is not only Giorgio, as Predappio's most public citizen, who falls victim to this association. I was told on countless occasions that it was a common habit for Predappiesi to lie about their origins when travelling outside of the town in order to head off the inevitable assumptions that outsiders would make about them. Not that such assumptions always lead to negative consequences: many Predappiesi have stories of discounts or other forms of preferential treatment at hotels when they show their passports, and the Italian police are famous in the town for displaying leniency to Predappiesi caught speeding, as are the military for giving an easy ride to Predappiesi conscripts.

Gianni, a local artist, has a favourite story of visiting a bar in Rome ("They're all Fascists there, you know," he says) and being overheard to pronounce his *s*'s in the idiosyncratic fashion of Emilia-Romagna. Upon revealing to his new Roman friends that he is from Predappio, he was instantly taken to be a *camerata* (a fascist term of address, akin to "comrade") and directed to a variety of restaurants in the city in which the mention of his hometown would earn him a very cheap dinner.

Gianni is not, in fact, a Fascist, or at least not according to any criteria that would make sense to anybody in Predappio or most people elsewhere. He has no compunction accepting a cheap dinner from self-proclaimed Fascists because he is an easy-going man with almost nothing to say about politics, preferring instead to devote himself to his paintings. Mayor Giorgio may well be a "dickhead" in the opinion of many Predappiesi who did not vote for him, but nobody except an outsider going only by his place of residence would call him a Fascist. He has been a member of Italy's mainstream left-wing party – the successor to the Italian Communist Party – throughout his political career.

Of course, the association between Predappio and Predappiesi on the one hand, and Fascism on the other, is not really dependent on the thought that everyone in Predappio is actually a Fascist. Rather, in cases like these, Predappio and Predappiesi are indexes of Fascism to those around them. That is, the town, or the appearance of its inhabitants, seem to do the work of making Fascism itself present to others, for good or for ill, in the same way in which a swastika indexes the presence of Nazism (Shoshan 2016). In providing a discounted room rate or restaurant dinner, or in forgiving a speeding ticket to someone for no other reason than that they are from Predappio, one is somehow – among other things – doing a favour for Fascism. In addressing the mayor of Predappio as a "dickhead," one is striking a blow at Fascism, even if this particular mayor, like all his postwar predecessors, is an erstwhile member of the Communist Party. More obviously, Predappio also clearly has long had an iconic as well as indexical relationship to Fascism, from the early days of fascist picture postcards of Predappio under the regime, to a woman who caused international consternation by mocking up a representation of the Predappio skyline on a T-shirt in place of the Disneyland logo, above the word "Auschwitzland" (Heywood 2019).

In some senses, this and other forms of behaviour by visiting neo-Fascists in Predappio, as well as letters addressing its mayor as a "fascist dickhead," look like stereotypical instances of what we have come to associate with "free speech" – extraordinary and dramatic (and sometimes hateful) interventions in the public sphere (cf. Candea et al. 2021; Pipyrou and Sorge 2021). Such interventions have increasingly become indexes of the very concept of "free speech," as it feels more and more impossible to discuss the topic without immediately invoking racist demagogues, hate preachers, or Nazis marching in Illinois (to reach back to an older exemplar).

This perhaps helps in part to explain the lack of widespread anthropological interest in "free speech." Given our discipline's methodological and philosophical preference for the mundane, the everyday, and the quotidian, iconic controversies around "free speech" are often wont to pass above our heads, or beneath our noses. Forms of speech that have tended to interest anthropologists often – though certainly not always, as in studies of political oratory – look very different indeed to the bombastic rhetoric of many who claim to exercise "free speech." The traditional objects of anthropological interest in speech are instead – often carefully recorded and transcribed – instances of "ordinary language": of an initial consultation between a patient and a Mapuche healer (Guzman 2014), or the role ethnonyms have to play in stories of the past in an urban community in Pennsylvania (Smith and Eisenstein 2013), or the cultural significance of fricative voice gesturing in Korea (Harkness 2011), to take three random examples from the *Journal of Linguistic Anthropology*. This opposition – between the "ordinary language" anthropologists tend to study and specially marked and controversial instances of "free speech" – is reinforced by arguments around "free speech" that either presuppose or critique the idea that the subject of free speech – the free speaker – is an autonomous individual giving voice to an independent interiority (e.g., Fish 1994): "ordinary language" is social (and therefore real), whereas "free speech" is individual (and therefore a fantasy or ideology).

If in this sense we are wont to think of "free speech" as unworthy of attention, both because it is not "ordinary" enough and because the linguistic ideology of decontextualized individuals expressing an unmediated inner self is merely a chimera, it has in these regards something in common with other forms of speech or utterance: those Ludwig Wittgenstein famously characterized as instances of "language on holiday" – that is, language that is "free," if you like, in the sense of being somehow unmoored or divorced from its proper context, not doing the job it usually does. Perhaps the quintessential example is sceptical speech, forms of which are often imagined – like "free speech" – to be the polar opposite of "ordinary language," as when sceptical philosophy is conjured up as the latter's opposite, precisely because such sceptical forms seem untethered to any sensible ordinary context: we do not under normal circumstances question the existence of tables, tomatoes, or bits of wax in front of our eyes. To do so is to use language in a way that grinds against the context – that makes no sense in any language game except the peculiar one of philosophy.

The kind of "free speech" I examine in Predappio, being on the inflammatory topic of Fascism, is sometimes "free speech" in this sense of being marked as special or eventful or significant (as opposed to being ordinary), particularly when it is indulged in by neo-fascist visitors. It indexes those qualities of controversy and bombast that we have increasingly come to take as interchangeable with instances of "free speech" in action, despite being, in fact, more or less ordinary in Predappio because of the town's very particular history and status.

But what I primarily wish to explore here are ways in which this sense of "free speech" ties into forms of sceptical speech about Fascism by Predappiesi themselves – forms of speech that might look at first like instances of "language on holiday," but which make perfect sense in the very specific context of Predappio. To illustrate this second sense of "free speech," I return to the question posed by the story of the letter writer: How do you know a Fascist when you see one?

Two Senses of "Free Speech"

Speech about Fascism in all sorts of other contexts is very often fraught. There is also a recursive quality to its fraughtness insofar as not only can speech about Fascism be difficult, but it is also itself often invoked as an explanatory factor for that very difficulty: actors accused of restricting "free speech" are labelled "Fascist," as very often are those whose (racist, sexist, homophobic, xenophobic, etc.) speech is actually or potentially restricted in any given legal context.

This quality of fraughtness has an extended history, almost as long as the history of Fascism itself. Philosophers, historians, political scientists, and commentators of all varieties have argued endlessly over the proper use of the word Fascism (Heywood 2023a). George Orwell (1944) once called "What is Fascism?" the most important unanswered question of our time, and in recent years that question has suddenly seemed relevant to many across the world once more, as a flurry of new or familiar answers have emerged in response to an international resurgence of the far-right. There is now a Wikipedia page solely devoted to competing "Definitions of Fascism," and *Slate* magazine, for example, recently printed an excerpt from Passmore's *Fascism: A Very Short Introduction* (2002) as part of its academy series on Fascism, suggesting readers consult the extract to determine whether or not they were living in a "fascist state" (Passmore 2017). *The Atlantic*, noting the "elusiveness" of definitions of Fascism, interviewed historian Robert Paxton in search of a checklist of features with which to assess the extent to which Donald Trump is a Fascist (Green 2016). The pages of international news and commentary have recently been filled with speculation as to whether and how far France's National Rally (formerly the National Front), Germany's Alternative for Germany (AfD), or the Freedom Party of Austria "count" or do not "count" as "Fascist," and the word was in the running to be *Merriam-Webster*'s "Word of the Year" in 2016. There is even a name – "Godwin's Law" – for the predictability with which almost any prolonged internet argument will inevitably devolve into accusations of Fascism.

We might imagine three sorts of responses to Orwell's problem. One sort of response seeks to provide a definition of some sort, a "fascist minimum," in the words of one well-known such attempt (Eatwell 1996). This sort of response has been attempted by a number of historians and politicians, as well as by jurists, who have, in contexts such as postwar Italy and Germany, been charged with the task of identifying and rooting out the remains of fascist regimes.

Historians and other academics have defined Fascism as, among other things, a class-based response to the development of socialism (see, for instance, Poulantzas 1974; Trotsky 1944), a psychological phenomenon resulting from a kind of mass hysteria (Reich 1933), a species of "developmental dictatorship" as a politico-economic stage (Gregor 1979), a palingenetic type of ultra-nationalism (Griffin 1991), and a form of religion as a political movement (Gentile 1990), to name just a few.

This sort of response will sound uncompelling to many anthropologists. It would seem to rely on the same "descriptive fallacy" (Austin [1946] 1979) upon which the linguistic ideology behind many arguments about "free speech" also depends – that is, the view that what language does is pick out "meanings" or things in the world (see Sidnell in this volume). It would suggest that the sort of speech about Fascism with which we are concerned here is a simple matter of assessing the qualities of the object it picks out against a benchmark definition. This might be true of actual, ordinary usage if it were the case that there were broad and general agreement about such a benchmark definition. This is true, as J.L. Austin ([1946] 1979) points out in his "Other Minds" critique of scepticism, of the way in which we often use words: if a qualified ornithologist tells us that the bird at the bottom of our garden is a goldfinch because of its red head and distinctive eye markings, we will probably take them at their word rather than ask whether or not they can be sure it is a real goldfinch rather than a stuffed one.

The problem in the case of Fascism – and a lot of other cases beyond goldfinches – is that there is no such broad and general agreement on benchmark criteria. So simply asserting an abstract definition that bears no relation to the variety of ordinary usage will not tell us much. It does not tell us if "being the mayor of Predappio" is a necessary or sufficient criterion for identification as a "fascist dickhead" in the same way that distinctive eye markings are so for a goldfinch.

The second sort of response is one with which anthropologists and social scientists may well feel more at home. It is neatly encapsulated in an essay penned by Umberto Eco (1995) for the *New York Review*. Though the piece is in part an attempt to enumerate a list of basic features of what Eco calls "Ur-Fascism," it is most notable for the argument that Fascism, like "game" in Wittgenstein's writings, is a family resemblance term. That is, in ordinary language it is used not with the intention of picking out a definable and essential characteristic but to draw together a set of phenomena, none of which in fact share any single quality.

Fascism became an all-purpose term because one can eliminate from a fascist regime one or more features, and it will still be recognizable as fascist. Take away imperialism from fascism and you still have Franco and Salazar. Take away colonialism and you still have the Balkan fascism of the Ustashes. Add to the Italian fascism a radical anti-capitalism (which never much fascinated Mussolini) and you have Ezra Pound. Add a cult of Celtic mythology and the Grail mysticism (completely alien to official fascism) and you have one of the most respected fascist gurus, Julius Evola. (Eco 1995)

An argument such as Eco's – and the Wittgensteinian claims on which it is based – feels a great deal more fine-grained and more ethnographically sensitive than the first kind. Unlike definitional arguments, it reads not as an assertion ("Fascism is X") but as a description of fact, or ordinary language use ("This is just how we talk about Fascism"). I will return to this form of response in my conclusion.

In Predappio, the question of what is and is not Fascist is posed in a rather particular form, unsurprisingly, and its relevance has never been purely historical. As I will describe, some speech about Fascism in Predappio is definitionally assertive in the manner of the "fascist minimum"; there are also a great many arguments of the sort noted above over what the proper criteria for such a minimum definition are. But what I wish primarily to explore ethnographically here is a third sort of response to Orwell's question – one foreshadowed in the example of Austin and the goldfinch.

In the *Philosophical Investigations*, Wittgenstein famously described some forms of philosophy – and the scepticism Austin was targeting in "Other Minds" is certainly a form he would have had in mind – as instances in which language "goes on holiday" (§38). "Free speech" in this sense – that is, speech that has gotten free of its moorings, of convention and context – is misuse of language, and on most occasions asking a qualified ornithologist who points to a goldfinch in your garden how they know that the goldfinch is real or stuffed is an example.

But what if there are no qualified ornithologists on hand? What if we do not agree on which distinctive features function as benchmark criteria for the identification of goldfinches, or what if a range of such criteria exist and we do not know how to choose between them? If on every occasion on which an apparently qualified person identifies a real goldfinch, another equally qualified person denies that it is so, or denies that it is real, a reasonable response might well be to suspect that the word "goldfinch" has been invented to drive people mad and is incapable of describing any actually existing bird.

Today we find the equivalent of such a position actualized in arguments that take the apparent variety of Fascism's usage as evidence for its lack of legitimacy as a term in political debate. But in truth there has always been a sceptical undercurrent to debates about Fascism. In 1979, one prominent historian became so frustrated by the ambiguous use of the term in his discipline that he famously called for it to be banned from historical discourse (Allardyce 1979; see also Holmes 2000, 13). Orwell (1944) himself, in raising the question of "what Fascism is," was making nearly the same point in remarking that he had heard the word applied to "farmers, shopkeepers, Social Credit, corporal punishment, fox-hunting, bull-fighting, the 1922 Committee, the 1941 Committee, Kipling, Gandhi, Chiang Kai-Shek, homosexuality, Priestley's broadcasts, Youth Hostels, astrology, women, dogs and I do not know what else."

In this chapter, I describe an ethnographic equivalent of this sort of scepticism, a situation in which a form of "free speech" – scepticism as "language on holiday" – has become in a sense conventionalized, or been brought back to work, as it were. The work such scepticism does, in the very particular context that is Predappio, is to render less troubling the sorts of accusations – or claims to fellow feeling – we have seen expressed towards Giorgio and Gianni, and which are so commonplace in regard to Predappio. When everyone around you takes you and your town as indexical or iconic signs of Fascism, being sceptical about "what Fascism is" accomplishes particular effects by muddying the waters of that taken-for-granted relationship.

Paradoxically for an instance of "language on holiday," I argue that one such effect is to render what might otherwise be taken as a dramatic and extraordinary accusation ("free speech" in the sense of inflammatory, special, or significant speech, such as the claim that someone or something is Fascist) into rather ordinary, mundane, banal terms. The work scepticism does here, in other words, is not to turn the ordinary into the extraordinary (by, say, doubting the existence of a garden variety bird in front of one's eyes) but to turn the extraordinary into the ordinary (Clarke 2014; Heywood 2021, 2023b, 2024a) by substituting a highly charged category (Fascism) for something else: graspingness, political self-interest, family loyalty, and so on. The fascist goldfinch, it turns out, is almost always stuffed rather than real.

Such expressions of scepticism are instances of "free speech" in a number of complex senses: in being focused on the question of who or what is a Fascist, they are of course part of the controversial universe of fascist discourse and accusations of Fascism that so much contemporary "free speech" seems to be about, and thus far from "ordinary." Yet they are perfectly ordinary – in the sense of being commonplace – in Predappio, whose existence is so thoroughly saturated by Fascism and by arguments about it. Finally, as I have noted, though such expressions may be as sceptical as Austin's doubter of goldfinches, they are far from being "free" in the sense of "on holiday," or of not doing work in the context in which they emerge: they are aspirational attempts to disaggregate the indexical link between Predappio and Fascism – to "free" the former from the latter.

Fascists, Not Nazis

Attempts to adjudicate the question of who or what is Fascist have an especially complex history in Italy, where Fascism became, in effect, a criminal category after the fall of the regime. Article 30 of the Long Armistice between Italy and the Allies, signed on 29 September 1943, obliged the Italian government to "carry out all directives which the United Nations may call for, including the abolition of Fascist institutions, the dismissal and internment of Fascist personnel, the control of Fascist funds, the suppression of Fascist ideologies and teachings" (quoted in Domenico 1991, 22).

After the war, Provision XII of the 1947 Italian Constitution forbade the reorganization, "under any form whatsoever," of "the dissolved Italian Fascist Party." This provision was then clarified and somewhat extended in a 1952 law known as the "Scelba Law," which not only forbids the reorganization of the dissolved Fascist Party, but also "apologia" for it, as well as public demonstrations in favour of it. Yet these measures too have been undermined in a number of ways, most obviously by the 1946 Togliatti amnesty for convicted fascist criminals and associated legal reforms, which led to the release of 20,000–30,000 people, as well as the electoral successes of the neo-fascist Italian Social Movement (Movimento Sociale Italiano, MSI) in 1948 (Domenico 1991, 212–14; Parlato 2006, 2017, 44).

Moreover, several Italian courts have, over the years, issued a number of decisions that very much restrict – or simply confuse – the scope of the application of the Scelba Law and its constitutional antecedent, as I have described elsewhere (Heywood 2019). For instance, already by 1958, at the trial of three men – two of whom were indicted for performing the Roman salute and wearing a black shirt at Mussolini's tomb in Predappio – Italy's Constitutional Court ruled that the law could only apply in situations in which there was a realistic and intended prospect of the reconstitution of the Italian Fascist Party (Partito Nazionale Fascista, PNF) (see Sentenza Corte Costituzionale n. 74, 1958), not simply in cases in which "demonstrations" were made in favour of it. Similarly, in 1994, the Consiglio di Stato ruled that use of the *fasces* as a political symbol could not in and of itself constitute a breach of electoral law, given the symbol's longer historical association with ancient Rome (Maestri 2017). More recently, the criminal section of the Corte Suprema di Cassazione condemned two CasaPound militants for giving a Roman salute at a memorial day gathering, and then, in 2016, absolved seven other militants for performing exactly the same gesture at a larger such memorial event (Casarotti 2017). In Predappio, where Roman salutes are a regular occurrence, often in full view of police or Carabinieri agents, no one expects intervention from the judicial authorities (Heywood 2019).

Policemen may not consider themselves experts on identifying Fascists in the manner in which an ornithologist could identify a goldfinch, but other outsiders to Predappio do. On a large march marking the anniversary of Mussolini's seizure of power on 28 October 1940, I was watching a small group of men of varying ages wearing black fascist military uniforms, led by a shaven-headed man in his forties. As the troop neared Mussolini's mausoleum at the edge of the town, its leader called out to the group to begin marching in military step.

After a brief and obvious moment of confusion, a young man towards the rear of the group began to goose-step, before being instantly reprimanded by the troop leader: "No! That's their [the Nazis'] thing! We're Fascists, not Nazis!"

I was reminded of this minor display of technical discrimination ("goose-stepping" makes you a Nazi, not a Fascist, and the difference is important to some) a little later that same day as I stood on the street with some anti-fascist acquaintances of my friend Carlo, who had come to Predappio from Forlì to witness the extent of the turnout and to take their dog for a walk. As we stood and watched individuals and groups of people pass by, some of whom were returning to town from the mausoleum, on foot and by car, one acquaintance began reeling off ostensive definitions of her own: "That one's Fascist … that one too … probably that one … that one might not be …" I asked how she was able to tell who was a Fascist and who was not, and she listed some of what she took to be indexical signs: black clothing (not an essential criterion, of course, because anarchists wear black too), leather (also not essential), biker paraphernalia, shaven head (also not an essential criterion), fascist slogans printed on T-shirts, and origin of car licence plate. Later on Carlo gave me another example of a comparable practice from his days in the 1970s as a member of the left-wing group Lotta Continua, one adopted by leftist militants from Forlì looking for visiting Fascists to attack: a volunteer would wait by the side of the road below a local hilltop for a coach to pass by; when it did, the volunteer would raise his arm to give the Roman salute, and if the coachload of visitors did the same in response, he would signal to comrades at the top of the hill, who would promptly begin dropping rocks and boulders on the coach from above.

Historic Turncoat Number One

The search for a "fascist minimum" has, as I have been describing, an established history both in Italy and abroad. One might well imagine that Predappiesi would have elevated this search into a science: Where would one be more likely to find experts on what constitutes Fascism than in the birthplace of its founder, and a kind of Disneyland for neo-fascists across the world? Yet the brief examples I provide above all involve outsiders: neo-fascists seeking to distinguish themselves from Nazis, and anti-fascists looking to identify the enemy. Predappiesi themselves are remarkably reticent in applying this label.

That is not of course because of a shortage of candidates. The most obvious candidates are the visitors themselves, many of whom would quite happily self-describe as "Fascist." Predappiesi themselves, however, very rarely refer to their visitors with any variant of political characterization. In line with their wider response to the ritual marches I have outlined elsewhere (Heywood 2019, 2021, 2023b, 2024a, 2024b), the most commonly used term for these visitors is *nostalgici*, "nostalgics." This resembles Predappiesi descriptions of the marches themselves as "folkloric," "traditional," or "carnivalesque," and suggests the visitors are more like a troop of historical re-enactors than part of a political movement. As in Italian philosopher Benedetto Croce's famous characterization of Fascism as a "parenthesis" in the otherwise great history of Italy, the implication of calling the visitors "nostalgic" is that the object they venerate is dead and gone, a piece of history rather than a living political movement.

That is not to say that all the visitors are perceived in the same way. Massimo, for example, a restaurateur who owns an upmarket eatery very near to the cemetery containing Mussolini's mausoleum, distinguishes between "historic" and "nostalgic" tourists. The former come because they are in the area, and Mussolini's grave is simply a tourist destination to them like any other ("Like I'd go to Jim Morrison's grave, wherever that is"). They come with their families, and if they stop at his restaurant they ask polite questions about the local area and leave again without further ado. The "nostalgic" tourists are those who come in uniforms, who come for the organized marches, and who tend to appear as large groups of men on buses. If Massimo does not attempt to stop them, they will perform Roman salutes in his restaurant after visiting the tomb, and of this group he is rather wary (though not at all averse to taking their coin, as we have seen). At no point does he use the word "Fascist" or any variant thereof to describe them. Massimo does not identify "nostalgics" with Fascists; he distinguishes them from "historical" tourists on the basis of the kind of feeling they have about Italy's fascist period and the intensity of such feelings. Both groups are defined by their feelings about Fascism as a thing of the past, rather than either being isomorphic with it.

There are local candidates too. Sergio, for example, founded the local chapter of the MSI, the postwar reincarnation of the Fascist Party. I have heard him called an "old Fascist" on occasion, but invariably in a jocular tone and in contexts – discussions of the past – that suggest the label refers more to his history as a soldier and his recalcitrance after the war rather than to any present quality in him. He is a very genteel and extremely elderly man, and he is treated with the respect accorded to his age. Nothing about his politics excludes him from sociality with others in the town, and he himself keeps a trove of partisan songs dedicated to Predappio's first postwar mayor and former partisan leader (Heywood 2021).

Other obvious candidates are the owners of three "souvenir" shops (as they are widely known) that punctuate Predappio's main street. "Souvenir shop" is itself something of a euphemism, given that these shops sell repugnant pieces of fascist and Nazi paraphernalia. Here the label "Fascist" is used more frequently, at least in one case, as I discuss below. But even in these cases the waters may be muddied. The most obvious question – often raised by Predappiesi – is whether it is ideology or money (or some combination of the two) that motivates the shop owners.

Two of these proprietors are from Predappio, one of them now deceased. This latter is one whom a number of Predappiesi would willingly call a "Fascist": he effectively began the souvenir trade by selling postcards and relics near the cemetery on the days of the anniversary marches. "He was always a Fascist," Chiara, a town council employee tells me, "even before, even when he wasn't selling gadgets [another common euphemism for fascist paraphernalia]." Her father, a retired lorry driver, disagrees immediately: "No, I think it's for the money. It's not for the politics, it's the money." Angela, a cafe owner, says that when this proprietor opened the first souvenir shop, people in the town joked that he would be selling Che Guevara T-shirts if Predappio had been lucky enough to be Che's birthplace. But she also seconds Chiara's point: "He was always a Fascist though."

Federica, a retired schoolteacher who has taught most of the town's inhabitants, is similarly equivocal:

> Let's say that this guy was the most involved from the beginning, from the point of view of politics. But even he didn't only do this, he did other, normal things too [he owned a hardware store]. And I know his family, they are actually really good people. His wife bends over backwards to help. When I needed a flag in school, she would always find one for me and give me a good price. But it would really bother me every time I went to the shop and had to see all those other things.

The second proprietor from Predappio, still living, is one about whom Predappiesi are much more cynical. "He was in a totally different business," recounts Federica,

> selling chickens, owning poultry houses. But then he went bankrupt, found himself without work, and had the idea to take advantage of this situation and open the shop. So he reinvented himself selling Mussolini souvenirs, but without, I think, any specific political inclination. I mean, it was a way to survive.

Angela is less generous and makes no mention of bankruptcy:

> He had this poultry farm and he made so much money, because it was a huge business, and his brother had an amusement arcade in Predappio. So, when he got old and closed this down, the other one decided to open this shop. He was, how would you say, a "busy bee." He knows where the money is. But there is no ideology there. If tomorrow someone else is popular, he will change his whole business.

Chiara is similarly convinced: "There's definitely more self-interest than ideology in his shop. He saw the business, he did it for the money. I know the family, they have never been Fascists, and he was never involved in politics his whole life before this."

Though it is not the largest, this second shop is in some ways the most conspicuous, at least for pedestrians, since it sits in the middle of Predappio's main street, and the merchandise spills out onto the pavement outside. The owner, a short, grey-haired man with a handlebar moustache, is often at work behind the counter or tidying up the displays, and his compatriots usually greet him politely as they pass. Even Giorgio, the erstwhile left-wing mayor, says hello, and though he dislikes entering the shop in case he is photographed by journalists, I have known him to do so and to reluctantly share a small glass of Mussolini wine with the owner.

The last proprietor is not from Predappio, as Predappiesi will happily tell you, and therefore not seen as their responsibility. He is the most widely known of the three outside of Predappio – even though his shop is the smallest and the least noticeable – because he is also the owner of the Villa Carpena, a fascist-inspired "museum" to Mussolini a little way down the road from Predappio. His pecuniary motivations are taken for granted by most Predappiesi, and there is a degree of resentment at the fact that an outsider is profiting from the town's heritage.

Of course, self-interest and ideological conviction need not be mutually exclusive, and my point here is not about whether or not these men are, in fact, really Fascists. It is that Predappiesi frequently deploy monetary self-interest *as if it were* mutually exclusive with political beliefs. When Predappiesi speculate about the self-interest of these men they are not doing so in order to add "greed" to their charge sheets. They do so in order to dismiss them, with a snicker or a guffaw and a wave of the hand. There is nothing really special about them, is the implication; they are simply businessmen – unscrupulous, perhaps, but this is not an unusual assumption for Italians to make about businessmen in general. In other words, there is a degree of reluctance involved in attaching the label of "Fascist" to even those who might seem most obviously to merit it. But also, in line with Predappiesi attitudes more generally, the way in which that reluctance is evidenced is by opposing something pragmatic or ordinary – like "making a living," being a "busy bee," and knowing where the money is – to the high politics of Fascism.

One might imagine that this sort of distinction would at least lead one to a certain set of criteria with which to identify who is, in fact, a Fascist. If self-interest is a characteristic that excludes people from this set, then presumably there are nevertheless other, less self-interested individuals who fit more comfortably within it. What is doubted here may not be the nature of Fascism as real or stuffed, but the particulars of any specific instance of identification.

The problem, however, is that self-interest is frequently perceived to be at the heart of apparently genuine political convictions more generally. This is of course a broader Italian phenomenon, but it takes on a specific character in Predappio (Heywood 2021, 2023b, 2024a), evidenced by a fascination with stories of *voltagabbana*, or "turncoats," people known to have switched from one political side to another. The implication of such stories is that political affiliation usually runs only skin deep, and that beneath the colours of red or black is simple self-interest. This leads to an even more profound scepticism as to the possibility of identifying Fascism.

One favourite such story of "turncoats" is of Angelo Ciaranfi, the last democratically elected mayor of Predappio in 1920, before the advent of Fascism forced his resignation in 1922. After a few years under the regime, however, Ciaranfi underwent a conversion and joined the Italian Fascist Party. In order to make the strength of his new convictions clear, he even rewrote his will to include a codicil requiring him to be buried in a fascist black shirt.

Later still, "after the disaster and the tragedy of war and the failures of Fascism," runs a local history book,

> Ciaranfi, good old Ciaranfi, realized he'd made a serious mistake and turned on his feet politically again, joining the Italian Communist Party [Partito Comunista Italiano, PCI]. After the liberation of Predappio, he served in the administration of the first postwar democratic mayor, Giuseppe Ferlini. But those tumultuous years had no doubt radically transformed Ciaranfi's existence, like those of many other Italians, and it's probably for this reason that he forgot to rewrite his will. So, when he died in June 1948, and his testament obliged him to be buried in a black shirt, there was much consternation and embarrassment amongst his comrades, who were expecting to send him off draped in the red flag with the "Internationale" playing. In the end, and not without argument, it was decided that his body would lie in an open casket, and obligatory black shirt, for a brief private ceremony with the family, before being buried with casket closed in a civil ceremony, complete with the PCI band and the red flag.[1] (Capacci, Pasini, and Giunchi 2014, 219)

Many of my Predappiesi friends loved the story of Ciaranfi, his multiple switches of political allegiance, and his awkward funeral.

There are a number of other such stories that Predappiesi like to tell. One concerns a *repubblichino* (a soldier of the post-1943 German puppet government of the Republic of Salo, the RSI) returning to Predappio after the Axis surrender and being stopped on the road outside the town by a band of anti-fascists looking to exact punishment on any returning RSI soldiers they encountered. Among this band the *repubblichino* is very surprised to find his former battalion sergeant, who had deserted from the army of the RSI only a month before the end of the war (Capacci, Pasini, and Giunchi 2014, 216–17). Another favourite is very similar: in the early 1920s a local man refuses to sign up to the

---

1 All translations are my own.

Fascist Party and is regularly beaten up by local Fascists as a result. Finally, he converts, and with a convert's zealotry he even goes on to fight for the RSI after the fall of Mussolini in 1943. After the surrender in 1945 he returns to Predappio, and as in the previous story, is seized by a band of anti-fascists in the town upon his return. Upon realizing that one of the men about to beat him for being a Fascist was one of the men who used to beat him for not being a Fascist, he says calmly to the group, "All of you can punch me as much as you want, except him, he's already had his turn" (217).

But it is Mussolini himself who is perceived as a sort of "turncoat-in-chief." This is particularly striking given how often man and movement are intertwined in the case of Fascism. As Robert Paxton (2004, 9) has strikingly put it, speaking of the idea that Fascism ought to be identified with its leader, "this image, whose power lingers today, is the last triumph of Fascist propagandists. It offers an alibi to nations that approved or tolerated Fascist leaders, and diverts attention from the persons, groups, and institutions who helped him." Indeed, this co-mingling of Mussolini and Fascism is one of the things that makes Predappio, Mussolini's birthplace and home to his grave, such a powerful attraction for contemporary neo-fascists.

But if, for neo-fascists, this isomorphism brings some degree of clarity regarding what it is they come to Predappio to pay homage to, for Predappiesi themselves – with their intimate knowledge of Mussolini's opportunism and chameleon-like qualities – it only further muddies the waters of definition: "Historic turncoat number one in Predappio was Benito Mussolini, the Duce of Fascism, son of Alessandro Mussolini, anarchist socialist, and blacksmith of Dovia" note the authors of one local history book (Capacci, Pasini, and Giunchi 2014, 212).

Mussolini was a fervent socialist for much of his early life, and his father had been a socialist town councillor in Predappio. His departure from the Italian Socialist Party (Partito Socialista Italiano, PSI) and move to the far-right was a scandal, as it occurred while he was editor of *Avanti!*, the national party organ. When he first visited Predappio as Italy's Duce he had many of his erstwhile compatriots from the Socialist Party arrested for the day so that the disjuncture between his past and present politics would not be too overt (Heywood 2021). So, in addition to the comic stories of political turncoats above, Predappiesi have similar stories about Mussolini himself. In one, during a visit to the town, Mussolini stops a local character he recognizes from his days in the PSI to ask him what he thinks of the political situation, and the man replies (in dialect) that he has never liked the white poplar leaf ("la fója de farfaraz," a metaphor for a turncoat due to its tendency to change colour) and turns away (Capacci, Pasini, and Giunchi 2014, 203). In another, a godson of Mussolini is baptized by the Duce himself, when he was still a socialist, with the name of "Rebel." After the Lateran Pact with the Catholic Church, Mussolini tells the child's father that he must change his son's name, and the father replies that since, after all, Mussolini gave him the first name, he had better be the one to change it (214; see also Heywood 2021).

In other words, at the very heart of Predappiesi conceptions of Fascism is an even deeper scepticism about identifying it than that expressed by doubt over any particular characteristic. In these conceptions there is a sense in which Fascism was never, in fact, anything more than a cloak for the self-interest of Mussolini.

Conclusion: Ordinary Scepticism

Eco (1995) describes Fascism as an "all-purpose term." Writing about both an Italian and an international context, his point, broadly speaking, is that anti-fascism is a vital and important cause, and that we "know," in some sense, to what it is opposed. This is revealed not by some fact about Fascism, but – as is characteristic of this view of speech more broadly – by the ways in which we use the word "Fascism" in ordinary language. "Who are They?" Eco asks, posing the sceptical philosopher's question only rhetorically, and then giving us the ordinary language philosopher's answer: "They" are those whom we call "Fascist."

But who are "We"? In the context of Predappio, it is far from clear whether a sense of the indefinability of the word either stems from a feeling that people know a Fascist when they see one or serves the purpose of allowing them to pick out the family resemblances between different kinds of Fascist. Ironically, Predappiesi ordinary language about Fascism instead looks more like that of the sceptical philosopher. Either it questions the application of the term based on a particular characteristic or set of characteristics ("he's not Fascist, he's just self-interested"; "they're not Fascists, they're just nostalgic clowns"), or, as in the stories of Mussolini, Ciaranfi, and those above, it implies an even more profound scepticism: if a man wears a fascist uniform, serves the fascist regime, holds a Fascist Party membership card, and yet later is to be found proclaiming his anti-fascism and beating returning soldiers, what hope is there of ever answering Orwell's question? If Mussolini himself is thought to have founded Fascism in part because the French bribed him into supporting the Entente in the First World War, then what does it even mean to be a Fascist?

My argument here is that the "underlying feelings," as Eco puts it, revealed by Predappiesi ordinary language about Fascism revolve not around some unspoken notion of "Ur-Fascism" revealed by a "we-know-we-see-it" mentality. Instead, they revolve around a deep-seated and profound scepticism about whether or not anyone is "really" identifiable as a Fascist. Talking to people in Predappio about Fascism is a little bit like talking to an expert ornithologist who denies the existence of goldfinches. Each time you believe you have spotted a real one it is in fact revealed to be stuffed, possessing the appearance of "goldfinchness" but being something else entirely at heart.

Unlike the scepticism Austin describes though, this sort of scepticism is perfectly ordinary in Predappio, in the sense that it is common, usual, and conventional to express such sentiments. Indeed, one of the ways in which it becomes "ordinary" is by virtue of repetition – the quality "Fascist" is not repudiated in a single grand instance of scepticism (most people do not simply claim that there is no such thing), but rather slowly eroded as any given instance of Fascism is revealed to be, in fact, something else.

Moreover, this form of free or sceptical speech is not "language on holiday," but is doing a particular sort of work. At the heart of such work is Predappio's indexical and iconic association with Fascism in the wider Italian popular imaginary. The fact, in other words, that for most other people who have heard of Predappio one need look no further for a better example of something one could point to and label as Fascist than Predappio itself. As I noted at the outset of this chapter, outsiders who have heard of Predappio rarely share Predappiesi scepticism about identifying Fascism – indeed, they often take the town itself, its inhabitants, and its appearance as indexical and iconic signs of the regime. Roman neo-fascist restaurateurs provide cheap dinners to Predappiesi tourists, policemen forgive speeding tickets to Predappiesi drivers, and army sergeant-majors hand out the best jobs to Predappiesi conscripts. Meanwhile, others consign the whole town to the "toxic waste dump of history" for its associations with Fascism (Wu Ming 2017). Newspaper reports about the ritual marches in Predappio are much more likely to call the marchers "Fascists" than "nostalgics," and non-Predappiesi are usually shocked to discover that the town consistently elected left-wing mayors until 2019. Predappiesi experience this association on a very regular basis – they experience their home's saturation with the symbolism and architecture of the regime every time they step outside their front doors, they experience its status in the eyes of neo-fascists every day when they pass such visitors on the street, and they experience how it is perceived by other Italians every time they are asked where they are from and either lie or face the consequent judgment.

In response, Predappiesi scepticism attempts to untether Fascism from any real-world referent, and certainly from their home and from their most famous co-citizen, who emerges from their stories not as an ideologue or a militant but as just another self-interested opportunist, of whom there are many in Italian politics. So, the "ordinary scepticism" I describe here is not simply "ordinary" in the sense of being common and "everyday" in the town, but also "ordinary" in that its effect – like the effect of other aspects of Predappiesi life I have described elsewhere (Heywood 2021, 2023b, 2024a) – is to scale Fascism down to the colour of a shirt one wears for the convenience and benefits it confers. In this vision, the high (or low) politics of Fascism, and of accusations of

Fascism, come down simply to where people think their interests lie. This is a form of sceptical speech endowed with a particular meaning and purpose by the context in which it takes place.

Talk about Fascism by people in Predappio – rather than by visitors to Predappio – often turns out not to be "free speech" in the sense of dramatic, extraordinary interventions in public discourse. Much talk about Fascism in Predappio aims instead at the opposite, despite its topic: at the ordinary, the banal, and the quotidian. Moreover, it does not turn out to be "free" in the sense of being "language on holiday," despite the sceptical form it takes.

One might imagine ordinary language to be the opposite of "free speech," in both of the above senses – the opposite of both talk about extraordinary and controversial subjects such as Fascism, and of epistemic positions such as scepticism. Yet in Predappio both are combined, and both are perfectly ordinary. What this points to, I suggest, is the need for contextualization – not just of phenomena that seem to resist contextualization, like free speech, but also of phenomena that come with a built-in sense of *what context is*, as our own talk about the putative opposite of free speech – ordinary language – sometimes does.

7 The Imaginative Power of Language in the Vacated Space of "Free Speech" in Putin-Era Russia

CAROLINE HUMPHREY

Since all language use is subject to social conventions, political judgments, and linguistic means, what can "free speech" mean in practice but *freer* than in some other situation, a different place, or an earlier time? I use such a relative and temporal definition of the idea to discuss the issue of "free speech" in contemporary Russia. This chapter discusses the effects of the sudden advent of an era of free (or freer) speech – and later its reversal – on language itself. After repeated revolutions, thaws, openings out, and shutting downs, the "unfree situation" that Russians referenced in 1989–91 was not some other country but the previous era in their own history. Yet, in rejecting that Soviet language of the immediate past and creating "free" language and socio-linguistic manners, people necessarily drew upon verbal forms within their ken to represent their liberated ideas. And when, from the year 2000 onwards, repression and censorship clamped down yet again and that space of political expression was seized from above, there still remained the irrepressible inventiveness of ordinary people's talk. In each of these two political about-faces, the paradox is that linguistic practices that at first sight appear to be purely contemporary have in fact turned to deep and multifarious historical roots. What this chapter aims to contribute to the work of Russianist scholars is a perspective that explores the temporal dynamics of the senses of freedom given by "free speech."

The demise of the Soviet Union with its monolithic ideology and heavily policed terminology initiated an era when *glasnost'* (transparency) was declared and censorship ended; when multiple and discordant voices could be heard in public, political leaders could speak of unfamiliar ideas, and previously completely silenced topics surfaced into discussion one by one. The 1990s was certainly a time when speech, as a general term for communications of all kinds, was freer than it had been before. But "freedom of thought and speech" has a lowly place in the present Russian Constitution (it is cited in Article 29),[1]

---

1 See the European Commission for Democracy through Law (Venice Commission): Russian Federation Constitution (2021), available at https://rm.coe.int/constitution-of-the-russian -federation-en/1680a1a237.

and there has been nothing like the active lobby to support it that surrounds the First Amendment in the United States. From 2000 onwards there was a sharp reversal. Under Putin a series of legislative measures prohibited "undesirable content," "false fabrications," and "verbal crime" (Bogush 2017). These laws have distinctive contours: while racist, misogynistic, ethnic, and sexist invective normally goes unpunished and government ministers regularly engage in calumny and spin fabrications (Roudakova 2017, 218–20), censorship returned with an onslaught on overt criticism of state policies and actions, official versions of history, the president of Russia, and "Russia" itself. All such public critique is liable to criminalization and ongoing surveillance, at worst to assassination, prison, or exile. Yet, in private speech, there remains the great commotion of everyday life – vibrant, tangled, undisciplined – and its outbursts. Some of this found niches on the relatively freer internet, where until recently (2022 and the advent of war conditions), independent subjectivities could be expressed. Significantly, in print, as well as in public protests, there is a certain exhilaration in the invention of sideways, *non-overt* expression, in which Russians have honed techniques over the centuries. In short, if the freedom of "freedom of speech" is defined negatively as an absence of repression, it is at the point of extinction in present Russia; but if we look for freedom of speech in a delimited, positive sense, by which I mean the capacity to express one's ideas and feelings privately from a self-chosen, independent subject position,[2] then that, I suggest, is far from moribund.

Russia's switchback between authoritarian and volatile regimes has created a hostile terrain in which to perceive the kinds of "free speech" envisioned in influential Euro-American discussions, whether that refers to Foucauldian *parrhesia*, the direct speaking of truth to power, or the capacity for public democratic dialogue on political matters. What can be seen in Russia is the complicated, contradictory, and shifting coexistence of diverse political attitudes. Brave people took to the streets to protest notably in 2011–13 against election fraud, and in 2020–1 in support of Navalny and his anti-corruption campaign, but large swathes of the population and the media support the government on those issues, even if they wax indignant about certain local decisions, and many other citizens do their best to ignore politics altogether. Increasingly, writers and the intelligentsia have recourse yet again to various forms of indirectness, especially to what Russians call "Aesopian language," referring to the ancient Greek storyteller who used pointed animal fables to suggest uncomfortable truths about human society. Meanwhile, the state-approved media, such as the main TV channel Pervyi Kanal (Channel One), is pervaded by a crude simulacrum of plain speaking, staging shows in which "common sense" always wins out against "extremism."

---

2 See the discussion in Gerasimov et. al. (2013, 15–20) of Quentin Skinner's lecture entitled "So What Does Freedom Mean to Us?"

Nevertheless, as mentioned, counter-currents have emerged in what we might call living language, the inventive or taboo-breaking usages of the population at large. This chapter will attempt to explain how it is that certain (positive) kinds of freedom have come to be exercised in Russia *within the sphere of everyday language itself*. This is sometimes a matter of giving new meanings to signs that used to mark opposition to the Soviet government; but it has also taken the form of idiosyncratic and rebellious play against regulation as such, against the norms of language culture and their manifestation in the rules of grammar and orthography, occasionally in the end probing the very capacity of language to carry community-wide, generally understood meaning.

Political Change and Linguistic Normativity

Russian sociologists, linguists, and anthropologists have raised the issue of what has become known as the "public aphasia" of the post-Soviet era. This refers not to the psycho-linguistic impairments analyzed by Roman Jakobson ([1956] 2004) but to a general discursive paralysis caused by the lack of a language of disinterested public debate (Guseinov 2004; Ushakin 2009; Vakhtin and Firsov 2016). Ushakin (2009, 763), for example, mentions the lack of generalizing mental maps and an insufficiency of symbolic forms adequate to express the essence of the situation that had arisen. Vakhtin and Firsov (2016, 7) echo several other writers in arguing that Russian society has been trapped by the dichotomy between the old Soviet official formulae and irreverent assorted kitchen-table opinions, neither of which can form a basis for constructive public debate, and they suggest that this is evident in the inability of public figures to consider facts from multiple points of view, to converse democratically with one another, or to reach a reasonable compromise.

As Russia is not alone in the world in experiencing such effects, there must be other causes beyond the shock of 1991. But the outcome in Russia does play out in distinctive ways, notably the heightened presence of expletives, criminal jargon, and violent metaphors, even in ordinary conversation (Zemskaya 2004), a crude style that has been taken up in populist mode by politicians, including the president (Ryazanova-Clarke 2019). When truth-based, well-argued, and reasonable political discussion is side-lined into niche publications and academia, this leaves the public space of the "lack" to be occupied by some other kind of language. The Azeri linguist Gasan Guseinov (2017) argued that this is the smugly lying, boastful, and aggressive language that has taken over arenas such as mainstream TV and political electioneering. For calling this language "cloacal," Guseinov was attacked by a storm of xenophobic and nationalist invective from people who took him to be referring to the Russian language as such. He became the object, in effect, of the very "cloacal language" to which he was drawing attention. The word "language" here refers to the particular manner of communication or "language culture" (Gorham 2014, 56) of the mainstream populist media, politicking, and electioneering. Yet that sociolect, while dominant, is but one among many. It feeds into and is fed by the "living language" – the vast range of available words, jokes and puns, metaphors, poetic fragments, religious references, commonly understood allusions, curses, foreign borrowings, internet memes, or high-flown literary phrases available to the population. Ingunn Lunde (2009) has referred to this complex interaction as the demonstration of "performative metalanguage"; namely, the deliberate negotiation of language norms by both political figures and ordinary people by voicings that are in effect statements about language.

Some historical background is necessary to explain the virulence of the feelings aroused by the word "cloacal." In Russia, as Guseinov (2004, 23) argues, language was always thought of as a normative instrument whereby rulers could govern the consciousness of the people. But if during the tsarist centuries the idea was to enrich and purify language with the aim of improving the population's usage, after the Bolshevik Revolution this goal ran aground when the ruling language was suddenly supposed to represent the speech of the proletariat and peasants. "Free speech" made a sudden public appearance, taking the form of egalitarian straight talk (formerly seen as rudeness). Courtesy and euphemisms were scorned as repellent bourgeois hypocrisy. A distant European historical analogy is the seventeenth-century Quaker puritan rejection of politeness as untruth (Bauman 1983). A closer comparison could be made with the "monotonous violence" that appalled Germaine De Staël (1800) in the standardized rhetoric of the Jacobins in the French Revolution,[3] or the crudeness and invective of the Red Guards that marked the Cultural Revolution in China (Perry and Xun 1997). However, in Russia in the early 1920s, as in revolutionary France and China, the "liberated" harsh speech was not in fact the language of the working classes. It belonged, rather, to the political activists. Bolshevik linguistic norms involved not just a hard-nosed style but also a party-originated linguistic bureaucratism that still afflicts Russia today. A host of difficult-to-master acronyms (VChK, VKP(b), Ispolkom, Narkomfin, OGPU, and so forth) became required markers of revolutionary consciousness.

Yet socialist transformation required the development of a unified, homogenous language for everyone that was to be founded, as Maxim Gorky argued, on the exemplary breadth and richness of the Russian literary language that did not exaggerate or falsify the speech of the people (see discussion in Gorham

---

3 "At many times in our Revolution the most revolting sophisms alone filled certain speeches; party slogans, repeated endlessly by the orators fatigued ears and dried up hearts. There is variety only in nature; only true sentiments inspire new ideas. What effect could be produced by this monotonous violence, by these terms so strong that they leave the heart cold?" (De Staël 1800, 375; my translation).

2000, 142–4). It was the nineteenth-century classical poets and novelists, Gorky wrote, that formed the "beautiful (*prekrasnyi*) Russian language." The idea of the "great, mighty, just and free Russian language" extolled by Ivan Turgenev (quoted in Vereshchagin and Kostomarov 1979, 174) gave rise, on the one hand, to the canonized institution of the "literary language," which became a staple of Soviet schooling, and on the other to the idea that the ordinary speech of the masses spoken from the heart could only be an "imperfect manifestation" requiring correction (Gorham 2014, 10). One of the early actions of the Bolshevik government had been to institute a reform of pre-revolutionary written Russian. Ostensibly, this was to make it clear and simple so that peasants and workers would be able to master it easily, but the deeper aim was to mark a new era, to break with tsarist Russia: *everything* was now to be new, including language (Baiburin n.d.). The new orthography rapidly became a policed orthodoxy, with extraordinary scrutiny given to ideologically marked details. For instance, while it was best not to write about God at all, it became a punishable offence to write the word "god" (*bog*) with a capital letter "B" (*Bog*) unless this word came at the beginning of a sentence (Guseinov 2004, 48). With the Soviet party-state's determination to educate people in the feeling of common values, "every act of speech became a political act" (Guseinov 2004, 24). That is why, when the grip of the atheist Soviet ideology finally loosened at the end of the 1980s, it was indeed a tiny political freedom to be able to write "God" rather than "god." This was only a relative freedom, however, as the overarching language ideology remained in place: namely, the conviction, not unlike the institutionalizing of French by the Académie Française, that there is a glorious, correct, and proper Russian language, and that it must be defended. This idea was and continues to be manifested most prominently by the ramparts of the "literary language."

The letter *B/b* is an example of the widely employed concept of the ideologeme. Originating with Bakhtin, who used the term in a broad semiotic sense (any word as a social sign is an ideological phenomenon), *ideologeme* has come to refer more specifically to a symbol bearing ideological content (Kristeva 1986), or to the minimal unit of written or spoken language that the speaker or listener takes to refer to an imagined code of ideological norms and attitudes (Guseinov 2004, 27). To use a capital letter, or not, when writing the word *god* was – in either case – to employ a widely understandable ideologeme throughout the twentieth century. But what has happened since then, I will suggest following Lara Ryazanova-Clarke (2016), is that all ideologemes have been radically destabilized.[4] Native wit and invention have reshuffled them,

---

4 The letter *b* on its own, extracted from any word, can in the living language stand metonymically for many things (*baba*, "woman"; *baraban*, "drum"; *bomba*, "bomb," etc.). This propensity for playful association on letters of the alphabet was encouraged by the pervasiveness

stuck them into inappropriate contexts, and garbled them into ever-changing neo-abbreviations, such that any sense of their general meaningfulness threatens to be lost. It is amid these shifting sands that the present substitutes for free speech (in its negative freedom sense) now appear.

Subject Positions of Speaking Out

It was the notion of "linguistic aphasia" allegedly brought about by the drastic events of 1989–91, mentioned earlier, that first suggested to me that a historical approach is needed in order to understand contemporary linguistic tactics. I was reminded also of the temporal "aporias" invoked by John Borneman (2003, vii) in his edited volume about Germany, *The Death of the Father: An Anthropology of the End in Political Authority*, in which he refers to various kinds of bewilderment, such as the regime that ends without the death of its leader; the death of a regime that is not recognized by the populace; and the people's representation to themselves of the dawning of a new era when from an external perspective that change is difficult to recognize. However, while aporia indicates an impasse and aphasia denotes an absence – the post-traumatic lack of a language with which to create a meaningful and socially valuable narrative of the present (Oushakine 2000) – it was not the case that people in Russia were totally baffled or altogether silent in the 1990s. Rather, as Yermakov et. al. (2004) and others have richly documented, many assorted groups adapted Soviet-era linguistic habits of indirectness to handle relations with the "new" powers – the "aporia" in this case being that, while everyone realized that a new era had dawned, the leaders were not so new after all, since both Gorbachev and Yeltsin had been Soviet-ruling apparatchiks for decades. With the turning wheel of the Yeltsin–Putin–Medvedev–Putin-again eras, matters changed: there was an ever-faster process of resignifying of earlier ideologemes and mining of fresh ones, as will be described later in this chapter.

This issue of the temporality of "free speech" can be informed by arguments concerning the interpretation of protests in the Stalinist era. In his path-breaking paper on "speaking out," Jochen Hellbeck (2000) argued that influential Euro-American historians were wrong to assume that most Soviet citizens stood aloof from the values of the communist regime. He charged these writers with losing sight of the frames of meaning guiding individuals' articulations and actions, and which accorded people subjecthood only if they expressed themselves in ways that appeared to be dissonant with the regime. Focusing on non-compliance

---

of Soviet acronyms. An example is VKP(b), which correctly stands for the All-Union Communist Party (Bolshevik), where uninformed people would guess wildly at the reference of the "(b)" while others deliberately subverted it. In a widely known mocking etymology, this "b" stood for *blyad'* (prostitute) (Guseinov 2004, 49).

meant that the encompassing temporal dynamic of social mobilization characteristic of modern revolution was ignored. Hellbeck showed that most dissent in
the 1940s and 1950s was motivated by individuals' *self-creating involvement* in
the political system and their dismay that the original revolutionary values were
being cast aside by the Stalinist regime (73–4). These (doomed) working-class
"speakers out" credited the October Revolution with giving them the very capacity to speak and understand themselves (81–2). The gist of this argument can be
extracted from the era discussed by Hellbeck and shifted to later periods in Russian political life. The point is that we need to pay attention to the source(s) *from
whence* people derive their felt authority to speak out, and to enquire about in
what name and to what purpose they articulate their critical or uncomfortably off-
beat acclamation of the powers that be. In the late 1980s and early 1990s, it would
be anachronistic to assume that calls for "freedom" would refer to some default
"Western" concept; rather, for the great majority of people, "freedom" (*svoboda*)
would mean one of the kinds they had grown up with in Soviet schools, be that
the poetical freedom invoked by Pushkin or the Leninist "democratic freedom"
of a class (see Humphrey 2007; see also Kruglova 2017 on the continued salience
of everyday "vernacular Marxism" in present-day Russia).

The "death of the father" has not happened in Russia. He has just reappeared
in different guises. With chameleon Putin, various kinds of unfilial questioning
have also taken on new colours. Some of these now draw on global sources, from
American comics and Japanese anime to Russian folklore, films, and science
fiction. Nevertheless, if we return to the key question that concerned Hellbeck
(2000), the ideas in the name of which such communications happen, I suggest
that the most numerous, varied, fertile, and experientially vivid are those de-
riving from lives lived inside Russia itself, and that these cannot be understood
without knowledge of the revolutionary double bouleversement of the values
that were elevated as politically legitimate in twentieth-century Russian history.
In what follows I provide some examples, each of which is impossible to understand without their tortuous backstories. I do not claim they are representative or
especially important features in the vast and varied field of linguistic innovation.
The aim, rather, is to point to three kinds of transmutation – ploys with language
proper, shifts in language culture, and a combination of the two – that have surfaced in the (vacated) place of "free speech." These moves, it should be stressed,
are libertarian in the sense that they make willful play with the status quo of the
literary language and its culture; but it would be wrong to assume that they are
therefore necessarily politically progressive as that idea is understood in Europe.

The "Hard Sign"

"If you ask me how the [post-soviet] renaissance of Russia started, I'd say,
without thinking twice, with the hard sign" (Russian author quoted in Baiburin
n.d.; my translation). The letter *yer* in the Russian alphabet, called the "hard

Figure 7.1. The "hard sign."

sign" (figure 7.1), has no sound and functions only as an orthographical means of showing that the previous letter is pronounced distinctly and separately from what follows and to show the masculine gender of the word. How could such a seemingly insignificant and ethereal entity be reckoned so game-changing?

When the Bolsheviks rushed through their language reform in 1918, they abolished several supposedly redundant letters of the alphabet, including the hard sign when used at the end of words, though it was kept in order to separate certain sounds within a word. Ostensibly the edict was aimed to simplify the writing of Russian in order carry out the urgent task of achieving literacy among the population. The weightier political reason was to demonstrate a sharp break with the previous era. After the Revolution *everything* was to be different, including the alphabet. Lev Trotsky turned letters into ideologemes when he wrote that the hard sign and the other eliminated letters were the "aristocratic estate" in "our" alphabet, abolished by "our" October Revolution; they were *parasitical letters*, while all the other letters were necessary labouring letters (quoted in Baiburin n.d.). The reform was hotly opposed. As a Russian linguist commented,

> People of the old world grasped at the meaningless hard sign as their banner. Bourgeois newspapers continued to use it despite the ban. Finally, decisive methods were necessary: sailors from the Baltic Fleet were sent to the printing houses of Petrograd to cleanse them of the letter *yer* ... But wherever the White Armies resisted, where generals, factory owners, bankers, and landlords held out, the old hard sign went with them as their faithful ally. It advanced with Kolchak, retreated with Yudenich, fled with Denikin, and finally, with Baron Wrangel was killed off and consigned to the past. For several long years, this letter played the role of separator not only of sounds inside a word but, in the gigantic spaces of our country, it "divided" life and death, light and shade, the future and the past (quoted in Baiburin n.d.; my translation)

Throughout the Soviet era, putting the forbidden hard sign at the end of a word was an almost unthinkable, bizarrely dissident act.

With the demise of the Soviet Union, the hard sign, unlike the other banned letters, was joyfully resurrected. It became the indexical sign of a new (relative) freedom, enthusiastically attached to the names of the institutions that were the advance guard of capitalist enterprises: banks, trading businesses, private services, law firms, typographies. People would decide, for example, that their bank, correctly written банк, was now to be designated банкъ. One of the most influential newspapers of the new era, *Kommersant* (Коммерсант), added a hard sign to its name (Коммерсантъ) and then took to calling itself by the "Ъ" alone. It soon became evident that the hard sign, now fixed, against the rules of literary Russian, at the end of all kinds of inappropriate words, had many extra-linguistic connotations. One might imagine that a "meaningless" letter like the *er* would be a prime example of Ferdinand de Saussure's (1916) assertion of the arbitrary relation between the signifier and the signified. But the fault in that proposition, discussed in general terms in Jakobson (1966), is evident in the thoughts about deploying the hard sign expressed by contemporary Russian wordsmiths. Businessmen explaining why they use it in their brand name say it connotes firmness, uprightness, and determination like the shape of the letter (see Avetisyan 2016). If we follow Jakobson's (1966) rebuttal of Saussure, it is easy to see that the *er* as a written sign, with its jutting back edge, has an iconic and a symbolic character, reflecting both in its distinction from the "soft sign," which looks similar but lacks this jut,[5] and its function, to create "hardness" in the previous consonant.

Furthermore, the historical reference is lost on no one. To return to the issue of subject position raised by Hellbeck (2000), the hard sign ideologeme signalled not only a stance in favour of the new capitalism but also the desire to grasp a historically longer Russian identity. When applied to an institution like a bank, the hard sign is intended to convey the (illusory) message that this bank inherited the values of probity and reliability of Russia's flourishing pre-revolutionary international capitalism and has nothing in common with that treacherous sink of good money, the Soviet *sbergatal'naya kassa* (savings bank). And then, many present-day Russians have taken with alacrity to the idea that the hard sign ending was used to denote the male gender of a word. In this regard, the absence/presence of the hard sign has been attributed with magical social agency.[6] For example, alluding to the alleged Soviet policy of demoting men and advancing women in order to create the androgynous *Homo Soveticus*, the film critic Sandomirskaya wrote: "It turns out that having been

---

5 The soft sign imparts a softening *i* sound to the previous consonant. Jakobson (1966, 31–2) pointed to the numerous ways in which languages establish links between morphemes by binary or serial similar sound shapes (father, mother, brother) while distinguishing them by small significant differences. The hard and soft signs do this by means of graphic shapes.

6 Judith Butler (2021, xxi) discusses analogies in the United States concerning the fantasies brought into being by the extraordinary power attributed to dissident speech: "The criticism of racism will by some magic power take down white businesses; the criticism of rape will by some imagined power result in castration."

deprived of the hard sign to indicate the male gender, Soviet men were no longer in a position to preserve their gendered identity, which led to dire consequences" (quoted in Baiburin n.d.; my translation). The sexual connotations of the pairing of maleness and hardness are much celebrated in the triumphant return of the hard sign and enjoyed in innuendo, jokes, and stories. Meanwhile, the inoffensive, "feminine" soft sign, which has been used unchanged all along, has gone unnoticed. But the gendering of the hard sign presaged a corresponding spread of *feminitiva*, the adding of feminine diminutives to previously neuter words for professionals, such as *avtorka* (authoress) in place of *avtor*, *doktorka* (woman doctor), or *blogerka* (woman blogger). This trend is the opposite to that ongoing in Europe, and the new terms indeed sound ridiculous to many Russians, but they have been normalized in much of the media.

Khamstvo *("Malicious Boorishness")*

I now shift attention from ploys with writing to "language cultures," by which I refer to the numerous socially created linguistic practices that are identified as distinctive in Russia.[7] Guseinov (2012, 178) has observed that written freedom of speech (*svoboda slova*), as distinguished from private oral conversation, reached Russia only with the internet; meanwhile, he notes, for ordinary people dealing with that borderland between the personal and the social – from the school and the shop to the railway ticket office or the town graveyard – speech is made up of obliqueness and interjections, or chatter lubricated by swearing. Guseinov evidently considers this crudeness as just a careless use of language, but *khamstvo* (boorish, injurious talk) stands out as an objectionable contravention of social norms (210–14). The *kham* (boor) dispenses with euphemisms, politeness, and kindly gestures (not to mention the cheery emoticons scattered through written communications indicating that one does not want to offend one's respondent). This stark language culture is not linguistically free in the sense of coining new words, metaphors, or spinning flights of fancy,[8] yet I will argue that it has, like the "Aesopian language" mentioned below, a deeply rooted kernel of "freedom of speech" in a socio-historical sense. This is not just because the *kham* assumes the freedom to flout the everyday habits of consideration for others; rather, the paradox lies in the concept itself, which is said to be untranslatable, and for which "boor" is undoubtedly inadequate.

---

7 See the discussion in Gorham (2014, 5–9) on the distinction between language culture and language ideology, the former referring to distinctive attitudes and practices in using language and the latter to conceptions of the nature, form, and purpose of language as such.

8 It is because *mat* (swearing) has exactly these features, having long ago taken leave of crude sexual connotations by means of linguistic inventiveness, that Guseinov (2004, 165–72) argued for its importance in linguistic freedom.

Khamstvo hurts the people who are its objects and, in this respect, recalls the "injurious speech" analyzed by Butler (2021). But hate speech owned by white majorities in Western democracies, despite the occasional resignification of notable insults from negative to positive (such as "queer"), contains no substrate of liberation. Indeed, the very reverse. The concept of *khamstvo*, on the other hand, is founded on a convoluted history that includes a ghost of social release.

The word *kham* has a religious origin, referring to Ham (*Kham*), the son of Noah. The biblical text (Genesis 9:20–7) is succinct: after the flood, Noah takes to farming, creates a vineyard, but then gets drunk and is seen by Ham lying asleep in disgraceful nakedness. Ham speaks out and tells his brothers Shem and Japhet. They, in contrast, behave with respect, cover their father with a piece of cloth, and avert their eyes. When Noah wakes up, he curses Ham's son and all his descendants for Ham's transgression (looking and telling). In Russian exegesis, Ham not only "saw" Noah but also laughed scornfully at his sleeping father when telling his brothers. Ham thus stands for the lack of love and respect for the father and indeed for the use of speech in the desire to humiliate him in the eyes of others. The expanded social connotations of the story give further depth to the notion of *khamstvo*. Russian biblical explanation elaborates on the meanings given to the brothers' names and extended to their descendants: Shem is said to mean "name" and "honour," Japhet means "spreader" (of God's word), and Ham means "hot, burning, black, and dark complexioned" (Prajt 2017). As was also common in European medieval traditions, these designations gave religious legitimation to racial categorization, but in Russia they also served to denote the social hierarchy within the country. God is said to have decreed that Shem's descendants would lead, Japhet's would live with them, and Ham's would serve them both. In the nineteenth century, Russian nobles used the word *kham* to denigrate the ineradicable baseness and impudence of peasants, workers, servants, and lackeys; by the early twentieth century, the category included the *meshchanstvo* (the mixed lower-middle-class estate), characterized by the nobility as the "soul of pandering, lack of spirituality, and hooliganism, as an anarchic [social] wave" (quoted in Vojvodina 2010, 16; my translation).[9] By the time of the 1905 and 1917 revolutions, the insolence and defiance of the so-called *khams* was directly pointed towards social and economic liberation.

As an aside, if we think about the ancient precedent recalled in the notion of *khamstvo*, an analogous genealogy applies to the notion of "Aesopian language." For after all, who was Aesop? He is held to have been a repulsively ugly son of a slave. This was the lowly figure who is said to have invented the cautious

---

9 Merezhkovskii was the author of a famous 1906 article, "Gryadushchii Kham" (Coming Ham) that predicted the terrible triumph of *khamstvo* coming from the social depths.

language game of the politically powerless, the fable that turns to lions, hares, and frogs to depict right rule, cruelty, enslavement, and freedom. The advantage of the fable is that it allows the author's irony to be instantly retracted, for it is the *listeners* to the story who perceive the political analogy in the shenanigans of the animals (Clark 2021, 25). The fable is most effective as a weapon in despotic regimes, writes a nineteenth-century editor of the stories: "a tyrant cannot take notice of a fable without putting on the cap that fits" (quoted in Clark 2021, 25).

The Bolshevik Revolution brought the so-called *khams* triumphantly into power (Arctus 2017). In the view of many in the Christian noble and upper classes, once the "low people" were in charge, their God-decreed Ham-like un-worthiness and malicious disrespect would lead to the destruction of society. Indeed, society was overturned, and with it the direction of *khamstvo*, which almost immediately came to be identified no longer with rebellious insolence but with the *top-down* enaction of the *khams'* propensity to deride and humiliate. It was seen in the new bosses' use of insultingly vulgar language to bully subor-dinates, disloyal telling on rivals, gloating at others' failures, taking advantage of principled people's weaknesses, and so forth. Indignant people added another quality to the characteristics of the Soviet *kham* – their assumption that anything was allowed to them. In the 1990s many people hoped that this type of behaviour would disappear, but in the 2000s, as Guseinov (2012, 214) writes, "the *kham*, the *zhlob* (obnoxious aggressive person) – whether among officials and oligarchs or just among the ordinary people – arose again." Now *khamstvo* was perceived everywhere, in insolence from below and in brutal betrayal from above. People began to ask, is it something inescapable, an intrinsic fault of the Russian char-acter? A recent documentary film entitled *Pravda li, chto khamit' u nas v krove?* (Is it true that boorishness [hamming] is in our blood?), showing incidents of *khamstvo* in schools, hospitals, offices, and taxis, for example, interviewed soci-ologists, psychologists, journalists, and teachers asking each of them why they thought it was so prevalent (see Redactsiya 2021). They replied variously, but a thread runs through the responses that has to do with the current degraded culture of interpersonal communication, revealed most sharply in language.

The documentary film as well as linguistic monographs (e.g., Zemskaya 2004; Yermakov et. al. 2004) make evident how power and status are held in place through language. In post-socialist Russia, encounters between ordinary citizens and those of high rank still entail one-sided deference and formality. For example, written communications should be "translated" from ordinary language into the formulae of the bureaucratic sociolect. They take the modular forms of the complaint (*zhaloba*), the demand (*trebovaniya*), and the various kinds of request (*proz'ba*) – for "support," "cooperation," "permission," or "a decision." These are written by citizens, who will only receive curt but polished answers from above (if they receive an answer at all), in awkward, unpractised officialese (Yermakov et.al. 2004, 62–7, 77–9). Oral communications from below must take respectful forms and circumlocutions rarely used in everyday life, and bosses react sharply to over familiarity. Meanwhile, also retained from Soviet practice, still frequent modes between officials and direct subordinates are straight oral commands or deliberately belittling offhand obstructiveness. But today when older principles of precedence, such as governmental office, are challenged by newer ones, be that sheer wealth, threat of physical violence, technological expertise, or cosmopolitan education, the jarring incompatibilities of esteem multiply the occasions for susceptibility to insult and loss of face. Linguistically, disrespect can be expressed in a multitude of ways, from the insulting use of the informal "you" (*ty*), immodest use of the word "I" (*ya*), simply questioning why, or giving unwanted advice, to the minefield of forms of address. With the abandonment of "comrade," the Russian language has no polite term such as "sir" or "madame" for addressing an unknown person. All that is left is basic physical categories ("Young man, you are in my way," "Woman, you have dropped your glove") and, as was remarked in the documentary about *khamstvo*, this bluntness can be experienced as a tiny insult right there. As Butler (2021, 1–2) observes, "We ascribe an agency to language, a power to injure, and position ourselves as the objects of its injurious trajectory … To be called by a name is one of the first forms of linguistic injury one learns."

Khamstvo, however, is not fundamentally a matter of breaching codes of politeness. Rather, it is on one side a performative self-assertion and on the other a *diagnosis*, perhaps mainly of betrayal of a presumed trust, that is made from radically different social positions. From a subordinate's perspective, the *kham* is someone who has assumed a right to lord it that they do not deserve and does so in a harmful way. From above, the *kham* is a lowly person who "gets above themself," who acts independently when they should be grateful and keep quiet, still worse a whistle-blower or an "agitator" for some alien cause. In the documentary film, one rare man recognized himself to be a *kham*, if only in the eyes of the director-journalist, and he responded that acting in ways that happened to humiliate others was exactly his right.[10] "Isn't it natural," he exclaimed, "wouldn't any upstanding person respond to the knocks of the world frankly, by striking out?" (Redactsiya 2021). Here we can see that the ghost in present-day *khamstvo*, the biblical Ham, is still somehow present in one unresolvable paradox presented by the story: for honesty and frankness are regarded in Russia as virtues, and Ham told the truth, even if that was also precisely what he should not have done. Remembering that "the death of the father" has not yet taken place,

---

10 A post on one website comments: "Many people in Russia think that *khamstvo* is the manifestation of pure freedom … but attempts to defend the right to *khamstvo* are a true sign of the demise of [the culture of] dialogue. The *kham* does not listen and cannot bear any restriction on his own means of expression. Monologue-ism has become the mark of the times" (Vasilievich 2020; my translation).

I would therefore suggest that the continued acute sensitivity to *khamstvo* is an important factor, largely unnoticed by the external world, in Russian life; it mitigates against the despairing claim of those such as Roudakova (2017, 218–19) or Pomerantsev (2016) that epistemological commitment to truth has vanished in Russia. Truth, indeed, seems to be superfluous in politicians' performances and the pro-government media, but that is not the case among the people at large.

From Khamstvo *to the Irreverent Internet*

Since around 2000, communication on the internet has been freer than in the mainstream media, ranging from serious comment on events, to live observation blogs, to calls for action and support of victims, to irreverent mockery. Nevertheless, one would hesitate to call this democratic "free speech" in a political sense, since genuine dialogue with the powers (*sily*) is altogether absent and websites and blogs are subject to abrupt closure. Still, the internet abounds with diverse counter-cultural linguistic invention. For example, *padonskii yazyk* (the language of the scruffs, from *podonki*, "dregs, scum") has now gone out of fashion, but it was essentially an attack on social hierarchy by means of subverting the rules of the "great Russian language"; it was written in deliberately distorted, misspelled, ungrammatical Russian with ample use of swear words and criminal slang (Dunn 2006, 5; Lunde 2009). Certain of its memes, migrating to the right, became nationalistic slogans, such as "*Vypei iadu*" (Drink poison) during the Kremlin's ban on Georgian wines (Dunn 2006, 4), and some of its plays on words were taken up as populist gestures in arenas like President Putin's staged question-and-answer sessions with the people.[11]

Other more recent internet genres, far from being taken up by pro-government groups, are condemned as "the language of *khamstvo*." Writing in the patriotic journal *Russkii Mir*, the linguist Vladimir Yemel'yanko (2021) observes that a "mutant form" of language has developed on youth-oriented sites and in social media. This is *kheit*, from the English "hate." *Kheit* is conducted in an ever-changing vocabulary, mostly adopted from the West. Status in its battles

---

11 On Putin's staged "direct lines" and "conversations" with the people, see Gorham (2014, 152–3, 166–7). An account of the injection of the deliberately confusing "*medved*" into such an event can be found at "Preved!," Wikipedia, accessed December 2021, https://ru.wikipedia.org/wiki/Превед. *Medved* was an acronym for Mezhduregional'noe Dvizhenie Yedinstva (Inter-regional Movement for Unity, later to become the pro-government United Russia Party), which became a *padonskii* meme-brand in the form of an anthropomorphized brown bear (correctly written *medved* would have a soft sign, *medved'*). But *medved* also refers to Dmitri Medvedev, the politician. In one such staged show, a cheeky *padonskii* question prepared for Putin, "What do you think of *medved*?," was in the end replaced by "What do you think of the journal *Medved'*?"' Foreign journalists nevertheless assumed Putin was being asked about Medvedev, which, in a sense, he was.

depends on speedy abandonment of out-of-date words and mastery of the latest ones. As of 2021, *inflyuensery* have *follovery* and *kheitery*, and the norm is to reply to the sarcastic posts of the latter by *kholivar* (holy war). A *chel* – someone up with it, with good self-esteem but not too much *ChVS*[12] – should retaliate with a witty barb aimed to humiliate or *bodisheim* (body shame) the opponent. It is not clear, however, that *kheit* can be straightforwardly identified with Western "hate speech" as a social phenomenon, as the latter consists of easily understandable invective against mostly public targets, whereas *kheit* appears to be far more inward-looking and aimed at scoring against weaker members of the given online community.[13] The public resonance of the genre is limited by its barbarically foreign vocabulary, along with the coded and mysterious Russian neologisms it has invented. The result is a "language" that older generations cannot understand and suspect conceals a harmful activity. In Yemel'yanko's (2021, 20) view, the young practitioners see themselves as able to explore their own thoughts in *kheit* precisely because in this way they can fence themselves off from the world of adults, and he reports that teachers and parents see *kheit* as a "frightening foreign abracadabra." Thus, *kheit*, like *padonskii yazyk*, is a linguistic form in which deep alienation from an imagined "proper" society can be expressed by flouting linguistic normativity.[14] But such forms could be described as *over-free* speech, since by flying so far from general intelligibility they create only consternation in the population at large and fail to have a noticeable political effect. However, it is not the case that young people only take inspiration from Western social media, nor that they always want to keep their communicative inventiveness hidden from view; some of them have been taken onto the streets in mass demonstrations.

Protest Placards

The following observations concern the 2011–12 street protests against unfair elections, which I can discuss here because they have been extensively documented and studied (Breininger 2013; Arkhipova et al. 2014;

---

12 *ChVS* is the *kheit* acronym for "feeling of one's own importance" (*chuvstvo sobstvennoi vazhnosti*).

13 It is for this reason, the desire and ability to humiliate someone in a situation where respect would be expected, that Yemel'yanko (2021) identified *kheit* with *khamstvo*.

14 I am indebted to Tamiza Tudor for directing me to numerous examples of the creation of distinctive "languages" by which groups in Russian society are separating themselves. If one is *osob yazyk*, the deliberately obscure code of officials, most are the "secret languages" of youth, such as *solenyi yazyk* (salty language), *pesochnyi yazyk* (sandy language), and *kirpichnyi yazyk* (brick language). These work by regularly substituting certain consonants and adding vowels. In salty language, an *s* is added after every vowel and then the vowel is repeated, so *mama* becomes *masamasa*.

Akhmetova 2012). Hundreds of placards were held aloft. Unlike the 2020–1 pro-Navalny and anti-corruption protests, where there were few banners and those were printed, mainly with messages addressed to other demonstrators ("Don't be afraid, don't be silent"), in 2011–12 most banners were homemade, and many called out the authorities. They were extremely various, reflecting the heterogeneity of the crowd in occupation, ethnicity, age, and gender. They were noticeably literate, including quotations from Che Guavara, Vaclav Havel, Andrei Sakharov, and other icons of the left. They included accusations ("You stole our voice at the elections. We won't forget, we won't forgive"); allusions to symbolism ("White ribbon versus black belt");[15] insults ("Vova – *zhlob!*" [Putin's a slob!]); slogans ("Power to the People, Bear [*medved*] to the Circus," referring to Medvedev, the then president); exhortations ("Give us back our voice!"), and appeals to unity ("'Ъ" – thank you for being with us!"). An unsmiling elderly woman using a walking-frame hung a placard round her neck that stated, "I would exchange Putin for Khodorkovsky" (the jailed oligarch).[16]

The most popular genre of placard spoke to the theme of temporality that has been central to this chapter: the derivation from the past of an allegorical precedent through which to designate a political stance. In this case, the immediate reference was to a recent event, a statement by Putin in 2011. Most of the slogans and appeals mentioned earlier were like shouting into the wind, since the linguistic forms did not invite response and, in any case, it was certain that the powers, while no doubt watching, would not reply to any messages addressed to them. This case was different. By taking Putin's own words and inserting themselves into the image-world he had conjured up, these placard-bearers were in a fable-like way venturing a dialogical stance with the president.

The placards in question referenced *banderlog*, the Monkey People,[17] from Rudyard Kipling's *Jungle Book*. This set of stories was translated several times into Russian and became the subject of a popular Soviet film, so they can be seen as widely shared childhood knowledge. In Kipling, the *banderlogi* appear as unruly outcasts who do not obey the Law of the Jungle. They have no speech of their own but use the stolen words they overhear when they listen and peep. They are a horde with no leaders. They boast and chatter and pretend they are a great people. They are evil, dirty, shameless. In Soviet Russia, the word *banderlog* came to mean an aggressive, uncultured, clamorous, and dull-witted person, and it was sometimes used for *churki* (uncouth "apes" from the

---

15 The white ribbon was the symbol of the protesters; Putin is well-known to have a black belt in judo.

16 See "Slogans of the Russian Movement for Fair Elections," accessed December 2021, http://slogans10dec.blogspot.com/2012/01/24122011-pavel-otdelnov.html.

17 *Banderlog* is from the Hindustani *bandar* (monkey) and *log* (people).

southern republics of the USSR) (Akhmetova 2012, 288–9). In Kipling's story, the *banderlogi* steal Mowgli and take him to their cave. Mowgli is rescued by the python Kaa, who invited the Monkey People by saying, "Come close to me," but then hypnotized them and subsequently ate them.

In December 2011, during the presidential elections, Putin engaged in one of his "conversations" with the people. He said:

> There are those, of course, who hold Russian passports but act in the interests of a foreign state and on foreign money. We will try to make contact with them, but that is often useless or impossible. What to say in this situation? You know what can be said in the end: "Come close to me, *banderlogs*." From childhood, I have always loved Kipling. (quoted in Arkhipova 2014, 131; my translation; see also Akhmetova 2012, 287)

Immediately after Putin's broadcast, internet commentary cast him in the role of Kaa and the demonstrators as *banderlogs*. The narrative now spiralled on its own course. Kaa, a positive character in Kipling, was transformed into a negative one and renamed Puu. And while Kaa was a python, Puu became a boa constrictor, enabling the association in both English and Russian between "constrictor" and the idea of a restrictive authoritarian government (Akhmetova 2021, 290). Some of the placards echoed Kipling's old pejorative idea ("Russia is not India, and we are not *banderlogs*"). But the great majority identified with alacrity with the subject position of the monkeys and took the boa as the enemy: "Unite, Banderlogs! Chase the beast from its lair!" Referencing the dire state of the law, one placard read: "Jungle Law is for boa constrictors, people have the rule of law and fair elections." Several placards expressed the idea: "You have called us, Great Puu? We have come!"

Once the Puu/boa ideologeme was established, invention was free to play with the etymological link between *udav* (boa constrictor) and *davit'* (to pressurize, bear down on, stifle). Allusions were made to the illustrations from another childhood favourite, Antoine de Saint- Exupéry's *The Little Prince*, of the boa devouring its spoils, or sitting with an elephant inside it: quotations were pasted up and one placard depicted Kaa/Puu with Russia inside its stomach. The *banderlog* identity was equally fertile; one placard read "Macaques take revenge," and another with a picture of a chimpanzee face mocked Soviet style "internationalist" slogans with "Ardent greeting to my African comrades." Kipling's jungle scenario can be seen as an imaginative childhood paradigm that was dormant until it was ignited by Putin, but it was powerful in ways the president almost certainly did not anticipate. In response to the image of the snake-mesmerizer, which had been reinforced by the way Putin had slowly uttered the phrase, "Come one step closer to me," raising his hands to the audience as a hypnotizer does (Akhmetova 2012, 289), one woman's placard expressed a responsive subjectivity: "Their hypnosis is our terror (*strakh*)." Others waved challenge-banners: "Be afraid, the *banderlogs* have come!"[18]

A Brief Conclusion

This chapter has shown that with the imposition of punitive measures against "free speech" after 2000, many Russians have turned, perhaps paradoxically, to the resources of language itself – to express controversial ideas, to take a stance in society, or simply to use language as a performative in battling against conformity. I have argued that these linguistic resources can only be understood temporally, both as regards the political limits of operation at a particular moment and the historical sources of people's moral-political convictions. This argument applies equally to particularistic ploys, like the resignification of the hard sign to mark rejection of the Soviet and acclamation of the late tsarist eras, as to more general practices, such as the battles over social status, respect, and government probity seen in accusations of *khamstvo*. I have tried to provide some indication of the enormous riches of language (seen broadly) in a highly literate country like Russia, where allusion, metaphor, allegory, and references to myth and literature are part of everyone's lived experience from childhood and are widely shared. Only the existence of these common resources enabled Aesopian language and the fable of the jungle to be effective, to join thousands of people in pointed address to their political masters. The mass arrests that followed the 2011–12 protests show the response of the "father who did not die." Even now, in a tragic era when mere hints of independent thought are smothered, there is no better conclusion than the words of the Russian editors of the journal *Ab Imperio* in 2013:

> After all, the condition of freedom is not the absence of restrictions themselves (every organized society is based on restrictions), but the refusal to accept the predetermined nature of one's acts or decisions. When the only positive content of public life is borrowed from the past (as in Russia today), the only path of emancipation becomes not the overcoming of restrictions, but the production of new meanings and emotional bonds of our own in society. (Gerasimov et al. 2013, 20)

Acknowledgments

I am very grateful in particular to Tamiza Tudor, Mattei Candea, Ayur Zhanaev, John Dunn, and Biancamaria Fontana for materials, insights, and suggestions that helped me write this chapter.

---

18 All references to placards in this and the previous paragraph are from Akhmetova (2012).

PART TWO

Extending the Politics of Free Speech

8 Designing Limits on Public Speaking: The Case of Hungary

SUSAN GAL

Introduction

Anthropologists have long asserted that all speech – indeed all expression – is constrained by social and linguistic conventions – that is, by political and cultural principles. Linguistic anthropologists have noted, in addition, that statements about language and language use – for instance, as "free" and "unfree" speech – are never only about language and are never only statements; they are also forms of action. As statements, they are reflexive metadiscourse and entail evaluations of other features of social life than language; as action, they display and often transform aspects of speakers' identities, values, and institutions. Reflexive metadiscourse – talk-about-talk – defines the social scene of speaking while enabling speakers/listeners to take up ideological locations in such scenes and in social life more broadly. "Ideological" is here understood as a positioned stance, within a world of alternatives, and not a matter of truth or falsity. Ideologies, in this sense, are frames about linguistic and expressive practice, with consequences for all social projects – motivating, justifying, and changing them (Gal and Irvine 2019). Importantly, metadiscourses about speech and its limits are always comparative; they imply a differentiating vision, establishing relations of contrast and often disputes among ways of (non) speaking and among those who speak.

In any comparison, many possible dimensions of contrast and sameness can be defined. Comparison itself is ideological work, and techniques of comparison differ in their starting points and consequences (Gal 2016). Standardizing measurement that submits each example to the same widely agreed-upon and often quantitative scale is a technique that erases the interested viewpoint from which the measures are made. Nevertheless, there is always a perspective, a point of departure, even if hidden. Decisions must be made about what is worth measuring and with what metric. Another technique of comparison divides the world into binaries: modern/traditional, public/private, North/South, liberal/authoritarian. Though not necessarily a quantitative metric, it can be fitted with numbers. It is familiar in social science and ubiquitous in the social world generally. Notably, it is amenable to fractal recursions that redivide each side – for example, finding the modern in tradition, the public in the private, and so on. This often lines up with an us/them distinction in which the analyst participates. It can create hierarchical scales along which ethnographic examples are placed, valuing or critiquing one side or perhaps the binary itself (Gal 2002; Candea in this volume). Indeed, during the Cold War, the rubric "freedom of speech" became a brand of the United States and its allies (the self-styled "free world"). Fractal recursions of this contrast were evident as further subdivisions evincing the same distinction within both sides in that era. In this chapter, I offer a related comparison, finding similarity, not difference, in the handling of the Cold War divide (as pluralism vs. centralized control).

Within a single chronotope – Hungarian public talk in the early twenty-first century – I juxtapose three disputes about constraints on speech. In each, there is an element of "design," a matter of "form-giving" through situated action, with design defined as an "invasive mode of intervention in the world" (Murphy and Wilf 2021, 9). That is, each stretch of talk and action is arguably dealt with in a way that is planned and organized for expected effects. The reigning political party's interests are effectively imposed to control the speech, despite legal protections against such control by the government itself. The protections are loudly avowed but at the same time undermined, hollowed out, often *by legal means*. The overarching ideological distinction between pluralism and centralized control is still in evidence. Yet the three disparate examples suggest that the dedication to pluralism evident in Hungary before 2010 is systematically circumvented in practice by the Fidesz government that has gained power since then. Evidence for this emerges in the way otherwise disparate incidents unfold in quite similar ways.

In the first episode I describe, Hungary's Prime Minister Viktor Orbán declared in a 2022 public address that Hungarians do not want to live in a "mixed-race society." Much discussion followed, interpersonally and in mass media: Did Orbán overstep legal constraints against harmful speech in a liberal, pluralist society? This reverses the more common concern about speech limits imposed by governments – today, Orbán and his party are, in effect, Hungary's government. I examine the "recipient design" of the speech and the scandal it evoked. How was responsibility for it deflected and turned to Orbán's advantage? The second incident occurred in 2018, when a humorist-journalist published a brief, satirical analogy between ancient Hungarian chiefs who were plunderers and the current prime minister's family. Protection of the press against libel in such cases is inscribed in the Constitution. Yet anonymous citizens claimed to have been harmed, and the journalist was heavily fined by the Hungarian Supreme Court. I ask how this legal manoeuvre was designed and accomplished. In the final set of examples, the main independent Hungarian newspaper unexpectedly ceased operation from one day to the next in October 2016. Many citizens were shocked by the closure of the popular paper that often criticized the government. Official state news declared it folded due to bankruptcy. Readers did not know what exactly to protest in this and numerous similar cases of magazine and website closures. No laws were broken; no one's rights had been violated. Yet access to news and a range of opinion were drastically curtailed.

In tracking talk-about-talk in these incidents, the focus here is on discussions among literate Hungarians with higher education in person-to-person exchanges with me and in a range of mass media that I have followed for each example, including the reporting of the few independent websites and magazines that are still in operation. The events were all well-publicized, but puzzles and major disagreements remained in their characterization. They provide a glimpse of a wide-ranging design by Orbán's ruling party (Fidesz). The importance of a plurality of voices and opinions in public expression is explicitly endorsed by government spokespersons. Newspapers, websites, and TV and radio stations abound. Yet in the experience of participants and watchdog organizations, public speech is curtailed and central control exerted, but the government's responsibility for that constriction is hard to locate and everywhere denied.

This pattern is also evident – as observers of Hungary have noted – in legal, financial, scholarly, and artistic institutions whose routine activities have been diminished, defunded, and hollowed out through legislation. The institutions are not entirely destroyed – a carapace and an aura of legality remain. Yet organizations capable of shaping public opinion and previously run by trained personnel (theatres, museums, universities, the Academy of Sciences) are now managed by the ruling political party's loyalists, often without the relevant skills, and with changed agendas. Some observers have called this pattern "autocratic legalism," and it has been noted in polities in many regions. Popularly elected leaders, such as Prime Minister Orbán, use the rules and customs of a liberal order – the regulated and ideal separation of the economic, legal, and political sectors – to undermine that order's institutions (Corrales 2015). Kim Scheppele (2018, 545) summed up this irony when she observed that they "dismantle by law the constitutional systems they inherit" in order to entrench themselves in office for the long-run (see also Magyar 2013; Gal 2019). In the case of public speech, this might well be called "media capture" (Selva 2020). I attend to the communicative, language-related aspects – and the scalar reach – of these processes, showing how they rely on a delicate handling of expectations about ideological difference.

Ideologies and Metapragmatic Struggles

Sometimes, disputes about public speech are matters of clashing ideologies. Indeed, as Judith Irvine and I have argued, there are always alternative ideologies that can be invoked in any scene, and all ideologies are inherently contestable (see Gal and Irvine 2019). But Hungarian disputes today should be distinguished from the grand Cold War ideological confrontations in Hungary's past. Presuppositions and explicit statements of what could/should be expressed in Hungarian public life were quite different under state socialism – now often captioned as an "authoritarian state" – than after that system's demise. Public expression in state socialism, especially in its early days, was explicitly focused on a centralized shaping of citizen consciousness. For instance, the ruling parties in East Germany, Hungary, and Romania during the Cold War justified mass cultural production (the arts, schools, press and other mass media) as cornerstones of their programs of social engineering, very much a matter of design and planning (i.e., the inculcation of their avowed values and the manufacture of their own legitimation). What did not fit these goals was not allowed, and there were punishments. The black Ziguli car that arrived at the journalist's house at night to take him away was one result of overstepping party directives and expectations about what could be said during the height of the Cold War. In the West, this was stereotyped and derogated as "ideologically motivated interdiction" or "information dictatorship" and was usually called censorship (Boyer 2003).

Yet, as I have argued elsewhere (Gal 1991), the various rhetorical techniques used in Eastern Europe in later years of the Cold War – allegory, circumlocution, suppressed premises, indirection, wooden bureaucratic speech, "ready-made" shibboleths in talk (Boyer and Yurchak 2010), and "messages between the lines" – were not limited to state socialism. They were also evident in speech strategies of what was then called small-scale egalitarian societies (Brenneis and Myers 1984). Roland Barthes (1957) discussed many of them in explicating bourgeois images and formulas. And they were and continue to be evident in the hidden messages ("dog whistles") of public media in capitalist-democratic social orders as well, even if quite different contradictions were/are hidden from view in say, US public discourse, than in Hungary (Stone 2004; McIntosh and Mendoza-Denton 2020). By the 1980s, before the system's collapse in Hungary, canny observers and participants diagnosed a situation in which artists and writers were seduced into silent self-censorship in collaboration with, not against, state requirements. In short, the language ideologies of the late socialist period could be summarized as "the artist and the censor – the two faces of the official [state] culture – diligently and cheerfully cultivat[ing] the gardens of art together" (Haraszti 1987, 7).

Now, however, the general understanding avowed by domestic and foreign observers alike is that Hungary, as a member of the European Union (EU) and the North Atlantic Treaty Organization (NATO), is operating under the same ideological presuppositions and political dispensation about public expression as the rest – the West – of Europe. Pluralism and disparate voices are supposedly everywhere in evidence, opinions of the left as well as the right. That image enables Hungary to participate in the idealized and self-congratulatory story about European "freedom of speech." As the narrative goes: the dark repressive forces of church, bourgeois morality, and the state have been giving way, since the Enlightenment, to reason, progress, artistic creativity, pluralism, and democracy (Rosenberg 2021). Never mind that this is not an accurate reflection of European publics today. Hungary's post-1989 Constitution followed this idealized playbook, rejecting communist-era arrangements concerning speech by borrowing or building on Western models. It included safeguards for a range of political speech in public and a diverse, autonomous press. Accordingly, early generations of post-socialist artists, journalists, and political leaders celebrated "freedom of speech" and the achievement of a plurality of voices in Hungarian mass media.

But within these expectations, disputes have flared, especially since 2010 and the second rise to power of Victor Orbán's increasingly extreme-right Fidesz party. It seems fitting to analyze these disputes not as ideological clashes, in the Cold War mode, but as what Webb Keane (this volume) has called "metapragmatic struggles." These are struggles that occur while more encompassing ideological presuppositions are shared among disputants. Metapragmatic struggles, as I understand the term, draw on alternative ways to define the particular situation at issue within a generally accepted acknowledgment that there is/should be expression of diverse opinions about public policies, and that criticism of public figures is important in a democracy, even one explicitly labelled an "illiberal" democracy by Orbán himself. The question becomes: Is the current event at issue a case of politically or legally authorized and ethical expression, or some other type of situation? What is appropriate expression in the given situation? What values are enacted by the speech or event? Who or what is responsible for the systematic limits on expression that are noticed and experienced by some?

Definition of an ongoing social interaction, as managed by participants, constitutes a foundational topic in linguistic anthropology (Goffman 1981; Gumperz 1982; Duranti and Goodwin 1992). Metapragmatic categories name and frame relationships and ways to change them in an ongoing event. In a familiar example, two speakers in a Euro-American scene can transition from a relation of strangerhood to amicable acquaintanceship with a mere change of address forms (Silverstein 2003a). A simple matter of reducing the volume of one's voice can change a conversation from public to private. Keane's proposal of the term "metapragmatic struggle," however, aims to highlight how fraught these metapragmatically mediated changes can become when they are scaled up, entailing positions taken by groups, not individuals, and between opposed principles in confrontation. It dramatizes the high social and ethical stakes when cultural or political disputes pertain to key activities of an institution, and not to single events. The incidents I discuss are metapragmatic struggles in institutions of public speaking within an ostensibly shared ideological frame. Under the aegis of a presumed pluralism, how is centralized, government control manifested – and denied? How are news media captured by government control? These are semiotic aspects of "autocratic legalism." They are not a Hungarian specialty but rather occur widely. That is precisely the reason they are important.

Orbán Makes a Declaration

Prime Minister Viktor Orbán, in the hot July of 2022, made his annual, much-awaited public speech to a large gathering of Fidesz party members and sympathizers in a partially Hungarian-speaking town in Transylvania (Romania). His party had won a fourth consecutive landslide election in the spring on the basis of heavily gerrymandered voting. Sitting at a large table, outdoors and in shirtsleeves, Orbán joked: "In this heat we should all have 'Fidesz spritzers,' that's two thirds to one third." His audience laughed appreciatively. They did not need to be told that this is the right proportion of wine and water for "spritzers," a favourite drink, and that it was also the proportion of Fidesz's supermajority. "Which shows," Orbán added, "that some things are forever." In addition to homey evocations of food and drink, the speech also quoted English, Russian, and Latin phrases. The effect was of an expansive, folksy schoolmaster instructing his charges about history, economics, culture, and the war in Ukraine. World politics, he explained, operates like a layer cake, a *Dobos torta* (another favourite) in which a key part is the "icing." Orbán's own Marxist education, with a similar metaphor, would have called it superstructure: demography, migration, and gender. On these issues, he averred, the West's wrong-headed policies have put it in precipitous decline; people there are anxious, no longer controlling the world's energy supply and raw materials. They are no longer the admired "West" but now a "post-West" that has lost its values and is losing its position of global power.

That is where Hungary comes in. Loosely translating his points, I summarize: We continue to have more burials than births. If we don't change this, sooner or later "they" [migrants] will steal away our country, they will inundate and replace us.[1] Migration has divided Europe. In one half, Europeans and

---

[1] "Ellakják tőlünk a Kárpát-medencét" is a play on words equating "ellopják" and "ellakják" (an archaism for settle): "they will settle/steal the Carpathian Basin away from us."

peoples from outside Europe live together. They are a world of mixed races. Those countries are no longer nations, just conglomerations of peoples. They are a post-West. We, on the other hand, are where different peoples living in Europe mix with each other. We [the East] are now the real Europe. They [the post-West] want to force us to be like them. The ideological trick of the international left is to claim that there has always been a mixture of races in Europe. This is a cheat, an abuse of words, a semantic confusion.

The rest of the passage is worth quoting directly:

[Mi a] saját európai otthonában élő népeknek vagyunk keveréke ... ezek a népek, ráadásul, egy ilyen hungaro-pannon mártásban össze is olvadnak, egy saját, új európai kultúrát hozva létre. Ezért harcoltunk mindig ... Egymással hajlandóak vagyunk keveredni, de *nem akarunk kevert fajuvá válni.* (emphasis added)

We are a mixture of European peoples who are living in our own home ... moreover, we peoples melt together in a kind of Hungarian-Pannonian sauce, creating our own new European culture. This is what we have always fought for ... We are willing to mix with each other, but *we do not want to become mixed-race people.*[2]

The italicized words caused a scandal. The reaction was immediate, forceful, and international. But why? There is not much new here in content. His audience knew, as did all of Europe and beyond, that Orbán had for years spoken against multiculturalism, immigration, migrants, and the cultural policies of the EU. He had insisted on maintaining "ethnic homogeneity" in Hungary. Ironically, in Transylvania, where Orbán spoke, Magyar, Romanian, and German speakers have long cohabited, sometimes in conflict. That was presumably why the rejected "mixture" invoked past battles of "Europeans" against Islam and "Arab civilization."

Yet the targeting of Islam was not the first source of outrage. On the day of the speech, one of his closest advisors of twenty years – who is Jewish – resigned, saying these comments were Goebbels-esque, a reference to the chief propagandist of Hitler's Nazi Party. Soon the Academy of Sciences collected protest signatures, objecting to "race" on scientific grounds; a legal suit was filed against Orbán by a former member of Parliament for violation of a hate speech law that was and is on the books (the case was refused); opposition parties expressed rage and shame; Hungarian Jewish organizations reacted in anger, as did leading rabbis and Roma groups; the European Commission's vice-president called the speech "poisonous racism"; numerous European heads of state protested; and the US Embassy mentioned no names but

2 All translations are my own.

condemned "all ideologies, policies and rhetoric that give oxygen to the doctrines of hate and division." The American mainstream press was even more pointed in its sharply negative commentary.

Some observers in Hungary and elsewhere in Europe noted that the outrage responded to Orbán's new choice of words. He moved from earlier incitements against "migrants" to people of "mixed race," which echoed a discourse of race purity recalling anti-Semitic, Nazi rhetoric. This is the kind of talk, critics said, that leads to genocide wherever it is heard. For these critics, Orbán had crossed a line; he had "gone too far." Acknowledging and decrying the crimes of the Holocaust has become a leading index of European identity and even of virtue itself (Özyürek 2016). Therefore, Orbán's speech was a provocation that interpellated listeners well beyond the families of Holocaust survivors or groups engaged in memorializing genocide.

Given these reactions, it is worth focusing on what linguistic anthropologists call "recipient design." Speech is continually oriented towards addressees, and speakers are alert to potential uptakes, which influence their choices (Bell 1984). In this lecture situation, Orbán is the Goffmanian "animator" of the speech and is also its "principal" – that is, the social actor responsible for its message. But he was probably not the one who composed the words. Yet, as his aide of twenty years who resigned on hearing the speech also noted, his custom is to carefully read and edit the work of those who actually choose the words, what Erving Goffman called the "authors." And the authors had a problem: since the start of the war in Ukraine, the term "migrant" and its accompanying discourse have lost the negative aura so vehemently created by the Orbán publicity machine since 2015, when hundreds of thousands entered Europe via Hungary from the Middle East and beyond. My own observations confirm that many of those hostile to the waves of migrants from the east and south in 2015 were priding themselves in 2022 on their "openness" to helping those fleeing, migrating west in the wake of the war in Ukraine.

Other expected audiences were European leaders. For them, "mixed-race" discourse still carries the whiff of Nazi rhetoric and can be condemned as such, but this is not its major effect. Axes of differentiation have shifted in Western Europe. The difference considered "racial" in France, Germany, Italy, and Austria most saliently concerns postcolonial African, Caribbean, and Near Eastern migrants and their children. I was in Vienna when Orbán visited there just days after his speech and I noted the way his rhetoric spoke to rightist politicians, who sent approving messages, while enabling moderate ones to mouth anodyne virtue gestures condemning anti-Semitism. Orbán, along with his writers, doubtless expected this. However, the recipients for which the passage was most precisely designed were those in the American audience Orbán would face a few weeks later at the Conservative Political Action Conference (CPAC) in Dallas, Texas. At that gathering, he was a keynote speaker, a kind of mascot for American rightist politics. He alluded, in English, to his earlier speech: "the mainstream media will call me a racist and anti-Semite," as indeed they did, to the delight of many in his American archconservative audience. In the US, race is again quite a different matter than in Hungary or Western Europe. It is key to African-American and national politics. In the US, this rhetoric of "mixed race" is more likely to evoke former president Obama and his allies than the Holocaust.

It is a fair bet that Orbán's canny authors were well aware that discourses of "race," "racism," and "anti-Semitism" were different in Texas than in Transylvania. Despite distinct uptakes, however, the repetition can enhance circulation of discourses and may create political alliances across contrasting social spaces, as has been the case in discourses of anti-gender (Gal 2019; Graff and Korolczuk 2022). It is therefore relevant that by inviting an otherwise small-scale politician to its annual meeting, CPAC was recruiting an eager Orbán into their project to build a global movement of the political right, in a "culture war" around what they characterize as "God, homeland, family, freedom and anti-gender." These values are arrayed against what they label the "liberal values," such as equality, separation of church and state, and rule of law.

The specifically metapragmatic struggle around the Transylvania speech, however, was less grand, as revealed in subsequent commentary. The original audience welcomed the "no mixed-race" announcement, thereby aligning with Orbán's party. Yet the next day Orbán announced that "[his] government follows a zero tolerance policy on both anti-Semitism and racism," and the Prime Minister's Office announced the speech was really about "immigration and assimilation." A week later, Orbán met in Vienna with Austrian Chancellor Karl Nehammer (ÖVP), who said – as expected – "we in Austria utterly reject any trivializing of racism or even anti-Semitism." Orbán also spoke about the scandal to international news media:

> It sometimes happens that I formulate things in ways that can be misunderstood. This is about a civilizational position [in Hungary] … it is not about racism but about cultural differences … [As everyone knows] I define myself as an anti-immigration politician. This is not a racial [faji] question but a cultural question. In politics no approach based on biology is possible; what is possible is a cultural approach … We want to maintain our civilization as it now is.

It was all a misunderstanding! In Hungary meanings are different! These moves resemble "plausible deniability" as analyzed in other polities (Hodges 2020a), but its details closely track autocratic legalism. On the one hand, the Hungarian Constitution, as rewritten by Fidesz (!), prohibits speech that insults minority citizens (ethnic Germans, Jews, Roma). That is why a former Parliament member could attempt to sue Orbán for his speech. On the other hand,

Orbán's defence alludes to this very law as his "no tolerance" policy. With some listeners, he benefitted from the Nazi echo; with others, by distinguishing Ukrainian from Arab migrants. For yet others, ironically, the "cultural" explanation relied on Hungary's supposed cultural-linguistic exceptionalism in Europe, where observers cannot object to differences of "culture" and "civilization." However denied retrospectively, the chosen term – *faj*, "race" – did a lot of communicative work. It made Orbán recognizable to potential allies in the quite different context of US far-right politics. The reframings both stood by the law, and undermined it.

The Dangers of Satire

The second example involves an incident in which Prime Minister Orbán was the subject of talk, not the speaker. A journalist's opinion piece published in 2018 was found by the Hungarian Supreme Court (a body then newly reorganized and entirely restaffed with Fidesz loyalists) to violate a section inserted into the Fourth Amendment of the Constitution in 2013.[3] The relevant section states: "The right of freedom of expression may not be exercised with the aim of violating the dignity of the Hungarian nation or of any national, ethnic, racial or religious community. Persons belonging to such communities shall be entitled to enforce their claims ... [against those] violating their human dignity," or their community's reputation. It might seem that this insertion was designed for the protection of minorities in Hungary, but its only use has been – as in this case – for the protection of the majority. Anonymous complainants charged that the article in the online version of the independent weekly *HVG* had harmed Magyars (Hungarians). The initial court hearing the case and an appellate court dismissed the charge. The Supreme Court overturning the earlier decisions found the journalist guilty. Many legal discussions called the Court's act contradictory, illogical, mistaken, and a bad precedent. My observations are not about technical aspects of the law but rather the public metapragmatic struggle around the journalist and the court.

The Court's actions centred on a short satirical opinion piece by Árpád W. Tóta. The article was a commentary on an earlier news item. An EU commission had, that week, found Orbán's son-in-law guilty of the corrupt use of roughly US$32 million in EU funds. Yet the Hungarian (Fidesz-appointed) prosecutor declined to start any criminal procedure against the son-in-law,

---

3 This amendment (and its media details) was harshly criticized by many journalists, opposition parties, the EU, and the Venice Commission because it limits the powers of the Court and allows arbitrary judgments, including fines for "imbalanced" and "insulting" reporting. This touches on the provision discussed here.

finding that there had been no crime. Tóta's article was a response to this situation. He wrote – facetiously, satirically – that the EU seemed to be puzzled by the Orbán government's response, so he, the journalist, would offer to explain it, to interpret it. Even my quick translation here conveys the tone:

> Let me help you [EU] understand Orbán's message. He said: I'm going to continue to steal. Whatever money flows in next [from the EU], they [Orbán, his family, friends] would like to keep it, this is not a crime here [in Hungary]. They are ready to sign any postcard about liberal values and the rule of law, it doesn't cost a penny … but they do not intend to have their relatives and friends locked up. If this is what the rule of law dictates, the rule of law should go fuck itself. He [Orbán] didn't destroy it just for fun.

This might seem heavy-handed as commentary, but it was not the part of the article identified later as offensive. Tóta's next paragraph evoked the early medieval chieftain Árpád. He led the Magyars who invaded the Carpathian Basin, migrating from the east, between c. 900 and 950 CE. He and his tribesmen conducted close to fifty raids for booty on Western European targets. These raids – done either as hirelings of warring princes or on their own initiative – have long been called "adventures" by nationalist historians, who have both aggrandized these activities and minimized the harm done. Hence the title of Tóta's article: "Magyars Don't Steal, They Go on Adventures." In his piece, Tóta reached for a striking historical parallel to critique the inaction of the EU in the face of the accusations against the Orbán family:

> Árpád chieftain didn't drag all his marauders to military court for plundering the whole of Europe. He honoured them. The robbery, arson, and violence – the so-called adventures – were not stopped by European legal decisions either, but by the Battle of Augsburg. It was there that the *stinking Hungarian migrants* repeatedly claimed that ravaging villages and monasteries were not crimes. The European knights, however, didn't accept their rules of the game, nor their illiberal worldview, and put the broadsword into them from ass to mouth. After that, the *Hungarian bandits* bravely ran home where they told others that a fucking big beating would follow the next adventure. This was then understood, and they took up Christianity in a great hurry, for which today they are extremely proud. (emphasis added)

The analogy – though far-fetched – suggests what it would take to change Hungarian (non-)responses to EU charges of crime and corruption. Many people found the analogy amusing. Besides the implicit charge against Orbán, it reminded readers – just a few years removed from the migrant crisis of 2015 – that people calling themselves Magyars had been migrants of a sort centuries ago, and not very friendly ones. One might also take this as somewhat insulting to the EU, accusing it of not enough action in comparison to supposed predecessors.

But it was not the analogy that was the subject of the lawsuit. Only the italicized words were identified as offensive. "Migrant" had been a neutral word that became pejorative after the Fidesz propaganda campaign against migrants and asylum seekers in 2015. The problem, however, was not only the term "migrant" but also "stinking" [*büdös*]. This is used for halitosis and mildew, but is also a common pejorative in ethnic epithets. Interestingly, the suit was not brought by the apparent targets of the analogy (i.e., Orbán and his family, who remained silent) but by two anonymous Hungarians who charged that their human dignity was violated by these statements about their national group. It is unclear how labelling ancient Magyars as migrants (even as possibly an ethnic epithet) harmed the two complainants. Clearly, the consequence was the important thing: that Tóta and the *HVG* – all Hungarians themselves – were fined and seen to be fined several thousand dollars; they had to apologize and remove the words italicized above from all versions of this article in print and online.

It hardly seems necessary to point out that this is a metapragmatic struggle about how to characterize what was said and that the specific interpretations by the two parties collided. Tóta's strategy was to draw a parallel between the current period and the earlier "adventures." This is the familiar genre of historical analogy, here as satire. By contrast, the Court decontextualized the italicized words, considered only their referential meaning, and deliberately overrode the tropic voicing of the passage, while recognizing that it was a condemnation. The Court agreed that the article was "ironic." In their official decision, the judges wrote: "The expression of condemnatory opinion is a value protected by the freedom of expression, but the stylistic tool used to express it and the genre of irony cannot provide an unlimited exemption from liability for violating the human dignity of others." Linguistic anthropologists would quickly point out that the judges turned Tóta's playful parallel into a bit of serious folk nominalism. They took for granted that the Magyars of 950 CE were the "same" as the people called "Magyars" today, so that insult to one would violate the human dignity of the other. Surely, Tóta's parallel between Magyar chieftains of the tenth century and today's ruling family would not apply to *all* current Magyars (or all ancient ones either) who do not steal and raid. With a straight-faced opinion, they opposed the legal demands of "freedom of speech" with those protecting "human dignity" and decided in favour of the latter.

It is hard to believe, Tóta remarked in interviews, that the judges were quite so stupid and had never read Hungarian literature. Some of the greatest poets of Hungary, Tóta noted, are much admired for using irony and satire in political criticism of their country's leaders. The judges were probably just beholden to Orbán. As Tóta angrily pointed out, writers will henceforth have to resort to the "flower language" (i.e., coded messages) of the deepest communist period. But journalists, he insisted, will not stop writing criticism. Legal observers feared that the judicial opinion and steep fine would indeed "chill" even humorous criticism of the prime minister's family, despite supposed legal safeguards for criticizing public figures. Laws seemingly designed to protect ethnic minorities from insult were here the means for shielding the regime's leader and family from critics and, perhaps most consequentially, retaliating against the independent press. And that, arguably, was the main point. All of it entirely legal.

A Newspaper Disappears

The first two examples showed the consequences for individual expression differently finessed: echoes of racist discourse by the prime minister explained away; satiric criticism of the regime punished. My final example is about the institution of the press and information dissemination as a whole. Orbán complained, in the early years of his regime, about the non-state owned, independent press and its often critical assessment of government actions.[4] Later he borrowed an epithet from the American scene, calling his critics' comments (in English) "fake news." Surveillance and control of individual journalistic output, as in Tóta's case, is a labour-intensive undertaking. Criticism is more effectively countered by elimination of diversity in press organizations. This, however, is hard to justify while maintaining an ideology of constitutionally guaranteed press pluralism. Even according to its harshest critics, the geopolitical situation of Hungary demands at least the appearance of legitimating popular support (however gerrymandered) and legal process in domestic, regional, and international circles (Magyar 2013; Vásárhelyi 2017). How can the entire mass media of a country be centrally controlled under these circumstances?

In October 2016, the country's major independent newspaper, the popular and prestigious broadsheet *Népszabadság* (People's freedom) was suddenly closed down. Metapragmatic struggle occurred around exactly who did what to this paper that was critical of the government. There were protests and street demonstrations. Was the shuttering legal? Did it violate press freedom? In a metaphor based on economic markets, the press in Europe is often framed as a marketplace of ideas. Diversity of viewpoints is supposed to provide the basis for an informed citizenry. By contrast, closing down newspapers is a familiar tactic of twentieth-century repression on the left as well as right, as in the actions of a Hitler or a Stalin. Did this closure signal that Orbán's government was a repressive regime?

---

4 Early in the second Orbán regime (2010–14), media organs to the right of Fidesz were also targeted, but the strategy towards them eventually changed; Fidesz took up their extreme right positions. Independent organs that take left or centre-left positions remained targets.

That image of autocratic control is what the Fidesz government tried to avoid when it insisted that it had nothing to do with the paper's demise. Literalizing the metaphor of the free market of ideas, the official news agency declared that closing the paper was a rational economic decision by its owners. The paper was a market failure. One state official expressed puzzlement that some people would want the government to "save" the paper: that would interfere with press freedom, he said. Among the Fidesz-friendly internet comments at the time, the following was typical: "The Socialists have still not learned that you can't just shout and bluster against facts, or rather, you can, but with good democratic common sense the majority laughs, mocks and ridicules them." In short, the cruel, capitalist market creates hard choices; its impersonal workings were responsible for the closure of the *Népszabadság*. This was not the only kind of reaction. Some comments were dubious. On the same thread another asked: "Is it just an accident that all this [the financial failure] emerged about the *Népszabadság* after they published all those articles that were so painfully embarrassing for the [Fidesz] Party?" In the *HVG*, the independent weekly, an editorial opined on 26 October 2016: "Sure, we can listen to the self-important busy-bodies talk BS about losses, portfolios, strategy changes and markets, but what for? All this presumes there is a media market in Hungary. And there isn't one … [just] honest journalists trying to do their work. The concrete story is not about the economy or market logic but about power and those who are willing to serve as its flunkies." The losers, the editorial concluded, were the readers.

Indeed, the closing of the *Népszabadság* is only the most dramatic of moves in evidence since 2010 that have narrowed the range of public opinion in Hungary. A second is the economic pressure exerted by the Fidesz government on independent or critical media outlets in the form of targeted taxation, withdrawal of state advertising, and denial of licensing. A third is the unification of most news and information within a single organization dubbed a foundation. Such narrowing, or "media capture," has occurred all over central and eastern Europe (Selva 2020, 15; Dragomir 2019). Scholarly observers note that Hungary is most extreme. Mass media operate as part of a government-business collaboration that controls the flow of information and thus opinion formation. These developments are well-known. Detailed discussions have appeared in the *New York Times* and *The Guardian*, as well as in publications by watchdog organizations such as the International Press Institute and Human Rights Watch. My goal here is merely to exemplify these manoeuvres, and to show how they dovetail with the earlier examples discussed.

The demise of the *Népszabadság* is a salient case because its excellent journalists were able to enlist foreign colleagues who created an international scandal. It is ironic that this paper, the former organ of the Hungarian Communist Party became, after the system change, a symbol of press pluralism. In the early 1990s the newspaper was privatized, owned partially by the Socialist Party, a German conglomerate, and the editorial board, and it became the most popular national daily and a leader of public discourse. Its profile was centre-left, supporting but also critical of the left-liberal Hungarian governments of the 1990s and early 2000s. In international matters it backed the EU and many US policies. Between 2005 and 2015, the paper's ownership changed a dizzying number of times through foreign and domestic publishing and holding companies. In those years, in concert with all other print media, its circulation plummeted, but it held its own against other daily national papers. At the time of its closure, it was making new investments in colour printing and staff positions. As the journalists and staff said in interviews, they knew nothing about plans for closure; they were celebrating the move to new headquarters when the bad news came by courier. The reasons for the closure were mysterious to them. Their website and internet archive of muckraking journalism were low cost, they noted, so immediately closing them was hardly necessary for economic reasons.

But economic arrangements were crucial to the appearance of the final result. The paper had been sold to Vienna Capital Partners, a holding company that created a Hungarian subsidiary named Mediaworks Hungary. By 2016, that company already owned a great many national newspapers and magazines in Hungary as well as many of the county-level newspapers, which have political importance as the major sources of information in rural areas that have no internet access. Mediaworks shuttered the *Népszabadság*. A few days later, Mediaworks, itself a very large company, was sold to an Orbán friend who, since 2010 and with government support, had become, according to Forbes, the third richest man in the country.

The sudden and complete demise of the *Népszabadság*, however, was an unusual version of the larger pattern. Domestic or foreign owners have been more gradually encouraged to sell, usually to oligarchs close to Fidesz, once taxes are raised or revenues decline as the state removes its advertising. By 2016 it was widely recognized by media scholars that TV and radio stations airing programs unfriendly to the regime were not awarded renewals of their operating licences. Private businesses that advertised on those TV and radio stations would themselves be super-taxed; demands would be made for them to follow newly minted rules – often ones created to fit those firms in particular. Although targeted legislation is ostensibly illegal, no effective opposition was possible against Fidesz's parliamentary supermajority (Vásárhelyi 2017).

Websites were at first thought to be a safe resort for independent press organs that were otherwise put out of business. But they too came under media capture through the second manoeuvre of direct pressure to change editorial policy. An excellent illustration is the case of Origo.hu, as recounted in a meticulous *New York Times* report (Kingsley and Novak 2018). In 2013, Origo was the country's most read news website, famous for its hard-hitting investigative journalism. When its German owner received an additional US$100-million tax bill and faced renewal of its frequency licences, negotiations between the government and the owner commenced. One editor of the website resigned on hearing that there would be a government consultant who would call him to provide advice about news coverage. A replacement editor continued the muckraking policies but was fired a few months later, as the German company moved to safeguard its licence renewal and further broadband deals in Hungary. Origo had become a liability; the German firm agreed to sell to the highest bidder. A Hungarian company was able to make the highest offer because it was heavily supported by government funding. Unlike the *Népszabadság,* the Origo website stayed in operation and in private hands, but by 2015 it was transformed from vociferous critic to enthusiastic supporter of government policies, especially on controversial issues such as immigration. Government support from advertising continued to rise as Origo's backing of Fidesz became more and more enthusiastic.

An even larger manoeuvre is the dramatic conglomeration of news media in a single organization. After 2010, a set of Fidesz-friendly oligarchs started buying national daily papers, internet news sites, and some fifty regional papers. A new civic organization was announced in 2018, registered as the Central European Press and Media Foundation (CEPMF). Billed as a non-profit, on the model of NGOs in the US and Western Europe, its stated aim is to "assist in the strengthening of Hungarian national consciousness in the media." On its website, it promised to "defend the freedom and diversity of the press and ensure the conditions for free dissemination of information necessary for the formation of democratic public opinion." Within a few months, the wealthy Fidesz supporters who had bought media firms handed them to CEPMF. The free gifts included TV and radio stations, newspapers, websites, and magazines. Nearly 500 media outlets operate under CEPMF's control, all managed by a board of Orbán's close colleagues. This unifies media that were already government-aligned, obviating competition among them and simplifying oversight. It also presents independent media with a huge, powerful competitor. In December 2018, Orbán signed an order that declared the consolidation of broadcast, internet, and print publications to be of "national strategic importance in the public interest," exempting CEPMF from anti-trust regulations. In 2019, regulative organizations in Hungary and internationally reported that at least 80 per cent of Hungarian news media was at the disposal of the Orbán government; the CEPMF provides the same centrally composed and government-aligned content to all of them.

These strategic moves are well known. An anthropological view would add two analytical observations. First, metapragmatic struggles link the concentration of media ownership to the cases of individual speech. As linguistic anthropologists have pointed out (Du Bois 1993), many customary practices like divination erase human intention and hence responsibility from activities that have consequential results. The supposedly impersonal forces of the capitalist market are one such mechanism, familiar to Hungarians through the devastating effects of the post-socialist transition. The 2008 financial crisis also hit Hungary hard, so the narrative of economic failure remains plausible to large sectors of the population. After all, the story goes, newspapers have been failing all over the world; websites change hands everywhere. Thus, metapragmatic disputes continue about "what really happened" to favourite newspapers or websites and who is responsible. Second, the institutional form of the Central European Press and Media Foundation is noteworthy. The government argues that it is no different than foundations in other EU member states. Yet, far from being independent, as its self-advertising and comparison to other states would suggest, its origins, mode of operation, governance, and personnel suggest it is a governmental organization grafted onto the widespread institutional concept of an independent "foundation." It gains credibility and authority from that process of grafting (Gal 2019). Meanwhile, the few independent weeklies and websites that remain are useful to the government in claiming that no undue centralization has occurred.

Media capture parallels reorganizations in other opinion-forming social domains – theatres, museums, libraries, the Academy of Sciences, and the universities (Magyar 2013). The *Népszabadság* and the Central European University were eliminated altogether, but in most other cases, the funding is curtailed, the rules of operation, employment, and administration revised, salaries and values transformed and all put under direct Fidesz control. Only the facade of the institutional name and function remain, while the changes are dubbed routine improvements or matters of economic necessity.

Conclusion

My goal has been to adumbrate the design aspects of a set of seemingly disparate events to make visible the semiotic armature of autocratic legalism and media capture as they operate in Hungary. A glance at the differences among these examples points to a wide range of contexts. The cases span individual experiences and institutional transformation. They contrast in the scale and influence of participants involved: from the domestic libel accusation against one journalist, to the international scandal around the mass mediated speech of the prime minister, to the destruction of a privately owned newspaper and the conglomeration of the vast majority of the country's information media. Yet, when compared, it is their similarity in a number of ways that is of significance.

First, I have emphasized their shared location: a post-socialist chronotope in which the Cold War dichotomy between pluralism in expression and government censorship, especially violent suppression of critical opinion ("free world" vs. communism), is still palpable after more than thirty years. This is in part because the dichotomy is invoked in political campaigns by far-right politicians to threaten and impugn the intentions of leftist and centrist political parties. Moreover, because the European Union is once again casting a critical eye on media laws and practices across Central European member states, a semblance of genuflection is required to the self-congratulatory narrative of "freedom of speech," which is maintained as an ideal in the liberal tradition authorized by the EU and its allies. Under these constraints, Hungarian officialdom organizes its impression management around this dichotomy and handles the dichotomy with care, claiming to stand firmly on its "pluralist" side. Despite its declaration of "illiberalism," Orbán's government has maintained a semblance of legitimacy in the EU and internationally by working against the perception that it practises censorship in illegal and violent ways.

Accordingly, the incidents are similar in seeming to be pluralist yet providing evidence of imposed government control. To be sure, a fractal analysis of this ideological divide would predict the reiteration of state control within a pluralist context, but the Hungarian situation goes further. The relevance of the ideological distinction is both evident and loudly denied, as if to say: "No government control here, only a tolerant constitution; just an independent judiciary; only the impersonal market, the rights of entrepreneurial ownership, and the necessity of state taxation." The legal and judicial system that – in an ideal liberalism – would defend pluralism has been captured for state interests, and the capture erased or explained away as a matter of economic rationality and public interest. These effects are mediated and supported by metapragmatic struggles, disagreements about the definition of the situation. Listeners are invited to hear Orbán's "mixed-race" remark as innocent because his constitution protects ethnic minorities. Readers of the satirist-journalist are asked to believe that judicial decisions are separate from party interests. And yet, the outcome in both cases was the limitation of critical commentary about a leading politician – even in the time-honoured form of satire. The demise of an independent daily and the gradual elimination of independent opinion in most websites is said to be the result of market considerations. A foundation unifying nearly all of the country's information media and producing identical content for all is justified as a means to "serve, preserve and uphold balanced media in Hungary" by a member of the foundation's governing board on its website. The Fidesz government is legally separate from the foundation; it cannot be held responsible for the seamless support it receives from the messages disseminated by the foundation's media outlets.

A carapace of pluralism and legal protections produces, for many critical participants, the disconcerting effect of hollowed out institutions, their administrators, managers, and employees substituted, their values entirely replaced by government-supporting views on crucial issues such as immigration, racism, gender, and EU mandates. My examples are similar to each other and also emblematic of a wider situation in that government control was clearly imposed, yet no rights were violated, no laws overstepped. The "side" of pluralism in the wider ideological contrast was loudly affirmed by official voices. Yet limitation was evident. This is a different form of constraint on critical speech and writing than the frank censorship and violent enforcement familiar to historians studying the autocracies and dictatorships – communist or fascist – of the twentieth century. But it is nonetheless a limitation on any independent speech that is critical of central officialdom, and a form of limitation by no means special to Hungary.

9 Expression Is Transaction: Talk, Freedom, and Authority when Egalitarians Embrace the State

RUPERT STASCH

Participants in free speech debates usually see the very definition of their polity as being at stake in their struggles over what can be said. Yet putting language at the centre of political imagination is not unique to societies influenced by Athenian or liberal framings of "free speech" as a central focus of collective legal concern. For example, until the late twentieth century, Korowai people of Indonesian-controlled Papua were not involved with any state and had no tradition of conflict or conviction around "free speech." Even during the revolutionary political changes they have recently undergone through interaction with the Indonesian state, Christianity, international tourism, and global consumer culture, free speech has not become a significant focus of attention for them. Yet their political order *does* turn on freedom, as they distinctively understand it. And they often define their freedom-centred polity via models of speech.

This chapter contributes to this volume's comparative conversation by outlining main patterns in how Korowai understand politics, freedom, speech, and the connections between them. These patterns are interesting not only because of their difference from "free speech" formations discussed in other chapters but also because of their complexity. They are built upon internal tensions and ambiguities.

In the first half of my account, I discuss past Korowai political order by surveying some patterns of language use illustrative of the polity's definition through images of speaking. A more specific idea I develop is that it is useful to identify three characteristic forms of freedom in Korowai people's lives. One is rejection of being told what to do by others in favour of thinking and deciding for oneself. A second is pushy impingement onto others, but often with collective understanding that the targets bear responsibility for answering relational desires expressed through the violation, and with collective understanding that the aggressor is responsible for repair in the wake of the violation. A third form of freedom is self-restraint or self-lowering, which is also surprising and complex, because it sometimes amounts to active or "free" pursuit of desired effects via disavowing free ability to bring effects about.

I sketch past Korowai political order by describing these three modes of freedom, but also by exploring their interrelations. The three contradict each other, yet also interlock. They might even be different facets of a single commitment. In these and other ways, my account of this ethnographic example develops further a home truth of the anthropology of ethics, the anthropology of exchange, and linguistic anthropology: that people's cultural understandings are often centred not on freedom itself but on a relational complex it is part of (e.g., Laidlaw 2014; Wagner 1974; Silverstein 2003a). This complex might be understandings of what a rule, regularity, given, constraint, or limit is; understandings of what it is to act, choose, create, or violate; and understandings of how these are interdependent, or strangely identical.

Interwoven with this account of three modes of Korowai freedom, the chapter's first half also cumulatively sets out the theme signalled by my title phrase "expression is transaction." This is the idea that Korowai think of speech less as a matter of relations between speakers and their words (such as whether they have the right to say certain things) and more as a matter of speech's effects on addressees, and on speaker–addressee relations.

Following that overview of the old polity, this chapter's final sections look at the changes of the last two decades. These changes were caused by shifts in administrative and financial structures of the Indonesian state, as mediated locally by Korowai people's own political values. Looking at these recent shifts provides more nuanced evidence of the shape of those same political values, even as recognizing those earlier values is crucial to understanding how the changes have taken place. Overall, Korowai dramatically expanded the "self-lowering" mode of freedom, and they began newly accepting relations of verbal subordination out of desire to overcome even more painful subordination in matters of material wealth.

The Polity as "Talk"

An illustration of assimilating the polity to speech is the regular Korowai use of two words that normally have the general meaning "language, talk, discourse, voice, sound" (*aup, maüon*) to mean more specifically "conflict, uproar, controversy." For example, people commonly describe someone as "having a big talk" or being the "owner of an uproar" to say that that person has harmed others by marriage, adultery, theft, bodily violence, negligence, or just proximity to a loss. One man said about his relative's death from a snakebite, "I held the entire talk" (*aup sendipto nupto atibale*). He meant that he alone had been the target of others' angry grievances, and he had travelled around persuading them to accept their loss without payment. It is common for an "uproar" to become a hiatus in collective time, with everyone in a region of the landscape pausing their other social plans and travel activities to pay attention only to the dangers and demands of the conflict. Men intending to elope with a sweetheart might spend months building an extra-high house and laying in supplies in anticipation of the "uproar" expected to follow. Speaking the new lingua franca of Indonesian, Korowai translate usages of the two Korowai general words for "talk," when used specifically in the "uproar" sense, by the Indonesian word masalah, meaning literally "problem" or "offense." (I underline Indonesian words, while italicizing Korowai ones, because of the new lingua franca's important indexical associations with processes of change discussed later.)

Using general words for "talk" this way, Korowai describe political conflict *as* the speech of many people expressing grievances about an event. Often here "talk" is modified by "big, huge" (*xongel, baul, -tale*), further stressing that what makes something an "uproar" is the *amount* of talking. Discussing specific conflicts, people often speak as if that "uproar" is a character of its own, abstracted from actual people who talk.

Another political quality asserted by this idiom relates to how in speaking of a "controversy" or "big talk," people usually imply that the offender is answerable. This is surprising in light of a more basic characteristic of the same polity, namely, that Korowai reject authority relations, asserting instead that people have "their own thoughts" and act on that basis. Korowai do have a concept of relations of political authority, and the common way it is expressed is by the image of one person "hearing" (*dai-*) or "fulfilling" (*kümoxo-*) another person's "talk," complementary to that other person "giving talk" (*aup fedo-*) or "ordering" (*lanumoxo-*). The image of one person telling others what to do, and being obeyed, is for Korowai a political primal scene, which again illustrates the central place given to speech in the imagining of political life. A stereotype about what would happen to someone who told others what to do was that "they would have been shot." In fact, though, the more common response to pushiness was just to move away. Perhaps the most basic practical form by which Korowai enacted rejection of authority was the everyday practice of living far apart in small, lone households or household pairs, a kilometer or more from any neighbours. People explained this dispersion as helping them avoid others' intrusive requests. Korowai also had no named leadership roles. A further verbal routine in which Korowai express rejection of authority is their common pattern of disavowing knowledge of others' intentions, again in favour of recognizing that everyone has "their own thoughts" and decides things for themselves (Stasch 2008a).

A good indication of how mentally aware Korowai are of the *possibility* of authority relations is their recent pattern of identifying roles of boss and subordinate as the signature social form of "city people," meaning all Indonesians, international tourists, or other natives of capitalist consumption. In stereotype-laden talk about urban space, Korowai regularly describe its social order as consisting wholly of relations between "heads" and the subordinates who "fulfill their talk." Here, the Korowai word *xabian*, "head," is newly used to mean "boss" or "leader," in mimicry of Indonesian-language patterns, where previously it was used only to refer to anatomical heads or head-like objects. Korowai fascination with "boss" relations, as a point of knowledge about the alien world of cities, again reflects their heritage of vigilant rejection of authority structures.

I propose that rejection of subordination is a first prototypic image and idea of freedom as Korowai understand it. Hundreds of societies worldwide have historically been organized around rejecting authority relations, as summed up in the models of "anti-state" or "anarchist" societies promoted by Clastres (1977), Graeber (2004), and J.C. Scott (2009), and frequently discussed by ethnographers in terms of "egalitarianism" or a value of "autonomy." I use these last two terms myself in Stasch (2009) and my other earlier descriptions of Korowai political life, but in this chapter I use "freedom" to cover some of the same space. In tension with individualist ideas of freedom in liberal states, an interpretively challenging pattern in ethnographic work on polities of this kind is that their members tend to interweave preoccupation with freedom and social connection very closely.

The scenarios of "uproar" I outlined above are a case in point. In those cycles of rupture and repair, aggrieved people speak frankly and insistently; political conflict is a matter of edgy confrontation between persons with incompatible opinions; and breakdowns result from someone's willful act that others did not want or expect. Yet, even while living far apart, expressing their own wills, and not investing anyone with centralized control, the people embroiled in conflict did often understand themselves to be linked in a coordinated story, such that separate persons felt teleologically compelled to answer to others' calls for repair.

Additionally, episodes of "uproar" themselves present a complication for my claim just now that Korowai prototypically locate freedom in rejecting subjection to other people. An "uproar" is often the result of one person unilaterally subjecting others to his/her will. The fact that this is a well-recognized genre of social process means also that Korowai *do* see persons subjecting others to their will as being a regularity of life. I turn now to describing the general salience of acts of impingement and violation as a second prototypic model of freedom for Korowai, or as a further face of the first one. I highlight how this mode of freedom is often understood to be ambiguously relation-making and relation-asserting, alongside being harmful.

Anger and Asking: Free Speech as Violation

One prominent site of this salience in the old Korowai polity was widespread interpretation of social affairs in terms of "anger" (*xen*). This word is used not only for emotion expressed in speech and facial expressions but also for acts of bodily violence and any aggressive violation of others' desires. To characterize a person as "angry" usually means that he/she has angry verbal outbursts, *and* hits or shoots people, *and* is pushy in transactions. In relation to objects or animals, "angry" can also mean "sharp," "poisonous," or "dangerous." Speakers often hyperbolically describe individuals, whole social networks, or the entire populace as "unbelievably angry" (*xen bamondinda*). They also explain many specific acts of others or themselves by their "anger" (compare Rosaldo 1980; Schieffelin 1990, 112–35; J. Robbins 2004, 182–214).

Here is one man's 2017 reflection on his history of being socialized into "anger" across his upbringing, an account that is striking for the distance he registers between self and self:

> I had no anger when I was small. But my thoughts said, "Be like your father." Later my relatives told me not to. But it was as though my thoughts themselves kept ordering me, it was as if saying, "Okay you get angry!" ... Men don't have anger and strength when they are small. But their fathers show them anger and they become so. People without an angry father don't become angry.

While anger aligns with masculinity, women also enact this quality, even to the extreme of beating or killing someone. Chatting with a woman on her front porch, I watched her casually manage a conflict with her three-year-old son at the same time:

> She smacks him on the back for something. He cries intensely and tries many different ways of smacking her or threatening to. She parries. He becomes intensely plaintive, injured, and distraught at the maternal aggression, but then eventually transitions to laughter in the face of her parrying.

This is a common kind of interactional sequence, and in this case even the young toddler holds a reflexive model of bodily violence's orderliness and relation-making potential.

Many other acts align with "anger" in realizing, in less acutely harmful ways, an idea of freedom as an aggressive impingement into others' lives. Use of second-person imperative verb forms often have this feeling. Another example is "asking" for objects (*nexmo-*), often performed by the bare assertion "Hey, me!" (*nup-e*) or the imperative "Give to me!" (*nu fedom*). Such requests are often expressed in the presence of the desired object and are politically similar to "demand sharing" in the typification of Peterson (1993). Another ubiquitous verbal enactment of freedom is the formula *nayul*, "I don't want to," expressing Bartleby-style refusal in the face of somebody else's offer of food, suggested joint action, request for a gift, or other overture.

In sum, when deciding for oneself is so valued, to act socially is to violate. Everyday requests and exhortations break keenly felt rules of restraint towards others' property, or towards their space to make up their own minds, while refusals violate the felt desirability of being in concert. This theatricalization of freedom as harm and violation makes "freedom" a funny word for describing Korowai actions. But the theatricalization is refreshing to contrast with liberal models emphasizing the possibility of peaceable exercise of freedom, in which one's freedom only needs to be limited at outer extremes where it causes serious harm to others. By contrast, Korowai emphasize the destabilizing violence of very basic free acts.

Taboo and Avoidance: Good Speech as Unfree

Another area of linguistic reflexivity where there is strong association of free speaking with violation is practices of formal avoidance and taboo. Whatever Korowai are talking about in a given conversation, they are also generally being careful to avoid names of their in-laws, "secret names" of other persons or objects within earshot, and names of occult beings (Stasch 2003, 2008b, 2011b). Since many personal names or "secret names" are common nouns or other high-frequency words, conversations are often peppered with circumlocutions, allowing speakers to say what they need to about some topic without using the most routine terms for it. These circumlocutions index speakers' vigilance about avoidance for the sake of some other person or entity also happening to be present. In reflexive discussions of "avoiding" (*lexap-*), the word people use as its opposite is *ndambelüm*, or "indiscriminate, careless." To avoid is to enact a stance of prudence and carefulness towards one's own actions in relation to others.

One comparative point highlighted by the topic of "taboo" is that free speech ideas vary not only in ideas of freedom, speech, and the human polity but also in ideas of how speech connects to other levels of life. One past Korowai speech taboo was a general prohibition of any discussion of divinities, the world's creation, or its hidden foundations. About one type of these divinities, it was broadly thought that they were "angry" and "ashamed," and they could make Korowai sick if offended. Another common sentiment was that the world was likely to flip, flood, or burn following any anomalous event. Other religious practices, including towards the same divinities, were more optimistic and transactionally constructive. But in general, the question of whether people would even be free *to keep living* is often present in Korowai people's minds, and in the near background of questions of freedom in speaking. This tendency to see rules of daily action as life-and-death in consequences partly matches Sahlins's (2017) observation that people who sharply reject relations of authority among humans often nonetheless have experience of domination in their relations with divinities.

Korowai expect taboo or avoidance violations to cause automatic existential damage to the speaker, the named object or person, or the world. This is different from the interpersonal confrontations or embarrassment that might result from "anger" or "asking." Yet there is consistency across these. People's sensitivity to freely deciding for themselves, and their steady experiences of those decisions violating others' freedom in turn and provoking flare-ups, have likely supported their wider understanding of linguistic representation more generally as an edgy violation, best inscribed within gestures of indirectness and renunciation. Conversely, their ideas about the automatic effects of taboo violations are likely supported by the volatile effects of speech in interpersonal affairs. When speakers do "ask," they often refer to requested objects euphemistically as "a little something" or by another vague circumlocution, or alternatively by a more precise expression that names something much less valuable than what is actually being requested. Above, I outlined some patterns of Korowai expecting or even celebrating brashness as a moral quality of speaking. But a correlative of their sensitivity to speaking as violation, and of their attunement to the ever-present possibility of an outbreak of confrontational demands, is that speakers routinely strike stances of politeness and humility towards their addressees, even when making a brash request.

"Giving Up" as Another Freedom: From Violation to Unity

Korowai expectations of the regular occurrence of "uproar" and "anger" associate speech with violation, while their expectations of "avoiding," "taboo," and euphemistic indirection associate speech with restraint. These two clusters together suggest an understanding of speech and related actions as walking a single edge of the simultaneous potential of violation and restraint. Having already suggested that the violation side of this duality is an important form of "freedom" as Korowai live it, I now suggest that the restraint side is *also* a main form of "freedom" for them.

A good place to see this is the common act of "giving up" or "letting go" (*yaxtimo-*). Korowai perform this through the verb itself, such as by saying *yaxtimale*, "I give up, I let go, I release," but also through one-morpheme sentences such as *lefap*, "done, that's enough," or *yepelap*, "it's fine, nevermind, whatever." Often the resolution of an "uproar" is that the protagonist "gives up" their grievance. Sometimes they do so as a result of being paid, but other times they do it in a spirit of resignation and moving on. One woman explained that the practice of a man giving bridewealth to his wife's relatives is "for the purpose of saying 'it's done'" (*lefap dungalxe*). She meant that, thanks to the payments, the wife's relatives give up their anger about the husband taking her from their lives.

Since "giving up" is a reversal of one's own desires and resolve, when someone performs it out of resignation rather than following a payment, it has the air of something people are *compelled* into. Yet it is also a kind of act that is performed and narrated by Korowai with such regularity, and sometimes with a clear sense of valued moral or social effect, that it should be recognized as a performance of a kind of mixed, contradictory volition of what might be termed "freedom in unfreedom," or "freedom under constraint." To "give up" is to free an object, person, emotion, or situation from oneself; set oneself free from it; and set a relation free from the impasse it has reached. This is a reset to a different state through sacrificial lowering rather than aggressive impingement.

A telling reflection of how much Korowai engage life in these terms is that "giving up" is prominent in historical consciousness of the recent massive socio-political changes I describe in more detail later in this chapter. For example, Christian conversions or aggregations in villages are described as events of "giving up" anger. What foreigners call "pacification," Korowai describe as "giving up" the killing of witches or other evildoers. Those revolutions have been shaped by transactional sensibilities of small-scale kinship, in which "letting go" is a routine interpersonal move. These patterns are consistent with sensibilities documented by other researchers working in the New Guinea region.

Wardlow (2006) has written of the "negative agency" of Huli women of Papua New Guinea who withdraw themselves from valued norms in protest at others' failings in the terms of those same norms. Knauft (2002) developed a related idea of "recessive agency" to grasp stances of passivity or subordination taken by Gebusi people (also of Papua New Guinea), with the expectation that this would elicit a good transactional outcome from others. In the case of Korowai sensibilities, another prominent feature of their egalitarianism has been that people were fearful or ashamed to stand out as special. Conversely, they expected that highlighting one's lack of possessions, or other acts of lowering, would make others feel moved by love or pity (finop) to lift the humbled person up with reassuring praise or with a gift. In connection with name avoidance, we have already glimpsed that performing restraint was a way persons knew their relation to be good. In some areas, Korowai paradoxically considered that acts of self-limitation could be a way to create the life one wanted.

Two points can be appreciated from the juxtaposition of "giving up" with "anger" or "asking." First, these contrasting freedoms do not stand just as unconnected alternatives. It is true that certain Korowai are known for being pushy, and others for being accommodating. The same person might act these different ways in different contexts. But the different qualities also interlock. It is common for one person to "ask" or angrily impose his/her will, in response to which another "gives up, releases." Also common is for a person to "ask" or angrily threaten, then "give up" when others reject the request. Some acts of "asking" are simultaneously an aggressive intrusion and a humbling display of one's own poverty. Rules of verbal taboo are dual in similar ways. Taboo observance is an exercise of the qualified freedom to not act freely in hope of receiving good outcomes from powers bigger than humans know. Additionally, these taboos enable aggressive enactment of freedom through violation: alongside the careful restraint I emphasized above, Korowai everyday speech practices are also peppered with opposite acts of swearing blasphemously, shouting "hidden names" to damage someone or something in earshot, or purposefully uttering in-laws' names behind their backs to put them down.

A second conceptual point underlined by juxtaposition of "giving up" with aggressive modes of freedom is that, across both poles, Korowai understandings of freedom are not centred on individual persons, but rather this value commitment is part of a larger context, including coexisting other values, such as a commitment to relationships. It has been common for ethnographers to formulate dualities like "autonomy" and "relations" to make sense of political communities similar to Korowai (e.g., Read 1959; Munn 1986; Myers 1986; McDowell 1990; Kulick 1992; J. Robbins 2004). Building on that work, in my own writings I have argued that Korowai focalize qualities like autonomy, separation, avoidance, and otherness as the substance of relations, rather than as external to them (Stasch 2009). Consistent with this, we have been seeing here that both "angry" and self-lowering modes of freedom are highly relation-embedded. In fact, thinking of freedom as a social process rather than a condition of individuals is probably an important step towards being unsurprised by Korowai patterns of working with multiple models of "free" action, including some models in which freedom mingles with qualities of constraint or surrender.

An illustration of valuing relations is how often Korowai feel unable to refuse another's request for an object, or how frequently they feel spontaneously compelled to give to someone who has not even asked, despite the desirability of keeping the object for oneself. Here too I will give an example from new economic interactions. An important first mode of engagement with the cash economy for many Korowai has been hosting international tour groups (Stasch 2016). When a tour group stays for several days with a local kin network, often a specific Korowai man takes a central role in performing and mediating the tourism labour. When the visitors depart, this man usually receives an overall cash payment from the group's tour guide, sometimes hundreds or thousands of dollars in value. Often he will *entirely* divide the money out, including to persons who did no work. The man ends up empty-handed himself, despite having worked more than others (see figure 9.1). Similar patterns unfold in the dividing out of butchered game or garden produce. People often explain their compulsion to share by fear of being seen as stingy. But sharers also describe the desire to give as positively motivated by feelings such as "love" (*finop*). Self-lowering is transactionally effective in the first place because others feel moved to respond with giving and equalization. Even when Korowai act assertively to get something, they regularly say it is because they want to "be like

Figure 9.1. Bailum Lemaxa distributing to kin the cash proceeds of an Austrian tour group visit, then showing his own empty hands, August 2017. Credit: Rupert Stasch.

my relatives": the ground of free actions is often a relation-centred desire for what others are enjoying. So, too, as glimpsed in the toddler's transition from blows to laughter, or in the shared feeling that an "uproar" needs resolution, aggression can be understood as relation-making and relation-integral, rather than being outside of relations and fracturing them.

The links between seemingly contrastive modes of freedom like angry violation versus solicitous self-lowering, and between freedom and relations, not only complicate what freedom is but also complicate "power." To see this, I return now to freedom and power *in speech* by looking at ambivalences in Korowai imagery of "telling" and "listening," parallel to the ambivalences about asking and giving just outlined.

"Hear" as "Heed": Rejecting Authority but Valuing Unity

We saw earlier that a prototypic image of political control is one person telling a second person what to do; the second person then "heeds" or literally "hears" (*dai-*) that talk. My emphasis there was on Korowai rejection of this scenario of verbal command as a characteristic expression of their generally egalitarian, freedom-privileging political ethos. However, it is also common for Korowai to view positively the image of someone "hearing the talk" or "fulfilling the talk" of another (*aup dai-, aup kümoxo-*). I have already noted that a *concept* of subordination is implied by the existence of these expressions, as well as speaker-centred ones like *lanumoxo-*, "command," and *aup fedo-*, "tell, advise" (lit. "give talk"). But it is also a recognized and common kind of actual interaction for someone to give another advice, even though doing so is edgy. The fact that the general perceptual verb "hear" (*dai-*) carries a more focused political sense of "listen to, heed, obey" seems to imply a certain prototypic identification of the hearer role with meeting a speaker's desires (and this pattern is common cross-linguistically). Korowai do often express admiration for relations in which one spouse "listens to" another, a son-in-law "listens to" his mother-in-law, a child "listens to" its parent, and the like. The man who narrated to me his own socialization into the regular performance of rage did so after telling me about a time in his childhood when he was almost struck by an arrow his father had shot at his mother for "crossing his talk" (*aup laxabemo-*) rather than obeying. So there is actually a model of marriage as patriarchal subordination of wives to their husbands' orders, coexisting with other models such as spouses determining their own actions, or partners heeding each other mutually.

The expressions "hear talk" or "fulfill talk" are also used to rationalize adherence to a whole order of life. Persons describe themselves as "fulfilling the talk of my parents" to explain why they live on a clan-owned forest territory, build houses, exploit the land as they do, or follow certain kinship practices. They also previously explained collective conventions by saying they are "fulfilling the talk" of a world-creating demiurge, and today Christian faith is expressed as "hearing God's talk" or "hearing the Gospel" (lit. "listening to world talk, listening to cosmology"). These patterns align with the Foucault-influenced academic idea that an entire institutional and material order is a "discourse," as well as with the centrality of "Word" to Christian thinking about human relations with the divine. But the Korowai understandings are importantly centred on the position of hearers, and on their stance of *listening*.

Persons who describe themselves as obediently "hearing" or "fulfilling" other people's talk in these different areas often do so with an affirmative stance of pleasure or rightness. I see this affirmative embrace of "heeding" as a variation on the patterns of self-lowering discussed in the prior section. Writing about Yopno people of Papua New Guinea, Slotta (2023) has coined the phrase "anarchic listening" to describe a cultural climate of people in an egalitarian polity placing intense social and epistemological weight on hearing as an activity. Yopno understand attentive listening to be crucial to acquisition of important knowledge, but necessarily mediated by responsibility for filtering and weighing what is heard, and deciding for oneself what to do (see also Slotta 2014). For Korowai in many contexts, freedom and subordination do seem to flow together harmoniously in the form of persons willingly obeying someone in order to attain a larger condition of equality, joint flourishing, and valued social coordination. My interlocutors have sometimes explained "fulfilling" another's talk as something they do "from their own thoughts." The emphasis on the hearer's choice in aligning with another's speech is one solution to the puzzle of Korowai stridently rejecting the idea of being ordered about, but also celebrating relations in which one person fulfils the talk of another.

Yet there are also actual contradictions between the Korowai premium on freedom and situations where people perform and experience domination. Relatedly, "listening" or self-lowering are internally contradictory and ambivalent modes of freedom, as I have emphasized. These patterns parallel the ambivalence about speaker-centred freedom of anger or aggressive impingement that we saw in my initial account of feuding as a "big talk": free speaking harms or disrupts as well as creates, equalizes as well as subordinates. The broader tendency across these understandings of speech and freedom is that what people pay attention to as speech's truth is its transactional implications. What qualities of benefit, harm, reciprocity, and repair are flowing between the participants through what they say?

State Intrusion and Radical Political Change

Over the last few decades, Korowai political order has been fundamentally altered through engagement with the Indonesian state and other new intruding forces and people. The pace of change accelerated in the 2010s. For the next few pages, I set aside main topics of earlier sections of this chapter to describe the broad shape of these changes, and of the wider regional political processes to which Korowai are newly connected. Then I return to the earlier themes to consider how links between speech and politics in Korowai understanding have importantly played into the course of radical change.

Due to difficult terrain and lack of economic incentives, outsiders only began intruding into Korowai space in the 1980s, and at first only in the southwest portion of their overall five-hundred square mile territory. Northern and eastern Korowai began engaging with these new people and institutions still more recently, in the last twenty years. Different Korowai initially felt intense millennial fear and repulsion towards the new outsiders, and today they describe this involvement as having amounted to an epochal break in collective time. The new interactions could be periodized by types of strangers who were most important: the 1980s were a time of Dutch missionaries and Papuan church co-workers; the 1990s and 2000s were a time of international tourists; and the 2010s were a time of Indonesian government officials.

The biggest practical way Korowai engaged with all the new institutional forces was making "villages" (see figure 9.2). They associated this exotic type of space with imported consumer goods, living peaceably rather than jumping quickly to anger, and learning Indonesian. It was Korowai themselves who

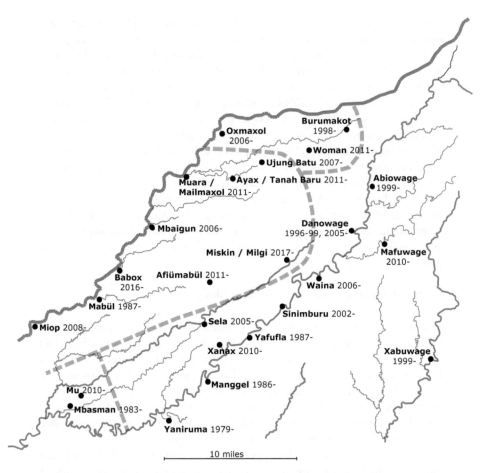

Figure 9.2. Selected Korowai villages, c. 2017. Dashed lines indicate differences in direction the villagers travel to reach their Regency seat. Credit: Rupert Stasch.

took the initiative in forming the new centralized settlements at different times across their overall region. State agents like police, civil servants, teachers, and health nurses rarely visited. In the 1990s, foreign missionaries were absent, and tourists were interested in traditional living conditions rather than villages. Yet while Korowai were the main agents of village formation, they held those villages at arm's length, in keeping with hostility to relations of subordination. We have seen that in their old order, Korowai lived out freedom through geography: they voted with their feet, residing far apart and changing who they lived with if they felt pushed around. Already in the 1980s, southwestern Korowai saw creating physical villages as entailing a later goal of government recognition of them as *administrative* units, involving installation of a "village head" and other officeholders. But in early years, Korowai often found ways to participate in villages while still spurning authority structures. For example, most people oscillated residentially between villages and the old type of space they call "forest," where small kin groups lived far apart on separately owned clan lands. Into the 2000s, villages were often empty, residents preferring to stay in their "forest" houses. But in recent times Korowai have taken up village living much more energetically. There are now about forty centralized villages found across every part of the region. By the time of my last visit in 2017, 90 per cent of Korowai were living in villages and visited forest territories mostly just on day trips. In tandem with this shift, Korowai also swung from shunning authority relations to embracing them, as I describe below. But first I need to consider the dramatic wider change of Indonesian state structures that has fed into this local shift.

Papua is best known internationally for its indigenous people suffering bodily domination by the Indonesian army and police and economic domination by civilian Indonesian migrants. Korowai people's location far from towns, and outside the reach of state institutions, meant that they had limited experience of these dynamics through the 1990s. However, conditions across rural Papua have been complicated over the last fifteen years, in ways not as well known to global academics and activists, by large policy structures known as "decentralization" and "special autonomy." Decentralization has been implemented across Indonesia, and its most visible form is the prolific subdivision of state administrative units at nested subnational levels of Province, Regency, District, and Village. When I began fieldwork in 1995, Papua's southern plain was one vast Regency, and its capital was located two hundred miles south of the Korowai area. After redistricting, Korowai are now divided between four Regencies, and each Korowai village orients to an elected "Regent" in one of four different administrative centres (see figures 9.2 and 9.3). These centres are all geographically distant, but much closer than the former one of Merauke.[1]

The policy of special autonomy has been implemented in relation just to Papua, with the purpose of dampening and disorganizing separatism. The

1   In 2022, Indonesia implemented in Papua a further major redistricting process at the next-highest territorial level of state administration, splitting a single existing "Province" into four. The four southernmost Regencies shown in figure 9.3 now together make up a complete province of their own, South Papua, whereas previously they were grouped together with twenty-four further Regencies, and their provincial capital was far to the north in Jayapura. This subdivision likewise brings the "Governor" level of electoral politics and funding streams much closer to Korowai than it previously was.

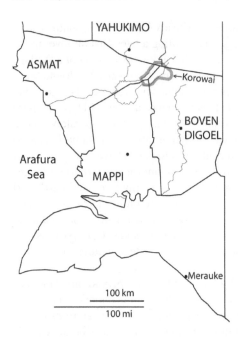

Figure 9.3. Korowai lands divided since 2002 across four Regencies, with Regency seats as dots. Credit: Rupert Stasch.

policy's main practical effect has been increased budget flows to government offices in Papua, and increased access of Papuans to civil servant jobs and elected high offices. Papuans widely say that special autonomy has failed in its supposed goal of improving their lives, such as through provision of health care, education, or entrepreneurial chances. Yet the paid jobs linked to new government administrative units, and the money controlled by those units' heads, have led local populations and their new elites to campaign for establishing their own new Villages, Districts, Regencies, or Provinces (Suryawan 2020; cf. Vel 2007; Eilenberg 2016).

Changes of electoral process additionally meant rural Papuans were newly invited into patronage relations of giving a Regent their votes in return for cash, consumables, and infrastructure, which he controls through the large sums now flowing through his administrative level. Another decentralization program was direct disbursement to villages of annual cash grants equivalent to many thousands of dollars, supporting small infrastructure and stimulus projects on the international model of "community-driven development." Papua is Indonesia's poorest region. The new financial flows implemented under decentralization and special autonomy have meant that many people on Papua's rural super-periphery have gone from cashless deprivation to sometimes having money for major purchases.

The recent Korowai swing almost wholly towards "village" living poses a puzzle of "anarchists for the state." Why would people who programmatically rejected authority relations now embrace them? From the preceding sketch of new Indonesian policies, an obvious answer is that money and consumer goods became suddenly available through state participation. This answer is true but incomplete. In the final sections, I describe how Korowai have actively sought relations of subordination to faraway government heads and adopted divides of ruler and ruled among themselves for the purpose of getting material resources. Importantly, the strength of their desires for new material resources and their ways of trying to get them were shaped by cultural sensibilities of their past polity.[2]

Self-Lowering towards Regents

While government structures have been changing, the new surge of local state formation has still been led by Korowai, who work very actively to make themselves visible on the state's terms. Faraway administrators still know little about actual conditions in the Korowai area. When they make a direct visit, they only come briefly to one of the four most connected villages. It is Korowai who have actively sought administrators' attention, such as by physically opening a village in the first place, compiling lists of residents to present to administrators, and lobbying intermediaries for help getting resources to support the further village-making process.

What most drives this movement towards the state is Korowai persons' profound sense of inferiority to "city people." I saw this self-deprecatory consciousness rise in the 2000s. During early involvement with missionaries, tourists, and Papuan church workers, specific Korowai persons often rejected foreign technologies and institutions, affirming the superiority of their own norms. In the mid-1990s when I first lived in the area as a PhD researcher, I rarely heard anyone voice collective self-deprecation. But across return visits in 2001 and after, I saw the rise of a widespread desire among Korowai that their land become a place of unlimited access to ready-made consumer goods on the model of the life they understand as being enjoyed by faraway "city people." It is difficult to exaggerate the intensity of most Korowai persons' feelings of deprivation and desire along these lines, echoing colonial and post-colonial experiences widely seen across Melanesia (e.g., Robbins and Wardlow 2005). Korowai have elaborated their imagery of city life based on what they have directly seen of city people's travel gear, houses, office jobs, or stockpiles of

---

2 This discussion parallels the differently-framed and more detailed accounts given in Stasch (2021, 2023).

consumer goods. Stereotypes about that easy life are also based on Korowai experience of consuming some types of new imported goods themselves, when they have access to them. But the feelings of yearning and inferiority are also shaped by prior sensibilities. One of these sensibilities was concern with material objects as media of aesthetic, personal, and relational value. (Notably, payment was very important in past Korowai social life. Current fascination with money builds partly on earlier foundations.) A related sensibility was intense attention to equality between kin. Korowai frequently explain desire for consumer goods as being driven by desire to "be like" tourists, city people, neighbouring ethnic groups, or their own relatives, whom they have seen enjoying those articles.

Korowai have transposed the political sensibilities of their past kinship life into the new macrostructure of their relations with global capitalism. Their expressions of the inferiority of their own lives are grounded in material experience, but also in the egalitarian moral psychology outlined above. This is most sharply illustrated by Korowai interest in client relations with "Regents" (Bupati), which amounts to applying the model of "asking" or "demand sharing" to the state.

In the 2010s, Regents were constantly discussed even by persons who had never seen one directly. Like the iconic figure of "tourists" (*tulis*), the Regent personifies urban consumer prosperity. For Korowai who have visited a Regency seat (Kabupaten), the commerce and infrastructure there represent what they hope their own villages will become. Local talk about the Regent commonly centres on his expected visit. During my 2011 and 2017 fieldwork, I was struck by how many kin networks across different parts of the landscape were preparing for Regent encounters. In 2011, no Regent had ever been to a local village, whereas by 2017 some had made flying visits to the most connected Korowai villages in their jurisdictions. But *rumours* of an imminent visit were a staple of life. Forest-dwelling Korowai travelled to villages based on such rumours, while villagers started new work of clearing vegetation and digging trenches along the visitors' expected promenade.

It is here that I can return to the themes of earlier sections of this chapter by outlining the centrality of *speech* to relations between Korowai and Regents, and particularly the transactional emphasis that Korowai place on speech, involving on their side prominent motifs of self-lowering. The standard script for a Regent's visit is that Korowai receive him with a martial dance procession in traditional dress, which has strongly sonic dimensions in the form of musical chanting of the non-semantic syllables *wo-wai*, punctuated by phases of low ululation and clattering of bundled arrows against bows. This is followed by these local residents listening in assembly to the Regent spell out his material promises to them, often in response to requests listed aloud to him by local spokesmen. The Regent's assistants usually make on-the-spot cash distributions to offset travel and food costs for the rural persons who have gathered. The encounter's emphasis on the Regent's answerability to villagers' desires rests on a wider understanding that his conferral of resources is a direct quid pro quo for having "given [their] voices" (*aup fedo-*) to the Regent in elections. The Korowai idiom of "give voices" to describe voting is a back translation of wider Indonesian usage, and there is a deeper history across Indonesia of state officials conferring development in exchange for iconic performances of local tradition. Korowai, from their own transactional starting points, find these wider templates very recognizable. An element they amplify is performance of material impoverishment through nudity and other bodily or technological motifs indexing lack and primitivity.[3] They extend to the Regent their cultural expectation that gestures of self-lowering are expected to move others to love and equalization. Also characteristic of Korowai sensibilities here is an understanding of positions of inferiority as also partly positions of strength. The martial processions, adapted from past feast performances, signify "we are from the forest" or "we have nothing," but they are also visually and vocally impressive – and politically intimidating. While Korowai audiences to a Regent strike stances of submissive hopefulness towards his ability to confer wealth, in their background discussions they assert that the Regent depends electorally on *them*, and so already owes them what they are demanding.

Long-distance relations with Regents also turn centrally on language, interpreted transactionally. I noted that submitting written lists of village residents is a major path for seeking state resources. This is followed by the further circulation of written reports that the villagers produce about their activities, and of printed signs sent back by officials for display next to new village infrastructure recording details of its funding. One telling performance of deprivation was the naming of the village of Miskin, founded in 2017. Normally, Korowai villages take their names from a nearby stream, but founders of this village cut to the chase by using the Indonesian word for "poor" or "poverty" (miskin). Their intended audience was the faraway Regent of Asmat, who would understand all the more clearly the deprivation and hope that was their core meaning in making a village. This move, like other acts of verbal self-lowering, had a precedent in past patterns of naming children after conditions of lack, such as "Famine," "Hungry," "Orphan," "Ugly," "Himself Alone," or "Houseless." This

---

3 Nudity and related technologies now bear an aura of pastness and inferior living, in part through extensive Korowai experience performing them for visiting tourists and film crews. See Stasch (2015) for the text of a Korowai spokesman's oration while giving a government visitor primitivity-marked technological objects and expressing the intention that the government should replace these with corresponding superior consumer goods.

was a way that a child's relatives deprecated their own conditions of life but also evoked positive emotions of compassion in other people who heard the name in use.

This section has traced how Korowai attraction to Regents reflects interplay between the changed state environment and past Korowai thinking about politics and speech. The "Regency" level of government is newly close and rich. People's heritage of intense egalitarian sensitivity in relations with close kin has now led Korowai to feel intense pain about their exclusion from the imagined wealth of city people. Desire to correct that inequality drives their enthusiasm for relations with Regents. At the centre of their overtures towards Regents are patterns of stylized performance of inequality, which Korowai are extending from past everyday kinship into the new governmental sphere. Besides the particular motif of self-lowering, a wider commonality between these Regent relations and patterns discussed earlier in this chapter is that questions of volitional freedom in speaking, and of speech's overall value, are heavily centred on its *transactional* implications. Rather than focusing on whether speakers have rights to say what they think or want, the first focus is on what an addressee will be moved by speech to do: the effects speaking has on what speaker and addressee will be to each other.

Listening to "Heads"

A last shift in power-marked roles that I will discuss is a newly embraced divide between "heads" and "community" among Korowai themselves. This was intertwined in the late 2010s with the rise of transactions known internationally as "community-driven development" and known in local administrative practice as "Village Block Grants" (Alokasi Dana Desa). Korowai call the transactions simply "work" or "wage labour," borrowing the Indonesian word kerja into Korowai-language frames like "take hold of work" (*kelaja ati-*) or "give wage labor" (*kelaja fedo-*). In ten villages I visited in 2017, with varied histories and administrative statuses, there was a striking uniformity of activity. Korowai gathered in increased numbers in villages, where they laboured together at projects like making new lanes, walkways, or permanent-materials houses. Village officeholders worked with intermediaries to report completed work to Regency centres. When grants came through, the leaders divided wages among the workers. To Korowai, the new material infrastructure was incidental to the more important labour-for-money exchange, and to the consumables bought with the pay.

What startled me was the widespread discussion of these activities in terms of an opposition between "heads" and "community" or "populace." The "heads" are men holding posts in the village administrative apparatus, for which they are paid a stipend (honor, *onol*). They tell the "community" what to do, meaning they organize their labour. Those addressees "hear" or "listen to" (*dai-*) the heads' talk, meaning they obediently do the work. Politics is again centrally imagined as a configuration of speech roles. Untalkative men stay away from these new leadership roles or leave them behind. People speak of "heads" by the Korowai word *xabian*, which I noted above has been newly used for the last twenty years to designate authority roles, imitating the Indonesian word kepala. By contrast with this longer-established pattern, explicit reference to a counterpart group of subordinate subjects is an innovation of the last few years. Speakers refer to the "community" by the newly borrowed Indonesian word masyarakat, and sometimes by the Korowai word *mayox*, "people." In 2017, when I first heard these references to villagers as basically "commoner" subordinates of the heads, it struck me as sharply breaking with past Korowai rejection of anyone's claims to tell others what to do.

Villagers without stipends resent exclusion from "head" roles. Often there is bad feeling about past labour that was never compensated by the heads. Some heads are artfully deferential and self-lowering towards the workers they direct, giving their leadership a kinship-inflected tone. Some also artfully manage money in ways that dull the new economic inequalities of this system. But when I put to Korowai my surprise at the division between "heads" and "populace," they agreed that it ran against their past principles, but they explained matter-of-factly that the purpose of accepting the division was to get money. A basic answer to the puzzle of "anarchists for the state" is that Korowai are embracing one relation of subordination in order to ease the larger, more painful one of collective exclusion from urban consumer prosperity. Under cover of a motive of gaining access to wealth, Korowai are accepting a new speech pattern of some men unilaterally announcing what other people should do.

Conclusion: Expression Is Transaction

The old Korowai understanding of freedom as a matter of having one's "own thoughts" and not being ordered about was part of a horizontal, dispersed institutional and economic order. The last sections of this chapter have described processes of that horizontal social space being newly integrated with vertical geopolitical structures of an altogether larger scale. There are at least two broad trends to how old, already complex Korowai understandings of freedom have been reorganized in that process. One is that in the duality of aggressive versus self-lowering modes of freedom, self-lowering has expanded, while aggressive self-assertion has become a bit less prominent (and in some cases, when it does occur, it has become even more ambiguously amalgamated with self-lowering). Another is that the politics of access and equality in material life has overshadowed issues of subordination in speech. Listeners newly accept the verbal instructions of political bosses when they understand this compliance will enable them to get money.

Elsewhere in Papua and in many cities across Indonesia (where Papuans migrate for university studies), security personnel or Indonesian civilians often violently stifle Papuan speech concerning their own domination by Indonesians and their desires for dignity or freedom in the face of it. The state also uses a law on "treason" (makar) to prosecute persons who question Papua's political integration in Indonesia. Even more widely, state propaganda at all levels – and particularly in the everyday work of police, military, and intelligence personnel – pervasively tags any discussion of issues of social justice or hardship by Papuans with the question of whether someone is "separatist" (separatis), an intensely condemnation- and stigma-attracting category in the wider mass political environment of Indonesian nationalism. Among Papuans in civic life, this results in intense self-restriction of speech and pervasive disparities between speech and consciousness, even among large numbers of Papuans whose actual personal convictions do not pose Papuan independence from Indonesia as the desirable or realistic way that goals of justice might be best met.

Across the last two decades, many Korowai developed the same forms of Papuan nationalist sentiment around this unjust order as are often found among rural Papuans at large. Often they acquired this consciousness through direct experience of ethnicized economic inequality during visits to towns. Other Korowai without wide travel experience acquired it mainly via energetic word-of-mouth reasoning and flow of information in conversation with neighbours or with each other. Many Korowai think of Papuan nationalist and separatist sentiment as something to be discussed secretly and knowingly among Papuans; in some interactions with ethnic Indonesians, Korowai feel intense hostility and mistrust, but again often keep those feelings verbally under wraps. Yet overall, the new Korowai consciousness of this conflict is focused intensely on the conflict itself, such as on material inequality between Indonesians and Papuans, on actual or potential violent fights, and on ideas about landownership and the conditions under which immigrant settlers should ever be present in other people's land. Issues of whether Papuans are allowed to express nationalist views do not rise to the level of being an important, attention-drawing dimension of the conflict, even among Korowai who have lived at length in towns (where coercive control of Papuan speech is more concentrated). I outline here this example of a proper "free speech" conflict just to highlight that discussions of "free speech" norms do exist in the wider geopolitical field in which Korowai live, and might become very important to some Korowai in the future, but they are not currently the kind of issue they focus on in thinking about relations between speech and politics, for the historical and contextual reasons I have set out across this chapter.

Yet Korowai reflexivity about speech, and their ideas of how a polity is made through models of speaking, have greatly influenced the reorganization of their political lives now taking place. A larger lesson of this chapter is thus about political change in interactions between social formations of radically different geopolitical scales. Namely, when a freedom-preoccupied egalitarian people move towards participation in state structures, this can be propelled not just by the state's features as an external condition but also by how those features enter into the already plural make-up of egalitarian relations in the smaller polity. In my account of the old Korowai polity, I highlighted freedom's complexity, such as the quite different forms it could take within the same people's lives, its cultural distinctiveness, and the contexts within which it was intrinsically defined. Recent embrace of the "head" versus "populace" division is one illustration of those complexities' importance to processes of change. The role divide of "head" versus "populace" has exploded because the image of people being told what to do, and doing it, already existed as an imaginable, attention-attracting kind of social form, charged with ambivalences. Korowai knew it when they saw it, and knew how to do it. Likewise, from a culturally distant position in which government and citizen is one domain of relations, and workplace hierarchy is another, it might be surprising that organizing *labour* for wages would be the type-case of political authority. But Korowai sensitivity to material goods as the deeper measure of people's positions with one another meant this was exactly the wedge-like context in which they could come to terms with a quasi-Hobbesian experiment in voluntary subordination to a ruler. Quite different situations examined by other contributors to this volume also illustrate this principle that a political system's plural, fractured composition is pivotal to how participants in it remake their lives in new contexts.

Acknowledgments

This chapter is based on ten months of fieldwork in the Korowai area in 1995–6, between one and two months each in 1997, 2001, 2002, and 2011, and about three months each in 2007 and 2017, as well as about one year of cumulative experience in Jayapura and other towns. I owe so much especially to those Korowai who shared their views with me in villages and in forest homes I visited in the 2017 fieldwork research that was a particularly focused on this chapter's topics. That fieldwork was possible thanks to financial support from the ERC grant "Situating Free Speech" and a US Fulbright Faculty Research Fellowship. I am very grateful to Matt Candea for his thoughtful, stimulating leadership of "Situating Free Speech," and for inviting me to be an associated researcher. I am equally grateful for the inspiring work and feedback of all other participants in the project's research and discussions, particularly Taras Fedirko for important help at a late stage.

10 Dissent, Hierarchy, and Value Creation: Liberalism and the Problem of Critique

NATALIE MORNINGSTAR

Freedom of Entry

In 2013, two artists were summoned to fix a problem. Property vacancy rates were at a post-recession high in Ireland, and Offaly County was one of the worst hit, the midlands region blighted by unoccupied buildings in newly developed town centres. Echoing similar strategies in other parts of the country, the County Council and Arts Council funded a contemporary art festival and invited both up-and-coming and established artists from the region and further afield. Their presence, it was hoped, might encourage residents to consume and become familiar with contemporary art, a project that funders hoped might stoke enthusiasm for a new arts centre planned in town. The two artists in question, Avril Corroon and Kerry Guinan, were more cynical. To them, this seemed like a familiar effort to deploy art as a political strategy through which funders and developers could regenerate depressed urban landscapes, adding value to derelict neighbourhoods while distracting from the fact that their solutions were temporary stopgaps for long-running structural inequalities.

Both third-year students at the National College of Art and Design in Dublin, Avril and Kerry were involved in activist campaigns critical of the then-government's response to the crash and speculative investment in the property market. At face value, they seemed like appropriate candidates for the job: young, politically engaged artists keen for the exposure a festival exhibition would bring and eager to address the infrastructural fallout of the recession. But the festival organizers were in for an unexpected twist.

The artists were given access to an unoccupied building in the centre of a town called Tullamore and told they could convert the space into a "pop-up exhibition" for the duration of the festival. While they were theoretically given free rein in designing the space, the festival curator evidently had in mind a familiar variety of contemporary art exhibition: a vacant, retail building through which the public might amble, lingering on pleasantly confounding art objects and, as the ideal vision would have it, enlivening a derelict site with their public presence and amenable discussion. Art, following this line of thinking, was a powerful tool for creating a sense of belonging and social effervescence in areas where the local community had been displaced by exclusionary processes of regeneration. Avril and Kerry were aware, and deeply critical, of this ambition, and as Kerry said, particularly of the role art was intended to play as an "instrument" through which to "legitimize" the processes of deurbanization, property speculation, and housing collapse – in which the funders were, in their view, complicit.

So, they took the concept of creative licence to its extreme logical conclusion. Once they were granted access to the building, they made a hundred copies of the keys and deeds and distributed them to households in a half-mile radius, along with a notice granting the recipients unconstrained access to the property, with which, they were told, they could do whatever they pleased. As they distributed envelopes through mail slots, residents emerged from their homes to enquire amongst themselves, in an image of public exchange markedly distinct from the one the festival organizers had in mind.

Later, as Avril and Kerry distractedly sipped coffees in a nearby shopping centre, a clearly piqued woman thundered past the window, notice in hand, and stormed into the local Citizens Information Centre. As it transpired, a group of residents had entered the building. Shocked and suspicious when his key actually opened the front door, one man called the landlord, who called the festival organizers. Within two hours of opening, the "exhibition" was shut down. Given one more chance to "put something in the room," Avril and Kerry offered the keys and deed, which were displayed in the shopfront window after their artistic intervention.

Subsequently entitled *Freedom of Entry*, this "art act" exhibits hallmark features of the genre of art to which my interlocutors ascribe. In 2016–17, I conducted fieldwork with left-wing artist-activists, the majority of whom lived, worked, and organized in a network of informal collectives, squats, and occupations that had cropped up in vacant sites in the years after the recession. All of them were invested in disruptive and uncomfortable genres of artistic production, and many of them lived in gentrifying neighbourhoods near controversial regenerations and social housing demolitions. Driven by event-based actions, art acts like the one described above are designed to confuse, interrupt, and reorder public space, often through what interlocutors described as "over-identification" with, or "over-performance" of, the object of critique. These art acts involve a selection of mundane objects and spaces, difficult to distinguish as "works of art," or of disorienting and satirical performances in the city streets. "Traces" of the act are often subsequently exhibited and discussed with other artists and members of the public in galleries and open question-and-answer sessions. The objective is thus to deploy art as a means through which to draw attention to, and provide a forum for discussing, the limits of contemporary governance, drawing on humour, parody, and absurdity. The goal is to jar a public audience into internalizing novel critical views of everyday life and considering possible alternatives.

As I have argued elsewhere (Morningstar 2021), artists' engagement with public space, and their style of critique, is a classic instance of what Michel Foucault describes as cynical *parrhesia*. *Parrhesia* is often defined as the "duty" (Foucault 2019, 65) to speak truth to power from a position of inferiority, and it is thus a productive tool for thinking about the politics of public expression and free speech, as this volume argues. However, another vein of Foucault's thinking on *parrhesia* is less concerned with speech than with the political potential of controversial public spectacle. Foucault's thinking on this subject is concerned with the long tradition, from ancient cynicism to modern art, political radicalism, and religious reformism, of manifesting politically dangerous ideas in public space not only through "critical preaching" and combative "dialogue" but also through "scandalous behaviour" (169). What makes these parrhesiastic forms cynical is the impulse to maintain a polemical attitude in relation to social norms and public figures and institutions. Through the display of unpleasant forms of taboo, absurdism, or contradiction, the cynical parrhesiast can galvanize a public audience, encouraging spectators to "internalize" the parrhesiast's cynical attitude and to become capable of viewing the world afresh through cynical eyes (181). As Foucault observed, in many modern and contemporary artistic movements, this is accomplished by mobilizing public culture against itself, treating art as a tool for critiquing cultural production from within. In Ireland, as elsewhere, this means appealing to forms of intentionally anti-social cultural production like the art acts described above: instead of facilitating a pleasurable encounter between artist and audience, the artist turns art itself into a conduit for staging a cynical revelation.

That said, the parrhesiast is a contradictory public figure, and the artist is a clear example of the reasons why. The parrhesiast is both a person of sufficient "status" (Foucault 2019, 118) that they can command the attention of a wide public and those in power, and one who makes themselves vulnerable to marginalization and the anger of a crowd (44). This chapter is interested in what this fact means for the contemporary status of critique – ranging from artistic rebellion to provocative speech – in liberal democracies. My focus is not on *parrhesia* per se but on a related problem: the question of how we should make sense of the fact that in liberal democracies, public criticism, even when it appears risky or provocative, can function to consolidate the critic's prestige, cement social hierarchies, and energize the elites nominally targeted with criticism. To address this, I set two bodies of literature, one anthropological and one sociological, in conversation with Foucault's thinking on liberalism.

First, I examine the work of Dominic Boyer and Alexei Yurchak on over-identification and the politics of indistinction in socialist, Soviet, and post-Soviet contexts (Boyer 2001; Yurchak 2003, 2008a, 2008b, 2013), and, more recently, in Euro-American liberal democracies (Boyer 2013; Boyer and Yurchak 2008, 2010). It is worth noting that these anthropologists have acted as a direct inspiration for some of my interlocutors, who – like Kerry – are aware of Yurchak's use of the word "over-identification" and of the artistic movements these anthropologists describe. Drawing on Natalia Roudakova's (2017) critique of this body of work, I argue that the parodic forms of over-identification Boyer and Yurchak describe should, however, be contextualized differently in liberal democracies versus in Soviet and post-Soviet contexts. In order to expand on why, I turn to Luc Boltanski, Eve Chiapello, Arnaud Esquerre, and Laurent Thévenot's work on capitalism, critique, and value (Boltanski and Thévenot 2006; Boltanski and Chiapello 1999, 2005; Boltanski and Esquerre 2015, 2020). These sociologists of critique argue that capitalism is distinctive for its ability to consume critique and transform it into a source of value creation or enrichment for a wealthy class.

In this way, their account of provocative public criticism chimes with Foucault's understanding of liberalism. Foucault (2008, 27) observed that one of the core features of liberalism, as distinct from the forms of statecraft that preceded it, is the explicit emphasis placed on "limit[ing] the exercise of government power internally." Liberalism is, as Foucault writes, remarkable for the serious attention it places on practising the "art of the least possible government" (28) or of "frugal government" (29). However, Foucault also notes that this limitation on governance is *itself* a technique of rule, an intensification of forms of rule that rely on explicit shows of force and a strategy for "perfecting" these forms of statecraft more fully (28). Moreover, liberalism accomplishes this by protecting certain "sites of truth" (30) – spaces in which truth is thought to emerge under natural and just conditions, outside state interference. Foucault was interested in how the market functioned as one such site of truth. I am interested here in how free speech and provocative public spectacle serve a similar function. As many vocal critics of free speech argue, the notion of free speech is perhaps best understood as an ideal type, a powerful political concept that serves the interests of some over others and can function to undercut public criticism and political action (Roberts 2004; Jack 2004; Fish 1994). Taking inspiration from these and other thinkers, I argue that we should recentre analyses of power asymmetry, political interest, and value hierarchies in ethnographies of the liberal democratic public sphere.

Ultimately, then, the above sociologists of critique offer essential context for Boyer's and Yurchak's accounts of parody as a reaction against a narrowing of hegemonic discourses and ideologies in liberal democratic public life. They demonstrate that capitalism and liberalism thrive on such critical practices.

More than this, the rise of cynical varieties of public criticism demonstrate that it is democracy, not liberalism or capitalism, that is at risk. To this end, I conclude by reflecting on the late work of critical historian of liberalism, Domenico Losurdo (2011), who insists that contemporary Euro-American politics are characterized by a renewed tension between liberal and democratic principles.

The Docklands

On an uncharacteristically balmy Saturday in autumn 2016, I stood under the bike shelter at a tram stop in central Dublin. A thin haze of rain came in fits and spurts, and as I stood sipping tepid coffee from a thermos, a small crowd began converging. Some were tourists, clad in the unmistakable leprechaun-dotted poncho then on sale at most corner shops in the city centre. They smiled hesitantly at each other, striking up quiet conversations about the weather or the surrounding area. The neighbourhood was distinctive for the metal and glass skyscrapers and hotels that punctured the skyline, jostling up against neoclassical and Georgian buildings in the city's historic quarter. The other arrivals, however, were of a different sort. Styled in muted monotones and minimalist fashions, they were immediately recognizable as art enthusiasts. As they gathered in groups of familiar acquaintances, they chatted comfortably. This latter group would be the critical mass of the audience at an experimental art production programed as part of a festival.

After purchasing tickets, we were given no other information than that we would have to meet at a given location in the financial quarter. The area is remarkable for its recent rapid redevelopment. It is the part of the city in which a striking number of tech companies, start-ups, and luxury hotels and flats have replaced small businesses, public housing estates, industrial facilities, and brownstone row-houses – all hallmarks of Dublin's historically working-class neighbourhoods. Equally controversial, several new builds in the area were left vacant or underused after the recession, and at a time in which housing was prohibitively expensive and scarce. It was in the vacant and partially constructed ground floor of one such building that we were – at this point unknowingly – to attend a "pop-up" performance, the subject of which was the "invasion" of corporate development and the toll the housing and financial crisis had taken on the millennial generation, now in search of both work and stable housing in Ireland.

As the clock ticked past the meeting time, the crowd became restless. People began ambling outside the shelter. One man craned his head this way and that, peering through gold-rimmed glasses, while his companion scrolled perfunctorily through her Instagram feed, propped up on the seat of a locked bicycle. Just then, a woman appeared around the corner of a nearby building and approached the crowd. She was slight and wearing a lavender leotard, a spray of reeds and flowers belted around her waist. Her face was solemn and her gait steady and deliberate, and as she approached the group, each person's attention was progressively trained on her. When she was in speaking distance of the crowd, she stopped and cryptically gestured for us to follow her.

As we drew near the base of the building, the artist turned to face the crowd and explained the structure of the event. After following her to the backside of the building, we would be let into the foyer of a luxury apartment complex under construction. After that point, a performance would start, and we would be told where to go next. On the way to the entrance, the ground would be strewn with the flowers tied around her body, carefully selected, she explained, from the various invasive species multiplying in the docklands due to the environmental disruption caused by rapid development. This would be our "trace" left on this "private landscape" and its "invisible strictures" – normally inaccessible to anyone who didn't pay to use it – the only remnants of a site-specific performance as ephemeral as the urban landscape, and one through which, it became increasingly clear, we were meant to critically engage with the consequences of exclusionary redevelopment. She went on to explain that this critical encounter was a privilege: that they had gotten "special permission" to host the show in this setting and that we would be part of a select group of people fortunate enough to witness this "out-of-place" artistic incursion onto the urban landscape.

We followed her past a series of pristine, identically apportioned new studio apartments, very few of which were occupied. A young man in a white-collared shirt, socks, and underpants ironed a pair of trousers while watching football on TV. As we approached, he looked up sheepishly, surprised at the crowd of strangers sidling past his window. As we entered the foyer, we were met with a handful of festival volunteers wearing matching T-shirts, each of whom checked our tickets and silently corralled us along a bank of newly installed windows, stickers still plastered across their panes. The interior of the building was bare concrete, with a few pieces of construction equipment and cans of paint concealed behind a makeshift barrier made of plastic wrap and reflective silver panelling, a sequence of abstract video clips flickering on and off in quick succession on the cling-film surface. The building was labyrinthine, with several semi-finished rooms partially concealing the full extent of the space. Each audience member appeared as confused as the next, though for many, the mystification was clearly cause for excitement. As we gathered, the group maintained an inquisitive silence.

Standing before us was a man dressed in shades of natural greens, greys, and blues and wearing a deadpan expression with his gaze trained on the wall behind us. Slowly, one by one, six performers emerged from behind the walls, all dressed in the same muted tones, and assembled around the first man. As each performer arrived, they silently laid a hand on his face. They then began to sing softly, their voices amplifying strangely in the cavernous space.

In turn, each performer then removed their hand, and with it their voice, before assembling in a line facing diagonally away from the audience. From this point onward, the performance became increasingly abstract. Punctuated by several reprisals of the singers' initial piece, the performers began unravelling a tape deck while holding tape in their mouths, forming a heap of dismantled cassettes that would subsequently be tangled and untangled at various points throughout the performance. In another sequence, the woman who guided us to the building walked around the room straightening the backs of her slowly slumping companions as another woman rubbed soap on the windows. One performer then made extreme convulsive motions with her arm before striding purposefully away from the audience, as two performers began singing about the River Liffey flowing "deeply, swiftly," about "water rushing in," an apparent reference to the momentum behind the initial speculative years of the crisis. As the piece neared its conclusion, two men took off their shirts and drank water frantically from two cups, spilling almost all of it on the floor at their feet and choking – seemingly genuinely – on their own saliva.

The Contradictions of Cynical Critique

Elements of the performance were recognizable as a critique of the years leading up to and after the recession. Empty policy promises sung out in chorus and performances of the artists' bodies being burdened and overwhelmed by substances could be interpreted as commentary on the unstinted – and in the artists' view, unnatural – flow of unsustainable forms of capital investment into the city. What words were sung or spoken were shot through with the language of invasion and flooding, unsustainability and panic. More straightforwardly, the performance was designed to spotlight an unused, high-value site at the centre of recent redevelopment, one to which the audience would not otherwise have access, and which was therefore singled out as a physical manifestation of the unequal distribution of wealth and resources. By granting us privileged access – for the price of a €14 ticket – the performance was escalating the very logic subject to criticism: that space is not a public resource but a luxury to be bought, a reality that would feel very real to those in the room who had come of age during the housing crisis and who held precarious, project-based employment in the creative sector.

Yet in other respects, the performance was cryptic and insular. At times, it felt more about platforming the artists' idiosyncratic experiences of the recession, on the assumption that their role as artists left them especially capable of communicating this in a revelatory fashion. For the same reason, for some in the room, the performance appeared less illuminating than confounding. It was thus the case that the event generated a combined sense of exclusivity, obscurity, and critical awakening, and it did this by marking out a physical space in the city, and a social encounter, as simultaneously revelatory, bewildering, and anointed.

Indeed, the production of extraordinary and clandestine spaces and social scenes was a feature of artists' lives more generally in the post-recession period. Often, they socialized in semi-hidden cafes or art spaces, tacitly acknowledged as sites where artists might gather. Yet like the performance I attended in the docklands, these spaces were also frequently funded or maintained by the Dublin City Council (DCC), and the artists in them the recipients of other forms of state-subsidized support. Indeed, in the years after the recession, as vacant spaces proliferated in the wake of a series of bankruptcies and foreclosures, the DCC explicitly turned to artists to revitalize these vacant spaces. Through programs such as Per Cent for Art Scheme and Creative Ireland, as well as "creative city" development models (Florida 2002, 2005, 2008; Kong 2014; Kong and O'Connor 2009; Lawton, Murphy, and Redmond 2010), the state explicitly framed artists as powerful allies for revitalizing the economy and increasing property values in so-called blighted neighbourhoods. It was thus precisely when artists' public criticism was most relevant to the transformations affecting everyday people's lives that they became politically "instrumentalised" (Guinan 2016).

Artists were keenly aware of this fact, which caused enormous concern: many commented on the ironic ease with which they could take up alternative forms of work and life and produce anti-cultural artwork during periods of economic downturn, as it was during these periods that they were of greatest economic and social utility to the state. Artists attributed this to what they called "co-optation," or the inevitability that sincere but aggressive forms of public criticism would be absorbed by policy programs as evidence of the health of the public sphere and the edginess and desirability of contemporary artistic production in Ireland rather than treated as truly subversive, impactful claims about those in power. As one artist interlocutor, Aaron, noted, the "creative futuristic thinking" increasingly dominant in city planning, tech, and finance meant that developers, politicians, and other stakeholders were adept at repurposing the language of creativity precisely to undercut the political punch of public criticism. Aaron had experienced this first-hand when the DCC had earmarked his arts space as part of a Strategic Development Zone, a designation nominally designed to platform creative enterprise, community building, and cultural production, but which functioned practically to facilitate the coercive eviction and sale of his thriving community arts space to the CEO of a major Silicon Valley tech company. As Aaron knew well, those in power were adept at speaking the language of creativity and dynamism in order to consolidate wealth and power: to use his words, "creativity and the language of creativity can be very quickly and easily co-opted to justify development patterns that curtail the very thing they pretend to ride on."

Aaron used the example of the "creative workspace," popular in creative and tech start-ups at the time, to further elucidate his point. These spaces would adopt the rebellious DIY and punk aesthetics common in artist studios, galleries, and other creative spaces to attract young workers and add an ephemeral sense of hipness and social value to the surrounding area. These spaces would present as being all about creativity, independent thinking, and free play, and yet they would function practically to exploit young workers employed on temporary contracts for start-ups platformed to kick-start economic growth in declining neighbourhoods – often in proximity to social housing estates undergoing forced evictions and derelictions. These spaces would push a "hang out culture" and a "cool, creative, and egalitarian" (Gill 2002) ethos to encourage forms of work that would otherwise appear straightforwardly troubling. Putting on the exaggerated tones of a cool, creative "tech bro," Aaron drawled, "Stay until 8 o'clock! Hang out! Why would you go home? You can eat here! Come meditate with me! It's *cool!*" For Aaron, this was one of innumerable examples in which the façade of artistic rebellion and creative innovation could be converted into a form of explicit value creation. In the process, any genuinely dangerous ideas or potential that lay in the artistic movements or spaces from which these aesthetics were borrowed would be overwritten by a spirit of "hipness."

This process tightly tracks Boltanski and Chiapellos's account of how critique functions as an engine of value creation in capitalist contexts. Boltanski and Chiapello's (2005, 163) work is focused on "capitalism's amazing ability to survive by endogenizing some of the criticisms it faces." They describe how capitalism actually "needs enemies, people who have a strong dislike for it and who want to wage war against it" (163). Crucially, it is through consuming its enemies that capitalism gains the kind of moral foundations that appear absent when it is treated, as Foucault argues, as a site of natural or spontaneous truth: capitalism's critics are "the people who provide it with the moral foundations that it lacks" (163). In *The New Spirit of Capitalism*, Boltanski and Chiapello (1999) describe how artistic critique in particular has therefore been thoroughly incorporated in the last several decades. This form of criticism "vindicates an ideal of liberation and/or of individual autonomy, singularity, and authenticity" (Boltanski and Chiapello 2005, 176) and has become central to the new management practices of the late twentieth and early twenty-first centuries that push a reimagination of the labourer as a wellspring of inspiration, flexibility, and dynamism. As a result, though artistic criticism was once central to left-wing radical activist ideologies, "supporters of artistic criticism have been co-opted into the power elite" (178). Artistic criticism has thus steadily transformed from a form of dissidence to an extraordinarily powerful tool through which to harness a certain kind of citizen-subject and manage workers in capitalist economies: it has become a technique of value creation and of rule.

In their recent book, Boltanski and Esquerre (2020) describe this process as a cornerstone of what they call an "economy of enrichment." They use this term to describe "the forms of wealth creation that are based on the economic exploitation of the past" (Boltanski and Esquerre 2015, 76). The rise of economies of enrichment signal, for them, a macroeconomic trend: "towards an economic order organized around the production of expensiveness" for a "wealthy class" keen on objects with an "aura" of "exceptionality" that mark them out as singular, unique, and distinctive (80). Among the examples given are a range of "exceptional items sought by a well-to-do public ... for example, art objects or antiquities, luxury goods, houses associated with artists or architects, and so on" (Boltanski and Esquerre 2020, 21). These objects are not valued for their use but for the distinction they confer on those who transact them, which occurs by raising the publicity and uniqueness of the (aspiring) elite consumer. For them, this trend unites the rise of finance capitalism characteristic of neo-liberalism and the celebrity culture and publicity politics sociologists have argued increasingly shape public and private life. As they note, along with an economy of enrichment, we also witness the rise of an "economy of attention," as "increasing importance is attributed not only to the objects themselves but also to the universes in which the objects are conceived and in which they circulate – and above all to the human beings surrounding them, whether these be 'creators' ... or 'personalities'" (23).

One need not go far to see the logics of enrichment in action. The examples they give are familiar, of arts spaces or monumental architecture employed to re-enliven urban centres that have suffered a decline in secure manufacturing employment (e.g., the construction of Gehry's Guggenheim Museum in Bilbao, the reinvention of Nantes as a city of art). Even where enrichment appears future oriented, there is a sense that these projects root a given space in a historical narrative about the identity, heritage, tradition, or authenticity of a place, which then adds value. A core argument of Boltanski and Esquerre's book is thus that we are not witnessing post-industrialization but a displacement of industrial production to the Global South and the margins of the Global North, with the spaces that once functioned as the engine room of industrial capitalism reclaimed for the enrichment of a wealthy global class, and upwardly mobile consumers keen to jockey for publicity through proximity to sources of distinction.

As noted above, in Ireland, this has taken shape through the explicit incorporation of pop-up and temporary arts projects in derelict properties as part of an entirely explicit set of policies that fund short-term creative enterprises and arts spaces to return property value and cultural caché to neighbourhoods earmarked for regeneration. The vignette with which this chapter opens is a case in point. In this sense, artists, their work, and their use of space can be understood as an exemplification of the possibilities and limits of critique in liberal democracies. Artists actively sought out spaces at the margins of controversial redevelopments, where they hoped they might exploit the cracks in ambitious policy programs to probe political alternatives. Yet their presence in these spaces was overtly "co-opted" for the purposes of economic revitalization, their anti-cultural critical attitudes deployed as a desirable paradigm for critical citizenship – precisely because this critique wasn't thought to pose any real threat, and their presence could be explicitly incorporated in policy documents as evidence of "vibrancy" and "community." Indeed, in a variety of policy initiatives in the years after 2008, the then-government frequently cited the profusion of artists and artistic spaces in the city as evidence of Dublin's status as a European capital of culture – a cosmopolitan city capable of attracting a creative and upwardly mobile consumer base who might be lured in by the ephemeral sense of the city's cultural magnetism. This was true even as the cost of living was rising to record heights, outpaced only by those recorded in the current cost-of-living crisis, and the housing crisis was among the most acute in Europe.

Thus, artistic critique – however parodic, satirical, or non-sensical – was easily exploited by political figures for whom a demonstration of the proliferation of radical criticism could be leveraged as evidence of the health of the public sphere, as a tool for generating value, *and* as a tactic to distract from simmering underlying structural inequalities. At the same time, and to make matters more complicated, artists' ability to engage in critical public expression in the first instance was conditional on being granted a platform, public funding, and a critical voice by the same well-positioned actors. Artists were therefore cynical. Critique was double-edged: it acted as a tantalizing conduit to sincere truth-seeking, which they imagined undertaking on behalf of an equally cynical and downtrodden public, yet by virtue of its relative exclusivity, their critique was also a confirmation of the hierarchies that continued to structure the public sphere. This fact would sometimes convince them that there was little point in artistic criticism, as it ultimately appeared to serve the powerful. Staying quiet and remaining "hidden in plain sight," as Aaron put it, was sometimes the safest route to protecting alternative forms of work and life from the logics of co-optation.

Critique and Value Creation

In order to unpack this vexed relationship between critique, hierarchy, and value it is worth turning to a recent body of comparative anthropological work on artistic production, dissidence, and public criticism. My focus here is on what is distinctive about the relationship between critique, hierarchy, and value creation in liberal democratic contexts, which these anthropologists illuminate through comparison with ethnographic accounts of critique under illiberal conditions. Boyer and Yurchak's work is especially illustrative. They have explored how we might theorize forms of dissidence not easily classed as opposition or resistance. To do so, they have examined the conditions of possibility of dissent in political contexts in which the constraints placed on public expression are sufficiently punitive that dissidents have been forced to explore ways of rendering their activities unintelligible to state surveillance. From the perestroika USSR to German Democratic Republic (GDR) Berlin, these are spaces in which overt displays of hostility towards those in power is not an option, as they would be met with violent retribution (Yurchak 2013; Boyer 2001). Moreover, owing to the formal consistency, or hegemony of form, of political ideologies and discourses, all overtly "political" action is absorbed by hegemonic discourses, interpolated as either consistent with or a threat to state ideology. It is in contexts like these that we see the rise of *stiob* – absurd, parodic overidentification with the object of criticism. By over-performing the absurdities of political discourse, dissident artistic movements can carve out a space of indistinction resistant to the logics of state surveillance.

A clear and crucial difference between a liberal democratic context like Dublin and the perestroika USSR or GDR Berlin is, of course, the extent and quality of political repression in the public sphere. Yet there is also a striking similarity between these contexts. As Boyer and Yurchak (2008, 2010) argue, both exhibit a "hegemony of form" in public discourse and political ideologies (see also Boyer 2013). Indeed, it is for this reason that they claim we are witnessing an uptick in parodic, absurd critique in Euro-American liberal democracies. They attribute this to a narrowing of what are considered acceptable forms of public criticism and political ideologies. Following this reading, liberalism is, as in the late years of the Soviet Union, undergoing a self-imposed collapse, whereby its core ideological values and discursive practices are becoming overly formally consistent and hollowed out, rendering them ripe for parodic criticism. This literature thus sees this style of parodic critique as a warning bell for the health of the liberal democratic public sphere.

Yet as Natalia Roudakova (2017) notes, the above analysis is less focused on how or why these forms of criticism gain ascension or the relationship between critique and hierarchy. In her recent ethnography of truth-seeking in the press in Russia, Roudakova insists that this fact cannot be overlooked. Indeed, she argues that without appreciating the ways in which social class impacts on the kind of critique one finds plausible, we could not understand the contemporary erosion of truth as a value in Russian public and political life. Roudakova examines how hierarchy relates to cynical forms of critique like *stiob*. As Roudakova writes, *stiob* was not just a canny strategy for protecting critique, pursued at the margins by side-lined dissident actors: "*stiob* also worked as a class and education marker among soviet artists and intellectuals. Instantly recognizing *stiob* for what it was, Soviet intellectuals could mark their distance from the presumably naïve others who might be confused by the ambiguity of *stiob*" (182). *Stiob* was thus an ambiguous tool of disorientation, one Roudakova argues became increasingly compelling to "friends of power" (181) after the collapse of the Soviet Union. This "new *stiob*" (181) is an intensification of the form Yurchak describes among Soviet dissidents in that it has lost any elements of sincerity. It is marked by a distinctively cynical orientation not only to those in power, but to all ideological commitments. It "mocks from no place of conviction; it is passionless mockery" (183). Roudakova thus offers a counter-interpretation of *stiob* as not only a tool for carving out a space of indistinction but also for accumulating prestige and vying for power. The *stiob*-like cynicism of friends of power has functioned in Russia and further afield as an intermediary between elite actors and the public. As Roudakova argues, "friends of power" – especially "cultural producers" (181) – become key mediators between "the cynicism of the powerful and the powerless" (181). These intermediary critics are significant because they are able to command the attention of and maintain popularity with "nonelite audiences," as both express the same "variety of cynicism" and therefore appear to share interests (181). These kinds of critics can therefore straightforwardly serve the powerful, who can platform these actors strategically to tactically exploit feelings of disenchantment and, ultimately, to consolidate power.

If we return to the sociologists of critique discussed above, this analysis has clear ramifications beyond illiberal Russia. Roudakova helps us understand how cynical criticism, of the type my interlocutors practise, could be politically useful for the elite actors targeted by their critique. These artists are, in some regards, "friends of power." They may not act as ideological mouthpieces of the political class in the way that partisan journalists do in illiberal Russia, but they are platformed by the actors and institutions in relation to which they maintain a polemical, cynical attitude. The DCC, developers, politicians, and arts institutions offer them a soapbox on which to practise a form of public criticism that serves those political actors precisely *because* they are the target of criticism. It appears to prove that those in power facilitate space for dissent, and it generates for those actors enormous capital, in the form of property wealth and immaterial assets. This is by no means the artists' fault, and it occurs despite artists' often most vigorous attempts to resist this process. It is nonetheless an extremely important and distinctive problem that besets critique in liberal democracies. In liberal democratic states, criticism does not need to toe the party line, so to speak, for it to serve political interests. The expression of bracing public dissent can itself function as a route to value creation and as a politically expedient confirmation of the health of the public sphere. A key difference between liberal and illiberal states is thus indeed that dissent is institutionally protected in the former and often radically constrained in the latter. This fact of course matters. But so too does another important truism: that publicly platformed dissent can itself be harnessed with extraordinary ease for purposes other than those that serve the interests of the critic – whether that be the people or the artist. Criticism is, in other words, entirely political, and our attention should therefore always be on whose interests it serves.

Conclusion

This chapter has focused on a predicament: that critical public dissent serves as a hyper-effective form of value creation in liberal democracies. Public criticism emerges here as double-edged: though it might elsewhere function to effectively pressure political actors, it can also enrich the elite actors targeted with criticism. What this chapter should reveal to us is that liberalism does not come with protections against this problem baked in. If we want to protect liberal values, and to extend them to a more universal democratic public, we cannot turn to capitalism to achieve this. In what remains, I want to step back and consider the implications this state of affairs has for Euro-American democratic politics. To do so, I turn to the work of critical historian of liberalism, Domenico Losurdo.

Losurdo offers a powerful rereading of liberalism as a political project. Losurdo (2011) argues that beginning in the eighteenth century, liberals were less concerned with extending freedom universally than with wresting power from an absolute monarch, with liberalism imagined as a bulwark against both "monarchical" and "democratic absolutism." Thus, it was not considered a problem that freedom was never extended to all citizen-subjects. Instead, monumental concessions were justified, with limits placed on who would enjoy the benefits of a liberal society, whether in factories in England, workhouses in Ireland, or on plantations in the United States. This trend continued apace throughout the twentieth century, with freedom and equality consistently ringfenced for a select class of liberal citizen-subject. In the period after the Second World War, and in the wake of a growing tide of workers and civil rights struggles, liberalism was forced into a temporary agreement with the universalist ambitions of democratic politics. But in the last several decades, Losurdo argues, we have once again returned to pre-war levels. Losurdo (1994) calls this the "purge" of democracy from liberalism.

Following this reading, liberalism is not only a set of institutions and practices designed to safeguard against the tyranny of the majority. It is a political project that serves the interests of some, and which has only extended freedom further when met with genuine confrontation. Indeed, as Losurdo (2011, 299, 49) argues, liberalism was only ever implemented within a "restricted sacred space" for a "community of the free" and withheld from those who occupied "the profane space" of servitude and labour. Moreover, the expansion of this sacred space of liberalism has most frequently occurred through co-optation by the elite of desirable actors. As Azzarà (2011) argues, Losurdo demonstrates that, historically, it has often been the case that "an enlargement of the sacred space could only occur by means of a selective co-optation from above operated by the ruling classes, rather than an autonomous pressure from below carried out by excluded social groups or subjugated nationalities" (Losurdo 2011, 168, 280–5, quoted in Azzarà 2011, 106). This is not to say that upward pressure – through protest, direct democracy, or dissent – has not yielded landmark political achievements, but it is to suggest that where these achievements are won, it is often because widening the "community of the free" is seen to advantage those who have already gained entry. What follows is that liberalism will always yield a political battle between the interests of "the recognised and the unrecognised" (Azzarà 2011, 104) – those who have gained entry and those who have not, those who feel they can command attention and those who feel they cannot.

We can understand the contemporary critics I describe here as in a crucial intermediary position between the recognized and the unrecognized. While elsewhere these artists' work and public criticism has been a crucial contribution to landmark democratic achievements in Ireland (Morningstar 2024), they are also frequently confronted with the problem that prominent actors are adept at co-opting critique and transforming it into a source of value creation. If we combine this fact with Losurdo's claims about the contemporary cleavage between liberalism and democracy, the significance of this should be apparent. The channels to direct democratic participation are narrowing, and where that perception gains popular traction, people are more vulnerable to political ideologies that promise either to puncture the boundary between the recognized and the unrecognized, or to allow those already inside the sacred realm to police its boundaries. To gloss these reactionary movements as anti-liberal populism misses the point. Populism isn't a threat to liberalism but rather a direct consequence of it. It is what happens when the channels to direct democratic participation appear closed, when the failure of liberalism to extend freedom and equality on a truly universal scale becomes too conspicuous to be ignored, and when the dividing line between the recognized and the unrecognized is under question.

11 The People's Radio between Populism and Bullshit

HARRI ENGLUND

Free speech has its dedicated media genre in the talk radio that puts the *vox populi* on air, a genre that has from its American origins onward attracted a wide variety of formats across the globe (Loviglio 2005). The broadcast of the voices of "the people," whether through phone-ins or interviews in the streets, often has at least an implicit ambition to counter the rhetoric peddled by other voices on the radio, such as those belonging to politicians, civil servants, and experts of various description. In this chapter, I consider two instances of the people's radio in strikingly different historical settings. A popular and long-standing program on Finland's national broadcaster contrasts in many ways with the work performed at the service of the people by a Zambian radio personality at a provincial and privately owned station. Apart from the obvious differences, some of which will be enumerated below, the comparison is an opportunity to pose questions about the role of radio journalists in mediating particular forms of free speech and *vox populi*. The comparison is, in effect, between the decision by a Finnish radio journalist to hide the true identity of a man in the street and the determination of her Zambian counterpart to expose such a figure as a fraudster. The comparison does not reveal the Zambian journalist as more morally upright than the Finnish one, but it does present a case for nuancing the apparent populism of *vox populi*.

Whatever else it has come to mean, "populism" might seem to take us beyond the general condition attributed by Mazzarella (2004) to mass media, namely, the need to mask the very act of mediation. By his own more recent admission, "populism marks ... a challenge to mediation as such ... by dreaming of a direct and immediate presencing of the substance of the people" (Mazzarella 2019, 49). And yet, in so far as the history of *vox populi* is virtually as long as that of the radio, the novelty of the challenges to mediation must not be overstated. Comparative work is required to identify variable responses to those challenges across time and place. The responses reveal historically specific imaginations not only of "the people" but also of how the very truth of *vox populi* has been variably mediated. Such comparative work will be hampered if certain high-profile twenty-first-century expressions of populism in the Global North assume unduly iconic qualities. After all, as Samet (2019, 11) puts it, "no two populisms are exactly alike," which undermines the easy dismissal, so instinctive to professional intellectuals, of populism as either far-right or far-left lunacy. A focus on those whose professional vocation it is to mediate *vox populi* over the airwaves can bring ethnographic and historical nuance to a topic that too readily evokes categorical pronouncements.

The comparison between the Finnish and Zambian populisms revolves around the radio journalists' different attitudes to truth in their pursuit of *vox populi* – a difference between complicity and exposé. Here the bluntness of populism as a concept requires further work for it to be of comparative use. Frankfurt's (2005) famous thesis on "bullshit" as a particular attitude to truth (and lies) has its problems, starting with the concept's pejorative connotations, but it may convey something important about a form of persuasion that often attends populism. Propelled by his conviction that "indifference to truth is extremely dangerous" (Frankfurt 2002, 343), Frankfurt identifies as the bullshitters those whose relation to both truth and lies is incidental. In so far as they tell lies, they do so "incidentally or by accident" (341). This was Frankfurt's response to G.A. Cohen's charge that "he assigns no distinctive goal to the bullshitter that would distinguish him from the liar" (329). While the liar has the goal of inducing his/her listener to believe in something that the liar knows is false, Frankfurt's bullshitter appears to leave the question of the truth value open.

The tactic of deception may apply to both the bullshitter and the liar – although the former's indifference to the truth can also mean that he/she says something true just as accidentally as he/she may utter falsehoods. What is of comparative interest is that such indifference may arise from a variety of concerns and aspirations that require ethnographic work to be understood rather than being dismissed on philosophical or political grounds. How bullshit might contribute to experiences of authenticity – and be in some sense "true" – is a genuinely important question in its own right and one that cannot be addressed without empirical research. By the same token, how a commitment to the truth as exposé, even when it appears to contradict *vox populi*, may inform the people's radio is a question that opens up comparative prospects. It is a comparison that attempts a certain symmetry – neither instance should be seen as historically or paradigmatically more exemplary of the key notions, whether the people's radio and *vox populi* or indeed populism and bullshit. The wide dispersal of these notions is precisely what makes the comparison pertinent.[1]

---

1 For an extensive discussion of how such comparison might differ from the us–them comparisons in anthropology, see Candea (2018).

This chapter explores how the effects of bullshit are recognized and appropriated or rejected by people whose professional vocation it is to work for the people's radio. As such, one of the issues to be addressed is whether or not radio journalists become complicit in the bullshit of their interlocutors in order to achieve the goal of authentic expression. For while "the bullshitter may not deceive us, or even intend to do so," his/her deception is essentially about his/her enterprise. "His [sic] only indispensably distinctive characteristic is that in a certain way he misrepresents what he is up to" (Frankfurt 2005, 54). When journalists at the people's radio are aware that what they help to reach a wider audience is bullshit, but nevertheless proceed to transmit it, they become complicit in the bullshitter's enterprise. For all their commitment to the people's radio, they become bullshitters themselves. When, on the other hand, they see as their vocation to expose bullshit as a form of fraud, even when committed by the proverbial man in the street, the *vox populi* they serve to mediate assumes a different aspect.

The Sonic Affordances of *Vox Populi*

Whatever the notoriety gained by politically explicit talk radio in the United States, radio's affordances as a medium have long sustained a sense of intimacy with its audiences unparalleled by other electronic media, old or new. Those affordances include its technological propensities, from its portability and relatively inexpensive infrastructure to its versatility in changing media environments. They also include, crucially, the human voice in its multiple affective registers. As Arnheim (1936) noted during radio's early existence, it "talks to everyone individually, not to everyone together." In another passage from this early history, Benjamin ([1931] 2008, 392) also recognized a parallel between the human voice and the association of radio listening with intimate spaces: "The radio listener, unlike every other kind of audience, welcomes the human voice into his house like a visitor."[2]

In a broader discussion of the senses and mass media, radio's partiality to aurality pits it against vision in what Sterne (2005, 15) has criticized as the "audiovisual litany." Where vision removes us from the world, hearing immerses us in it, with the result that "vision is most frequently deemed to be the quintessentially modern sense, one that is alternately demonized by critics and

---

2   In so far as Benjamin ([1931] 2008) assumed domestic spaces as the main sites of radio listening, he did so without knowledge of where it often took place when the radio was introduced to Africa – chiefly courts and local governmental headquarters. The role of radio listening in fostering sociality beyond the domestic unit has continued in many African settings until the present (Spitulnik 2002; Larkin 2008).

celebrated by those who associate vision with reason and clear thinking" (Kunreuther 2014, 94; see also Weidman 2006). As far as bullshit goes, therefore, both vision and aurality have their ways of exposing it for what it is. Yet radio, through its sonic affordances, would seem to do so through a particularly compelling appeal to authentic experience. At the same time, the audiovisual litany stands to be modified precisely because technological and sonic affordances do not alone determine the extent to which radio is experienced as a "medium of directness" (Kunreuther 2014, 151). Important also is the claim a particular radio genre might make to such authenticity, and how it makes it under specific historical conditions of broadcasting and publicness.

The radio genre of *vox populi* has existed in Zambia and Finland under the variable conditions of political and economic populism. While in Zambia the rise and demise of Michael Sata's government in the 2010s has already led to reflections on "post-populism" (A. Fraser 2017), in Finland, as in many other Northern European countries, populism continues to be associated with the confrontational politics of the New Right, whether as elected opposition or as vigilantes (Wahlbeck 2016). The populism of *vox populi*, both as a political trope and a radio genre, goes beyond either of these instances in the two countries. Appeals to the people – or *povo*, drawing on the Portuguese term used by the Marxist-Leninist liberation movement in neighbouring Mozambique – had been issued by Zambia's "humanist" and "socialist" leaders in the early decades of its independence, while an agrarian imagery of the people was until recently a plausible political trope in Finland, a relative newcomer to large-scale urbanization. These broad patterns of populism do little, however, to nuance the specific ways in which radio journalists in the two countries have seen their own role in mediating the truth of *vox populi*. The comparison that follows reveals, among other things, the extent to which serving the people can either uphold or unmask the fictions of *vox populi*.

The People's Radio in Finland and Zambia

Since its inception in 1979, *Kansanradio* (The people's radio) in Finland has broadcast every week the voices of its listeners, currently as a thirty-minute, pre-recorded assemblage of phone calls as well as letters and emails read out by its hosts. While the early broadcasts could include interviews with civil servants and various experts, in addition to lengthy conversations between the hosts and their listeners, the current format involves a faster pace by which the different contributions are made to follow each other, usually with no attempt to solicit expert views. The hosts' conversational tone and colloquial language remain crucial, however. Some of the phone calls they broadcast are monologues spoken to the program's answering machine, while others are dialogues recorded during the hosts' weekly three-hour slot for taking calls. With some

400,000 listeners in a country of 5 million people, *Kansanradio* is one of the most popular programs on Radio Suomi, the national broadcaster's mainstream channel. Its reputation for being the program of choice among elderly Finns is borne out by the dominant role played by elderly voices talking about their concerns with, among other things, pensions, care provisions, unfamiliarity with computers and the internet, alongside comments on both current affairs and personal matters from ill health to relationship troubles. Although the hosts invite humorous and quirky contributions, complaints fuelled by disaffection, even anger, are more common (Englund 2018a).

Speaking in dialects, using vernacular expressions, and emanating from elderly men and women often calling from the remote parts of the vast country, the voices on *Kansanradio* are distinct from the more rehearsed talk heard elsewhere on the Finnish airwaves, however casual its tone may be. The difference is, in effect, between an apparently nostalgic sound of the people as rural folk and the ostensibly current urban lingo preferred by several other, often commercial radio stations. Precisely because *Kansanradio* has developed a unique soundscape of elderly voices, it attracts not only keen listeners but also caricatures and hoax calls.

A regular topic during my fieldwork with the hosts in 2015–16 was the extent to which callers could be trusted to be what they claimed to be. Jaana Selin, a woman who was approaching retirement age after having established herself as the program's stalwart, and Olli Haapakangas, a man in his thirties co-hosting the program on temporary contracts with the broadcaster, shared with me stories about both familiarity with regular callers and embarrassing incidents when an unsuspecting journalist had taken seriously what turned out to be a hoax. Apart from receiving opinions that they found reprehensible, the hosts also had to contend with calls coming from drunk or mentally unstable people. With her experience as a host, Selin elaborated on her methods of verifying the callers' authenticity. They included less an effort to seek independent confirmation of what she had been told than applying her own sensibilities to an evolving conversation. Critical, she said, was to keep the conversation going long enough, especially when the interlocutor appeared to put forward facts about personal lives. Selin would eventually hear if the interlocutor's grip was "waning" (*herpaantua*) when she carried on with the topic. Whether the call was put on air or not, she and Haapakangas avoided openly interrogating their callers, committed as they were to *Kansanradio*'s ambience of intimacy and conviviality.[3]

---

3 The co-hosts did have their differences in style, with Haapakangas preferring a more interventionist approach to the opinions expressed by listeners. It was, however, a matter of growth in his role as he gradually came to realize that being "more clever" (*fiksumpi*) than his listeners could put them off and contradicted the program's egalitarian ethos.

The case I discuss below shows that Selin's time-honoured method of listening had not prepared her for identifying a regular caller as a bullshitter until she met him in person. For all her skills at deploying the radio's sonic affordances, it was vision – the act of seeing this caller – that revealed to her the truth about him. Rather than rejecting his calls from then on, Selin became complicit in his bullshit by continuing to broadcast his contributions. To understand this approach to the effects of bullshit, it is useful to consider a very different approach adopted by Gogo Breeze, a Zambian radio grandfather broadcasting at the privately owned Breeze FM in the country's Eastern Province (see Englund 2018b). By using the term *gogo*, a Chinyanja word for grandparent, Grayson Peter Nyozani Mwale conveyed in his radio name an effort to address a public of kinsfolk. As his listeners' grandfather, he was, as befits the role, variously ludic and stern in his encounters with them and entirely unaffected by the kind of egalitarianism that made *Kansanradio*'s hosts tread carefully when they were confronted with dubious opinions and characters.

During my research with him between 2012 and 2018, people in Eastern Province turned to Gogo Breeze in search of the sort of practical advice and moral guidance that an elder could provide.[4] The element of *vox populi* nevertheless drove Gogo Breeze's work as it did *Kansanradio*, not confined to the format of one program but through the letters, phone calls, SMS messages, and chance encounters he broadcasted over a variety of programs. Whether it was the letters program (*Makalata*) or the interviews and chats he recorded for programs such as *Landirani alendo* (Welcome visitors) and *Chidwi pa anthu* (Interest in people), he addressed and investigated grievances put to him by listeners struggling with economic problems and all manner of personal issues. Unlike the hosts of *Kansanradio*, he spent more time in the streets, offices, shops, markets, and villages than in the broadcasting house to meet his listeners and their adversaries in person. The soundscape he produced for broadcast may have been richer than the one on *Kansanradio*, but common to both was the abundance of vernacular expression and dialogue between the radio hosts and their listeners.

For all his desire to listen to and assist his public of grandchildren, Gogo Breeze was no less plagued by concerns with hoaxes and fraud than were his Finnish counterparts. But where the general adherence to rules and transparency in Finland appeared to inspire trust even in interpersonal encounters, public controversies framed in terms of corruption and fraud were something of a national pastime in Zambia. Accordingly, Gogo Breeze could be relentless in his pursuit of fakes, fraud, and bullshit in Frankfurt's sense, not only among the

---

4 I discuss elsewhere (Englund 2018b) the apparent paradox that a media figure based on elderhood could have such a vast following in a popular culture otherwise saturated with youthful styles and aspirations.

employers and authorities who had inflicted harm on his radio grandchildren but also among the grandchildren themselves. When he could not trace people's complaints to genuine instances of exploitation or misfortune, he could be scathing about their attempts to use poverty as an excuse for self-pity, victimhood, or deception. His popularity on air appeared to withstand – or perhaps was even enhanced by – the stern tone with which he delivered his judgments on "laziness" (*ulesi*) and "lies" (*mabodza*).[5]

Vox populi on Gogo Breeze's programs had little sense of populism as deference to "the people." It is this propensity to publicize their activities as potentially fraudulent and to talk about them in the idiom of lies rather than bullshit that offers an opportunity to contrast Gogo Breeze's work with the approach taken by *Kansanradio*'s hosts. In both cases, the interesting question is what happens *after* it has been established that the interlocutor's intent has been to bullshit.

Mauno Voutilainen

Selin's surprise, if not shock, mentioned above was about the identity of a prolific contributor to *Kansanradio*. For a number of years, Mauno Voutilainen had called the program from Jyväskylä in Central Finland, always introducing himself as "Mauno Voutilainen from Jyväskylä," and always calling the program's answering machine rather than when its host was on the line. It enabled Voutilainen to speak without interruption and prevented the hosts from applying Selin's method to establish how genuine the caller was. So convincing was Voutilainen's performance as an elderly, somewhat parochial man that Selin found it hard to believe her eyes when he was introduced to her as one of their regular callers at a public meeting that *Kansanradio* had arranged in Jyväskylä.[6] Another man had brought to her a well-dressed middle-aged man, who turned out to be Voutilainen. His comportment and mode of speech were

---

5 Chinyanja-speakers are generally less taken with profanities than Finnish-speakers, and hence it would be difficult to provide a direct translation for "bullshit" as an idiom for deception in that language. Chinyanja does have a rich vocabulary for such idioms, of which *mabodza* as "lies" is perhaps the strongest in its assertion of truth values. A common verb for "deceiving" is *kunyenga*, which can also be used to describe seduction. *Kupusitsa* is the causative of *kupusa*, "to be stupid," and therefore conveys deception as a matter of making someone else stupid. The opposite is *kuchenjera*, "to be clever" or "cunning," whether for good purposes or bad, and it can also be used to mean "being alert." Noteworthy is also how *katangale*, now the most common Chinyanja word for "corruption," was originally used to describe deception by which traders would try to sell less than what was apparent to their customers. On Finnish-speakers' choice between the different types of bodily waste for "bullshit," see note 9 below.

6 Although the hosts did not venture out of their broadcasting house to gather material for the program, *Kansanradio* did arrange "market-square meetings" (*toritapaamisia*) during the summer time, where people could meet the hosts.

radically different from what he had used when calling the program. Selin realized that he was "pulling off a role" (*vetää roolia*) on *Kansanradio*, but it did not deter her from continuing to include his calls on the program.

Selin and her colleagues came to learn that Voutilainen had acquired considerable provincial fame, if not notoriety, independently of his appearances on *Kansanradio*. He had been convicted in his youth of burning down his school, which had led to a period in care and further disruption in his education. By his late forties, when he began to call *Kansanradio* regularly, he had adopted the role of a "lifestyle unemployed" (*elämäntapatyötön*) who lived off the benefits of the Finnish state. A part of his role was to complain about the lack of reasonable opportunities for an elderly man, whether on the job market or in romantic pursuits. A bachelor, Voutilainen made public his efforts to find a woman through notices in the provincial newspaper *Keskisuomalainen*. He also patronized this newspaper by offering frequent, daily commentary on its online fora for news and articles, with the number of his contributions running into tens of thousands by the early 2010s. Although the substance of his contributions to *Kansanradio* did not differ markedly from these online comments – revolving around Finland's employment policies and his personal difficulties – the voice he used on air made him sound at least twenty years older than the middle-aged provincial celebrity he was locally. As Haapakangas pointed out to me, when Voutilainen got excited about his topic, his voice could drop a little to make him sound more "normal." Yet as Selin's surprise indicated, so genuine was his voice on *Kansanradio* that few listeners without knowledge of his actual identity would have heard him as anyone else than the old man he projected. After Selin's revelation, his contributions continued to be aired as before, and no one suggested that he should be asked to speak in his normal voice or that his performances should be excluded.

From my conversations with Selin and Haapakangas, it became clear that they regarded Voutilainen as a useful bullshitter, one who approximated the authenticity that they wished the program to be known for. Not only did his personal past become known to them, they also came to learn that Voutilainen's sisters were leading perfectly comfortable middle-class lives as medical doctors. Although Voutilainen's reputation started to gain national recognition through his appearances on *Kansanradio*, many listeners remained unaware of it and attributed to him the old man's habitus. For example, when Voutilainen called to comment on a proposal to reintroduce public works as a measure against unemployment, he later received criticism for being out of touch with technological developments.[7] The proposal on *Kansanradio* had been to bring

---

7 Voutilainen's contribution was broadcast on 21 February 2016, and the responses to him a week later on 28 February 2016.

back *risusavotta*, a historical term for work parties clearing the forest. Voutilainen admonished the caller for harking back to the 1950s when such work parties may have been feasible, while at present they would do little else than provide free labour to landowners with forests. Two responses to him were broadcast the following week, the first of which argued that the wood obtained through such work would now be processed to produce pulp that could be sold. This caller affirmed that "nowadays *risusavotta* is not what Mauno knows from fifty years ago when the sticks were gathered and burnt."[8] The second response suggested that *risusavotta* may have been used metaphorically for various kinds of collective effort and asked "Mauno" to "read between the lines" (*lukea rivien välistä*). The responses alluded to familiarity with Voutilainen by using his first name, but they also supported his self-portrayal as an old man standing to be corrected about how the world was.

Bullshit, in any of its Finnish vernacular variants, was not how the hosts would describe *Kansanradio*'s content.[9] They were proud of its remit to put on air the voices of those who were otherwise absent from the broadcaster's airwaves. Voutilainen's voice fitted into this remit perfectly. He was not the only caller who had become a household name on the program, but the hosts were not aware of anyone else who was "pulling off a role" like he did. Nor was their acceptance of Voutilainen's role the only aspect of their work to which Frankfurt's notion of bullshit might apply. While many of *Kansanradio*'s occasional listeners seemed to believe it was a live program, the seamless flow of talk was a carefully crafted product that depended on the hosts' skills to generate experiences of authenticity. Those skills included their own uses of language and their capacity to sustain conversations with callers whose views and lives in the remote parts of Finland could differ from their own in the capital. On the other hand, what to include from the abundant calls, letters, and emails they received, and in what sequence to put them on air, were editorial matters that the immediacy of the contributors' voices served to hide. The truth value of what the hosts were told was certainly of interest to them, and Haapakangas would sometimes contrast, in his conversations with me, his use of Google search with Selin's apparently more casual attitude to the verification of facts. Yet if the effect of authenticity required a certain deception about the hosts' enterprise, they were prepared to let *Kansanradio* bullshit its public.

---

8 My translation. "Nykyään risusavotta ei ole sitä mitä Mauno tietää viiskymmentä vuotta sitten, että risut kasattiin ja poltettiin."

9 Although "bullshit" finds its literal equivalent in vernacular Finnish (*häränpaska*), the purposeful action it denotes often comes to be expressed through another form of bodily waste. *Kusettaminen* summons human urine as the substance by which others are deceived.

Joseph Lungu

In contrast to Selin and Haapakangas, Gogo Breeze had no inclination to efface his own presence on air. Authenticity was less a matter of letting listeners' voices speak for themselves and more about confronting or endorsing those voices with grandfatherly authority. Key to achieving this sense of authenticity, again in contrast to editing *Kansanradio*, was Gogo Breeze's frequent encounters out in the streets, offices, and villages. Many of the exchanges he recorded during these excursions went on air because of the entertaining interactions they involved, not because he had necessarily set out to expose injustices and abuse. So common, however, were various forms of fraud and deceit in everyday life that even the most innocuous and well-meaning inquiries into interlocutors' activities could turn into investigations of deception. Such interactions were at their most entertaining when they lasted for several minutes and included a number of twists and turns as the participants variously tried to answer and evade the radio elder's questions.

Among the contrasts that can be drawn between *Kansanradio* and Gogo Breeze's work, the place of bullshit in their respective editorial practices is of particular comparative interest. Instructive is the way Gogo Breeze often sought to define fraud and deception as lies instead of allowing them to exist as useful bullshit. The encounter to be discussed here took about eight minutes of broadcast time and began as a casual conversation between Gogo Breeze and a young man he had met outside the Breeze FM building.[10] It transpired that the young man, whose name was Joseph Lungu, was helping one of the presenters at the radio station to sell chickens in the street. In ways that are impossible to convey fully in writing, the interaction had humorous aspects beyond the emerging sense of Lungu's involvement in fraudulent activity. His mixing of Chinsenga, a language not taught at school and of few resources in print, with slang expressions in the lingua francas of English and Chinyanja, coupled with a voice that clearly emanated from a young man, gave the sonic impression of someone who genuinely belonged to the streets, cunning in some ways but also eventually reduced by the radio elder to an unthinking youngster on the brink of damaging his own prospects.

Gogo Breeze sounded at first favourable to Lungu's explanation for his presence in the street. "A very good thing" (*nkhani yabwino kwambiri*), he commented on Lungu's business, but it was the answer to his question of "how is the trade?" (*malonda akuyenderani bwanji?*) that instigated their exchange about the honesty of Lungu's business practice. In what he might have intended as an expression of mere modesty, Lungu used a Chinsenga/Chinyanja

---

10 Broadcast on *Landirani Alendo*, 19 January 2012.

slang version of the English word *short* to assert that he did not have as much money as he would have expected. Gogo Breeze's attempts to find out why this was the case were met with lengthy pauses, which prompted him to turn the Chinsenga/Chinyanja word *kushota* into the causative *kushotetsa*, suggesting that Lungu had deliberately made the money run short. Lungu's protestations of innocence resulted in a series of questions about both his own circumstances and the prices of the chickens he had sold. Throughout the exchange, listeners could follow how the young man struggled to answer Gogo Breeze's increasingly penetrating questions, and how he contradicted himself. The pauses and the filler expressions such as *ah*, *ee*, *mm*, and *awa* added to the sonic sense of cunning giving way to a somewhat vacuous disposition.

Gogo Breeze gave Lungu ample opportunity to admit that he had spent money on food, drink, and girlfriends, but to no avail. Particularly entertaining was the moment when Lungu sounded indecisive about the price he had asked for the chickens, making Gogo Breeze exclaim, "Now you are telling me many words!" (*Lomba mwandiuza mawu angapo!*). His threat of the police arresting Lungu soon gave way to amicable queries about Lungu's prospects for marriage. Gogo Breeze's use of the name Tibetche for his purported girlfriend made them both laugh, but Lungu denied that he had pocketed the missing money to prepare for marriage. Gogo Breeze's mood shifted between disapproval and geniality, but grandfatherly opprobrium became more dominant the longer they talked. "Why are you boys dishonest/untrustworthy on small things?" (*Chifukwa chinji inu anyamata musakhulupirika pa zinthu zazing'ono?*), he asked with some exasperation and repeatedly urged Lungu to be trustworthy. A grandfatherly understanding of what young men aspired to informed his question of whether Lungu would merely be cultivating sweet potatoes after failing at this first attempt to sell chickens on someone else's behalf. Instead of beginning to save money for marriage and perhaps more ambitious business ventures, Lungu came across as shortsighted in his handling of money. Although Gogo Breeze failed to establish the actual reason for the missing money, he elicited the promise from Lungu that he would return the money to the owner of the chickens.

Gogo Breeze refused to turn his interlocutor into a subject of charity. Nor did he begin with the assumption that the business had to be treated with suspicion. The discovery of fraud was an emergent property of the interaction, a consequence of interrogation that was driven by grandfatherly authority rather than by a charitable disposition. It was in his experience of the many forms of insincerity produced by poverty and socio-economic inequality that Gogo Breeze found reason to probe the young man's claims. Yet just as he was not a Good Samaritan finding a poor person in the street, nor was he an investigative journalist on a mission to expose fraud. It bears repeating that the burden he carried was that of a grandfather, an elder at once compassionate and stern,

forever mindful of his obligation to provide moral education. Laughing together, such as when he suggested that Tibetche was Lungu's girlfriend, was
consistent with the amity and intimacy of the grandparent–grandchild relationship. It served to reject the other positions Gogo Breeze might have occupied
in this exchange, whether as the Good Samaritan or the investigative journalist.
Towards the end of their exchange, he suggested that Lungu wanted Gogo
Breeze to assist him by paying the missing money, but Gogo Breeze refused
the prospect by inviting him to plan how he would return the money. Rather
than allowing Lungu to occupy the position of a subject awaiting charity, the
radio grandfather allocated to him the responsibility to rectify the fraudulent
activity. It is important to note that Lungu himself anticipated to meet this
responsibility partly through his relationship to his mother. She would lend
him some of the money that was missing. The radio grandfather's allocation
of responsibility did not make Lungu an autonomous individual but mediated,
as a grandparent might be expected to do, the social position within which the
young man could exercise his responsibility.

Moral Authority and *Vox Populi*

Radio journalists and anthropologists might plausibly view both Mauno Voutilainen and Joseph Lungu as bullshitters rather than as liars. Where Voutilainen projected an elderly man commenting on issues close to him, Lungu
came across as a young, inexperienced hustler genuinely puzzled as to why the
money he had made was less than expected. It is unlikely that either of them
had specifically embarked on telling lies, but both were engaged in deceiving
the radio journalists and their audiences about the nature of their enterprises.
The key comparative question has revolved here around whether, and why,
bullshit has been compatible with the pursuit of *vox populi* over the airwaves.
In other words, once an activity has been recognized as bullshit by those exposed to it, the anthropologist may move on to investigate how and why instances of bullshit attract different responses from people who may in principle
share similar attitudes to it, such as radio journalists.

   Certain contrasts between the Finnish and Zambian cases presented here
are stark. Particularly stark is of course the contrast between the Finnish radio hosts' tolerance of bullshit and the Zambian radio host's attack on it –
stereotypes about the attitudes towards transparency in public life in the two
countries would further underline the contrast. Equally superficial would be to
explain the contrast as a reversal that proves the stereotype. More interesting
from an anthropological point of view is the place of advice and moral guidance in the respective radio journalists' pursuit of *vox populi*. *Kansanradio*'s
hosts subscribed to the general ethos in Finnish public-service broadcasting
not to give anyone advice, let alone interfere in the voices they broadcast with

moral views of their own. "The people" were expected to speak for themselves, and public broadcasting had to ensure that their voices could be heard by officials, business leaders, and politicians, whose responsibility it was to draw conclusions from what was being aired. Gogo Breeze, by contrast, devoted himself to the cause of moral guidance in no uncertain terms. Much as he also considered himself to be at the service of the people in order to bring authorities to task, so too was justice best achieved, in his ethos of public service, by his insisting on the morally upright behaviour of all those, however humble, he met in the street. The different styles between the radio hosts could thus result in real differences in editorial choices and in what that "the people's radio" sounded like in Finland and Zambia.

There was, at the same time, something eminently comparable about the way in which the radio hosts' interlocutors were understood to occupy social positions through which the truth of *vox populi* could be identified and evaluated. Voutilainen "pulled off" his role well enough to fool *Kansanradio*'s hosts about his social position and to provide the authentic-sounding voice they desired for the program. Lungu, on the other hand, with his self-reported financial incompetence, failed to convince Gogo Breeze of the social position he tried to project and became subject to a series of questions that emanated from the radio grandfather's understanding of what young street hustlers would normally try to do. Note the sonic sense in which the two bullshitters' social positions became apparent to the radio hosts and their audiences. Voutilainen sounded like a humble elder, while Lungu's slang expressions, pauses, and hesitation when caught in Gogo Breeze's crossfire made audible his social position as a cunning hustler.

Voutilainen conveyed rather more talent for bullshit than Lungu did – his project was not so much to deceive as to inhabit, over the airwaves, the social position of a parochial old man. It was only when *Kansanradio*'s host had seen him that Voutilainen was revealed as a bullshitter. Complicity arose from the host's decision to continue to broadcast his contributions with no overt editorial intervention. Gogo Breeze, on the other hand, made exposé his central modality of mediating the *vox populi*. His inquisitive approach to those he met contrasted with the approach taken on *Kansanradio* and had less need for vision as a revelatory sense. After all, Lungu looked every bit as much a struggling street vendor as a hapless hustler. Responsibilities associated with the radio hosts' own social positions drove their divergent approaches, from the Finnish hosts' self-effacing protocols to Gogo Breeze's relentless interventions.

The anthropologist must, however, resist the temptation to conclude by exposing these approaches to bullshit as themselves based on a certain deception about the mediated nature of whatever authenticity the radio hosts wished to transmit. The populism of *vox populi* draws too readily condescension from professional intellectuals. Resisting critical anthropology's own preferred genre of exposé is to open up richer prospects for comparison, not merely of *vox populi* itself but of populism more broadly. High-profile political populisms in the twenty-first century, whether in the Global North or South, need not exhaust the variable aspirations and fears invested in the idea of "the people." In the mundane work of the people's radio, the anthropologist can find empirical instances for a careful study of populisms in their historical contexts. The modest comparison presented here shows the different directions a professional vocation may take as it seeks to put *vox populi* on the air. In the end, it is the attitude to bullshit that reveals whether populism masks unstated motives behind reverence for "the people" or advances moral education by a figure of authority.

12 Environments for Expression on Palestine: Fields, Fear, and the Politics of Movement

AMAHL BISHARA

What we can safely say depends on where we are – but not in a simple way in which place can be reduced to jurisdiction or state sovereignty. States can influence what is sayable beyond their boundaries, too, because of the ways in which people move and because of the interdependence writers and speakers have with one another. States and non-state entities – corporations but also "non-profits" – can also essentially work in concert to undermine the ability of people to speak truth to power. Inextricable from these dynamics is the racialized positionality of the speaker. If Ruth Wilson Gilmore (2007) thinks of race as that which makes people additionally prone to death at the hands of or in ways sanctioned by the state, we can extrapolate that those in additional risk of physical harm are often at additional risk of being hurt for what they say or in other ways being limited in what they say. A critique of "free speech" as situated clearly in democratic states – a "free world" brightly separated from other parts of the world – is an important insight of the anthropology of expression, which can put "familiar debates about freedom of speech into a broader comparative frame" (Candea et al. 2021). I argue here that comprehending these geographical and racialized dimensions of expression is crucial for anyone who writes with any comfort in the United States about global issues, because we are so often "writing alongside" those with less freedom than ourselves – people upon whom our own apparent independent ability to express ourselves often is conditioned, or with whom it is entangled.

Palestine is a telling location through which to explore the contours of what is regarded in rights talk as a "universal" right to freedom of expression. What can be said about and by Palestinians is limited in such different ways across various places. Military occupation – Israel's heavily armed and racialized form of control over Palestinians in the West Bank and Gaza Strip – produces physical threats to journalists and others involved in expressive acts. On 11 May 2022, an Israeli soldier shot and killed Al Jazeera journalist Shireen Abu Akleh while she was reporting from the West Bank city of Jenin. She had been wearing a helmet and a protective vest marking her as a journalist. She was one of at least twenty Palestinian journalists killed by Israel between 2000 and 2022 (Halpern, Zeveloff, and Mahoney 2022). At once a national icon and fond household presence, Shireen Abu Akleh's loss had painful resonances that were both public and intimate. Palestinians in multiple cities participated in her funeral, and she was quickly memorialized in murals and billboards in many cities (Al Jazeera 2022). Her killing is a sharp example of how individual cases of violence or restriction can have immense impacts on societies. But for communities under threat, even less profound losses can have collective effects. Restrictions on expression often compound each other. I have written elsewhere about the physical violence faced by Palestinian journalists with an eye to how this violence shapes journalism and the production of political knowledge (Bishara 2013). I focus here on the forms of restriction on expression that operate across borders. In addressing these more subtle threats, I seek to explore the global atmosphere of threats to Palestinian expression that is another part of the context for outright violence.[1]

Racialization poses different threats across various subject positions and state borders. I have thought of Palestinians – especially those living under military occupation – as "epistemic others" (Bishara 2013) who are limited in three ways in their ability to express themselves. First, and here especially I am building on the work of Edward Said (1978), they are seen as less trustworthy due to long-standing orientalist associations between Arabs and lying or "florid" speech. Second, they are stateless, and political speech is integrally linked to and often validated by citizenship status. Third, they have been racialized as associated with terrorism during the "War on Terror," which we can think of as neither beginning with President Bush's declaration of that war in September 2001 nor as ending with the US pulling out its troops from Afghanistan twenty years later. But it is not only Palestinians whose ability to engage in political expression about Palestine is limited – non-Palestinians are also impacted – and among Palestinians, the right to speak is graduated by many factors.

Pierre Bourdieu (1993, 2005) offers a window onto understanding how expression and knowledge production are linked to specific institutions and restricted by associated forms of power. Bourdieu's concept of a field organizes

---

[1]   In grief, I note that I substantially finalized this chapter well before Israel killed over one-hundred Palestinian journalists in its war on Gaza (Committee to Protect Journalists 2024). This extreme violence – including the deadliest ever period for journalists since the Committee to Protect Journalists (CPJ) began recording such killings in 1992 – is a terrifying backdrop to the pressures and menaces described here, and we will need to reckon with these unbearable losses for a long time to come.

an analysis of how disciplines, professions, media worlds, and other spaces of knowledge production are both related to broader fields of power and also somewhat independent from them. This independence means they partially can challenge prevailing systems of power – but it also means that they can have their own versions of hierarchy that can be oppressive in their own ways. Bourdieu's (1993, 38, 49, for example) schematic charts position positive and negative poles to distinguish how certain artistic fields are aligned with capital and related to other prestige systems. They allow for a clear mapping of spaces for cultural production. However, these charts can obscure how profoundly place-bound much of our expression is. Overlaid on Bourdieu's neat charts, we need checkpoints and border control! We need oceans and interrogation rooms!

I am inspired to think about US academia as a site of political practice by Lara Deeb and Jessica Winegar's 2016 *Anthropology's Politics: Disciplining the Middle East*, an oral history and analysis of Middle East anthropology in the United States that accounts for how US politics and trends in the neo-liberal university have shaped the experiences of scholars of various genders, classes, races, ethnicities, and generations. The cultural and ideological relationship between Israel and the United States has endured during the first decades of the twenty-first century, alongside newly intensified forms of Islamophobia and structures of "state security" that especially police the movement of brown and Black people. How is speaking truth to power on Palestine different but similar in the United States than in Israel or the West Bank or Europe?[2] How are these environments for expression distinct but related? How is freedom of expression influenced by the circulation of legal frameworks and state speech and also of actual people? When does mobility open up possibilities for expression and when does movement – or the possibility of movement – undermine the potential for expression?

Regarding Palestine, it is especially important to consider a category of "state speech." Building on the work of Judith Butler (1997), I think of this as what states or their representatives can declare without evidence and without rigorous research but which is nevertheless effective because it is a state that declares it. State speech works on at least three levels. First, states have an effective power to influence discourse because those speaking on behalf of the state automatically command an audience. Second, they are usually distinctly able to take action to make statements effective: to issue permits, make arrests, inhibit movement, and more. Third, they can produce data – through censuses

---

2   The legal and cultural landscape of restriction on Palestinian political expression is different in Europe, and the focus of this chapter is on the traffic between Israel and the United States. For more on Europe, see Atshan and Galor (2020) and Doughan (2022).

or police reports, for example – to solidify social facts. To put it in J.L. Austin's (1975) terms, they have the bureaucracy and the army to make their own felicity conditions. The speech of authorities can drive news events that have widespread implications, even when they are not followed by full-fledged legal processes (Cody 2023). States are at the centre of security discourses that operate on a global scale to reproduce logics of racialized separation (Besteman 2020). Therefore, their declarations about security have power that operates beyond the borders of single states.

For those concerned with speech about Palestinians, the key examples are when Israel (or another state) determines something to be a statement in support of terrorism, or when an Israeli official deems something anti-Semitic. Both of these categories are ones about which, it often seems, there can be no legitimate debate. Yet these categories have become blurred in pro-Israeli discourse, as Israeli officials deem both rhetoric that questions the legitimacy of Israel as a Jewish state and the act of boycott tantamount to terrorism and anti-Semitism. Because Israel operates in a world of states, and because discourses on terrorism and anti-Semitism are both mediated and indeed legislated in interconnected ways across many countries, Israel's declarations on these topics have influence beyond its borders. Potentially, they also can be checked or questioned if Israel declares something to be a terrorist act or entity in a way that ultimately does not make sense to others – but this has often been an uphill battle given Israel's position of privilege in defining anti-Semitism and terrorism as a post-Holocaust Jewish state in the Middle East. For the sake of space, I will not take on in-depth debates about the definitions of either terrorism or anti-Semitism here. Instead, in this chapter, I especially consider how limits on expression are shaped in academia and related spaces of apparently privileged expression in ways related to cross-border movement of ideas, money, and people.

Reflecting on Academic Practice

As an anthropologist of Southwest Asia and North Africa who lives and works in the United States, my intellectual work involves a constant toggling across spaces where, it can seem, different things are sayable. As a committed ethnographer, I often feel I cannot say anything without moving across spaces and listening to many people. Anthropologists have long thought about our debts to our interlocutors and to the communities with which we work, and there have been active conversations in anthropology and beyond about citational politics and the imperative to cite women and non-binary scholars, scholars of colour, and others. It is essential that we as writers account for not only our privilege in terms of our social positions but also our specific obligations as knowledge producers. As ethnographers working on politically urgent topics, we often must rely on adjacent forms of knowledge production to make our arguments in the strongest possible ways. So much of what I write depends on the research and hard work of Palestinians and Israelis who do the daily work of cataloguing Israeli violence. This, for me, entails a deep set of responsibilities to these people and indicates, if not a common cause, a camaraderie of sorts across various forms of difference.

These issues have been a backdrop to my recent book *Crossing a Line: Laws, Violence, and Roadblocks to Palestinian Political Expression* (2022), which addresses the different *environments for expression* for Palestinian citizens of Israel (in Israel's 1948 territories) and Palestinians in the Israeli-occupied West Bank. I think of those two environments as distinct but related because they are both under Israeli sovereignty (though under two disparate legal regimes). Here, I expand and reflect on that material in two ways. First, I move beyond these two apparently distinct jurisdictions that are actually under a single sovereign by looking at expression across state boundaries, under different state sovereigns (primarily the United States and Israel). Second, I reflect on my experience as a scholar and consider the university in general as a site for intellectual production that is nevertheless shaped by dynamics of other states' restrictions on expression.

Reflection on our citational practices initiates a deeper awareness of accountability that we have as writers. One way of asking about this accountability is to consider our company as we write. In my writing about journalism (Bishara 2013), "writing alongside" was for me a way of conceptualizing a relationship distinct from "writing up," as described by Laura Nader (1974). Journalists have similar social power as anthropologists, and our writing overlaps in ways that can create tensions over our different audiences and norms. The special practice of "writing alongside" I am describing in this chapter is also a writing *across* borders and lines of social power. I am encouraged in this conception of "writing alongside" by anthropological approaches to expression that recognize that "the model of a self-owning, rights-bearing individual subject of free speech is only one of multiple possible ways in which human societies have thought about and organised the relation between speech and freedom" (Candea et al. 2021).

While the focus in my book is on Palestinian political expression, and while the assumption of the book is that it is crucial for Palestinians to be able to speak to each other and as a collective despite their different political statuses, I could not have written the book without a number of Jewish Israelis and Israeli institutions. This includes institutions and individuals of a variety of political stances, including stances of "objectivity." Some I would regard as closely aligned with the politics of the Palestinian activists about whom I write, such as Zochrot, the Jewish Israeli organization that promotes Israeli memory of the Palestinian Nakba, or mass dispossession, of 1948. It also includes institutions that are important critics of the Israeli state though they are not necessarily aligned with the politics of the Palestinian activists about whom I write, such as Israel's premiere human rights organization B'Tselem. Finally, it includes Jewish Israeli reporters working for a variety of Israeli newspapers that are not explicitly oriented towards a fundamental critique of the Israeli state. While some of the journalists are major public figures and important critics of the Israeli state whom I have admired and followed for decades, like Amira Hass and Gideon Levy of *Haaretz*, others emerged as personas for me as I wrote my book. I imagined Nir Hasson, also of *Haaretz*, on the streets of Jerusalem, at night, reporting on right-wing crowd violence against Palestinians. I knew there were a variety of reasons I would not be in his place. This citational practice may seem unremarkable, but in an era when and at a site where different groups may adhere to separate truths (Stein 2021), my dependence on Jewish Israeli knowledge producers of various institutional and mostly likely ideological positions is important to recognize. Still, the energy of this chapter focuses on Palestinian knowledge producers, because, as subjects often racialized as threats by the Israeli and US states, they face the most profound risks.

"Writing Alongside" Threatened Human Rights Activists

Palestinian human rights organizations occupy an essential position in an ecology of human rights knowledge production, as they can begin conversations and document abuses in ways that push other national and global non-governmental organizations (NGOs) to continue their advocacy. Indeed, we have seen this in the last few years as B'Tselem, Human Rights Watch, and Amnesty International have all built on the cases made by Palestinian human rights organizations, arguing that Israel is an apartheid state.[3] For my research, the most important among these human rights organizations have been Adalah: The Legal Center for Arab Minority Rights in Israel, based in Haifa, and BADIL Resource Center for Palestinian Residency and Refugee Rights, Defense for Children International Palestine, and Addameer Prisoner Support and Human Rights Association, all based in the West Bank.

As I was completing my book, two of these organizations – Defense for Children and Addameer – were among six Palestinian organizations declared

---

3 For example, eight Palestinian human rights organizations submitted a major report about Israeli apartheid to the UN Committee on the Elimination of Racial Discrimination in 2019 (Al-Haq 2019), and then the Israeli human rights organization B'Tselem (2021) and Human Rights Watch (2021) and Amnesty International (2022) followed soon after. Each presented their own research, and taking the lead of Palestinian organizations is hardly automatic, but after decades of documentation and argument led by Palestinian human rights organizations (L. Allen 2013), this new consensus has grown.

to be terrorist organizations by Israel.[4] The accusations stretched credulity. They were purportedly linked to allegations that individuals at the organizations were involved with fundraising for a leftist Palestinian political party, the Popular Front for the Liberation of Palestine (PFLP), which the United States, the EU, and Israel had all labelled as a terrorist organization. This is part of a broader criminalization of Palestinian politics that we can see inside Israel's 1948 territories and in the West Bank and Gaza.

The Israeli declaration had several kinds of impacts, but one was epistemic. With these accusations, various realms of knowledge production collided. There is the open and accessible world of human rights knowledge production, where publicity is often the point and can be protective. There is the academic mode of production, where there can be a collusion between a neo-liberal "marketplace of ideas" and demand to produce, on the one side, and activist scholars' interest in making heard stories of injustice and struggle, on the other. Both of these contrasted starkly with the field of knowledge production of the Israeli state's declaration, in which information is produced through violence and made to be effective not because it is rigorously presented, but because it is stated with force to back it up. It is not transparent but deployed with a combination of secrecy and accusation. The human rights, academic, and activist realms can be described in terms of the theories of the public sphere, geared towards deliberation, but the Israeli declaration left little to deliberate. Yet – and this is the key point – these environments are interconnected.

Analysts see Israel's declaration of these six organizations as terrorist groups to be part of a lengthy campaign to derail their work. Israel had long accused such organizations of "delegitimizing Israel," a vague accusation that seems to miss that human rights organizations are charged with criticizing oppressive states. Ramping up accusations, in May 2021, Israel circulated a dossier to European officials accusing these Palestinian human rights organizations of being involved with funding terrorism, but the officials were unconvinced. Rather than convince, then, the Israeli state declared. In October 2021, Israel pronounced the six organizations to be terrorist organizations according to Israel's 2016 Counterterrorism Law. Both culturally and legally, when Israel makes such a declaration, it must be attended to both inside and outside of Israel. According to joint reporting by the online publication *The Intercept* and the Israeli news magazine *Local Call*, the details of the dossier presented to Israeli officials were gained under circumstances of torture of two accountants who had worked with one of the organizations. Interrogation sessions lasted as long as twenty-two hours at a time. According to his lawyer, accountant Said

---

4   The other four groups were Bisan, Al-Haq, the Union of Palestinian Women's Committees, and the Union of Agricultural Work Committees.

Abdat was interrogated while his hands were tied behind his back and his feet were also tied, in a position known by generations of Palestinian prisoners as a *shabah*, a stress position. Interrogators also threatened harm to his family during the interrogation. Abdat fainted more than once but received no medical care (Abraham, Ziv, and Rapoport 2021). Again I underscore that we are very far from the modes of knowledge production that would be accepted by my university's Institutional Review Board.

The details of the allegations were compiled in a document marked "classified," but by the fall of 2021, they were being widely circulated. This exemplifies the ways in which secrets can be deployed to wield more power than information that circulates freely, producing impunity for the producers of secrets and deepening senses of insecurity for those who are their targets.[5]

The declaration of the six organizations as terrorist organizations was quickly condemned by international human rights organizations as well as by twenty-four leading Israeli human rights organizations (Zaher 2021). But the declaration nevertheless had momentous potential influence. It could have impacted data collection for an investigation of the International Criminal Court into the Israeli crimes in the West Bank and Gaza that began in 2021. As Michael Sfard, an Israeli lawyer representing Al-Haq, commented, "It all starts and ends with the fact that these organizations are seen as promoting a boycott of Israel and the investigation of war crimes at the International Criminal Court … The attack on them is a political one under the guise of security" (quoted in Abraham, Ziv, and Rapoport 2021). This also has the potential to disrupt hundreds of Palestinian lives – people who depend on these organizations for their livelihood, as well as communities of human rights workers. According to the 2016 Israeli Counterterrorism Law, all of these organizations' activities have been criminalized, and their equipment and assets could be seized, and their staff arrested (Zaher 2021).

This tactic for defunding and delegitimizing Palestinian human rights organizations is related to "lawfare," the strategy of using legal cases as a weapon in conflict that has been widely used against Palestinian advocates, especially to combat their speech and association (Guinane 2021). While the designation occurs under the purview of Israel's 2016 Counterterrorism Law, there is little legal process involved; security logics often undermine legal processes (Shenhav and Berda 2009; Dorsey and Díaz-Barriga 2015). Designation of an organization as a terrorist organization in Israel happens without a prior hearing; then the minister of defence may hear a petition from the organization to reverse its own decision, but this may involve secret evidence on the part of the

---

5 See Tate (2007) for a different process of production of impunity, and Paz (2021) on the production of collective anxiety as a result of the discretionary circulation of secret information.

state, as could a legal petition to the Israeli Supreme Court. As Eliav Lieblich and Adam Shinar (2021) write, "The Counterterrorism Law provides a vestige of due process but in fact allows Israel's security apparatus almost unfettered discretion."

Importantly, the incontestability of these laws relies on cultural assumptions that can feel universal in "the free world," that terrorism can never be considered legitimate (Li 2019). Yet "terrorism" is too often left undefined. In the case of these six organizations, there are no allegations of them having funded violent acts, and certainly not violent acts against civilians (the requirement of many definitions of terrorism), only that some funding in some cases might have been geared towards cultural activities like dance lessons or summer camps organized by the PFLP (Abraham, Ziv, and Rapoport 2021). In a powerful report for the Charity and Security Network, lawyer and free speech advocate Kay Guinane (2021, iv) writes of lawfare as a tactic increasingly used to threaten civil society in two ways, as "driven by authoritarian leaders seeking to restrict civic space in order to repress political dissent, and by counterterrorism measures passed in the wake of the 9/11 attacks." Yet the key point here is that the "War on Terror" as a discursive formation exposes the lack of a bright line between democratic and non-democratic contexts. Discourses of security also often blur this line. Anti-Palestinian agendas have been a core of antiterrorism law, used to repress dissent over many decades (Li 2024).

The impact of such declarations reaches beyond state boundaries. They are made effective through donors' sense of fear and legal liability. As Diala Shamas of the Center for Constitutional Rights writes:

> The US Departments of Treasury or State need not themselves designate these human rights groups for there to be significant fallout from Israel's claims. Launching these allegations alone, with or without substance, can cause serious and crippling isolation of the designated groups. Third parties – funders, institutions, advocates, students – fear they might be violating some law, or that they could subject themselves to resource-intensive lawsuits to defend themselves from allegations of supporting a designated group. Those of us who advise Palestinian rights groups and engage in advocacy for Palestinian rights suspect that this is exactly the intended consequence. Indeed, each time there is a new report purporting to uncover terrorist ties to Palestinian rights groups – no matter how implausible the accusations – my organization receives calls from individuals and institutions alike concerned about their potential liability in light of this new, or newly packaged, information. (Shamas 2021)

Whether as a distraction campaign that takes resources away from other important issues or as a threat to these organizations' funding, the terrorism designation is a debilitating attack.

There is also speculation (and fear) that this attack on Palestinian human rights organizations is but a first step towards a crackdown on Israeli human rights organizations like B'Tselem. While a scholar's risk of citing these organizations pales in comparison to the dangers faced by the organizations themselves or to their funders, some scholars may also experience a sense of risk. In an atmosphere in which an NGO maintains a website slandering scholars for their criticism of Israel, some junior or vulnerable scholars may fear citing "terrorist" information. If the alternative is to cite only Israeli or international human rights organizations, this serves to reinforce dynamics in which Arab sources are less trusted than Israeli, European, or North American ones. This can perpetuate a troubling and historically engrained cycle. This all underscores how these environments for expression are interrelated across geographies and modalities of writing.

Nevertheless, the declaration of these six organizations as terrorist organizations might be a kind of a limit case: the declaration has created a backlash in the United States and Europe and (re)exposes the racialized and problematic labelling of Palestinians as terrorists. We are currently in the middle of this story, and it will be important to watch as it unfolds. By the summer of 2022, ten European countries had decided to restore funding to the organizations (Kuttab 2022; Lis 2022).

Transnational Approaches to Boycott, Divestment, and Sanctions

The Boycott, Divestment and Sanctions (BDS) movement is especially illustrative of the ways in which speech is at once territorialized but not bound to the jurisdictional laws of where one is primarily located. Academic boycott is a means of speaking collectively, of drawing people's voices together against repressive policies. Boycott campaigns, in contrast to state declarations of terrorism, often gather tremendous evidence and a chorus of voices to press people into deliberation and action. Recent campaigns in the United States have strived to have a politics of voice that resists racialized logics of expertise and mobility by working intersectionally against US racism and settler colonialism and by foregrounding the perspectives of Palestinians in Palestine.[6] Boycott campaigns are not without risk for their leaders. One's stance on the boycott can have different impacts depending on one's location. The BDS movement is a Palestinian-led campaign launched in 2005 that calls for these three (nonviolent) tactics to be used to isolate and put pressure on Israel until it ends its

---

6 See, for example, the website of the Anthropologists for the Boycott of Israeli Academic Institutions (https://anthroboycott.wordpress.com) and analysis of the campaign by Allen, Segal, and Winegar (2023), Bishara (2023), and Deeb and Winegar (2017).

military occupation of the West Bank and Gaza, treats all of its citizens equally, and honours the right of Palestinian refugees to return.[7] Boycott campaigns are one way in which both individual academics and academic associations can express solidarity with a Palestinian-led campaign. Recent boycott victories include votes from the American Studies Association (ASA) in 2013, the Middle East Studies Association (MESA) in 2022, and the American Anthropological Association (AAA) in 2023 to implement an academic boycott.

However, there has been a coordinated global campaign against the use of boycott as a tactic, a campaign that attempts to undermine the Palestinian consensus on BDS. In the occupied territories of the West Bank and Gaza, boycotting Israeli goods is widely recognized as a positive strategy to the extent that that is possible, given the prevalence of Israeli goods in Palestinian markets, which is a product of Israeli occupation. However, according to a 2011 Israeli law, support for the boycott by Israeli citizens can lead to legal sanction (Lis 2011). In the United States, too, thirty-four states had anti-boycott laws as of November 2021 (Foundation for Middle East Peace 2021). As Human Rights Watch (2019) has found, "Anti-boycott laws in the US are part of an increasingly global campaign by Israel and its supporters to combat perceived supporters of the Boycott, Divestment and Sanctions (BDS) movement." On this issue, as on many others, right-wing activists arrive in jurisdictions ready to submit bills for voting. These anti-boycott bills do not necessarily represent local debates or priorities. As local press institutions are hollowed out and become polarized along similar lines as the national press in the United States, thorough consideration of these bills can be difficult to engineer. Organizing against them, while certainly possible, requires work from local organizations that are closely following local legislation and are able to mobilize the right people to confront the law, as I witnessed as residents of my state waged not one but two successful campaigns against such laws (Massachusetts Peace Action 2019).

Anti-boycott laws can provide a purportedly "pragmatic" logic against boycotts, as opposed to arguments based in principles. In the recent AAA campaign, one anti-boycott argument, refuted by boycott organizers, was that a boycott resolution would make it impossible for the AAA to hold meetings in certain places that had anti-boycott laws in place. According to a close analysis, the laws would not prohibit the conferences being held in such states in any case (AnthroBoycott n.d.). However, for those accustomed to facing

---

7   See the websites of the key boycott institutions, the BDS movement (https://bdsmovement
    .net) and the US Campaign for the Academic and Cultural Boycott of Israel (https://usacbi
    .org), as well as analysis of the history and contemporary importance of the boycott movement
    by Feldman (2019) and Takriti (2019).

no interruption to the usual business of the academy, who have internalized the sense that the academy is a free space for the exchange of ideas – rather than a field of struggle for such freedoms, as Bourdieu (1993) might have it – conceiving of what it might mean to face restrictions on where a conference could be held was a plausible reason to vote against a boycott. For those in support of a boycott, the laws were a related injustice that needed to be addressed. The campaign raised the possibility that the association would need to think about the politics of location more consistently in planning where to hold its conferences in order to press for academic freedoms, the right to boycott, and the rights to expression and education more broadly.

Zooming out, we can see that anti-boycott laws in Israel and the United States create a tension between activist Palestinians under occupation who are strongly inclined to support BDS and Palestinians in Israel or Palestinians and their allies the United States who can be isolated by boycott politics and who can also perceive certain kinds of support for BDS as risky. Here again, though, tides may be turning, if the recent academic institutional votes are any indication.

Points of Entry: Rhetoric and Visas

It is those most viscerally committed to Palestinian rights who are sometimes most threatened in these networks of restrictions on expression and mobility. Israel, as the effective sovereign power over not only its 1948 territories but also the territories Israel occupied in 1967, controls access for many Palestinians to their families and to their hometowns. For generations of Palestinians, border stories are constitutive of Palestinian identities. These are the lucky Palestinians who have even the possibility of access, unlike most Palestinian refugees in the Arab world beyond historic Palestine. Delays and searches at Ben Gurion Airport are rites of passage for young Palestinians as they travel alone. Travellers tell their stories with a certain sense of wearing a badge of honour, sometimes recounting their clever retorts or sincere challenges to the border control officers, or the camaraderie or shared anxiety they found with others in the small rooms where they waited. In this sense, border stories propel expression.

Yet it is less often acknowledged that border experiences can set limits on the expression of Palestinians and others. State deployment of information and control of mobility can produce anxiety and fear in targeted communities (Paz 2018, 137). Passport control is another site at which state and – as we will see – non-state actors threaten freedom of expression even beyond their borders. Once again, these logics of exclusion are at odds with expectations about open spaces of discourse in democracies. Universities (especially in the United States) rely on a sense of global connection, and scholars value global circulation of their ideas, so these limitations on movement interrupt utopian views of the academic environment for expression. Restrictions on movement interlace the domestic and international politics of Israel and the United States and their two related but distinct racialized hierarchies. Though exclusion happens at the level of the individual, such cases contribute to perpetuating an atmosphere of fear and anxiety around critique of Israel, especially for Palestinians and other Arabs. These dynamics again illuminate how free expression is territorialized, but not bounded to state sovereigns in any simple way.

As of a 2017 Israeli law, support for the BDS movement could lead to prohibitions on entering Israel for non-Israelis.[8] Israel denied a work visa to the director of the Human Rights Watch Israel and Palestine desk, Omar Shakir, in 2017, and the Israeli Supreme Court upheld a deportation order in 2019 (Human Rights Watch 2019). In many circles, each activist who embarked to Israel and each group of students or church or synagogue delegation became a new test case for the law. Rumours circulated of border patrol officers doing Google searches of would-be travellers. People had their theories of how Israel's passport control officers operated – but even expressing the theories effected Israel's threats and intimidation against critics because they work by circulating fear.

Then in 2018, *Haaretz* published evidence that Israel had an unlikely source for its information on whom should be excluded from entering Israel: the website Canary Mission (Landau 2018). Canary Mission is a US-based anonymous webpage, established in 2015, that slanders students, professors, and others for criticism of Israel, deeming their statements to constitute anti-Semitism or support for terror. Canary Mission targets many Arabs, Muslims, and other people of colour, posting their pictures along with statements twisted to sound nefarious (Jewish Voice for Peace 2016). This has negative effects on students' reputations and can impact factors like admission to graduate schools and attaining jobs. This, then, is a case of Israeli officials effectively using anonymous rumours to make decisions about visas – based on people's purported expressions. Canary Mission can post whatever it likes with no repercussions, but those advocates for Palestinian rights risk bans on entry (and more) if they are caught in Canary Mission's net. While Israel has for decades used security files to hide information from those accused, this use of unverified information from a non-government source seemed especially egregious and presented itself as a new level of threat to those watching the developments.

And then there were more high-profile cases of visa refusals. In the fall of 2019, Israel declared it would prohibit entry of US Congressperson Rashida

---

8 The 2017 law built upon the 2011 law that made supporters of boycott subject to civil liability in Israel (Redden 2017).

Tlaib because of her support for the BDS movement. This was unprecedented because Tlaib was to go as part of a congressional delegation. Tlaib's status as the only Palestinian American member of Congress and as one of the "squad" of four progressive women of colour who were regularly targeted by then US president Trump are necessarily part of this story. Trump had harassed Tlaib in the past, and he goaded Israeli Prime Minister Benjamin Netanayhu on in the visa denial, tweeting, "It would show great weakness if Israel allowed Rep. Omar and Rep. Tlaib to visit" (Kershner, Stolberg, and Baker 2019). The Israeli government reversed its decision and said it would allow Tlaib to visit, but the case exemplified how even when they are elected, even when they are representatives of Israel's most powerful ally, women of colour are prone to be racialized and gendered in order to discredit and marginalize their voices. Muslim Americans and Palestinian Americans are often racialized as risky (Rastegar 2021), and they often experience a sense of never quite belonging in the United States (Cainkar 2009; El-Haj 2015). For Arab Americans who watched Tlaib's and Omar's inaugurations into the US Congress with awe, their racialized exclusion from a basic privilege of US citizenship – mobility, entry into the territory of one of the US's closest allies, whose budget the Congress indeed supports generously – exacerbated a sense of threat and exclusion.

Travel has been inhibited in the other direction as well. Limitations on travel did not only have to do with criticism of Israel but were also reinforced by an underlying logic that saw Arabs as dangerous. In May 2019, the United States denied entry to Hanan Ashrawi, who has for decades been a prominent "voice for peace," a negotiator, a Palestinian parliamentarian, a NGO founder, and a frequent guest at US universities. As a woman in her seventies holding a PhD in English from the University of Virginia, she hardly fit the profile of a security threat. She accounted the problem to Trump, writing, "His administration does not have the tolerance or capacity to engage in fact-based dialogue. It combats meaningful discussion because it has no interest in respectful negotiations and sees no value in international engagement" (Ashrawi 2019). She also pointed out that she was one of several Palestinian leaders and activists who had recently experienced visa denials. While Trump may have exacerbated matters, the US has denied visas to Arab and Muslim intellectuals for decades, as with the visa denials of Tariq Ramadan and Adam Habib (Schmidt 2010).

For me, one of the most illustrative cases was of a denial of entry to a Palestinian student entering Harvard. In the fall of 2019, after he had already been through all the security checks entailed with attaining a visa, after he had received that visa in his passport and travelled to Boston's Logan Airport, customs officials interrogated Ismail Ajjawi about other people's Facebook posts that they found on his digital wall. He was only allowed entry after a long ordeal that stretched out over several days (Kaleem 2019). His ordeal demonstrates a criminalization of a Palestinian *conversation*: Ajjawi was not even being penalized for what he said, but rather for what others said to him. Indeed, from the time when he initially attempted to enter the United States to when he was later allowed in, his number of Facebook friends fell from 752 to 299, suggesting unfriending was a way of making his profile more palatable to border control.

These cases demonstrate that limitations on speech are racialized during the long "War on Terror," that they are enforced while people are in motion, that they impact not only individuals but collectives, and that while they are related to state control, they effectively operate across borders.

What Does It Entail to Engage Expression as a Site of Struggle?

Palestinian activists understand these restrictions on collective expression in a deeply engrained way. Over decades of experience with international law, they have seen purportedly universal liberal principles falter again and again when Palestinians try to put them into action (L. Allen 2020). While they may continue to engage institutions of international law, they may in other cases attempt a collective refusal of the conditions of participation placed upon them. This refusal resonates with other refusals of settler colonial order (Simpson 2014). These refusals are public challenges to these racialized controls on movement and expression.

In 2020, Palestinian civil society organizations came together to reject a new wave of conditions on European funding. Foreign funding of civil society institutions is a vivid example of how limitations on expression can operate in a manner that is territorialized but operates across international lines. Palestinian institutions of civil society are integral for documenting Israeli violence, asserting Palestinian collective rights, and creating spaces for the practice of Palestinian heritage. They also constitute a relatively reliable segment of the economy upon which many members of the tenuous middle class rely. Because of Palestinian statelessness and the investment of the "international community" in having some form of stability in the region, much of the work of Palestinian civil society is made possible through foreign funding. There have long been conditions on that funding, including, by the early 2000s, requirements from the United States Agency for International Development (USAID) and the US State Department to isolate "terrorists," very broadly defined. But these restrictions had not extended to European funding, until more recently. As a statement signed by dozens of Palestinian institutions of civil society asserted,

In recent years, Israeli and Zionist campaigns targeting Palestinian civil society, and its national non-governmental organizations, have escalated. In conjunction with this, funding constraints from various donors have escalated, which include conditions that we have resisted such as preventing engagement in the Palestinian Boycott, Divestment and Sanctions Campaign (BDS), the defense and promotion of the right of return, and programs and projects in areas such as the Gaza Strip, or Palestine 1948 (Israel). These conditions have reached an unacceptable level that stipulates the signing of the provisions on preventing terrorism that affect the history and struggle of our people. (BADIL 2020)

Funders have become complicit in Israel's attempt to impose fragmentation of Palestinians into separate societies and struggles in the West Bank, Israel, and the West Bank. European restrictions labelled a number of Palestinian political movements to be terrorist and required civil society organizations receiving funding to screen people and organizations as potential terrorists. In response, the Palestinian organizations, led by the refugee rights organization BADIL, declared, "Palestinian political factions and forces are not terrorist organizations, and their popular, national, and legal statuses are not determined by a European document" (BADIL 2020). They pledged to "abstain from signing any conditional funding agreement that includes the anti-terrorism policies" and asked other Palestinian organizations to do the same, "to stand against and resist the criminalization of Palestinian history" (BADIL 2020). For cash strapped organizations, this was a strong stance to take. It was something akin to going on a strike, threatening one's own (organizational or economic) health to make a collective statement about injustice and pervasive threat. It was a recognition that if a single institution refused to accept the new conditions, it would mean nothing, but together the refusal could have political significance.

Compare the underlying logic here to that of those who assert boycotting Israeli institutions is unacceptable because it limits the expression of Israeli academics who are not the central perpetrators and who should, according to this logic, be able to express themselves as individuals in ways that are unimpeded.[9] The Palestinian stance of refusal sees the ability to express one's self collectively and individually as a possibility only through ongoing struggle – and here I am channelling not only Palestinian language about the "national struggle" but also Bourdieu's (1993, 40) language about "the struggle for the dominant principle of hierarchization" within a field. It moreover recognizes that significant limitations and suffering may be necessary for a collective statement to be heard and for the long-term accomplishment of a goal of justice. Those opposing a boycott of Israel, on the other hand, see any small impediment to individual expression, and even any small stigma attached to it, to be unacceptable, even though the jobs and core ability to conduct and publish research of Israeli academics are not threatened by institutional boycotts.

---

9   See Wind (2024) for an important critique of this argument.

In another contrast to those opposing an academic boycott of Israel, scholars at the University of Toronto supported censure of their own university – tantamount to a boycott – when the University of Toronto pulled a job offer to law scholar Valentina Azarova for her past writings on Palestine. In the summer of 2020, Azarova had been a top choice of a hiring committee for a position at the University of Toronto as director of their International Human Rights Program. Deans and university lawyers had been working closely with her to get her residency and work-authorization permits in place, and she was expected to relocate by the end of 2020. Then, apparently, a donor blocked her hire because of her legal work earlier in her career on behalf of Palestinian rights. Once again, visas played a role in the logic of ceasing the offer, though in a different way: procedural issues related to the work visa initially provided cover for the university's political decision.

As a result of research into the issue by University of Toronto scholars, the real reasons behind rescinding the offer came to light. In April 2021, the Canadian Association of University Teachers (CAUT) called for a censure of the University of Toronto, only the third time they issued such a censure. Many scholars at the University of Toronto saw the disruption of the offer as an affront to the university's values of academic freedom at their institution and thus to their own academic freedom. They supported the CAUT's censure, publishing a "How to" censure guide and documenting the case extensively. Censure, they noted, would involve refusing speaking engagements, appointments, distinctions, and honours from the University of Toronto until the censure was lifted (Censure UofT 2021). The case generated global publicity, including an article by Masha Gessen (2021) in the *New Yorker*.

In this case, the collective action accomplished its goal. As a result of the campaign, the university finally made the offer to hire Azarova in September of 2021 (too late for her to actually join the university), and the CAUT censure was lifted in November 2021. Yet scholars at the University of Toronto have not ceased their struggle to make space for Palestinian voices and critique of Israel, having launched their Hearing Palestine initiative to strategize for a long-term hub for the study of Palestine at the University of Toronto. The multifaceted organizing of scholars at the University of Toronto underscores that the struggle for freedom of expression and for broader forms of justice can involve both the work of refusal – such as boycott and censure – and also the positive work of creating spaces for expression.

Conclusions

As a Palestinian scholar based in the United States, and in particular as an anthropologist who is committed to learning from and with Palestinians in the region and also Israelis about Israeli violence and Palestinian struggles for justice, this returns me to a sense of what my responsibilities are: to make transparent the relationships on which I rely to do my work, to make clear how we as speakers write and speak on unequal terrain for expression, and to strive continually to make that terrain more equitable. Just because I am in a country that rates high in measures of "liberal democracy" according to many indices, and just because I have university tenure that should guarantee me certain kinds of academic freedom does not mean that I am untouched by these restrictions. I say this not to point out my vulnerability but instead to underscore the interconnectedness of various environments for expression. University spaces – even relatively privileged ones like mine – are not islands of free expression, because there are no such islands. Geopolitics and racialized logics of the long "War on Terror" ensure that unfreedoms leak and proliferate, and passports offer little protection. Again, we can return to the killing of Palestinian journalist Shireen Abu Akleh. Not only did being a US citizen not protect her from a soldier's bullet, but her US passport has as yet not made it possible for her family to see her killers held accountable.

While the University of Toronto case came to a relatively swift conclusion, the same cannot be said of the restrictions on funding of Palestinian civil society institutions. Indeed, as I discussed above, rather than have these restrictions lifted following their 2020 campaign, Palestinians saw Israel attempt to expand the number of organizations regarded as terrorists in 2021. In 2022, Israel issued a new military order stipulating that Palestinian institutions of higher education must receive Israeli permission for the "foreign" faculty they hire and even must submit to a limit on the number of foreign students they admit, another way in which a limit on mobility hampers free expression in higher education (Bishara 2022; HaMoked 2022; Hass 2022). As I have demonstrated here, these are not distant threats to freedom of speech in an isolated place where freedoms have long been squelched. They are threats that can circulate the globe due to racialized definitions of who is a terrorist and who might be a speaker of truth. Palestinian organizations know their ability to engage in free expression is conditioned by traffic in money and ideas from Israel to the European Union and the United States and back to the occupied Palestinian territories. They are willing to organize to maintain whatever tenuous ability to mobilize that they have under Israel's military occupation. Scholars at the University of Toronto recognized that their academic freedom was contingent on that of all members of their community. They all recognize that freedom of expression is a site of struggle, territorialized but not bounded by states. With creativity and perseverance, on our own and in concert, we must all do the same.

PART THREE

Narrating, Witnessing, Troubling

13 Freedom of Speech in Jeju Shamanism

HEONIK KWON

In November 1989, the world was riveted by the powerful drama unfolding in the city of Berlin. While the wall that had divided the city since 1961 was crumbing in the hands of ordinary Berliners, an event that subsequently became the shining marker of the end of the Cold War, people elsewhere were witnessing their own era-ending, epoch-changing dramas. In Taiwan, the change was principally about the country's celebrated transition to political democracy after four decades of life under the authoritarian Kuomintang (KMT) military rule. This transition involved, crucially, the lifting of the curtain of silence about the 2/28 Incident, the tragic episode of state violence and white terror in 1947–8 (Shih 2014). During the same period, the people of Jeju, a beautiful island near South Korea's maritime border with Japan, were experiencing their own era-ending drama, which was, as in Taiwan (and in Myanmar and in Indonesia, too), also part of the country's transition to political democracy following the popular uprising in 1987 against the decades-long military rule. This drama involved opening a wall, although here as in Taiwan, the wall was a less materially tangible one compared to that in Berlin – the wall of silence that had enveloped the islanders' everyday lives for the past four decades. The opening began with an act of speaking out, which entered the public sphere in 1989.

Called *Ijesa malhaemsuda* (Now we speak out) in the islanders' distinct indigenous language, this publication consisted of twenty eyewitness accounts of the political violence of 1947–9, the time typically referred to as the April Third Incident, or simply 4/3.[1] The incident refers to an armed uprising by a small and poorly armed group of local communists on 3 April 1948, first directed against several police outposts across the island. It also included numerous civilian killings that devastated the island communities following the uprising, caused principally by brutal counterinsurgency military campaigns

---

1 This and other related episodes introduced in this chapter draw upon Kwon (2020, chap. 6).

and, in part, by counteractions by the communist partisans. The counterinsurgency campaigns had been initially launched by the United States Military Government of Korea (1945–8) that was occupying the southern half of the Korean peninsula following the end of the Pacific War.

The 4/3 incident in Jeju, together with the Taiwanese 2/28 Incident, the Malaysian Emergency, and the First Indochina War, speaks closely to the prevailing, precarious condition of the postcolonial world in the early Cold War. The time refers to the few years following the March 1947 pronouncement of the Truman Doctrine that defined America's place in the post–Second World War world order as the paramount leader in the global fight against international communism. Considering the subject of this volume, we may define this condition in terms of a clash between two different ideas of freedom. One of them is in the sense of Truman's Saving Freedom (the idea that only the United States can afford to defend the Western tradition and the principle of freedom nurtured in this tradition), and also in that of Eisenhower's Crusade for Freedom (which expresses the political idea of the Free World with the religious idea of freedom from tyranny – thus, freedom from communist tyranny) (Scarborough 2020). The other idea of freedom is according to the ideal and imperative of decolonization (i.e., freedom from colonial domination) in the progression of which "freedom," in the sense of Saving Freedom, took up a relatively marginal space compared to another freedom (from oppression and inequality, see below) long propagated by the Crusade for Freedom's antagonist – "tyranny" – since the Russian Revolution in 1917 (Preston 2012; Kirby 2002). Freedom had different colours during this epoch, eventually taking on bifurcating meanings between, in the words of the historian Odd Arne Westad (2005), the Empire of Liberty and the Empire of Equality. Freedom, which was understood at the geopolitical centre by either of these two empires, furthermore, was also not the same as the freedom desired by many nations in the postcolonial periphery of the bipolarizing world order.

The above is familiar to most of us who experienced a small part of the "age of extremes" in the twentieth century (Hobsbawm 1995), although the era's clashing ideas of freedom and their enduring ramifications in contemporary political lives may not be clearly cognized in our encounter with the world by means of ethnographic engagement. As I mentioned elsewhere (Kwon 2010), an understanding of Cold War history, and its relevance for coming to terms with some of the key concepts in contemporary anthropological research, is still in its infancy within the discipline (see also McGranahan and Collins 2018). The recent political history of the concept of freedom is an important subject for an investigation of the idea of free speech. Important to this investigation are not only the bifurcating political meanings of freedom, mentioned above, but also collusions between the religious and the political in the constitution of the freedom concept. The terrain for this investigation is vast. What concerns this chapter is how the idea manifests itself in a specific local situation at a particular historical moment – such as in Jeju at the end of the Cold War.

∗∗∗

Ijesa malhaemsuda was a culmination of the long-standing political activism of the island's writers, journalists, and dissident intellectuals against the military-led authoritarian rule. It presents views of the 4/3 crisis from a variety of actors – for instance, a secondary school student in town, a village farmer, a former prisoner, and a former partisan fighter. Each of the twenty testimonies provides a rare glimpse of the previously unknown historical reality, and as a whole they are meant to offer a view of the era from multiple perspectives. What is of interest for this chapter is the fact that a story from a local *simbang*, a common reference among the islanders to a specialist in shamanism, a strong tradition in Jeju, acts as the lead testimony, ahead of all other original accounts. It is as if the *simbang*'s story was meant to be a general introduction to the rest of the stories that follow. The *simbang* says:

> Nearly every family keeps some grievous spirits of the tragic dead from the time. If you listened to their stories, you would discover that nearly all the dead were innocent people. They were neither on that side nor on this side. Ensconced in between the two sides, they were simply trying to escape a brutal fate. Some escaped to the mountains to preserve their lives and never came back; other met death while staying quietly at home. Each time I opened a *kut* [shamanic rite], I heard these stories. In *kut* for families who had people working for the police or the government, you would hear more about people killed by the mountain side [mountain-based communist partisans]. In other homes, stories were mostly about the victims of the government side. Many dead had no this or that side origin. I heard from a man [this man's spirit] how his death had been caused by his relative-in-law. His relative had had a grudge against him because of an old marriage dispute between the two families. (Jeju 4·3 Yŏnguso 1989, 21–2)

The making of these testimonies, first in the space of a local newspaper and shortly afterwards as a book, is regarded among the island's intellectuals as one of the most important public events in recent decades and as an event that put an end to the island's long-held silence about its past experience. Such public historical testimonial actions advanced in Jeju earlier and more forcefully than in other parts of South Korea (in relation to the grassroots experience of Korea's civil war in 1950–3, to which the 1948 crisis in Jeju was, in many ways, a prelude). What is interesting about *Ijesa malhaemsuda*, however, as already mentioned, is more than its exemplary status as an act of historical witnessing in the chronological sense.

The efficacy of shamanism as an initiatory act in historical testimony draws upon the islanders' everyday lives during the long Cold War. The anthropologist Kim Seong-nae notes the unique place of the local religious culture of shamanism in the history and legacy of political violence. Kim (1989) conducted fieldwork in a coastal village on Jeju at the end of the 1980s. Her research initially focused on gender questions in the islanders' cultural life, especially the significance of shamanism in the daily lives of the island's women. This shamanism is a religious form existing alongside rituals of ancestor worship, which also takes up an important place in the routines of the islanders' family and communal lives. The anthropologist changed her research focus, however, after discovering fragmented traces of historical violence in the shamanic rituals she was attending. Kim had no knowledge of the 1948–53 violence at that time, nor had she encountered any traces of this tragic past outside the ritual context. Through this experience, Kim (2013) later came to conclude that shamanism in Jeju is a powerful, distinct institution of historical memory.

Kim's (1989) ethnography focuses on the ritual act called locally "the lamentations of the dead." In a family-based performance, the lamentations of the dead typically begin with a tearful narration of the moments of death, the horrors of violence, and expressions of indignation against the unjust killing. Later, the ritual performance moves on to the stage where the spirits, exhausted with lamentation and somewhat calmed, engage with the surroundings and the participants. They express gratitude to their family for caring about their grievous feelings, and this is often accompanied by magical speculations about the family's health matters or economic prospects. When the spirits of the dead start to express concerns about their living family, this is understood to mean that they have become somewhat free from the grid of sorrows, which the locals call a "disentanglement of grievous feelings."

The act of disentanglement is never complete, however. On the next occasion that the family hosts a spirit consolation rite, therefore, it is likely that a similar scene of the spirits of the dead expressing sorrows be repeated, although over time the expression may become less intense. The ritual for lamenting souls is a type of ancestral rite in that it invites primarily the spirits of the dead related in ties of kinship to the ritual-hosting family. Spirits who appear in the ancestral ritual within a *kut*, however, are not the same as those invited to the domestic ancestral death-day commemorative rite called *jesa*. The category of ancestors in the former context is broader in scope than that in the latter. The difference has several distinct, although ultimately interrelated, aspects.

First, the institution of *jesa* is typically restricted to the family's genealogical past traced according to the dominant lineage ideology, which in this case is patrilineal descent (although exceptions do exist). The idea of ancestors in shamanism, in contrast, is open to the ritual host's broad historical relational milieu, including matrilateral and sometimes affinal ties. Observers of

Korea's traditional popular religions explain the difference between these two institutions of death commemoration in several ways. Laurel Kendall (1985) highlights the aspect of gender – the fact that shamanic rituals tend to attract particularly active participation by women, although not exclusively so, in contrast to the ancestral rites of *jesa*, in which male descendants usually take up the organizing role. Also relevant is the deep political history of Korea's kinship system – the fact that this system was primarily of a bilateral character before Korea's neo-Confucian revolution of the thirteenth century onward. As Martina Deuchler (1995) shows, this revolution was both political and social in character, with the aim of realizing a new political order through a radical reform of the existing loose, flexible bilateral kinship order to one that takes patrilineal descent as the singularly meaningful organizing ideology. Key to this revolution was the transformation of the ancestral rite to an institution that was exclusively for the patrilineal genealogical past. Seen together, these two points about the difference between *jesa* and *kut* show that the category of ancestors in *kut* is relatively free from the ideology of the dominant moral order compared to that within the institution of *jesa*, whether we consider this relative freedom in a sociological (as an aspect of gender) or historical (an incomplete neo-Confucian revolution) perspective.

In the Jeju tradition, moreover, it needs to be noted that ancestral rites themselves have a thematically related property, referred to popularly as the "*jesa* unknown even to the crow." The crow here is understood to be a type of messenger between this world and the other world, and the cultural form addressed as such refers to domestic death-remembrance rites that, although formally akin to the *jesa* proper, depart from the latter in substance. The *jesa* unknown to the crow is open to memories of the dead that are not part of the family's ritual obligation (i.e., those who died without descendants or affinal relatives, or even former neighbours who are obliterated). It is also performed rather secretly (so the idea of being unseen even to the watchful eyes of the crow) by an individual or by a very few individuals who feel close to the deceased, in contrast to the *jesa* proper that is a public as well as a domestic event, being open to and often involving a broad descent group. In the aftermath of the 4/3 violence, accordingly, a number of Jeju families took to this ritual form while trying to account for the death of their close relations whose memories were politically sensitive and publicly sanctioned against – that is, as a way of countering the crisis in the ritual order generated by the tragedy of mass death and the ensuing political repression. In this sense, we may argue that the shamanic ancestral rite incorporates both the *jesa* proper and the informal crow-know-not *jesa* practices. In other words, the structure of "the lamentations of the dead" features a relative freedom from the imperatives of the dominant moral and political order, in comparison to that of the ancestral death-day rite.

This idea of freedom, and the related structural difference between the two traditionally pre-eminent institutions of death commemoration, explains how Kim Seong-nae came to discover shamanism in Jeju as a distinct theatre of historical memory. If *kut* was relatively free from the dominant ideology of the neo-Confucian moral order in traditional times, the same can be said about the modern times and with regard to the dominant ideology of anti-communism in the second half of the twentieth century.[2] A similar idea may apply to the organization of *Ijesa malhaemsuda*, which advances the structural specificity of shamanism in the domain of death commemoration to an initiatory act of historical truth telling – that is, in relative freedom from the prevailing atmosphere of the political society that sets ancestors who are acceptable in public memory (those killed by the communist partisans) against those who are not (e.g., those who fell to the state's counterinsurgency violence).

***

Much more can be said about this freedom that emanates from the lamentation of the dead. On the one hand, it is clear that this ritual context is not separable from the shape of the broad global political arena that I illustrated earlier with the Truman Doctrine of 1947. Historians argue that it was a decisive event in the history of the Cold War that radicalized, militarized, and globalized the bipolar conflict of the second half of the twentieth century. It was also a signal to the coming-of-age of the US as a global military empire. According to new studies of this epoch, the process was both a political and a religious event in the sense that "freedom" as in Truman's Saving Freedom or in Eisenhower's Crusade for Freedom (or his Freedom in the World) becomes more intelligible, if approached as a concept having double meanings of the religious and the political (Preston 2012; see also Kwon and Park 2022, 17–22). In this light, Andrew Preston writes of an epic drama of "America's Mission." The idea of "mission" in this context runs along a tightrope between the secular (pursuit of aggressive and sometimes expansionist liberalism, as in Manifest Destiny – the idea that the United States is a uniquely virtuous nation and, as such, has the calling to save the world) and the religious (defending the freedom of religion and reaching the unreached, as Upholders of Spiritual Values and Defenders of the Faith). Hence, the idea of mission has both literal and

---

2 This closely relates to the key message from the currently vibrant anthropology of ordinary ethical life. Although there are several diverging and sometimes mutually conflicting trends in it, this field is very much focused on eliciting normative qualities embedded in human life that are distinct from (or subdued under) the moral directives and dictates emanating from the dominant ideology of a political society. Most notably, see Lambek (2010a) and Keane (2016).

metaphorical meaning in this context, shifting its semantic life between the two spheres, secular and religious, time and again – despite the founding constitutional creed of separation between church and state. Relatedly, the effort to understand the freedom of speech as demonstrated in Jeju shamanic rituals involves paying attention to how this global political project was manifested differently between the centre of Cold War geopolitics and their distant postcolonial peripheries. In the latter, the Cold War was hardly a "cold" war but rather an enduring crisis of civil war or other exceptional conditions akin to a perpetual civil war, in which the political idea of freedom often took on a much more radical meaning than in the Western world (Kwon 2010). The last was amply shown in the Jeju crisis, where the most brutal counterinsurgency violence against the islanders was committed by the paramilitary groups of the Christian youth displaced from their homes in the northern region of Korea, then under Soviet occupation. For these religious youth groups, freedom from communism and the freedom of faith were indistinguishable and made up an identical whole.[3]

---

3 Korea's northern regions, especially those in the northwest where Pyongyang, the capital of North Korea today, is located, were the original stronghold of Protestant missions, primarily those from America's northern Presbyterian society, to the extent that before the 1940s the city of Pyongyang used to be referred to as the Jerusalem in the East. Between 1945 and 1953, a large number of these Northwest Christians, as they were called, left their homeland, threatened by the revolutionary campaigns, first during the Soviet occupation and later by the North Korean state. An estimated 7,000–10,000 of them, nearly half of the total number of Korean Protestants at that time, joined the exodus to the US-occupied south. The Korean War caused great suffering to the Koreans, and Korea's Christian population was no exception to this. Institutionally, however, the war also provided a great momentum for vitality and growth to Korea's Protestant movement. The Christian movement in the northwest region was strong in the early twentieth century, not only with Presbyterian missions but also with the modernizing elite. Some of these god-fearing, educated, politically moderate, and entrepreneurial Christians, who were also the economic elite and opinion leaders in Pyongyang and its environs, on encountering and suffering the heavy-handed revolutionary politics in their northern home, especially the sweeping land reform that shattered not only their own but also their churches' economic basis, transformed into some of the most fervent and militant anticommunist warriors in the postcolonial era. The experience of the Korean War further radicalized their politically charged religious commitment. The war was a radical existential crisis for the Christian refugees from northern Korea, understood as a possible permanent loss of a secure home after the loss of their original homes in the north. This existential status, however, both religious and political, was also hugely advantageous on the south side of the 38th Parallel in the early Cold War. The US Military Government saw the Northwest Christian refugees as the natives it could work with. These were people who shared with Americans Christian values and enmity against God-denying communism – in contrast to many other native political leaders they encountered in Korea whom that government regarded as too left-leaning or too nationalistic (meaning, in this context, to put the ideal of national liberation ahead of the imperative of struggle against international communism).

In parallel with these historical horizons of global and local proportions, moreover, an understanding of freedom found in the lamentation of the dead rituals equally requires a further in-depth view of the ritual world. One important concept in this matter might be *sovereignty* – referring to the fact that in Korea's shamanic culture, beings in the other world, or supernature, whether they are powerful mythical spirit figures or more human-like ancestral spirits, are all stubbornly autonomous and self-determining entities in their own right and relationally sovereign existents.[4] The same idea applies to the categorical interiority of ancestors – namely, between spirit entities that have the right to join the ritual milieu of *jesa* and those that are excluded from this milieu of remembrance for various reasons. Hence, this idea entails that when spirits take on narration and thus assert their right to speak out (in the context of the lamentation ritual), they do so as fully sovereign beings (within the cosmopolitical world of shamanism), and their right to speak is an inalienable right (again within this world).

The points raised above are all worth careful consideration; for now, suffice it to say that the idea of freedom that is elicited in the rituals involving lamenting and speaking spirits of the dead is in touch with both notions of freedom, as discussed above. One of these is freedom as in the ideology of Saving Freedom, which constitutes the broad historical milieu within which the lamenting spirits had become an otherworldly existence as such in the first place. The other is freedom that has long existed in the tradition of the ritual form and in its given cosmopolitical order, which makes even the socially or politically excluded spiritual beings a sovereign existence in their own right and thereby allows them the equal right to speak in the (ritualized) public space (see Kwon and Park 2022, 136–56). This phenomenon resonates with what the notion of *isegoria* has in store – the idea of freedom that sublimates *equality* of all speakers (rather than freedom of speech as such) in the freedom to speak (see the introduction to this volume). What is clear is that when these spirits speak out, we need to attend to their locution with both of these separate ideas of freedom, geopolitical and cosmopolitical, in mind.

---

4 This idea of a democratic supernatural world order with reference to Korea's shamanism tradition is from one of South Korea's most prominent anthropologists and folklorists, Yim Suk-jay (1903–98). I discuss his original contribution to the anthropology of religion in Kwon and Park (2022, chaps. 5, 6).

14 Truth of War: Immersive Fiction Reading and Public Modes of Remembrance in an English Literary Society

ADAM REED

"Unequal Commemoration": Some Historical Context for a Contemporary Concern

I want to begin by going back to Remembrance Day 1981. Or rather back to the political and public furore surrounding that year's commemoration in London, as recalled by Patrick Wright. The furore in question, which at the time dominated newspaper headlines, spoke to a peculiar set of British concerns, not just about war remembrance and truth-telling but also about class and competing positionings of the nation as "a key figure in ... politics" (P. Wright [1985] 2009, 127). In retelling that story now, it is hard to fully grasp the heat behind the dispute. However, as Patrick Wright ([1985] 2009, 125) points out in *On Living in an Old Country*, the furore did in many ways crystallize terms of national debate about how to "invoke the authenticity of history and tradition." It also illustrated something crucial about shifting contexts for "a sense of the past as present" (138), which for Wright exemplified that wider historical moment when Margaret Thatcher's government came to power and ushered in a new monetarist regime.

The news story itself centred on reported events at the Cenotaph, the UK's national war memorial and the site of public wreath-laying by leaders of the country's main political parties every 11th of November. More specifically, controversy swirled around the choice of coat worn by Michael Foot, the leader of the Labour Party. Although newspapers couldn't agree on what type of outer garment it was – some claimed a duffle coat, others that Foot was wearing a donkey jacket (a woollen workwear jacket with leather or PVC shoulder pads) – there appeared to be consensus that the item concerned was conspicuously untailored. And just as importantly, that it was dark or mottled green in colour rather than formal black. For many commentators, such dress was disrespectful and "distinctly out of place" (P. Wright [1985] 2009, 121). In fact, some adjudged Foot's choice of apparel to be an affront to the solemnity of the state occasion. Even more seriously, accusations circulated that it was an insult to veterans, especially those on parade at the Cenotaph. As the same newspapers highlighted, this included a few remaining survivors of the Western Front, the conflict that first inspired the annual ceremonials and with which Remembrance Day is still most strongly associated. Wright ([1985] 2009, 125) himself recalls the poignant sight of these men, as he has it, the last "moving figures of a directly experienced and passionately remembered First World War." But Foot's appearance at the Cenotaph prompted some newspapers to invite their readers to also feel a sense of outrage on those old soldiers' behalf.

The Labour leader's opponents, and particularly Thatcher's Conservative Party, naturally sought to make political capital from the incident. However, what interests Wright ([1986] 2009, 122) is the fact that the furore also "represented a [very contemporary] clash between opposed modes of public remembrance." On the one hand, one could discern the Establishment mode of remembrance, invested in the idea of history as tradition and in the ceremonial production of authenticity (123). "Traditional authenticity exists in the present: it is bestowed upon the dead in ceremonies through which the present also reaffirms its continuity with the past," Wright argues. He continues: "Establishment remembrance raises the dead ritualistically in order to reposition them at the heart of what it simultaneously reaffirms as the 'nation'" (123). By contrast, the oppositional mode of remembrance taken to be indexed by Foot's appearance at the Cenotaph sought to attach authenticity to a "more direct and partisan *identification* with some especially among 'those who have fallen'" (123; original emphasis). From this perspective, the Labour leader presented "as bearer and manifestation of the history of the common people, of the aspirations, consciousness and courage which have produced and sustained the labour movement." Wright adds, "In these terms it is a question of *where* one stands rather than of the ceremonial steps one might go through" (123; original emphasis).

And what intrigues further is the broader context in which both these modes of remembrance sit, especially what Wright identifies as a renewed energy invested in the cultivation of that relationship to a national past. The early 1980s is a period, for instance, of accelerated discussion about National Heritage in Britain, not just the issue of preservation itself but also of what should be defined as part of that heritage worth preserving. As Wright ([1985] 2009, 212) famously describes, it is additionally a time in which the "subjective side" of that orientation to the past came to the fore. As well as "an inclination to value the past, to notice and cherish it," Wright observes something further, an original desire "to move into it and maintain it as a presence in our lives." In what follows, Wright sets out to explore the diverse ways in which the sense of the past gets intimately experienced, "glimpsed as both other and miraculously still present." But at the same time, he seeks to challenge the innocence of such feelings, to problematize some of the possibilities attached to reports "of an alienated past which keeps breaking into view" (212).

The relevance of Wright's reflections and their contextualization in competing modes of war remembrance has in recent years taken on new force. Indeed, despite the effect of pastness attached to retelling the events of Remembrance Day 1981 (a dispute over a coat seems in many ways absurd), that furore maintains a presence in British political memory, including within contemporary debates about how to figure the nation. Sometimes the nod is quite explicit. We might fast forward, for instance, to Remembrance Day 2018, when in a febrile post-Brexit referendum environment, the then current leader of the Labour Party, Jeremy Corbyn, was taken to task in some quarters of the media for wearing a raincoat or hooded anorak at the Cenotaph. Only a few years before, a minor scandal had erupted over whether Corbyn had "bowed properly" after laying down his wreath. Identified as taking Labour back to its leftist roots, rightly or wrongly associated with the figure of Michael Foot and with the party of that period, part of the tension in these news stories revolved around whether the choice of jacket was a deliberate reference to 1981. Was Corbyn making a statement about where he stood? Not just in relationship to the Establishment mode of remembrance and the question of whom he identified with among "those who have fallen" but also in relationship to the struggle of the labour movement itself and the party's politics post–Tony Blair? Conservative-leaning political commentators certainly hoped so, since they wanted to cement the connection to further the public association with Foot, widely portrayed in the press as a failed leader, and to raise again the issue of Corbyn's views on Britain's wars. If Foot's supposedly too-casual attire revealed his attitude – as Wright ([1985] 2009, 121) points out, the duffle coat could also be read as having connotations with peace campaigning and the early protests of the Campaign for Nuclear Disarmament – then Corbyn's anorak might do the same. Opinion pieces that circulated at the time stressed the Labour leader's reported pacifism and his general reluctance to name a historical conflict that he was willing to justify.

However, in the end, these associations lacked the heat of 1981, perhaps partly because Foot and the events back then at the Cenotaph no longer loomed so large in the public imagination. Or alternatively, because the terms of what was at stake in opposed modes of war remembrance had moved on. As Wright ([1985] 2009, 229–31) himself indicated, politics of race as well as class were vitally implicated in the ways in which relationships to a national past got invoked in the 1980s (see Nassy Brown 2005). But forty years on, this was even more clearly the case. Indeed, by the time of Corbyn's wreath-laying, oppositional truth-telling about war, and especially the First World War, centred squarely on the twin issues of racism and equality.

In the last few years, calls for decolonizing schools' teaching of the First World War have become considerably louder. Some national newspapers have given much space to newly published academic and popular histories of the

First World War, which uncover the role of African and Asian soldiers in the British Imperial Army and of non-combatant Chinese labourers on the Western Front (cf. S. Das 2014, 2018; Olusoga 2014; Bourne 2019). Also institutionalized in a new online section of the British Library's collection devoted to the First World War, those histories have been reported in terms of what they have to say about forgotten voices, methods of mobilization and unfair treatment within the Imperial Army. Especially in left-leaning newspapers such as *The Guardian*, emphasis has typically fallen on the "brutality" of those who commanded them but also upon the "sacrifice" and "bravery" of those who served "in the face of prejudice" (Sherwood 2018). But the real heat in this development has centred on complaints of "unequal commemoration of troops" and particularly the "racist treatment of black and Asian war dead" (*The Guardian* 2021). This was crystallized in the widely circulated conclusions of the report of the Commonwealth War Graves Commission (2021), in which attention fell on the fact that colonial troops were sometimes buried in mass graves, or more often in graves without any marked headstones that acknowledged the individual's service. The findings led Boris Johnson, the Conservative prime minister, to publicly declare in 2021 that he was "deeply troubled" by the failure to honour these soldiers.

Alongside the focus upon racist treatment of the war dead, discussion has flared up around the issue of equal honours for all ranks as well as for those possibly suffering shellshock and executed for "cowardice" or "desertion" during the First World War. The latter call led to the earlier construction in 2001 of a Shot at Dawn Memorial within the UK's National Memorial Arboretum and to a 2006 government announcement of pardon for these executed soldiers. Indeed, across all these examples it is notable the extent to which the reconfiguration of truth-telling about war returns to the issue of the care for the dead. While a full decolonizing of the school curriculum might remain contested and unlikely, it seems that consensus has shifted over who should be commemorated in modes of public remembrance. In fact, one can envisage a future in which questions of belonging and relationship to a national past become increasingly addressed through the expansion of war dead able to be positioned at the heart of the nation. In this curious settlement, Wright's ([1985] 2009) original contrast between competing modes of public remembrance blurs somewhat. Or, depending upon one's view, the oppositional mode gets swallowed up into a new Establishment praxis.

Accepting the Game of *Parrhesia*

As already mentioned, much of the recent debate about unequal commemoration centres squarely on the question of the truth of war and the right to speak frankly and freely about what *really* happened. With this in mind, I want to consider discussion and practice linked to modes of public remembrance as kinds of a "parrhesiastic game," a phrased coined by Foucault (2011, 12–13) in order to draw attention to the quality of specific relationship between truth-teller and addressee, which he likens to a "bond" or "pact." In this relationship, emphasis typically falls on the courage exhibited by the truth-teller, who in Foucault's account risks not only their life but additionally the breaking or ending of relationship itself (11). While the stakes are not quite so dramatic, I believe that one can certainly see a parrhesiastic logic to these decolonizing critiques: that is, an urging to speak the truth of the forgotten, even at the risk of puncturing a national self-image. Indeed, a similar logic can be identified in the stress behind the wider oppositional mode of remembrance, as Wright ([1985] 2009) recounts it. Declaring where one stands, for instance through an interpretation of the classist or imperial context of war, provides clear examples of that spoken frankness. Albeit Wright's story reminds us that truth-telling is not just about speech. Neither Foot nor Corbyn say anything at the Cenotaph. If they do participate in a parrhesiastic game, which is never entirely obvious, then their actions (i.e., wearing an inappropriate coat or not bowing properly) vitally rely on the sympathetic or unsympathetic interpretation of others.

One might very reasonably dismiss the idea that such silent gestures can be incorporated into the quality of a frank relationship that concerns Foucault, which is absolutely about the act of utterance. Nevertheless, it is important to acknowledge that Foucault's (2011) account does open a space for us to consider and take more seriously the positionality of addressee or the experience of truth-receiver. For in the ancient Greek or Roman examples that he provides, truth-telling can only occur if someone "accepts the game of *parrhesia*; they must play it themselves and recognize that they have to listen to the person who takes the risk of telling them the truth" (12). Indeed, the presumption of that move is essential to the nature of the bond or pact that Foucault wishes to describe and valorize. It is also central to the concern of this chapter. In what follows, I am precisely interested in the terms of that bargain or pact seen from the perspective of those who claim to receive the truth of war from another and hence perhaps to accept or play the game of *parrhesia*. Foucault frames that experience through the dominant metaphor of listening, but I want to excavate a bit further the nature of that relationship by considering a very different context for truth reception, this time grounded in the action of reading.

The recent public debates about unequal commemoration prompted me not just to go back to *On Living in an Old Country* but also to return to the ethnographic work I had already done on the intersections between war remembrance and fiction reading in an English literary society. As I have previously explored, members of the Henry Williamson Society have an emotional attachment to the period of the First World War (see Reed 2011). This is partly developed through special interest and acquired general knowledge about the conflict. It also sometimes emerges out of a desire to understand better the experience of close or more distant kin (fathers, uncles, grandfathers, great-grandfathers, etc.) who fought in that war. More broadly, the connection centres on the individual reading and shared rereading of five long novels that form part of a fifteen-volume historical novel saga known as *A Chronicle of Ancient Sunlight*. Written in the decades just after the Second World War, these war books are amongst the best-known works by Henry Williamson (1895–1977), regularly cited by historians. Central to that appreciation is a sense of the novels as an exercise in documentation; the Williamson readers I knew liked to refer to "Henry the chronicler." Observers commend the books for their detailed description of war both on the Western Front and on the "home front" in Britain, praise invariably underwritten by the widely acknowledged status of the author as himself a veteran of that conflict. In fact, Williamson's own memories of trench warfare, including audio and filmed recordings of his reflections on experiencing the famous Christmas Truce of 1914, continue to be featured in televised broadcasts and documentaries often planned to coincide with Remembrance Day or with other important anniversaries of the war.

A further reason to return to that ethnographic work lies in the unusual angle or entry-point it provides into any discussion about public modes of remembrance and relationships to national pasts. For the white men and white women who made up the membership of the literary society crucially participated in "uncritical" reading practices. The term is coined by Michael Warner (2004, 19) as an attempt to positively situate forms of fiction reading beyond critical reading, and to reflect that these practices too are "embedded within and organized by ethical projects for cultivating one kind of person or another." Amongst the best-known qualities of uncritical reading, Warner cites examples of "identification, self-forgetfulness, reverie, sentimentality, enthusiasm, literalism, aversion, distraction" (15). In this chapter, I will mainly just refer to immersive reading experiences, which may include elements of most of the above. More particularly, I will examine those simulated, almost first-person sensations of going into battle that literary society members regularly claimed as an effect of reading the war books, and which for them also underpinned the truth of those books' accounts. While never exactly asserting an equivalence to what Wright ([1985] 2009, 125) describes as the "directly experienced and passionately remembered First World War" of veterans, these uncritical reading experiences nonetheless complicate the assumptions behind Wright's depiction of opposed modes of remembrance and more widely his account of the "subjective side" of orientations to the past. And they provide a helpful sideways perspective for considering the terms of national debate today.

Likewise, I would argue that a look at uncritical reading practice complicates an understanding of how the process of truth-receiving operates. Rather than a model that envisages the straightforward acceptance of someone else's frank or risky speech, where the truths about war contained in that speech also define the risks attached to listening, I explore a model that assumes truth-telling undergoes a form of transmutation through its reception. Or where the riskiness attached to truth-receiving lies elsewhere, less in what the utterance or text contains and far more in what happens to the figure who apparently consumes it. Although the Williamson readers I knew certainly valued their favourite author as a kind of truth-teller, celebrating and worrying over his frankness in equal measure (see Reed 2022, 2023),[1] their precise role or position in any parrhesiastic game is far harder to pin down. Or perhaps better put, the game they do play confuses that boundary. As we will see, this is because Williamson readers claim to not just receive a true account of the First World War but in some fashion to live it or to find themselves unwittingly immersed in its unfolding drama.

Charging up That Hill

For many Williamson readers, the immersive experience of trench warfare properly began when reading the volume *How Dear Is Life* ([1954] 2010), and more particularly the first description of going into battle. In this much-cited passage, the historical saga's chief protagonist, Phillip Maddison, joins a charge up the hill at Wytschaete, or "Whitesheet," as the British troops renamed it, part of a series of piecemeal attacks following the First Battle of Ypres in 1914. It is worth, I think, quoting a brief extract in full.

> Mr. Ogilby was moving his sword from his head towards the right. They were too far to the left. Right incline! shouted Baldwin's voice only just audible in the noise. Right incline! How thin his own voice felt. He could now hear machine-guns firing. Each bullet passed with a sharp hissing. He broke into a sweat. Why was Baldwin kneeling down? He seemed to be sick. Then he saw that he was vomiting blood from his mouth. He fell sideways, hands clutching face, fingers streaming bright red jerking blood.

---

1 In the 1930s Williamson turned towards British Fascism and in the later volumes of his historical saga presented a revisionist history of Britain at war. While not exactly a fascist reading of the home front during the Second World War, those volumes do present an unorthodox account, one whose "truths" many of the Williamson readers remain uncomfortable with or even sometimes disturbed by. Indeed, it is notable that very few of them claim experiences of immersion linked to those later war volumes or anything like the intensity of identification derived from the war books of the Western Front. I have elsewhere discussed the Williamson readers' response to the author's Fascism, including the politics of explanation (see Reed 2022, 2023). But for the purposes of this chapter, which centres on the earlier volumes about the First World War, I merely want to note that in the minds of readers, Williamson's riskiness is not associated with Fascism or historical revisionism linked to that ideology.

> Movement thereafter for Phillip became automatic. He was stumbling over brown furrows of a ploughed field, near a tall hedge red with hawthorn haws. There were stacks at the far end of the field, and a windmill. Near the windmill was a farmhouse, with a red roof. He was a walking mass of perspiration. A jumble of memories rose before him, his head was filled with a high singing note, a steel wire seemed to make him go on after each automatic bending down, arms shielding face, from great black metallic-rending crumps in the field. (Williamson [1954] 2010, 257)

The passage is in many ways typical of the war books. A vivid sense of the action is accompanied by a strong narration of Maddison's internal state, albeit delivered by a narrator in the third person, and by detailed reference to what is happening to those around him. For instance, the reader knows that the fallen man, Baldwin, was Phillip's closest mate in the battalion, and that Mr. Ogilby had been their commanding officer since training days back in England. Likewise, in the lines that continue this passage, we are provided with Maddison's interspersed memories of home. These are indicative of a wider structure in the war books that consistently juxtaposes moments at the front not just with moments back in reserve lines but also with moments set in Maddison's family home or in his place of work, which is a clerk's office in a City of London insurance company. We also know that Phillip is part of a territorial battalion and more broadly of an army that is increasingly composed of volunteers and, as we go on to learn, from 1916 onwards of conscripted men too.

But let's return to the attack itself, for that's precisely what Williamson readers regularly did. Indeed, in our conversations and interviews, members of the literary society consistently narrated back the experience of first reading that passage, both its eventfulness and initiatory role in developing an individual and shared understanding of the truth of war. I offer a few examples of those commentaries below. As well as illustrating the tone and shape of their uncritical reading, the selected examples are indicative of at least two forms of dominant narrative. One, in which that immersive reading cements but also dramatically alters the terms of interest in the First World War, and another, in which it drags an interest out of a reading subject previously disinclined or actively hostile to hearing more about that historical conflict. Both instances are, I think, important to consider when reflecting upon the Williamson readers' attitude to past-present alignments and to public modes of remembrance.

Joe Madden, only in his mid-thirties when we met, was a great deal younger than the average literary society member, but the commentary he offered was very familiar. In his case, it was couched in a broader account of how he discovered the works of Williamson. For it was a happenstance reading of *How Dear Is Life* that also began that journey. Browsing one day in his local library in Sutton, Joe came across a book that immediately grabbed his attention. The cover presented a graphic depiction of battlefield shell holes, raging fire and thick smoke, and two soldiers staggering to make their way forwards with another body portrayed sinking into a crater. When Joe turned the book over, he discovered that the image came from a painting appropriately enough entitled *L'Enfer* (Hell) by a French war artist whose name he didn't recognize. He also didn't know the author's name. However, Joe decided to borrow the book since he had what he termed a "subliminal interest" in the First World War, partly prompted by the knowledge that his grandfather fought in it and by a general thirst for history, the subject he studied at university.

"So, I started reading it, and it wasn't a modern guts epic of the First War at all," Joe observed. "It just begins with somebody [Phillip Maddison] going off to his first day at work, this character all fidgety and nervy, and my reaction then was one of irritation." Joe admitted that he was half-tempted to put the book away. "Anyway, suddenly in quick succession the War starts," and unexpectedly Joe found himself completely absorbed.

> All the while there's a momentum, and the momentum builds up, builds up, a real quickening, absolute quickening pace right up until the charge up Whitesheet hill. And that had a terrific effect, for me a feeling that I was going up the hill as well, that I was there … And then just as abruptly, it doesn't end in what people might imagine, like a bayonet fight or even a shoot-out. No, suddenly it's just crouching down in this ditch and spending hours there, doing nothing. People get killed, yes, within a few yards of him, but nothing happens, nothing that we might expect happens. And that's good, it keeps certainly me as a reader on my toes, interested in what is going to happen next.

As we can see, Joe's commentary includes reflections on the quality of Williamson's writing, both its effectiveness in making Joe feel that he was there, charging up that hill, and in breaking his expectations as a reader by following that attack with a period of relative inaction. The latter move keeps Joe on his toes, invigorates the reader in a different way, but each element is held responsible not just for making the passage engaging but also for making it true. Indeed, Joe's commentary reinforces the sense of Williamson as artist and truth-teller.

However, regardless of how those sensations of immersion occurred, Joe wanted also to acknowledge the reality or autonomy of that first-person reading experience and more particularly what it was like to feel that "I was going up the hill as well, that I was there." This included registering the initial reading as an event, a significant happening in his life. While the trajectory behind other Williamson readers' engagement with this passage varied greatly (not many of them, for instance, started their reading of the fifteen-volume historical saga at volume four), that reported sense of viscerally sharing an individual experience of going into battle was common.

For Gary White, getting to the war novels was initially quite a disappointment. "When I started reading the *Chronicle* it got to *How Dear Is Life* and Phillip was enjoying his life in the insurance office," Gary explained, "and I was thinking, well this is quite cosy, I'm enjoying the detail of this life as lived." As Gary highlighted, part of his pleasure derived from the fact that at that point he too worked in the City of London; although born and raised in Newcastle, Gary had been employed in the information technology section of one of the financial district's banks for nearly seventeen years. When I first met him, by then in his late forties, Gary had left the bank due to ill health, but he still lived in a small, terraced house in Sydenham, a London suburb. "Then Phillip joins the Territorials and ends up in France," Gary continued, "and I thought, as I was reading it, I was thinking, oh no, not the First World War! Well maybe he [Williamson] will miss it out." As Gary explained, he had had his fill of learning about that conflict at school, and he had always remained suspicious of the motivations behind the annual ceremonials of Remembrance Day. His concern soon disappeared though. For despite himself, "once Phillip got a bit of action I was utterly hooked." Quite uncharacteristically, Gary discovered a passionate interest in the war and the experience of its trench soldiers. Indeed, the following year he proposed to his wife that they go on holiday to the battlefields of the Western Front. "So, we went there, and it was absolutely amazing, absolutely marvellous," Gary recalled, "and I've been back since, I don't know how many times more."

That story too was familiar. Many of the Williamson readers I knew had similarly felt compelled to visit the battlefields after reading the war books (Reed 2011, 153–4). Both Joe and Gary had also joined one of the occasional battlefield tours organized by the literary society. But like Joe, Gary was most keen to emphasize the extraordinary experience of that first reading of the battle scene at Wytschaete, to give an account of what it was like. He too placed stress on the pace and energy of the passage, on its emotional intensity, and on the sensation of being there:

> When the [battalion] go into action, there's an urgency that takes you along with it. And Henry talks of running up the hill and shouting to everybody. And you think, oh my God, I can feel that I'm there. I can hear this crackle, which gets more horrific the closer one gets, until Phillip's actually thrown into it, and it's even more desperate than he thought.

As Gary reported it, immersive sensations of identification blurred the distinction between any described experience of literary character and what in the moment felt like the first-person experience of the reader. But in his version, it also blurred the distinction between the experience of Phillip Maddison and the war experience of the author. This confusion was captured in the slippage of describing the passage as if it were Henry's own account of running up that hill and going into battle. The blurring was a common occurrence among the Williamson readers, in this case exacerbated by the shared knowledge that as a young volunteer Williamson did participate in the Wytschaete attack and that it was indeed his first experience of battle.

In fact, Gary's commentary offered something further; a hint at another common suggestion, that the veracity of the passage and its immersive experience could also be confirmed by the retrospective judgment of the reader and more particularly by self-enquiry. Here, the reader or addressee of Williamson's realism introduces what appear to be external criteria for assessing that truth about war. Indeed, a strange transitivity emerged in the ways in which Gary and other readers typically did this. Immediately after the charge up Wytschaete hill, for instance, Gary told me that he was left breathless and questioning, "surely it couldn't have been this bad, surely that can't be true." But upon further reflection he concluded it must be. By way of justification, Gary offered me the following statement: "To a large extent Maddison's me, when he's going through this absolute funk, as he calls it, before a battle, because I'd be exactly the same as well, you know." The observation begins with what sounds like a reiteration of the rewards of identification or first-person immersion generated by reading the passage but then ends by suggesting a reversal of sorts. It is the self-knowledge that Gary would have acted the same way that for him reaffirms the authenticity of the protagonist's actions and emotions, and hence the truth of what Gary felt and witnessed during that immersed reading. This kind of minor confirmatory work happened all the time.

More broadly, members of the literary society kept circling around and back on the quality of immersion, not just upon the issue of whose experience it was but also what, in a spatio-temporal sense, was exactly happening. "That was my first encounter, I subsequently realized, of the fourth dimension," Joe explained to me. "You know there was a distortion of time and place, normal rules seem to be broken." Although for him firmly located in the powers of Williamson as writer, Joe kept returning to its realization in his own reading experience:

It's about this ability in the writing to create a sequence, an instance that is timeless, timeless. And perhaps the best way I can express this is to mention again the charge up Whitesheet, which seems to last forever, is an entirely emotional experience, a personal experience in Phillip Maddison's eyes ... and for the reader as well. I mean the ability of the reader to step in, to be beside him, to experience without necessarily understanding what is going on, that adds to the authenticity.

For other members, the immersed experience of war left them equivocating over the position of the reader. "I'm very much outside looking in," Ali Meadows insisted. "I'm not in it, I'm definitely outside." By way of illustration, she then drew a comparison to the quality of memory, which led her to reflect in turn on dreaming and in the process to revise her original statement:

> It's a sense of being there without being there. If you imagine back on any event, it's not the event so much [that you recall]. You can't remember exactly what somebody was wearing, you can't remember exactly what was said, but you have a sort of sense of the occasion, you have a sort of feeling, don't you? ... It's almost identical [to dreaming]. I mean that's actually quite a good analogy in a way, because you haven't been there, but you feel that you have been there in some way. No, I'm not actually physically there, Ali isn't standing there [or running up that hill]. It's an Ali that's not really me. I am an onlooker, like when you're dreaming and you are not really yourself, you are still slightly removed, I think.

As an illustration of the kinds of experiences prized by uncritical reading and of the kind of projects "for cultivating one kind of person or another" embedded within reports of immersion, two things immediately stand out. First, the experiences described are crucially uncontrolled. There is a clear emphasis common to many forms of uncritical reading on the "abnegation of agency" (Warner 2004, 18). But second, and at least for the Williamson readers less common, typical elements of immersion, such as identification, reverie, and self-forgetfulness, seem in these reports to often resolve into shifting accounts of what it was like for the reader *as reader* to be present at this first attack. This is unusual. As I have described at length elsewhere (see Reed 2011), both men and women at the literary society more regularly place a premium on the rewards of occupying or being possessed by a first-person stance and outlook ascribed to someone else, normatively understood as belonging either to the chief protagonist or to "Henry." So, whether figured as charging up the hill with the rest of the battalion or "being there without being there" as if in a dream, one might expect readers to claim the same. Some do. But, as we have seen, others seem to suggest a certain autonomy from the outlook of character or authorial figure (i.e., Joe steps in *beside* rather than from *inside* Phillip Maddison; Ali's status is strangely doubled, at once present but slightly removed, yet even that version that is "not really me" remains "Ali"). That fact speaks volumes, not just about the peculiar quality of immersion observed when reading the war books but also about the Williamson readers' general perspective on war remembrance, in both its subjective and public modes.

Commemoration after Immersion

Williamson readers have, as one might expect, a diversity of opinions about the rights and wrongs of various historical conflicts. A significant minority hold pacifist views or come from pacifist family backgrounds, such as Quakerism. Others support the notion of a just war but may argue over whether the First World War fits those conditions. In this regard, Williamson's truth-telling is not definitive. In fact, the holders of any of these positions claim the author as an inspiration, just as they typically claim to have had their position on the First World War complicated by the war books. This is possible because the truth of war is partly received via immersion; as we have seen, Williamson is appreciated for the experiences he provides readers as much as for or even more than for what he tells them about that conflict. But one might reasonably enquire what all this means for public modes of remembrance and the kinds of debates about the national past and commemoration of the nation's war dead with which we opened.

Well, it's important to register the fact that Williamson readers do still appear concerned both with the ceremonial steps one goes through and with the public issue of where one stands. Individuals generally observe the solemnities of Remembrance Day each year, and aspects of the steps attached to that state occasion get integrated into the ceremonial activities of the literary society. An important feature of every annual general meeting, for instance, is a visit to Henry Williamson's grave in the North Devon village of Georgeham. This visit typically closes the meeting and involves the laying of a poppy wreath on the headstone (red poppy wreaths are conventionally laid at the Cenotaph and other war memorials on Remembrance Day). Similarly, when the literary society organizes a battlefields tour, the visit is usually peppered by two-minute silences and wreath-laying ceremonies. These might be at the graves of individual soldiers that fought alongside Williamson or were otherwise related to the author, or alternatively at the gravesides of soldiers known to appear as characters in the war books, such as the historical person behind Phillip Maddison's fallen mate, Baldwin (Reed 2011, 158). Trips often occur to remoter battlefield sites, too, including that at Wytschaete, linked to action in the novels. Members also typically take time out to pay respects at the graves of their own kin. Collectively, they additionally visit the larger Commonwealth War Graves commissioned cemeteries in Belgium and France as well as major war memorials like the Menin Gate in Ypres, where respects are paid more broadly to "our boys."

However, reproduction of what Wright would term key features of the Establishment mode of remembrance always come with caveats. In invoking "our boys," members certainly intend to mark those war dead that in their minds naturally belong to the nation and hence can be spoken of as "ours." Note, this does not usually include war dead of the wider British Imperial Army, neither white solders of settler colonies such as Canada or Australia nor Black and Asian colonial troops. But at the same time the designation suggests something further: a commitment to commemorate "ordinary" men and particularly those from "ordinary" backgrounds unexpectedly caught up in the conflict (like the novel-cycle's protagonist, Phillip Maddison). Often the emphasis goes further and stresses a desire to especially commemorate those from the labouring classes, that is, agricultural or factory workers. While there is no serious attempt to make a connection to the broader struggles of the labour movement, there does appear a concern to understand the First World War as a "manifestation of the history of the common people" (P. Wright [1985] 2009, 123). This includes an assumption of that mode of remembrance as in some sense oppositional.

"Well, I'm totally against war," one Williamson reader in his early seventies named Ted Glass told me, "but the Great War attracts me because of the heroism of the men who fought it." Ted then clarified what he meant: "I'm talking about men with very little education, who led a normal working-class life and who found themselves suddenly pitchforked into this dreadful, horrendous affair on the Western Front." It's clear from Ted's further reflections that these were also men that he closely identified with. Although occupying a low-level salaried post in a telecommunications firm for most of his working life, Ted didn't go to university; in fact, he was born and brought up in a working-class area of South London. Other literary society members had different backgrounds, for instance raised into middle-class families or through their careers moving into the professional classes, but that attachment to ordinary men previously living ordinary lives and, on that basis, facing the extraordinary hardships of trench warfare remained.

If, in their public modes of remembrance, the Williamson readers stood in this fashion with "our boys," it is important to highlight that because of immersion that relationship was perceived to undergo significant transformation. This was in large part because uncritical reading gave them the sensation of actually being there or, in the words of Ali Meadows, "being there without being there." So, instead of merely symbolically standing with "our boys" through acts of public remembrance, readers had the visceral experience of literally standing beside them on the battlefield. And since that reading experience could also feel quite like a dream or personal memory, the issue of remembrance itself became further complicated. The classic questions attached to public modes of remembrance, such as how one commemorated the war dead or who among the war dead one commemorated or what truths one commemorated on such occasions, were to a certain extent supplanted by the overriding truth of what one remembered first-hand, or at least in the modality of the first person. Whether charging up that hill in the guise of Phillip Maddison or of "Henry," or perhaps even more extraordinarily there beside that character or authorial figure in the first-person guise of the reader, members in a sense performed and shared a dual role: as simultaneously the commemorated and the commemorator.

That difference marked not just the relationship to public modes of remembrance but also the divergent relationship expressed to national pasts. As several members of the literary society emphasized, in the case of the First World War, that relationship was based much more on a "feeling" than on a particular historical interest. Or as Steve Spencer, in his late fifties when we first met, put it, reading the war books clarified that what at first appeared an interest was in fact a feeling. "I was shocked in a way to find that I had this feeling about the war, about the time and the period, you know this feeling of being there." The point was drawn out through a commonly made contrast. "Now, I'm interested in the Second World War and still am, but it's the First [World] War which has the chill, which has the identification." Steve also clarified what precisely that dominant feeling was: fear. "I got physically frightened reading those books," he told me. "It was revelatory." By way of exemplification, Steve referred back to the experience of reading the passages about Maddison's first action, including the charge up the hill at Wytschaete. But instead of the battle itself, it was the description of the lead-in, travelling up to the front line in recommissioned buses, that he kept returning to. "I remember feeling it was almost impossible," Steve recalled. "It was so difficult to read on sometimes, the strength of the emotion, the strength of apprehension and the strength of foreboding were simply unbearable."

This time the immersive principle was apparently clear. "You know Phillip Maddison was me. It wasn't necessarily what he said or did, but everything he felt I felt were my feelings." On the face of it, this was a quite normative claim to character identification, or to being there in the first-person guise of the chief protagonist, but in Steve's mind there was a further twist. For what truly caused that sensation to be revelatory was not the fact that through immersion Steve experienced Maddison's feelings first hand, but rather that Steve experienced those feelings as his own feelings or, perhaps better put, as feelings he had somehow had before. "Now is that the power of the writing?" Steve mused. "Or is it this genetic link? You know the words leapt out at me, grabbed me by the throat and showed me I was there." Steve repeated the final stress to make the emphasis clear. "I knew all about it, he didn't need to tell me, I already knew" (see Reed 2011, 153). Although most members of the literary society skirted around such bold statements, the implication persisted that this feeling of being there, or of being there without being there, might be based on some other, even stronger claim. Steve's musings next prompted him to tell me about "an ancestor," his father's uncle who fought in the trenches and came back shell-shocked. "I don't think he spoke more than half a dozen words from that day, when he was invalided out of the army, to the day he died." Had Steve's feelings of being there been passed down from this great uncle, through their genes so to speak? Or alternatively, were those feelings the result of a more mysterious process than either the power of writing or a genetic link, for example, something closer to reincarnation? "I guess I'm trying to avoid telling you what I think, that in some way I can't explain I was perhaps there," Steve concluded. "That's fanciful, isn't it? And you know I can't believe it. But," Steve added, "if I try to think of any reason, that's the only thing that I can think of."

Conclusion: Britain's War Dead

The notion that Steve had already felt the fear and other feelings of being there that he reported feeling (again) when immersed in the war books opened up a set of intriguing possibilities. For instance, that the war experience of his ancestors lived on through him, or that Steve had, in some fashion, once been one of Britain's war dead. The latter possibility was in his mind reinforced by the fact that only certain passages in the war books produced those feelings. It was just the pages in and around Maddison's first experience of battle in 1914 that made Steve feel that way. This led him to speculate that perhaps he once might have been killed on those battlefields.

But Steve also admitted that these explanations were "fanciful." Like other Williamson readers, he was prepared to concede that the feelings of being there might be the effect of the power of the writing. For instance, as I have discussed elsewhere (Reed 2011, 97), sensations of déjà vu were commonly claimed by members of the literary society. This was especially so when reflecting upon the quality of experience linked to first visiting "Williamson Country" or the English literary landscapes associated with the author's many other novels. Likewise, the treatment of ancestors was more conventionally directed towards the burning question of what fathers or grandfathers or great uncles went through in the First World War. Indeed, I recall one moving conversation with a very old member of the literary society who told me that his reading "had probably finally answered the questions which I really wanted to ask my father." Here, the war books stood as a replacement for the commonly reported silence of kin, but in a manner that satisfied because of immersion or of the crucially first-person impressions of trench warfare that they provided. Historians might express cynicism about the "myth of silence," highlighting that of course some veterans did speak and a few, like Williamson, famously so. However, from the members' perspective, this somewhat missed the point. It was the silence towards specific addressees that mattered, and especially the refusal to tell sons or daughters or grandchildren directly what happened. As the Williamson readers liked to emphasize, their favourite author provided the perfect example. For despite speaking frankly about the conflict in five long books, Williamson never spoke about his war experiences to his own adult children.

Of course, the significance of being there or being there without being there also relied on a wider genealogical sense or reasoning. In addition to gaining access to a simulated version of what their fathers or other ancestors went through during the First World War, those immersive experiences enabled the Williamson readers to reassess where they came from. As Cannell (2011, 472) points out, genealogical work in British contexts often centres precisely on a certain kind of "care for the dead," which itself typically turns out to be a process of self-discovery. Cannell bases her observations not just on ethnographic work with amateur genealogists in England but also on a reading of a very popular television show, *Who Do You Think You Are?* Each episode of the program traces the family tree of a different British celebrity and invariably concludes with a denouement that selects a particular previously unknown ancestor as a figure that affirms the identity of that celebrity or otherwise explains who they are. The effect, Cannell suggests, is to "enliven" the dead as persons and to "reconnect" them to the living as kin (465), a process that also introduces a powerful sense of reciprocity or reverse agency – that is, the re-enlivening of the living as a certain kind of person. As discussed elsewhere (Reed 2019, 76), Williamson readers incorporate that logic into aspects of their literary society work, most notably the research performed on minor characters in the novels. However, what strikes me here is not just the way in which the principle of immersion complicates that sensation of the dead as continuing to impact the living – that is, when the living person concerned claims to experience through Henry either the first-person outlook and emotions of that dead person or of someone who stood beside that person on the battlefield – but also the ways in which that logic might motivate wider public commemoration of the war dead.

The lines of the "Ode of Remembrance," a condensed version of Laurence Binyon's poem "For the Fallen," get read aloud at every Remembrance Day service. Indeed, the words are ingrained into the ceremonial steps of what Patrick Wright describes as the Establishment mode of commemoration, but they are also repeated at the little graveside ceremonies conducted by literary society members at battlefield cemeteries (Reed 2011, 158). The final, most recalled line of the "Ode of Remembrance" provides a template for acts of public remembrance and for a nation defined through its relationship to its war dead. "At the going down of the sun / and in the morning / We will remember them." In Wright's ([1985] 2009, 123) eyes, the instruction connects to the more sinister project of raising "the dead ritualistically in order to reposition them at the heart of what it [i.e., the state] simultaneously reaffirms as the 'nation.'" Yet the observations of Cannell (2011, 473) suggest something further. According to the kind of genealogical reasoning that she describes, both I and we also remember so as to enliven the dead to reconnect with us and hence demonstrate, as Cannell has it, the dead's own "token of care, a gift of kinship continued into the future."

Of course, appeal to such a genealogical sense is replete with exclusionary dangers. As Jacqueline Nassy Brown (2005, 8–9) points out, the British preference for idioms such as "born and bred," grounded in that genealogical sense, feeds an ideology of place that has been central to the politics of race and citizenship in the UK. But, as noted right at the beginning of this chapter, it appears that care for the dead (and perhaps the dead's care for us) is right at the heart of much of our contemporary debate about war remembrance. This includes the heated discussion about unequal commemoration and the racist treatment of Black and Asian war dead.[2] A decolonizing moment it might be, certainly an invigoration of truth-telling about the First World War. Yet it also seems to me a moment in which that genealogical sense has itself been reinvigorated, placed even more centrally in competing positionings of the nation, including those powerfully invoked through oppositional modes of remembrance. As Cannell (2011) astutely noticed, this is nowhere more evident than in programs such as *Who Do You Think You Are?*, which provide a successful and very popular formula for nation-building through genealogical research. Indeed, the conscious attempt in recent years to diversify the program's range of celebrities has led precisely to fresh narrations not just of who those celebrities discover themselves to be through the ancestors they choose to highlight or to be enlivened by but also of who we discover ourselves to be as a nation. That sometimes includes a story about forgotten war dead who fought or died bravely and, as colonial troops in an imperial war, did so in the face of prejudice.

Most members of the literary society recognize the importance of these genealogical stories, as they continue to recognize and invoke attachments to place through idioms such as "born and bred." Many also acknowledge the importance of new histories, for instance revealing the vital role of Chinese labourers in sustaining trench systems or the sacrifice of colonial troops from the Caribbean on the Western Front. But, and this is perhaps essential to the way in which nation-building works through a genealogical sense, Williamson readers typically do so without imagining that they themselves are reconnected or shaped by those particular ancestors or war dead. Instead, the reconnection, where recognized, occurs between fellow citizens who, while not sharing the same ancestors or the same histories, do share an equivalent sense of the impact

---

2 As Nassy Brown (2005, 20–3) also highlights, the racist treatment of Black and Asian war dead was not just about colonial troops. In the First World War, African seamen who had been based in Liverpool and started families there joined the merchant navy particularly, and also got drafted into the standard navy for the duration of the conflict. This was a participation in the war effort that the "Liverpool-Born Black" community Nassy Brown worked with in the 1990s regularly invoked and expressed pride in, as well as expressing their outrage at the lack of public recognition.

of enlivening the dead and of the dead in turn enlivening them. So, while these debates might not result in an official expansion of Britain's war dead, they do appear to suggest an expansion of the ancestors that matter in any discussions about who we are as a nation.

In many ways, adding uncritical reading or the immersive experience of war to the mix only reinforces that sense of what we might term genealogical exceptionalism. Although troops from the "Indian Corps" fought very close, if not exactly alongside the battalion of Maddison (or in historical vein, that of Williamson) during the charge up the hill at Wytschaete, none of the Williamson readers I met mentioned them in their reports of being there or being there without being there. Certainly, there was no suggestion that readers might occupy the first-person outlook and emotions of those colonial troops. This might be, as the Williamson readers would themselves highlight, because the author did not write that truth of war or the experience of those soldiers into his historical saga. The war books do include the odd brief encounter between Maddison and fellow front-line soldiers from India, but generally those colonial troops remain unindividuated. The Williamson readers' lack of identification with colonial troops might also be the result of a sense of discomfort. That is, less at the proposition itself (though I don't discount that possibility) and more at the issue of whether it is appropriate for the entirely white membership of a literary society to claim such immersive first-person feelings.

As we have seen, central to those immersive feelings and to the sense of the war books' truthfulness was the sensation of fear. Of course, that emotion has its own complicated place in the history of racism and in the wider politics of race (see Sara Ahmed 2004). But the fears that the Williamson readers reported feeling during those immersed states was not so obviously racialized. It wasn't organized, for instance, around a visceral fear of others. Instead, readers tended to emphasize an overriding sense of fright or foreboding and a concern for immediate self-preservation, without necessarily "othering" someone else as the source or cause of that affective state. Indeed, in their minds, fear of this sort was essentially democratic. In the kind of parrhesiastic game that we might imagine the Williamson readers played, it was the one great equalizer across divisions of rank, class, and nation (and by implication, race, too). Regardless of whatever else differentiated them (i.e., prejudice, anger, humiliation, or even bravery), it was assumed that all trench troops felt that fear or that in those circumstances everyone would be fearful. That is the simple truth of war, or the truth that the Williamson readers claimed to inhabit and hence accept as a consequence of their uncritical reading.

There are, of course, grounds to be sceptical about a union of equality centred in the universal experience of fear. But what, we might finally ask ourselves, are the *real* risks in this particular parrhesiastic game? After all, none of these readers actually risk their lives. None of them really witness others being shot at close quarters or blown to bits on the battlefield. And none suffer the trauma of war. Indeed, one might point out that in many ways this game appears a rather comfortable exercise. For after being there, or being there without being there, readers have the luxury of closing the book and making themselves a cup of tea and going about their normal lives.

That's certainly the case. Yet one suspects that this kind of observation betrays a prejudice towards the forms of ethical project and kinds of relationship to truth that uncritical reading supports. I refer here not just to its typical emphasis on the "abnegation of agency" (Warner 2004, 18), nor just to its concrete and apparently "fanciful" practices of identification, self-forgetfulness, reverie and distraction, and so on, but also to the issue of pretence itself. This includes the presumption that simulated risks matter or can constitute the basis for a genuine parrhesiastic game.

One might challenge that scepticism by highlighting how the effects of uncritical reading display riskiness elsewhere, for instance by undercutting narratives of bravery, such as those typically associated with both Establishment and oppositional modes of public remembrance. Or alternatively, by focusing on the kinds of "real" risks uncritical readers might suffer as a result of immersion.[3] One might acknowledge, for example, the riskiness of inhabiting fears that do not belong to one, especially if those fears destabilize the reader's sense of themselves as certain kinds of persons. A member of the literary society confided, for instance, that his immersive experience of charging up Wytschaete hill made him realize that he was a coward, and that if he had been there, he probably would have been shot at dawn for desertion. This was received as an uncomfortable truth. But these moves distract from the fact that simulated risks and the immersive states that accompany them are what motivate Williamson readers to receive and accept the truth of war. And what ultimately shape how and what they remember.

Acknowledgments

I would like to thank the members of the Henry Williamson Society, and especially Williamson's official biographer, Anne Williamson. Grateful thanks also go to Gregory Bablis, Matei Candea, Alexander Edmonds, Paolo Heywood, Toby Kelly, Thalia Ostendorf, and Shari Sabeti for their careful comments on earlier drafts.

---

3 Of course, uncritical reading has long been associated with existential risk in the minds of its observers. Take, for instance, the observations of Frances Wilson (1999, xxi), who warns that absorbed readers might become irredeemably diverted by acts of identification, and hence unable to return to the same self again. For Wilson, that riskiness is part of the positive frisson of immersion, as one imagines it might also be for Warner (2004, 18) when he invokes the "abnegation of agency" as a core experience in the self-cultivation of the uncritical reader.

15 As It Were: Narrative Struggles, Historiopraxy, and the Stakes of the Future in the Documentation of the Syrian Uprising

ANDREAS BANDAK

Thirteen years can seem like an eternity when viewed in relation to the Syrian tragedy. It is hard to fathom the immensity of the hopes unleashed in March 2011 and now, these many years later, to reflect on what has passed. Not only were the hopes of the demonstrators thwarted and willfully destroyed by the Syrian army supported by Russian and Iranian forces, but the narrative of an otherwise, of a different way forward, is now also being actively silenced by the Syrian regime. In a sense, the active and ongoing writing of history has taken a novel form in the aftermath of the Syrian uprising as evidence, testimony, and historical experience have been documented so abundantly by way of cameras and cell phones and through memories graphically engraved on the bodies and minds of the Syrian population (Bandak 2014; Bandak, Crone, and Mollerup 2024; Wedeen 2019; McManus 2021).

In this chapter, I consider the struggle over a narrative that now takes place in relation to the bourgeoning production of Syrian documentaries (cf. Wessels 2018; Della Ratta 2018; Tarnowski 2021; Weiss 2022), but which also has been evident in the production of Syrian TV serials (Salamandra 2019). As such, this chapter meditates on the role of speech, freedom, and history in the aftermath of an uprising that turned into what Syrian intellectual Yassin al-Haj Saleh (2017) has termed a tragedy. My central concern is to unravel the changing registers of historical experience and the narrative efforts placed in keeping particular pasts alive in order to make way for the future. Inspired by Simon Coleman (2011), I reflect on this as a particular form of historiopraxy, which rearranges and reorders experiences as they oscillate between the singular and the collective, the particular and the generic, in the wake of violence and atrocities committed on a massive scale. As a central trope, I consider the wording "as it were." According to the *Cambridge Dictionary*, "as it were" sometimes is used after a figurative or unusual expression.[1] "As it were" in this sense may not just point to how things actually were but also to how they potentially could be. This play between actuality, factuality, and potentiality is critical for the work on the past both in the aftermath of severe crisis and tragedy but also in any ordinary sense. Accordingly, the freedom to tell and keep particular pasts alive is a burden, which demands the work of a Penelope, a constant reweaving and retying of memory and narrative in the meeting with the gradual changes of actual remembrance and the passing of generations with different stakes in what took place.

Taking my point of departure in ongoing research on Syrian image production and memory work, I reflect on material collected over the last years among exiled Syrians. This chapter opens this exploration by engaging the work of Syrian documentarists Ali Atassi and Rami Farah, who both have won international acclaim for their films. My entry to this discussion has been prepared by long-term fieldwork in Syria before the uprising in 2011, subsequent fieldwork in Lebanon, and current ethnographic work in Jordan and Denmark on displaced Syrians (cf. Bandak 2014, 2015a). Centrally, this chapter argues that the changing tempo of conflict allows for novel engagements with the past, both the past considered historical and more increasingly the past considered as the personal and private registers of experiences and memories not neatly folded into any grand narrative. The chapter accordingly is an attempt at excavating what Reinhart Koselleck (2018) aptly has described as sediments of time, exploring the forms of sedimentation of time that Syrians reflecting on the past are starting to embark on in their engagements with what came to pass. Tracking the unfolding human powers of making history, of unleashing destruction as well as coming to terms with defeat and disappointment, is but a feeble attempt at orienting the scholarly debate towards the writing and rewriting of history, as well as engaging with what Syrian playwright Mohammad Al Attar refers to as an attempt to create a "realistic narrative of hope, and not a nostalgia of the revolution" (Jadalliya 2021). Freedom of speech in this context, I posit, takes on a particular salience as a narrative effort of keeping alive what came to pass not submitting to the Syrian regime's deliberate attempts at creating its official representation of history. Keeping open the possibility for speech outside and contrary to the regime's discourse, speech of the events, personal stakes, and the price paid on the part of the Syrian population are critical for the general conversation instigated by Syrian cultural producers such as Atassi and Farah when they reflect on their own roles in the course of events. As such, this freedom to narrate is critical as it invites a pensive engagement with not just what was but also with what still eventually may come.

1   *Cambridge Dictionary*, s.v. "as it were," accessed 4 June 2024, https://dictionary.cambridge .org/dictionary/english/as-it-were#google_vignette.

Pensiveness and Spaces of Reflection

A central concern of this chapter is to reflect on the role of history for exiled Syrians who are reflecting on the recent past. History of and reflections on the past take on a particular salience when people experience major upheavals. For Syrians – as for Egyptians, Tunisians, and Yemenites – a high-pitched sense of not merely witnessing history but actively writing it with one's actions was a marked experience in late 2010 and the early part of 2011 (Schielke 2017; Armbrust 2019; Porter 2017; al-Khalili 2021). At that time, taking the streets was by many actors seen as the only right thing to do. In Eelco Runia's (2014, 18) insightful treatment, such sublime historical events present a certain "readiness to put a way of life, a culture, on the line." To some extent, this was a time of and for actions and not one of reflection and pause. As Paul Virilio (2006) points out, revolutions are about speed and tempo, to allow for drastic accelerations towards change. The moment of the uprising allowed Syrians to see themselves as one, as one of the slogans frequently chanted had it: "Wahid, wahid, wahid, al-shab al-suri wahid!" (One, one, one, the Syrian people are one!)

In a Syrian context, what moved people may not have been the same in the southern city of Deraa as in cities such as Homs, Hama, and Aleppo. However, the initial feeling that past and entrenched forms of politics were about to fall led to an outpouring and a coming together of people more collectively. New alliances and friendships were forged (Brønds 2017), and different and repressed memories were resuscitated from neglect. As Salwa Ismail (2018) has shown, past violence from the 1980s was readily readdressed in light of the regime's violent assault on the uprising in the present. Early 2011 was a moment of change.

With the passing of time, the tempo and immediacy of events changed. After an initially peaceful start, the regime responded with enormous vehemence, and violence became integral not just to the crushing of the revolution but also to various factions taking up arms in response to it. The Syrian situation became increasingly protracted. The regime's brutalization was met by the radicalization of contingents of Islamic factions in parts of Syria. With the lack of actual engagement from the United States and European powers, the regime, greatly helped by Iranian forces and, from September 2015, by Russian forces, slowly succeeded in defeating the uprising. Accordingly, the world witnessed a massive displacement and upheaval of Syrians inside the country, with refugees flowing into neighbouring Lebanon, Jordan, and Turkey, and into Europe, Canada, and the United States. With the protracted nature of the Syrian tragedy, the tempo today, thirteen years after the hopeful beginnings, is not marked by urgency of action but by the slower pace of reflection or a living on with what came to pass (see Bandak and Anderson 2022; Bandak 2024). Some Syrians keep the past open by referring to "al-thawra" (the revolution), while others now talk about "al-ahdath" (the happenings) as a piecemeal way of getting on with life. As Theodor Adorno (1978) points out in *Minima Moralia*, such reflections on a damaged life open up different registers of thought. More particularly, they open up a space of pensiveness, which albeit painful and hurting, is a critical move towards keeping the past alive without falling prey to either cynicism or uncritical forms of nostalgia, regret, and remorse. "Pensiveness" is a term I take from Jacques Ranciére, who addresses the virtue of such slow engagement. In his *The Emancipated Spectator*, Ranciére (2009, 107) describes pensiveness as a certain state of being overtaken by thoughts: "In pensiveness, the act of thinking seems to be encroached upon by a certain passivity." Such thinking opens spaces of possibility, where a coming to terms with and through narrative as well as visual representation are worked out not in order to accept what has happened but in order to understand it.

Ethnographically, pensiveness is not a virtue for the few; rather, it is a condition, which all actors in different ways may find themselves thrown into, certainly in the aftermath of war and tragedy. Engaging the Syrian tragedy necessitates what Veena Das (2007) describes as a descent into the ordinary, which may lead to a different form of meditation on the ways taken during conflict, or what could – or should have been known – and what to retain for keeping the past for future reengagements. In Runia's (2014, 6) apt phrasing, "coming to terms with a historical trauma is the result of answering the commemorative question 'Who are we that this could have happened?'" Answering such a hard question forces us to move between what happened, accepting the course of events, and keeping the promise, which initially sparked the fatal events (Haugbølle and Bandak 2017). Accordingly, we need to assert a particular tension between the ending, *eschaton*, and the end, *telos*, in order to reflect on the work of time and the lasting imprint of what happened on the sediments and sedimentation that are taking place in the aftermath of the Syrian uprising. Pensiveness, I posit, is critical to keep open the factuality of past events, while admitting to the changing registers of experience and circumstances being lived through in the time coming after what happened.

Sediments of Time and the Rewriting of History

One key feature of history is to single out and sort things, events, and persons' deeds for later evocation. In Hannah Arendt's (1958, [1961] 1993) profound reading of ancient and modern concepts of history, we see how the role of memory is critical, that history, albeit changing in scope and character, needs to keep store of deeds, of immortalizing them to safeguard them for posterity (see also H. White 1980; Hartog 2015). In Arendt's ([1961] 1993) treatment of the modern concept of history, she argues for a disregard of taking sides, be that in national interest, or in one's own favour. She deliberately advocates for discarding "the alternative of victory or defeat, which moderns have felt expresses the 'objective' judgment of history itself, and does not permit it to interfere with what is judged to be worthy of immortalizing praise" (51). Where this may be an obvious lesson for critical scholarship, it is a hard ideal to aspire to, when located in a context of immediate war, conflict, and tragedy.

Reinhart Koselleck (2018) extends a similar line of thought across several of his brilliant essays in the recently released *Sediments of Time: On Possible Histories*. In this collection published posthumously, Koselleck unravels the diverse configurations of time and experience also known in his seminal *Futures Past* (2004). Koselleck (2018, 105) has observed that particular events in history have marked the consciousness on either side of a divide, or in his wording, "participants experienced particular thrusts of events as high points of all previous histories, whether they belonged to the victors or the vanquished, although the vanquished were often compelled to write better, more clear-sighted histories." In his understanding, history is constantly being rewoven and rewritten.

The clear and neat division between winners and losers in the game of history is further complicated by Koselleck (2018, 215) when he asserts that "not every victory remains a victory, nor every defeat a defeat." The malleability of experience, but also the ongoingness of time, complicates the neatness of such binary categorizations. Or, as Koselleck continues: "It thus is not just victory or defeat but also the kind of victory and the kind of defeat that lead to numerous refractions in the formation of consciousness, such that it becomes difficult to define minimal commonalities of collective spaces of consciousness" (215). Adding to this insight, we could also point to the work of David Scott (2014, 29) in deciphering the failed Grenada Revolution (1979–83), of which he writes: "They succeeded. They failed." The tragic experience of failing happened against the background of hopes and a social experiment, which attests to the human freedom and capability of initiating actions, actions with dire consequences that never quite could be anticipated.

The relationship between past, present, and future also has been pressing in recent anthropological work. Eric Hirsch and Charles Stewart (2005) advocate for ethnographies of historicity (see also C. Stewart 2016). The move towards addressing historicity is one that they advance in order to elucidate the ways temporal ordering are made sense of in social terms. Hirsch and Stewart (2005, 262) write that "'historicity' describes a human situation in flow, where versions of the past and future (of persons, collectives or things) assume present form in relation to events, political needs, available cultural forms and emotional dispositions." They deliberately contrasts the notion of "history" as an adding up of events with "historicity," which, as they explain, "focuses on the complex temporal nexus of past-present-future. Historicity, in our formulation, concerns ongoing social production of accounts of pasts and futures" (262).

In discussing this conceptualization, Coleman (2011) has proposed the term "historiopraxy." According to Coleman, historiopraxy is formulated to hone in on the agency that social actors have in using their pasts to move towards or even jump into the future. In his formulation, historiopraxy relates to the notion of historicity, however, as he points out: "What I preserve for historiopraxy is a stronger, proleptic sense of *making* the future, or more precisely of creating a present that, from the perspective of the future, will be recognized to *have been* a radical transformation" (435). Where Coleman underscores such agentive uses of the past, of historiopraxy, I find it useful to see the discrepant dimensions he finds in his material. Coleman asserts that historiopraxy can alternate between a "making" of history and an "invoking" of history. These modalities both imply action and recourse to the past, however the degree to which agency is asserted varies.

In these different conceptualizations, we see that the ordering of time actively involves actors, who use and mobilize the past in orienting their present and future. The circumstances for doing so, however, allow for plural engagements with the past, and even plural pasts to coexist (Henig 2018). This is where the aftermath of historical events situates actors with disappointed hopes and hence private and individual memories, which no longer are carried forward by a strong social impetus. In D. Scott's (2014, 6) eloquent wording: "What we are left with are *aftermaths* in which the present seems stricken with immobility and pain and ruin; a certain experience of temporal *afterness* prevails in which the trace of futures past hangs like the remnant of a voile curtain over what feels uncannily like an endlessly extending present." Such afterness may easily draw people towards grief and mourning over what was. This is almost unavoidable. However, in the active rethinking and grappling with what came to pass, there is also a remedy of reasserting the value of what happened even if nothing ended as was hoped for, which perhaps also points to the more general point observed by Arendt (1981, 103): "Every thought is an afterthought."

Engaging Ali Atassi: "We Lost the Battle for Freedom ... but We Didn't Lose Our Narrative!"

In late April 2021, I hosted a meeting on Zoom with Beirut-based Syrian journalist and director Ali Atassi. We met for the first time some years back at a workshop but had not been in contact since then. Atassi is known for his critical role in making documentaries featuring Syrian intellectuals, such as Riyad al-Turk, both in 2001 with *Ibn al-Am* and also more recently in 2012 with *Ibn al-Am Online*, but also for initiating Bidayyat, literally "Beginnings," launched in 2013, a collective of artists and intellectuals who assist Syrian artists and filmmakers (see https://bidayyat.org). On an overall level, the Syrian tragedy sparked an enormous effort to document the uprising and the destinies and stories of Syrian actors from all walks of life. Bidayyat has had a central role in educating and forming part of the conversation as the Syrian uprising turned violent and the regime brutally forced Syrian activists and civilians to flee.

In an interview with SyriaUntold (Milani and De Angelis 2020), Atassi explains: "With the outbreak of the Syrian revolution in 2011, a new generation emerged in covering the hopes and tragedies of the Syrian revolution. A new space to rebel and create emerged, which accompanied the birth of a new cinematic language, different ways of filming, and different forms of cinematic expression. These ways of making cinema were different from the approach of the [government-affiliated] General Organization of Cinema, which focused on fictional movies with higher budgets." The documentary that serves as a background for the conversation with Atassi is his *Baladna Rahib* (Our terrible country) that features the prominent Syrian intellectual and regime critic Yassin al-Haj Saleh. Al-Haj Saleh (2017) is known as a persistently outspoken critic of the regime, who both in Arabic and in translated works has called for an understanding of the regime's nefarious politics. The film is a moving testimony to al-Haj Saleh's clarity and courage as it follows him in the early phases of the uprising, his cordial and trustful cooperation with the young activist Ziad al-Homsi, and his move from besieged parts of Damascus to his childhood city of Raqqa only to finally be forced into exile and arrive in Turkey.

The film is moving on many accounts. It is moving because al-Haj Saleh with enormous clear sightedness and dignity is presented as he is forced to leave his wife and partner Samira Khalil. It is moving because the film follows al-Haj Saleh on his path, which ends up not as a victory but as the defeat of his dreams and hopes for a peaceful revolution. The film is also moving since many viewers will know that Samira was abducted in 2013 and never heard from again. The film is moving because we follow the demise of a dream, a hope, and a future, which seemed to be within grasp at that moment. The documentary allays these hopes and follows al-Haj Saleh on his travels through a country that is being destroyed first by the regime and later by the so-called Islamic State, also known under the acronym ISIS. What we watch is a futures past in Koselleck's (2004) sense, a particular moment with a specific horizon of expectation and space of possibility.

In the film, we meet not only al-Haj Saleh but also the young activist Ziad al-Homsi, who at this point is in his early twenties. Al-Homsi's cordial and respectful relationship with al-Haj Saleh is similarly touching. The two men from different generations share the same hopes, and also come to share the same fate while travelling towards Raqqa. We hear their profound conversations on what is happening, while we as viewers are situated in a markedly different present. We know that their moment in the unfolding chain of events is carrying them towards tragedy, while we are witnessing the enormous dignity with which they both carry on their assiduous labour of thinking and remembering despite the violence and destruction they face.

When I meet with Atassi, he is very frank and forthcoming in our conversations. He explains how he felt "a need to document" Yassin al-Haj Saleh and his life. At the same time, he is also aware of the specificities of the film being somehow his own personal view of al-Haj Saleh. Further to this, Atassi explains that as seen from today the enterprise back then was marked by "not very rational decisions." The sense of time was different, Atassi says: "We thought it was a matter of weeks, not months, back then!" In a sense, it all just unravelled. He pauses and says: "We were anticipating something different!"

Atassi explains al-Haj Saleh's decision to actually travel to Raqqa at that point. "We thought it would take some days, but it ended up taking weeks!" Further to this, Atassi explains how ISIS was taking over Raqqa with dire consequences for Yassin's brothers. To add to this, Atassi explains about his choice to go on a journey on his own to meet with al-Haj Saleh and al-Homsi in Raqqa under the control of ISIS. Laughing, he explains how he had to grow a full beard to go to Raqqa incognito. "Today I see it as stupid!" he exclaims. After a short pause, Atassi asserts the following: "We have to see it from the perspective of that moment … It was a particular moment …" In this way he explains how things were done at that moment, which now in retrospect appears rather differently.

Atassi elaborates on the film, explaining that it is "not only about the journey, but how I as a director in the editing room tell the story." In that vein, Atassi asserts that the film gestures at what he calls a "public visibility of the left in society." In the course of the conversation, Atassi focuses on two scenes from the film, which he sees as highly important. These scenes are both tracking al-Haj Saleh's engagement with ordinary people. In the first scene, he ends up in a heated discussion with an elderly man and a restaurant owner in Gaziantep. The second scene takes place in Duma, in greater Damascus, where al-Haj Saleh is trying to convince people to engage in a cleaning-the-street project with very little success.

Attasi asserts that his film is a documentation of a period marked by secular and peaceful movements just before they were overtaken by jihadist groups and a wider radicalization. He explains about Yassin's approval of the film, when he first watched the final cut in Istanbul. Later, he was less happy about it, or in Atassi's formulation: "Yassin would tell his story differently!"

Towards the end of our conversation, Atassi raises an important point: "We need a self-conscious reflection on our own roles. We were not able to face our own destiny. And we have to reflect on the enemies within and outside, which allowed this to pass." Atassi thinks for a short while before continuing: "Now is a time of reflection and critique. We lost the battle for freedom … but we didn't lose our narrative! What we are doing now is about what narrative, which will prevail." A little later, when responding to some of my questions on the important changes in visual culture and what these changes imply for the possible audiences, perspectives, and identifications, Atassi says: "We have archives, people, and narratives! We have different tools beyond the cinema … It is about a narrative battle. We need to be more honest, to discuss and complicate the established narrative … We are building for the future." After a short pause, Atassi asserts: "In the Syrian case, reality sometimes is beyond fiction! This is why we make documentary films."

Engaging Rami Farah: "Yes, We Lost. But We Still Have Our Memory"

Indeed, the Syrian reality does seem to transcend fiction in the wake of the horrors that were unleashed. However, the actual engagement with concrete persons is a highly important avenue for not just Ali Atassi but also prominent documentarists such as Waad al-Khatib, Abdullah al-Khatib, Yasmin Fedda, Firas Fayad, Ossama Mohammad, Obaidah Zeitoun, and Rami Farah. All these documentarists have made heartbreaking films covering the realities of the Syrian tragedy. All documentaries assert the need to take stock of what happened both for individual lives as well as for the broader context and story of the Syrian tragedy. In the following, I focus on the work of Rami Farah in order to reflect on the ways he is addressing the need for engaging memories of the past in their own right but also from the side of ordinary citizens and exiled Syrians.

On a Thursday morning in mid-May 2021, we in the research group had scheduled a Zoom conversation with Farah. We had long awaited this moment, as the COVID-19 pandemic restrictions made it impossible for us to meet physically when Farah, supported by International Media Support, was editing his film in Copenhagen at the Kong Gulerod Studio in December 2020. Farah was living in Paris and had over the last couple of years established himself as one of the most important and reflective Syrian documentarists of his generation with his films *A Comedian in a Syrian Tragedy* (2020) and *Our Memory Belongs to Us* (2021).

Both films elucidate significant aspects of the Syrian tragedy, in particular the changing temporal dynamics following enforced exile and displacement. The first film focuses on the famous Syrian actor Fares Helou, which the film follows as he joins the revolution, comes under attack from the regime, and ends up fleeing Syria to France. The film follows this forced move, which also has become Farah's own fate. Farah's own voice is important in the film, even if we hardly see him in front of the camera.

While still in Syria, we follow Helou in his endeavour of building an art space in al-Bustan. The art space is to be an open space for artists doing all sorts of exhibitions and performances. The energy Helou is putting into the makings of the space is palpable. However, with his speaking up against the regime, thugs send a strong message by destroying his art space. In the next scenes, Helou talks on the phone with various persons from the regime who either try to sweet talk him into coming back to their ranks or with sheer force try to cajole him into submitting to authority. He is targeted as a popular figure, but also as a Syrian hailing from a Christian background and, accordingly, critical of the regime narrative and its framing of the entire revolution as being just about Islamic extremists, not a popular and peaceful protest movement.

Later, we follow Helou in Paris. He stays with a Syrian acquaintance, who starts to question his narrative. Hence, the reflection on whether the revolution was worth its price is forced upon Helou. Devoid of the fame and importance bestowed upon him in Syria, Helou's life in Paris is somewhat more humble. Life goes on, surely, but life in exile is markedly different from the hopes and elated spirits of the early revolution. The film presents an uprooted figure who is tied to the revolutionary moment but appears to be cut loose and trying to find his footing in France.

Farah's second film is rather different. It presents three Syrian men in exile, namely, Odai, Rani, and Yadan, whom Farah summons to meet him in Paris to talk about what happened in Syria. The three men live in different European countries, and the film therefore brings them together to reflect on these events. All three were activists in the uprisings in Syria in Deraa. They were engaged in filming and documenting the unfolding events as they unravelled in 2011 and 2012. Yadan had arranged to bring the entire collection of digital files out of Syria to Jordan, and later, in 2013, he entrusted the digital collection to Farah. Hence, Farah received the entire collection of some 12,756 videos in order to make a film out of them. A copy of the digital collection was also passed on to Dima Saber at Birmingham City University so she and Paul Long could make a digital archive (Saber 2020; Saber and Long 2017). For this film, Farah had arranged for four days of collective watching of these videos on the stage of a Parisian cinema. This microcosm of friends on stage, reorganizing events and talking about their hopes, their fears, and the lost friends and loss of home presents a cathartic moment. The three men reassert their memories through their laughter and tears. Poignant scenes abound, and Farah frequently figures on the stage talking with Odai, Rani, and Yadan about the footage and their reactions to it. At different times, Yadan asks for the camera to stop filming, which Farah respects. The film accordingly gives respect, autonomy, and dignity back to these three ordinary persons. Significantly, the film ends by Farah asserting his voice and narrative alongside those of Odai, Rani, and Yadan. One of their friends, Abu Nimr, who is a major presence in the film, was killed while documenting what was happening, and his death was captured on camera. As the three men are about to watch this scene, Yadan asks Farah not to show it, saying, "I don't want to remember him that way!" Farah respects this choice. However, after ending the scene on the stage in Paris, the film ends with this very scene of Abu Nimr being shot dead by a sniper as he crosses a dangerous street. Farah's voice concludes the movie, saying: "I chose to remember."

In our conversation, Farah reflects on the stakes of Syrian archiving processes but also of generations holding different positions and memories regarding what happened. "The older generation lived in Syria and has to reconstruct their memories now," he comments. He then goes on to say: "The younger generation, by contrast, has a different memory. Their memory structure is different." As he explains, they did not hold any memories before the bombs struck. He elaborates on how he sees the idea of images as evidence and proof as particularly important before, when it all happened. Things are different now, he says: "Now, after ten years, it is a different approach, it is about our own archive, our own narratives, and not about collective experience."

Farah asserts that his own ambition is to "give the narrative back." This ambition ties in to what Farah wants to accomplish with the film: "The film is both for now and for the future." This implies making the international community aware of the persisting role of the regime in perpetrating violence. He explains how allowing embassies to reopen in Syria will give legitimacy and authority to the regime. "It is also important to show the film in Denmark with the current situation," Farah asserts, pointing to the fact that the Danish authorities at the time of writing still intend to send back Syrians to the Damascus area as it is deemed a "safe" area contrary to all official reports. Farah pauses before he goes on: "It is also important for my daughter, she needs to understand how it all was." Farah recounts how his own family was displaced from the Golan Heights in 1967. "I had questions for my parents, and I expect my daughter will have [questions for] me as well."

Farah points to the problematic situation regarding the active denial currently orchestrated by the Syrian regime. "The statue which was taken down in Deraa is now back up ... We need to keep [hold of] these moments," Farah explains, referring to one of the opening scenes in the film that shows the statue of Hafiz al-Assad being taken down.

Regarding the second film, Farah explains how he was in Copenhagen in 2013 meeting up with Signe Byrge Sørensen from the Danish Film Institute. However, what for him was a straightforward story was less easy to communicate. Supported by his partner Lyana Salem, who co-produced the film, Farah explains the idea of getting Odai, Rani, and Yadan to meet him in Jordan and film their conversation. They were supposed to meet for Yadan's wedding, but only Yadan was able to make it on a theatre stage in Jordan. Odai and Rani were Skyped in. "I studied theatre, and I feel secure on the stage ... As a dancer, I toured the world and performed in many different places. I feel at home on the stage. It is taking me out of time and space, whether Odai, Yadan, and Rani were in the Netherlands, the UK ... We wanted to take the persons out of their context ... This film gave us the tools to do this." Salem joins in, describing their film as "history telling," which "was about the revolution, how it started, how it became militarized, Islamized, internationalized."

At this point in the conversation, I comment on the dignity of the characters presented in the film, observing that they all come across very powerfully and with dignity. Farah responds: "I was observing and just following Fares, we were experiencing the end of the Syrian regime!" He sighs. "I was naïve, I didn't see what was happening." He explains the details around the second film as being very different: "I had 12,756 videos and four days of shooting. Here it was on how their lives were affected." He elaborates further on this: "We chose 18 March because it was [then that] the statue was destroyed ... It was a start [for them] to narrate their own stories, to fix the narrative and give dignity back to people!" Salem joins in again: "All became equal after the revolution, and even more so in France." She adds: "You lose your ground beneath!" Reflecting on this, she continues: "The revolution and [what comes] after is always different. Yes, we lost. But we still have our memory. It is the most important tool."

The footage allowed for a different form of intervention and telling of the past. One specific impetus was to circumvent the traffic in what Farah calls "graphic images." Farah and Salem both point to the way Syria has been turned into a global repository of images of destruction and violence. "My nightmares need not be relived in the context of films," Farah says, then continues: "People are traumatized as they are denied memories." He ties this back to his second film and their method of elicitation: "On stage in the theatre there is a space of reflection between them and the screen." Salem adds to this: "This led us to make this film, to keep the violent photos out. To keep it out in order to reflect on it." She continues this line of thought: "We need to control the memories. We need to confront what happened to us!"

As It Were: Critical Events and the Work of Time

In the work of Syrian documentarists such as Ali Atassi and Rami Farah, we see the changed conditions for narrating what happened in Syria. The revolutionary present is long gone, but its aftereffects are still alive, albeit on a much more personal level. The general problem here is how to keep and protect such memories, to keep that reality alive and present the narratives of what happened without romanticizing them. As such, the narrative efforts in these critical works attest to a freedom of speaking up but also speaking out after what came to pass. Here, documentaries present themselves as a particular way to narrate events, to make feelings palatable, and to offer a space of pensiveness. The various engagements with the past in the work and reflections of Atassi and Farah gives what Catherine Z. Elgin (2017) has called "epistemic access" to the efforts of living with what happened. It does so by opening up our understanding to the work of time on the experiences and narratives of what was. It does so by playing with the fidelity of staying true to the memories and documentations of particular persons' lives in the unfolding of events, while situating those present times as forms of futures past. Fixing the narrative, as formulated by Lyana Salem and Rami Farah, accordingly plays on the ambiguity of "as it were": trying to speak even if such an attempt may be less solid when moving to personal and intimate terrains. By moving from the collective to the personal, the narrative forms and memories also move towards new articulations, where pause and reflection become critical.

In my conception, the modality of "as it were" is a productive way to think about the relationship between actuality, factuality, and potentiality. As time passes, what happened in the Syrian context is articulated in new ways, and the narrative becomes more fragmented and personalized, as evidenced by the documentaries by Farah and Atassi. Here, the "as it were" plays on the ambiguity of the "as if," which Lisa Wedeen (1999, 2019) so aptly describes in her important works on Syria. A politics of "as if" in Wedeen's reading is based on the fact that much of Syrian politics has been based on a symbolism, where people would act "as if" they revere the leader and state, while for many this was hardly the case. For some of Syria's minorities, such as many Christians, the vision of a multicultural state was indeed a possible aspiration in the years preceding 2011. In moments of crisis, the "as if" frequently risks collapsing into an "as is" – that the reality at hand actually could promise something if not good, then at least workable (Bandak 2015b; see also Bandak 2014, 2015a). With the "as it were," my contention is to open up for the reconstructing and reworking of the past that now takes place in the memory work of exiled Syrians. These memories draw from what happened but also often inadvertently play with that reality, changing one's position, making one either more or less responsible for what actually took place. In that sense, I see "as it were" as contrasted with "as it was," which appears "solidly" to be grounded in fact. The "as it were" is in this context a persistent attempt to speak about what happened, to retain that freedom, all the while one is moving into new terrains. In moving to the modality of "as it were," we are afforded a different frame, which engages the temporal ordering and allows the work of time to become visible by playing off on the intersecting yet diverse registers of the past, present, and future, but particularly so in the attempts to put them into words. The "as it were" operates as a particular form of freedom of speech that opens up the personal and private registers and continuously attempts engaging what happened, without the fixity of an official form of narrative, and perhaps even allows for a certain playfulness.

Venna Das (2000, 59; 2007, 80) eloquently captures the relationship between temporality and narrative in her work on violence in an Indian context. When attending to violence and unsettling forms of brutality, Das contends, we may

need to stand back and avoid easy conclusions and fast opinions. In her formulation, what is of concern is "the *work* of time, not its image or representation."
A general line of thought is that a coming to terms with what has passed, implies a descent into the ordinary. Hereby we are pointed to the critical role that
stories have in establishing a sense of control over one's narrative, a point that
anthropologist Michael Jackson (1998, 2002, 2005) has unravelled across his
oeuvre (see also Lambek 2010). Jackson frequently points to Arendt's (1958)
reading of the human condition as constantly torn by situations in which the
human actor finds himself/herself an object of others' decisions and actions,
and the reverse, situations in which the human actor finds himself/herself to
be the subject and narrator of his/her life. Thus, Jackson designates this hard
balance as an existential imperative, which is a trait seen cross-culturally, albeit
circumstances and articulations obviously vary. Violence inscribes memories
vividly on the bodies and minds of the victims and witnesses. Violence freezes
the normal flow of experience and articulation, arresting time's flow. Simultaneously, what comes after attests to life as ongoing, even if guilt, shame, and
uneasiness with having survived may mark those who live on. Time, inadvertently goes on, but it is never quite the same. Violence accordingly affords
a particular haunting of memories, as what one would want to leave behind
may constantly be reactivated, willingly or unwillingly (Bandak and Coleman
2019; Bryant 2010; Knight 2021).

The need for time to move on also presents a paradox as, in moral terms, a
moving on cannot happen without, in some measure, learning to live with one's
actions and their consequences. One of the key faculties allowing for such a
transition is storytelling. Storytelling and speech allow the work of time to happen in a retaking of one's own narrative, even though that may be messy and require constant effort to achieve. For Venna Das (2007, 87) this implies that "time
is not purely something represented but is an agent that 'works' on relationships – allowing them to be reinterpreted, rewritten, sometimes overwritten –
as different social actors struggle to author stories in which collectivities are
created or re-created."

Time may indeed work on the consciousness of both individual actors as
well as the broader social webs in which one is inscribed. Acknowledging that
one was and forever will be marked by the events of a moment as decisive as
the Syrian uprising is a starting point for engaging personally with the ways
"history" happened and one's role in it without falling into unwanted forms
of nostalgia and romanticizing. Nostalgia may frequently be seen as patently
bound to an idealized past, on fantasies with no bearing on the future as when
Appadurai (1996, 77) talks of "imagined nostalgia" as a nostalgia "for things
that never were" (see also Özyürek 2006). However, following Svetlana Boym
(2001, 41ff), we need to discern different forms of nostalgia, as she points to
both a restorative and a reflective modality of nostalgia. Critically, she points

out that restorative nostalgia is bound to the re-establishment of a past order that evokes national pasts as well as national futures. Reflective nostalgia has a different openness to it as it points to aspects of memory in cultural and individual terms. In Boym's formulation: "Re-flection suggests new flexibility, not the reestablishment of stasis. The focus here is not on recovery of what is perceived to be an absolute truth but on the meditation on history and passage of time" (49). As such, Boym points to the role of such reflective nostalgia being to allow for critical thinking even if it may frequently be fragmentary and inconclusive. Reflective nostalgia is a going-back that allows for a moving forward, not a going-back in order to turn back time. Nostalgia in its reflective modality opens up for a meditation on the relation between past, present, and future. However, this happens not because of ease and accommodation with the past but rather because of the pain and "defamiliarization and sense of distance that drives them to tell their story, to narrate the relationship between past, present and future" (50).

Such reflective work, and such freedom of reflection, has certainly come at a high cost for Syrians in or outside the country's national boundaries. However, by allowing reflective re-engagements with the past, the sedimentation of what took place can be given a more mature and conscious form, and perhaps, perhaps, also become the potential for new forms of freedom and experimentations beyond the fixity and unfreedom of the Syrian regime. This, *as it were*, would allow for the work of time but also for an active reworking of time.

Acknowledgments

Beyond being presented on the online seminar organized by the editors, this contribution was presented in the European Association of Social Anthropologists (EASA) Media Network e-seminar series organized by Nina Grønlykke Mollerup, and in the online seminar at L'École des hautes études en sciences sociales (EHESS) organized by Emma Aubin-Boltanski. I thank Christa Salamandra, Simon Coleman, Daniel M. Knight, John Postill, Emma Aubin-Boltanski, and David Zeitlyn for their comments. My gratitude goes to Ali Atassi, Rami Farah, Lyana Salem, Dima Saber, Signe Byrge Sørensen, Christine Crone, Stefan Tarnowski, and Lisa Wedeen as well as Adam Reed and Matei Candea for careful engagements. My research for this article was funded by the collective project Archiving the Future: Re-collections of Syria in War and Peace, Sapere Aude Starting Grant no. 9062-00014B financed by the Independent Research Council Denmark.

16 Historical Vertigo: Art, Censorship, and the Contested History of Bangladesh

LOTTE HOEK

Swift and Total

In February 2016, as the world's contemporary art elite gathered in Dhaka, Bangladesh, an exhibition was closed down without warning. Titled *Age of Saturn*, the exhibition filled two gallery floors with photographs, lightboxes, a film, many documents and objects, two tables and chairs, a sculpture, and an ongoing performance. Accompanying the show was a detailed thirty-page catalogue, in which the artist and his collaborator laid out the principles of the show (O. Chowdhury and Zaman 2016). The exhibition and its written guide had been put together with extreme precision. And then it was over. The censorship was swift and total. Artist and curator scattered. Discontent in the small but significant art world in Dhaka rumbled in the distance, and eventually the gallery that had hosted the show was closed down.

Age of Saturn narrated the encounter between artist Omar A. Chowdhury and a distant family member against the backdrop of Eastern Bengal's twentieth-century history. Sadia Rahman (2016, 1), the curator of the exhibition, notes in her foreword to the catalogue that *Age of Saturn* was "created in close collaboration with the political and economic historian Dr. Shahidul Zaman, [and] the show explores important questions of how one can experience, or re-experience history and one's own past." In the end, both *Age of Saturn* and the events it set in motion significantly probed the possibilities for such historical narration under conditions of violence, displacement, and censorship. The thorough political reconfiguration of Bangladesh's twentieth-century history was a central plank in the consolidation of power during the fifteen years of authoritarian rule under Sheikh Hasina's Awami League government (2009–24). Described as a "hybrid" regime, "characterized by a mixture of institutional features of democracy with institutions of an autocracy" (Riaz 2019, 15), public expression had been a particular target for violent state control (Hasan 2019; Khan 2021; Shoesmith and Genilo 2013). Enforced disappearances and heavy-handed repression of political mobilization in any form sat alongside an increased self-censorship borne from the resulting climate of fear (Riaz 2019, 35; Ruud and Hasan 2022). Within this authoritarian retooling of the public sphere in Bangladesh, the events of the past have become an area of heightened political intervention and censure. Sewing the narrative of the nation's liberation ever closer into the mythology of the ruling party, utterances related to Bangladesh's history, its key moments, and its central actors had become especially tightly controlled and heavily policed. Omar A. Chowdhury's *Age of Saturn* approached this history artistically and reaped the consequences.

How does creative expression become possible and even useful in such circumstances? While contemporary Bangladesh may bring a particular sort of urgency to this question, it is one that many face in different ways in the global reconfiguration of communication technologies and their profound reshaping of politics and governance (Sundaram 2020). In a fundamental sense, such conditions pertain everywhere. In his account of politics as "the conflicts and undecidability lying at the heart of the social world," Thomas Blom Hansen (1999, 18) urges us "to recognize that the very reason why discourses of order and technologies of government try to fix and authorize certain forms of knowledge and certain taxonomies is that these schemes are fundamentally inadequate and impossible." Constraints on expression and incitements to standardized speech are therefore an inevitable part of any social order and sedimented in institutional forms and legal frameworks, including censorship (see Candea et al. 2021; Kaur and Mazzarella 2009). But these sedimented forms are also inevitably inadequate to the task of papering over the unsettled nature of the social, and therefore require ideology which, "through the enactment of repetitive practices, rituals, routines, and institutions offers a framework, a discipline, a direction, and a mechanism for simplification of the social world, which by virtue of its mere form or convention reduces contingency and temporarily "sutures" the fundamental lack in the subject" (Hansen 1999, 64). In contemporary Bangladesh, these processes are highly visible in relation to its twentieth-century history, given the unsettled nature of the young nation-state's historical narrative and the ongoing struggle to consolidate power through enforcing particular versions of that narrative. Artistic practice such as that displayed in *Age of Saturn*, and the confounding censorship it faced, exposes this unsteady terrain of ideology and excess.

In this chapter, I analyze the exhibition *Age of Saturn* and its convoluted aftermath of censorship and repression. I do not consider its closure a straightforward case of censorship in which creative or "free" expression was constrained. Instead, taking my cue from *Age of Saturn*'s distinctly unreliable narrator, I theorize the experience of censorship when accounting for one's relationship to history as a dizzying, disorienting feeling that impels and propels, rather than stalls, one's unsteady account of the past. The story of *Age of*

Saturn's closure could only be experienced or retold by any of those involved in the same disorienting manner as the show's artistic account of Bengal's history itself. This is because both stories (that of this particular show's closure and that of Eastern Bengal's history generally) are fundamentally shaped by a cascading range of repressions at the heart of the subject, by the social relations in which they are placed, and by the politics that tries to create ideological closure on this unsettled ground. Just as we are unable to give an account of ourselves (Butler 2005), so our accounts of history are caught up in partial, censured, incomplete, and inherited speech. I argue that any attempt at recounting a story of censorship and repression inevitably becomes entangled with those repressions. I suggest that *Age of Saturn*'s artistic choices allow this process to become visible both in terms of the way it presents the theme of a subject's relationship to history as well as in the effects of the censoring of the show. To do so, I present a close reading of the content and closure of *Age of Saturn* and show how these elicited a set of disorientations that befell artist, collaborators, spectators, and authorities, as well as myself as I tried to narrate and analyze these events. I will describe that disorientation as "historical vertigo." Historical vertigo is such a condition of disorientation that befalls one when narrating a history that can only be experienced and told within the terms of its own repression or censorship. That is, it can only be told in a dizzying, uncertain manner.

Age of Saturn

When I'd met Omar just before the opening of *Age of Saturn* in Dhaka in early 2016, he had enthused about finding the exact right colour of paper for the printing of the text that was to accompany the exhibition: a deep indigo and a glowing mustardy ochre. He'd been up and down Old Dhaka, to all the printers, to find the exact paper quality he wanted. The old city had long been the home to many printing presses, and they continued to thrive despite the fact that printing anything, on paper or online, had become a blood sport in Bangladesh.

Age of Saturn opened in late January 2016 and the catalogue was indeed resplendent. It contained an artist's statement, laying out the background and conceptual orientation of the show. Incorporating quotes from Heidegger, Levinas, and Hobsbawm, the text narrates the personal history of Dr. Shahidul Zaman. This text formed the backbone of the show and was captured in the many objects that were exhibited at the Daily Star-Bengal Arts Precinct in Dhaka's central Tejgoan area. Everything exhibited across the two floors of the gallery space demonstrated the artist's obsessive attention to detail and precision. From the tightly edited thirty-five-minute documentary film to the precisely controlled performance piece executed by men in military uniform, everything was closely orchestrated and planned.

Age of Saturn tells the family history and personal trajectory of a cousin of the artist's father, a Dr. Shahidul Zaman. Omar reconnected with Dr. Zaman after he moved to Bangladesh from Australia, where Omar had been raised. Lengthy conversations offered Omar a means to approach the history of Bengal that he felt a part of but did not fully grasp. Delving into the complex history of Eastern Bengal through this familiar other, Omar explains how his meetings with Dr. Zaman precipitated in him "a sense of drifting in history and a bodily re-experiencing that unsettled my sensorial certainty" (O. Chowdhury and Zaman 2016, 3). As Omar sat with Dr. Zaman in Dhaka's golden afternoon light, he noted that it "felt like I was listening to a virtuoso storyteller who traversed ages and different epistemological universes" (O. Chowdhury and Zaman 2016, 3). *Age of Saturn* provided the means by which this historical realization could be worked through and given public expression in the form of an exhibition.

Age of Saturn is more than the excavation of the personal past. To understand a personal life as it illuminates a collective experience and history is cast by Omar as a public duty. This is what Omar writes about his responsibility to history (see O. Chowdhury 2019): "The history is out on the streets, it's all still unresolved and flailing around. The history is debated and fought over with menace and a ferocity that's heartbreaking." And, "I guess I feel a special responsibility to raise these questions again in all their variegation and uncertainty. That the answers that people have settled on and are trying to bind each other with leads us to more bloodshed and backwardness and disorientation." The embattled history of Eastern Bengal, and the fear and violence that it has caused and continues to incite, has been a site for reflection and expression for scholars and artists alike (Mohaiemen 2014; Mookherjee 2015; Murshid 1996; Toor 2011). For Omar, there are two questions that occupy the foreground in *Age of Saturn*: How can you experience and understand your own connection to history when that history is kept at a distance from you, violently policed, and in many ways irretrievable? What tools might an artist have to give shape to their own place within this history, in the face of both disruptive dislocations wrought by a postcolonial history of migration, displacement and silence, as well as a public history now violently retold?

A framed set of documents in the *Age of Saturn* exhibition shows a map of all Bengal, including West Bengal and Assam, overlaid by the Urdu and Bengali alphabets, both doubled. It is captioned "Combine (Pre-history 2)." Alongside it are photographs, one of which is captioned, "Possibly a photograph of Dr. Zaman's father in the 1950s. Dr. Zaman is not sure if this is his uncle or his father. His uncle was heavily involved in the Language Movement. His father was not." It sits alongside a poem from a journal described as "centre-right." The panel drives quick and deep into the undisputed heart of the history of Eastern Bengal: the relation of language and religion to the identity of the populations there, and their capacity to constitute a cohesive people or nation. The panel foregrounds the question of the participation in the language struggle, the singular marker of the righteous in the increasingly melodramatic narration of the history of Bangladesh, in which right and wrong are starkly separated between martyrs and freedom fighters on one side and collaborators on the other. But while the question is raised, no clear answer is forthcoming from Omar's composite. Instead, the letters in Bengali and Urdu scripts are doubled, unfocused, while the captions bring further uncertainty and disrupt clear alignment with martyrs or collaborators.

Was it the father? Or the uncle? A creeping sense of doubt suffuses the whole exhibition. The catalogue admits that it is unclear whether a particular meeting happened at all; a caption notes the lack of certainty about another detail. I looked and looked again at a reproduction of a table of contents page from a *Journal of Asian Studies* issue from 1991 contained in one of the framed composites in the show. A familiar essay by Philip Lutgendorf from that year sits alongside an article authored by Dr. Zaman on elite control in Eastern India. It is not only the texts in the show that precipitate this uncertainty. A large part of the mezzanine was taken up by a performance piece titled "System Decay and Its Origin" in which a uniformed man on a platform stands to attention and on occasion reads out texts into a microphone. As described by Omar, it is a "performance-installation that essentialises the facades, infrastructure, and processes of various colonial systems. The treatment of the user is based on chance and pre-determined heuristics. Derived from the research of Dr. Shahidul Zaman" (O. Chowdhury 2018, 12). That is, the uniformed man's movements, posture, and words are dependent on circumstances. While white visitors are spoken to in one way, given access to the platform he is standing on, Brown or Black visitors are spoken to in a different way and not given access to the platform. The viewer's encounter with this soldier is entirely shaped by their own personal characteristics, including race, gender, dress, and comportment. Combined, the uncertainty of the texts and images, alongside the modulation of the experience of the viewer, induced hesitation and doubt in me as I moved around the exhibition. Writing in my notebook, hiding behind my camera, I steadied myself.

An even greater sense of dislocation was precipitated by the exhibition in those familiar with the art world in Bangladesh. Upon entering the gallery, they came face to face with portraits of Dhali Al Mamoon. The images of this prominent visual artist and professor at the Fine Arts Institute at the University of Chittagong stand in for the body of Dr. Zaman in *Age of Saturn*. Dhali Al Mamoon's personal documents are woven into the show. His portraits are enlarged on lightboxes. Personal photographs of the artist and his family are included in the framed composites and catalogues. Dhali Al Mamoon is also the unwavering focus of the film *Memoirs of Saturn* that runs in a loop in

Figure 16.1. Omar Adnan Chowdhury. Photograph (Future), Text, Tables and Chairs 40pp, 10" x 6.5", full colour, softcover, old tables and chairs (variable dimensions). Installation view. Image courtesy of Omar Adnan Chowdhury. Photograph by Omar Adnan Chowdhury.

the exhibition. Following the minimal daily movements of its protagonist, the camera meticulously tracks its subject. The viewer sees Dhali Al Mamoon at a desk, walking through the streets, reading a paper, but never hears him speak. Instead, a voice-over recorded by Omar overlays the finely edited film and narrates the daily life, history, and personal thoughts of Dr. Zaman. As Dhali Al Mamoon is quite a recognizable public figure, especially familiar to participants in Bangladesh's vibrant art world, the effect is one of deep disorientation.

Age of Saturn mobilizes a familiar documentary register. Its materials are archival documents and personal photographs, and its references are to libraries and scholarly engagement. Two desks and chairs await visitors who can sit down with the relevant texts and read them for historical illumination (figure 16.1). The film's crisp imagery and slow contemplative tempo, staying close to its quiet protagonist at all times, fit the genre of the documentary film. Nonetheless, doubt and uncertainty, a sense of losing your footing, accompany you as you make your way through the exhibition. "I began to sense in me a vague apprehension, which manifested itself as a feeling of vertigo. The outlines on which I tried to focus dissolved," writes W.G. Sebald ([1990] 1999, 33), in *Vertigo*, his novel about, among other things, memory. This is the experience that *Age of Saturn*, focused on memory, history, and identity, induces. In this way, *Age of Saturn* precipitates that "sense of drifting in history and a bodily re-experiencing that unsettle[s] ... sensorial certainty" (O. Chowdhury and Zaman 2016, 3) in those who came to see the exhibition. To visit *Age of Saturn* was to experience a "vague apprehension manifesting as dizzying vertigo."

History and Parafiction

An acute sense of disorientation has also animated academic and artistic practice that engages unresolved history. Archival materials, documentary modes, and investigative approaches have come to inhabit galleries and biennials as artists and scholars feel around the edges of their methodologies for means appropriate to the expression of, and enquiry into, the many violent and bloody seams of the past and its heavy hold on the present. Under the constellation of imperialism, the devastations of extractive capitalism, and racist epistemologies, recourse to the traditional means of research and representation appear inadequate, impoverished, and themselves a reprisal of that violence. Instead, scholars find means to exceed the settled archive and expand the possibilities for historical narration by cultivating the capacity to "access not what is *in* the archive but to this invaluable option of seeing in a non-imperial way and partaking in the actualization of non-imperial archival modalities" (Azoulay 2017, 9), and to "creatively disorder the institutional fictions and the violent abstractions authorized as fact and truth" (Hartman 2021, 129). Relatedly, artists have turned to a multiplicity of archives, finding raw materials in historical documents, scientific findings and oral histories for installation works or artists' films. Where artists have turned to archives, scholars have embraced speculative and creative practices to explore their research questions. Each provide different modalities to give shape to a subject's relationship to history.

Contemporary art practice in Bangladesh has been one of the sites in which it has been possible to raise the contradictions and discontentment with the overdetermined and partial account of the history of Bangladesh in a truly variegated, material manner. It has been so since democracy was restored in Bangladesh after the fall of the Ershad regime in the late 1980s and is exemplified by the film *Muktir Gaan* (1995) by Tareque Masud and Catherine Masud. Excavating the history of the Liberation War, they turned to a complex blend of documentary footage, reconstruction and speculation, to present a hugely powerful and influential film about 1971 (Mohaiemen 2016). In fine art, this work has been undertaken prominently in recent years by Naeem Mohaiemen. He straddles the domain of personal recollection and public history in *Rankin*

Street, 1953 (2013) and *United Red Army (The Young Man Was, Part I)* (2012), in the face of ossifying and streamlined public historical narratives. He too finds that "when I probe family history, nothing seems settled" (Mohaiemen 2014, 51). But whereas Mohaiemen's work aims to excavate facts and illuminate hidden connections, often turning to public events such as in his works *Last Man in Dhaka Central (The Young Man Was, Part III)* (2015) or *Two Meetings and a Funeral* (2017), the self-evident falsehoods and creeping sense of doubt in *Age of Saturn* do not in any way point in the direction of recuperating a hidden historical reality, however messy or unsettled. Instead, Omar's documentary and archival style captions, voice-over, and imagery sows doubt and confusion about the historical artefacts and accounts offered. The fundamentally unstable ground presented in *Age of Saturn* casts a light of uncertainty not only on its own narrative but also on linear histories and documentary forms more generally, whether presented in the gallery or elsewhere.

Age of Saturn is an elaborate work of para-fiction, a form of artistic production in which "fictions are experienced as fact" (Lambert-Beatty 2009, 54). As Omar phrases it in a gallery talk from 2014, parafiction "combine[s] and re-purpose[s] fictional, documentary, and experimental techniques to create a rich, philosophical and phenomenological enquiry" (Momentum Worldwide, n.d.). Rather than tell visitors to the exhibition the complex and contradictory facts of the history of Bengal, *Age of Saturn* invites viewers to experience this history's complexities phenomenologically and in the present. The work is set beyond the domain of the particular facts of that history, even though the exhibition is made up out of scraps and forms that could easily be true, could very well be true, and some of which are definitely true.

Discussions of parafiction have focused on the ways they may encourage a critical and doubtful stance in a citizen surrounded by misinformation, political interest, and corporate hoodwinking. It is thought that "the experiences of deception and doubt we are put through by parafictional experiments prepare us to be better, more critical information consumers, and therefore citizens" (Lambert-Beatty 2009, 77). But in Omar's work, the parafictional is not posited as the domain of a clairvoyant artist serving up enlightenment for the edification of blinded others. *Age of Saturn* is neither self-congratulatory nor unambiguous. The doubt and uncertainty of the exhibition is not merely induced in me as I walk through the exhibition but instead is centrally present in the narrator's voice. Omar's emphasis is on the torturous ways of self-knowledge and the tentative exploration of personal histories that are inevitably also public and in a profound sense inaccessible with any form of personal agency.

Age of Saturn most acutely brings to mind Walid Raad's fictional collective, the Atlas Group, in which the artist developed a series of works that document the civil war in Lebanon. Here, too, fictional archival materials, such as documents, films, images, and papers, were attributed to non-existent personae and, despite this lack of facticity being repeatedly acknowledged, the overwhelming experience of viewers was one of veracity. The body of work associated with the Atlas Group raises key questions around historiography and the archive, particularly in the context of violence and trauma (A. Gilbert 2016; Korola 2021). Like in *Age of Saturn*, "various misdirections in Raad's work expose the fictional elements in reconstructions of the past (especially personal ones) while undermining the presumed authority – Raad's own first and foremost – to write a definitive historical account" (A. Gilbert 2016, 4). The use of the renowned Bangladeshi artist Dhali Al Mamoon to give shape to Dr. Zaman connects the work directly to Raad's *Hostage: The Bachar Tapes* (2000), in which "Raad cast ... an actor [widely] recognizable in Lebanon" (Lambert-Beatty 2009, 76).

While Omar uses the parafictional form, his choice of Dhali Al Mamoon points his work in a different direction than parafiction as a critique of historiographic practice. The focus in *Age of Saturn* is on an established artist, public intellectual, and university professor, who might be well recognized within the Bangladesh art world but is not the household name a popular actor might be. The *Memoirs of Saturn* film's slowly unfolding imagery and the reflective voice-over brings out textures of Chris Marker's creative documentary form. Extreme precision – also found in other works by Omar, such as *Vastness in Eclipse* (2014), described as being set in "an anachronistic Bengali village" (O. Chowdhury 2018, 31) – and ultra-high definition imagery, betray a deep formal quality in Omar's work. In our conversations, we have spoken more than once about the cinema of Apichatpong Weerasethakul, the treacly temporality of which is echoed in *Age of Saturn*. Like Weerasethakul's films, Omar's work induces an uncertain dwelling on the edges of a surreal immersive and visceral experience in the viewer, who is thrown back onto their experiencing body to make sense of the work phenomenologically.

The title of the exhibition, *Age of Saturn*, states explicitly the artist's indebtedness to W.G. Sebald, for his melancholy exploration of art, history, and memory; his use of visual imagery with text; and the concretization of history in objects. As Janet Carsten (2007, 8) notes about Sebald's work in her *Ghosts of Memory*, a wandering protagonist searches for a meaningful life that is out of reach once "the chains of connection to one's own past have been broken." Little describes Omar's work more effectively. For Omar, too, the past appears out of reach and needs to be reconfigured, made phenomenally present, to come to a self-understanding. To "point the camera at the world and see how it 'breathes me,'" is how Omar explained his position once, underscoring how his work is about self-knowledge as refracted through a material engagement with the world.

Colonial violence, capitalist extraction, authoritarian censure, and migratory dislocation have deprived Omar of a connection to the history of Bengal. His artistic practice is a means of reconstituting such a connection and its exhibition gives others access to it. As he phrased it: "These layered and elusive installations are attempts to travel through time and into the lives of others – into what I feel was taken from me" (O. Chowdhury 2018). The focus in *Age of Saturn* is therefore not on the nature of archival material. Instead, the relationship of the subject to history proposed in *Age of Saturn* is closer to how Veena Das (2007, 97) describes the distinction between phenomenal and physical time, in which "the simultaneity of events at the level of phenomenal time that are far apart in physical time make the whole of the past simultaneously available." *Age of Saturn* conjures such disparate events into the phenomenal time of the exhibition and makes them simultaneously present in the material form of the show's objects, images, and sounds. Like for Sebald's protagonist in *The Rings of Saturn*, the confrontation with a history of destruction, motivated by the opacity of one's own past, describes Omar's self-exploration in *Age of Saturn*. Here, the Australian artist of Bengali heritage in the diaspora returns to a family history in Bengal that is fundamentally irretrievable, equally personal as it is collective, and violently embattled. The material objects in the show conjure up the events of physical time into the present phenomenal time in the gallery. These visual and material objects anchor the protagonist across a timeline and set these up for an encounter with a visitor to the gallery, for whom the events of the past are made coeval in the space of the gallery and made personal through the figure of Dr. Zaman. The account and experience produced out of these elements is fictional, but for that matter no less truthful in articulating the history of Bengal as a phenomenal, personal reality.

Access to a phenomenal and personal historical reality is premised on the availability of a double, or an "other," through which this history can be experienced. Most obviously in *Age of Saturn*, this "other" is Dhali/Zaman. Omar takes Dhali/Zaman to enquire into his own history, as "without the impression of ourselves in the face of the other, one lacks the dialectical setting in which languages evolve" (J. Siegel 1999,108). In *Age of Saturn*, this doubling is squared, as the Dhali/Zaman pairing encounters Omar/Omar, where the artist splits himself too, frequently referring to "Omar" in the third person when discussing the exhibition with me or in public talks. This recurrent doubling and pairing not only sets up a dialectal movement between the poles of this encounter. The excesses produced through this mimesis (Taussig 1993) unleash "the generative potential of imitation in transforming the 'original'" (N. Chowdhury 2020, 33). The "other" as interlocutor allows the experience of an occluded history in the present. But this doubling sets signifiers askance of their signifieds, generative of a disorienting momentum that was to overwhelm the show's various protagonists.

Uncanny Pressure

For all the work and care that had gone into the exhibition, it was not to be. Mere days after opening, the exhibition was shut down. No formal notice or legal case was brought, no plain-clothes officers appeared, nor did "digital vigilantes" (Lacy and Mookherjee 2020, 283) show up on Omar's timeline. Small pressures at first: requests for lines in the catalogue to be rephrased, maybe to be cut out entirely. Omar tells me he did sit down with the catalogues. A panel to be reordered, perhaps taken out entirely? Phone calls, a nervous curator, a request to speak with the director of the gallery. Discontent, anger, despair with collaborators on the show. Personal relationships irrevocably in tatters. There was pressure on the art foundation, on the gallery, the collaborators, the curator, on the director, and an inordinate amount of pressure on the artist. The show closed well before its time and was dismantled.

Was the pressure self-induced? Was it panic? Was it brute force? Even six years after the fact, Omar describes the pressure in uncertain and contradictory terms, indeed as if "the outlines on which [he] tried to focus dissolved" (Sebald [1990] 1999, 33). In our conversations, Omar guesses at what it was he said or did that sparked offence or concern, and to whom exactly, and how this was then expressed back to him and his collaborators. The evanescence of the offence and the resulting pressures make the censorship appear eerie in Omar's tentative retelling of what happened. It resembles acutely what Freud ([1919] 2003, 150) describes as the uncanny: the perception of the effects of forces that you don't quite understand or perceive but know or fear to be there. The effects of the unseen forces of censorship were undeniably present for Omar and all involved in *Age of Saturn*. In the immediate aftermath of the exhibition's closure, the curator resigned from her post and the artist left, first escaping into the countryside, later moving to Europe. The gallery space itself no longer exists.

For whom was *Age of Saturn* so disconcerting? That *Age of Saturn* would have been at the very least uncomfortable for Dhali Al Mamoon is obvious to see. It is Dhali Al Mamoon's image, and that of those who are closest to him, that are insouciantly used throughout the exhibition. Again, Freud's ([1919] 2003, 141–2) description of the *Unheimlich* reads apposite to the events as they unfolded: "those motifs that produce an uncanny effect ... involve the idea of the 'double' (the *Doppelgänger*) ... that is to say, the appearance of persons who have to be regarded as identical because they look alike ... Moreover, a person may identify himself with another and so become unsure of his true self; or he may substitute the other's self for his own." *Age of Saturn* is suffused with this experience. Dhali Al Mamoon's image stands in for the fictional Dr. Zaman, but the boundaries between the two are blurred. Omar appears here, too, as a double of himself, as both the artist whose show this is and the fictional interlocutor of the fictional Dr. Zaman, who both stand in for the encounter between Dhali Al Mamoon and Omar, the two artists who did meet and talked extensively. Zaman qua Dhali is also history's double, allowing Omar-the-artist to encounter his own dislocated history as he speaks with and tries to understand Dhali/Zaman. The exhibition's objects are the result of that encounter. Freud ([1919] 2003, 142–3) understands our internal double to be our conscience, which makes us "capable of self-observation." In *Age of Saturn*, Dhali/Zaman is that double through which Omar/Omar can observe himself in history.

While Dhali Al Mamoon had participated in the design and execution of the exhibition and works of art, coming face to face with himself may have unsettled him. Dhali Al Mamoon eventually had a famous human rights lawyer send a "cease and desist" letter to Omar. In the exhibition, Dhali Al Mamoon's image is put into relation with other texts and images, intertexually and intermedially. Alongside the composites and objects, there are many close ups of his face, enlarged and glowing on the light boxes. The meaning that emerges from this dense and highly orchestrated concatenation of images, texts, and objects is of course plural but, within the reductive reading regimes of regional and political history in contemporary Bangladesh, it also hits the exact wrong notes. These dissonant notes unsettle other signs. Once you put "Muslim League" (the political party on the wrong side of Bangladesh's history) in one of the boxes, it comes to contaminate the meaning of all else, as "the object of a sign – what it is a sign of – is never simply a static anchor for signification" (Keane 2022, 411), not even when it is your own face. Dhali Al Mamoon's image, so evidently indexical, is reassigned and mystified in the show. Speculation on the question of consent and the nature of the collaboration that preceded the exhibition is foreclosed by the "cease and desist" letter, despite the significant weight these questions have continued to hold for Omar. I find myself abiding by this injunction as I choose images to accompany this chapter, despite the letter not being addressed to me. What I can gauge from our conversations and my own eerie sense of pressure to "desist" is the lack of control that ensued for both artists involved. An uncanny experience of overwhelming but opaque forms of censure has enveloped us all.

As scholars of censorship in South Asia have suggested, culture is shaped by the spoken and unspoken, written and unwritten, rules around public expression, which are only partially mapped by formal legislation (Mehta 2021). This ambiguity, tacking between explicit law and implicit and ambiguous modes of enacting those laws, coincides with the ways in which political anthropologists have explained the fluidity and opacity of the state and sovereignty as a palimpsest of institutional forms, everyday practices, and shared imaginations (see, inter alia, Abrams 1988; Bryant and Reeves 2021; A. Gupta 1995; Mathur 2015). To approach sovereignty requires ethnographic attention to its effects (Trouillot 2001, 126) and the ways it inhabits our imaginations (Hansen and

Stepputat 2001). It is a classic description of an uncanny experience, where unseen forces have effects in the world, inhabiting our imagination. Censorship, as a practice of the state, is similarly best approached through the uncanny effects resulting from different modes of "public regulation" that work "to create value ... out of a delicate balance of incitement and containment" (Kaur and Mazzarella 2009, 9).

The narrative around the historical emergence and development of Bangladesh is a central focus of the mobilization and management of mass feeling, a delicate balance of "incitement and containment." There are many modes and forms through which this historical narrative was publicly managed by the Awami League regime. A huge repertoire of public cultural forms, from festivals and songs to advertising and exam questions, was mobilized to make this history stick in the most encompassing, singular, and self-evident way possible. Nusrat Chowdhury (2020) shows how this has led to an "obsessive visual canonisation" (42) in the "political iconographic culture" (39) of Bangladesh. She tracks how the effervescence of public iconography amounts to "the 'monumentalised reproducibility' of sovereign power" (34). It resonates with what Boyer and Yurchak (2010, 204) describe as a "highly institutionalized and monopolized" public culture, which, they argue, invites responses that inhabit its hypernormalized discursive forms. Parafiction is one such form.

What the combination of the extraordinary outpouring of history-related public cultural forms with the enhanced repertoire of regulation and censorship in Bangladesh suggests is that what was policed here were the ways in which the events of the past could be made "simultaneously" and affectively available. The concern was not only or primarily with rewriting the history textbooks or the revelation of new facts to continue older contestations, modes of historical narration that stay within what Trouillot (1995, 73) might indicate as a "thinkable." The revision that is at work in *Age of Saturn* and that generates a disorienting form of pressure and censure is the rearranging of the relationship between phenomenal and physical time, so that "the simultaneity of events at the level of phenomenal time" (V. Das 2007, 97) break through into the palpable all at once. To arrogate to oneself the capacity to arrange such a sensory experience of the past, evocatively and melodramatically, risks censorious responses. *Age of Saturn* incurred a form of censorship that was experienced as an uncanny pressure that overwhelmed and incorporated those involved. The affective productions of the history of Eastern Bengal by the artist and by the state induce parallel forms of vertigo, as truthful untruths not only cast doubt on established modes of knowing the past but also intervene in the ways in which those historical events may be sensed in the present. It is not only indicative of Omar's own attempt to make sense of his place within the history of Bengal, guided by interlocutors such as Dhali/Zaman, but also of his understanding of an individual's relationship to time and the past in general.

Vertigo and Momentum

I am frequently overcome by a sense of vertigo when trying to think about Omar's work. By the winter of 2018, Omar was an artist resident at the Rijksakademie van Beeldende Kunsten in Amsterdam. I visited him in his studio and he showed me new works, as well as the remnants of his latest exhibition. We talked for what felt like hours. I watched parts of his new installation film *Augustijn* (2018) in which Omar follows a young Muslim convert in his small hometown in Flanders. I was mesmerized by a scene in which the protagonist voices the call to prayer. "Did you know he was going to do that," I ask naively, captured by the familiar documentary style. "I can't possibly comment," Omar grins. A little later in the conversation, when talking about *Age of Saturn*, Omar mentions the correspondence between Dr. Zaman and his wife. I tell Omar about some work on fan mail I'd been doing around the same time and ask him how he managed to get hold of these letters. He looks at me, possibly perplexed. I feel the ground shift under me. There is no Dr. Zaman, why am I asking these questions *as if* there were? As we know from Gell (1999), art works are "the objectification of complex intentionalities" (212) and "one responds to an artwork as a co-present being, an embodied thought" (199). The art work functions like "a trap or snare that impedes passage" (213) as it makes a viewer ponder or marvel. I was quite certainly ensnared by Omar's complex works of art, in which the question of truthfulness, history, and reconstruction are mobilized in such a way that I wavered unintentionally between belief and disbelief.

I recognized this uncertain dislocation in Omar too when we spoke on another occasion about the reasons *Age of Saturn* was closed down. Running through the possible scenarios and counterfactuals, he too seems drifting in an account that may or may not have much reality to it, even if it feels truthful and is viscerally real. Omar cannot account for what happened to the show and to "Omar," his double who has been swept up in its afterlife. Omar/Omar too is ensnared, interpellated, and propelled by *Age of Saturn*. Sometimes I wonder whether Omar willed the censorship upon himself rather than it having emerged from the outside. Did he purposefully provoke his collaborators, the gallery, baiting the prominent art world figures who had gathered in Bangladesh in February 2016 for the Dhaka Art Summit? Or did the nerves about this playful but serious approach to hugely significant others, delving with them into collective and personal pasts, rattle him and all those around them once the show came together? These unsteady grounds of uncertainty and disbelief arise from the engagement with historical enquiry, with the face of the "other," with the state. The effects of all these unseen forces are made palpable in the unsettling experience of censorship.

The force exerted on the exhibition, curator, and on the artist, did not dissipate in the moment of the show's collapse. Instead, it energized it, animated the narrative and its characters into a new movement, illustrating the well-documented productivity of censorship (Kuhn 1988). In the act of censorship, the project was given new life, animating it beyond the control of any of its protagonists. Once in Amsterdam, Omar continued his engagement with Dr. Zaman in three further exhibitions titled *Echo, Saturn – Prologue* (2018), *Echo, Saturn* (2019), and *Echo, Saturn – The Courts* (2021). These exhibitions and other artefacts that are part of the *Saturn* universe have continued the unfolding of Dr. Zaman's story with further facts and fictions that delve into the history of Bengal. Omar himself appears entirely interpellated by Dr. Zaman, Dr. Zaman's presence now taking control of Omar's work. As Omar said to me, "I often felt very much and I still feel with Saturn now, that I'm led by the movement of this story." He appears unable to shake Dr. Zaman's grip on his imagination. What was repressed returns as an echo, continuing to shape Omar's artistic practice. Dr. Zaman even pulls two reviewers for the Dutch newspaper *De Volkskrant* into his orbit, as they mistake Dr. Zaman for Omar in their review of *Echo, Saturn* (Bem and Van Leeuwen 2019). The continued elaboration of *Saturn*'s universe is propelled by the weights put on it in the extraordinary pressure cooker of Bangladesh's conflicted and high-pitched relationship with its own history and the way in which the various repressions in the original exhibition have returned and motivate Omar. The generative potential of mimesis creates effects that continue to appear as uncanny encounters with the limits of historical enquiry.

The Narrator

Any attempt at recounting a story of censorship and repression inevitably becomes entangled with those repressions. Untangling is impossible. In an essay for the journal *Wissen Der Künsten* published in the winter of 2019, Omar presents a presumably fictional email exchange with a colleague, in which he writes about his experience of the censorship of his show in Dhaka. Not only does he identify three layers of censure (from the state, from the institution, from the artist collaborators) that led the show to close, but he also presents an intricate drawing (figure 16.2) that appears to map the central ideas behind the show (O. Chowdhury 2019). At its heart is the artist himself, his identity fractured. Around him are the Rings of Saturn, each a layer that allows this identity to be reconstituted and recounted, in a revisionist history of the self and its relationship to place and time. As Omar noted in an erstwhile version of his webpages "I'm an immigrant from historical Bengal – a vanished, decolonized place. Disoriented by this geographic and temporal rupture I make meta-fictional environments that house tightly-coupled fields of objects, actions and representations … These layered and elusive installations are attempts to travel through time and into the lives of others – into what I feel was taken from me"

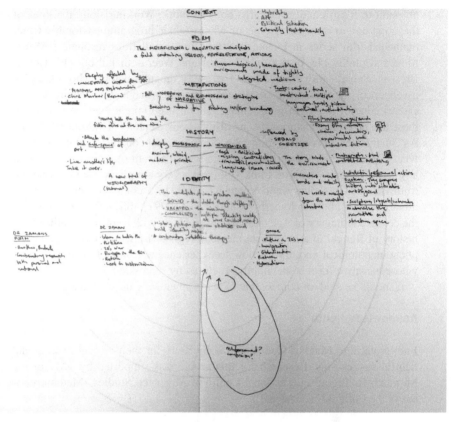

Figure 16.2. Omar Adnan Chowdhury. Diagram. Pen on paper. 2019. Image courtesy of Omar Adnan Chowdhury.

(O. Chowdhury 2018). As in Sebald's work, the debris of the past provides a means of immersing and steadying yourself within the flow of time while never conjuring a cohesive account of the past or your place within it. The diagram cannot undo the disorienting grip of historical vertigo that besets any account of the fate of *Age of Saturn* or the histories of Bangladesh it investigates.

The body of work that falls within the *Saturn* universe is playful and unsettling. But it is nothing if not deeply earnest at the same time, its central themes so profoundly pointing to the violence and dislocations of the twentieth-century history of Bengal that it cannot be simply understood to be a prank, playing with a bewildered audience asked to drop its lazy disinterest and passive complicity. The diagram, the learned interlocutors, the high-definition imagery, all point to a profoundly formalist body of work. Working along the lines of the great auteur-directors (some of whom Omar programmed for his Cinematheque film series in Dhaka in 2015), his installations resonate with the films and philosophy of not only Marker and Weerasethakul but also Robert Bresson, Satyajit Ray, Mani Kaul. The use of amateur actors, who often play a version of themselves, in sparse and sometimes magical environments, the critical edge of the avant-garde image, all suffuse Omar's work. It is through these that he crafts "histories that no history book can tell" (Trouillot 1995, 71). As Omar states, "I couldn't think of a more incorrect conclusion to make about what a cinema does than to assume it tells us the truth or records the truth in any way. If that's what you think you have a very simplistic idea of what the truth is" (O. Chowdhury and Vinen n.d., 44). In a context where history is mostly spoken about in hyperbole, Taussig's (1999) public secret exemplified, the censored imagery of *Age of Saturn* presents us with truthful untruths of the history of Bengal in a formalist cinematic register by which Omar presents a phenomenological enquiry on how to experience and inhabit historical time whose narrative form is inevitably structured by repression.

It should be said, of course, that Omar is an entirely unreliable narrator.

Acknowledgments

I am grateful to Magnus Course and Toby Kelly for their critical reading and helpful suggestions. Research for this article was supported by TM7 of the Merian – R. Tagore International Centre of Advanced Studies "Metamorphoses of the Political" (ICAS:MP).

PART FOUR

Therapies, Individual and Collective

17 Free Speech, without Listening? Liberalism and the Problem of Reception

MICHAEL LEMPERT

"Free speech" is guilty of misdirection. It would have us focus on expression while ignoring the simultaneous and complementary role of *listening*. Recent public-sphere debates over free speech, for instance, not only challenge the commonplace of deliberative democracy that it is good to talk to people you disagree with; they also ask whether the right to speech can be revoked – by boycott, deplatforming, or firing – when an individual is said to cause harm or jeopardize safety. Online and off, and across the political spectrum, people ask whether "cancelling" individuals curtails free speech and is bad for liberalism or whether such selective disengagement upholds liberal-democratic values by stopping harmful speech and amplifying marginalized voices. These debates overwhelmingly focus on expression even as they rely on unexamined semiotic ideologies of reception – including when, how, and why to *listen*. They are as much about opening up new forms of reception or protecting people from things they may hear or read as they are about curtailing or promoting speech, and it is to the other side of free speech that I want to turn.

It is hardly a surprise to find the spotlight trained on talk and other modalities of "expression." Apart from the specific liberal-democratic legacy of investment in speech and "voice," there are any number of semiotic ideologies – often criticized but still with us – that privilege speaking and imagine discourse as the linear, unidirectional transfer of information from "sender" to "receiver"; listening tends to be ignored as mere passive reception. Scholarship on social interaction has often stressed that listening is not the mere absence of talk. Listening makes conversation possible, not just through the sheer force of receptive co-presence but also through the way interactants sustain and alter the flow of talk through embodied and verbal displays of attention and reaction. A more "distributed," "ecological" conception of discursive interaction can remind us to attend to the centrality of listening practices in liberal democratic projects, including those concerned with freedom of expression.[1]

---

1 On ecological and distributed perspectives on conversation, see, for example, Goodwin (2018), Erickson (2004, 2010), and Bavelas, Coates, and Johnson (2000).

To sharpen our sense of why an anthropology of freedom of speech should overcome its speaker-centricity and open itself to receptivity in all its ethnographic and historical complexity, this essay juxtaposes a few scenes wherein receptivity stands out as problematic, either because it is hard to cultivate or because it isn't entirely clear what *kind* of receptivity is needed.

The first scene, drawn from the immediate postwar period in the United States, centres on Kurt Lewin, an influential researcher of group dynamics who was anxious to shore up democracy from below, as it were – in daily face-to-face interactions. Lewin and his students studied what made some interactions democratic and others authoritarian and applied their science to leadership training. In an effort to prefigure democratic lifeways within their own scientific practice, the Lewinians also worked on themselves. They felt obliged to break down the hierarchical relationship of observer to observed in favour of multidirectional "feedback" – a kind of receptivity that was much broader than just face-to-face listening.

The second scene jumps ahead about two decades to the storied discursive institution of second-wave feminism, the "consciousness-raising" (CR) group, which experimented with prefigurative disciplines of audition – especially interactional techniques of listening – aimed at promoting what was sometimes called "internal democracy." In the early years of CR, contestation erupted in radical feminist circles over how best to listen to other women, contestation that centred on what I term "deliberative" versus "validational" registers of listening. Was it okay to interrogate a woman's testimony in collective pursuit of the truth? Or was such questioning androcentric and in need of replacement with a feminized – and psychotherapeutically inflected – register that unconditionally validated what women said?

Similar contestation over deliberative and validational listening recurs in my third scene, which returns us to the present, focusing especially on questions of (il)liberal listening on campuses post-2016. When you listen across difference, as is often urged, are deliberative responses always appropriate, or only under some circumstances? More deeply, deliberative democracy sees dialogue as an unconditional good, but must you feel obligated to listen to those with whom you may strongly disagree – or, worse, to those whose speech you find harmful? On campuses "active bystander workshops" address an equally pressing question: How should students, faculty, and staff respond when they hear or overhear troubling talk, such as verbal microaggressions? I show how these questions related to receptivity are central to liberal contestation over "free speech," "harmful speech," and "cancellation," all of which focus on expression but rely on ideologies of reception.

There are certain historical links among the scenes constructed here, but rather than stitch them together, my purpose is largely comparative. I use these three moments to suggest the enduring if variable place of listening in liberal-democratic projects while inviting us to appreciate – ethnographically, semiotically, and historically – how listening is configured, enacted, construed, and contested as part of a broader politicization of interaction in socio-historical life.

Liberal Listening

As trope and as topic of study, listening has of course been reclaimed many times before. Feminist methodologies for recovering women's "voices" have at times embraced the trope of listening, for instance. Sound studies has explored how the material affordances of media technologies shape listening practices. Sensorial ethnographers and ethnomusicologists in anthropology have stressed the importance of the sonic and its receptivity. Steven Feld (2015) coined "acoustemology" to capture the way knowing the world can occur centrally through listening. Some linguistic anthropologists have written about the cultural pragmatics of listening and silence, while others have traced the discursive formation of a listening subject.[2] Quite a few have studied the way democratic ideals – and fears of authoritarianism – have inflected ideas about what "democratic communication" is and should be, as with postwar Frankfurt School anxieties about the corrosive power of mass media on susceptible audiences or utopian multimedia experiments from the same period that media historian Fred Turner (2013) has called "democratic surrounds." The Habermasian legacy has argued that intersubjective communication and argument undergirds liberal-democratic life, yet his work, like most, remains uncritically speaker-centric.[3] A handful of political theorists of deliberative democracy – many directly inspired by Habermas – have recently recognized the need to take listening seriously, arguing, for instance, that it isn't enough for informal and formal deliberation to be procedurally "inclusive" of different sociological categories of people, as many insist, because you can always ignore what people say. As Mary Scudder (2020, 16) suggests, listening is how we give – and show – "fair consideration" to others' expressive inputs, for it is "*in* listening [that] we constitute the deliberative act."[4]

---

2 In sound studies, see, for example, Helmreich (2010, 2016); on receptivity and technologically mediated hearing and listening, see Larkin (2014), Semel (2022), Hsieh (2019, 2021); on listening and silence, see Bauman (1983), E.T. Hall (1969), Maltz (1985); for ethnographies of listening, see Bendix (2000), Erlmann (2004); for a genealogy of a "listening subject," see Inoue (2003, 2006); on listening as ethical subject formation, see Hirschkind (2008); and for conversational-analytic studies of listening in interaction, see Gardner (2001).

3 Of the many critical engagements with Habermas, it is telling that few questioned his speaker-centricity; for an important early exception, see Graham (1993). While Habermas (1974, 1984, 1995) reimagined critical rationality as a product of discursive interaction, his vision of argument was ultimately that of monadic speakers who symmetrically alternate turns of *talk*.

4 See also Bickford (1996) and Dobson (2014). For a review of listening in deliberative theory, see Morrell (2018).

As this form of political theory is self-consciously normative, it does not muck about in context. It does not ask what listening – and receptivity more broadly – is taken to be in a given case, and how, why, and with what effects people practise it or avoid it. These are rarely settled issues for actors themselves, of course. In an ethnographic study of a popular Finnish radio show, Harri Englund (2018) explores how the hosts agonized over questions about how best to tell the truth while respecting a diversity of opinions. Through careful interaction with guests and through equally careful editing, the hosts tried to fashion a multivocal dialogue of viewpoints. They thought a lot about reception. One radio host, for instance, reported being "haunted by personal qualms about failing to sustain dialogue on air when interlocutors' views sounded outrageous to him" (102), for he came to realize that "a need to be heard, rather than bigotry, drove many of the contributions" (106). Stressing this "need to be heard," Englund reminds us of the need to consider the entwinement of listening and speech in liberal practice.

In "Can the Subaltern Listen?," James Slotta (2017) draws listening fully out from the shadows. He unsettles universalizing liberal political assumptions by stressing how listening rather than speech is treated as a vehicle for self-determination among people from the Yopno Valley in Papua New Guinea. Subaltern studies, Slotta recounts, embraced the trope of voice in thinking about what is involved in restoring agency to marginalized groups; from this perspective, the converse – listening – appears as if it were always only "an act of deference or even submission." Slotta's ethnographic counter-example details the way Yopno draw on local-cultural sensibilities about the power of "listening well" to control their future.

Even in cases where listening is not explicitly thematized, we can usually find tacit but important assumptions about listening that sometimes start to come into focus for actors themselves. After the Unite the Right white supremacist rally in Charlottesville, Virginia, in 2017, local linguistic anthropologists Lise Dobrin and Eve Danziger (2017, 372) noticed this happen in public-sphere debates about the distinction between hate speech and free speech, observing that people "seem ready to move beyond the speaker-centric view of speech as something individuals produce, and think about the wider setting that makes communication – including reception and interpretation – possible within a free society." They continue: "Note that the hearer has an important role to play in all of this." Of late, the issues of reception and "listening" have indeed surfaced in public contestation over free speech, reminding anthropologists of its relevance.

Let me stress immediately that by foregrounding listening, my intent is not to reinstate the sender-receiver model by arguing that one side has received short shrift. Instead, I seek both to decentre "speaking" and to call attention to the way that "listening" – while itself a reductive, ideological abstraction – can be objectified by actors, troped upon, even technologized. We must remember that the seemingly elementary dyadic relation of "speaking" and "listening" is an ideological construct, a selective and value-laden configuration and elaboration of communicative acts and associated participant roles.[5] We must recognize further that most investments in listening involve a broader ideological investment in *interaction* itself as an epistemic and technical object. To know listening is to know something about interaction in the round. Indeed, we will see below how an interest in listening rests on a reflexive orientation towards social interaction as both ideological site and object to know, and control.[6]

Let me also stress the need to leave "listening" capacious, in order to invite careful ethnographic attention. Erving Goffman famously demonstrated that "speaker" and "hearer" are analytically coarse terms that need to be resolved into finer participant roles,[7] but we can't just drop "listening," to the extent that it has been abstracted out and imbued with significance. Like "voice" or "dialogue," "listening" is often a highly resonant trope and needs to be appreciated as such, coarseness and all.

Nor can we assume in advance what listening even involves. In many cases, listening may well prototypically mean *aural* receptivity to the spoken word. Receptivity quickly touches on much more than hearable speech, especially as interactants draw inferences about listeners based on *how* they listen and respond to their speech (through so-called backchannel vocalizations like *mm* and embodied gestures like head nods that are produced while someone else talks) and what they say next. That is, interactants often treat listener reactions and responses as indexicals that reveal the degree or quality of "involvement" or intersubjective "understanding."[8] Still, invocations of listening often have less to do with observable communicative behaviour and more with, say, the moral condition of the soul or heart or mind that makes a person "receptive" to a message or person or truth. For facilitators of conversations about race, for instance, we sometimes hear appeals to "deep listening," which is less about techniques and more about an internal state of readiness and openness that

---

5 For an introduction to participant roles, see Sidnell (2014).

6 As Gal and Irvine (2019, 168) suggest, ideological sites should not be defined by their literal socio-spatial location and extension but rather by the way they involve and invite *joint attention* by social actors.

7 Cf. Webb Keane's (2016) stress on the interactional dimensions of ethical life. In revisiting the notion of "dignity" (110, et passim chap. 3), for instance, he emphasizes how this moral concept gets actualized in the communication of deference and demeanor (see also Goffman 1974, 1981). As Charles Goodwin notes (2006, 20–1), Goffman (1981) made finer distinctions among speaking-based participant roles (namely, between author, animator, and principal) than he did for listening.

8 Compare with Goffman's (1957) foundational essay on "involvement" obligations in social interaction.

then makes interactional receptivity possible. As we will see next, quite often listening is more than an interactional practice and instead part of a highly distributed project of cultivating receptivity in domains, modalities, and media other than exclusively the face-to-face.

Freedom as Feedback: Postwar Listening for Leaders circa 1947

In the years after the Second World War, "small group" analysis, as many called it, became a social science boom industry in the United States. Often laboratory-based, technophilic, and technocratic, this new interdisciplinary science studied social interaction in groups that ranged in size from two to about twenty individuals. Disarming by name, small group science had big ambitions. It could analyze any form of interaction, from chess matches to marital disputes, in contexts ranging from cockpits to classrooms. A theme issue of the *American Sociological Review* from 1954 gathered more than a dozen papers that together made "the case for the study of small groups" (Strodtbeck 1954). How *practical* this new form of study was, editor Fred Strodtbeck crowed. Whatever small group analysis meant – and it certainly wasn't unified in theory or method – it was clear that it would be good for social engineering and hence good for postwar social science patronage.

More than a few held that knowledge about group dynamics could help stem authoritarianism and grow democracy, and nobody drew out this potential more than the German Jewish émigré and social psychologist Kurt Lewin (1890–1947). Lewin became a major figure in small group science and founded the interdisciplinary Research Center for Group Dynamics at the Massachusetts Institute of Technology in 1945. After his sudden death in 1947, the centre relocated to the University of Michigan.

So confident was Lewin (1945, 131) about the relevance of his science that he alarmed some of his peers with what he came to call "action research." "The main methodological interest," Lewin wrote of his centre at the Massachusetts Institute of Technology, would be "the development of group experiments and particularly change experiments." In labour relations, Lewin's group engaged in industrial consulting at a factory in rural Virginia.[9] It tried to heal race relations and curb anti-Semitism. Above all it promoted democracy in interpersonal life.

In his far-reaching essay on Lewin, Matthew Hull (2010) rightly conceives of Lewin's science as what he calls a democratic technology of speech. As

---

9 See Chris Kelty's (2019) thoughtful discussion of Lewin's application of his science to industry.

speech was only half the story, let us stretch this and term it a democratic technology of interaction. Following Latour, technology doesn't name a thing with definable properties but rather an orientation and aspiration that, Hull explains, "guides efforts to demarcate and isolate some sociomaterial process or entity from its myriad connections, especially with humans, in order to make it transferable and usable across different social boundaries" (259). Technologizing a thing means that you try to cut away figure from ground and hold the two apart to such an extent that you can imagine a discrete technology – tool, machine, method, etc. – that humans instrumentally "use," that can be "applied," that can be felt to have "effects" on an independent existing world. Hull outlines Lewin's science of interpersonal democracy in relation to wartime and postwar America and then traces how it was translated and ported over to South Asia in the decolonizing years after the Second World War, such as through Ford Foundation–funded efforts to bring "democratic group life" to Delhi.

Here, let us return to a few highlights that illustrate how this technology was first developed. Lewin's first step towards a democratic technology of interaction began in the 1930s. While a professor at the Iowa Child Welfare Research Station, he worked closely with students Ronald Lippitt and later Ralph White to develop experiments that led to publications in 1938 and 1939 that studied clubs of ten-year-old boys and tested the effects of three different leadership styles: "authoritarian," "democratic," and "laissez-faire" (Lewin, Lippitt, and White 1939).[10]

Lewin (1939, 273) wrote, "On the whole, everything was kept constant except the group atmosphere," to see what difference this made. The democratic leader gave options, for instance, and made "all policies a matter of group discussion." The research burned with relevance. Which group climate incited "rebellion against authority, persecution of a scapegoat, apathetic submissiveness to authoritarian domination, or attack upon an outgroup?" (271). And was there something quietly, dangerously seductive about authoritarianism? It was impossible to miss the allegory of the essays, as one was published some six months before Kristallnacht, another four months before Germany invaded Poland.[11] More than an urgent morality play, more than a refutation of Nazism and Fascism, Lewin offered a way to intervene. The Lewinians concretized democracy, materializing this ideological formation in interaction. They made it palpably small, which opened the possibility not just for knowledge and prediction but also, crucially, for control.

---

10 See also F. Turner (2013, chap. 2); Bradford (1974); R. White and Lippitt (1960).
11 In 1944, Lewin learned that his mother had perished in a concentration camp in Poland (Marrow 1969, 141).

A Democratic Laboratory in the Wild

If you knew what democratic life looked like face-to-face, what steps could you take to reproduce it? Of course you could share knowledge in the usual ways. At the Chicago Rotary Club, for instance, the Lewinians discussed their findings with film clips, charts, and graphs (White and Lippitt 1960, 10). A far more ambitious solution came in the form of a large annual training "laboratory" for group interaction that Lewin's centre began holding in summers at an old private school in Bethel, western Maine, a remote village of some 2,000 located in the foothills of the White Mountains. The lab would recruit leaders from across the nation.

The two-week National Training Laboratory (NTL) on Group Development, as it was called, was held in late June 1947, just months after Lewin passed away. The centre was never shy about the lab's commitments. One topic was "understanding and working in terms of an explicit democratic philosophy and ethics of change" (NTL 1947, 69). The lab ended on 4 July, Independence Day.

The NTL's 1947 report outlined the mission. The first goal was "to provide research scientists with an opportunity to communicate scientific knowledge of group dynamics to key education and action leaders." The second was "to provide an opportunity for observing, experiencing, and practising basic elements of the democratic group process which are relevant to educational and action leadership." They invited some 133 delegates who hailed from twenty-nine states and four foreign countries (6).[12]

The Bethel lab built on prior work, including Lewin's own experimentation with group "climate." Years earlier, Lewin had democratized his own team. In Berlin he had tried to cultivate a non-hierarchical climate for intellectual discussion. At the heart of this experiment was a discursive ritual. Called *die Quasselstrippe* – "chatter box" or more literally "chatter line" (the analogy here may be to the way people gab on the telephone) – the practice was meant to be an incubator of creativity and open-mindedness (see Marrow 1969). He had launched this in response to what he saw as stifling apprenticeships in which students studied at the feet of analysts like Freud and Adler. This took place in a café located across the street from none other than the Berlin Psychological Institute (Ash 1992, 201). When Lewin relocated to Iowa, he recreated the ritual on the top floor of a restaurant to which his students would bring lunches (Marrow 1969, 88).

---

12 While the Lewinian's early focus on the boy's clubs suggested a familiar gendering of the political as a "male"-coded domain, women were invited to the first national training laboratory, and these participants were not all wives of male invitees. I thank Matthew Hull for alerting me to the gendering of the political in Lewin's science.

Much as they had learned to engineer their own climate and modify experimentally the climate of the boy's club, so at Bethel the Lewinians knew they needed to construct an environment conducive to democracy, and this required work.

It helped that Bethel was, in ritual fashion, a place set apart. This "intensive practice laboratory in human relations skills, isolated from the pressures of daily work and living, may prove to be the most effective means of learning how to bring behaviour into line with the difficult demands of democratic ideology" (NTL 1947, iii). This freedom from everyday pressures – including the stresses of a hierarchical workplace at home – recalls Jamie Cohen-Cole's argument about the importance of leisure for cultivating liberal-democratic scholarly lifeways (see Cohen-Cole 2009, 2014). Bethel had its recreational activities like square dancing that "gave all delegates a chance to swing partners and *do-se-do*" (NTL 1947, 31). It had its "communal dining hall" (30) and centralized living quarters that allowed participants to "live together" (4–5). "Informal singing" and music would erupt spontaneously before and after meals.

The school's built environment did need tweaks. It had fixed desks. The organizers unbolted and removed them. In their place they found "beautiful oval oak tables that could seat about 20 persons" (Bradford 1974, 44). Wherever possible, seats would be arranged in circles, and everyone would cultivate mindfulness about the inclusive power of the pronoun *we*. Visitors were discouraged from dropping by unannounced, "for much of the value of the experience would depend on the gradual development of intimate group relations and a very cohesive group structure" (Bradford 1974, 16).

The daily log kept for one training session monitored this cohesion. "Group level of morale in Workshop lower today," the journal read just a few days in, though there was a glimmer of "good progress in strengthening group feeling." There were ups and downs, frustrations, even power struggles. By Thursday of the retreat, "sometimes we had attempts at pretty autocratic or formalized leadership," but they "did not get away with it." By Friday of the retreat, "two members had previously seemed to be vying for leadership role" and "today they seemed united against two members: less 'we-ness.'" One day the conveners felt the sting of criticism: "Got rather frank and personal in our evaluation today. We took it, but some of us felt a little sore." A week later, the meetings hit bottom, scoring their lowest rating, "yet by [getting] out a lot of aggression against each other and the leadership," this "cleared the way to move ahead." Indeed, by 3 July, the "final evaluation session was almost a spiritual experience" (Bradford 1974, 139–42).

Spiritual was only half the story. Bethel was a teetotaling town, and that wouldn't be conducive to "we-feeling." Martha Bradford – the wife of Leland Bradford, the director of adult education from Washington, DC, who was both a Bethel trainer and a lab co-organizer – managed the lab's small library. She also did the "Berlin Run" – to Berlin, New Hampshire – twice a week to ferry booze across state lines. While the locals "usually retired around 9 pm, our group often began drinking and singing into the early morning" – which predictably caused some strain with the community, and when "one participant drove his car around the Academy's racing track, leaving deep ruts in the track and grass," the conveners were sure they'd never be invited back (Bradford 1974, 48).

How would you know if this lab had worked, beyond notes in a journal and ruts in the grass? The conveners had welcomed the delegates with an "informal tea" and supper, and not long after subjected them to "pre-measurements" so you could later see if they changed. For practical reasons, only a handful underwent the full battery of testing, which they did along with the faculty (Bradford 1974, 45). But all were assessed before and after by means of a questionnaire and interview.

The Ideology Questionnaire netted the demographics. Then came seventy-four statements to be evaluated with a five-point scale. Many questions concerned the group discussion itself. Do "group members have a responsibility to draw into the group discussion those who are not participating?" Is it "all right to interrupt other people, if one has an important idea to put across?" (Bradford 1974, 107–11).

The Ideology Interview got personal. "Do you have, or have you ever had, servants working in your home?" "How do you think servants ought to be treated?" "What traits should a good wife have?" "Do you think that character traits are fixed or changeable?" And so on. And, to the crux of the matter: "How should a leader behave in a democratic group?" And a hypothetical that left nothing to chance: "Suppose there was a dictator who would use the techniques of changing people without regard for their welfare ... how would you feel about that?"

As the Bethel lab drew to a close, there was the "Final Ideology and 'Change' Interview," which probed the delegates' sense of change. Tellingly, the interviews also solicited feedback on the lab itself and on its trainers. For instance: What were [the trainer's] "assets as a leader" compared to others? "What do you consider his liabilities?" "What sort of relationship would you say exists between you and him?" (Bradford 1974, 105).

The Bethel lab didn't rely only on surveys and interviews. In tow were interaction scientists, led by Harvard's Robert Freed Bales, who would observe in real time how the delegates behaved. Observers were instructed to code the "smallest discriminable act" (NTL 1947, 127). They would remain alert to signs of democratic and anti-democratic tendencies. Bales was using a list of twenty distinct communicative actions to score. One was "autocratic manner," which included "giving bald commands or directions, implying no autonomy for the other" as well as "denying permission, blocking, restricting, prohibiting, disrupting activity" (127).

Yet here again, it wasn't only the expert observers who got to say what had happened. Immediately after each discussion, participants filled out forms that asked how they felt things went. Their "post-meeting reactions" were assessed and plotted over time, so that you could see the changing "temperature" of the group as it warmed, cooled, and warmed again (NTL 1947, 138). At Bethel, observation and assessment were to come from all directions as ongoing, multi-directional "feedback." It was feedback that nurtured self-awareness and sensitivity, which were capacities deemed critical to democratic intersubjectivity.

After Bethel was over, the faculty leaders subjected each other to feedback by drawing on what the delegates had said. They reviewed evaluations, which were sometimes indicting: "very self-assertive," "interrupts frequently," "argues often with one individual ignoring the effects on the group" (Bradford 1974, 160). They debated whether the assessments were fair, and each trainer got a chance to say how they thought things went. And all of this feedback-on-feedback was audio recorded and transcribed. Perhaps if they had time in the future, they would return to this transcript and go meta yet again to see what these discussions revealed about their interaction styles and group dynamics. Endless reflection, feedback forever.

Democratic life wasn't easy. It wasn't simply a matter of doing some communicative actions and not others, because, as an interactional culture, democracy needed constant receptivity. Accountability to others, an openness to feedback, a keen sensitivity to interpersonal action-and-reaction and the way that contributed to group climate – all this constituted the communicative habits of a self-regulating democratic culture.[13] Like a servomechanism, like feedback in its cybernetic sense, one had to be responsive to others. Cultivating receptivity was critical to the Lewinian democratic technology of interaction.

Epistemologically, ethically, and politically, the Lewinians felt they *owed* receptivity to the leaders they sought to know, and change. This required a measure of intellectual vulnerability. They should be willing to field questions and receive comments and candid evaluations, and such "feedback" should in principle be able to come from anywhere and anyone. The liberal receptivity they aspired to cultivate was not primarily about "listening" in a limited, interactional sense; that is, listening as an act and as a participant role to be enacted in face-to-face interaction. It was more varied, distributed, and multimodal.

---

13 The Lewinian training labs have been cited as a source for the widespread corporate practice of "360-degree feedback" in human resource management (Slater and Coyle 2014). As Kelty (2019, 96) writes, when the Lewinian's democratic technology was trained on the workplace – rather than on cultivating leaders – you could see this effort as a form of "governing through freedom" (to use Peter Miller and Nikolas Rose's [2008] expression, specifically), as "the crafting of a new kind of subject" who was "exhorted to be democratic, independent, autonomous, and eventually entrepreneurial."

Receptivity could indeed mean giving subjects a chance to talk and making sure that one sat and listened well. But it could also mean having them fill out paper surveys and evaluations. At its deepest, receptivity also required an internal willingness to *learn* empirically about oneself, about how one "actually" affected other people interpersonally and, when necessary, a willingness to try new things, to adjust – to improve – one's behaviour. As a feat of interpersonal engineering, it was as if the Lewinians had been trying to correct the imbalanced ratio of "expression" to "reception" so that humans would be better able to mutually know and adjust to one another. At the very least, the very act of *trying* to be more receptive conveyed that you were willing to treat them like a colleague, which would thus prefigure a future of more open, trusting, and communicatively intimate social relations.

Feedback should not be accepted uncritically, however. It was still just data. You had to think and assess and weigh it all. If possible, you should also triangulate, collecting data from different vantage points so that you might converge on the truth. The climate that these social engineers of group dynamics sought to construct was not unlike Lewin's old chatter line in that it facilitated not just free-flowing talk and information but potentially argumentative communication. The receptivity implicit in the Lewinian democratic technology of interaction was, in a word, *deliberative*. It did not require that you unconditionally support others and suspend your forensic concern for the truth.

Second-Wave Listening for Women

As we leap forward now two decades and encounter a very different manifestation of liberal receptivity, the "consciousness-raising" (CR) sessions developed by feminists in the late 1960s and early 1970s, two important differences from the Lewinians stand out. With CR, receptivity is prototypically interactional. It is about "listening" face-to-face. Second and more importantly, it was at first a live question as to what *kind* of receptivity was needed. For many feminists the "deliberative" kind felt troubling, even androcentric. Rather than listen with an ear towards deliberating critically about truth and falsity, many sought what we might term a *validational* register of listening that owed much to a psychotherapeutic sensibility and that has arguably continued to inform contestation over (il)liberal listening today.

As an interaction ritual, the carefully orchestrated "small group," as consciousness-raising was often called early on, came to feature ostentatiously inclusive methods that were central to its prefigurative design.[14] As some of the

---

14 For a semiotic treatment of what I have been loosely calling, after Boggs (1977), the "prefigurative" dimensions of interaction ritual, see especially Stasch (2011a) and Silverstein (2004). On the historical instability and plasticity of prefigurative rituals, see Lempert (2012).

guides to CR put it, the group should be a "safe" space, a "free" space, in which each woman got a chance to speak and nobody would be judged. With its special interpersonal methods, the feminist small group foregrounded interaction itself as a domain of social life, making interaction's normative expectations stick out so that they could be critiqued and ritually transformed. Interdiscursively, the feminist small group contrasted poetically with "ordinary" (androcentric and patriarchal) conversation in which women routinely experienced subordination and marginalization.

CR groups met weekly, not in labs but in members' homes, and ranged from as few as five or six to as many as twelve or fifteen (see, for example, Carden 1974, 34; O'Connor 1969, 5, 15; 1970; Jenkins and Kramer 1978, 70). With no men present, women would be free to explore issues each week.[15] "Why did you marry the man you did? How do you feel men see you? How do you feel about housework? ... What did you want to do in life?" (Sarachild 1970). By sharing feelings and personal experiences, members would learn about their collective condition.

While ferreting out the indexical meaning of feelings, much as you might do in therapy, this anti-therapy therapy reversed the directionality of causation. Feelings supplied insight into the political, pointing not inward towards ingrained mental states but outward towards patriarchal relations. "Our Politics Begins with Our Feelings" is the title of a statement presented by Lynn O'Connor at a 1970 San Francisco meeting of a Women's Liberation group known as the Redstockings West. "Our first task is to develop our capacity to be aware of our feelings and to pinpoint the events or interactions to which they are valid responses" (O'Connor 1970, 1). When you followed the indexical route from feelings to sources, these sources were not revealed to be individual pathologies like "masochism, self-hate, or inferiority" but rather "a response to some behavior that was in fact designed to humiliate, hurt and oppress us" (1).

CR groups were largely white and tended to draw women of class and educational privilege, which meant that the intense homosocial intimacy that CR members could experience was not simply a performative effect of talking together. Their sense of connection and shared plight was aided by "real" (offstage) similarity – similarity based not on being members of a monolithic, universally oppressed class called "women" but on being a raced and classed subgroup whose commonalities were created in part by postwar suburbanization and redlining, which ensured that these women looked alike and shared a lot well before they set foot in each other's homes. CR groups could also shut their doors whenever they felt they got too big, which, in practice, could be

---

15 On CR groups that did experiment at including men, see Nachescu (2006).

used for gate-keeping.[16] Their contradictions and exclusions notwithstanding, by 1970, feminist small groups populated major cities across the United States and rapidly became the celebrated interactional technology of second-wave feminism, the "cornerstone" of the whole movement (Dreifus 1973, 5).

Feminists claimed CR as their own while acknowledging that its influences were many. Some credited the Maoist practice of "speaking bitterness" as a source of inspiration, and despite early disavowals by feminists promoting CR, the practice drew deeply on a psychotherapeutic sensibility. Less acknowledged at the time was CR's indebtedness to the New Left circles of the early 1960s, with their prefigurative desire to democratize participation – including how they interacted at their own meetings.[17]

CR's "origins" were discussed and disputed at the time it was popularized, and the practice itself was a moving target. CR underwent changes as it spread. It started in radical feminist circles, yet after 1970, liberal organizations like the National Organization for Women (NOW) started to use CR largely as a means of recruitment, and CR often started to look more like a "support group" or a "study group" for women, to the dismay of CR's early architects and promoters.[18] As Anne Enke (2007) stresses, given how decentred the women's movement was, CR was flexible. It could be tailored for local contexts.

As the small group practice spread and evolved, its participation structure experienced ideological elaboration, regimentation, and contestation. Normatively, CR group institutionalization tended to make the practice ever more finely equalitarian. As an early essay about CR noted, the practice experimented with "internal democracy," which involved settling a topic of discussion in advance and ensuring that everyone got a chance to speak. "Some of the rules include no leadership, speak in circles, no one talks a second time until everyone has had her turn, no challenges of the veracity of members' statements, theoretical analysis of a topic only after all have spoken" (Dreifus 1973, 16). In some cases, speaking tokens were distributed, to be cashed in whenever one talked and counted at the end of the session to see who had talked more, and less. Just as one must speak from personal experience, one should ask only clarifying questions of others, thus never "challenging another woman's experience"

---

16 See Nachescu (2006) who discusses the racial and class-based exclusions of CR while recovering less visible Black and Chicana CR groups. See also Thomlinson (2012). For early reflections on CR's exclusions, see Black feminist Celestine Ware (1970, 35, 108–18), also discussed in Nachescu (2006, 58–62, 143–7).

17 On CR's relation to therapy, see Herman (1995) and Rutherford and Pettit (2015). On CR's roots in the New Left, see Evans (1979, 134–5), Gitlin (1987, 357), and Loss (2011, 292).

18 On CR's movement from radical to liberal circles and its increased resemblance to therapeutic genres, see Rosenthal (1984). Nachescu (2006, 15) suggests that it was white feminists who were more alert to and troubled by the likeness between CR and therapy, because Black feminists, for instance, didn't have the same history of access to therapy.

(Dreifus 1973, 22). Great care was taken to ensure that each member respected a woman's autonomy and her inviolable personal experience, that each listened well and validated others.[19]

Its heterogeneity notwithstanding, CR had crystallized as a "method." Kathie Sarachild [1973] 1978), who had chartered feminist consciousness-raising in late 1968, had contempt for what she saw as such procedural fetishism. For her, giving unconditional support to others was never the point. The aim was to learn from others empirically so that you could generalize and produce knowledge that would then inform and incite political action. Her framing for CR was deliberative. In fact, Sarachild's own small-group facilitation style reportedly could feel "confrontational," as "she did not hesitate to challenge ... testimony." Her remarks reveal contestation over what feminist small-group participation should look like, with some within the movement using the gender binary to distinguish "soft" from "hard" CR.[20]

The soft variety won out. CR became seen as a self-consciously feminized organizational ritual (even as men and others experimented with the genre). It was feminized not simply because of the "absolute dictum" that men be excluded (Dreifus 1973, 21) but especially because of its design. The cultivated inclusiveness, the epistemic personalization, the attentiveness and validation of the feelings of each and every member – all amounted to a prefigurative gender politics. At its most utopian, CR became a feminist counter-institution – the mirror-image opposite of all the competitive, hierarchical, androcentric organizations that demeaned, subordinated, and silenced women. Women would "develop a group process not predicated upon dominance and subordination" (O'Connor 1970, 1; Echols and Willis 1989, 186). As Pamela Allen's (1973, 272) influential essay branded it, CR aspired to be a "free space": "the small group is especially suited to freeing women to affirm their own view of reality and to think independently of male-supremacist values."

(II)liberal Listening for Students, Post 2016

If we return, finally, to the present, we discover tensions reminiscent of the early feminist tension between soft and hard CR, between validational and deliberative listening, respectively. Receptivity here still prototypically means interactional and especially face-to-face listening, yet contestation over receptivity today is far more distributed than this, manifesting itself most notoriously in the interactive virtual environs of social media, but also – in terms of higher-education

---

19 For a notable first-hand case study of CR communication, see Susan Kalčik (1975, 4–6).
20 On soft and hard CR, see Dreifus (1973, 13–14). On Sarachild's confrontational style, see Echols and Willis (1989, 88).

campuses – in numerous sites, from library catalogues (see efforts to remediate "harmful language in library metadata") to campus building names and statues that commemorate people with troubling pasts and that are felt to cause ongoing harm for vulnerable recipients. Even as the sites of liberal receptivity are many and hence far exceed the hearing and overhearing of "speech" in co-present interaction, the face-to-face retains a special importance.

On campuses – and elsewhere – countless in-person community "conversations" and "dialogues" were convened after the 2016 presidential election with the aim of cultivating democratic sensibilities through speaking across differences. At the University of Michigan where I teach, public messaging entreated students to "engage civilly." In the lead up to and aftermath of that divisive election, as our campus was rocked by acts of intimidation and racist flyering, large university posters cast in Michigan's totemic blue and maize made pleas for respectful engagement while the campus scrambled to offer opportunities for students to come together face-to-face as a community. Whatever else such appeals were meant to do, they seemed to cue well-rehearsed ideals of deliberative democracy, where decision-making depends on a willingness to talk and argue and *listen*. This stance usually has an implicit ethical grounding. You should listen not for reasons of etiquette – to avoid being, say, a "conversational bore" (to recall a figure from twentieth-century etiquette manuals, which referred to someone who failed to take turns reciprocally, failed to yield the floor and listen); nor do you listen strategically, out of self-interest, to find fault or plan what point to make next. Instead, you listen because you remain *open* to the possibility that you might change your mind as a result of the very dialogue in which you are engaged. Some call this *deliberative listening*, and I will do the same.[21]

---

21 See especially Morrell (2018). To be clear, by captioning varieties of listening in this chapter, I mean to call attention to their status as historically emerging interactional "registers" of listening. Naming them as distinct has heuristic benefits but should not be taken to mean that such registers exist as sharply defined repertoires akin to well-developed speech registers, such as Received Pronunciation, which have both inventories of features and a high degree of social recognizability *as* registers. Asif Agha's (2007) processual notion of *enregisterment* is critical here, as it allows for various states of formation. Agha also recognizes the multimodality of register, for unlike the sociolinguistic usage of the concept, he does not limit register to speech and writing. While I cannot develop this argument here, register is arguably also useful for the way it highlights a range of practices on which social actors can draw – albeit with different degrees of fluency – as they navigate different pragmatic contexts, since speakers are exposed to and acquire experience with numerous registers during the course of socialization. Compare with "genre," which has also been used to conceptualize distinct forms of listening (e.g., Kapchan 2017, 5–6; Marsilli-Vargas 2014, 2022). See especially Xochitl Marsilli-Vargas's (2014, 2022) work on psychoanalytic listening in Argentina, where she writes of "genres of listening" akin to "speech genres" described in linguistic anthropology and the ethnography of communication. In her book length treatment, she mobilizes the notion of genre to explore a widespread psychoanalytic culture of listening in Buenos Aires.

Yet many now dispute whether deliberative listening is an unmitigated good and instead ask whether public condemnation and selective disengagement – "cancelling," as this has been contentiously captioned – can be a positive refusal to stay silent in the face of injurious communication and a way to redirect attention to and amplify minoritized voices. Liberalism is again cued here, albeit different aspects of it; this, despite the fact that advocates of these views rarely recognize the liberal dimensions of these stances and instead often target capital-L liberalism as a pernicious ideological formation to be transcended.[22] Relevant here is the long liberal legacy of interest in "harm" (notably, Mill's harm principle) and the associated issue of when to curtail individual freedoms, while the paired tropes of "voice" and "amplification" cue the liberal-democratic problem of representation in a multiracial politics of recognition.

Let us hold off on exploring such tensions directly and instead turn sideways and consider other pedagogic and institutional practices on campuses that feature liberal listening. We might compare cancellation with other progressive interventions on campuses such as "active bystander intervention," for instance. This training has its origins in efforts to stem sexual violence. It mobilizes social-psychological literature on passivity to equip future passers-by with strategies that will allow them to overcome this natural if moral weakness and *do* something (without jeopardizing one's own safety). This type of training has been extended to cover not just physical but also verbal harm of many kinds. As a pedagogy, it coaches participants in how to react when they hear or overhear a verbal microaggression, for instance, such as a tacitly racist remark. The point is to cultivate sensitivity towards the harms of speech and behaviour with the hope that this training might translate into reactive and proactive behaviour. You should learn to recognize and anticipate how seemingly mundane expressions can harm vulnerable receivers – and you should be vigilant, not only by monitoring your own talk but also by intervening when you hear or overhear something troubling.[23] This training ethicalizes communication deemed harmful and advocates new sequential normativities of interaction that concern what you – as hearer or overhearer – should do "next." This training does not advocate public shaming or firing, yet it is similarly *allocentric* in seeking to hold others "accountable" for what they say while making *you* accountable for your own reaction – or inaction. Indeed, while the Lewinians sought continual 360-degree feedback, because that is what democracy as an intersubjective practice demanded, bystander training seems to demand continual 360-degree "accountability." After all, keeping others accountable includes

---

22 On the way liberal assumptions inform recent efforts at scholarly decolonization despite the criticism and disavowal of liberalism, see Yasmin Moll (2023).

23 On the ethicalization of social interaction, see Lempert (2013) and Keane and Lempert (2023).

a willingness to be held accountable by others. Let us broadly and provisionally call this form of receptivity *interventionist listening*.

A third register of listening is rather different. In its focus, it is egocentric rather than allocentric and has a strong psychotherapeutic sensibility. It is strongly reminiscent of CR in that it involves validating rather than questioning another's experience. Many argue that when people of colour tell those with white privilege about their experiences with everyday racism, for instance, the latter should affirm rather than question because the event should not be framed as deliberative. It's not a debate, not a time to interrogate a person about evidence, and so on. There are various names proposed for this, but let us call this, again, *validational listening*.

Consider, for instance, one of the many advice pieces written on mainstream media platforms for people aspiring to be white allies, during the intense waves of anti-racist activism that followed the brutal police murder of George Floyd. A July 2020 piece from CNN, "How to Talk with Your Black Friends about Race," combined first-person reflection from a Black author with advice from experts. "If your friend is open to talking, it's important to listen without trying to invalidate his experiences," one recommends. "Don't ask a bunch of pointed questions about how they're doing or request they explain their feelings," the author writes, because – quoting another expert – "that kind of prodding can 'feel invasive,'" because "to experience racism is trauma" (Rogers 2020). At work here is an effort to promote an interpersonal stance that is not forensic or deliberative. (It may be no accident that some of this advice resembles calls to *believe* victims who bring forth allegations of sexual violence, as it may well be that the transposition from physical to verbal harm here was effected first in relation to harm against the female body.) This discipline of listening involves self-restraint. You should take care to mute yourself – to cede the floor, to let others speak, to avoid "interruption."[24] It is through such restraint that you can support those who experience harm and allow their voices to resonate within and without.[25]

This inflection of listening owes much, I think, to a broadly psychotherapeutic take on listening that was popularized in part through the spread of feminist CR and through its subsequent institutionalization in diverse domains of life. But this is no simple story of the spread if not triumph of psychotherapeutic registers. In practice, this register of listening has had its own host of problems. It has been no easy substitute for deliberative listening, not even for its advocates. Pragmatically, therapeutic framings of communicative behaviour tend to be highly unstable and in some cases can be construed as patronizing and

---

24 On the politicization of "interruption" in second-wave feminism, see Lempert (2024).

25 On the importance of listening and being "heard" as a way of addressing social injustice and trauma, see Stauffer (2015).

even harmful. As a metadiscursive framing, this mode of listening – insofar as it is socially recognizable as "therapeutic" in register – risks inviting an asymmetrical definition of the situation that can undermine the listener's proclaimed state of status-lowered "openness" and "vulnerability." That is, insofar as validational listening is felt to resemble the receptivity of a therapist seated before a (vulnerable?) client, this willy-nilly raises the listener: it invites you to see an asymmetry in expertise and status. Worse, validational listening can also invite you to think that it is the speaking individual alone – and not the listener – who is saddled with pathology: it is *their* problem, not a problem whose etiology is sociogenic. (Recall, again, feminists who insisted that their small group practice may resemble therapy but, unlike therapy, CR did *not* promote "adjustment" to unjust social regimes – to patriarchy.)

Needless to say, in tentatively distinguishing among three registers of listening – deliberative, interventionist, and validational – I do not wish to suggest a high degree of regimentation, as if these were isolable "kinds" that can be included in an inventory. (You can find public-facing scholarship that does offer neat inventories of listening without providing evidence as to whether and, crucially, *for whom* these exist as distinguishable forms.) Nor do I wish to suggest that such forms of listening occur separately, as alternatives, in practice. Some, for instance, do advocate for exclusively validational listening in some contexts, yet this register does not usually occur on its own; rather, it usually precedes deliberative engagement. The recipe, at base, is simple and familiar. First, listen attentively and validate; *then* it's okay to pursue the truth.

Of late, blends of validational and deliberative listening seem particularly volatile. Consider a scene from the Netflix series *The Chair* (2021), set at Pembroke University, a fictitious northeastern Ivy League institution. Irreverent English professor Bill Dobson finds himself in crisis after he gets video recorded and memed on social media for allegedly "using" a Nazi salute during a classroom discussion of Fascism and absurdism. His administration pleads with him to issue a carefully worded written apology. He doesn't take the advice. Instead, he decides to convene a student town hall to speak directly with concerned students.

"Obviously I am not a member of the Jewish community, and I'm not in a position to tell you what is or is not offensive," he leads. "But I am a member of the Pembroke community, and I want to understand your point of view." "No Nazis at Pembroke," one student throws out. "Hate speech has no place here," another says. "Are you harboring neo-Nazi sentiments?" yet another presses. After some exchanges with the crowd that begin to get testy, he voices the tried-and-true value of deliberative freedom: "The university should be a place to uphold free discourse, the exchange of ideas without fear."

Yet the discussion only gets more heated. At last Dobson stops holding back. He defends his action. "If you are suggesting that what I did is the same as propagating neo-Nazism, that's inaccurate. That is a willful misrecognition of what was clearly –" A student cuts him off with a question as outrage builds. Finally, a student who will hear no more asks him curtly, "Are you going to apologize?" Dobson pauses to gather himself. Fateful orchestral music swells. "I am sorry if I made anyone feel –" He cannot finish. The students will not listen. His speech gets broken up by noise and jeers, during which one student says pointedly, and on the nose, "You're minimizing your responsibility by saying you're sorry for how we *feel*."

Note the appeal to interior states ("feelings"). No apology so framed could be performatively felicitous, even with the causative *made* ("I *made* you feel") through which Dobson assumes some responsibility. To be sure, this is itself a cliché; to acknowledge "how you feel" in an apology is a therapeutic bromide. But in this context, given the widespread semiotic distinction between "intention" and "impact" familiar in progressive circles and taught on campus through workshops of various kinds, appeals to feelings can be particularly fraught. In soft CR the situation had been different. "Feelings" were a desired epistemological object – something you drew out in small group practice. Once elicited, feelings were to be validated, even if their *significance* in terms of sexism would need to be uncovered so that everyone grasped what these feelings "really" indexed.

Courts of law sometimes adjudicate intent, just as people sometimes strain to spell out what people intended, but some argue that you cannot adjudicate "impact" the same way, in large part because the evidence for impact is positional and experiential; in effect, impact is something that only those harmed by speech can reliably report, and in this way impact is not up for debate; it is not a deliberative object open in principle to all. Without delving deeper into this contestation over harmful speech, let me say only that *any* appeal to inner states by someone accused of causing harm creates the possibility of *different* and possibly competing interpretations of action – and this smuggles deliberation back in. After all, appeals to interiority can imply – and often do imply – that it is possible to *adjudicate* among perspectives and arrive at a truth, even if that truth is a perspectivalist one, namely, that people can experience "the same" speech or behaviour differently. Ultimately, then, it does not matter what Dobson intended, what lurked in his heart or mind; nor does it matter what social and semiotic circumstances ("context") surrounded and inflected his ill-fated Nazi salute. In this fictional, filmic universe anyway, context doesn't matter; what matters is only the isolable sign and its impact on vulnerable others.[26] Dobson does try to acknowledge and apologize for impact – if

---

26 For ethnographic cases in which people are held responsible for the effects of speech rather than on their original "intentions," see Rosaldo (1982) and Duranti (1993a, 1993b). On the way discrete, isolable signs can be treated as intrinsically performative, irrespective of "context," see Luke Fleming's discussions of "rigid performativity" in taboo language in Fleming (2011) and Fleming and Lempert (2011, 2014).

only impact on "feelings" – but his apology isn't accepted, nor is his attempt to contextualize his actions. Dobson's apology is rejected by the students as profoundly insincere.

I recall this televisual scene in part to sample some of the current contestation over receptivity – especially what many take to be an inability or unwillingness to listen – but also, more broadly, to illustrate how people have been reflecting on and objectifying "listening" as a problem to understand and address. If we turn back a few years, stirrings of such contestation over liberal listening can be found in any number of Op-Eds and published letters. In "Listening to Ta-Nehisi Coates While White," for instance, the *New York Times* conservative commentator David Brooks (2015) went meta about receptivity. "I suppose the first obligation is to sit with it, to make sure the testimony is respected and sinks in," he writes, before asking (rhetorically), "But I have to ask, am I displaying my privilege if I disagree? Is my job just to respect your experience and accept your conclusions?" For Brooks, the answers to both were a resounding no. He went on to disagree – while still claiming to have been genuinely affected by Ta-Nehisi Coates's "testimony." Brooks seems to sit squarely in the deliberative always-everywhere camp, yet he entertained, if only for a moment, what is now a familiar progressive position, that differences in social and positional identities can and should affect how you listen. That was 2015. The contestation since has intensified.[27]

Conclusion

The differences among the three scenes juxtaposed here remind us how liberal receptivity can be variously imagined and configured. As for modalities, for the Lewinians, receptivity came in the form of panoramic 360-degree "feedback" that could take the material form of face-to-face talk but also of ratings from paper instruments like a survey. For CR, receptivity was more modular, concentrated as it was in an interpersonal ritual. Receptivity manifested itself especially in the technique of "listening well" to other women in small groups, a practice that could be evaluated based on how you reacted and responded to someone else's talk. On campuses, liberal receptivity takes many forms but it is interpersonal "listening" that remains important if not prototypical.

---

27 This chapter was written before the wave of violent crackdowns on students protesters in the United States who criticize Israeli policy in its war in Gaza. In the name of curbing anti-Semitism and ensuring community "safety," universities have called in police who have used pepper spray, tear gas, tasers, and zip ties to arrest unarmed students and faculty – including many who are themselves Jewish. Many have noted how this reveals a familiar irony: that liberal norms of "free speech" are selectively applied, and so dropped when they aren't expedient. Some have also noted how progressive discourses on receptive "harm" and "safety" have been recruited to argue that vulnerable others should not have to hear – let alone listen to – speech that makes them feel "uncomfortable" or "unsafe."

All three scenes reveal the struggle to meet the demands of liberal receptivity. These demands at times could be considerable, sometimes because it was hard to execute, and sometimes because it wasn't clear what it looked like and sounded like to "listen well."

Indeed, a tension common to my last two scenes has been the changing valence of deliberative responsiveness. Some have asked whether deliberative listening is appropriate in some contexts but not others. Some have wondered whether this register of listening should be replaced or supplemented with some kind of (feminized) validational receptivity that affirms and supports speakers in part by restraining from interrogating alter's truth claims. Brooks's (2015) restraint in his Op-Ed letter was held for a while but remained sequentially "first"; *after* showing his receptivity – how the book affected him, how he "learned" much from it – he then turned decisively to argue with it, with the disjunctive *but* as the hinge. Is a phase of receptive restraint that gives way to critical probing okay, then? Or would *any* deliberative action – any questioning of alter's claims, however brief – upset the whole tilt of the event, making it potentially harmful?

These are questions that should be addressed ethnographically, which I cannot do here, but we should at least sense how, in general, "the interpersonal" (as a constructed "domain" of political action and ideological site) has resurfaced, even as many on and off campuses remain ambivalent about its relative importance and vexed about the relationship between the "interpersonal" and the "institutional," as this interscalar antinomy has long been called. Indeed, all three scenes involve the objectification of social interaction as an ideological site of great importance. For the Lewinians, who were confident democratic engineers of the interpersonal, this objectification involved marshalling social-scientific knowledge on small-group dynamics while simultaneously lowering themselves and opening themselves to democratizing feedback, for they, too, would need to listen well. Participants in feminist consciousness-raising sessions were equally preoccupied with "internal democracy" as well as with the co-present interpersonal practice of listening to other women. In this they made the interpersonal political.[28] Campus DEI-themed workshops have been acutely concerned as well with interpersonal harms caused by speech and behaviour.

Together, these scenes of liberal listening should serve as a caution. They should remind us that we must not take literally and uncritically the overt focus

---

28 I adapt here Carol Hanisch's famous second-wave adage "the personal is political." For a historical account that traces how the interpersonal became political through feminist research on interaction, see Lempert (2024).

on expression in captions like "free speech." We should not let the speaker-centricity of free speech cause us to neglect the interactional breadth of liberal-democratic practices and projects, because, after all, without listening, who would free speech be *to* or *for*?

Acknowledgments

This chapter was originally written for the conference "Freedom of Speech: Anthropological Perspectives" (Cambridge University, June 2021), for which I thank organizers Matei Candea, Taras Fedirko, Paolo Heywood, Adam Reed, and Fiona Wright. A revised version was presented in October 2021 at the Sociology Workshop on Aesthetics, Meaning, and Power (SWAMP), Department of Sociology, University of Virginia. There I want to acknowledge especially Fiona Greenland, Richard Handler, and Isaac Reed, as well as Eve Danziger, Lise Dobrin, and Dan Lefkowitz. For valuable feedback on this chapter, I also thank James Slotta and Fiona Wright. I owe a special debt to Yasmin Moll, who read drafts and helped me think through issues raised in the chapter. In 2021, I began a collaborative, team-based ethnography that explores tensions over (il)liberal listening on a university campus, in sites such as active bystander trainings, student educational theatre, anti-racist and DEI workshops, and classes that teach students how to facilitate dialogues across difference, for which I thank support from the Wenner-Gren Foundation. I do not incorporate findings from this in-progress fieldwork here but wish to acknowledge my research team – Benjamin Davis, Alex Forrest, Cameron Johnson, Greta Kruse, Tina Zou, and Charles Zuckerman – and weekly "Listening Lab" for many stimulating conversations about listening. Portions of this chapter were adapted with permission from Lempert (2024).

18 An American Canard: The Freedom of (Therapeutic) Speech

E. SUMMERSON CARR

Whether imagined under domes, on ivied campuses, or in blood-drenched streets flooded with insistent chants and livid signs, the exercise of free speech in the United States is commonly understood as a decidedly public affair. Yet we should remember that, for decades, countless Americans have been exhorted to verbally reveal what they really think and how they really feel – or *speak freely* – in the relative privacy of professional psychotherapy sessions.[1] To be sure, in the United States, free speech is not just a sign of a healthy democracy but also an act and evidence of healthy personhood. Accordingly, American individuals are regularly evaluated and sometimes putatively cured by speech that apparently springs forth from inner selves, unfettered by the authority of others. As I've argued in other work, American psychotherapies are especially revealing sites to examine how ideals of free speech – and the semiotic ideologies that underlie them – are reproduced, managed, and even distilled (cf. Carr 2011, 2023).

While the reader may doubt the suggestion that we can learn about the politics of free speech by looking at the dynamics of psychotherapies, many prominent American psychologists lend credence to this thesis. For instance, consider how father of client-centred therapy, Carl Rogers, laced the keywords of American democracy – or what Nancy Fraser calls "folk paradigms of justice" (Fraser and Honneth 2003) – through the description of his therapeutic program. More specifically, Rogers (1961) conceived of himself as creating the dialogic conditions

---

1 As the opening dome-to-bloody street metaphor means to signal, Americans' access to psychotherapy as a more-or-less productive site of expression or reformation has always been radically classed, racialized, and gendered. Consider – just for example – those who voluntarily access something like client-centred therapy in the confines of insurance-covered therapists' offices relative to those who are relinquished, court-ordered, or otherwise mandated to psychological care. As Susan Gal (2002) has noted, the semiotic production and reinforcement of the public/private distinction is always a matter of other lines of difference.

for clients to see themselves as free and to speak accordingly, a therapeutic project that he called "self-actualization." That this project coincided with growing anti-authoritarian sentiment, stoked by the Cold War on the one hand, and global challenges to white supremacy and colonialism on the other, was no accident.

On a mild June day in 1962, in front of an audience of at least 500 students, faculty, and onlookers gathered at the University of Minnesota Duluth, the famous psychologist seized upon this growing sentiment and framed his therapeutic program in triumphantly democratic terms. Referencing current events, from civil rights and decolonization movements to Westerners' growing interest in existentialism and Zen Buddhism, Rogers noted:

> As I endeavor to understand this vigorous new cultural trend, it seems to me to be the voice of subjective man speaking up loudly for himself. Man has long felt himself to be a puppet in life, molded by world forces, by economic forces. He has been enslaved by persons, by institutions, and, more recently, by aspects of modern science. But he is firmly setting for a new declaration of independence. He is discarding the alibis of "unfreedom." He is choosing himself, endeavoring to become himself: not a puppet, not a slave, not a copy of some model, but his own unique self. I find myself very sympathetic to this trend because it is so deeply in line with the experience I have had working with clients in therapy. As one therapist has said, the essence of therapy is the client's movement from feeling unfree and controlled by others to the frightening but rewarding sense of freedom to map out and choose his new personality. (*Dialogue* 1976)[2]

Here, we see how Roger scales up from the clinical to the political by way of recognizably democratic ideals. We can hear echoes of Fanon, if in less elegant and more ambiguously racialized terms, as Rogers avers that "man" has been "enslaved" "by persons, by institutions, and ... by aspects of modern science," uniformly cast as "alibis of unfreedom." Notably, therapy and therapists – or at least ones working in the Rogerian vein – are exempted from this

---

2 The 1962 debate was titled, "A Dialogue on Education and the Control of Human Behavior," which was recorded and released by the American Academy of Psychotherapists. It was eventually transcribed, and reprinted in Kirschenbaum and Henderson (1989), though the transcriptions here and that follow are my own, based on the AAP recordings (Rogers and Skinner 1976) and cited herein as *Dialogue* 1976. Kirschenbaum (1979) details the format of the debate in his intellectual biography, *On Becoming Carl Rogers*. He explains that it allowed for fifteen minutes of opening remarks by each man, followed by seventy-five minutes of discussion. The first evening was capped by a discussion by an invited panel and small group discussion among audience members. The next morning, Skinner and Rogers resumed for another seventy-five-minute session, took an hour of questions from the audience, and offered brief closing remarks.

conglomerate of tyrannical forces, framed instead as paving the way for "clients' movement from feeling unfree and controlled by others to the frightening but rewarding sense of freedom" (*Dialogue* 1976). No longer "puppets" nor "slaves," "unique selves" set forth from the Rogerian therapeutic encounter psychically prepared to speak freely, even "declar[e] their independence," as autonomous and healthy-minded Americans. In these paradigmatically democratic terms, Rogers spent the next two days outlining his central therapeutic premise, elaborated over his many writings (e.g., Rogers 1946, 1951, 1961, 1980), that clients will "self-actualize" so long as professionals abstain from (overt) evaluation and direction. And, as he repeatedly implied, client speech – once liberated from professional influence – was both the means and the evidence of their democratic/therapeutic development.

Sitting across from Rogers on the Minnesotan stage was the equally famous, if far more controversial American psychologist, B.F. Skinner.[3] Over the course of the debate, the men offered starkly divergent epistemological premises about and attendant ethical positions on the locus of human behaviour, the nature of language, and the proper ground of psychology, frequently trading razor-sharp barbs. Doubtlessly emboldened by the support of the university-based audience, Rogers spared no time going on the attack, associating Skinner's behaviourism with authoritarianism and repeatedly suggesting that the freedom of speech and therefore the liberty of subjects was at stake in Americans' choices of interventions. Certainly, what Rogers idealized as unencumbered self-expression, Skinner (1957) understood as verbal behaviour that is always shaped by the environment, past and present, including one's immediate interlocutors. The behaviourist focused on engineering ideal – even utopian – environments, where speech was valued for the quality of associations and interactions it helped forge – or, for what speech communally produced rather than what it individually expressed. So, whereas Rogers's brand of psychotherapy was premised on the idea that the professional, as an external authority, should minimally influence what clients say so as to understand their speech as free, Skinner maintained that ethical professionals should consciously and explicitly help craft conditions, or positively reinforce, speech and other behaviour.

Though the Rogers-Skinner debate highlighted, even diagrammed, several fundamental and enduring contradictions in American democracy, in this

---

3 This was the third, and the most intensive, of the public engagements between the two men. It was organized by University of Minnesota Duluth students who – having learned that Skinner would be receiving an honorary degree at a nearby college and thus travelling to the area from his post at Harvard – invited Rogers, who was then teaching at the nearby University of Wisconsin-Madison, to join Skinner for a "dialogue." It was apparently important to the organizers that the event be relatively unscripted and provide opportunity for impromptu discussion between the men and with the audience (Kirschenbaum 1979).

chapter, I am especially interested in Skinner's evocation of a canard: a fabrication at the heart of the cherished ideal of free speech and a telling theme in his exchange with Rogers. In short, Skinner suggested that *speech is "free" only to the extent that the social circumstances of its production are obscured from view.*

The remainder of this chapter elaborates on this charge. I argue that in the debate between these two American psychologists, we can discern the ideological labour involved in making American speech apparently free and evaluate the costs of doing so.[4]

Delving into the terms of the debate and drawing as needed on the two psychologists' respective published works, I focus on how Rogers's highly conventional formulations about language and its functions squared with his those of his opponent. Writing against "mentalist" approaches, Skinner worried that asocial conceptions of language have limited, even dangerous, political utility. Presaging his 1971 treatise, which argued that the American tendency to attribute causality to the individual hindered both science and politics, including efforts to build a just society that optimizes and equalizes people's ability to thrive, Skinner asked Rogers – and the legions of Americans who shared his views – to think "beyond freedom and dignity" when it comes to questions of speech (Skinner 1971).

Free Speech: Duck or Rabbit?

The Rogers-Skinner debate was charged in large part because neither of the psychologists were the least bit shy about embracing the practical and political implications of their disciplinary concerns.[5] If they agreed on little else, both readily conceded that the psychological is political, if with some notable caveats.[6]

Consider, too, that in mid-twentieth-century America, political questions were commonly couched in psychological terms, with many Americans

---

4 On the *metalinguistic labour* involved in a genealogically connected American therapeutic project, see Carr (2006, 2011, 2021).

5 Both Rogers and Skinner ran active research labs and did not hesitate to generalize their findings to actual practice (Kirschenbaum and Henderson 1989). However, Skinner – unlike Rogers – was not a practising psychotherapist; he nevertheless was keenly interested in the practical implications of his theory of behaviour, especially in the field of education. As in therapy, Skinner argued, the teacher's job is "to ... shape behavior – to build it up and strengthen it, rather than to find it already in the student and draw it out [as Rogers claims]" (Kirschenbaum and Henderson 1989, 118).

6 For instance, Skinner certainly would have objected to the idea that his lab experiments were mediated by politics as much as Rogers declined to see the directive and even authoritative elements of his therapeutic style.

viewing the Cold War as a battle between the safeguarding of freedom of thought and the active suppression of it. B.F. Skinner's radical behaviourism was commonly associated with the latter tendency, and not just by the FBI who assembled an ample file on the social scientist (see Wyatt 2000), but also by his scholarly colleagues who increasingly regarded Skinner's scholarly program as narrow and rigid (Cohen-Cole 2014, 124–5; see also Hull 2010, 258).[7]

Rogers was certainly among the most critical of those colleagues, whose suspicions of Skinner seemed as grave, if not as potentially consequential, as those of federal authorities. As the father of client-centred therapy put it on that stage in Duluth during his lengthy opening remarks, which he prepared in advance of the debate:

> ... to the extent that the behaviorist point of view in psychology is leading us toward a disregard of the person ... toward the control of the person by shaping his behavior without his participant choice, or toward minimizing the significance of the subjective ... I question it very deeply. My experience leads me to say that such a point of view is going against one of the strongest undercurrents in modern life and is taking us down a pathway with destructive consequences. (*Dialogue* 1976)

The displacement of the individual will as causal agent, of course, was profoundly disturbing to Rogers whose therapeutic program depended on the idea that people should be authors of their own acts, and their behaviour traceable to sources within themselves (i.e., "participant choice").[8] Throughout the debate, Rogers repeatedly returned to the idea that "minimizing the significance of the subjective" is as much of an anathema to politics as it is to psychotherapy.

Later in the debate, Skinner would more directly counter this formulation. He would also, with remarkable poise and precision, defend his own program and position. However, demonstrating that he was an astute student of verbal behaviour, Skinner began the debate by commenting on its very own (operant) conditions. He placed particular emphasis on the rhetorical force of his

---

7 Nevertheless, Skinner's ideas enjoy continued influence if in modified form. To be sure, the third wave behavioural therapies have enjoyed tremendous success, having been widely institutionalized and trained, though they typically restore some notion of a willful interiority – "cognitively" or otherwise – that radical behaviourists were criticized for evacuating. By contrast, since the mid-twentieth century, Rogerian therapy has been relatively uncontroversial, and virtually synonymous with ethically sound, politically progressive psychotherapeutic practice.

8 Note that Rogers was in seminary before earning his PhD in psychology. Whether or not the soul was in question for Rogers, he was deeply invested in the idea that the course of individual action is driven from within.

opponent, bolstered as it was by the conventional assumptions about language, autonomy and interiority that Rogers shared with the audience. After genteelly greeting the moderator and his opponent, who had clearly come out swinging, Skinner wryly noted:

> I always make the same mistake. In debating with Carl Rogers, I always assume that he will make no effort to influence the audience. [*Laughter from audience*] And then I have to follow him and speak, as I am speaking now, to a group of people who are very far from free to accept my views. [*Loud and extended laughter from audience*] In fact, I was just reminded of a story that I once heard about Carl Rogers, and I will tell it now hoping to confirm or have him deny it. I suppose it is apocryphal. At least I'm sure it has grown in its dimensions. (*Dialogue* 1976)

Note how, before recounting the story, Skinner diagrams his critique of Rogers's premises about the freedom of speech. He swiftly dismisses any implication that the debate is simply the ideas of two men spontaneously spilling out of their heads into words, which then simply flow from the stage into the audience. Instead, Skinner craftily points to the rhetorical dimensions of Rogers's opening statement, noting how – despite protestations to the contrary – the father of client-centred therapy is quite adept at influencing others when he speaks. In a backhanded compliment, he goes further to suggest that Rogers is so persuasive that he has effectively conditioned the audience to be "very far from free to accept [Skinner's] views." Judging from their laughter, the irony was not lost on the audience. And while some may have thought it unfair to compare the conditions of public debate and ostensibly private therapeutic exchange, Rogers opened that door himself by claiming that his "experience working with clients" resonated with, and perhaps even exemplified the cultivation of the freedom of American speech and speakers. Skinner continued:

> The story as I heard it is as follows: Carl Rogers was never much of a duck hunter, but he was persuaded upon one occasion to go duck hunting. Uh, he and some friends went into a blind and sat through a dreary cold early dawn, and no ducks arrived until the very end of the time when shooting was possible. Finally, one lone duck came in, and his friends allowed him to shoot, and he did. At the same time, along the shore a few hundred yards away, another man shot at the same duck. The duck fell. Plop! Dr. Rogers got out of the blind and started toward the duck. The other man got out of his blind and started toward the same duck. They arrived at the same moment. Dr. Rogers turned to him and said, "You *feel* that this is *your* duck." [*Loud, widespread laughter*] (*Dialogue* 1976)

Part of why Skinner's story is so funny is because it restages a classically Rogerian engagement well outside the confines of the therapy room, if still within an ostensibly dyadic exchange. As the audience clearly recognized, the tale's narrative climax – "You *feel* that this is *your duck*" – is a signature Rogerian *reflection*, a tentative statement about an interlocutor's feelings. In Rogerian therapy, such reflections serve as denotative checkpoints, opportunities to assess "whether [the therapist's] understanding of the client's inner world is correct" (Rogers 1986, 375).

Indeed, reflections are arguably the central technology of Rogers' highly influential approach to psychotherapy. According to the legions of American psychotherapists who make prominent use of the Rogerian-style speech act today, reflections are superior to questions, which can appear probing and diag-nostic. They are also preferred to directives, which baldly project professional authority. That said, as tentative guesses, much like questions in intonational disguise, reflections (like "you *feel* this is *your duck*") both elicit more speech and, when skillfully placed within therapeutic dialogue, can also *direct* that speech, prompting the client to elaborate, equivocate, and revise what they are about to say in particular ways (see Carr 2021, 2023). As Skinner might put it, reflections are more-or-less positive reinforcements – operant conditions which his opponent misrecognized or refused to acknowledge.

Just a few years after the debate, Rogers's own students confirmed Skinner's humour-veiled charge, finding evidence for the directive nature of Rogers's "reflective listening." Transcribing and analyzing their former professor's psychotherapy sessions, they showed how Rogers selectively reinforced some client statements, while remaining silent in the face of others (Traux 1966; Traux and Carkhuff 1967). Audaciously, Traux (1966, 1) not only found "significant reinforcement effects in client-centered therapy," he also framed this as a point scored for Skinner, writing, "the findings suggest that the therapist, in this case Rogers, implicitly alters (or controls) the patient's behaviour in the therapeutic setting. To this extent, then, the evidence weighs in favour of the view proposed by Skinner rather than Rogers" (7). In other words, Rogers's students suggested, reflections are an effective, if highly subtle – and perhaps even surreptitious – means of acquiring a proverbial duck.

This research flew directly in the face of Rogers's (1947, 359) claim that the client-centred therapist "helps maximize the freedom of expression by the individual." After all, Rogers claimed that to offer verbal direction is to interfere with the process of self-actualization and, by extension, to vi-olate the principle of individual freedom. His students' research also con-tradicted his own studies of client-centred therapy transcripts, summarized in his 1947 address as the retiring president of the American Psychological Association and later published in *American Psychologist*. There, Rogers (1947, 358) claimed that it was a "fortunate characteristic" of the record-ings that he studied "that the verbal productions of the client are biased to a minimal degree by the therapist." He even went so far to claim that "material from client-centered interviews probably comes closer to being a 'pure' expression of attitudes than has been achieved by other means" (358).[9] As we will see, Skinner would proceed to disabuse his opponent from this claim, and – moreover – the very possibility of "pure" expression. What patients say in therapy, Skinner would argue, is always influenced by their professional interlocutor, whether that interlocutor denies it or not. This is not only because speech is inherently interactional, and even the most subtle verbal cues spawn responses in others; it is also because the authority structure of professional exchanges and cultural norms of comportment in and out of the therapy room shape what people say and otherwise do.[10]

Indeed, the duck story is all-the-more effective because it parodies a way of approaching interaction that is blind to a whole host of salient features of the environment in which that interaction takes place. In this case, the duck-hunting in Rogers's reflection circumvents all the features of the duck hunt as a set of conditions in a communally shared environment, in which one might make and lay claims (e.g., that Rogers "was never much of a duck hunter"; that the day was dreary, cold, and virtually duckless; that Rogers's friends had "allowed him to shoot" once a duck finally arrived; that there were several other blinds from behind which other and likely more experienced hunters shot; that there were a set of structuring norms and social dynamics of duck hunting, including competitive ones). Rogers's reported reflection evacuates these conditions, channelling them into an affirmative statement of what his duck hunting opponent *feels*, which Rogers claims to both immediately recognize and apparently decline to counter.[11] Yet, as the audience's roar was soon to signal, Skinner's punchline was yet to come. He continued:

> The reason that I was reminded of that story was that the *end* of it is that Dr. Rogers brought the duck home. [*More loud laughter*] I shall do my best to prevent a similar outcome. [*Skinner joins in audience's laughter*] (*Dialogue* 1976)

---

9 Rogers (1947, 358) immediately added, in a dazzling spin of his data: "One can read through a complete recorded case or listen to it without finding more than a half-dozen instances in which the therapist's views on any point are evident."

10 As Benjamin Smith (2005, 264) puts it, "the participant structure of a Rogerian session tends toward the complete collapse of anything beyond whatever roles are established via the client's speech."

11 Apparently, Rogers later commented that he thought the duck hunting story was confined to his family, and expressed wonder at how Skinner had ever heard word of it (Kirschenbaum 1979). At the debate, Rogers conceded, "there's a great deal of truth in story," while correcting what he recognized as the "punchline": he and the other duck hunter had "resorted to a procedure very highly regarded in scientific circles – we flipped a coin, and that proved that I had shot the duck" (*Dialogue* 1976).

If a witty and dismissive way to follow Rogers's strident opening treatise, the implication is quite a serious one. That is, Rogers's style of professional interaction and his approach to politics is not naïve but sneakily manipulative, allowing the storied therapist-hunter to take the (proverbial) duck home. Indeed, by way of the duck story, Skinner raised the question of just what his opponent may be hiding, suggesting that even the most putatively unmediated "ways of being with people" have directive elements, whether the practitioner admits it or not (Carr 2023). And, as the debate continued, Skinner would return repeatedly, if often implicitly, to the suggestion at the heart of the duck story: that the production of one democratic ideal – *freedom of speech* – too often depends on the suppression of another – *transparency in governance.*

Cold War, Cold Therapies

Skinner's duck story was a clever way to humorously pad his trenchant critique of Rogers, which he proceeded to elaborate on over the course of the debate. It was also a remarkably cool response to some very serious, even threatening, charges on the part of his opponent. After all, in his opening statement, Rogers had not only implied that Skinner was "pathetic" but had also figured the behaviourist as decidedly anti-American.[12] Indeed, before his opponent even had a chance to speak, Rogers had swiftly inventoried the democratic ideals, beginning with freedom and ending with personal responsibility that Skinner's behaviourism presumably violated:

> Here are some of the words and concepts that I have used which are almost totally without meaning in the behaviorist frame of reference: *freedom* is a term with no meaning; *choice,* in the sense I have used it, has no meaning ... *Purpose, self-direction, value* or *choice* – none of these has any meaning; *personal responsibility* as a concept has no meaning. (*Dialogue* 1976)

Significantly, for the most part, Skinner did not shy away from what supposed to be an incriminating characterization of his views, loaded up as they were with social salience.[13] At one point, Skinner even confessed, "I don't believe in the notion of personal responsibility," underscoring that all

---

12 Specifically, Rogers stated: "Some of the most pathetic individuals I know are those who continually attempt to understand and predict their behavior objectively" (*Dialogue* 1976). Not surprisingly, Skinner seemingly declined to take the insult personally.

13 Skinner later added that it was therefore exceedingly difficult for American psychologists to understand people from "other areas of the world" who did not share this peculiar conception of self (*Dialogue* 1976).

behaviour – including speech – is always co-produced and environmentally conditioned. More specifically, while Skinner made clear that people should be held accountable for the consequences of acts that they could reasonably foresee, he unashamedly confirmed Rogers's charge that "when people have been induced to behave in particular ways, without aversive consequences entering into the picture, there is no meaning to the conception of personal responsibility" (*Dialogue* 1976).

Of course, Skinner was keen to the fact that Rogers's critical characterization of behaviourism reflected the "national tendency ... to suppose that the individual ... has something inside himself which is very important. (*Dialogue* 1976). Nevertheless, as a devout empiricist, Skinner eschewed all attempts to find causes within the black box of individual psyches, instead seeking explanations for behaviour in the observable history of interaction.[14] Thus, in response to Rogers, Skinner bemoaned that his colleagues fetishized autonomous purpose, inferring "inner processes" *as cause* and thereby systematically overlooking the contextual factors that shaped the course and consequences of human behaviour. These views made him not just a behaviourist, but a decidedly radical one as well. And while acknowledging that "strangely enough, it is the community that teaches this individual to "know himself" (Skinner 1953, 261), as if this project was of the highest ethical order, Skinner maintained that causality – and therefore the possibility for freedom – was to be found in the history of behavioural interactions and not within people (cf. Bateson 1971; Foucault 1977; Johnson 1988; Latour 2005).

In this sense, Skinner was arguably quite broad in his view of psychology, focusing as he did on the environmental conditions, past and present, that produced behaviour, as well as on the pragmatics of how problem behaviour might be conditioned otherwise. In the lab, Skinner had found that observable historical reinforcements that produced extant behaviours; as a utopian, he imagined how interaction might be otherwise engineered. He was therefore steadfast in his thesis that "man ... [is] the product of past elements and forces and the determined cause of future events and behaviors," and that "isolating the originating event [of behavior] as something to do with inner experience" was a methodological error with profound real-world implications (*Dialogue* 1976; see also Skinner 1953, 1971). So, as the debate went on, Skinner made clear that more than a pilfered duck was at stake. By the second day in Duluth, he was working to make clear that mentalism – exemplified by Rogers if shared by most of their American audience – was not just a psychological error

---

14 Importantly, this did not mean that Skinner denied the existence or experience of inner life; rather, Skinner resisted its epistemological primacy.

but a political one as well. After all, political economic conditions shape who experiences what kind of problems and punishments, making freedom and freedom of speech a deeply stratified affair. And while Skinner didn't explicate the raced, classed, and gendered nature of operant conditions, his experiments – including his labour-saving "baby box" (see below) – suggest that he understood that "self-actualization" was not just an epistemologically problematic goal, but one that set many up for failure by not attending to stark differences in the environmental shaping of human subjects.

So while speech could never be "free" for Skinner, he also acknowledged that it is freer for some than others and accordingly imagined remedies for such inequities. Notably, here, we should consider that Skinner was deeply attuned to the question of reflexive calibration of social interaction, and particularly social interventions, such as early education and psychotherapy. Having spent his career demonstrating that all animals can learn – he taught pigeons to play ping pong and dance, after all – Skinner asserted that a distinguishing feature of humans, as a kind of animal, is our capacity for reflection. At baseline, this means we can observe the consequences of our own responses to a set of environmental stimuli and, when yielding unpleasant or harmful responses in others, reorient and anticipate how to respond differently in the future. Denying one's part in the ongoing orchestration of social life is to deny responsibility *for others*.

Skinner used his own reflections on his scholarly behaviour as an example, refusing to attribute his momentous academic achievements to his own mental attributes, despite his critics' frequent goading. Indeed, when asked during a video-recorded interview in his office at Harvard University if as author of his own writings he should take credit for them, an eighty-four-year-old Skinner went on to detail the operant conditions that allowed him, with reflection, to be productive as a scholar – the arrangement of his desk, the time of day in which he set to work, the presence or absence of others – suggesting all those conditions were as responsible for scholarly production as he, as an individual organism, was himself (Skinner 1988). His achievement was only in reflecting and experimenting with these conditions. (Along the same lines, Rogers repeatedly baited Skinner at each one of their meetings whether he was simply "emitting sounds" because "his past environment had operantly conditioned his behavior in such a way that it was rewarding to make those sounds," to which Skinner cheerfully replied that he thought Rogers's "characterization" of his presence was "very close" indeed) (*Dialogue* 1976).

Part of Skinner's point was that too many individuals were ready to take undue credit for the fortunes of their environmental conditions – particularly, perhaps, white male academic luminaries like he and his opponent in Duluth. In an "effective world," Skinner later continued, "the reasons for admiring will disappear" (*Dialogue* 1976). Acknowledging that many would feel this as a loss, Skinner maintained that we should evaluate our responses in terms of the good they produce in the world rather than in the myopic terms of personal achievement. For instance, Skinner explained that if someone were to provide evidence that his words or actions were angry ones, he would take that seriously and work to adjust his responses in the future. Indeed, this sort of reflective calibration to the flow of human behaviour was not an exercise in "self-control" as much as a matter of personal ethics. For Skinner, it was rather a way of being responsive to others, the community of actors who shape and are shaped by one's actions, including one's words.

Yet there was even more at stake in clinging to mentalist explanations of social exchange. Skinner also implied that the failure to reflect or acknowledge the influence one had on others was a pathway to potential tyranny. After all, the flipside of taking personal credit for environmentally produced achievements is holding certain individuals accountable for environmentally produced problems. Here, claims to have transparent access to the interiors of individuals – such as Rogers's (1947, 360) assertion that he had been "admitted freely into the backstage of the person's living" and that he had "repeatedly peered through ... psychological windows into the personality" (360) – could get dangerous, particularly when in the wrong hands. Locating problems within personalities rather than within behaviour could and regularly did lead to stigma, stratification and unjust punishment, enduring concerns that Skinner worked to address over the course of his career. Being reflexive, then, means being aware of and precise about how one's own responses affect others, particularly if one is in an authoritative position. Especially concerned about the dangers of blind authority, Skinner conducted and imagined experiments with the firm conviction that no human intervention should have surreptitious elements.

From the beginning to the end of the two-day debate, Skinner remained unmoved from his thesis "the inner events which seem so important to us are not essential to action and probably do not, in any important case, precede action" (*Dialogue* 1976). And whereas Rogers (1946, 416) insisted that therapists accept the "principle that the individual is basically responsible for himself," Skinner (1953, 382–3) made it clear that the goal of interventions is precisely to direct, or positively "condition" people to act in responsible ways relative to others. Thus, for Skinner, the pressing question was not *whether* to direct people, but how to do so in positive, productive, and non-punitive ways. This question drove the history of Skinner's experiments – including utopian ones – which would add fuel to the firestorm of criticism. Importantly, those experiments hinged on a theory of language that sought to relocate the freedom of speech from more-or-less liberated American individuals to more-or-less receptive, cooperative American communities wherein people were free to the extent they could exercise reflexive self-control.

Skinner's Utopia: Beyond the Autonomous Speaker in the Freedom of Speech

Perhaps Skinner's placid demeanour throughout the debate derived from the fact that he was no stranger to virulent criticism, especially after the 1948 publication of his utopian novel, *Walden Two*. In it, Skinner imagined a community where punishment had no place, gender equality reigned, and positive reinforcement of children began at birth, with the aim of fostering self-control and cooperation and eliminating competitive individualism. Prominent critics cast this unapologetic behaviourism not just as anti-democratic but as distinctly un-American as well (Nye 1992; Richelle 1993; Rutherford 2006). Across his many public-facing writings, Skinner's central thesis of *operant conditioning* was commonly received as an attack on the cherished ideal that American individuals are authors of their own acts, whose participation in public life is unmediated by external authorities. Some went so far as to translate operant conditioning as "another word for Nazism" (Lancelot quoted in Richelle 1993, 4).[15]

While historians argue that the skepticism of experts reached new heights post–Second World War, the American public's critique of expert authority was quite selective. Thus, while readers were lapping up Dr. Spock's now in-famous child-rearing advice, they chafed at the *Ladies Home Journal* article in which Skinner described the "air crib" that he designed for the care of his second baby daughter and for his wife, whose maternal labour he was moti-vated to save (see Skinner 1945). The air crib was enclosed, like the traditional crib, with three opaque sides and a plexiglass front that allowed the baby visual stimulation but also provided light and sound control. Equipped with a rotating linen-like plastic sheet, the crib also diminished the amount of laundry gener-ated and therefore parental labour required (Nye 1992). Some critics charged that the "baby box" (as the title of the *Ladies Home Journal* article dubbed it) was simply a larger version of the box Skinner had created for his pigeons (see Bjork 1997). And while others may have bristled at the feminism of the invention, the air crib was also undoubtedly controversial for simply drawing attention to extant conventions of infant control.

Arguably, Skinner's conception of freedom was implicit in the crib's de-sign. While it obviously – like other cribs – confined its infant inhabitants, it

---

15 As Rutherford (2006) adroitly explains, this criticism co-existed with ample application of Skinnerian ideas about behaviour modification across numerous fields. And while third-wave behavioral therapies – like cognitive behavioural therapy – have enjoyed tremendous success, in part because of their relative efficiency and cost-effectiveness, they have been cleansed of the most politically problematic implications of Skinner's radicalism, most centrally his displacement of an internal motor of human action (see Carr 2023).

maximized opportunity for their stimulation and comfort. Just as importantly, it freed mothers from the more unpleasant tasks of caregiving, suggesting that one actor's freedoms hinge on others. In other words, Skinner's air crib indicated that freedom was a feature of the interaction of mother, child, and crib, buoyed by the elimination of more averse if implicit methods of control.

Interestingly, especially vitriolic commentary arose around Skinner's use of the word "experiment" in the article, which appeared to turn his own daughter into an object of his expertise and to even suggest that human babies, like any other animal (read: pigeon), could be positively conditioned given an ideal environment. As the vaguely understood nature of Skinner's scientific program of behaviourism coalesced with the public focus on the externally uninhibited cultivation of open American minds (Cohen-Cole 2014), the directive nature of Skinner's child-rearing, labour-saving device was considered problematic while Dr. Spock's pointers on child rearing remained implicit and normatively acceptable.

Over the course of several decades, a tellingly broad range of prominent political figures expressed outrage over Skinner's rejection of the ideal of the sovereign will and the free-thinking subject, as well as his interest in designing environments to stimulate pro-social behaviour. For instance, within months of Noam Chomsky's (1971, 22) scathing review of Skinner's *Beyond Freedom and Dignity* in the *New York Review of Books*, which compared a Skinnerian world to "a well-run [if punishment free] concentration camp," Spiro Agnew (1972, 22) issued a warning to the American public that "Skinner attacks the very precepts on which our society is based" and seeks to perform "radical surgery on the national psyche" – a psyche that the Cold War American public increasingly insisted should be recognized, not directed.[16]

As an assistant professor at the Massachusetts Institute of Technology, Chomsky had other bones to grind with Skinner as well. After all, Skinner (1957, 2) understood speech as "behavior reinforced through the mediation of other persons," which could deal a substantial blow to the young linguist's emerging theory of universal grammar. Skinner's 1957 book, *Verbal Behavior*, was interested in the conditions, including community-specific norms and as well as speech of other speakers, that shape the actual production of verbal behaviour (familiar fodder for linguistic anthropologists, one might say). *Verbal Behavior* can also be read as a sustained attack on mentalist views of language, including Chomsky's formal theories of universal grammar (which Skinner never explicitly addressed). After all, *Verbal Behavior* refuses the idea that

---

16 According to Rutherford (2006), Agnew's speech was originally delivered at the Farm Bureau of Chicago and reprinted later in *Psychology Today*.

the speaking subject is simply spilling grammatical rules, stored in the mind, out into the world. Skinner insisted that like any other behaviour, speech was subject to environmental conditioning, past and present, including, of course, *language socialization* (see Schiefflin 1986).

In his lengthy review of the book, Chomsky (1967, 43) nevertheless protested that while "the manner in which such factors operate and interact in language acquisition is completely unknown," and that "reinforcement" is one among many "important factors," one should conclude that "it is clear that what is necessary in such a case is research, not dogmatic and perfectly arbitrary claims, based on analogies to that small part of the experimental literature in which one happens to be interested."

While Skinner never replied to or directly engaged Chomsky, he was apparently speaking as much to him as to Rogers when he opened the second day of the Duluth debate by remarking:

> I have written a rather long and, I am told, very difficult book which attempts to account for verbal behavior on the part of the speaker, without invoking, one, the notion of meaning; two, the earlier notion of idea or proposition, or three, the more recent notion of information. These three terms all make a fundamental mistake in supposing that there is one kind of cognitive activity which is not itself verbal, which happens before verbal behavior, and that verbal behavior becomes simply the symptom of symbol. (*Dialogue* 1976)

Though there is much to say about this pregnant passage, here it is important to emphasize Skinner's efforts to dislodge the freedom of speech from the inside of speakers who are more-or-less constrained in pouring inner meaning, proposition, or information into words. This, Skinner maintained, overlooked where and how freedom might be cultivated. He insisted, instead, that freedom of speech is always a communal affair – a dynamic set of conditions that positively reinforces some verbal behaviour and discourages others, for better and for worse. As Skinner put it in Duluth: "In general, while those who deal with experience are likely to make a great deal of inner stimulation, those of us who deal with behavior are much more likely to talk about the common elements to the verbal community" (*Dialogue* 1976). Thus, while both his rivals repeatedly claimed, if in different terms, that Skinner's thesis downplayed the creativity of human self-expression, it is far more accurate to say that he concertedly attacked the chimera of the autonomous speaker.

Recall that Rogers was deeply committed to the notion of language-as-inner reference, a language ideology that enjoys widespread uptake in the United States as well as special prominence in therapeutic institutions (Carr 2006, 2011). As noted above, for Rogers to assert that his clients were liberated subjects, unmediated by his professional presence, he had to regard their speech as free and pure expression. For the utopian Skinner, by contrast, the measure of democratic speech is never about the expression of the psychic interior of individual speakers; since freedom emerges in interaction, verbal behaviour, like all other behaviour, should socialize people into the shared norms of a just, democratic society, and do so transparently. These very different, if not directly antithetical, ideas about language not only organize the epistemologies, ethical stances, and democratic ideals of opposing American therapeutic approaches. They also provide some glimpses into the tensions and contradictions of broader American conceptions of the freedom of speech.

Conclusion: If Free Speech Walks Like a Duck, and Talks Like a Duck, It May *Not* Be a Duck

Over those two mid-century summer days in Duluth, Minnesota, much to his popular opponent's dismay, Skinner held firm that the relative freedom of speech is an affordance of systems that reinforce it to greater or lesser degrees, rather than a latent psychic quality of any one individual participant in it. On that stage, Skinner dared to insist that human behaviour, including speech behaviour, is driven by something other than the inner forces of individuals themselves. This audaciously implied, as Rogers rightly extrapolated, that human speech is unfree *if* freedom is narrowly conceived as an unfettered expression of a psychic interior.

Consider one last exchange, in which Rogers challenged Skinner to explain to a Freedom Rider as "a locus of unique forces which have predetermined him to move southward to site in certain illegal places," to which Skinner confidently responded: "There are many cultures which would never produce Freedom Riders at all" (*Dialogue* 1976). Clearly, given his experimental and utopian projects, this should not be read as an avowal of the state of American democracy, as Skinner then saw it. Rather, it is a reminder that the freedom of speech and other behaviours are the creatures of the ongoing experiment of American democracy. America's most prominent radical behaviourist called on fellow citizens to reflexively calibrate, rather than obscure or deny, the conditions that foster free speech, with freedom always measured by what is produced rather than simply expressed.

Indeed, by pointing to the paradoxes involved in directing ostensibly autonomous subjects and co-producing putatively free speech, Skinner and his duck story did more than critically highlight the political limitations of an asocial view of speech as autonomous self-expression. He also proposed an alternative approach to American political life that recognizes and values the social indices of verbal behaviour, and carefully crafts the conditions for transparent, reflexive, and responsive democratic exchange.

19 Therapeutic Politics and the Performance of Reparation: A Dialogical Approach to Mental Health Care in the UK

FIONA WRIGHT

A young woman is sitting on a chair, arms crossed in front of her, her back facing a room full of people she has never met before and who know nothing of her life. Beside her sits her father, and on the other side, her mother. Facing them, towards the audience of mental health professionals in training, sit a psychiatrist and a mental health nurse, their chairs turned to form a circle enclosing this intimate yet very public dialogue. The young woman, Anne, starts to speak, nervously, laughing quietly as she remarks on the way she has positioned herself to sit with her back towards all these strangers. She pauses and then continues, the psychiatrist and nurse looking at her warmly and listening, nodding regularly in agreement and encouragement, and the family talk among themselves following Anne's lead for the best part of half an hour before the nurse offers any response. We hear about Anne's struggles while she still went to school, the tensions in her family, her attempts to make sense of what was happening in her life, and her eventual diagnosis of bipolar disorder during a brief but distressing stay in the acute psychiatric ward of a hospital. Her parents' interjections as she speaks – remarking about their feelings when Anne hit certain lows, and communicating their support for her but also their fears, their desires for her life, and their ideas about what might make things better for her – are offered with their voices louder and more confident than that of Anne, but sometimes they waver, pausing as they gather themselves when on the verge of tears.

The nurse starts to speak only when Anne talks of their first encounter, around fifteen months before today's meeting, when they had started to work together in the therapeutic practice of "Open Dialogue" that they are now engaged in demonstrating for this audience of training practitioners. They smile at each other, mutually reflecting on what they describe as the "journey" they had been on to reach the point that Anne is considering moving away from her parents and going back to education. Having started from the aftermath of her detention and forced treatment under the UK's Mental Health Act, and her parents' shock and feelings of helplessness in the face of her emotions and behaviours, they describe some of the difficulties and processes of trans-formation they had each faced. Anne talks about her pleasure in discovering that she could form relationships of trust with the nurse and the psychiatrist, having previously experienced mental health care professionals as complicit in her suffering – not listening to her but rather imposing on her both their understandings of her problems and medication that she didn't want to take. The psychiatrist smiles listening to this, reflecting on how she, too, had experi-enced their relationship as a revelation – that gaining Anne's trust through their conversations had changed the way she thinks about how she interacts with all her patients. She also describes how in her own life she had experienced challenges as a mother, trying to balance the urge to protect her child with the need to let them make their own decisions and choices, and she shares how she had felt an emotional connection with Anne's parents in light of this shared life experience. The five of them continue to talk in this way – between poignant reflections, gentle humour, and moments of delicacy and sadness – for around another forty minutes as those gathered around the circle listen and watch, seemingly absorbed in the ebbs and flows of this conversation.

The conversation – dialogue, in the terms of its participants – took place as part of a training program in which mental health practitioners in the UK were learning the language and techniques of a therapeutic approach called Peer-Supported Open Dialogue. The audience to the dialogue of Anne, her family, and the practitioners working with her, were among the several hundred mental health care professionals from across the UK, who since 2014 have been undertaking such training programs. In these programs, trainees are encouraged to question the premise and use of their clinical expertise, to challenge hierarchical relationships among mental health professionals, as well as between professionals and service users, and to fundamentally reorient their approach to psychological distress by undermining their own sense of certainty about what it is to experience mental ill health. Psychiatrists, psychologists, nurses, social workers, occupational therapists, peer support workers, and others, have all been among those to embark on what they often refer to as their "journey," training and starting to practise, in this approach. Central to Peer-Supported Open Dialogue, or "POD," are the practitioners' endeavours to learn a different kind of therapeutic language, in which the words of service users and their family and friends are placed at the centre of therapeutic sessions through a particular set of linguistic and embodied techniques. As a way of trying to avoid the deficiencies of mental health care typical in "treatment as usual," in POD, several practitioners will meet with a service user and members of their "social network" (this can refer to anyone the service user wants to bring to a session, but generally – in discussion and in practice – means members of their family) in the midst of crisis. In this meeting, practitioners will attempt to create an encounter in which diagnostic categories and questions about medication are secondary to a focus on the words and feelings of the service user, their family members and friends, and indeed also on the affective responses of the practitioners. The approach seeks to avoid, as far as possible, the potential violence of involuntary hospital admissions and coercive treatment that are otherwise so common in service users' trajectories through mental health care services.

I followed the attempts of mental health practitioners to reorient their professional lives in this way over a two-year period, doing ethnographic research at training sessions, public events, and in staff meetings and supervisions. Learning the language of POD requires an intensive and often personally challenging process of *un*learning of clinical expertise and identity, as many practitioners describe it, with training programs using techniques such as mindfulness meditation, group role-play sessions, and explorations of trainees' own family and social histories, in order to lead practitioners to experience forms of relationality and vulnerability that are to be the basis of their new style of working with service users. These programs rely heavily on the performance of the approach in "live" dialogues, sometimes with networks appearing as guests in the training program and making themselves vulnerable by entering into a dialogue in front of an audience of trainees, as Anne and her family did. Or these live dialogues feature participants in the program themselves experimenting with the genre as they reflect in front of the rest of the group about their personal and professional experiences, and often about their experience of the training program and the process of re-education they are going through. This dialogue format was rarely absent from any POD event, whether a clinical session, a team meeting, a training program, or public-facing events such as the POD annual conference: a performance of affects and embodied responses among speakers and listeners is central to how POD attempts to have both healing and persuasive effect.

The dialogue as a performative act, voiced by participants seated on chairs in a circle facing each other, is a key embodied and linguistic form in which anyone who becomes involved in POD is required to become fluent – the way in which one introduces oneself (first names, no titles, often with a personal anecdote or detail about one's life), how to use body language to indicate one's willingness to listen and be open to others (leaning forward, arms open), what kind of words to choose (talking about how you feel listening to the words of another person rather than talking about what you interpret of their situation). As such, these dialogues require a kind of public vulnerability, an exposure of the self and an affective relationality that is felt to be unfamiliar in these kinds of therapeutic and professional spaces. There are often emotional moments, and personal revelations that feel weighty. With speakers often referencing a past state of affairs, a more coercive or damaging one, they require an empathetic response that creates a new kind of relationship among the participants. These encounters are thus transformative of the people involved, and work to create the sense of a broader social project of which they are all a part. The regular and repeated performance of these dialogues takes on the form of a ritualized language and space through which people become emotionally and professionally invested in Peer-Supported Open Dialogue, and which signals the coming into being of a movement pushing for systemic reform in mental health care services.

In this chapter I reflect on how the set of embodied linguistic practices that form the basis of this therapeutic space are informed by political ideals of collective repair in the face of systemic suffering, and professionals' complicity with that suffering. In tune with other chapters in this section, I suggest that this particular manifestation of therapeutic speech, and its ideas of liberation from suffering, reflect the political paradigms and debates of its time. In this case, the practices of speaking, listening, and response at play, and their capacities to do or undo harm, to be more or less free from harmful social practices, have much in common with what has been described as the "rupture-repair-redemption paradigm" (Drabinski 2013) of moves to promote reconciliation in post-conflict settings. In a similar vein to Michael Lempert's tracing of the cultivation of "receptive co-presence" thought to be required for the right kind of listening in postwar American liberal democracy (this volume), and Summerson Carr's study of American psychotherapies as dynamic sites manifesting political questions and free speech ideals (this volume), here I consider the form of truth-telling engendered in POD as a manifestation of an embodied mode of reckoning with past harms requiring a form of performed public vulnerability through words spoken and received. These modes of publicity and vulnerable testimony recall those that have become emblematic of a global reparative politics.

The specific ways in which mental health practitioners and service users are invited to publicly stage a recalibration of their relationships, and its potential to repair harms done, are akin, I submit, to how perpetrator-victim relationships are framed in the forms of reparation considered to be possible through practices of public testimony and witnessing. As I will elaborate in what follows, the ways in which POD imagines power relationships to be manifested and potentially changed through specific speech and listening practices reflects how therapeutic speech practices are imagined here not only as addressing the subjective or interpersonal domain, but as themselves having political effects. I will argue, in this vein, that not only has politics taken on the language of the therapeutic, as is commonly suggested (and mostly in the sense that this is to the detriment of collective political struggles), but that therapeutic speech practices work with and on bodies and subjectivities that are presupposed as the basis of reparative politics. Thus, to consider the idea of social and political repair in the wake of harm done, we need to attend not only to the truth-telling speech that is thought to expose wrongdoing, but to the ways those who speak and hear it are invited to be in relation with one another in and through these speech practices.

Crucially, in POD, the performed public dialogues often involve both a reckoning with the past and a performance of an alternative social and therapeutic orientation in the present. Those who have experienced mental health services first hand often speak of the harm done to them through the failings of the system of care as it has existed in the wake of deinstitutionalization and the rise of biomedical, rather than psycho-social, approaches to psychological distress, as well as in the undermining of even those services under austerity politics and its stripping back of mental health care services over the past decade in the UK (F. Wright 2022). Narratives of suffering under a broken, neglectful system, as well as in the face of cruel encounters with individual professionals working within it, are often prominent in how people frame their experiences of psychological suffering and any forms of healing they have experienced. Understandings of the harms people have suffered while under the care of the UK's state mental health services are discursively linked to a view of those services as themselves being in crisis, a condition that is linked with the ways in which coercive treatment and detention in psychiatric wards can be experienced as violent and retraumatizing. POD is often then introduced as a form of redress, sometimes even redemption, when these experiences of suffering can be bracketed as in the past, or at least as in the process of being worked through.[1] Through the approach a new language and embodiment of relational, vulnerable selves – mutually implicated in distress and enabled to address it – emerge in the present as performed in the dialogue.

This ritualized mode of therapeutic speech carries strong echoes of similarly collective and performative forms of testimony and truth-telling in post-conflict and settler colonial settings, where truth and reconciliation commissions (TRCs) have often been at the forefront of movements for justice and reparation. Partaking in a globalized genre of witnessing, in what John Borneman (2002) described as a form of "cultivated listening" that is made essential to the kind of truth-telling emerging in these modes of speech, POD's dialogues

---

1 POD as it is being introduced in the UK is a particular version and development of Open Dialogue – a therapeutic method developed in Finland's Western Lapland region since the 1980s – and follows its core principles and practices (Seikkula 2011; Seikkula and Arnkil 2006, 2014). Two key adjustments to POD in the UK context have been (1) the involvement of peer support workers, practitioners who are explicitly recognized as having "lived experience" of mental health difficulties and services themselves, and who use this experience in their therapeutic encounters with other service users; and (2) the practice of mindfulness by POD practitioners (Razzaque 2015, 2018).

share with the politics of TRCs the premise that a social and political transformation will be brought about through these ritualized speech performances. In POD gatherings, participants often spoke about their practice with reference to political movements, one trainer referring to the need to challenge suffering within mental health care as the "last great struggle" in the civil rights movement. Another spoke about POD's dialogical methods as being not just about psychological distress but as connected to a democratic deficit evidenced in political events such as the Brexit vote and Donald Trump's election as US president, suggesting that the modes of listening and responding practised in POD could be the basis of a revitalized polity as well as having individual therapeutic effects. Central to the link I am drawing between this global politics of reparative speech and POD's dialogical therapy, and to the link POD practitioners themselves drew between their therapeutic speech and notions of being implicated in a wider social nexus, is the notion of an accountability made public, the performativity of words that, by being spoken in a particular way before an audience, invoke specific interpersonal and thus political effects. For the truths told in this genre involve risk in the exposure of participants' past and present vulnerability, their capacity to be injured by the forms of care and coercion described but also, in the case of the mental health practitioners involved, their modes of complicity with these practices and the transformation they undergo in acknowledging and addressing their own positions within this system.

As in Drabinski's (2013) analysis of the politics of reconciliation, in this case too, the close study of the "kinesics of truth-telling speech" – the gestures, the words, the tone of the telling – reveals that the embodied performances of telling these truths, and of reforming selves and relationships, are critical in these moments' ritual efficacy. Consider the following scene, in which forms of speech and listening constitute a ritualized inversion of a normalized hierarchy between practitioner and service user, considered as effective in the reconfiguration of power relationships within the therapeutic practice. In front of a room crowded with practitioners training in POD, two women sit on chairs, elevated on a stage, one empty chair between them. Jenny – a woman whose experiences of being subject to mental health care services, including sometimes coercive treatment that she brings to her work as a peer support worker in a POD team – is interviewed by Rachael, a psychologist. Their conversation lasts the best part of an hour before they take questions from those in the room. Narrating what she describes as her "journey" through several psychological crises, family breakdowns and moments of abandonment, and her attempts to enter and re-enter paid work, Jenny talks at length and with ease in a manner that she is clearly accustomed to. Rachael does not need to ask much, only offering brief responses, voicing empathy and sharing the feelings evoked for her by listening to Jenny's narrative. Details of Jenny's time spent in an acute psychiatric ward, "pacing the halls," being put on and taken off various psychotropic medications with each subsequent admission and change in doctor, form the backbone of her account. A social worker who looks beyond medication to help her with her benefits and housing, and a psychiatrist who takes a critical view of the long list of diagnoses and treatments she has endured and takes her off all of her medications, offering his time and sitting with her unmedicated self simply in order to listen, appear as key figures whose presence prefigure the therapeutic relations to which the POD trainees in the room are invited to aspire. After a short pause, a moment of silence, Rachael asks, "Can I just reflect?" Jenny nods and Rachael, pointing to the unoccupied chair in between them, becomes tearful and says, "Just thinking about the voices not in the room ... I just feel really sad sitting here."

Rachael's invoking the "voices not in the room" and linking her emotional state to their absence connected the dialogue between her and Jenny to the more standard circular format of POD and its staging of particular relational forms. For while there had been a back and forth between Jenny and Rachael, parts of their conversation felt much more "monological," in POD's terms, in that Jenny spoke at length, uninterrupted, as an "expert by experience," using the time given to her to speak in front of this audience to inform them of her experiences. It was clear that it was not the first time she had given an account of herself in that way, and that she had become one of those people whose suffering in relation to mental health services was regularly mobilized to invite a certain kind of self-reflection on the part of its practitioners – someone whose "lived experience" was considered the basis of a privileged form of truth-telling thought to have the capacity to shake up long-standing inequalities in whose voice is heard and legitimized in relation to psychological distress. Where "monological" modes of speaking (those that involved the practitioner speaking from a privileged position of expertise, by, for example, the clinician giving advice, talking about treatment plans, or initiating new subjects the network members have not brought up) were discouraged during the POD training program, here it served a rhetorical purpose, inverting how power relations were understood in the POD community to place the service user in the position of monological authority in relation to the practitioners.[2] The "voices not in the room" imagined by Rachael were those other service users who had not been able to speak publicly of their distress as Jenny had, and perhaps their family members, even those occupying the position that Rachael did of the therapist whose role it is to facilitate the voicing of suffering. In calling forth those absent voices, Rachael brings the relationships among people occupying

---

2 For ethnographies of the monologic, and a discussion of the relationship between monological and dialogical speech, see Tomlinson and Millie (2017).

these various positions into the conversation, inviting the audience of practitioners to relate to Jenny's story as a part of the dialogical mode of communication in which they are being trained. She invokes a wider community in which relationships of responsibility and complicity are to be renegotiated through certain linguistic formulations and the delivery of them in particular embodied ways.

This wider community is one bound through the expression of affect, as is reflected in the way Rachael chokes on her words above, tears forming as she is moved by the relations she makes part of her conversation with Jenny. Showing one's vulnerability and exposing one's emotional responses were core aspects of dialogical communication taught to the practitioners undertaking the POD training. As well as staged dialogues between people like Jenny and Rachael, as described above, practitioners, in particular, were thought to need particular training in both feeling and expressing their emotions. The training program assigned considerable space for reflection and public speech of a kind imagined to allow affects to seep through an otherwise detached persona who has been professionalized not to show their own vulnerability. For example, in the "fishbowl" slots, often timetabled at the end of a day or week of the training program, those attending the program would sit in a large circle around a small inner circle or four of five chairs, where there was a microphone ready to be passed on to the next person who would come to occupy one of the central chairs in order to share some feeling or reflection on their experience in the training in front of the whole group. These were often moments of intense collective feeling, in which those picking up the microphone would give voice both to a confessional practice (speaking of the harm they feel they have been party to in the past) and to their own emotional response to this reckoning.

For example, Benjamin, a clinical psychologist, spoke during one fishbowl about how during the training he had come to recognize that he had been "dead to [his] own feelings" in his professional practice, and after the training felt that he had been given a way to bring his emotions and vulnerabilities into his work that would help to create a therapeutic relationship with service users. Another trainee, social worker Amanda, broke down in tears as she spoke about the discomfort she had felt for many years in relation to things she witnessed, as well as in her own practice, at work, and that with the mode of being in dialogical relation with service users enabled by POD, she would finally be able to practise "with integrity." These forms of communication that particularly encouraged practitioners to publicly speak of their implication in the doing of harm, and a commitment to a different future practice, served to underline the structural designs of these speech practices, in that through embodying and performing a vulnerable self, the directionality of the psychological and affective impact of the therapeutic practice is destabilized. This redirection of harm through public, truth-telling speech, is considered in POD to be central in remaking a dialogical community of speakers and listeners whose shared vulnerability facilitates psychological repair.[3]

These speech practices – the words participants are invited to speak, and the affective and embodied expressions and practices that are considered necessary to deliver and to listen to them – bear strong resemblance to those of TRCs. Ronald Niezen (2016, 925–6, 930) describes how Canada's TRC on Indian residential schools affirmed the "survivor" as its dominant category of victimhood through specific forms of giving testimony. Much like the scenes described above, people were invited to sit in chairs in a circle, with audiences around them listening, while former students narrated histories of traumatic events of abuse and humiliation, so much so that those without such traumatic experiences were reluctant to take up the microphone. As Niezen argues, such practices do much more than simply provide a space in which certain truths can be told. Rather, they shape what forms of truth will be recognized as such, through inviting certain categories of person ("survivor" and "perpetrator") to perform an affective and embodied form of speaking and listening considered as authentic in that context. These forms become exemplars as forms of truth telling that can both uncover hidden histories and provide a form of healing (Shaw 2007).

The politicized ideal of reparative speech as it is manifested in these kind of spaces, as well as in POD, then, involves an elaborate set of practices around the words spoken, which produces a certain framing of ethical and affective relations among its speakers and listeners. The intended result is a recalibration of those relationships based on the ritualized telling of painful histories. As Borneman (2002, 289; emphasis in original) suggests, witnessing here "involves the listening and speaking of at least two parties, and its intended end is *truth-telling* ... giving voice to individuals who have been silenced, but here I want instead to concentrate on witnessing as an act of listening, on the relation of speaking to the listener, a third party after a violent conflict." As Lempert (in this volume) similarly argues, listening "is not passive but interactive, involving soliciting, questioning, and weighing competing accounts, as well as hearing. Listening can be learned and cultivated, and some individuals are far better at it than others. I am suggesting here that we rethink the very practice of listening – both what should be listened for, and who might be the best practitioners of listening after violent events" (Borneman 2002, 293). Similar to POD's emphasis on listening as central to effective dialogue, Borneman's (2002) interest in finding better forms of listening itself echoes a broader cultural investment in listening as ethical and political practice, in which the idea

3 For a more extended discussion on understandings of the relationship between speech, harm, and affect in late liberalism see F. Wright (forthcoming).

that how one positions oneself as listener will affect what kind of redress can be done in light of harms done, and one's complicity with them. In POD, the rotation of trainees from the position of speaker, giving voice to one's role in sometimes harmful practices, to that of listener, the witness to fellow practitioners' similarly confessional accounts, works to create a community of truth-tellers who are such only insofar as they also hear and hold each other accountable. Thus here, too, listening comes to hold an ethical and political quality as a crucial element in the dialogical form that is held up as the grounds of reparative speech practices.

Scholars of TRCs in the arena of global politics have analyzed how the therapeutic logic of speech events in post-conflict settings or in the aftermath of founding historical violence works to create the effect of a scene of reparation: as if something previously whole had been broken by violence, and is repaired in the ritual moment – when justice is done – and wholes are once again made. The "rupture-repair-redemption" paradigm (Drabinski 2013) works on the premise that it is the act of truth-telling through the exposure and transformation of vulnerable, injured subjects that can repair a broken community and move a collective towards justice and democratic futures. As Richard Wilson (2001, 98) notes, TRCs and human rights hearings in post-conflict settings were "emotionally intense public ceremonies which generated collective moral values and sought to inculcate them in all who participated." The moral and political force of this embodied and affective relationship to truth and repair are also connected to its pitfalls – the ways in which it sidelines enduring structural violence and may prioritize certain forms of performed, public victimhood which eclipse people's ongoing struggles. If it is the "triumph of the therapeutic" (Torpey 2001) in these domains of political transformation after violence that is often analyzed as a problematic feature of TRCs, what of the translation back into the therapeutic domain of this politicization of healing speech? For, in Peer-Supported Open Dialogue, the voice of the therapeutic encounter is charged with a moral and political force, seeming to borrow from the ways in which politics has been spoken in the language of healing.

In one way of understanding such practices, TRCs are seen to be indicative of an increasingly dominant mode of politics in which psychological and bodily states come to the fore, at the cost of thinking about systems, structures, and histories. In this analysis, we lose out on the collective ability to effect systemic change, because of the limiting of the field of political struggle to the inter-subjective, therapeutic realm. There is another way in which we might view these embodied performances, though, and here it is important to think about how these dialogues have travelled – from the scene of therapy, to the domain of politics and justice, and back again. In the retranslation back into the domain of injured and healing selves and relationships, the practice of performing vulnerability and the exposure to risk involved in truth-telling has lent words and gestures a different quality, a political force. The healing promise of the therapeutic space also becomes a mode of addressing the harms done beyond the personal relationships being voiced between the people sitting in the circle of a dialogue. So it is not only, as Drabinski (2013, 119) argues about the politics of reconciliation, that "we have to live with, and sometimes as, this body who is performing and gesturing such sadness. All of this violence haunts us yet at the same time promises to transform our possibilities as a polity." Rather, or also, this polity is invoked and transformed in the reconfigurations of embodied selves and relationships that are performed in the dialogical approach to psychological harm and distress that I have described in this chapter. POD's performed vulnerability can be understood as a ritualized mode of therapeutic speech that partakes in a global politics of testimony and witnessing, in which what is remade, or repaired, is the very idea of political community, and not only the psychological states of its members. In this sense injuries and vulnerability become part and parcel of what is considered as the healing capacity of truth-telling speech – reparation as a process of speaking the truth of violence done, and embodying the broken foundation on which relationships can be transformed.

As scholars have noted, this modality of truth-telling speech – that of authentic testimony and confession – both has a grounding in Christian discourses on suffering, forgiveness, and redemption (Derrida's "Globalatinization" [Drabinski 2013, 120]) and is merged with a notion of reconciliation that is vague enough that it can appeal to different groups of people with various agendas (R. Wilson 2001, 101–10). Thus, its uptake and transformation in POD can be married with an eclectic array of founding texts and approaches to the therapeutics (in POD these include Bakhtin's thought on dialogism, theories and practices from systemic family therapy, and Buddhist meditation). In common, however, these political forms presuppose the possibility of repair based on the exposure of the truths of rupture through words spoken and heard, a paradigm mirrored in therapeutic forms that view their work as the repair of community and polity, as well as intersubjective healing. Speaking and listening in the truth-telling forms of Peer-Supported Open Dialogue is thus as much the enactment of an imaginary of reparative citizenship, as it is a therapeutic mode seeking to facilitate repair within and between those who perform its language of vulnerable testimony.

20 Secrecy, Curse, Psychiatrist, Saint: Scandals of Sexuality and Censorship in Global/Indian Publics

SARAH PINTO

> In dealing with an open-secret structure, it's only by being shameless about risking the obvious that we happen into the vicinity of the transformative.
> – Eve Kosowsky Sedgwick, *Epistemology of the Closet* (1990)

To get it out of the way, let's begin with a hateful portrayal. The farcical 2014 Bengali film *Obhishopto Nighty* (The cursed nighty) follows the absurdities that ensue when a nightgown cursed to awaken sexual appetites is passed from woman to woman across contemporary Kolkata. Entangling realities and meta-realities, the film's fantastical and exhilarating message of sexual liberation is paired with a critique of censorship and its bureaucracies, as ludic scenes are interrupted by a censor board sitting beneath giant scissors streaked with blood. Amid all the fun, there is a sour note in the form of a crass portrayal of a non-binary character, a newspaper editor whose queerness is played for a laugh as their over-the-top desires draw revulsion from the main character. The character is an undeniable send-up of filmmaker Rituparno Ghosh, who died a year before the film was released. The film's thinly veiled mockery – so homophobic, so shocking – so spoiled the reception of the film that it became the topic of most of the film's (limited) media coverage, including an account of filmmaker Aparna Sen's dramatic walkout on a screening (*Times of India* 2014).

For a film that (cl)aims to expose the hypocrisies of sexual repression, is this hypocrisy? The ugly limit of progressive critique? Or is it obvious – a step too far in a film that makes fun of everyone (as though all mockery is the same)? Or does it point to an encompassing logic, one that both impels and interrupts concepts of "freedom of speech"? Or is it simply a map of permissible and impermissible desires in post-millennial West Bengal?

A few other themes are worth consideration. First, *secrecy*, which is here associated with things spectral. The accursed nighty falls into the hands of an ingénue actress, Brishti/Apsara, who, when wearing it can bypass her moral and physical aversion to the grotesque movie producers who want her to barter sex for film roles; in short, the nighty helps her put out. When a reporter, Apu, learns that Brishti/Apsara "broke a record" by signing twelve films in one night, he seeks out her secret and discovers the nighty. The article he writes goes viral and the city is hysterical with a sex panic-cum-scandal (pun intended – and used in the film's marketing) with sightings of the nighty (which Apsara has lost). Apu learns from a fortune teller about the nighty's dark past (a dying lounge singer cursed the nighty as revenge on her lover/murderer). Together Apu and Apsara essentially exorcise the nighty, rendering it useless. At one level, the plot's architecture is Freudian, its therapeutic that of the hysterical symptom. But there is also the matter of the *curse* – a second key theme. Aligning repressed speech with repressed desire, vignettes show the undoing effects of sexual liberation (generated by a curse), embodied as both symptom and secret by the nighty. Curse, secret, symptom – tangles of agency and its absence, twisted sisters of expression – propel a message about free expression and the agentive subject.

Perhaps in atonement for *Obhoshopto Nighty*, or basic irony, Parambrata Chatterjee, the actor who portrayed Apu, starred in *Samantaral* (2019) about a male-presenting person whose mental illness-like symptoms are revealed to masquerade the film's central secret: that she is transgender and wishes to live as a woman. Though the secret of her gender identity is initially *understood* by another female character, the secret is *explained* to the audience by a psychiatrist, in a minor but pivotal role. And so we arrive at a third element: the *psychiatrist*. At key moments of *Obhoshopto Nighty*, the film-within-a-film (if that is what it is) stutters to a freeze-frame, and the censor board – comprised of a businessman, fire chief, sociologist, "film and theater personality," and psychiatrist – debate the scene's merits according to their specialization: the sociologist elucidates the ills of modern society, the psychiatrist describes psychological syndromes. In one subplot, a middle-aged singer besotted with Rabindranath Tagorea asks a wall-sized photograph of the bard, "Who sings your songs best?" The photo replies, "Tumi, tumi, tumi" ("You, you, you," in the familiar form). The film stops and we are back in the cutting room, where the actor asks, "How can they make this kind of joke about Tagore?" The psychiatrist explains, "This is the idea of the woman, not of Tagore … You can call this a kind of hallucination. You can call it Extra-Tagore Syndrome." (The actor insists they "beep" Tagore's "tumi," asking, "How can you interfere with a cultural icon?")

In Bengali films, psychiatrists pop up everywhere. Occasionally villains, they are more often sympathetic characters who propel the plot through discovery and exegesis, *explaining* (diagnoses), *contextualizing* (behaviours), *educating* (about mental health), and *enabling* (characters to solve dilemmas). The quality of their speech is remarkably consistent, aligning truth with transformation, freedom with therapeutics, producing speech that is often semi-concealed and ephemeral, along the way, to the side, dislodged from the permanence of publicity. In few cases does their language attach to either "Western" or "Indian," "secular" or "religious" forms (compared to the diacritical quality of psychiatrist characters in certain Hindi films; Pinto 2014). In *Obhoshopto Nighty*'s censor-board scenes, the psychiatrist contributes to the film's economy of knowledge with absurd theories that encompass another economy of knowledge – that of the secret that orients the primary plot. Playing with the proximity of cultural offence and social/psychological explanation, he is both made fun of and part of a larger poking fun at sexual prurience and wounded cultural sentiments, whose capacity to violence is made vivid by the massive scissors. (Is it an accident, perhaps, that the derided gay character is an editor?)

What happens if we take seriously the way these elements hang together – not just sex and the scandal of making it public, and not just critique of censorship and offensive speech (obvious bedmates, or nighty-sharers), but another set of things: psychiatrists, secrets, curses, what, for now, I'll call (imperfectly) "homosexuality," and what is sometimes, as in *Obhishopto Nighty*, collapsed with it, what for now I'll call (imperfectly) "transgender"? How might these elements, enchained, help us reckon with the relationship between "freedom of speech" (a supposedly atemporal liberal form) and "secrecy" in its temporally, culturally, and representationally located forms?

Historically, Indian film censorship has focused on sexuality, regulating pleasures in visual form that, in the early decades of the twentieth century, attached to questions of class and the varying ability of audiences to "recognize" and thus "be offended by" sexual innuendo (Mazzarella 2013; Mazzarella and Kaur 2012). Towards the end of the twentieth century, questions of censorship increasingly figured as a "cultural offence," which came to be sutured less to heterosexual sex acts (like kissing) than to portrayals of homosexuality, though, of course, these have long been conjoined, as in the simultaneous obscenity trials of Ismat Chugtai and Saadat Hasan Manto in 1944. Beyond film, economies of secrecy and exposure figured in scandals over "cultural offense," and censorship involved as much a politics of reading and revising as speaking/showing. In censorship of books, scholarship, and other literary portrayals, diverse qualities of secrecy did more than invite corrective work; they become the voice of correction. It is at these junctures – and their obvious/unobvious scenes of contraction – that "homosexuality," as a discrete identity/form, became especially potent, through and against diverse registers of what we might call "queer."

Suggesting campy pleasures, *Obhishopto Nighty* invites us in and betrays us. If its colourful indie absurdities entice us into circuits of reading by breaking and re-erecting boundaries between reader and text (fourth walls would be too easy), its sudden homophobia/transphobia requires we take seriously what such critical economies traffic in. It raises the possibility that the arrangement – sex is a problem of publicity and its political and social conditions – recognizable in the history of censorship *of* film in India can be productively reversed when it comes to portrayals of censorship *in* (this) film: publicity, and its contours may be a product of the way certain instantiations of "sex" motivate economies of concealment and disclosure. This analytic choreography is drawn from the early work of Eve Kosowsky Sedgwick, notably the book *Epistemology of the Closet* (1990), whose argument can be summarized as follows: since the end of the nineteenth century, "energy of attention and demarcation ... has been impelled by the distinctively indicative relation of homosexuality to wider mappings of secrecy and disclosure, and of the private and the public" (71). As such, "the most crucial sites for the contestation of meaning" in the twentieth century are "indelibly marked with the historical specificity of homosocial/ homosexual definition," including "secrecy/disclosure and private/public" at the heart of chains of associated pairings (72). What "history of readings" (Sedgwick's phrase) might be propelled by the problem of *Obhishopto Nighty*?

This chapter offers one possibility, shifting from film to text, by revisiting an academic scandal of the 1990s, the 1890s text it debated, a culturally adjacent (1890s) text, and a recent film that reconceives the second 1890s text. Sedgwick (1990) is part of this history in compounding ways, offering both contexts and metatexts that allow us to trace mobilities that are at once "of" as well as "in" their time. I borrow that cadence from Mazzarella and Kaur (2012, 6) who note that censorship in India "is not just *in* but *of* the public sphere," constituting what "public" might come to be and who has rights to it, a thing not just of censor board screening rooms but publics more generally (see Mazzarella 2013). As such, formal censorship is a "particular," even "privileged" form of a "more general set of practices" of "cultural regulation" (Mazzarella and Kaur 2019, 9), "public cultural interventions" that may seem diametrically opposed – a readerly dilemma akin to that of *Obhishopto Nighty*. Among the products of these intervention is a sense of the obvious, the open secret, a form Sedgwick (1990, 8) considered an integral effect of the epistemology of the closet, by which "particular insights generate, are lined with, and at the same time are themselves structured by particular opacities." Important to that passage is its emphasis on the particular. The open secret is not one thing but many, its public one of contradictory "interventions" – like moral opprobrium and liberal understanding. With particularities in mind, we might ask less if a thing is obvious *or* contradictory, and, instead, what forms of the obvious are transferrable and transformable.

Scandal

In the last years of the twentieth century, the field of religious studies, especially the corners concerned with Hinduism, was wracked with debate over the 1995 publication of *Kali's Child: The Mystical and the Erotic in the Life and Teachings of Ramakrishna*, by Jeffrey Kripal. Based on Kripal's PhD dissertation, *Kali's Child* re-examined biographical and religious writings about the nineteenth-century Bengali sage Ramakrishna, arguing that, contrary to the orthodox view of the Ramakrishna Order, the saint's mysticism was driven by Tantric concepts and practices, mystical experiences fuelled by homoerotic energies. Through psychoanalytically informed analysis of passages from the *Kathamrita*, the hagiographic text on Ramakrishna's life written by his follower Madhusudan Gupta (or M.), Kripal argued that a better understanding of mysticism, especially its tantric forms, might come from exploring the ways "homosexual" erotics shape transformative religious experiences. Kripal focused on sections of the *Kathamrita* designated "secret teachings," accounts of Ramakrishna's experiences of the goddess Kali and interactions with his devotees. Kripal (1998, 5)[1] argued that these had been obscured in "bowdlerized" translations and the transformation of Ramakrishna's teachings into the asceticized, masculinized vision of Hinduism established by Ramakrishna's successor, Vivekananda, and promoted by the Order.

Kripal's (1998) observations were neither entirely new nor surprising, though the frank discussion of the homoerotics of mysticism was considered innovative for Hindu studies. Initially, *Kali's Child* was well received in academia, receiving the History of Religions Prize from the American Academy of Religion and positive reviews from prominent scholars (Haberman 1997; Parsons 1997; John Hawley 1998; Radice 1998; Urban 1998). Most academic reviewers felt that *Kali's Child* raised important questions, initiated conversations about mysticism and homoeroticism, and rigorously read important texts. Some noted that Tantrism was a metonym for larger disciplinary concerns, and that, in Kripal's hands, the *Kathamrita,* was a site of scholarly "recovery" and dismantling of puritanical revisionism (Patton 2019). By "recovering" aspects of Ramakrishna's life and teachings, Kripal had restored the freedom and exuberance lost in "the straightlaced, socially conscious asceticism through which Vivekananda brought Ramakrishna to the world" (John Hawley 1998, 404), and his effort to "penetrate the layers of pious obfuscation and reverential distortion" had "recover[ed] the original Bengali texts" (Urban 1998, 318).

---

1   From this point onward, references to *Kali's Child* are to the second (1998) edition of the book, which includes Kripal's preface responding to the events described here. For a more thorough review of the debate, see Brian Hatcher (1999).

Meanwhile, fires of criticism were being lit in reviews accusing Kripal of sensationalism, mistranslation (Oppenshaw 1995; Ray 1997), "monocausal reductionism" (Larson 1997, 658), and failing to consult the Ramakrishna Order (Larson 1997). Members of the Order wrote painstaking rebuttals, arguing that poor understanding of Bengali had led Kripal to impose homoerotic desires and actions on the saint (Ātmajñānānanda 1997). Calls were raised for the book to be banned, letters were written asking the University of Chicago to renounce approval of Kripal's dissertation. Perhaps the most inflammatory, or at least most infamous, response was a full-page review in Calcutta's *The Statesman* newspaper written by Narasingha Sil (1997), also author of a psychoanalytically informed biography of Ramakrishna (Sil 1991), which had connected the saint's religious experiences with childhood abuse. In his review, Sil (1997) lobbed insults accusing Kripal of attacking Hindu culture, having poor knowledge of Bengali, exhibiting crassness, and producing a work that was, in the final words of the review, "plain shit." *The Statesman* published initial responses, but following a flood of letters took the remarkable step of closing the conversation in a 1997 Op-Ed titled "And Now Let It Rest." While diatribes against *Kali's Child* continued in print (Tyagananda 2000; Tyagananda and Vrajaprana 2010), they began to find a home on the internet, amid the consolidation of Hindu nationalist voices on new websites that collated, facilitated, and amplified diverse accusations of cultural offence, notably in US academia.[2]

In several essays and in the preface to the second edition of *Kali's Child*, Kripal responded to his critics, apologizing for certain mistranslations and defending his arguments, the soundness of his translation, and validity of his analytic. For Kripal and his supporters, the debate emphasized the fortress of policed speech, puritanical thinking, and historical revisionism that surrounded Ramakrishna, and Hinduism more generally. It was the critics, Kripal wrote, who reduced a complex discussion of mysticism to a pointed discussion of Ramakrishna's sex-life.

Many agreed that what Kripal "exposed" was hardly news. In an illuminating essay, Brian Hatcher wrote,

> While Kripal makes much of the way Ramakrishna's secrets have been concealed by his followers, one would have to say that they have done a somewhat poor job of concealing; after all, one can purchase the complete Bengali

2 As Patton (2019, 238) argues, the "second wave of critique [was] conducted largely on and through the internet," and "evolved into an institutional critique" by conjoining instances with scholars' home institutions. Rajiv Malhotra's Infinity Foundation hosts the Sulekha website that continues to hold an archive of critiques of Kripal's work, and is a key node in a network supporting Hindu nationalist causes in the US and funding university endeavours.

utterances of Ramakrishna right in the foyer of the Ramakrishna Institute in Gol Park. (1999, 178)

Ramakrishna was always "the problem child," Hatcher (1999, 168) wrote, situating the conflict in the religious schools at issue – the neo-Vedantic nondualism and cultivation of *sadhana* (awareness) espoused by the Ramakrishna Order, and the Tantric practices focused on Kali and involving the transcendent power of sexual energies adopted, albeit ambivalently, by Ramakrishna. Because the asceticism of the Order could not accommodate Ramakrishna's "mansion of fun" (Ramakrishna's description of life with devotees), "any attempt to foreground the fact of Ramakrishna's powerful Tantric devotion to the mother will be met with the [Vendantic] denial [*neti, neti*]: 'not this, not this'" (Hatcher 1999, 168).

At the heart of Kripal's argument was an observation about both the nature of Ramakrishna's speech and the structure of the *Kathamrita*. Kripal (1998, 4) described the *Kathamrita* as "a reluctant text," its five volumes cyclically retracing the same four years (1882–6), gradually revealing the secrets at the heart of Ramakrishna's philosophy, with "more culturally acceptable" teachings appearing in its earlier volumes, and "'secret' dimensions" in "the background" in later volumes. Secrecy in Ramakrishna's life and words was less an act of concealment than an economy of exposure, a structure of speech through parables and brief descriptions that "simultaneously revealed and concealed ... mystic-erotic energies [Ramakrishna] neither fully accepted nor understood" (5), including a "profound ambivalence" to Tantra that may have been even a "secret even to himself" (4). In this dynamic economy of knowledge, homosexuality was "triply concealed," first by/from Ramakrishna himself, second in the "complex cyclical structure" of the *Kathamrita*, and third in its "bowdlerized" translation (5). This structural sense of secrecy informs Kripal's use of secrecy as method, an analytic of reading as exposure that draws on the counter-normative quality of Tantrism and its famously esoteric language of "complex sexual metaphors" (31) that requires "tortuous hermeneutical strategies" to examine (32). For Kripal, the "study of secrets" is also a "study of the history of these secrets" (27), the latter of which includes the "appropriat[ion of secrets] by the larger culture" (7). Reckoning with the mystical structure of the secret makes it, for Kripal, amenable to psychoanalysis, whose hermeneutics he found compatible with Tantrism.

The place of psychoanalysis in the larger debate is perhaps counterintuitive if it is expected that what is offensive about psychoanalytic scholarship is its Western origins. Kripal's use of psychoanalysis did trouble critics, but not because it was culturally inappropriate. After all, not only had Sil (1991) published a decently received psychoanalytic account of Ramakrishna, but psychoanalysis has long been a mainstay in public intellectual writing in India.

Rather, as one reviewer put it, psychoanalysis was reductionist *in this instance* because, when applied to textual sources and not "patients," it could not *elicit* speech, but only *read* (versus Kripal's view that psychoanalysis opened texts to creative hermeneutics; see Ray 1997). Unlike an analysand, the argument went, a text cannot "talk free," making the reader responsible for ensuring that the "identifications" they observe "are generally accepted in the given culture" (Ray 1997, 102). Through a dynamic, reversible relationship between cultural offence, majoritarian "identifications," "analysis," and "free speech," critics rejected Kripal's arguments, not on the ground that his *speech* was too *free*, but for using a too *constraining* method of *reading*.

According to Laurie Patton (2019, 233), "At stake [in the Kripal case] are two competing interpretive publics: the Indian and the Euro-American (although mostly American) scholarly tradition and the interpretive tradition of the Ramakrishna order." But other, more readerly, mappings than "collision" require confronting the debate's cruder sentiments. It goes nearly without saying that the angriest critiques burn with horror at homosexuality, which, while evident in certain print essays (especially the painstaking examination of Kripal's translation), is especially (also obviously) so on the internet, where overt homophobia rings – ironically? obviously? – through Hindutva appropriations of the language of post-colonial identity politics, appropriations that decry "cultural appropriation" in calls for that scholarship be retracted. These assertions at the core of what Lawrence Cohen (2012, 106; emphasis in original) describes as the "painful" part of the story, acts of reading that transcend sides, conjoining "Kripal's argument and the critical, often quite wounded responses to it as twinned sites of *accusation*." A hermeneutic of accusation depends on and produces homosexuality as "specie-fied" (Sedgwick 1990, following Foucault) acts, feelings, and energies to be concealed/exposed, in which accusation and "recovery" are part of the same economy of knowledge, operations of language to be decoded. In the *Kali's Child* debate, circuits of accusation/recovery are closed in (direct-seeming) exchanges between Sil and Kripal: to Sil's suggestion that Kripal's writing exposed his own latent desires, Kripal (1998, xxi) accused his critics of "a deep cultural rejection of homosexuality" (certainly true) by referring to Christopher Isherwood, whom Kripal described as "openly homosexual," and who, a reader had once told Kripal, would likely have loved *Kali's Child* (xiv). Kripal (1998, xiv) recalled that Isherwood (1965) had written that in his own biography of Ramakrishna he would have liked to discuss Ramakrishna's sexuality but could not because of the project's endorsement by the Order.

The point, of course, is not that Kripal was as homophobic as his detractors, but that the structure of accusation, as L. Cohen (2012) describes, works through scenes that are not only about respectable publics and wounded cultural sentiments but also which articulate knowledge dynamics, seemingly forcing diverse "publics" into collision – as pointed out by Patton (2019) – while showing them to share an economy of exposure. L. Cohen (2012, 106) writes, "At the least, *Kali's Child* is spectacularly inattentive to the historical formation of effeminate and homosexual accusation (and self-accusation) in the late colonial period and subsequently ... The tragedy is that Kripal's analyses are often spectacularly insightful in attending to the poetics of ecstatic experience, but the denunciatory field in which they locate themselves may render them illegible to a self-respecting public."

In 1990s India, "boundaries of public civility and decorum were constantly being challenged" in "key areas" that included homosexuality, while media coverage of calls for censorship (notably of Deepa Mehta's film *Fire*) produced the "dramaturgical standardization" of an "overdetermined clash" along lines of insider/outsider, religion/secularism, India/the West (Mazzarella and Kaur 2013, 3). As queer identities consolidated in cosmopolitan languages through HIV/AIDS activism and opposition to Section 377 (the "anti-sodomy" section of the Indian penal code that criminalized sex outside of "laws of nature"), new vocabularies also named sexual pluralities in challenges to cosmopolitan, elite constructions of "gay" identity (Reddy 2005; L. Cohen 2005).[3] While there is no question that the strongest critiques of *Kali's Child* were freighted with Hindutva homophobia, there is less evidence that emerging queer activism, consolidation of censorship around homosexuality, or even the homophobia of Kripal's strongest critics figured for his defenders. Brief mentions of this context feel partial and unfinished. For instance, though Patton (2019, 238–9) names "gay and lesbian" activists as one of "three public spheres with three very different sets of rules" that "collided" in the Kripal case, she writes nothing further about those activists or the context they might provide. Kripal himself is a lone voice in this regard, and even that voice, crucial though it was, was conditioned by particular opacities. The phrase "openly homosexual," describing Christopher Isherwood as a would-be supporter, is, like so much else, both of its time and in it.

Secret

According to Sumit Sarkar (2019, 188), the language of the *Kathamrita* should be understood in relation to the social context of Ramakrishna's followers – largely non-elite urbanites struggling under colonial rule, a middling class of "clerks" whose office jobs moved the machinery of colonial bureaucracy and

---

3 The "controversy" over Deepa Mehta's 1996 film *Fire* is a touchstone in this history. See
   B. Bose (2000), John and Niranjana (2000), Kapur (2000), H.S. Gill (2017), and Naim (1999),
   though this is not an exhaustive list.

for whom cosmopolitan possibilities were in view but out of reach. Allured by the Ramakrishna's rustic rejection of elite pretensions, they were drawn to teachings that rearranged the socio-political terms of language by upsetting distinctions between orality and literacy and between high and low cultures (Sarkar 1992, 1546). As Bengali literature moved towards a "greater chastity and decorum," Ramakrishna's rebuke of "the printed word" and English-educated elites, his "earthy and unsophisticated" parables, his vulgarities and colloquialisms were "an additional attraction" to followers for whom Bengali literary styles "may have felt slightly oppressive" (Sarkar 1992, 1546). Sarkar reminds us that we only know what we know about Ramakrishna from these disciples, and that while the *Kathamrita* was likely mostly "true," it was also "a site of *bhadralok* appropriation"; the text of M., the Calcutta clerk, "simultaneously illuminat[ing] and obscur[ing]" (Sarkar 1990–1, 99). Both account and product of its social landscape, the *Kathamrita* was written in the form of diary notes, "displays of testimonies to authenticity" in which "secret talks" were carefully located (Sarkar 1992, 1544).

In a moment uncommented upon by reviewers, Kripal (1998) mused over a familiar (at least in Bengali literary circles) point of contact: that Freud's writing, in *Civilization and Its Discontents* (1989), on the "oceanic feeling" came out of the writings of (and correspondence with) French writer and "mystic" Romain Rolland on Ramakrishna. If, as Kripal reminds his readers, psychoanalysis was already influenced by Ramakrishna, its own methods for working with secrecy long connected to his teachings, we might also consider other historical circuits in which language was a scene of transformation. Which brings us back to Tantra, and the social world of the *Kathamrita*. Sarkar reminds us, in an intertextual reading, that the *sandhya-bhasa* (twilight language) of Tantra is not the same as the *guhya katha* (secret words) of the *Kathamrita*. Describing Ramakrishna's language,

> Closer, in its use of everyday images drawn from rural life and labour, to the language of lower-caste sects than to the formal *sutra bhasya* format of high-brahmanical exegesis, its meaning always remained single and on the surface. *Sandhya-bhashya* had been marked by a richness and fluidity of metaphor: the boatman, the river, or caged bird of the Bauls can be understood in many different ways. Metaphor, in contrast, is rare in Ramakrishna: its place is taken by clearcut analogies or parables, with the intended message often carefully verbalized. (2019, 206)

While commentators in the 1990s considered Tantra's centring of heterosexual sex at odds with Kripal's reading, in later decades, anthropologists interested in moral and pedagogical aspects of queer life in South Asia saw Tantra as informing "possibilities and limits of advice and self-transformation on the social margins" (L. Cohen 2012, 101). While Tantra's relationship to queer lives is, of course, connected to its figuring of the censorious (that which is forbidden becomes the means of liberation from morality), more important in these discussions are modes of language, in which pedagogic possibilities hinge on distinctions and transitions between literal and metaphoric understandings (Saria 2021). Verses in the "code" of *sandhya bhasa* offer possibilities of suggestion, play, and concealment and, at the same time, the possibilities of *literal* readings, allowing, as Vaibhav Saria (2021, 159–60) argues, queer pedagogies that mobilize forbidden forms of sex (such as incest) to be "liberated from and beyond morality."[4] Reading beyond economies of concealment and exposure, and not for "secrecy" but for "talk," figures the possible as not hidden in metaphor but, at times, literal, less an open secret than an "out" from the very moral economies that produce such codes (cf. Saria 2021; L. Cohen 2012). What would it mean to imagine these possibilities for Tantra into the "reluctant" text that is the *Kathamrita*? Might we contrast these forms of reading/hearing/doing with notions of concealment and revelation, accusation and recovery that traffic in open secrets and point, again and again, at that sedimented thing "homosexuality"? What intertextual circuits are thinkable?

Among these is the possibility that a rejection of depth for surfaces, metaphor for the literal, and formality for the direct could be – paradoxically/obviously – a foundation for "secret talk." If we put to the side the idea that secrecy is necessarily a matter of concealed (true) interiors, and consider the way "secret talk" might be created through textual management of diverse language potentialities, we meet the possibility that the *Kathamrita* may be at once a text (one of many) *of* a moment and an *account* of a moment (one of many) in which certain uses of language, including some associated with Tantra, those that may bear possibilities for queer instantiations of life "beyond" moral codes (Saria 2021), were made over as secrecy of a slightly different, slightly literary sort, an idiom with the ability to move. Perhaps the kind of secrecy the *Kathamrita* instantiated, in its speech (Ramakrishna's) and structure (M.'s), was at once an embrace and rejection of the diverse and particular possibilities of the literal, already bound up in a cosmopolitan world order against which it would come to be read, and through which accusations and recoveries would come to be made. Or is this fantasy an artefact of the intertextuality of the 1990s scholarly world? When Sarkar (2019, 197) observes that *Kathamrita* discussions of Tantric terms are labelled "secret matters," he adds a footnote: "I

---

4 In a delightfully nested set of citations, I cite Saria (2021, 159–60), who cites Siegel (1978, 188), who cites Bharati (1970, 171) on this point.

would like to acknowledge my indebtedness to this point to the ongoing work of Jeff Kripal, Chicago University research scholar."

Boon

To traverse the 1890s and 1990s may, thus, be to traverse the boiling down of that punctum in the textual history of secrecy into the dangerous secret of homosexuality, a traversal that includes in its timeframe the history of Section 377. Adjacent to the *Kathamrita*, other sources fill in some of that passage, taking us elsewhere than the transformation of the *Kathamrita* into the teachings of Vivekananda (certainly an important element), and pointing at another, even more open, secret at stake in *Kali's Child* and the *Kathamrita*, a fact that, in the 1990s, was treated as an evidentiary subset of the "secret" of homosexuality: Ramakrishna's bodily transgressions of gender. Biographies and psychoanalytic treatments of the life of Ramakrishna prior to *Kali's Child* considered Ramakrishna's adopting of female dress and instances of bodily gender crossing as at once elements of his mysticism and evidence of, variously, confused sexual identity, childhood trauma (Sil 1991), and psychoanalytic diagnosis (Kakar 1991). In Hindu figurations more broadly, sexuality and gender identity are variously collapsed and parsed in diverse literatures in which queer components and gender transgression are read as at once enabling and troubling heteronormative aspects of kinship, religion, and law (Ramberg 2014). In the play *Chitra*, published in Bengali in 1892 and English in 1905, Rabindranath Tagore (1914) retells the Mahabharata romance of Princess Chitrangada, a story whose actions and moral message depend on the concealment and exposure of ("true") gender, conflated with beauty and ugliness. In the Mahabharata, the back story to the actions of the play figure Chitravahana, king of Manipur, the first to bear a daughter in a royal lineage afforded the boon of bearing one child, a son, in each generation. With the responsibility of sustaining the royal lineage, Chitravahana raises Chitrangada as a son, concealing the secret of her gender so she might serve as heir.

Tagore's play begins with Chitrangada in male form describing to demigod Madana her meeting and rejection by Arjuna, a Pandava brother exiled to the Manipur forest. She begs Madana to make her female (to have "perfect beauty") for one day, but Madana grants a greater boon: a year in female form. When Chitra meets and enchants Arjuna, she worries over her secret: her imminent return to masculinity. Arjuna, smitten, vows to "dissolve" his promise of chastity and Chitra, ashamed that in "disguise" she led him astray (made him "blind to the light of the deathless spirit!") begs Madana to revoke the boon. She declares she will reveal her "true self," "a nobler thing than this disguise." On their last day together, Chitra in female form and Arjuna meet a group of peasants whose village is threatened by attackers and who bemoan the absence of their protector, Chitra, who, they have been told, is travelling on pilgrimage. Arjun wonders at the character of this Chitra – why would such a protector abandoned his responsibilities? What other needs would he have? Angry, Chitra replies, "Her needs? Why, what has she ever had, the unfortunate creature? Her very qualities are as prison walls, shutting her woman's heart in a bare cell. She is obscured, she is unfulfilled." Chitra asks Arjuna if he can bear seeing her true self. Arjuna responds, "A time comes when [Truth] throws off her ornaments and veils and stands clothed in naked dignity. I grope for that ultimate you, that bare simplicity of truth." Chitra opens her cloak to reveal her true form, full of "flaws and blemishes," lacking in "loveliness," and offers the "gift" of the "heart of a woman," "an imperfection which yet is noble and grand." She explains that she is carrying Arjuna's child, who will carry on the line of the King Chitravahana. Arjuna declares, "Beloved, my life is full."

Tagore's *Chitra* is a tale of self-knowledge, a theme familiar in his other works; self-knowledge is soteriological, truth connected to a self freed from deceptive trappings. Spiritual awakening and truth are revealed through and against the economies of secrecy and deceit that are made necessary by gods' deals with mortals, their boons and curses. Costume and curse are aligned, individual freedom connected to social freedom and, especially, to reform of gender inequities. While the ability to cross (or layer) gender allows for self-discovery through love, it also facilitates the continuation of law in the form of kinship and kingdom. In many Hindu texts and narratives involving "gender crossing," it is not simply that one's "true self" is recognized in having one's "true gender" acknowledged, but that gender switching is the framework for larger dharmic struggle. Tagore's *Chitra* presents both social transformation and the continuation of law through the management of secrets of gender in a plot dense with therapeutic transformation and discovery.

On the one hand, there is a vast distance between Tagore's beatific *Chitrangada* and the "rather crude, if charismatic" Ramakrishna (Hatcher 1999) and his Tantric uses of gender transformation to discover the Mother in all women. On the other hand, if as Kripal (1998, xvii) points out, "Freud, Ramakrishna, and the modern category of mysticism … share a common synchronistic history," we can add to that synchrony *Chitra* and its Bengali and international publics. In both cases, while Tagore's writing is rich with feminist messages and female heroines, it is less easily appropriated for a history of queer life. Such limits appear at the point at which gender switching becomes something more than narrative mechanism, at which it represents the limit of the literal. In 1914, a *New York Times* review titled "Tagore's Ideal Woman" with the subheading "Under the Guise of an Old Hindu Legend, He Touches Modern Feminism," read,

We did not look for an Oriental, even though a seer, to write a book (especially twenty-five years ago, when this was written) that might serve as evangel to the most advanced among Occidental women – yet this is just what Rabindranath

Tagore has done. By "advanced," be it understood, we are not referring to that group of biological freaks to whom the term is sometimes applied, but to the sane and sincere women who are endeavoring – whether by advocating political equality with men or by opposing it is a detail – to secure the highest good for their sex. (1914, BR129)

Again the question – what is obvious, what contradictory? By 1914, for an international readership with ample room for both Tagore's *Chitra* and Ramakrishna's teachings (as presented by Vivekananda on his American tours), we find, as the limit-point for liberatory uses of gender transgression, the "biological freak," read out of a therapeutic economy of secrecy and exposures. What transformations, if any, are left between this censorious parsing of sexual types and the liberatory/hateful messages of *Obhoshopto Nighty*, whose opening epigraph is an invocation of freedom from another twentieth-century mystic – Khalil Gibran?

Therapy

Texts can be read in diverse ways. Another reading of Tagore's 1914 play, the film *Chitrangada: The Crowning Wish*, directed and starred in by Rituparno Ghosh (the subject of *Obhishopto Nighty's* mockery) was released in 2012 to critical acclaim. An account of a choreographer's staging of Tagore's dance-drama, the film weaves the story of Chitrangada into the life of a choreographer, Rudra Chatterjee, who begins but ultimately withdraws from gender affirmation surgeries. Ghosh's film nests temporalities – the clinical temporality of the hospital where Rudra recovers from one surgery and awaits another, the worldly temporality of Rudra's life leading up to the surgery, and the dance-drama of *Chitra's* mythic stagings.[5] The clinical temporality opens with a shot onto the Kolkata skyline from Rudra's hospital window and a conversation with a counsellor, Shubho, the film's Madana. In encounters of profound therapeutic intimacy and care, Rudra and the counsellor witness the second temporality, walking along the edges of remembered scenes as Rudra recounts events – dinner table conversations with disapproving parents, an affair with Partho a drug-addicted drummer, rehearsals, and performances. Rudra describes deciding to undergo surgery to "become a woman" so as to adopt a child with Partho, because the government does not allow two men to adopt. After Rudra's first surgery, Partho reveals that he is leaving Rudra for a female

---

5   Pronoun usage in this film is challenging to translate from Bengali, which does not gender pronouns or verb forms. Across the film's timeframes, Rudra variously refers to themself as man and woman, and, in an early scene, insists the nurse stop using the honorific "Sir," raising questions about pronoun uses in English that Bengali largely avoids.

dancer in the troupe, with whom he is having a child, a betrayal layered with the additional shame of Partho's rejection of Rudra's post-operative body – "The man I loved was not this half-thing. If I have to have a woman then I want a real woman not, a synthetic one."

Ultimately, Rudra decides not to undergo vaginal construction surgery, choosing instead to have breast implants removed. This decision is not portrayed as a return to a hegemonically defined male body, indeed, the film never portrays Rudra has having such a body or identity; Rudra is confidently non-binary throughout the film. Instead, the decision is portrayed as affirmation of a self and gender not defined by state, kinship, or intimate mandates. Indeed, the idea of surgical gender affirmation is rendered insufficient, even violent, in contrast with a subtler, more malleable sense of gender, sexuality, and identity, replete with possibilities for care and acceptance. It is not a teleological body/ gender that forms the narrative of transformation, but the *work* of gendering which, aligned with remembering, entails reversals and returns. In the final exchange between Rudra and the counsellor, the film declares its in-motion approach to self-realization. Throughout the film, Rudra has been receiving mysterious, koan-like text messages from an unknown caller. The final message asks, "Why is a building called a building even after it is complete?" Rudra, reading the SMS, says, "No transition is ever complete, it's an ongoing process,"[6] punctuating a discussion of the impossibility of self- and other-knowledge, an impossibility that contains the possibility for intimacy.

In its final moments, *Chitrangada: The Crowning Wish*, writes across the screen, "Be what you wish to be," even as its plot suggests that both "being" and "what one wishes" are ambiguous, incomplete, and unfinished work. Perhaps, the transformative work across genders that allows a malleable selfhood to be realized, with gender is a tool, not an endpoint. Or, a slightly different reading finds an assertion of the validity and beauty of non-binary gender identities. By either reading, this is not a coming out narrative. Indeed, moments of revelation are scenes of betrayal, in a larger narrative that is not driven by revelation or accusation. Rudra's gender identity is never concealed, nor is it at risk of discovery. As such, this film can be contrasted with recent Bengali and Hindi films portraying queer life through narratives of social acceptance, coming out narratives, in which transgender and gay characters are vehicles for (cis, straight) heros' moral transformation.

In a remarkable sequence, Rudra suggests to Shubho that they may not have fully understood Chitrangada and the way her life was directed by her father.

---

6 A configuration that would not work in Bengali, leading us to consider the possibilities and con- straints inherent to, variously, the Bengali and English metaphors for transformation and their associated histories, a longer conversation. I am grateful to Brian Hatcher for pointing this out.

When Shubho asks if Rudra would like to "stage Chitrangada again," Rudra responds, "I mean, the production was fine, it had gloss, it had spectacle, but how much it reflected the soul of Chitrangada, I'm not sure. Now it seems to me that I don't know her well enough." This moment contains much that makes this film stand to the side of heremeneutics of concealment and exposure. Here is a possibility of return, of rereading, revision, open-ended interpretation. Here is a form of understanding to the side of revelation or accomplishment. Here, too, collaboratively with the psychotherapist, is an alternate reckoning of the therapeutic possibilities of speaking, alternate to an analytic of recovery.

Structure and Shape

Chitrangada: The Crowning Wish (which prompted no censorious ire) brings us back to our original cultural product, with which it is representationally bound. Contained between the aesthetic polarities of *Obhishopto Nighty* (and its readerly juxtaposition of the obvious/contradictory) and *Chitrangada: The Crowning Wish* (which proposes a theory of reading as revision) is the recursive relationship between the 1890s of Ramakrishna, M., and *Chitra* and the 1990s of Hindutva censorship and academic scandals. Between these scenes is a twentieth century containing not only Section 377, the rise of Hindu nationalism, and transformations in publics that made cultural diacritics all, but encounters via "psy" therapeutics, such as that which arguably made both "gender switching" and psychoanalysis part of Bengali cultural patrimony, in which psychoanalyst Girindrasekhar Bose proposed to Freud that things might be different in India, where analysands did not fantasize about killing their fathers, but about switching genders (cf. Hartnack 2001).

Here, Sedgwick's *Epistemology of the Closet* (1990) becomes relevant as both context and meta-text, orienting scholarship in the decade of queer theory it inaugurated, the decade that included *Kali's Child* (1998), by reading literatures from the decade of Kripal's key source, authors (Melville, James, Proust) whose work bore the imprint and effect of the epistemological pressures that shaped the "gender, sexual, and economic structures of the heterosexist culture at large," concepts of public and private, secrecy and exposure that were "oppressively, durably condensed in certain figures of homosexuality" (Sedgwick 1990, 71). It almost goes without saying that the Kripal affair unfolded as though a Sedgwickian script. Yet Sedgwick's vocabulary for a "history of secrecy" (a concept Kripal also claimed) was absent from the academic conversation her language undoubtedly shaped. I don't mean to suggest a citational failure, or that one academic field failed to account for what was happening in another, but I do think that the strange way that Sedgwick's literary vision described the arc of the *Kali's Child* narrative gives us a particular point of entry to larger conversations. For one thing, her arguments are relevant to both "thens" – the 1990s of *Kali's Child* and proliferations of recovery/accusation that produced "the homosexual" as both problem and solution for "India," and the 1890s timeframe of Kripal's and Sedgwick's literary sources.

Kripal raises the possibility that Ramakrishna's visions influenced Freud but leaves fewer lines of contact with textual worlds that might situate M., author of the record of Ramakrishna's life, in a reading Bengali public or articulate with other literary sources, sources in which secrecy (in diverse, particular forms) that may have mattered (in diverse, particular ways, including not at all) to Ramakrishna's devotees, clerks and elites, readers and cultural producers (like playwright Girish Chandra Ghosh). It takes but a modicum of literalizing to imagine, at the dawn of a century when Bengali texts and their envoys were attracting audiences in Europe and North America, while English literatures were established elements of Indian education, a trans-local sense of reader-ship, that cross-cut with the filters, appropriations, and diacritics of reading under Empire, the possibility of what Lisa Lowe (2015) calls intimacies across continents. Or to find both a global literary form and an anticipation of political needs in Ramakrishna's and M.'s transformations (if that is what they were) of Tantrism into "secret talks." Such political expediencies may have include the orienting arrangement of social and moral worlds under colonialism, famously articulated by Partha Chatterjee (1993), the public, male domain of politics and colonial rule, and the private, female, "spiritual" space where anti-colonial sentiments could grow. And they certainly included the ways secrecy and dis-closure were paramount to both a colonial state enacting sedition laws to quell counter-revolutionary action and to anti-colonial actors and the covert speech they generated, secrets in plain sight in Bengali theatre and communicated by revolutionaries who found solace with charismatic sages.

By locating her account as "Euro-American," Sedgwick (1990) invites us to ask whether and how the "epistemology of the closet" obtains "elsewhere." While the political and literary conditions surrounding *Kathamrita* might be read as points of difference, or at least variation, from Sedgwick's epistemol-ogy of the closet, their status as "different" differs from the (more radical) sense of difference that orients the *Kali's Child* scandal and readings of it. Thinking with literary form allows us to extend that story beyond the censorial repressions that mark the internationalization of Hindutva in the 1990s (and the transformation of Ramakrishna's message in the early 1900s), and to avoid the unhelpful argument that the true "western" or "foreign" subject in the *Kali's Child* case was not Kripal, but his detractors, speaking for a Hinduism they misrepresented, and the equally unhelpful suggestion that their condemna-tions were at odds with "civilizational" (in Cohen's terminology) sources more accepting of sexual and gender diversity. Forms of secrecy that circuited the 1890s and 1990s are as complexly "Indian" as they are both "Euro-American" and features of that modern thing, "world literature."

It could be pointed out that "the closet" is a Western formulation, as unfamiliar in South Asian, where queer possibilities for expression and exposure are not restricted to notions of "gay" identity or "coming out." But what is Tagore's *Chitra* if not a coming out story, of a kind? At the same time, what kinds of "coming out" are permitted/established through long-standing tropes of gender reversal? Might the same element that produces anxiety about the limits of feminism in one context (the *New York Times* review) generate different illuminations/opacities in another, even as it links them in global literary circuits? What might it do to include *Chitra* into Sedgwick's canon, and its readers and arrangements (beauty/plainness, curses/boons) into her "chain of binaries" (public/private, outside/inside)? Whose sexual politics, whose history of secrecy, would it expand? Would it alter or reinforce the sense of a world connected-up by identically named legal codes criminalizing queer forms of sex (Section 377 remained in place across the British postcolonial world), in which the closet was/is widely recognizable as a "history of judicial formulations" that "codifie[d] an excruciating system of double binds" (Sedgwick 1990, 70)? Sedgwick (1990, 56) describes the closet as "that curious space that is both internal and marginal to the culture: centrally representative of its motivating passions and contradictions, even when marginalized by its orthodoxies," in which what is at issue is not (only) "homosexuality 'itself'" but the "management of information about it" (70). That such a set of creations was and is "different" in India is true; that it was and is connected to broader systems of regulation through colonial law is also true. But also possible is that if the closet – a constantly moving production – follows trajectories that absorb and reallocate speech and its forms, bending towards diverse senses of the political, it draws on diverse energies and passions, including those that hew to "civilizational" texts and "turn" to ambiguous and diverse ("religious") narrative particularities otherwise unrecognizable in liberal formulations, secrets and curses, the therapeutic voice and cryptic actions of a saint.

How does this circuit between 1890s and 1990s matter now, in, if not a post-closet world, then a world in which such a thing is imaginable? There are two immediate responses: *Obhishopto Nighty* – a perturbing representation of a view to that horizon. And *Chitrangada: The Crowning Wish*, a portrayal not conditioned by – yet taking readerly interest in – secrecy and exposure, curses and boons, where relationships between gender expression and forms of law are formed between persons with bodily stakes in each other, and therapeutics revisit but do not reveal. In its alternate theory of reading, understanding can be revised, decisions reversed. There is risk here, but it is not the risk of exposure. It is the risk of relationships, of, in Rudra's words, "suffering" another person, risking what never feels obvious.

Acknowledgments

The author wishes to thank Brian Hatcher for generously sharing archival materials and knowledge of the debate over *Kali's Child*, as well as for thoughtful insights and suggestions about this chapter. Thank you also to Aniket De, Aidan Schaffert, Dwai Banerjee, and Sarah Luna for invaluable comments, and to the editors of this volume for their helpful guidance and feedback.

References

Abraham, Yuval, Oren Ziv, and Meron Rapoport. 2021. "Secret Israeli Document Offers No Proof to Justify Terror Label for Palestinian Groups." *The Intercept*, 4 November 2021. https://theintercept.com/2021/11/04/secret-israel-dossier-palestinian-rights-terrorist.

Abrams, Philip. 1988. "Notes on the Difficulty of Studying the State." *Journal of Historical Sociology* 1 (1): 58–89. https://doi.org/10.1111/j.1467-6443.1988.tb00004.x.

Abu-Lughod, Lila. 1986. *Veiled Sentiments: Honor and Poetry in a Bedouin Society*. Berkeley: University of California Press. https://doi.org/10.1525/9780520965980.

Adorno, Theodor W. 1978. *Minima Moralia: Reflections on a Damaged Life*. London: Verso.

Agha, Asif. 2004. "Registers of Language." In *A Companion to Linguistic Anthropology*, edited by Alessandro Duranti, 23–45. New York: Blackwell.

– 2007. *Language and Social Relations*. Cambridge: Cambridge University Press.

Agnew, Spiro T. 1972. "Agnew's Blast at Behaviorism." *Psychology Today* 4: 84–7.

Agrama, Hussein. 2012. *Questioning Secularism: Islam, Sovereignty, and the Rule of Law in Modern Egypt*. Chicago: Chicago University Press.

Ahmed, Sara. 2004. "Affective Economies." *Social Text* 22 (2): 117–39. https://doi.org/10.1215/01642472-22-2_79-117.

Ahmed, Shahab. 2016. *What Is Islam? The Importance of Being Islamic*. Princeton, NJ: Princeton University Press.

Ajidarma, Seno Gumira. 1999. "Fiction, Journalism, History: A Process of Self-Correction." Translated by Michael H. Bodden. *Indonesia* 68: 164–71. https://doi.org/10.2307/3351300

Akhmetova, Maria. 2012. "And the Banderlog Have Come: Vladimir Putin's Statement and the 'Folk Placard.'" *Forum for Anthropology and Culture* 8: 287–302.

Akhtar, Iqbal. 2016. *The Khōjā of Tanzania: Discontinuities of a Postcolonial Religious Identity*. Leiden: Brill. https://doi.org/10.1163/9789004292888_001.

Alatas, Ismail Fajrie. 2021. *What Is Religious Authority? Cultivating Islamic Communities in Indonesia.* Princeton, NJ: Princeton University Press.

al-Bulushi, Samar. 2014. "Peacekeeping' as Occupation: Managing the Market for Violent Labor in Somalia." *Transforming Anthropology* 22 (1): 31–7. https://doi.org/10.1111/traa.12026.

al-Haj Saleh, Yassin. 2017. *The Impossible Revolution: Making Sense of the Syrian Tragedy.* London: Hurst.

Al-Haq. 2019. "Palestinian, Regional, and International Groups Submit Report on Israeli Apartheid to UN Committee on the Elimination of Racial Discrimination." Al-Haq, 12 November. https://www.alhaq.org/advocacy/16183.html.

Al Jazeera. 2022. "Photos: Murals Mark 100 Days since Shireen Abu Akleh's Killing." Al Jazeera, 18 August 2022. https://www.aljazeera.com/gallery/2022/8/18/photos-murals-mark-100-days-since-shireen-abu-aklehs-killing.

al-Khalili, Charlotte. 2021. "Rethinking the Concept of Revolution through the Syrian Experience." *Al-Jumhuriya.* 5 May 2021. https://aljumhuriya.net/en/2021/05/05/rethinking-concept-revolution-through-syrian-experience.

Allardyce, Gilbert. 1979. "What Fascism Is Not: Thoughts on the Deflation of a Concept." *American Historical Review* 84 (4): 367–88. https://doi.org/10.2307/1855138.

Allen, Lori. 2013. *The Rise and Fall of Human Rights: Cynicism and Politics in Occupied Palestine.* Stanford: Stanford University Press.

– 2020. *A History of False Hope: Investigative Commissions in Palestine.* Stanford: Stanford University Press.

Allen, Lori, Daniel Segal, and Jessica Winegar. 2023. "The AnthroBoycott Collective and Organizing Against Apartheid – An Interview with Daniel Segal and Jessica Winegar." MERIP. 9 August. https://merip.org/2023/08/anthroboycottinterview/.

Allen, Pamela. 1973. "Free Space." In *Radical Feminism,* edited by Anne Koedt, Ellen Levine, and Anita Rapone, 271–9. New York: Quadrangle Books.

Al-Nimr, Nimr. 2012. "He Will Be Eaten by Worms and Suffer the Torments of Hell in His Grave" (speech). Memri TV, 27 June 2012. https://www.memri.org/tv/saudi-shiite-cleric-nimr-al-nimr-rejoices-death-saudi-crown-prince-nayef-he-will-be-eaten-worms.

Amnesty International. 2022. "Israel's Apartheid against Palestinians: Cruel System of Domination and Crime against Humanity." Amnesty International, 1 February. https://www.amnesty.org/en/documents/mde15/5141/2022/en/.

Anderson, Benedict. 1991. *Imagined Communities: Reflections on the Origin and Spread of Nationalism.* Rev. ed. London: Verso.

Anderson, Jane, Hannah McElgunn, and Justin Richland. 2017. "Labelling Knowledge: The Semiotics of Immaterial Cultural Property and the Production of New Indigenous Publics." In *Engaging Native American Publics: Linguistic Anthropology in a Collaborative Key,* edited by Paul V. Kroskrity and Barbra A. Meek, 184–208. London: Routledge.

AnthroBoycott. n.d. "Corrections to the Misinformation in the AAA Executive Board's 'Points to Consider.'" Anthropologists for the Boycott of Israeli Academic Institutions. Accessed 31 July 2024. https://www.anthroboycott.org/resources /correcting-aaa-points-to-consider.

Appadurai, Arjun. 1996. *Modernity at Large: Cultural Dimensions of Globalization.* Minneapolis: University of Minnesota Press.

Arctus. 2017. "The Russian Revolution Was the Uprising of the Russian *khams*" [in Russian]. *Live Journal*, 3 June 2017. https://arctus.livejournal.com/360591.html.

Arendt, Hannah. 1958. "The Modern Concept of History." *The Review of Politics* 20 (4): 570–90. https://doi.org/10.1017/S0034670500034227.

– 1981. *The Life of the Mind*. Boston: Houghton Mifflin Harcourt.

– (1961) 1993. *Between Past and Future. Eight Exercises in Political Thought*. New York: Penguin Books.

Arkhipova, Aleksandra, Anton Somin, and Aleksandra Sheveleva. 2014. "Shershavym yazykom plakata: Oppozitsionnyi diskurs na protestnykh aktsiyakh." In *"My ne nemy": Antropologiya protesta v Rossii 2011-2012 godov*, 125–48. Tartu: Nauchnoe Izdatel'stvo.

Armbrust, Walter. 2019. *Martyrs and Tricksters: An Ethnography of the Egyptian Revolution*. Princeton, NJ: Princeton University Press.

Arnheim, Rudolf. 1936. *Radio*. Translated by Margaret Ludwig and Herbert Read. London: Faber and Faber.

Asad, Talal. 1993. *Genealogies of Religion: Discipline and Reasons of Power in Christianity and Islam.* Baltimore, MD: Johns Hopkins University Press.

– 2003. *Formations of the Secular: Christianity, Islam, Modernity*. Stanford: Stanford University Press.

– 2013. "Free Speech, Blasphemy, and Secular Criticism." In *Is Critique Secular? Blasphemy, Injury, and Free Speech*, by Talal Asad, Wendy Brown, Judith Butler, and Saba Mahmood, 14–57. New York: Fordham University Press. https://doi .org/10.2307/j.ctt1c5cjtk.5.

– 2015. "Thinking about Tradition, Religion, and Politics in Egypt Today." *Critical Inquiry* 42 (1): 166–214. https://doi.org/10.1086/683002.

– 2018. *Secular Translations: Nation-State, Modern Self, and Calculative Reason*. New York: Columbia University Press.

Asad, Talal, Wendy Brown, Judith Butler, and Saba Mahmood. 2013. *Is Critique Secular? Blasphemy, Injury and Free Speech*. New York: Fordham University Press. https://doi.org/10.2307/j.ctt1c5cjtk.

Ash, Mitchell G. 1992. "Cultural Contexts and Scientific Change in Psychology: Kurt Lewin in Iowa." *American Psychologist* 47 (2): 198–207. https://psycnet.apa.org /doi/10.1037/0003-066X.47.2.198.

Ashrawi, Hanan. 2019. "I Am a Palestinian Negotiator. I Was Denied a Visa – and I Think I Know Why." *Washington Post*, 3 June 2019. https://www.washingtonpost .com/opinions/2019/06/03/i-am-palestinian-negotiator-i-was-denied-visa-i-think-i -know-why.

Associated Press. 2022. "Jan. 6 Committee Hearings – Day 8." *PBS Newshour*, last updated 21 July 2022. https://www.pbs.org/newshour/politics/watch-live-jan-6-committee-hearings-day-8.

Atlas Group Archive. *Journal of Visual Culture* 20 (2): 455–77.

Ātmajñānānanda, Svāmī. 1997. "Scandals, Cover-Ups, and Other Imagined Occurrences in the Life of Rāmakṛṣṇa: An Examination of Jeffrey Kripal's *Kālī's Child*." *International Journal of Hindu Studies* 1 (2): 401–20. https://doi.org/10.1007/s11407-997-0007-8.

Atmakusumah, ed. 1992. *Mochtar Lubis: Wartawan Jihad*. Jakarta: Harian Kompas.

Atshan, Sa'ed, and Katharina Galor. 2020. *The Moral Triangle: Germans, Israelis, Palestinians*. Durham, NC: Duke University Press.

Austin, John Langshaw. (1946) 1979. "Other Minds." In *Philosophical Papers*, edited by James Opie Urmson and Geoffrey Warnock, 76–117. 3rd ed. Oxford: Clarendon Press.

– 1957. "I.—A Plea for Excuses: The Presidential Address." *Proceedings of the Aristotelian Society* 57 (1): 1–30. https://doi.org/10.1093/aristotelian/57.1.1.

– 1962. *How to Do Things with Words*. Oxford: Clarendon Press.

– 1975. *How to Do Things with Words: The William James Lectures Delivered in Harvard University in 1955*. New York: Oxford Paperbacks.

Avetisyan, Roxana. 2016. "'Ъ' and 'ѣ' as Signs of the Elite: Foppiness on the Old Rules of Russian Spelling" [in Russian]. *LIFE*, 10 October 2016. https://life.ru/p/913952.

Aziz, Sahar F. 2003. "The Laws on Providing Material Support to Terrorist Organizations: The Erosion of Constitutional Rights or a Legitimate Tool for Preventing Terrorism?" *Texas Journal on Civil Liberties and Civil Rights* 91 (1): 45–92.

– 2021. *The Racial Muslim: When Racism Quashes Religious Freedom*. Berkeley: University of California Press.

Azoulay, Ariella. 2017. "The Imperial Condition of Photography in Palestine: Archives, Looting, and the Figure of the Infiltrator." *Visual Anthropology Review* 33 (1): 5–17. https://doi.org/10.1111/var.12117.

Azzarà, Stafano. G. 2011. "Settling Accounts with Liberalism: On the Work of Domenico Losurdo." *Historical Materialism* 19 (2): 92–112. https://doi.org/10.1163/156920611X573815.

Bacqué, Raphaëlle, and Ariane Chemin. 2016. "Islam et laïcité: Le schisme de la gauche." *Le Monde*, 5 May 2016. https://www.lemonde.fr/idees/article/2016/05/05/laicite-le-schisme-de-la-gauche_4914258_3232.html.

BADIL. 2020. "Against Terrorism and Against Conditional Funding: Statement of the Palestinian National Campaign to Reject Conditional Funding." Press release. BADIL Resource Center for Palestinian Residency and Refugee Rights. https://www.badil.org/press-releases/585.html.

Baiburin, A. n.d. "Materialy k kul'turnoi istorii "tverdogo znaka." Electronic Resource [in Russian]. Accesssed 12 December 2021. http://www.elzabair.ru.

Bakhtin, Mikhail M. 1981. *The Dialogic Imagination.* Austin: University of Texas Press.

Bandak, Andreas. 2014. "Of Rhythms and Refrains in Contemporary Damascus: Urban Space and Christian-Muslim Coexistence." In "Unity and Diversity: New Directions in the Anthropology of Christianity," edited by J. Robbins. *Current Anthropology* 55 (S10): 248–61.

– 2015a. "Reckoning with the Inevitable: Death and Dying among Syrian Christians During the Uprisings." In "Death and Afterlife in the Arab Uprisings," edited by A. Mittermaier. *Ethnos: Journal of Anthropology* 80 (5): 671–91.

– 2015b. "Performing the Nation: Syrian Christians on the National Stage." In *Syria from Reform to Revolt.* Vol. 2, *Culture, Society, and Religion.* Edited by Christa Salamandra and Leif Stenberg, 195–229. Syracuse, NY: Syracuse University Press.

– 2024. "Syrian Futures: Percolation, Temporality and Historical Experience in the Plural." *History and Anthropology.* https://doi.org/10.1080/02757206.2024.2346885.

Bandak, Andreas, and Paul Anderson. 2022. "Urgency and Imminence: The Politics of the Very Near Future." *Social Anthropology/Anthropologie sociale* 30 (4): 1–17. https://www.berghahnjournals.com/view/journals/saas/30/4/saas.30.issue-4.xml.

Bandak, Andreas, and Simon Coleman. 2019. "Different Repetitions: Anthropological Engagements with Figures of Return, Recurrence and Redundancy." *History and Anthropology* 30 (2): 119–32. https://doi.org/10.1080/02757206.2018.1547900.

Bandak, Andreas, Christine Crone, and Nina Grønlykke Mollerup. 2024. "Re-Collections: Images beyond the Archive." *Visual Anthropology* 37 (1): 1–18. https://doi.org/10.1080/08949468.2023.2285211.

Bánkuti, M, G. Halmai, and K.L. Scheppele. 2012. "Hungary's Illiberal Turn: Disabling the Constitution." *Journal of Democracy* 23 (3): 138–50. https://doi.org/10.1353/jod.2012.0054.

Barendt, Eric. 2005. *Freedom of Speech.* Oxford: Oxford University Press.

Barthes, Ronald. 1957. *Mythologies.* Paris: Éditions du Seuil.

Bateson, Gregory. 1971. "Steps to an Ecology of Mind." Chicago: University of Chicago Press.

Bauman, Richard. 1983. *Let Your Words Be Few: Symbolism of Speaking and Silence among Seventeenth-Century Quakers.* New York: Cambridge University Press.

Bauman, Richard, and Charles L. Briggs. 1992. "Genre, Intertextuality and Social Power." *Journal of Linguistic Anthropology* 2 (2): 131–72. https://doi.org/10.1525/jlin.1992.2.2.131.

Bavelas, Janet, Linda Coates, and Trudy Johnson. 2000. "Listeners as Co-Narrators." *Journal of Personality and Social Psychology* 79 (6): 941–52. https://doi.org/10.1037/0022-3514.79.6.941. Medline: 11138763.

Bayly, Christopher A. 2011. *Recovering Liberties: Indian Thought in the Age of Liberalism and Empire.* Cambridge: Cambridge University Press. https://doi.org/10.1017/CBO9781139012140.

Bejan, Teresa M. 2020. "Free Expression or Equal Speech?" *Social Philosophy and Policy* 37 (2): 153–69. https://doi.org/10.1017/S0265052521000091.

Bell, Allan. 1984. "Language Style as Audience Design." *Language in Society* 13 (2): 145–204. https://doi.org/10.1017/S004740450001037X.

Bell, Duncan. 2014. "What Is Liberalism?" *Political Theory* 42 (1): 682–715. https://doi.org/10.1177/0090591714535103.

Bem, Merel, and Anna van Leeuwen. 2019. "Bij de Open Studios van de Rijksakademie lijkt het of de kunstenaar net even is weggelopen." *De Volkskrant*, 21 November 2019. https://www.volkskrant.nl/cultuur-media/bij-de-open-studios-van-de-rijksakademie-lijkt-het-of-de-kunstenaar-net-even-is-weggelopen~b0c4e097/.

Bendix, Regina. 2000. "The Pleasures of the Ear: Toward an Ethnography of Listening." *Cultural Analysis* 1: 33–50.

Benjamin, Walter. (1935) 1968. "The Work of Art in the Age of Mechanical Reproduction." In *Illuminations: Essays and Reflections*, edited by Hannah Arendt. Translated by Harry Zohn. New York: Schocken.

– (1931) 2008. "Reflections on Radio." In *The Work of Art in the Age of Its Technological Reproducibility, and Other Writings on Media*, edited by Michael W. Jennings, Brigid Doherty, and Thomas Y. Levin. Translated by Rodney Livingstone, 391–2. Cambridge, MA: Harvard University Press.

Benson, Susan. 2006. "Injurious Names: Naming, Disavowal, and Recuperation in Contexts of Slavery and Emancipation." In *An Anthropology of Names and Naming*, edited by Gabriele vom Bruck and Barbara Bodenhorn, 179–99. Cambridge: Cambridge University Press.

Benveniste, Émile. (1956) 1966. "The Nature of Pronouns." In *Problems in General Linguistics*, translated by Mary Elizabeth Meek, 217–22. Coral Gables: University of Miami.

– (1956) 1966. "Subjectivity in Language." In *Problems in General Linguistics*, translated by Mary Elizabeth Meek, 223–30. Coral Gables: University of Miami.

Berlin, Isaiah. 1969. *Four Essays on Liberty*. Oxford: Oxford University Press.

Bernstein, Andea, and Ilya Marritz. 2022. *Will Be Wild*. Podcast, 12 episodes. Produced by Wondery. https://wondery.com/shows/will-be-wild/.

Besteman, Catherine. 2020. *Militarized Global Apartheid*. Durham, NC: Duke University Press.

Bharati, Agehananda. 1977. *The Tantric Tradition*. New York: Doubleday

Bhojani, Ali-Reza. 2015. *Moral Rationalism and Shari'a: Independent Rationality in Modern Shi'i usul al-Fiqh*. Abingdon: Routledge.

Bickford, Susan. 1996. *The Dissonance of Democracy: Listening, Conflict, and Eitizenship*. Ithaca, NY: Cornell University Press.

Bigelow, Whitney. 2021. "Grappling with Governing: Sen. Mike Lee's View of Trump from 'Unelectable' to 'Captain Moroni.'" *The Daily Universe*, 11 January 2021. https://universe.byu.edu/2021/01/11/senator-mike-lee-on-trump-from-unelectable-to-captain-moroni.

Bishara, Amahl. 2013. *Back Stories: U.S. News Production and Palestinian Politics.* Stanford: Stanford University Press.

– 2022. *Crossing a Line: Laws, Violence, and Roadblocks to Palestinian Political Expression.* Stanford: Stanford University Press.

– 2023. "Decolonizing Middle East Anthropology: Toward Liberation in SWANA Societies." *American Ethnologist* 50 (3): 396–408. https://doi.org/10.1111/amet.13200.

Bjork, Daniel W. 1997. *B.F. Skinner: A Life.* Washington, DC: American Psychological Association.

Blanchard, Taryn Sheridan. 2019. "Free Expression Activism in a (Post)Modern World of Risk and Uncertainty." PhD diss., University of Toronto.

Boggs, Carl. 1977. "Marxism, Prefigurative Communism and the Problem of Workers' Control." *Radical America* 6: 99–122.

Bogush, Gleb. 2017. "The Xriminalisation of Free Apeech in Russia." *Europe-Asia Studies* 69 (8): 1242–56. https://doi.org/10.1080/09668136.2017.1372733.

Bok, Sissela. 1989. *Lying: Moral Choice in Public and Private Life.* New York: Vintage Books.

Bollinger, Lee C. 1991. *Images of a Free Press.* Chicago: University of Chicago Press.

Boltanski, Luc, and Eve Chiapello. 1999. *The New Spirit of Capitalism.* Translated by Gregory Elliott. London: Verso.

– 2005. "The New Spirit of Capitalism." *International Journal of Politics, Culture, and Society* 18 (3): 161–88. https://doi.org/10.1007/s10767-006-9006-9.

Boltanski, Luc, and Arnaud Esquerre. 2015. "Grappling with the Economy of Enrichment." *Valuation Studies* 3 (1): 75–83. https://doi.org/10.3384/VS.2001-5592.153175.

– 2020. *Enrichment: A Critique of Commodities.* Translated by Catherine Porter. Cambridge: Polity Press.

Boltanski, Luc, and Laurent Thévenot. 2006. *On Justification: Economies of Worth.* Translated by Catherine Porter. Princeton, NJ: Princeton University Press.

Borneman, John. 2002. "Reconciliation after Ethnic Cleansing: Listening, Retribution, Affiliation." *Public Culture* 14 (2): 281–304. https://doi.org/10.1215/08992363-14-2-281.

–, ed. 2003. *The Death of the Father: An Anthropology of the End in Political Authority.* New York: Berghahn Books.

Bose, Brinda. 2000. "The Desiring Subject: Female Pleasures and Feminist Resistance in Deepa Mehta's Fire." *Indian Journal of Gender Studies* 7 (2): 249–62. https://doi.org/10.1177/097152150000700207.

Bose, Shila. Letter to the Editor. *The Statesman,* 7 February 1997.

Bourdieu, Pierre. 1991. *Language and Symbolic Power.* Transalted by Gino Raymond. Cambridge, MA: Harvard University Press.

– 1993. *The Field of Cultural Production.* New York: Columbia University Press.

– 2005. "The Political Field, the Social Science Field, and the Journalistic Field." In *Bourdieu and the Journalistic Field,* edited by Erik Neveu and Rodney Benson, 29–47. Cambridge: Polity Press.

Bourne, Stephen. 2019. *Black Poppies: Britain's Black Community and the Great War.* Cheltenham, UK: The History Press.

Bowler, Kate. 2014. *Blessed: A History of the American Prosperity Gospel.* Oxford: Oxford University Press.

Boyer, Dominic. 2001. "Foucault in the Bush: The Social Life of Post-Structuralist Theory in East Berlin's Prenzlauer Berg." *Ethnos* 66 (2): 207–36. https://doi.org/10.1080/00141840120070949.

– 2003. "Censorship as a Vocation: The Institutions, Practices, and Cultural Logic of Media Control in the German Democratic Republic." *Comparative Studies in Society and History* 45: 511–45. https://doi.org/10.1017/S0010417503000240.

– 2013. "Simply the Best: Parody and Political Sincerity in Iceland." *American Ethnologist* 40 (2): 276–87. https://doi.org/10.1111/amet.12020.

Boyer, Dominic, and Alexi Yurchak. 2008. "Postsocialist Studies, Cultures of Parody and American Stiob." *Anthropology News* 49 (8): 9–10. https://doi.org/10.1111/an.2008.49.8.9.

– 2010. "American Stiob: Or, What Late-Socialist Aesthetics of Parody Reveal about Contemporary Political Culture in the West." *Cultural Anthropology* 25 (2): 179–221. https://doi.org/10.1111/j.1548-1360.2010.01056.x.

Boym, Svetlana. 2001. *The Future of Nostalgia.* New York: Basic Books.

Bradford, Leland P. 1974. *National Training Laboratories: Its History, 1947–1970: Originally National Training Laboratory in Group Development and Now NTL Institute for Applied Behavioral Science.* Bethel, ME: Bradford.

Breakell, Sue. 2015. "Archival Practices and the Practice of Archives in the Visual Arts." *Archives and Records* 36 (1): 1–5. https://doi.org/10.1080/23257962.2015.1018151.

Breininger, Olga. 2013. "Banderlogs and Network Hamsters: The Language of Political Protest in Russia." *Open Democracy*, 28 March 2013. https://www.opendemocracy.net/en/odr/banderlogs-and-network-hamsters-language-of-political-protest-in-russia/.

Brenneis, Donald L., and Fred R. Myers, eds. 1984. *Dangerous Words: Language and Politics in the Pacific.* New York: New York University Press.

Broadwater, Luke. 2021. "Here Are 7 Republicans Who Voted to Impeach Trump." *New York Times*, 13 February 2021. https://www.nytimes.com/2021/02/13/us/politics/republicans-vote-to-impeach.html.

Brody, David, and Scott Lamb. 2018. *The Faith of Donald J. Trump: A Spiritual Biography.* New York: Broadside Books.

Brønds, Thomas. 2017. "The Most Beautiful Friendship: Revolution, War and Ends of Social Gravity in Syria." *Middle East Critique* 26 (3): 283–96. https://doi.org/10.1080/19436149.2017.1331517.

Brooks, David. 2015. "Listening to Ta-Nehisi Coates While White." *New York Times*, 17 July 2015. https://www.nytimes.com/2015/07/17/opinion/listening-to-ta-nehisi-coates-while-white.html.

Brown, Keith. 1998. "Macedonian Culture and Its Audiences: An Analysis of Before the Rain." In *Ritual, Performance, Media*, edited by F. Hughes-Freeland, 160–76. London: Routledge.

Brown, Wendy, Judith Butler, and Saba Mahmood. 2013. Preface to *Is Critique Secular? Blasphemy, Injury and Free Speech*, by Talal Asad, Wendy Brown, Judith Butler, and Saba Mahmood, vii–xxii. New York: Fordham University Press. https://doi.org/10.2307/j.ctt1c5cjtk.3.

Bryant, Rebecca, and Madeleine Reeves, eds. 2021. *The Everyday Lives of Sovereignty: Political Imagination beyond the State*. Ithaca, NY: Cornell University Press.

B'Tselem. 2021. "A Regime of Jewish Supremacy from the Jordan River to the Mediterranean Sea: This Is Apartheid." B'Tselem, 12 January. https://www.btselem.org/publications/fulltext/202101_this_is_apartheid.

Bunn, Matthew. 2015. "Reimagining Repression: New Censorship Theory and After." *History and Theory* 54 (1): 25–44. https://doi.org/10.1111/hith.10739.

Burge, Ryan. 2020. "Could Democrats Win Over Mormon Votes? Here's Where They Diverge from Evangelicals." Religion Unplugged. 26 May. https://religionunplugged.com/news/2020/5/26/could-democrats-win-over-mormon-votes-heres-where-they-diverge-from-evangelicals.

Butler, Judith. 1997. *Excitable Speech: A Politics of the Performative*. London: Routledge.

– 2005. *Giving an Account of Oneself*. New York: Fordham University Press.

– 2013. "The Sensibility of Critique: Response to Asad and Mahmood." In *Is Critique Secular? Blasphemy, Injury, and Free Speech*, by Talal Asad, Wendy Brown, Judith Butler, and Saba Mahmood, 101–36. New York: Fordham University Press. https://doi.org/10.2307/j.ctt1c5cjtk.5.

– 2021. *Excitable Speech: A Politics of the Performative*. New York: Routledge Classics.

Buttu, Diana. 2022. "Anti-BDS Laws and the Politics around Them." *This Is Palestine – The IMEU Podcast*. 9 June 2022. https://imeu.org/basic_page/4832.

Cainkar, Louise A. 2009. *Homeland Insecurity: The Arab American and Muslim American Experience after 9/11*. New York: Russell Sage Foundation.

Cameron, Deborah. 1995. *Verbal Hygiene*. London: Routledge.

Candea, Matei. 2018. *Comparison in Anthropology: The Impossible Method*. Cambridge: Cambridge University Press.

– 2019a. "The Duelling Ethic and the Spirit of Libel Law: Matters and Materials of Honour in France." *Law Text Culture* 23: 171–97.

– 2019b. "Silencing Oneself, Silencing Others: Rethinking Censorship Comparatively." *Terrain* 72. https://doi.org/10.4000/terrain.18773.

– Forthcoming. "Reason, Honour and Carnival: French Law, Danish Cartoons and the Anthropology of Free Speech." *Comparative Studies in Society and History*.

Candea, Matei, Fiona Wright, Paolo Heywood, and Taras Fedirko. 2021. "Freedom of Speech." In *The Open Encyclopedia of Anthropology*, edited by Felix Stein.

Facsimile of the first edition in *The Cambridge Encyclopedia of Anthropology*. https://www.anthroencyclopedia.com/entry/freedom-speech.

Cannell, Fenella. 2005. "The Christianity of Anthropology." *Journal of the Royal Anthropological Institute* 11 (2): 335–56. https://doi.org/10.1111/j.1467-9655 .2005.00239.x.

– 2011. "English Ancestors: The Moral Possibilities of Popular Genealogy." *Journal of the Royal Anthropological Institute* 17 (3): 462-80. https://doi.org /10.1111/j.1467-9655.2011.01702.x.

– 2017. "Mormonism and Anthropology: On Ways of Knowing." *Mormon Studies Review* 4 (1): Article 2. https://scholarsarchive.byu.edu/msr2/vol4/iss1/2.

Capacci, Palmiro, Rolando Pasini, and Virna Giunchi. 2014. *La fója de farfaraz: Predappio, cronache di una communitá viva e solidale*. Cesena: Il Ponte Vecchio.

Carden, Maren Lockwood. 1974. *The New Feminist Movement*. New York: Russell Sage Foundation.

Carmi, Guy E. 2008. "Dignity versus Liberty: The Two Western Cultures of Free Speech." *SSRN Electronic Journal*. https://doi.org/10.2139/ssrn.1246700.

Carr, E. Summerson. 2006. "Secrets Keep You Sick: Metalinguistic Labor in a Drug Treatment Program for Homeless Women." *Language in Society* 35 (5): 631–53. http://www.jstor.org/stable/4169533.

– 2011. *Scripting Addiction: The Politics of Therapeutic Talk and American Sobriety*. Princeton, NJ: Princeton University Press.

– 2021. "Learning How Not to Know: Pragmatism, (In)Expertise, and the Training of American Helping Professionals." *American Anthropologist* 123 (2): 1–13. https:// doi.org/10.1111/aman.13598.

– 2023. *Working the Difference: Science, Spirit, and the Spread of Motivational Interviewing*. Chicago: University of Chicago Press.

Carr, E. Summerson, and Michael Lempert, eds. 2016. *Scale: Discourse and Dimensions of Social Life*. Oakland: University of California Press.

Carsten, Janet. 2007. *Ghosts of Memory: Essays on Remembrance and Relatedness*. London: Blackwell Publishing.

Casarotti, L. 2017. "Giurisprudenza: Una questione cultural e sociale." http:// anpiprovincialepavia.blogspot.com/2017/11/giurisprudenza-una-questione -culturale_11.html. (site discontinued)

Censure UofT. 2021. "In Support of the CAUT Censure of the University of Toronto." https://censureuoft.ca/.

Chace, Zoe. 2018. "The Impossible Dream." *This American Life*. Podcast #642. 6 April 2018. https://www.thisamericanlife.org/642/the-impossible-dream.

Chait, Jonathan. 2015. "*Charlie Hebdo* and the Right to Commit Blasphemy." *Intelligencer*, 7 January 2015. https://nymag.com/intelligencer/2015/01/charlie -hebdo-and-the-right-to-commit-blasphemy.html.

Chakrabarty, Dipesh. 2008. *Provincializing Europe: Postcolonial Thought and Historical Difference*. Princeton, NJ: Princeton University Press.

Charkavarthy, N.S. Letter to the Editor. *The Statesman*, 18 February 1997.

Chatterjee, Partha. 1986. *Nationalist Thought and the Colonial World: A Derivative Discourse*. London: Zed Books.

– 1993. *The Nation and Its Fragments: Colonial and Postcolonial Histories*. Princeton, NJ: Princeton University Press.

Chemerinsky, Erwin. 2020. "The Philosophy That Makes Amy Cony Barrett So Dangerous." *New York Times,* 21 October 2020. https://www.nytimes.com /2020/10/21/opinion/supreme-court-amy-coney-barrett.

Chemin, Ariane. 2015. "Polémique dans la famille Charlie Hebdo." *Le Monde*, 14 January 2015. https://www.lemonde.fr/societe/article/2015/01/14/polemique-dans -la-famille-charlie-hebdo_4556428_3224.html.

Chomsky, Noam. 1967. "A Review of B.F. Skinner's *Verbal Behavior*." In *Readings in the Psychology of Language*, edited by Leon A. Jakobovits and Murray S. Miron, 142–3. New York: Prentice-Hall.

– 1971. "The Case against B.F. Skinner: Review of *Beyond Freedom and Dignity* by B.F. Skinner." *The New York Review of Books*, 30 January 1971, 18–24.

Chowdhury, Nusrat Sabina. 2019. *Paradoxes of the Popular: Crowd Politics in Bangladesh*. Stanford: Stanford University Press.

– 2020. "A Second Coming: The Specular and the Spectacular 50 Years On." *South Asia Chronicle* 10: 31–58.

Chowdhury, Omar Adnan. 2018. "Online Portfolio." Accessed 15 June 2022. https://omarchowdhury.com/files/Portfolio%20Omar%20Chowdhury.pdf (site discontinued).

– 2019. "Memoirs of Saturn." *Wissen Der Künsten* 8. https://wissenderkuenste.de /texte/ausgabe8/memoirs-of-saturn/.

Chowdhury, Omar Adnan, and Kate Vinen. n.d. Interview with Omar Chowdhury (transcript). 4A Centre for Contemporary Asian Art.

Chowdhury, Omar Adnan, and Shahidul Zaman. 2016. *Age of Saturn*. Dhaka: Bengal Foundation.

Christensen, Kevin. 2021. "The Bulwark Compares Romney and Lee, and Mentions Captain Moroni." *Mormon Dialogue* (forum). 8 January 2021. https://www .mormondialogue.org/topic/73459-the-bulwark-compares-romney-and-lee -and-mentions-captain-moroni.

Clark, T.J. 2021. "Masters and Fools." *London Review of Books* 43 (18): 22–6.

Clarke, Morgan. 2014. "Cough Sweets and Angels: The Ordinary Ethics of the Extraordinary in Sufi Practice in Lebanon." *Journal of the Royal Anthropological Institute* 20 (3): 407–25. https://doi.org/10.1111/1467-9655.12117.

Clastres, Pierre. 1977. *Society against the State*. New York: Urizen Books.

Clifford, James. 1997. *Routes: Travel and Translation in the Late Twentieth Century*. Cambridge: Harvard University Press.

CM. 2015. "In the Wake of Charlie Hebdo, Free Speech Does Not Mean Freedom from Criticism." *Hooded Utilitarian* (blog). 7 January 2015. https://www

.hoodedutilitarian.com/2015/01/in-the-wake-of-charlie-hebdo-free-speech-does
-not-mean-freedom-from-criticism.

CNN. 2018. "Read Sen. Jeff Flake's Speech Criticizing Trump." CNN.com. 17 January
2018. https://edition.cnn.com/2018/01/17/politics/jeff-flake-speech/index.html.

Cody, Francis. 2015. "Populist Publics Print Capitalism and Crowd Violence beyond
Liberal Frameworks." *Comparative Studies of South Asia, Africa and the Middle
East* 35 (1): 50–65. https://doi.org/10.1215/1089201X-2876092.

– 2023. *The News Event: Popular Sovereignty in the Age of Deep Mediatization.*
Chicago: University of Chicago Press.

Cody, Francis, and Alejandro I. Paz. 2021. "Securitizing Communication: On the
Indeterminacy of Participant Roles in Online Journalism." *Journal of Linguistic
Anthropology* 31 (3): 340–56. https://doi.org/10.1111/jola.12339.

Coetzee, J.M. 1996. *Giving Offense: Essays on Censorship.* Chicago: The University
of Chicago Press.

Cohen, G.A. 2002. "Deeper into Bullshit." In *Contours of Agency: Essays on Themes
from Harry Frankfurt*, edited by Sarah Buss and Lee Overton, 321–39. Cambridge,
MA: MIT Press.

Cohen, Lawrence. 2005. "The Kothi Wars: AIDS Cosmopolitanism and the Morality
of Classification." In *Sex in Development: Science, Sexuality, and Morality in
Global Perspective*, edited by V. Adams and S. Pigg, 269–303. Durham, NC: Duke
University Press.

– 2012. "The Gay Guru: Fallibility, Unworldliness, and the Scene of Instruction."
In *The Guru in South Asia*, edited by L. Cohen, J. Copeman, and A. Ikegame,
97–112. New York: Routledge.

Cohen-Cole, Jamie. 2009. "The Creative American: Cold War Salons, Social
Science, and the Cure for Modern Society." *Isis* 100 (2): 219–62. https://doi.org
/10.1086/599554. Medline: 19653489.

– 2014. *The Open Mind: Cold War Politics and the Sciences of Human Nature.*
Chicago: University of Chicago Press.

Colclough, David. 2005. *Freedom of Speech in Early Stuart England.* 1st ed.
Cambridge: Cambridge University Press.

– 2009. *Freedom of Speech in Early Stuart England.* Illustrated ed. Cambridge:
Cambridge University Press.

Cole, David. 2003. "The New McCarthyism: Repeating History in the War on
Terrorism." *Harvard Civil Rights-Civil Liberties Law Review* 38 (1): 1–30. https://
doi.org/10.2139/ssrn.383660.

Coleman, Simon. 2011. "'Right Now!': Historiopraxy and the Embodiment of
Charismatic Temporalities." *Ethnos* 76 (4): 426–47. https://doi.org/10.1080
/00141844.2011.580354.

Committee to Protect Journalists (CPJ). 2024. "Journalist Casualties in the Israel–
Gaza War." Last updated 23 July 2024. https://cpj.org/2024/07/journalist-casualties
-in-the-israel-gaza-conflict.

Commonwealth War Graves Commission. 2021. *Report of the Special Committee to Review Historical Inequalities in Commemoration.* Maidenhead: Commonwealth War Graves Commission.

The Compass. 2009. "The Name That Must Not Be Said Out Loud." 20 January 2009. https://www.thecompassnews.org/2009/01/the-name-that-must-not-be-said -out-loud.

Cook, Michael. 2000. *Commanding Right and Forbidding Wrong in Islamic Thought.* Cambridge: Cambridge University Press.

Corrales, Javier. 2015. "Autocratic Legalism in Venezuela." *Journal of Democracy* 37: 38–45. https://doi.org/10.1353/jod.2015.0031.

Crapanzano, Vincent. 2000. *Serving the Word: Liiteralism in America from the Pulpit to the Bench.* London: The New Press.

Crenshaw, Kimberlé Williams. 1993. "Beyond Racism and Misogyny: Black Feminism and 2 Live Crew." In *Words That Wound: Critical Race Theory, Assaultive Speech, and the First Amendment*, by Mari J. Matsuda, Charles R. Lawrence III, Richard Delgado, and Kimberlé Williams Crenshaw, 111–32. Boulder, CO: Westview Press.

Darnton, Robert. 2015. *Censors at Work: How States Shaped Literature.* Reprint ed. New York: W.W. Norton.

Das, Santanu, ed. 2014. *Race, Empire and First World War Writing.* Cambridge: Cambridge University Press.

– 2018. *India, Empire, and First World War Culture: Writings, Images and Songs.* Cambridge: Cambridge University Press.

Das, Veena. 2000. "Violence and the Work of Time." In *Signifying Identities. Anthropological Perspectives on Boundaries and Contested Values*, edited by Anthony Cohen, 59–73. New York: Routledge.

– 2007. *Life and Words: Violence and the Descent into the Ordinary.* Berkeley: University of California Press.

Dasgupta, Birsa. 2017. *Obhishopto Nighty.* Shree Venkatesh Films Pvt.

Dave, Naisargi N. 2012. *Queer Activism in India: A Story in the Anthropology of Ethics.* Durham, NC: Duke University Press

Debenport, Erin. 2015. *Fixing the Books: Secrecy, Literacy, and Perfectibility in Indigenous New Mexico.* Santa Fe, NM: School for Advanced Research Press.

Deeb, Lara, and Jessica Winegar. 2016. *Anthropology's Politics: Disciplining the Middle East.* Stanford: Stanford University Press.

– 2017. "Middle East Politics in US Academia: The Case of Anthropology." *Comparative Studies of South Asia, Africa and the Middle East* 37 (1): 103–12. https://doi.org/10.1215/1089201x-3821333.

DeFrancis, John. 1977. *Colonialism and Language Policy in Viet Nam.* The Hague: De Gruyter Mouton.

Delgado, Richard. 1993. "Words That Would: A Tort Action for Racial Insults, Epithets, and Name Calling." In *Words That Wound: Critical Race Theory,*

Assaultive Speech, and the First Amendment, by Mari J. Matsuda, Charles R. Lawrence III, Richard Delgado, and Kimberlé Williams Crenshaw, 89–110. Boulder, CO: Westview Press

Della Ratta, Donatella. 2018. *Shooting a Revolution. Visual Media and Warfare in Syria*. London: Pluto Press.

Denery, Dallas G. 2015. *The Devil Wins: A History of Lying from the Garden of Eden to the Enlightenment*. Princeton, NJ: Princeton University Press.

Deseret News. 2016. "In Our Opinion: Donald Trump Should Resign His Candidacy." Editorial. *Deseret News*, 8 October 2016. https://www.deseret.com/2016/10/8/20598212/in-our-opinion-donald-trump-should-resign-his-candidacy/.

De Staël, Germaine. 1800. *De la littérature considéré dans ses rapports avec les institutions sociales*. Paris: Bibliothèque Charpentier.

Deuchler, Martina. 1995. *The Confucian Transformation of Korea: A Study of Society and Ideology*. Cambridge, MA: Harvard University Press.

Devecchio, Alexandre, and Eleonore de Nouël. 2018. "Mark Lilla/Laurent Bouvet: 'La France résistera-t-elle au multiculturalisme américain?'" *Figaro Vox*, 19 October 2018. https://www.lefigaro.fr/vox/societe/2018/10/19/31003-20181019ARTFIG00004-mark-lillalaurent-bouvet-la-france-resistera-t-elle-au-multiculturalisme-americain.php.

Dobrin, Lise M., and Eve Danziger. 2017. "'Free Speech' in Times of Conflict." *Anthropology News* 58 (6): 371–4. https://doi.org/10.1111/AN.710.

Dobson, Andrew. 2014. *Listening for Democracy: Recognition, Representation, Reconciliation*. Oxford: Oxford University Press.

Domenico, Roy. 1991. *Italian Fascists on Trial, 1943–1948*. Chapel Hill: University of North Carolina Press.

Dorsey, Margaret, and Miguel Díaz-Barriga. 2015. "The Constitution Free Zone in the United States: Law and Life in a State of Carcelment." *Political and Legal Anthropology Review* 38 (2): 204–25. https://doi.org/10.1111/plar.12107.

Doughan, Sultan. 2022. "Desiring Memorials: Jews, Muslims, and the Human of Citizenship." In *Jews and Muslims in Europe: Between Discourse and Experience*, edited by Ben Gidley and Samuel Sami Everett, 46–70. Leiden: Brill. https://doi.org/10.1163/9789004514331_004.

Douthat, Ross. 2015. "Opinion | Checking Charlie Hebdo's Privilege." *New York Times*, 18 April 2015. https://www.nytimes.com/2015/04/19/opinion/sunday/ross-douthat-checking-charlie-hebdos-privilege.html.

Drabinski, John. 2013. "Reconciliation and Founding Wounds." *Humanity* 4 (1): 117–32. https://doi.org/10.1353/hum.2013.0010.

Dragomir, Marius. 2019. *Media Capture in Europe*. Centre for Media, Data and Society. https://cmds.ceu.edu/article/2019-05-27/media-capture-europe-mdif-publishes-new-report-dragomir.

Dreifus, Claudia. 1973. *Woman's Fate: Raps from a Feminist Consciousness-Raising Group*. New York: Bantam Books.

Du Bois, John W. 1993. "Meaning without Intention: Lessons from Divination." In *Responsibility and Evidence in Oral Discourse*, edited by Jane H. Hill and Judith T. Irvine, 48–71. New York: Cambridge University Press.

Dunn, John. 2006. "It's Russian – but Not as We Know It." *Rusistika*, 31: 3–6.

Duranti, Alessandro. 1993a. "Intentionality and Truth: An Ethnographic Critique." *Cultural Anthropology* 8: 214–45. https://doi.org/10.1525/can.1993.8.2.02a00050.

– 1993b. "Intentions, Self, and Responsibility: An Essay in Samoan Ethnopragmatics." In *Responsibility and Evidence in Oral Discourse*, edited by Jane H. Hill and Judith T. Irvine, 24–47. New York: Cambridge University Press.

Duranti, Alessandro, and Charles Goodwin, eds. 1992. *Rethinking Context: Language as an Interactive Phenomenon*. Cambridge: Cambridge University Press.

Eatwell, Roger. 1996. "On Defining the 'Fascist Minimum': The Centrality of Ideology." *Journal of Political Ideologies* 1 (3): 303–19. https://doi.org/10.1080/13569319608420743.

Echols, Alice, and Ellen Willis. 1989. *Daring to Be Bad: Radical Feminism in America, 1967–1975*. Minneapolis: University of Minnesota Press.

Eco, Umberto. 1995. "Ur-Fascism." *New York Review*, 22 June 1995. http://www.nybooks.com/articles/1995/06/22/ur-fascism.

Eilenberg, Michael. 2016. "A State of Fragmentation: Enacting Sovereignty and Citizenship at the Edge of the Indonesian State." *Development and Change* 47 (6): 1338–60. https://doi.org/10.1111/dech.12272.

Elgin, Catherine Z. 2017. *True Enough*. Cambridge, MA: MIT Press.

El-Haj, Thea Renda Abu. 2015. *Unsettled Belonging: Educating Palestinian American Youth after 9/11*. Chicago: University of Chicago Press.

Englund, Harri. 2006. *Prisoners of Freedom: Human Rights and the African Poor*. Berkeley: University of California Press.

– 2018a. "The Front Line of Free Speech: Beyond *Parrhêsia* in Finland's Migrant Debate." *American Ethnologist* 45 (1): 100–11. https://doi.org/10.1111/amet.12602.

– 2018b. *Gogo Breeze: Zambia's Radio Elder and the Voices of Free Speech*. Chicago: University of Chicago Press.

Enke, Anne. 2007. *Finding the Movement: Sexuality, Contested Space, and Feminist Activism, Radical Perspectives*. Durham, NC: Duke University Press.

Erickson, Frederick. 2004. *Talk and Social Theory: Ecologies of Speaking and Listening in Everyday Life*. Cambridge, MA: Polity Press.

– 2010. "The Neglected Listener: Issues of Theory and Practice in Transcription from Video in Interaction Analysis." In *New Adventures in Language and Social Interaction*, edited by Jürgen Streeck, 243–56. Philadelphia: John Benjamins Publishing Company.

Erlmann, Veit, ed. 2004. *Hearing Cultures: Essays on Sound, Listening, and Modernity*. New York: Berg.

Errington, J. Joseph. 1988. *Structure and Style in Javanese: A Semiotic View of Linguistic Etiquette*. Philadelphia: University of Pennsylvania Press.

Evans, Sara M. 1979. *Personal Politics: The Roots of Women's Liberation in the Civil Rights Movement and the New Left*. New York: Knopf.

Fahmy, Khaled. 2018. *In Quest of Justice: Islamic Law and Forensic Medicine in Modern Egypt*. Berkeley: University of California Press.

Fassin, Didier. 2015. "In the Name of the Republic: Untimely Meditations on the Aftermath of the *Charlie Hebdo* Attack." *Anthropology Today* 31 (2): 3–7. https://doi.org/10.1111/1467-8322.12162.

Favret-Saada, Jeanne. 2016. "An Anthropology of Religious Polemics: The Case of Blasphemy Affairs." *HAU: Journal of Ethnographic Theory* 6 (1): 29–45. https://doi.org/10.14318/hau6.1.003.

Fedirko, Taras. 2020. "Self-Censorships in Ukraine: Distinguishing between the Silences of Television Journalism." *European Journal of Communication* 35 (1): 12–28. https://doi.org/10.1177/0267323119897424.

– 2021. "Liberalism in Fragments: Oligarchy and the Liberal Subject in Ukrainian News Journalism." *Social Anthropology* 29 (2): 471–89. https://doi.org/10.1111/1469-8676.13063.

Fedirko, Taras, Farhan Samanani, and Hugh F. Williamson. 2021. "Grammars of Liberalism." *Social Anthropology* 29 (2): 373–86. https://doi.org/10.1111/1469-8676.13061.

Feld, Steven. 2015. "Acoustemology." In *Keywords in Sound*, edited by David Novak and Matt Sakakeeny, 13–21. Durham, NC: Duke University Press.

Feldman, Ilana. 2019. "Reframing Palestine: BDS against Fragmentation and Exceptionalism." *Radical History Review* 2019 (134): 193–202. https://doi.org/10.1215/01636545-7323685.

Fish, Stanley. 1994. *There's No Such Thing as Free Speech, and It's a Good Thing, Too*. New York: Oxford University Press.

Fisher, Max. 2015. "What Everyone Gets Wrong about Charlie Hebdo and Racism." *Vox*, 12 January 2015. https://www.vox.com/2015/1/12/7518349/charlie-hebdo-racist.

Flaherty, Colleen. 2018. "The N-Word in the Classroom." *Inside Higher Education*, 11 February 2018. https://www.insidehighered.com/news/2018/02/12/two-professors-different-campuses-used-n-word-last-week-one-was-suspended-and-one.

Fleming, Luke. 2011. "Name Taboos and Rigid Performativity." *Anthropological Quarterly* 84 (1): 141–64. https://doi.org/10.1353/anq.2011.0010.

Fleming, Luke, and Jack Sidnell. 2020. "The Typology and Social Pragmatics of Interlocutor Reference in Southeast Asia." *The Journal of Asian Linguistic Anthropology* 2 (3): 1–20. https://doi.org/10.47298/jala.v2-i3-a1.

Fleming, Luke, and Michael Lempert. 2011. "Introduction: Beyond Bad Words." *Anthropological Quarterly* 84 (1): 5–14. https://doi.org/10.1353/anq.2011.0008.

– 2014. "Poetics and Performativity." In *Cambridge Handbook of Linguistic Anthropology*, edited by N.J. Enfield, Paul Kockelman, and Jack Sidnell, 485–515. Cambridge: Cambridge University Press.

Flood, Finbarr Barry. 2018. "Bodies, Books, and Buildings: Economies of Ornament in Juridical Islam." In *Clothing Sacred Scriptures: Book Art and Book Religion in Christian, Islamic, and Jewish Cultures*, edited by David Ganz and Barbara Schellewald, 49–68. Berlin: De Gruyter.

Florida, Robert. 2002. *The Rise of the Creative Class: And How It's Transforming Work, Leisure, Community and Everyday Life*. New York: Basic Books.

– 2005. *Cities and the Creative Class*. New York: Routledge.

– 2008. *Who's Your City?: How the Creative Economy Is Making Where to Live the Most Important Decision of Your Life*. New York: Basic Books.

Foucault, Michel. 1976. *Histoire de la sexualité*. Vol. 1, *La volonté de savoir*. Paris: Gallimard.

– 1977. *Discipline and Punish: The Birth of the Prison*. New York: Pantheon.

– 1983. "Discourse and Truth: The Problematization of Parrhesia. Six Lectures Given by Michael Foucault at the University of California at Berkeley, Oct.–Nov. 1983." Explore Parrhesia. https://foucault.info/parrhesia/.

– 1984. *Histoire de la sexualité*. Vol. 3, *Le souci de soi*. Paris: Gallimard.

– 1997. *Ethics: Subjectivity and Truth*. Edited by Paul Rabinow. Translated by Robert Hurley. New York: New Press.

– 2001. *Fearless Speech*. Edited by Joseph Pearson. Los Angeles: Semiotext(e).

– 2008. *The Birth of Biopolitics: Lectures at the Collège de France, 1978–1979*. Edited by Michel Senellart. Translated by Graham Burchell. New York: Palgrave Macmillan.

– 2011. *The Courage of Truth (The Government of Self and Others II): Lectures at the Collège de France, 1983–1984*. Edited by Frédéric Gros. Translated by Graham Burchell. New York: Palgrave Macmillan.

– 2019. *Discourse and Truth and Parresia*. Edited by Henri-Paul Fruchaud and Daniele Lorenzini. Translated by Nancy Luxon. Chicago: University of Chicago Press.

Foundation for Middle East Peace. "State Anti-Boycott Bills: Explicit Conflation of Israel and Settlements." Last updated 19 November 2021. https://fmep.org/wp/wp-content/uploads/BDS-laws-Israel-territories.pdf.

Frankfurt, Harry G. 2002. "Reply to G.A. Cohen." In *Contours of Agency: Essays on Themes from Harry Frankfurt*, edited by Sarah Buss and Lee Overton, 340–4. Cambridge, MA: MIT Press.

– 2005. *On Bullshit*. Princeton, NJ: Princeton University Press.

Fraser, Alastair. 2017. "Post-Populism in Zambia: Michael Sata's Rise, Demise and Legacy. *International Political Science Review*" 38 (4): 456–72. https://doi.org/10.1177/0192512117720809.

Fraser, Nancy. 1990. "Rethinking the Public Sphere: A Contribution to the Critique of Actually Existing Democracy." *Social Text* 25/26: 56–80. https://doi.org/10.2307/466240.

Fraser, Nancy, and Alex Honneth. 2003. *Redistribution or Recognition? A Philosophical Exchange*. Translated by Joel Golb, James Ingram, and Christiane Wilke. London: Verso.

Freud, Sigmund. (1919) 2003. *The Uncanny*. Translated by David McLintock. London: Penguin Books.

Friedrich, Paul. 1979. "Structural Implications of Russian Pronominal Usage." In *Language, Context, and the Imagination: Essays by Paul Friedrich*, edited by Anwar S. Dil, 64–125. Stanford: Stanford University Press.

Gade, Anna M. 2004. *Perfection Makes Practice: Learning, Emotion, and the Recited Qur'ān in Indonesia*. Honolulu: University of Hawai'i Press.

Gal, Susan. 1991. "Bartók's Funeral: Representations of Europe in Hungarian Political Rhetoric." *American Ethnologist* 18 (3): 440–58. https://doi.org/10.1525/ae.1991.18.3.02a00020.

– 2002. "A Semiotics of the Public/Private Distinction." *differences* 13 (1): 77–95. https://doi.org/10.1215/10407391-13-1-77.

– 2016. "Scale-Making: Comparison and Perspective as Ideological Projects." In *Scale: Discourse and Dimensions of Social Life*, edited by E. Summerson Carr and Michael Lempert, 91–111. Berkeley: University of California Press.

– 2019. "Making Registers in Politics." *Journal of Sociolinguistics* 23 (5): 450–66. https://doi.org/10.1111/josl.12374.

Gal, Susan, and Judith T. Irvine. 2019. *Signs of Difference: Language and Ideology in Social Life*. Cambridge: Cambridge University Press. https://doi.org/10.1017/9781108649209.

Gardner, Rod. 2001. *When Listeners Talk: Response Tokens and Listener Stance*. Philadelphia: John Benjamins Publishing Company.

Gell, Alfred. 1999. "Vogel's Net: Traps as Artworks and Artworks as Traps." In *The Art of Anthropology: Essays and Diagrams*, 187–214. London: The Athlone Press.

Gentile, Emilio. 1990. "Fascism as Political Religion." *Journal of Contemporary History* 25 (2): 229–51. https://doi.org/10.1177/002200949002500204.

Gerasimov, I., Glebov, S, Kaplunovski, A., Mogilner, A. and Semyonov, A. 2013. "The Alien Origins of Freedom." *Ab Imperio* 1: 15–20. https://doi.org/10.1353/imp.2013.0012.

Gernelle, Etienne. 2020. "Plenel et Despentes, la gauche anti-'Charlie.'" *Le Point*, 2 September 2020. https://www.lepoint.fr/editos-du-point/plenel-et-despentes-la-gauche-anti-charlie-02-09-2020-2390062_32.php.

Gessen, Masha. 2021. "Did a University of Toronto Donor Block the Hiring of a Scholar for Her Writing on Palestine?" *The New Yorker*, 8 May 2021. https://www.newyorker.com/news/our-columnists/did-a-university-of-toronto-donor-block-the-hiring-of-a-scholar-for-her-writing-on-palestine.

Ghosh, Rituparno. 2012. *Chitrangada: The Crowning Wish*. Shree Venkatesh Films.

Ghoshal, Aparna. Letter to the Editor. *The Statesman*, 17 February 1997.

Gilbert, Alan. 2016. "Walid Raad's Spectral Archive, Part I: Historiography as Process." *e-Flux Journal*, Issue #69. https://www.e-flux.com/journal/69/60594/walid-raad-s-spectral-archive-part-i-historiography-as-process/.

Gilbert, Nora. 2013. *Better Left Unsaid: Victorian Novels, Hays Code Films, and the Benefits of Censorship*. Stanford: Stanford University Press.

Gill, Harjant S. 2017. "Censorship and Ethnographic Film: Confronting State Bureaucracies, Cultural Regulation, and Institutionalized Homophobia in India." *Visual Anthropology Review* 33 (1): 62–73. https://doi.org/10.1111/var.12122.

Gill, Rosalind. 2002. "Cool, Creative and Egalitarian? Exploring Gender in Project-Based New Media Work in Euro." *Information, Communication & Society* 5 (1): 70–89. https://doi.org/10.1080/13691180110117668.

Gilmore, Ruth Wilson. 2007. *Golden Gulag: Prisons, Surplus, Crisis, and Opposition in Globalizing California*. Berkeley: University of California Press.

Gitlin, Todd. 1987. *The Sixties: Years of Hope, Days of Rage*. New York: Bantam Books.

Givens, Terryl L. 2013. *The Viper on the Hearth: Mormon Myths and the Construction of Heresy*. Oxford: Oxford University Press.

Go, Julian. 2008. "Global Fields and Imperial Forms: Field Theory and the British and American Empires." *Sociological Theory* 26 (3): 201–29. https://doi.org/10.1111/j.1467-9558.2008.00326.x.

Go, Julian, and Monika Krause. 2016. "Fielding Transnationalism: An Introduction." *The Sociological Review Monographs* 64 (2): 6–30. https://doi.org/10.1111/2059-7932.12000.

Goede, Marieke de. 2018. "The Chain of Security." *Review of International Studies* 44 (1): 24–42. https://doi.org/10.1017/S0260210517000353.

Goffman, Erving. 1957. "Alienation from Interaction." *Human Relations* 10 (1): 47–60. https://doi.org/10.1177/001872675701000103.

– 1974. *Frame Analysis: An Essay on the Organization of Experience*. New York: Harper Colophon Books.

– 1981. *Forms of Talk*. Philadelphia: University of Pennsylvania Press.

Goodwin, Charles. 2018. *Co-Operative Action*. Cambridge: Cambridge University Press.

– 2006. "Interactive Footing." In *Reporting Talk: Reported Speech in Interaction*, edited by Elizabeth Holt and Rebecca Clift, 16–46. Cambridge: Cambridge University Press.

Gopalakrishnan, L. Letter to the Editor. *The Statesman*, 7 February 1997.

Gordon, Sarah Barringer. 2002. *The Mormon Question: Polygamy and Constitutional Conflict in Nineteenth-Century America*. Chapel Hill: University of North Carolina Press.

Gorham, Michael S. 2000. "Mastering the Perverse: State Building and Language 'Purification' in Early Soviet Russia." *Slavic Review* 59 (1): 133–53. https://doi.org/10.2307/2696907.

– 2014. *After Newspeak: Language Culture and Politics in Russia from Gorbachev to Putin*. Ithaca, NY: Cornell University Press.

Graan, Andrew. 2022. "Marketing Logics and the Politics of Public Spheres: On Discursive Engineering and Enclosure." *Journal of Linguistic Anthropology* 32 (2): 301–25. https://doi.org/10.1111/jola.12360.

Graeber, Dan. 2020. "Paula White's 'Victory' Prayer about Trump, Africa Goes Viral." *International Business Times*, 5 November 2020. https://www.ibtimes.com/paula-whites-victory-prayer-about-trump-africa-goes-viral-watch-3076940.

Graeber, David. 2004. *Fragments of an Anarchist Anthropology*. Chicago: Prickly Paradigm Press.

Graff, Agnieszka, and Elżbieta Korolczuk. 2022. *Anti-Gender Politics in the Populist Moment*. Routledge: New York.

Graham, Laura. 1993. "A Public Sphere in Amazonia? The Depersonalized Collaborative Construction of Discourse in Xavante." *American Ethnologist* 20 (4): 717–41. https://doi.org/10.1525/ae.1993.20.4.02a00030.

Green, Dominic. 2016. "The Elusive Definition of 'Fascist.'" *The Atlantic*, 18 December 2016. https://www.theatlantic.com/politics/archive/2016/12/fascism-populism -presidential-election/510668.

Gregor, A. James. 1979. *Italian Fascism and Developmental Dictatorship*. Princeton, NJ: Princeton University Press.

Griffin, Roger. 1991. *The Nature of Fascism*. London: Pinter Publishers.

Grossarth, Eric. 2022. "Capital Riot "Captain Moroni" Expected to Reach Plea Agreement." *East Idaho News*, 13 January 2022. https://www.eastidahonews .com/2022/01/capitol-riot-captain-moroni-expected-to-reach-plea-agreement.

The Guardian. 2021. "Racist Treatment of Black and Asian War Dead Is Acknowledged at Last." *The Guardian*, 22 April 2021. https://www.theguardian.com/uk-news/2021 /apr/22/racist-treatment-of-black-and-asian-war-dead-is-acknowledged-at-last.

Guinan, Kerry. 2016. *The Impact and Instrumentalisation of Art in the Dublin Property Market: Evidence from Smithfield, Dublin 1996–2016*. Dublin: Self-published.

Guinane, Kay. 2021. *The Alarming Rise of Lawfare to Suppress Civil Society: The Case of Palestine and Israel*. Washington, DC: The Charity & Security Network. https://charityandsecurity.org/wp-content/uploads/2021/09/The-Alarming-Rise-of -Lawfare-to-Suppress-Civil-Society.pdf.

Gumperz, John J. 1982. *Discourse Strategies*. New York: Cambridge University Press.

Gupta, Akhil. 1995. "Blurred Boundaries: The Discourse of Corruption, the Culture of Politics, and the Imagined State." *American Ethnologist* 22 (2): 375–402. https:// doi.org/10.1525/ae.1995.22.2.02a00090.

Gupta, Meghnad. Letter to the Editor. *The Statesman*, 7 February 1997.

Guseinov, Gasan. 2004. *D.S.P. Sovetskie ideologemy v russkom diskurse 1990-x*. Moscow: Tri Kvadrata.

– 2012 *Nulevyye nakonchike yazyka : Kratkii putevoditl' po russkomu diskursu*. Moscow: Delo.

– 2017. "V rossii lyudy prinimayut nasilie kak proyavlenie osobogo prava vlasti." *Realnoe Vremya*, 29 June 2017. https://realnoevremya.ru /articles/69107-gasan-guseynov-o-diskurse-mrakobesiya-leksikonk-stalina.

Guzman, Jennifer R. 2014. "The Epistemics of Symptom Experience and Symptom Accounts in Mapuche Healing and Pediatric Primary Care in Southern Chile." *Journal of Linguistic Anthropology* 24 (3): 249–76. https://doi.org/10.1111 /jola.12055.

Haberman, D.L. 1997. "Review: Kali's Child: The Mystical and Erotic in the Life and Teachings of Ramakrishna." *The Journal of Asian Studies* 56 (2): 531. https://doi .org/10.2307/2646302.

Habermas, Jurgen. (1962) 1989. *The Structural Transformation of the Public Sphere.* Translated by Thomas Burger. Cambridge: Polity Press.

– 1974. "The Public Sphere: An Encyclopedia Article (1964)." *New German Critique* 3: 49–55. https://doi.org/10.2307/487737.

– 1984. *The Theory of Communicative Action.* Boston: Beacon Press.

– 1995. *Justification and Application: Remarks on Discourse Ethics.* Translated by Ciaran P. Cronin. Cambridge, MA: MIT Press.

Haeri, Niloofar. 2003. *Sacred Language, Ordinary People: Dilemmas of Culture and Politics in Egypt.* New York: Palgrave Macmillan.

Hall, Edward T. 1969. "Listening Behavior: Some Cultural Differences." *The Phi Delta Kappan* 50 (7): 379–80.

Hall, Stuart. 2001. "Constituting an Archive." *Third Text* 15 (54): 89–92. https://doi .org/10.1080/09528820108576903.

Halpern, Orly, Naomi Zeveloff, and Robert Mahoney. 2022. "Deadly Pattern: 20 Journalists Died by Israeli Military Fire in 22 Years. No One Has Been Held Accountable." *Committee to Protect Journalists* (blog). 9 May 2022. https://cpj.org /reports/2023/05/deadly-pattern-20-journalists-died-by-israeli-military-fire-in-22 -years-no-one-has-been-held-accountable/.

HaMoked. 2022. "HaMoked to the Minister of Defense: The Revised Procedure for the Entry of Foreigners to the oPt Is Still Fundamentally Flawed and Must Be Frozen until It Is Amended." HaMoked. 14 September. https://hamoked.org /document.php?dID=Updates2327.

Hankins, James. 2019. *Virtue Politics: Soulcraft and Statecraft in Renaissance Italy.* Cambridge, MA: Harvard University Press.

Hansen, Thomas Blom. 1999. *The Saffron Wave: Democracy and Hindu Nationalism in Modern India.* Princeton, NJ: Princeton University Press.

Hansen, Thomas Blom, and Finn Stepputat. 2001. *States of Imagination: Ethnographic Explorations of the Postcolonial State.* Durham, NC: Duke University Press.

Haraszti, Miklós. 1987. *The Velvet Prison: Artists under State Socialism.* New York: Basic Books.

Harkness, Nicholas. 2011. "Culture and Interdiscursivity in Korean Fricative Voice Gestures." *Journal of Linguistic Anthropology* 21 (1): 99–123. https://doi .org/10.1111/j.1548-1395.2011.01084.x.

Hartman, Saidiya. 2021. "Book Forum: Intimate History, Radical Narrative." *The Journal of African American History* 106 (1): 127–35. https://doi.org /10.1086/712019.

Hartnack, Christiane. 2001. *Psychoanalysis in Colonial India.* New Delhi: Oxford University Press.

Hartog, Francois. 2015. *Regimes of Historicity. Presentism and Experiences of Time.* New York: Columbia University Press.

Hasan, Mubashar. 2019. "Who Suppresses Free Speech in Bangladesh? A Typology of Actors." In *Transnational Othering – Global Diversities*, edited by Elisabeth Eide, Kristin Skare Orgeret, and Nil Mutluer, 155–70. Gothenburg, Sweden: Nordicom.

Hass, Amira. 2022. "Israel to Decide for Palestinians Which Foreign Lecturers Can Teach at West Bank Universities." *Haaretz*, 8 March 2022. https://www.haaretz .com/israel-news/.premium-israel-to-decide-which-foreigners-can-teach-at-west -bank-universities-1.10662018.

Hatcher, Brian. 1999. "Kālī's Problem Child: Another Look at Jeffrey Kripal's Study of Śrī Rāmakṛṣṇa." *International Journal of Hindu Studies* 3 (2): 165–82. https:// doi.org/10.1007/s11407-999-0002-3.

Haugbølle, Sune, and Andreas Bandak. 2017. "The Ends of Revolution: Rethinking Ideology and Time in the Arab Uprisings." *Middle East Critique* 26 (3): 191–204. https://doi.org/10.1080/19436149.2017.1334304.

Hawley, John Stratton. 1998 "Kālī's Child: The Mystical and the Erotic in the Life and Teachings of Ramakrishna by Jeffrey J. Kripal," *History of Religions* 37 (4): 401–4. https://doi.org/10.1086/463515.

Hawley, Joshua. 2019. "The Age of Pelagius." *Christianity Today*, 4 June 2019. https://www.christianitytoday.com/ct/2019/june-web-only/age-of-pelagius-joshua -hawley.html.

Hazareesingh, Sudhir, and Julie Clarini. 2017. "'Charlie' contre 'Mediapart' vu du Royaume-Uni : 'Une discussion consternante.'" *Le Monde*, 15 November 2017. https://www.lemonde.fr/idees/article/2017/11/15/charlie-contre-mediapart-vu-du -royaume-uni-une-discussion-consternante_5215163_3232.html.

Hellbeck, Jochen. 2000. "Speaking Out: Languages of Affirmation and Dissent in Stalinist Russia." *Kritika: Explorations in Russian and Eurasian History*, n.s., 1 (1): 71–96. https://doi.org/10.1353/kri.2008.0143.

Helmreich, Stefan. 2010. "Listening against Soundscapes." *Anthropology News* 51 (9): 10. https://doi.org/10.1111/j.1556-3502.2010.51910.x.

– 2016. "Gravity's Reverb: Listening to Space-Time, or Articulating the Sounds of Gravitational-Wave Detection." *Cultural Anthropology* 31 (4): 464–92. https://doi .org/10.14506/ca31.4.02.

Henig, David. 2018. "Prayer as a History: Of Witnesses, Martyrs, and Plural Pasts in Post-War Bosnia-Herzegovina." *Social Analysis* 61 (1): 41–54.

Herman, Ellen. 1995. *The Romance of American Psychology: Political Culture in the Age of Experts, 1940–1970.* Berkeley: University of California Press.

Heryanto, Ariel, and Stanley Yoseph Adi. 2002. "Industrialized Media in Democratizing Indonesia." In *Media Fortunes, Changing Times: ASEAN States in Transition.* Edited by Russell H.K. Heng, 47–82. Singapore: Institute of Southeast Asian Studies.

Heywood, Paolo. 2015. "Freedom in the Code: The Anthropology of (Double) Morality." *Anthropological Theory* 15: 200–17. https://doi.org/10.1177/1463499614568498.

– 2018. "Making Difference: Queer Activism and Anthropological Theory." *Current Anthropology* 59 (3): 314–31. https://doi.org/10.1086/697946.

– 2019. "Fascism, Uncensored: Legalism and Neofascist Pilgrimage in Predappio, Italy." *Terrain* 72: 86–103. https://doi.org/10.4000/terrain.18996.

– 2021. "Ordinary Exemplars: Cultivating the Everyday in the Birthplace of Fascism." *Comparative Studies in Society and History* 64 (1): 91–121. https://doi.org/10.1017/S0010417521000402.

– 2023a. "Are There Anthropological Problems?" In *Beyond Description: Anthropologies of Explanation*, edited by Paolo Heywood and Matei Candea, 25–44. Ithaca, NY: Cornell University Press. https://doi.org/10.1515/9781501771583.

– 2023b. "Out of the Ordinary: Everyday Life and the 'Carnival of Mussolini.'" *American Anthropologist* 125 (3): 493–504. https://doi.org/10.1111/aman.13850.

– 2024a. *Burying Mussolini: Ordinary Life in the Shadows of Fascism.* Ithaca, NY: Cornell University Press.

– 2024b. "Making Fascism History in the 'Land of the Duce.'" In *New Anthropologies of Italy: Politics, History, and Culture*, edited by Paolo Heywood, 105–21. Oxford: Berghahn Books.

Hill, Jane H., and Judith T. Irvine, eds. 1993. *Responsibility and Evidence in Oral Discourse.* New York: Cambridge University Press.

Hirsch, Eric, and Charles Stewart. 2005. "Introduction: Ethnographies of Historicity." *History and Anthropology* 16 (3): 261–74. https://doi.org/10.1080/02757200500219289.

Hirschkind, Charles. 2006. *The Ethical Soundscape: Cassette Sermons and Islamic Counterpublics.* New York: Columbia University Press.

– 2008. "The Ethics of Listening: Cassette-SermonAudition in Contemporary Egypt." *American Ethnologist* 28 (3): 623–49. https://doi.org/10.1525/ae.2001.28.3.623.

Hoài Thanh, and Hoài Chân. (1942) 1999. "Một thời đại trong thi ca." In *Thi Nhân Việt Nam, 1932–1941.* Hanoi: Văn Học.

Hobsbawm, Eric. 1995. *Age of Extremes: The Short Twentieth Century, 1914–1991.* London: Abacus.

Hodges, Adam. 2020a. "Plausible Deniability." In *Language in the Trump Era: Scandals and Emergencies*, edited by Janet McIntosh and Norma Mendoza-Denton, 137–48. New York: Cambridge University Press. https://doi.org/10.1017/9781108887410.009.

– 2020b. *When Words Trump Politics: Resisting a Hostile Regime of Language.* Stanford: Stanford University Press.

Holbraad, Martin. 2017. "The Contingency of Concepts: Transcendental Deduction and Ethnographic Expression in Anthropological Thinking." In *Comparative Metaphysics: Ontology after Anthropology*, edited by Pierre Charbonnier, Gildas Salmon, and Peter Skafish, 133–58. London: Rowman and Littlefield.

Holmes, Douglas R. 2000. *Integral Europe: Fast Capitalism, Multiculturalism, Neofascism*. Princeton, NJ: Princeton University Press.

Holmes, Oliver Wendell. 1918. *US Reports: Schenck v. United States, 249 U.S. 47*. Supreme Court of the United States.

Hornsby, Jennifer, Louise Antony, Jennifer Saul, Natalie Stoljar, Nellie Wieland, and Rae Langton. 2011. "Subordination, Silencing, and Two Ideas of Illocution." *Jurisprudence* 2 (2): 379–440. https://doi.org/10.5235/204033211798716826.

Howe, Ben. 2019. *The Immoral Majority: Why Evangelical Christians Chose Political Power over Christian Values*. New York: HarperCollins.

Hsieh, Jennifer C. 2019. "Piano Transductions: Music, Sound and Noise in Urban Taiwan." *Sound Studies: An Interdisciplinary Journal* 5 (1): 4–21. https://doi.org/10.1080/20551940.2018.1564459.

– 2021. "Making Noise in Urban Taiwan: Decibels, the State, and Sono-Sociality." *American Ethnologist* 48 (1): 51–64. https://doi.org/10.1111/amet.13003.

Hull, Matthew. 2010. "Democratic Technologies of Speech: From WWII America to Postcolonial Delhi." *Journal of Linguistic Anthropology* 20 (2): 257–82. https://www.jstor.org/stable/43104263.

Human Rights Watch. 2019. "Israel: Supreme Court Greenlights Deporting Human Rights Watch Official." *Human Rights Watch* (blog). 5 November 2019. https://www.hrw.org/news/2019/11/05/israel-supreme-court-greenlights-deporting-human-rights-watch-official.

– 2021. "A Threshold Crossed: Israeli Authorities and the Crimes of Apartheid and Persecution." Human Rights Watch. 21 April 2021. https://www.hrw.org/report/2021/04/27/threshold-crossed/israeli-authorities-and-crimes-apartheid-and-persecution.

Humphrey, Caroline. 2007. "Alternative Freedoms." *Proceedings of the American Philosophical Society* 151 (1): 1–10. https://www.jstor.org/stable/4599040.

Hunter, Emma. 2017. "Languages of Freedom in Decolonising Africa." *Transactions of the Royal Historical Society* 27: 253–69. https://doi.org/10.1017/S0080440117000123.

Huỳnh Sanh Thông. 1987. *The Tale of Kiều: A Bilingual Edition of Nguyễn Du's Truyện Kiều*. Translated by Huỳnh Sanh Thông. New Haven, CT: Yale University Press.

Idowu, Ronke. 2020. "'I Hear the Sound of Victory,' Trump's Spiritual Adviser Prays as Biden Inches Closer to 270." *Channels TV*. 5 November 2020. https://www.channelstv.com/2020/11/05/i-hear-the-sound-of-victory-trumps-spiritual-adviser-prays-as-biden-inches-close-to-270/.

Inoue, Miyako. 2003. "The Listening Subject of Japanese Modernity and His Auditory Double: Citing, Sighting, and Siting the Modern Japanese Woman." *Cultural Anthropology* 18 (2): 156–93. https://doi.org/10.1525/can.2003.18.2.156.

– 2006. *Vicarious Language: Gender and Linguistic Modernity in Japan*. Berkeley: University of California Press.

Isherwood, Christopher. 1965. *Ramakrishna and His Disciples*. New York: Simon and Schuster.

Ismail, Salwa. 2018. *The Rule of Violence. Subjectivity, Memory and Government in Syria*. Cambridge: Cambridge University Press.

Iteanu, André. 2015. "Recycling Values: Perspectives from Melanesia." *HAU: Journal of Ethnogrphic Theory* 5 (1): 137–50. https://doi.org/10.14318/hau5.1.007.

Jack, Gavin. 2004. "On Speech, Critique and Protection." *Ephemera: Theory and Politics in Organization* 4 (2): 121–34. https://ephemerajournal.org/sites/default/files/2022-01/4-2jack.pdf.

Jackson, Michael. 2002. *The Politics of Storytelling. Violence, Transgression and Intersubjectivity*. København: Museum Tusculanum Press.

– 2005. *Existential Anthropology. Events, Exigencies and Effects*. New York: Berghahn Books.

Jadalliya. 2021. "Live Event – Syria Ten Years On: Art, Journalism, and the Struggle over Narrative." 18 March 2021. https://www.jadaliyya.com/Details/42502.

Jakobson, Roman. 1966. "Quest for the Essence of Language." *Diogenes* 51: 21–37. https://doi.org/10.1177/039219216501305103.

– (1956) 2004. "Two Aspects of Language." In *Literary Theory: An Anthology*, edited by Julie Rivkin and Michael Ryan, 2nd ed., 76–80. London: Blackwell.

Jamieson, Neil. 1993. *Understanding Vietnam*. Berkeley: University of California Press.

Jeju 4·3 Yŏnguso. 1989. *Ijesa malhaemsuda* (Now we speak out). Seoul: Hanul.

Jenkins, Lee, and Cheris Kramer. 1978. "Small Group Process: Learning from Women." *Women's Studies International Quarterly* 1: 67–84. https://doi.org/10.1016/S0148-0685(78)90379-2

Jewish Voice for Peace. 2016. "Canary Mission." *Jewish Voice for Peace* (blog). 13 May 2016. https://www.jewishvoiceforpeace.org/2016/05/canary-mission/.

John, Mary E., and Tejaswini Niranjana. 2000. "Mirror Politics: Fire, Hindutva and Indian Culture." *Inter-Asia Cultural Studies* 1 (2): 374–9. https://doi.org/10.1080/14649370050141267.

Johnson, Jim. 1988. "The Sociology of a Door Closer: Mixing Humans and Non-Humans Together." *Social Problems* 35 (3): 298–310. https://doi.org/10.1525/sp.1988.35.3.03a00070.

Jones, Megan Sanborn. 2018. *Contemporary Mormon Pageantry: Seeking after the Dead*. Ann Arbor: University of Michigan Press.

Kakar, Sudhir. 1991. *The Analyst and the Mystic: Psychoanalytic Reflections on Religion and Mysticism*. New Delhi: Penguin.

Kalčik, Susan. 1975. "'... Like Ann's Gynecologist or the Time I Was Almost Raped': Personal Narratives in Women's Rap Groups." *The Journal of American Folklore* 88 (347): 3–11. https://doi.org/10.2307/539181.

Kaleem, Jaweed. 2019. "He Got into Harvard. And Now He Finally Got into the United States." *Los Angeles Times,* 3 September 2019. https://www.latimes.com/world-nation/story/2019-09-03/ismail-ajjawi-harvard-student-palestinian.

Kalmbacher, Colin. 2021. "Man Who Allegedly Dressed as Book of Mormon Figure Who Raised Armies against Tyrants Arrested Over Jan. 6 Attack." *Law Crime*, 15 July 2021. https://lawandcrime.com/u-s-capitol-siege/man-who-allegedly-dressed-as-book-of-mormon-figure-who-raised-armies-against-tyrants-arrested-over-jan-6-attack/.

Kant, Immanuel. 1991. *Political Writings*. Edited by H.S. Reiss. Translated by H.B. Nisbet. 2nd ed. Cambridge: Cambridge University Press.

Kapchan, Deborah. 2017. *Theorizing Sound Writing*. Middletown, CT: Wesleyan University Press.

Kapur, Ratna. 2000. "Too Hot to Handle: The Cultural Politics of 'Fire.'" *Feminist Review* 64 (1): 53–64. https://doi.org/10.1080/014177800338963.

Karpiak, Kevin. 2015. "On Charlie Hebdo: Metaphor and the Tyranny of Secular Liberalism." *Anthropoliteia* (blog). 12 January2015. https://anthropoliteia.net/2015/01/12/on-charlie-hebdo-metaphor-and-the-tyranny-of-secular-liberalism.

Kaur, R., and Mazzarella, W. 2012. *Censorship in South Asia: Cultural Regulation from Sedition to Seduction*. New Delhi: Routledge.

Kaviraj, Sudipta. 1997. "Filth and the Public Sphere: Concepts and Practices about Space in Calcutta." *Public Culture* 10 (1): 83–113. https://doi.org/10.1215/08992363-10-1-83.

Keane, Webb. 1996. *Signs of Recognition*. Berkeley: University of California Press.

– 1997. *Signs of Recognition: Powers and Hazards of Representation in an Indonesian Society*. Berkeley: University of California Press.

– 2002. "Sincerity, 'Modernity,' and the Protestants." *Cultural Anthropology* 17 (1): 65–92. https://doi.org/10.1525/can.2002.17.1.65.

– 2007. *Christian Moderns: Freedom and Fetish in the Mission Encounter*. Berkeley: University of California Press.

– 2009. "Freedom and Blasphemy: On Indonesian Press Bans and Danish Cartoons." *Public Culture* 21 (1): 47–76. https://doi.org/10.1215/08992363-2008-021.

– 2013. "On Spirit Writing: The Materiality of Language and the Religious Work of Transduction." *Journal of the Royal Anthropological Institute* 19 (1): 1–17. https://doi.org/10.1111/1467-9655.12000.

– 2014. "Rotting Bodies: The Clash of Stances toward Materiality and its Ethical Affordances." *Current Anthropology* 55: S312–S321. https://doi.org/10.1086/678290.

– 2016. *Ethical Life: Its Natural and Social Histories*. Princeton, NJ: Princeton University Press.

– 2018a. "Divine Text, National Language, and Their Publics: Arguing an Indonesian Qur'an." *Comparative Studies in Society and History* 60 (4): 758–85. https://doi.org/10.1017/S0010417518000282.

– 2018b. "On Semiotic Ideology." *Signs and Society* 6 (1): 64–87. https://doi.org/10.1086/695387.

– 2022. "Peirce among the Muslim Saints' Graves in Java." In *Philosophy in Fieldwork: Critical Introductions to Theory and Analysis in Anthropological*

Practice, edited by Nils Bubandt and Thomas Schwarz Wentzer, 406–23. London: Routledge.

Keane, Webb, and Michael Lempert. 2023. "Making the Ethical in Social Interaction." In *The Cambridge Handbook for the Anthropology of Ethics*, edited by James Laidlaw, 231–50. Cambridge: Cambridge University Press. https://doi .org/10.1017/9781108591249.009.

Keijer, Kees. 2021. "Kunstenaar Omar Adnan Chowdhury houdt van ontregelen, zoveel is zeker." *Het Parool*, 10 September 2021. https://www.parool.nl/kunst -media/kunstenaar-omar-adnan-chowdhury-houdt-van-ontregelen-zoveel-is -zeker~bf1ac5b4.

Keller, Aaron. 2021. "Capitol Siege Defendant Who Admitted Tasing Michael Fanone Files Court Documents Suggesting He Was 'Acting Upon' Donald Trump's 'Authorization.'" *Law Crime,* 18 October 2021. https://lawandcrime.com/u-s -capitol-siege/capitol-siege-defendant-who-admitted-tasing-michael-fanone-files -court-documents-claiming-he-was-acting-upon-donald-trumps-authorization/.

Kelty, Christopher. 2019. *The Participant: A Century of Participation in Four Stories*. Chicago: University of Chicago Press.

Kendall, Laurel. 1985. *Shamans, Housewives, and Other Restless Spirits: Women in Korean Ritual Life*. Honolulu: University of Hawai'i Press.

Kershner, Isabel, Sheryl Gay Stolberg, and Peter Baker. 2019. "Israeli Decision on Omar and Tlaib Inflames Politics in Two Countries." *New York Times*, 15 August 2019. https://www.nytimes.com/2019/08/15/world/middleeast/trump-israel -omar-tlaib.html.

Khan, Naveeda. 2021. "Marginal Lives and the Microsociology of Overhearing in the Jamuna Chars." *Ethnos: Journal of Anthropology* 88 (5): 927–48. https://doi.org/10 .1080/00141844.2021.1936116.

Kim, Seong-nae. 1989. "Lamentations of the Dead: The Historical Imagery of Violence in Cheju Island, South Korea." *Journal of Ritual Studies* 3 (2): 251–85. https://www.jstor.org/stable/44368940.

– 2013. "The Work of Memory: Ritual Laments of the Dead and Korea's Cheju Massacre." In *A Companion to the Anthropology of Religion*, edited by Janice Boddy and Michael Lambek, 223–38. Chichester: Wiley Blackwell.

Kingsley, Patrick, and Benjamin Novak. 2018. "The Website That Shows How a Free Press Can Die." *New York Times*, 24 November 2018. https://www.nytimes .com/2018/11/24/world/europe/hungary-viktor-orban-media.html.

Kirby, Dianne. 2002. "Harry Truman's Religious Legacy: The Holy Alliance, Containment and the Cold War." In *Religion and the Cold War*, edited by Dianne Kerby, 77–102. New York: Palgrave Macmillan.

Kirschenbaum, Howard. 1979. *On Becoming Carl Rogers*. New York: Delacorte Press.

Kirschenbaum, Howard, and Valerie Land Henderson, eds. 1989. *Carl Rogers – Dialogues: Conversations with Martin Buber, Paul Tillich, B.F. Skinner, Gregory Bateson, Michael Polanyi, Rollo May, et al.* Boston: Houghton, Mifflin and Company.

Knauft, Bruce. 2002. *Exchanging the Past: A Rainforest World of Before and After.* Chicago: University of Chicago Press.

Knight, Daniel M. 2021. *Vertiginous Life: An Anthropology of Time and the Unforeseen.* New York: Berghahn Books.

Kong, Lily. 2014. "Transnational Mobilities and the Making of Creative Cities." *Theory, Culture & Society* 31 (7–8): 273–89. https://doi.org/10.1177/0263276414549329.

Kong, Lily, and Justin O'Connor. 2009. *Creative Economies, Creative Cities: Asian–European Perspectives.* London: Springer. https://doi.org/10.1007/978-1-4020-9949-6.

Korola, Katerina. 2021. "Blue Like the Mediterranean: The Work of the Monochrome in the Atlas Group Archive." *Journal of Visual Culture* 20 (2): 455–77. https://doi.org/10.1177/1470412921995222.

Koselleck, Reinhart. 2004. *Futures Past: On the Semantics of Historical Time.* New York: Columbia University Press.

– 2018. *Sediments of Time: On Possible Histories.* Stanford: Stanford University Press.

Kripal, Jeffrey J. 1998. *Kali's Child: The Mystical and the Erotic in the Life and Teachings of Ramakrishna.* 2nd ed. Chicago: University of Chicago Press.

Kripke, Saul A. 1980. *Naming and Necessity.* Cambridge, MA: Harvard University Press.

Kristeva, Julia. 1986. *The Kristeva Reader.* New York: Columbia University Press.

Kruglova, Anna. 2017. "Social Theory and Everyday Marxists: Russian Perspectives on Epistemology and Ethics." *Comparative Studies in Society and History* 59 (4): 759–85. https://doi.org/10.1017/S0010417517000275.

Kuhn, Annette. 1988. *Cinema, Censorship and Sexuality.* London: Routledge.

Kulick, Don. 1992. *Language Shift and Cultural Reproduction: Socialization, Self, and Syncretism in a Papua New Guinea Village.* Cambridge: Cambridge University Press.

Kunreuther, Laura. 2014. *Voicing Subjects: Public Intimacy and Mediation in Kathmandu.* Berkeley: University of California Press.

Kuruvilla, Carol. 2020. "D.C. Church 'Outraged' That Trump Used It as Photo-Op." *HuffPost*, 2 June 2020. https://www.huffingtonpost.co.uk/entry/st-johns-fire-protest-donald-trump_n_5ed53051c5b645ff4afb19b2?ri18n=true.

Kuttab, Jonathan. 2022. "An Update on Israel's Terrorist Designation for Palestinian Civil Society Organizations." Arab Center Washington DC. 3 August. https://arabcenterdc.org/resource/an-update-on-israels-terrorist-designation-for-palestinian-civil-society-organizations/.

Kuttig, Julian, and Sarker Shams Bin Sharif. 2022. "The Everyday Politics of Rumours and Information: Bangladesh's Hybrid Media System and Party-State Corporatism." In *Masks of Authoritarianism: Hegemony, Power and Public Life in Bangladesh*, edited by Arild Engelsen Ruud and Mubashar Hasanm, 19–35. Singapore: Palgrave Macmillan.

Kwon, Heonik. 2010. *The Other Cold War.* New York: Columbia University Press.

– 2020. *After the Korean War: An Intimate History*. Cambridge: Cambridge University Press.

Kwon, Heonik, and Jun Hwan Park. 2022. *Spirit Power: Politics and Religion in Korea's American Century*. New York: Fordham University Press.

Lacy, Mark, and Nayanika Mookherjee. 2020. "'Firing Cannons to Kill Mosquitoes': Controlling 'Virtual Streets' and the 'Image of the State' in Bangladesh." *Contributions to Indian Sociology* 54 (2): 280–305. https://doi.org/10.1177/0069966720917923.

Lại Nguyên Ân. 2013a. "Phan Khôi với phong trào Thơ Mới." *Tìm Lại Di Sản: Tiểu Luận – Phê Bình*. Ho Chi Miny City: Culture and Arts Publishing House.

– 2013b. "Bài thơ "Tình già" và một mối tình thời trẻ." *Tìm Lại Di Sản: Tiểu Luận – Phê Bình*. Ho Chi Minh City: Culture and Arts Publishing House.

Laidlaw, James. 1995. *Riches and Renunciation: Religion, Economy, and Society among the Jains*. Oxford: Oxford University Press.

– 2002. "For an Anthropology of Ethics and Freedom." *Journal of the Royal Anthropological Institute* 8 (2): 311–32. https://doi.org/10.1111/1467-9655.00110.

– 2014. *The Subject of Virtue: An Anthropology of Ethics and Freedom*. New York: Cambridge University Press. https://doi.org/10.1017/CBO9781139236232.

Lambek, Michael, ed. 2010a. *Ordinary Ethics: Anthropology, Language and Action*. New York: Fordham University Press.

– 2010b. "Towards an Ethics of the Act." In *Ordinary Ethics: Anthropology, Language and Action*, edited by Michael Lambek, 39–63. New York: Fordham University Press.

Lambert-Beatty, Carrie. 2009. "Make Believe: Parafiction and Plausibility." *October* 129: 51–84. https://doi.org/10.1162/octo.2009.129.1.51.

Landau, Noa. 2018. "Official Documents Prove: Israel Bans Young Americans Based on Canary Mission Website." *Haaretz.com*, 4 October 2018. https://www.haaretz.com/israel-news/.premium-official-documents-prove-israel-bans-young-americans-based-on-canary-mission-site-1.6530903.

Langton, Rae. 1993. "Speech Acts and Unspeakable Acts." *Philosophy and Public Affairs* 22 (4): 293–330. https://www.jstor.org/stable/2265469.

Larkin, Brian. 2008. *Signal and Noise: Media, Infrastructure, and Urban Culture in Nigeria*. Durham, NC: Duke University Press,

– 2014. "Techniques of Inattention: The Mediality of Loudspeakers in Nigeria." *Anthropological Quarterly* 87 (4): 989–1016. https://doi.org/10.1353/anq.2014.0067.

Larson, Gerald James. 1997. "Polymorphic Sexuality, Homoeroticism, and the Study of Religion." *Journal of the American Academy of Religion* 65 (3): 655–65. https://doi.org/10.1093/jaarel/65.3.655.

Latour, Bruno. 2005. *Reassembling the Social: An Introduction to Actor-Network-Theory*. Oxford: Oxford University Press.

Laursen, John. 1996. "The Subversive Kant: The Vocabulary of 'Public' and 'Publicity.'" In *What Is Enlightenment? Eighteenth-Century Answers and Twentieth-Century*

Questions, edited by James Schmidt, 253–69. Berkeley: University of California Press.

Lawrence, Charles R., III. 1993. "If He Hollers Let Him Go: Regulating Racist Speech on Campus." In *Words That Wound: Critical Race Theory, Assaultive Speech, and the First Amendment*, by Mari J. Matsuda, Charles R. Lawrence III, Richard Delgado, and Kimberlé Williams Crenshaw, 53–88. Boulder, CO: Westview Press.

Lawton, Philip, Edna Murphy, and Declan Redmond. 2010. "Examining the Role of 'Creative Class' Ideas in Urban and Economic Policy Formation: The Case of Dublin, Ireland." *International Journal of Knowledge-Based Development* 1 (4): 267–86. https://doi.org/10.1504/IJKBD.2010.038039.

Leibovich, Mark. 2020. "Romney, Defying the Party He Once Personified, Votes to Convict Trump." *New York Times*, 5 February 2020. https://www.nytimes.com/2020/02/05/us/politics/romney-trump-impeachment.html.

Lempert, Michael. 2012. *Discipline and Debate: The Language of Violence in a Tibetan Buddhist Monastery*. Berkeley: University of California Press.

– 2013. "No Ordinary Ethics." *Anthropological Theory* 13 (4): 370–93. https://doi.org/10.1177/1463499613505571.

– 2024. *From Small Talk to Microaggression: A History of Scale*. Chicago: University of Chicago Press.

Lester, Rebecca J. 2005. *Jesus in Our Wombs: Embodying Modernity in a Mexican Convent*. Berkeley: University of California Press.

Lewin, Kurt. 1939. "Experiments in Social Space." *Harvard Educational Review* 9 (1): 21–32.

– 1945. "The Research Center for Group Dynamics at Massachusetts Institute of Technology." *Sociometry* 8 (2): 126–36. https://doi.org/10.2307/2785233.

Lewin, Kurt, Ronald Lippitt, and Ralph K. White. 1939. "Patterns of Aggressive Behavior in Experimentally Created 'Social Climates.'" *The Journal of Social Psychology* 10: 271–99. https://doi.org/10.1080/00224545.1939.9713366.

Li, Darryl. 2019. *The Universal Enemy: Jihad, Empire, and the Challenge of Solidarity*. Stanford: Stanford University Press.

– 2024. "Anti-Palestinian at the Core: The Origins and Growing Dangers of U.S. Antiterrorism Law." Center for Constitutional Rights and Palestine Legal. https://ccrjustice.org/sites/default/files/attach/2024/02/Anti-Palestinian%20at%20the%20Core_White%20Paper_0.pdf.

Lieblich, Eliav, and Adam Shinar. 2021. "Counterterrorism Off the Rails: Israel's Declaration of Palestinian Human Rights Groups as 'Terrorist' Organizations." *Just Security*, 24 October 2021. https://www.justsecurity.org/78732/counterterrorism-off-the-rails-israels-declaration-of-palestinian-human-rights-groups-as-terrorist-organizations/.

Lis, Jonathan. 2011. "Israel Passes Law Banning Calls for Boycott." *Haaretz*, 11 July 2011. http://www.haaretz.com/news/diplomacy-defense/israel-passes-law-banning-calls-for-boycott-1.372711.

– 2022. "Germany, Israel to Explore Funding Options for Projects by Outlawed Palestinian NGOs." *Haaretz*, 11 February 2022. https://www.haaretz.com/israel -news/.premium.HIGHLIGHT-germany-working-with-israel-to-fund-projects-run -by-terrorist-palestinian-ngos-1.10605551.

Loss, Christopher P. 2011. "'Women's Studies Is in a Lot of Ways – Consciousness Raising': The Educational Origins of Identity Politics." *History of Psychology* 4 (3): 287–310. https://doi.org/10.1037/a0024799. Medline: 21936235.

Losurdo, Domenico. 1994. *La seconda Repubblica: Liberismo, federalismo, postfascismo*. Turin: Bollati Boringhieri.

– 2011. *Liberalism: A Counter-History*. Translated by Gregory Elliott. London: Verso.

Louden, Robert B. 1986. "Kant's Virtue Ethics." *Philosophy* 61 (238): 473–89. https:// doi.org/10.1017/S0031819100061246.

Loviglio, Jason. 2005. *Radio's Intimate Public: Network Broadcasting and Mass-mediated Democracy*. Minneapolis: University of Minnesota Press.

Lowe, Lisa. 2015. *The Intimacies of Four Continents*. Durham, NC: Duke University Press.

Lunde, Ingunn. 2009. "Peformative Metalanguage: Negotiating Norms through Verbal Action." In *From Poets to Padonki: Linguistic Authority and Norm Negotiation in Modern Russian Culture*, edited by Ingunn Lunde and Martin Paulson, 110–28. Bergen: University of Bergen.

Luong, Hy Van. 1990. *Discursive Practices and Linguistic Meanings: The Vietnamese System of Person Reference*. Amsterdam: J. Benjamins Publishing.

Maasson, Jeffrey. 1980. *The Oceanic Feeling: Origins of Religious Sentiment in Ancient India*. Dordrecht: D. Reidel.

MacIntyre, Alasdair. (1981) 2006. *After Virtue: A Study in Moral Theory*. London: Duckworth.

MacKinnon, Catherine A. 1985. "Pornography, Civil Rights, and Speech." *Harvard Civil Rights-Civil Liberties Law Review* 20 (1): 456–9.

– 1993. *Only Words*. Cambridge, MA: Harvard University Press.

MacKinnon, Catherine A., and Andrea Dworkin. 1997. *In Harm's Way: The Pornography Civil Rights Hearings*. Cambridge, MA: Harvard University Press.

Maestri, Gabriele. 2017. "Quando il problema non è il (solo) fascio." I simboli della Discordia, 13 June 2017. http://www.isimbolidelladiscordia.it/2017/06/quando-il -problema-non-e-il-solo-fascio.html.

Magyar, Bálint, ed. 2013. *Magyar Polip: A Posztkommunista Maffiaállam*. Budapest: Noran Libro.

Mahler, Thomas. 2017. "Mediapart contre 'Charlie,' une querelle 'si française'?" *Le Point*, 22 November 2017. https://www.lepoint.fr/debats/mediapart-contre-charlie -une-querelle-si-francaise-22-11-2017-2174284_2.php.

Mahmood, Saba. 2005. *Politics of Piety: The Islamic Revival and the Feminist Subject*. Princeton, NJ: Princeton University Press.

– 2013. "Religious Reason and Secular Affect: An Incommensurable Divide." In *Is Critique Secular? Blasphemy, Injury, and Free Speech*, by Talal Asad, Wendy Brown, Judith Butler, and Saba Mahmood, 64–100. New York: Fordham University Press. https://doi.org/10.2307/j.ctt1c5cjtk.5.

Maji, Debasish. 1997. Letter to the Editor. *The Statesman*, 11 February 1997.

Malka, Richard. 2020. "Procès 'Charlie': Ces complices intellectuels qui ont du sang sur les mains." *Le Point*, 12 August 2020. https://www.lepoint.fr/societe/me-richard -malka-la-situation-est-bien-pire-qu-il-y-a-cinq-ans-12-08-2020-2387585_23.php.

Maltz, Daniel N. 1985. "Joyful Noise and Reverent Silence: The Significance of Noise in Pentecostal Worship." In *Perspectives on Silence*, edited by Deborah Tannen and Muriel Saville-Troike, 113–37. Norwood: Ablex Publishing Corporation.

Mangan, Dan. 2021. "Trump Bible Photo Op Not Reason Cops Violently Cleared George Floyd Protest Outside White House, Feds Claim." *CNBC*, 9 June 2021. https://www.cnbc.com/2021/06/09/protestors-cleared-outside-white-house-for -fence-not-trump-photo-op.html.

Marr, David. 1971. *Vietnamese Anticolonialism, 1885–1925*. Berkeley: University of California Press.

– 1981. *Vietnamese Tradition on Trial, 1920–1945*. Berkeley: University of California Press.

Marrow, Alfred J. 1969. *The Practical Theorist: The Life and Work of Kurt Lewin*. New York: Basic Books.

Marsilli-Vargas, Xochitl. 2014. "Listening Genres: The Emergence of Relevance Structures through the Reception of Sound." *Journal of Pragmatics* 69: 42–51. https://doi.org/10.1016/j.pragma.2014.03.006.

– 2022. *Genres of Listening: An Ethnography of Psychoanalysis in Buenos Aires*. Durham, NC: Duke University Press.

Massachusetts Peace Action. 2019. "Anti-Boycott Bill Surfaces Again; Let's Defeat It Again." MAPA. 16 October. https://testsite2.masspeaceaction.org/anti-boycott -bill-surfaces-again-lets-defeat-it-again/.

Mathur, Nayanika. 2015. *Paper Tiger: Law, Bureaucracy and the Developmental State in Himalayan India*. Cambridge: Cambridge University Press.

Matthiesen, Toby. 2013. *Sectarian Gulf: Bahrain, Saudi Arabia, and the Arab Spring That Wasn't*. Stanford: Stanford Briefs.

Mazumdar, Swaraj. 1997. Letter to the Editor. *The Statesman*, 11 February 1997.

Mazzarella, William. 2004. "Culture, Globalization, Mediation." *Annual Review of Anthropology* 33: 345–67. https://doi.org/10.1146/annurev.anthro.33.070203.143809.

– 2013. *Censorium: Cinema and the Open Edge of Mass Publicity*. Durham, NC: Duke University Press.

– 2019. "The Anthropology of Populism: Beyond the Liberal Settlement." *Annual Review of Anthropology* 48: 45–60. https://doi.org/10.1146/annurev-anthro -102218-011412.

McDowell, Nancy. 1990. "Person, Reciprocity, and Change: Explorations of Burridge in Bun." In *Sepik Heritage: Tradition and Change in Papua New Guinea*, edited by

N. Lutkehaus, C. Kaufmann, W. Mitchell, D. Newton, L. Osmundsen, and M. Schuster, 343–50. Durham, NC: Carolina Academic Press.

McGranahan, Carol, and John F. Collins, eds. 2018. *Ethnographies of U.S. Empire*. Durham, NC: Duke University Press.

McHale, Shawn. 2004. *Print and Power: Confucianism, Communism and Buddhism in the Making of Modern Vietnam*. Honolulu: University of Hawai'i Press.

McIntosh, Janet, and Norma Mendoza-Denton, eds. 2020. *Language in the Trump Era: Scandals and Emergencies*. New York: Cambridge University Press. https://doi.org/10.1017/9781108887410.

McKinnon, Susan, and Fenella Cannell, eds. 2013. Introduction to *Vital Relations: Modernity and the Ppersistent Life of Kinship*, 14–49. Santa Fe: School for Advanced Research Press.

McManus, Anne-Marie. 2021. "'On the Ruins of What's to Come, I Stand': Time and Devastation in Syrian Cultural Production since 2011." *Critical Inquiry* 48 (1): 45–67. https://doi.org/10.1086/715985.

McWhorter, John. 2021. "How the N-Word Became Unsayable." *New York Times*, 30 April 2021. https://www.nytimes.com/2021/04/30/opinion/john-mcwhorter-n-word-unsayable.html.

Mehta, Monika. 2021. "Censorship." *BioScope: South Asian Screen Studies* 12 (1–2): 49–52. https://doi.org/10.1177/09749276211026105.

Mendoza-Denton, Norma. 2020. "The Show Must Go On." In *Language in the Trump Era*, edited by Janet McIntosh and Norma Mendoza-Denton. New York: Cambridge University Press.

Milani, Maya, and Enrico De Angelis. 2020. "From Exile in Beirut, Cinematic 'Beginnings': A Q&A with Syrian Film Company Bidayyat's Founder Mohammad Ali Atassi." SyriaUntold, 17 July 2020. https://syriauntold.com/2020/07/17/from-exile-in-beirut-cinematic-beginnings.

Mill, John Stuart. (1859) 1989. "On Liberty." In *On Liberty, with the Subjection of Women and Chapters on Ssocialism*, edited by Stefan Collini, 1–115. Cambridge: Cambridge University Press.

Miller, Peter, and Nikolas Rose. 2008. *Governing the Present: Administering Economic, Social and Personal Life*. Cambridge: Polity Press.

Miskawayh, Ahmad Ibn Muhammad. 1968. *The Refinement of Character: A Translation from the Arabic of Ahmad Ibn Muhammad Miskawayh's* Tahdhīb al-akhlāq. Translated by Constantine Zurayk. Beirut: American University of Beirut.

Mitchell, David. 1999. "Tragedy in Sumba: Why Neighbours Hacked Each Other to Death in a Remote Part of Indonesia." *Inside Indonesia* 58: 1–6.

Mohaiemen, Naeem. 2014. *Prisoners of Shothik Itihas*. Basel: Kunsthalle Basel.

– 2016. "Simulation at Wars' End: A 'Documentary' in the Field of Evidence Quest." Bioscope: *South Asian Screen Studies* 7 (1): 31–57. https://doi.org/10.1177/0974927616635933.

Moll, Yasmin. 2017. "Subtitling Islam: Translation, Mediation, Critique." *Public Culture* 29 (2): 333–61. https://doi.org/10.1215/08992363-3749093.

– 2023. "Can There Be a Godly Ethnography? Islamic Anthropology, Decolonization and the Ethnographic Stance." *American Anthropoligst* 125 (4). https://doi.org /10.1111/aman.1391.

Momentum Worldwide. n.d. "Form As Being – Omar Chowdhury in Dialogue with Mark Gisbourne." Accessed 6 June 2024. https://vimeo.com/119846178.

Mookherjee, Nayanika. 2015. *The Spectral Wound: Sexual Violence, Public Memories, and the Bangladesh War of 1971*. Durham, NC: Duke University Press.

Morningstar, Natalie. 2021. "Bad *parrhesia*: The Limits of Cynicism in the Public Sphere." *Social Anthropology* 29 (2): 437–52. https://doi.org/10.1111 /1469-8676.13036.

– 2024. "Critique Refigured: Art, Activism, and Politics in Post-Recession Dublin." *Journal of the Royal Anthropological Institute*. https://doi.org /10.1111/1467-9655.14097.

Morrell, Michael E. 2018. "Listening and Deliberation." In *The Oxford Handbook of Deliberative Democracy*, edited by André Bächtiger, John S. Dryzek, Jane J. Mansbridge, and Mark Warren, 237–50. Oxford: Oxford University Press.

Mottahedeh, Roy. 1985. *The Mantle of the Prophet: Religion and Politics in Iran*. New York: Simon and Schuster.

Moya, Ismaël. 2015. "Unavowed Value: Economy, Comparison, and Hierarchy in Dakar." *HAU: Journal of Ethnographic Theory* 5 (1): 151–72. https://doi.org /10.14318/hau5.1.008.

Mukhopodhyay, Jyoti. 2001. *Śrīrāmakṛṣṇēr samakāmitā o yaunabhāba ēkaṭi biśba-bitarka: Hritbik, Boi Mela* (Sri Ramakrishna's homosexuality and sexuality: A global debate). Ritvik: Book Fair.

Munn, Nancy D. 1986. *The Fame of Gawa: A Symbolic Study of Value Transformation in a Massim (Papua New Guinea) Society*. Cambridge: Cambridge University Press.

Murphy, Keith, and Eitan Wilf. 2021. Introduction to *Designs and Anthropologies: Frictions and Affinities*, 1–20. Albuquerque: University of New Mexico Press.

Murray, D.W. 1993. "What Is the Western Concept of the Self? On Forgetting David Hume." *Ethos* 21 (1): 3–23. https://doi.org/10.1525/eth.1993.21.1.02a00010.

Murshid, Tazeen M. 1996. *The Sacred and the Secular: Bengal Muslim Discourses, 1871-1977*. Dhaka: Oxford University Press.

Myers, Fred. 1986. *Pintupi Country, Pintupi Self: Sentiment, Place, and Politics among Western Desert Aborigines*. Washington, DC: Smithsonian Institution Press.

Nachescu, Voichita. 2006. "Becoming the Feminist Subject: Consciousness-Raising Groups in Second Wave Feminism." PhD diss., State University of New York at Buffalo.

Nader, Laura. 1974. "Up the Anthropologist – Perspectives Gained from Studying Up." In *Reinventing Anthropology*, edited by Dell Hymes, 284–311. New York: Vintage Books.

Naim, C.M. 1999. "A Dissent on 'Fire.'" *Economic and Political Weekly* 34 (16/17): 955–7. https://www.jstor.org/stable/4407870.

Nakassis, Constantine V. 2013. "Citation and Citationality." *Signs and Society* 1 (1): 51–77. https://doi.org/10.1086/670165.

– 2018. "Indexicality's Ambivalent Ground." *Signs and Society* 6 (1): 281–304. https://doi.org/10.1086/694753.

Nassy Brown, Jacqueline. 2005. *Dropping Anchor, Setting Sail: Geographies of Race in Black Liverpool*. Princeton, NJ: Princeton University Press.

National Training Laboratory (NLT). 1947. *Preliminary Report of the first National Training Laboratory on Group Development, Held at Gould Academy, Bethel, Maine*. Bethel, MA: NTL.

New York Times. 1914. "Tagore's Ideal Woman." 22 March 1914, BR129.

Newman, Andrew J. 2001. "Fayd al-Kashani and the Rejection of the Clergy/State Alliance: Friday Prayer as Politics in the Safavid Period." In *The Most Learned of the Shi'a: The Institution of the Marja' Taqlid*, edited by Linda S. Walbridge, 34–52. Oxford: Oxford University Press.

Niezen, Ronald. 2016. "Templates and Exclusions: Victim Centrism in Canada's Truth and Reconciliation Commission on Indian Residential Schools." *Journal of the Royal Anthropological Institute* 22: 920–38. https://doi.org/10.1111/1467-9655.12497.

Noyce, David, and Peggy Fletcher Stack. 2022. "'Mormon Land': A 'Divinely Inspired' Constitution – Where Such Talk Began and Why It Matters Now." *Salt Lake Tribune*, 29 June 2022. https://www.sltrib.com/religion/2022/06/29/mormon-land-divinely-inspired.

Nunès, Eric. 2015. "Dans les collèges et lycées, le soutien à 'Charlie Hebdo' loin de faire l'unanimité." *Le Monde*, 14 January 2015. https://www.lemonde.fr/societe/article/2015/01/14/a-l-ecole-il-faut-faire-comprendre-que-la-laicite-est-notre-fondement_4555679_3224.html.

Nye, Robert D. 1992. *The Legacy of B.F. Skinner*. New York: Brooks/Cole.

O'Connor, Lynn. 1969. "Defining Reality." *Tooth & Nail* 1 (1): 7–11. https://cache.kzoo.edu/items/e80b0579-107b-448b-be29-bc7477ce6bd5.

– 1970. "Our Politics Begin with Our Feelings" (also known as the "Redstockings West Manifesto"). Statement presented at San Francisco Meeting of Women's Liberation, 21 March. https://cache.kzoo.edu/items/0ef57567-ccbf-4026-b17d-4b41d25e30bb.

Olusoga, David. 2014. *The World's War: Forgotten Soldiers of Empire*. London: Head of Zeus.

Onishi, Norimitsu. 2010. "Arrests for a Revealing Dance Pit Flesh against Faith." *New York Times*, 20 January 2010. https://www.nytimes.com/2010/01/20/world/asia/20bandung.html.

Oppenshaw, Jeanne. 1995. "Review: Kali's Child: The Mystical and the Erotic in the Life and Teachings of Ramakrishna." *Times Higher Education Supplement*. 15 December.

Orsi, Robert. 2004. *Between Heaven and Earth: The Religious Worlds People Make and the Scholars Who Study Them*. Princeton, NJ: Princeton University Press.

Orwell, George. 1944. "What Is Fascism?" *Tribune* (London), 24 March 1944.

Oushakine, Serguei. 2000. "In the State of Post-Soviet Aphasia: Symbolic Development in Contemporary Russia." *Europe-Asia Studies* 52 (6): 991–1016. https://doi.org/10.1080/09668130050143806.

Özyürek, Esra. 2006. *Nostalgia for the Modern: State Secularism and Everyday Politics in Turkey*. Durham, NC: Duke University Press.

– 2016. "Export-Import Theory and the Racialization of Anti-Semitism: Turkish- and Arab-Only Prevention Programs in Germany." *Comparative Studies in Society and History* 58 (1): 40–65. https://doi.org/10.1017/S0010417515000560.

Pal, P.S. 1997. Letter to the Editor. *The Statesman*, 11 February 1997.

Parikh, Anar. 2018. "Race Is Still a Problem in Anthropology." *Anthrodendum*, 9 April 2018. https://anthrodendum.org/2018/04/09/race-is-still-a-problem-in-anthropology.

Parlato, Giuseppe. 2006. *Fascisti senza Mussolini: Le origini del neofascismo in Italia, 1943–1948*. Milan: Il Mulino.

– 2017. "Delegitimation and anticommunism in Italian neofascism." *Journal of Modern Italian Studies* 22 (1): 43–56. https://doi.org/10.1080/1354571X.2017.1267981.

Parsons, William B. 1997. "Psychoanalysis and Mysticism: The Case of Ramakrishna." *Religious Studies Review* 23 (4): 355–61.

Pasamonik, Didier. 2007. "Procès des caricatures: Charlie Hebdo gagne son procès." *ActuaBD*, 22 March 2007. https://www.actuabd.com/Proces-des-caricatures-Charlie -Hebdo-gagne-son-proces.

Passavant, Paul A. 2002. *No Escape: Freedom of Speech and the Paradox of Rights*. New York: New York University Press.

Passmore, Kevin. 2002. *Fascism: A Very Short Introduction*. Oxford: Oxford University Press.

– 2017. "Is This Fascism?" *Slate*, 20 January 2017. https://slate.com/human-interest /2017/01/define-fascism-why-nailing-down-a-comprehensive-theory-of-fascism -has-been-so-historically-difficult.html.

Patton, Laurie L. 2019. *Who Owns Religion? Scholars and Their Publics in the Late Twentieth Century*. Chicago: University of Chicago Press.

Paxton, Robert O. 2004. *The Anatomy of Fascism*. London: Penguin.

Paz, Alejandro I. 2018. *Latinos in Israel: Language and Unexpected Citizenship*. Bloomington: Indiana University Press.

– 2021. "North Atlantic Public Opinion and the Israeli Security State: The Case of Valentina Azarova at the University of Toronto." Paper presented at the American Anthropological Association Annual Meeting, Baltimore, MD.

Peed, Matthew J. 2005. "Blacklisting as Foreign Policy: The Politics and Law of Listing Terror States." *Duke Law Journal* 54 (1321–1354): 35.

Peirce, Charles Sanders. (1906) 1933. *Collected Papers of Charles Sanders Peirce*. Vol. 4, *The Simplest Mathematics*. Edited by Charles Hartshorne and Paul Weiss. Cambridge, MA: Harvard University Press.

– 1955. *Philosophical Writings of Peirce*. Edited by Justus Buchler. New York: Dover.
– 1966. *Charles S. Peirce: Selected Writings (Values in a Universe of Chance)*. Edited by Philip P. Wiener. New York: Dover.
– 1976. *The New Elements of Mathematics*. Vol. 4. Edited by Carolyn Eisele. The Hague: De Gruyter Mouton.
– 1998. *The Essential Peirce, Selected Philosophical Writings*. Vol. 2, *(1893–1913)*. Bloomington: Indiana University Press.
Perry, Elizabeth J., and Li Xun. 1997. *Proletarian Power: Shanghai in the Cultural Revolution*. Boulder, CO: Westview Press.
Perry, Samuel L. 2019. "What Arouses Evangelicals? Cultural Schemas, Interpretive Prisms, and Evangelicals' Divergent Collective Responses to Pornography and Masturbation." *Journal of the American Academy of Religion* 87 (3): 693–724. https://doi.org/10.1093/jaarel/lfz024.
Perugini, Nicola, and Neve Gordon. 2015. *The Human Right to Dominate*. New York City: Oxford University Press.
Peters, John Durham. 2005. *Courting the Abyss: Free Speech and the Liberal Tradition*. Chicago: University of Chicago Press.
Peterson, Nicolas. 1993. "Demand Sharing: Reciprocity and the Pressure for Generosity among Foragers." *American Anthropologist* 95 (4): 860–74. https://doi .org/10.1525/aa.1993.95.4.02a00050.
Phan Khôi. 1928. "Tư tưởng của Tây phương và Đông phương" (Western and Eastern styles of thinking). *Đông Pháp thời báo*, 774 (27 September 1928); 776 (2 October 1928).
– 1929a. Chữ trinh: Cái tiết với cái nết (Chastity: Purity and virtue). *Phụ nữ tân văn*, 21 (19 September 1929).
– 1929b. "Cái ảnh hưởng của khổng giáo ở nước ta" (The influence of Confucianism on our country). *Thần chung*, 213 (1 Ocotber 1929) to 249 (18 November 1929).
– 1930a. "Vấn đề cải cách" (The problem of reform). *Trung lập*, 6218 (9 August 1930); 6220 (12 August 1930); 6221 (13 August 1930); 6223 (18 August 1930).
– 1930b. "Nói thế nào là khiếm nhã" (What is rude speech?). *Phổ thông*, 72 (26 September 1930).
– 1930c. "Phép làm văn, Bài thứ II: Cách đặt đợi danh từ" (Rules of writing, article two: Ways of using pronouns). *Phụ Nữ Tân Văn*, 73 (9 October 1930), 13–14.
– 1931a. Gia đình ở xứ ta, nay cũng đã thành ra vấn đề rồi (The family in our country has now also become a problem). *Phụ nữ tân văn*, 83 (21 May 1931).
– 1931b. "Một cái tục, nếu không bỏ đi thì bất tiện: Tục kiêng tên" (A custom, which if not abandoned, becomes inconvenient: The custom of name taboo). *Phụ Nữ Tân Văn*, 90 (9 July 1931), 5–8.
– 1932a. "Ân và Tình" (Grace and affection). *Phụ nữ tân văn*, 116 (14 January 1932).
– 1932b. "Một lối 'thơ mới' trình chánh giữa làng thơ" (Style of "new poetry" presented to the poetic community). *Phụ nữ tân văn* 122 (3 October 1932), 15–16.
– 1933. "Luận về khí tiết" (Essay on moral integrity). In *Những áng văn hay: Thử phê bình nhơn vật và văn thơ cổ kim*, 21–7. Hanoi: Nam Ký thư quán.

- 1936. "Tự do gì lại có tự do xin?" (What kind of freedom is a freedom that one asks for?). *Sông Hương* 16 (14 November 1936).
- 1937. "Nhà nho với dân chủ" (Confucianism and democracy). *Đông Dương tạp chí*, 33 (25 December 1937).
- 1939. "Lịch sử tóc ngắn" (A history of short hair). *Ngày nay*, 149 (15 February 1939).
- 1956. "Phê bình lãnh đạo văn nghệ" (Critique of the leadership of the arts). *Giai phẩm*, Fall 1956.
- 2018. *Ảnh Hưởng Khổng Giáo Ở Nước Ta* (The influence of Confucianism in our country). Edited by Lại Nguyên Ân. Ho Chi Minh City: Ho Chi Minh City Literature and Arts Publishing House.

Phan Thị Mỹ Khanh. 2017. *Nhớ Cha Tôi, Phan Khôi* (Memories of my father, Phan Khôi). Ho Chi Minh City: Da Nang Publishing House.

Pinto, S. 2016. "'The Tools of Your Chants and Spells': Stories of Madwomen and Indian Practical Healing." *Medical Anthropology* 35 (3): 263–77. https://doi.org/10.1080/01459740.2015.1081902. Medline: 26263046.

Pipyrou, Stavroula, and Antonio Sorge. 2021. "Emergent Axioms of Violence: Toward and Anthropology of Post-Liberal Modernity." *Anthropological Forum* 31 (3): 225–40. https://doi.org/10.1080/00664677.2021.1966611.

Pomerantsev, Peter. 2016. *Nothing Is True and Everything Is Possible: The Surreal Heart of the New Russia*. London: Faber and Faber Limited.

Popli, Nik, and Julia Zorthian. 2023. "What Happened to the Jan. 6 Rioters Arrested Since the Capitol Attack." *Time*, last updated 26 May 2023. https://time.com/6133336/jan-6-capitol-riot-arrests-sentences.

Porter, Ross. 2017. "Freedom, Power and the Crisis of Politics in Revolutionary Yemen." *Middle East Critique* 26 (3): 265–81. https://doi.org/10.1080/19436149.2017.1328875.

Post, Robert C. 1986. "The Social Foundations of Defamation Law: Reputation and the Constitution." *California Law Review* 74 (3): 691–742. https://doi.org/10.2307/3480391.

–, ed. 1998. *Censorship and Silencing: Practices of Cultural Regulation*. Los Angeles: Getty Research Institute.

Poulantzas, Nicos. 1974. *Fascism and Dictatorship: The Third International and the Problem of Fascism*. London: Verso.

Prajt. 2017. "The Damnation of Ham" [in Russian]. *Live Journal*, 4 December 2017. https://prajt.livejournal.com/86861.html.

Pramoedya Ananta Toer. 1985. *Sang Pemula dan Karya-Karya Non-Fiski (Jurnalistik), Fiksi (Cerpen/Novel) R.M. Tirto Adhi Soerjo*. Jakarta: Hastra.

Preston, Andrew. 2012. *Swords of the Spirit, Shield of Faith: Religion in American War and Diplomacy*. New York: Anchor Books.

Proust, Marcel. 1982. *A Search for Lost Time: Swann's Way*. Translated by James Grieve. Canberra: Australian National University.

Radice, William. 1998. "Review: Kali's Child: The Mystical and the Erotic in the Life and Teachings of Ramakrishna." *Bulletin of the School of Oriental and African Studies* 61 (1): 160.

Rahman, Sadia. 2016. Introduction to Omar Chowdhury and Shahidul Zaman, *Age of Saturn*. Dhaka: Bengal Foundation.

Ramberg, Lucinda. 2014. *Given to the Goddess: South Indian Devadasis and the Sexuality of Religion*. Durham, NC: Duke University Press.

Ranciére, Jacques. 2009. *The Emancipated Spectator*. New York: Verso.

Rastegar, Mitra. 2021. *Tolerance and Risk: How U.S. Liberalism Racializes Muslims*. Minneapolis: University of Minnesota Press.

Rathnam, Lindsay Mahon. 2023. "The Marketplace of Ideas and the Agora: Herodutus on the Power of Isegoria." *American Political Science Review* 117 (1): 140–52. https://doi.org/10.1017/S0003055422000661.

Ray, Rajat. 1997. "Review: Kali's Child: The Mystical and the Erotic in the Life and Teachings of Ramakrishna." *The Indian Economic and Social History Review* 34 (1): 101. https://doi.org/10.1177/001946469703400108.

Razzaque, Russell. 2015. "Mindfulness and Open Dialogue: A Common Foundation and a Common Practice." *Context*, 138: 145–6.

– 2018. "Open Dialogue and the Impact of Therapist Mindfulness on the Health of Clients." *OBM Integrative and Complementary Medicine* 3 (1). https://doi.org/10.21926/obm.icm.1801001.

Read, Kenneth E. 1959. "Leadership and Consensus in a New Guinea Society." *American Anthropologist* 61 (3): 425–36. https://doi.org/10.1525/aa.1959.61.3.02a00060.

Redactsiya. 2021. "Pravda li, chto khamit' u nas v krove?" YouTube video, 58:56. 2 December 2021. https://youtu.be/R0QPYht-zuw.

Redden, Elizabeth. 2017. "Israel Bars Boycotters." *Inside Higher Ed,* 10 March 2017. https://www.insidehighered.com/news/2017/03/10/scholars-speak-out-against-new-law-barring-supporters-boycotts-entering-israel.

Reddy, Gayatri. 2005. *With Respect to Sex: Negotiating Hijra identity in South India*. Chicago: University of Chicago Press.

Reed, Adam. 2011. *Literature and Agency in English Fiction Reading: A Study of Henry Williamson Society*. Manchester: Manchester University Press, and Toronto: University of Toronto Press.

– 2019. "Minor Character Reading: Tracing an English Literary Society through its Culture of Investigation." *PMLA* 134 (1): 66–80. https://doi.org/10.1632/pmla.2019.134.1.66

– 2022. "Sympathy for Oswald Mosley: Politics of Reading and Historical Resemblance in the Moral Imagination of an English Literary Society." *Comparative Studies in Society and History* 64 (1): 63–90. https://doi.org/10.1017/S0010417521000396.

– 2023. "Explaining the Politics of the Author." In *Beyond Description: Anthropologies of Explanation*, edited by Matei Candea and Paolo Heywood, 221–40. Ithaca, NY: Cornell University Press.

Reich, Wilhelm. 1933. *The Mass Psychology of Fascism*. London: Souvenir Press.

Riaz, Ali. 2019. *Voting in a Hybrid Regime: Explaining the 2018 Bangladeshi Election*. Singapore: Palgrave Pivot.

Richelle, Marc. 1993. *B.F. Skinner: A Reappraisal*. Hillsdale, NJ: Erlbaum.

Riess, Jana. 2021. "At the Capitol, We Saw the Best and the Worst of U.S. Mormonism." *Salt Lake Tribune*, 8 January 2021. https://www.sltrib.com /religion/2021/01/09/jana-riess-capitol-we-saw/.

Rizvi, Sayyid Muhammad. 1998. "The Historical Meeting with Ayatullah Al-Uzma Sayyid 'Ali As-Sistani." Al Ma'Arfi. 3 September. https://al-m.ca/sachedina-meeting -with-ay-sistani.

Robbins, Ira P. 2008. "*Digitus Impudicus*: The Middle Finger and the Law." *UC Davis Law Review* 41: 1403–86.

Robbins, Joel. 2004. *Becoming Sinners: Christianity and Moral Torment in a Papua New Guinea Society*. Berkeley: University of California Press.

– 2013. "Monism, Pluralism, and the Structure of Value Relations: A Dumontian Contribution to the Contemporary Study of Value." *HAU: Journal of Ethnographic Theory* 3 (1): 99–115. https://doi.org/10.14318/hau3.1.008.

Robbins, Joel, and Holly Wardlow, eds. 2005 *The Making of Global and Local Modernities in Melanesia: Humiliation, Transformation, and the Nature of Cultural Change*. Burlington, VT: Ashgate.

Roberts, John Michael. 2004. "John Stuart Mill, Free Speech and the Public Sphere: A Bakhtinian Critique." *Sociological Review* 52 (1): 67–87. https://doi .org/10.1111/j.1467-954X.2004.00474.x.

Rogers, Carl. 1946. "Significant Aspects of Client-Centered Therapy." *American Psychologist* 1 (10): 415–22. https://doi.org/10.1037/h0060866.

– 1947. "Some Observations on the Organization of Personality." *American Psychologist* 2 (9): 358–68. https://doi.org/10.1037/h0060883.

– 1951. *Client-Centered Therapy: Its Current Practice, Implications, and Theory*. London: Constable.

– 1961. *On Becoming a Person: A Therapist's View of Psychotherapy*. London: Constable.

– 1980. *A Way of Being*. New York: Houghton Mifflin Company.

– 1986. "Reflection of Feelings." *Person-Centered Review* 1 (4): 375–7.

Rogers, Carl, and B.F. Skinner. 1976. *A Dialogue on Education and the Control of Human Behavior: A 6-Cassette Audio Album*. Edited by Gerald A. Gladstein and Otto Pollak. New York: Jeffrey Norton Publishers.

Rogers, Kristen. 2020. "How to Talk with Your Black Friends about Race." CNN.com, 6 July 2020. https://www.cnn.com/2020/07/06/health/how-to-talk-about-race-with -black-friends-wellness/index.html.

Roland, Alan. 1998. "Ramakrishna: Mystical, Erotic, or Both?" *Journal of Religion and Health* 37 (1): 31–6. https://doi.org/10.1023/A:1022956932676.

Romboy, Dennis. 2021. "Why Mitt Romney Loses Points with Utah Republicans, Scores Big with Democrats." *Deseret News*, 24 January 2021. https://www.deseret

.com/utah/2021/1/24/22242586/mitt-romney-poll-disapproval-mike-lee-republican
-donald-trump-election-fraud-joe-biden-democrat.

Romney, Mitt. 2020. "Romney Delivers Remarks on Impeachment Vote." Mitt
Romney US Senator for Utah (website). 5 February 2020. https://www.romney
.senate.gov/romney-delivers-remarks-impeachment-vote/.

Rosaldo, Michelle Zimbalist. 1980. *Knowledge and Passion: Ilongot Notions of Self
and Social Life*. Cambridge: Cambridge University Press.

– 1982. "The Things We Do with Words: Ilongot Speech Acts and Speech Act
Theory in Philosophy." *Language in Society* 11: 203–37. https://doi.org/10.1017
/S0047404500009209.

Rosenberg, Ian. 2021. *The Fight for Free Speech: Ten Cases That Define Our First
Amendment Freedoms*. New York: New York University Press.

Rosenthal, Naomi Bruan. 1984. "Consciousness Raising: From Revolution to
Re-Evaluation." *Psychology of Women Quarterly* 8 (4): 309–26. https://doi.org
/10.1111/j.1471-6402.1984.tb00639.x.

Roudakova, Natalia. 2017. *Losing Pravda: Ethics and the Press in Post-Truth Russia*.
Cambridge: Cambridge University Press.

Runia, Eelco. 2014. *Moved by the Past: Discontinuity and Historical Mutation*. New
York: Columbia University Press.

Rutherford, Alexandra. 2006. "The Social Control of Behavior Control: Behavior
Modification, Individual Rights, and Research Ethics in America, 1971–1979."
Journal of the History of the Behavioral Sciences 42 (3): 203–20. https://doi
.org/10.1002/jhbs.20169.

– 2009. *Beyond the Box: B.F. Skinner's Technology of Behavior from Laboratory to
Life, 1950s–1970s*. Toronto: University of Toronto Press.

Rutherford, Alexandra, and Michael Pettit, eds. 2015. *Feminism and/in/as Psychology*.
Special Issue of History of Psychology 18 (3).

Ruud, Arild Engelsen, and Mubashar Hasan, eds. 2022. *Masks of Authoritarianism:
Hegemony, Power and Public Life in Bangladesh*. Singapore: Palgrave Macmillan.

Ryazanova-Clarke, Lara. 2004. "Criminal Rhetoric in Russian Political Discourse."
Language Design 6: 141–60.

– 2016. "Distorted Speech and Aphasia in Satirical Counter-Discourse: Oleg
Kozyrev's 'Rulitiki' Internet Videos." In *Public Debate in Russia: Matters of (Dis)
order,* edited by Nikolai Vakhtin and Boris Firsov, 265–80. Edinburgh: Edinburgh
University Press.

– 2019. "Russian Linguistic Culture in the Age of Globalization: A Turn to Linguistic
Violence." In *Russian Culture in the Age of Globalization*, edited by Vlad Strukov
and Sara Hudspith, 264–90. London: Routledge.

Saber, Dima. 2020. "'Transitional what?': Perspectives from Syrian Videographers
on the YouTube Take-Downs and the 'Video-as-Evidence' Ecology.'" *(W)archives.
Archival Imaginaries and Contemporary Wars*, edited by Daniela Agostinho, Solveig
Gade, Nanna Bonde Thylstrup, and Kirstin Veel, 385–408. London: Sternberg Press.

Saber, Dima, and Paul Long. 2017. "'I will not leave, my freedom is more precious than my blood': From Affect to Precarity: Crowd-Sourced Citizen Archives as Memories of the Syrian War." *Archives and Records* 38 (1): 80–99. https://doi.org /10.1080/23257962.2016.1274256.

Sachedina, Abdulaziz A. (1998) 2011. "What Happened at the Meeting of Ayatollah Sistani and Sachedina." Internet Archive. https://web.archive.org /web/20111011121547/http://www.uga.edu/islam/sachedina_silencing.html.

– 2023. "Open Letter to Respected Community Members. Fairfax, VA, 28 July 2023. https://mcusercontent.com/e0a4b75019d25ad4dca022117/files/8aa46b0b-b933 -5765-2cf7-0f227c3d7f90/Dr_Sachedina_2_Letter.03.pdf.

Sahlins, Marshall. 2017. "The Original Political Society." *HAU: Journal of Ethnographic Theory* 7 (2): 91–128. https://doi.org/10.14318/hau7.2.014.

Said, Edward W. 1978. *Orientalism.* New York: Random House.

Salamandra, Christa. 2019. "Past Continuous: The Chronopolitics of Representation in Syrian Television Drama." *Middle East Critique* 28 (2): 121–41. https://doi.org /10.1080/19436149.2019.1600880.

Samet, Robert. 2019. *Deadline: Populism and the Press in Venezuela.* Chicago: University of Chicago Press.

Sarachild, Kathie. 1970. "A Program for Feminist 'Consciousness Raising.'" In *Notes from the Second Year: Women's Liberation, Major Writings of the Radical Feminists,* edited by Shulamith Firestone and Anne Koedt, 78–80. New York: Radical Feminism.

– (1973) 1978. "Consciousness-Raising: A Radical Weapon." In *Feminist Revolution: An Abridged Edition with Additional Writings, Redstockings of the Women's Liberation Movement,* 144–50. New York: Random House.

Sarahtika, Dhania. 2018. "From 'Drill Dance' to 'the Dribble': Dangdut Twerking through the Ages." *Malay Mail,* 13 March 2018. https://www.malaymail.com /news/life/2018/03/13/from-drill-dance-to-the-dribble-dangdut-twerking -through-the-ages/1596827.

Saria, Vaibhav. 2021. *Hijras, Lovers, Brothers: Surviving Sex and Poverty in Rural India.* New York: Fordham University Press.

Sarkar, Sumit. 1990–1. "Ramakrishna and the Calcutta of His Times." *India International Centre Quarterly* 17 (3–4): 99–121. https://www.jstor.org /stable/23002455.

– 1992. "Kaliyuga, Chakri, and Bhakti: Ramakrishna and His Times." *Economic and Political Weekly* 27 (29): 1543–59, 1551–6.

– 2019. *Essays of a Lifetime: Reformers – Nationalists – Subalterns.* Albany, NY: State University of New York Press.

Saussure, Ferdinand de. 1916. *Cours de linguistique générale.* Complied by Charles Bally and Albert Sechehaye. Paris: Payot.

Saxonhouse, Arlene W. 2006. *Free Speech and Democracy in Ancient Athens.* Cambridge: Cambridge University Press.

Scarborough, Joe. 2020. *Saving Freedom: Truman, the Cold War, and the Fight for Western Civilization*. New York: Harper.

Schauer, Frederick. 1982. *Free Speech: A Philosophical Enquiry*. Cambridge: Cambridge University Press.

Scheppele, Kim Lane. 2018. "Autocratic Legalism." *University of Chicago Law Review* 85 (2): 545–83. https://www.jstor.org/stable/26455917.

Schieffelin, Bambi. 1986. "Language Socialization." *Annual Review of Anthropology* 12: 163–91. https://doi.org/10.1146/annurev.anthro.15.1.163.

– 1990. *The Give and Take of Everyday Life: Language Socialization of Kaluli Children*. Cambridge: Cambridge University Press.

Schielke, Samuli. 2017. "There Will Be Blood: Expectation and Ethics of Violence during Egypt's Stormy Season." *Middle East Critique* 26 (3): 205–20. https://doi.org/10.1080/19436149.2017.1336023.

Schmidt, Peter. 2010. "U.S. State Department Ends Ban on 2 Prominent Muslim Scholars." *The Chronicle of Higher Education*, 20 January 2010. http://www.chronicle.com/article/u-s-state-department-ends-ban-on-2-prominent-muslim-scholars/.

Scott, David. 2014. *Omens of Adversity. Tragedy, Time, Memory, Justice*. Durham, NC: Duke University Press.

Scott, James C. 2009. *The Art of Not Being Governed: An Anarchist History of Upland Southeast Asia*. New Haven, CT: Yale University Press.

Scudder, Mary F. 2020. *Beyond Empathy and Inclusion: The Challenge of Listening in Democratic Deliberation*. New York: Oxford University Press.

Sebald, W.G. (1990) 1999. *Vertigo*. Translated by Michael Hulse. London: Harvills Press.

Sedgwick, Eve Kosofsky. 1990. *Epistemology of the Closet*. Berkeley: University of California Press.

Seikkula, J. 2011. "Becoming Dialogical: Psychotherapy or a Way of Life?" *Australian and New Zealand Journal of Family Therapy* 32 (3): 179–93. https://doi.org/10.1375/anft.32.3.179.

Seikkula, J., and T.E. Arnkil. 2006. *Dialogical Meetings in Social Networks*. London: Karnac.

– 2014. *Open Dialogues and Anticipations*. Helsinki: National Institute for Health and Welfare.

Seizer, Susan. 2011. "On the Uses of Obscenity in Live Stand-Up Comedy." *Anthropological Quarterly* 84 (1): 209–34. https://doi.org/10.1353/anq.2011.0001.

Sells, Michael. 2007. *Approaching the Qur'án: The Early Revelations*. 2nd ed. Ashland, OR: White Cloud Press.

Selva, Meera. 2020. *Fighting Words: Journalism under Assault in Central and Eastern Europe*. Reuters Institute Report. https://reutersinstitute.politics.ox.ac.uk/fighting-words-journalism-under-assault-central-and-eastern-europe.

Semel, Beth M. 2022. "Listening Like a Computer: Attentional Tensions and Mechanized Care in Psychiatric Digital Phenotyping." *Science, Technology, & Human Values* 47 (2): 266–90. https://doi.org/10.1177/01622439211026371.

Sen, Shyamal. 1997. Letter to the Editor. *The Statesman*, 18 February 1997.

Shamas, Diala. 2021. "The Downstream Effects of Israel's 'Terrorist' Designation on Human Rights Defenders in the US." *Just Security*, 4 November 2021. https://www.justsecurity.org/78884/the-downstream-effects-of-israels-terrorist-designation-on-human-rights-defenders-in-the-us/.

Shaw, Rosalind. 2007. "Memory Frictions: Localizing the Truth and Reconciliation Commission in Sierra Leone." *International Journal of Transitional Justice* 1 (2): 183–207. https://doi.org/10.1093/ijtj/ijm008.

Shenhav, Yehouda, and Yael Berda. 2009. "The Colonial Foundations of the State of Exception: Juxtaposing the Israeli Occupation of the Palestinian Territories with Colonial Bureaucratic History." In *The Power of Inclusive Exclusion: Anatomy of Israeli Rule in the Occupied Palestinian Territories*, edited by Adi Ophir, Michal Givoni, and Sari Hanafi, 337–77. New York: Zone Books.

Sherwood, Harriet. 2018. "Indians in the Trenches: Voices of Forgotten Army Are Finally to Be Heard." *The Guardian*, 27 October 2018. https://www.theguardian.com/world/2018/oct/27/armistice-centenary-indian-troops-testimony-sacrifice-british-library.

Shih, Fang-Long. 2014. "Transition to Democracy at the Expense of Justice: The 2-28 Incident and White Terror in Taiwan." Middle East Institute, 4 March. https://www.mei.edu/publications/transition-democracy-expense-justice-2-28-incident-and-white-terror-taiwan.

Shoesmith, Brian, and Jude William Genilo, eds. 2013. *Bangladesh's Changing Mediascape*. Bristol: Intellect.

Shoshan, Nitzan. 2016. *The Management of Hate: Nation, Affect, and the Governance of Right-Wing Extremism in Germany*. Princeton, NJ: Princeton University Press.

Sidnell, Jack. 2014. "Participation." In *The Pragmatics of Interaction*, edited by Jef Verschueren and Sigurd D'hondt, 125–56. Philadelphia: John Benjamins Publishing Company.

– 2023. "The Inconvenience of Tradition: Phan Khôi's Pragmatism and His Proposals for Modernizing Language Reform." *Journal of Vietnamese Studies* 18 (3): 56–97. https://doi.org/10.1525/vs.2023.18.3.56.

Siegel, James T. 1999. "Georg Simmel Reappears: 'The Aesthetic Significance of the Face.'" *Diacritics* 29 (2): 100–13. https://doi.org/10.1353/dia.1999.0013.

Siegel, L. 1978. *Sacred and Profane Dimensions of Love in Indian Traditions, as Exemplified in the Gītagovinda of Jayadeva*. Delhi: Oxford University Press.

Sil, Narasingha. 1991. *Ramakrsna Paramahamsa: A Psychological Profile*. Leiden: E.J. Brill.

– 1997. "The Question of Ramakrishna's Homosexuality." *The Statesman*, 31 January 1997.

Silva, Daniel, ed. 2017. *Language and Violence: Pragmatic Perspectives.*
Philadelphia: John Benjamins Publishing Company.

Silverstein, Michael. 1976. "Shifters, Linguistic Categories, and Cultural Description."
In *Meaning in Anthropology*, edited by Keith H. Basso and Henry A. Selby, 11–55.
Albuquerque: University of New Mexico.

– 2003a. "Indexical Order and the Dialectics of Sociolinguistic Life." *Language
and Communication* 23 (3-4): 193–229. https://doi.org/10.1016/S0271
-5309(03)00013-2.

– 2003b. "Translation, Transduction, Transformation: Skating 'Glossando' on Thin
Semiotic Ice." In *Translating Cultures: Perspectives on Translation and Anthropology*,
edited by Paula G. Rubel and Abraham Rosman, 75–106. London: Berg.

– 2004. "'Cultural' Concepts and the Language-Culture Nexus." *Current
Anthropology* 45 (5): 621–52. https://doi.org/10.1086/423971.

Simpson, Audra. 2014. *Mohawk Interruptus: Political Life across the Borders of
Settler States.* Durham, NC: Duke University Press.

Sinh, Vinh. 2009. "Introduction: Phan Châu Trinh and His Political Writings." In *Phan
Châu Trinh and His Political Writings*, by Phan Châu Trin. Edited and translated by
Vinh Sinh. Ithaca, NY: Cornell Southeast Asia Program.

Sistani, Sayyid Ali Al. 2019a. *The Recommendations of the Supreme Religious Authority
to the Speakers and Orators on the Occasion of the Coming Month of Muharram
1441.* Imam Ali Foundation. 24 August. https://www.najaf.org/english/1164.

– 2019b. *Response Concerning Spreading Issues about the Fundamental Beliefs of
the Faith (Usool-e-Deen) and the Practical Branches of Faith (Furoo'-e-Deen).*
Imam Ali Foundation. 14 February. https://www.najaf.org/english/1120.

Skinner, B.F. 1945. "Baby in a Box: The Mechanical Baby-Tender." *The Ladies Home
Journal* 62 (10): 30–1.

– 1953. *Science and Human Behavior.* New York: MacMillan.

– 1957. *Verbal Behavior.* New York: Appleton-Century-Crofts.

– 1963. "Operant Behavior." *American Psychologist* 18 (8), 503–15. https://doi.org
/10.1037/h0045185.

– 1971. *Beyond Freedom and Dignity.* New York: Knopf.

– 1988. *Philosophy of Behaviorism.* An interview conducted by Eve Segal, February
1988. YouTube. https://www.youtube.com/watch?v=NpDmRc8-pyU.

Skinner, Quentin. 2016. "A Third Concept of Liberty." In *The Liberty Reader*, edited
by David Miller, 243–54. New York: Routledge. https://doi.org/10.4324
/9781315091822-13. Medline: 28683449.

Slater, Rory, and Adrian Coyle. 2014. "The Governing of the Self/the Self-Governing
Self: Multi-Rater/Source Feedback and Practices 1940–2011." *Theory &
Psychology* 24 (2): 233–55. https://doi.org/10.1177/0959354313520087.

Slotta, James. 2014. "Revelations of the World: Transnationalism and the Politics
of Perception in Papua New Guinea." *American Anthropologist* 116 (3): 626–42.
https://doi.org/10.1111/aman.12114.

– 2017. "Can the Subaltern Listen? Self-Determination and the Provisioning of Expertise in Papua New Guinea." *American Ethnologist* 44 (2): 328–40. https://doi.org/10.1111/amet.12482.

– 2023. *Anarchy and the Art of Listening: The Politics and Pragmatics of Reception in Papua New Guinea*. Ithaca, NY: Cornell University Press.

Smith, Allan. 2022. "Rusty Bowers, a Jan. 6 Committee Star Witness, Loses GOP Primary in Arizona." *NBC News*, 3 August 2022. https://www.nbcnews.com/politics/2022-election/rusty-bowers-jan-6-committee-star-witness-loses-gop-primary-arizona-rcna40647.

Smith, Andrea L., and Anna Eisenstein. 2013. "Thoroughly Mixed yet Thoroughly Ethnic: Indexing Class with Ethnonyms." *Journal of Linguistic Anthropology* 23 (2): 1–22. https://doi.org/10.1111/jola.12012.

Smith, Barbara Herrnstein. 1993. "Unloading the Self-Refutation Charge." *Common Knowledge* 2 (2): 81–95. https://doi.org/10.1215/0961754x-7299138.

Smith, Benjamin. 2005. "Ideologies of the Speaking Subject in the Psychotherapeutic Theory and Practice of Carl Rogers." *Journal of Linguistic Anthropology* 15 (20): 258–72. https://doi.org/10.1525/jlin.2005.15.2.258.

Sorabji, Richard. 2021. *Freedom of Speech and Expression: Its History, Its Value, Its Good Use, and Its Misuse*. New York: Oxford University Press. https://doi.org/10.1093/oso/9780197532157.001.0001.

Spitulnik, Debra. 2002. "Mobile Machines and Fluid Audiences: Rethinking Reception through Zambian Radio Culture." In *Media Worlds: Anthropology on New Terrain*, edited by Faye D. Ginsburg, Lila Abu-Lughod, and Brian Larkin, 337–54. Berkeley: University of California Press.

Stampnitzky, Lisa. 2016. "The Lawyers' War: States and Human Rights in a Transnational Field." *The Sociological Review Monographs* 64 (2): 170–93. https://doi.org/10.1111/2059-7932.12007.

Stasch, Rupert. 2003. "Separateness as a Relation: The Iconicity, Univocality, and Creativity of Korowai Mother-in-law Avoidance." *Journal of the Royal Anthropological Institute* 9 (2): 311–29. https://doi.org/10.1111/1467-9655.00152.

– 2008a. "Knowing Minds Is a Matter of Authority: Political Dimensions of Opacity Statements in Korowai Moral Psychology." *Anthropological Quarterly* 81 (2): 443–53. https://doi.org/10.1353/anq.0.0009.

– 2008b. "Referent-Wrecking in Korowai: A New Guinea Abuse Register as Ethnosemiotic Protest." *Language in Society* 37 (1): 1–25. https://doi.org/10.1017/S0047404508080019.

– 2009. *Society of Others: Kinship and Mourning in a West Papuan Place*. Berkeley: University of California Press.

– 2011a. "Ritual and Oratory Revisited: The Semiotics of Effective Action." *Annual Review of Anthropology* 40: 159–74. https://doi.org/10.1146/annurev-anthro-081309-145623.

– 2011b. "Word Avoidance as a Relation-Making Act: A Paradigm for Analysis of Name Utterance Taboos." *Anthropological Quarterly* 84 (1): 101–20. https://doi.org/10.1353/anq.2011.0005.

– 2015. "From Primitive Other to Papuan Self: Korowai Engagement with Ideologies of Unequal Human Worth in Encounters with Tourists, State Officials, and Education." In *From "Stone-Age" to "Real-Time": Exploring Papuan Mobilities, Temporalities, and Religiosities*, edited by Martin Slama and Jenny Munro, 59–94. Canberra: Australian National University Press.

– 2016. "Dramas of Otherness: 'First Contact' Tourism in New Guinea." *HAU: Journal of Ethnographic Theory* 6 (3): 7–27. https://doi.org/10.14318/hau6.3.003.

– 2021 "Self-Lowering as Power and Trap: Wawa, 'White,' and Peripheral Embrace of State Formation in Indonesian Papua." *Oceania* 91 (2): 257–79. https://doi.org/10.1002/ocea.5310.

– 2023. "Anarchists for the State: From Egalitarian Opacity to Anticipating Thoughts of the Powerful." *Ethnos* 88 (4): 724–48. https://doi.org/10.1080/00141844.2021.2007155.

Stauffer, Jill. 2015. *Ethical Loneliness: The Injustice of Not Being Heard.* New York: Columbia University Press.

Steele, Janet. 2005. *Wars Within: The Story of "Tempo," an Independent Magazine in Soeharto's Indonesia.* Jakarta: Equinox.

Stein, Rebecca L. 2021. *Screen Shots: State Violence on Camera in Israel and Palestine.* Stanford: Stanford University Press.

Sterne, Jonathan. 2005. *The Audible Past: Cultural Origins of Sound Reproduction.* Durham, NC: Duke University Press.

Stewart, Charles. 2016. "Anthropology and Historicity." *Annual Review of Anthropology* 45: 79–94. https://doi.org/10.1146/annurev-anthro-102215-100249.

Stewart, Katherine. 2021. "The Roots of Josh Hawley's Rage." *New York Times,* 11 January 2021. https://www.nytimes.com/2021/01/11/opinion/josh-hawley-religion-democracy.html.

– 2022. *The Power Worshippers: Inside the Dangerous Rise of Religious Nationalism.* London: Bloomsbury.

Stewart, Michael. 1997. *The Time of the Gypsies.* Boulder, CO: Westview Press.

Stone, Adrienne, and Frederick Schauer. 2021a. Introduction to *The Oxford Handbook of Freedom of Speech*, edited by Adrienne Stone and Frederick Schauer, 60–81. Oxford: Oxford University Press. https://doi.org/10.1093/oxfordhb/9780198827580.013.33.

–, eds. 2021b. *The Oxford Handbook of Freedom of Speech.* Oxford: Oxford University Press. https://doi.org/10.1093/oxfordhb/9780198827580.001.0001.

Stone, Geoffrey R. 2004. *Perilous Times: Free Speech in Wartime from the Sedition Act of 1798 to the War on Terrorism.* New York: W.W Norton.

Strathern, Marilyn. 1988. *The Gender of the Gift: Problems with Women and Problems with Society in Melanesia.* Berkeley: University of California Press.

Strodtbeck, Fred L. 1954. "The Case for the Study of Small Groups." *American Sociological Review* 19 (6): 651–7. https://doi.org/10.2307/2087911.

Sundaram, Ravi. 2020. "Publics or Post-Publics? Contemporary Expression after the Mobile Phone." In *Data Publics Public Plurality in an Era of Data Determinacy*, edited by Peter Mörtenböck and Helge Mooshammer, 213–27. London: Routledge.

Suryawan, I. Ngurah. 2020. *Siasat Elite Mencuri Kuasa: Dinamika Pemekaran Daerah di Papua Barat*. Yogyakarta: Basabasi.

Tagore, Rabindranath. 1914. *Chitra: A Play in One Act*. New York: The Macmillan Company.

Takriti, Abdel Razzaq. 2019. "Before BDS: Lineages of Boycott in Palestine." *Radical History Review* 2019 (134): 58–95. https://doi.org/10.1215/01636545-7323408.

Talukdar, Geeta. 1997. Letter to the Editor. *The Statesman*, 18 February 1997.

Tarnowski, Stefan. 2021. "Both Authors and Authored." *Film Quarterly* 75 (2): 59–67. https://doi.org/10.1525/fq.2021.75.2.59.

Tate, Winifred. 2007. *Counting the Dead: The Culture and Politics of Human Rights Activism in Colombia*. Berkeley: University of California Press.

Taussig, Michael. 1999. *Defacement: Public Secrecy and the Labor of the Negative*. Stanford: Stanford University Press.

Thomlinson, Natalie. 2012. "The Colour of Feminism: White Feminists and Race in the Women's Liberation Movement." *History: The Journal of the Historical Association* 97 (327): 453–75. https://doi.org/10.1111/j.1468-229X.2012.00559.x.

Thompson, Laurence C. 1987. *A Vietnamese Reference Grammar*. Honolulu: University of Hawai'i Press.

Tilly, Charles. 2004. "Terror, Terrorism, Terrorists." *Sociological Theory* 22 (1): 5–13. https://doi.org/10.1111/j.1467-9558.2004.00200.x.

Times of India. 2014. "Aparna Sen slams Rituparno Ghosh's Caricature in Obhishopto Nighty." *Times of India*, 21 February 2014.

Tomlinson, Matt, and Julian Millie, eds. 2017. *The Monologic Imagination*. Oxford: Oxford University Press.

Toor, Saadia. 2011. *The State of Islam: Culture and Cold War Politics in Pakistan*. London: Pluto Press.

Torpey, John. 2001. "'Making Whole What Has Been Smashed': Reflections on Reparations." *The Journal of Modern History* 73 (2): 333–58. https://doi.org/10.1086/321028.

Tran, Ben. 2017. *Post-Mandarin: Masculinity and Aesthetic Modernity in Colonial Vietnam*. New York: Fordham University Press.

Trần Trọng Kim. (1930–2) 2012. *Confucianism*. In *Sources of Vietnamese Tradition*, edited by George Dutton, Jayne S. Werner, and John K. Whitmore, 414–23. New York: Columbia University Press.

Traux, Charles B. 1966. "Reinforcement and Non-Reinforcement in Rogerian Psychotherapy." *Journal of Abnormal Psychology* 71: 1–9. https://doi.org/10.1037/h0022912. Medline: 5902551.

Traux, Charles B., and R.R. Carkhuff. 1967. *Toward Effective Counseling and Psychotherapy.* Chicago: Aldine.

Trotsky, Leon. 1944. "Fascism: What It Is and How to Fight It." Marx-Engels Internet Archive. https://www.marxists.org/archive/trotsky/works/1944/1944-fas.htm.

Trouillot, Michel-Rolph. 1995. *Silencing the Past: Power and the Production of History.* Boston: Beacon Press.

– 2001. "The Anthropology of the State in the Age of Globalization: Close Encounters of the Deceptive Kind." *Current Anthropology* 42 (1): 125–38. https://doi.org/10.1086/318437.

Trudeau, Garry. 2015. "The Abuse of Satire." *The Atlantic*, 11 April 2015. https://www.theatlantic.com/international/archive/2015/04/the-abuse-of-satire/390312.

Turner, Fred. 2013. *The Democratic Surround: Multimedia & American Liberalism from World War II to the Psychedelic Sixties.* Chicago: University of Chicago Press.

Turner, Terence. 2009. "The Crisis of Late Structuralism. Perspectivism and Animism: Rethinking Culture, Nature, Spirit, and Bodiliness." *Tipití: Journal of the Society for the Anthropology of Lowland South America* 7 (1): Article 1.

Tyagananda, Swami. 2000. *Kali's Child Revisited or, Didn't Anyone Check the Documentation?* Boston: Ramakrishna Vedanta Society.

Tyagananda, Swami, and Pravajika Vrajaprana. 2010. *Interpreting Ramakrishna: Kali's Child Revisited.* Delhi: Motilal Banarsidass.

Urban, Hugh Bayard. 1998. "Review: Kali's Child: The Mystical and the Erotic in the Life and Teachings of Ramakrishna." *The Journal of Religion* 78 (2): 318. https://doi.org/10.1086/490220.

Ushakin, Sergei. 2009. "Byvshee v upotreblenii: Postsovetskoe sostoyanie kak forma afazii." *Novoe Literaturnoe Obozrenie* 100: 760–92.

Vakhtin, Nikolai, and Firsov, Boris, eds. 2016. *Public Debate in Russia: Matters of (Dis)order.* Edinburgh: Edinburgh University Press.

Vásárhelyi, Mária. 2017. "The Workings of the Media: A Brainwashing and Money-Laundering Mechanism." In *Twenty-Five Sides of a Post Communist Mafia State*, edited by Bálint Magyar and Júlia Vásárhelyi, 491–526. Budapest: Central European University Press. https://www.jstor.org/stable/10.7829/j.ctt1mtz64j.24.

Vasilievich, Alexey. 2020. "Who's the Boor Here? Seven Signs of Rudeness" [in Russian]. *Legal Social Network*, 20 October 2020. https://www.9111.ru/questions/7777777771038479.

Vel, Jacqueline. 2007. "Campaigning for a New District in West Sumba." In *Renegotiating Boundaries: Local Politics in Post-Soeharto Indonesia*, edited by Henk Schulte Nordholt and Gerry van Klinken, 91–119. Leiden: KITLV Press.

– 2008. *Uma Politics: An Ethnography of Democratization in West Sumba, Indonesia, 1986–2006.* Leiden: KITLV Press.

Venkatesan, Soumhya. 2023. "Freedom." In *The Cambridge Handbook for the Anthropology of Ethics*, edited by James Laidlaw, 251–80. Cambridge: Cambridge University Press.

Vereshchagin, E.M., and V.G. Kostomarov, eds. 1979. *Russkie poslovitsy, pogovorki I krylatye vyrazheniya.* Moscow: Russkii Yazyk.

Virilio, Paul. 2006. *Speed and Politics. An Essay on Dromology.* Translated by Marc Polizzotti. New York: Semiotext(e).

Viveiros de Castro, Eduardo. 2011. "Zeno and the Art of Anthropology: Of Lies, Beliefs, Paradoxes, and Other Truths." *Common Knowledge* 17 (1): 128–45. https://doi.org/10.1215/0961754X-2010-045.

Vojvodina, A.A. 2010. "Sotsial'naya doctrina Z. N. Gippius i D. S. Merezhkovskogo v kontekste razvitiya russkogo khristianskogo liberalizme." PhD diss., Kazan State University.

Wagner, Roy. 1974. "Are There Social Groups in the New Guinea Highlands?" In *Frontiers of Anthropology: An Introduction to Anthropological Thinking,* edited by Murray J. Leaf, 95–122. New York: Van Nostrand Reinhold.

Wahlbeck, Östen. 2016. "True Finns and Non-True Finns: The Minority Rights Discourse of Populist Politics in Finland." *Journal of Intercultural Studies* 37 (6): 574–88. https://doi.org/10.1080/07256868.2016.1235020.

Waldron, Jeremy. 2014. *The Harm in Hate Speech.* Reprint ed. Cambridge, MA: Harvard University Press.

Walton, G. Charles. 2011. *Policing Public Opinion in the French Revolution: The Culture of Calumny and the Problem of Free Speech.* Oxford: Oxford University Press.

Wardlow, Holly. 2006. *Wayward Women: Sexuality and Agency in a New Guinea Society.* Berkeley: University of California Press.

Ware, Cellestine. 1970. *Woman Power: The Movement for Women's Liberation, a Tower Public Affairs Book.* New York: Tower Publications.

Warner, Michael. 2004. "Uncritical Reading." In *Polemic: Critical or Uncritical,* edited by Jane Gallop, 13–38. London: Routledge.

– 2005. *Publics and Counterpublics.* Brooklyn, NY: Zone Books.

Warren, Martin L. 2009. "The Quakers as Parrhesiasts: Frank speech and plain speaking in the Fruits of Silence." *Quaker History* 98 (2): 1–25. https://www.jstor.org/stable/41947674.

Wedeen, Lisa. 1999. *Ambiguities of Domination. Politcs, Rhetoric and Symbols in Contemporary Syria.* Chicago: University of Chicago Press.

– 2019. *Authoritarian Apprehensions. Ideology, Judgment, and Mourning in Syria.* Chicago: University of Chicago Press.

Weidman, Amanda J. 2006. *Singing the Classical, Voicing the Modern: The Postcolonial Politics of Music in South India.* Durham, NC: Duke University Press.

Weiss, Max. 2022. *Revolutions Aesthetic: A Cultural History of Ba'thist Syria.* Stanford: Stanford University Press.

Welch, John, W. 1985. "Hugh Nibley and the Book of Mormon." The Church of Jesus Christ of Later-day Saints. https://www.churchofjesuschrist.org/study/ensign/1985/04/hugh-nibley-and-the-book-of-mormon.

Wessels, Joshka. 2018. *Documenting Syria. Filmmaking, Video Activism and Revolution*. London: I.B. Tauris.

Westad, Odd Arne. 2005. *The Global Cold War: Third World Interventions and the Making of Our Times*. Cambridge: Cambridge University Press.

White, Hayden. 1980. "The Value of Narrativity in the Representation of Reality." *Critical Inquiry* 7 (1): 5–27. https://doi.org/10.1086/448086.

White, Ralph K., and Ronald Lippitt. 1960. *Autocracy and Democracy: An Experimental Inquiry*. New York: Harper.

Whitman, James Q. 2000. "Enforcing Civility and Respect: Three Societies." *Yale Law Journal* 109 (6): 1279–393. https://doi.org/10.2307/797466.

"Why Did Mormon See Captain Moroni as a Hero?" 2016. Book of Mormon Central. 1 August 2016. https://knowhy.bookofmormoncentral.org/content/why-did-mormon-see-captain-moroni-as-a-hero.

Williams, Bernard. 2014. *Essays and Reviews: 1959–2002*. Princeton, NJ: Princeton University Press.

Williamson, Henry. (1954) 2010. *How Dear Is Life*. London: Faber and Faber.

Wilson, Frances. 1999. *Literary Seduction: Compulsive Writers and Diverted Readers*. London: Faber and Faber.

Wilson, Richard. 2001. *The Politics of Truth and Reconciliation in South Africa: Legitimizing the Post-Apartheid State*. Cambridge: Cambridge University Press.

Wind, Maya. 2024. *Towers of Ivory and Steel: How Israeli Universities Deny Palestinian Freedom*. New York: Verso Books.

Wittgenstein, Ludwig. (1953) 2009. *Philosophical Investigations*. Edited by Joachim Schulte and P.M.S. Hacker. 4th ed. Oxford: Wiley-Blackwell.

Woolard, K.A., and B.B. Schieffelin. 1994. "Language Ideology." *Annual Review of Anthropology* 23 (1): 55–82. https://doi.org/10.1146/annurev.an.23.100194.000415.

World Atlas. 2019. "List of Red States (Republican States)." 25 March. https://www.worldatlas.com/articles/states-that-have-voted-republican-in-the-most-consecutive-u-s-presidential-elections.html.

World Federation of KSIMC. 2019. Question to the Office of His Eminence Sayyid Ali Husayni Sistani. London, 12 February 2019. https://www.najaf.org/english/1120.

Wright, Fiona. 2022. "Making Good of Crisis: Temporalities of Care in UK Mental Health Services." *Medical Anthropology* 41 (3): 315–28. https://doi.org/10.1080/01459740.2021.2018586. Medline: 35060803.

– Forthcoming. "The Pedagogy of (Un)Safe Spaces and Therapeutic Speech: Containing the Permeable Subject In Contemporary Britain." *Current Anthropology*.

Wright, Patrick. (1985) 2009. *On Living in an Old Country*. Oxford: Oxford University Press.

Wu Ming. 2017. "Predappio Toxic Waste Blues." Wu Ming Foundation. 27 October 2017. https://www.wumingfoundation.com/giap/2017/10/predappio-toxic-waste-blues-1-di-3.

Wyatt, W. Joseph. 2000. "Behavioral Science in the Crosshairs: The FBI File on B.F. Skinner." *Social and Behavioral Issues* 10 (1): 101–9. https://doi.org/10.5210/bsi .v10i0.128.

Yemel'yanko, Vladimir. 2021. "Yazyk khamstva. Kak ostanovit' 'kholivar'?" *Russkii Mir*, January 2021, 18–20.

Yermakov, S.V., Kim, I.E., Mikhailoga, T.V., Osetrova, E.V., Sukhovol'skii, and S.B. 2004. *Vlast' v russkoi yazykovoi i ethnicheskoi kartine mira*. Moscow: Yazyki Slavyanskoi Kul'tury.

Yurchak, Alexi. 2003. "Soviet Hegemony of Form: Everything Was Forever, until It Was No More." *Comparative Studies in Society and History* 45 (3): 480–510. https://doi.org/10.1017/S0010417503000239.

– 2008a. "Necro-Utopia: The Politics of Indistinction and the Aesthetics of the Non-Soviet." *Current Anthropology* 49 (2): 199–224. https://doi.org/10.1086/526098.

– 2008b. "Suspending the Political: Late Soviet Artistic Experiments on the Margins of the State." *Poetics Today* 29 (4): 713–33. https://doi.org/10.1215/03335372-082.

– 2013. *Everything Was Forever, until It Was No More: The Last Soviet Generation*. Princeton, NJ: Princeton University Press.

Zaher, Sawsan. 2021. "Israel Has Outlawed Six Palestinian Human Rights Organizations. Why?" *OpenDemocracy*, 4 November 2021. https://www.opendemocracy.net /en/north-africa-west-asia/israel-has-outlawed-six-palestinian-human-rights -organizations-why/.

Zemskaya, E.A. 2004. *Yazyk kak deyatel'nost': morfema, slovo, rech'*. Moscow: Yazyki Slavyanskoi Kul'tury.

Zigon, Jarrett. 2007. "Moral Breakdown and the Ethical Demand: A Theoretical Framework for an Anthropology of Moralities." *Anthropological Theory* 7 (2): 131–50. https://doi.org/10.1177/1463499607077295.

Zinoman, Peter. 2002. "Introduction: Vũ Trọng Phụng's Dumb Luck and the Nature of Vietnamese Modernism." In *Dumb Luck: A Novel*, translated by Nguyễn Nguyệt Cầm and Peter Zinoman, 1–48. Ann Arbor: University of Michigan Press.

– 2011. "Nhân Văn–Giai Phẩm and Vietnamese 'Reform Communism' in the 1950s." *Journal of Cold War Studies* 13 (1): 60–100. https://doi.org/10.1162 /JCWS_a_00071.

Contributors

Andreas Bandak is Associate Professor and Director of the Center for Comparative Culture Studies in the Department for Cross-Cultural and Regional Studies at the University of Copenhagen. He specializes in the themes of temporality and exemplarity and in anthropological studies of Syrian pasts and futures. He is the author of *Exemplary Life: Modelling Sainthood in Christian Syria* (University of Toronto Press, 2022) and has edited several volumes, including *Ethnographies of Waiting: Doubt, Hope and Uncertainty* (Bloomsbury, 2018), *Different Repetitions: Anthropological Engagements with Figures of Return, Recurrence and Redundancy* (Routledge, 2021), and most recently *Porous Becomings: Anthropological Engagements with Michel Serres* (Duke University Press, 2024).

Ali-Reza Bhojani is Teaching Fellow in Islamic Ethics and Theology at the University of Birmingham and Honorary Research Fellow at the Al-Mahdi Institute. His research, teaching, and writing focuses on intersections between Islamic legal theory, theology, and ethics. His doctoral study, conducted at Durham University, was published as *Moral Rationalism and Shari'a* (Routledge, 2015). More recent publications include the co-edited volume *Visions of Sharī'a* (Brill, 2020).

Amahl Bishara is Professor of Anthropology at Tufts University and is affiliated with the Department of Studies of Race, Colonialism and Diaspora. She is the author of *Crossing a Line: Laws, Violence, and Roadblocks to Palestinian Political Expression* (Stanford University Press, 2022), concerning the different conditions of expression for and exchange between Palestinian citizens of Israel and Palestinians in the West Bank, and *Back Stories: US News Production and Palestinian Politics* (Stanford University Press, 2013), an ethnography of the production of US news during the second Palestinian intifada. She also writes about popular refugee politics in the West Bank, attending to struggles over and through media, water, space, and protest.

Matei Candea is Professor of Social Anthropology at the University of Cambridge. He is the author of *Corsican Fragments* (Indiana University Press, 2010) and *Comparison in Anthropology: The Impossible Method* (Cambridge University Press, 2019), and the editor of a number of volumes, including *The Social after Gabriel Tarde* (Routledge, 2010), *Detachment: Essays on the Limits of Relational Thinking* (Manchester University Press, 2015) with Jo Cook, Catherine Trundle, and Tom Yarrow, and *Beyond Description: Anthropologies of Explanation* (Cornell University Press, 2024) with Paolo Heywood.

Fenella Cannell is Associate Professor/Reader in Social Anthropology at the London School of Economics. She works particularly on social practices at the intersection between religion, kinship, and politics, and on unexpected aspects of lived Christianities. Her first book was *Power and Intimacy in the Christian Philippines* (Cambridge University Press, 1999). She has also published two edited collections: *The Anthropology of Christianity* (Duke University Press, 2006), and *Vital Relations* (University of New Mexico Press, 2013) with Susan McKinnon. She is currently writing and publishing on both American members of the Church of Jesus Christ of Latter-day Saints and Anglican cathedral spaces in the United Kingdom.

E. Summerson Carr is Professor at the University of Chicago, jointly appointed in the Department of Anthropology and the Crown Family School of Social Work, Policy, and Practice. She works between linguistic, medical, and sociocultural anthropology to illuminate the production and performance of expertise. Carr is author of *Scripting Addiction: The Politics of Therapeutic Talk and American Sobriety* (Princeton University Press, 2011) and *Working the Difference: Science, Spirit and the Spread of Motivational Interviewing* (University of Chicago Press, 2023), and co-editor of the volume *Scale: Discourse and Dimensions of Social Life* (University of California Press, 2016) with Michael Lempert. Her latest project examines canine labour in the US health and human services.

Morgan Clarke is Professor of Social Anthropology at the University of Oxford. He is the author of *Islam and New Kinship: Reproductive Technology and the Shariah in Lebanon* (Berghahn Books, 2009) and *Islam and Law in Lebanon: Sharia Within and Without the State* (Cambridge University Press, 2018), and co-editor of *Rules and Ethics: Perspectives from Anthropology and History* (Manchester University Press, 2021) with Emily Corran.

Harri Englund is Professor of Social Anthropology at the University of Cambridge and Fellow of the British Academy. He is the author of five monographs and several articles on vernacular confrontations with liberal democracy, human rights, freedom, and equality, including *Gogo Breeze: Zambia's Radio Elder and the Voices of Free Speech* (University of Chicago Press, 2018) and *Visions for Racial Equality: David Clement Scott and the Struggle for Justice in Nineteenth-Century Malawi* (Cambridge University Press, 2022).

Taras Fedirko is a political and economic anthropologist studying media, war, and oligarchy in Ukraine. He is Lecturer (Assistant Professor) at the School of Social and Political Sciences at the University of Glasgow and Associate Researcher with the Conflict and Civicness Research Group at LSE Ideas. He studied social anthropology at Durham University and held postdoctoral positions at Cambridge University and the University of St. Andrews. He currently leads the Monitoring Actors and Networks in Ukraine project, a research group studying the informal economy of the Russo-Ukrainian War.

Susan Gal is Mae and Sidney G. Metzl Distinguished Service Professor at the University of Chicago in the Departments of Anthropology and Linguistics. She writes about the semiotic power of political talk, and about linguistic variation and valuation in controversies of gender, ethnicity, and regionalism in Europe. She has written several books, most recently *Signs of Difference: Language and Ideology in Social Life* (Cambridge University Press, 2019), co-authored with Judith T. Irvine, which sets out an approach to perspective and social action in the language and ideology of social life. Her current work focuses on authoritarian discourse.

Paolo Heywood is Associate Professor of Social Anthropology at Durham University. He took his undergraduate and postgraduate degrees at Cambridge University, where he was Junior Research Fellow. He is the author of *After Difference: Queer Activism in Italy and Anthropological Theory* (Berghahn Books, 2018) and *Burying Mussolini: Ordinary Life in the Shadows of Fascism* (Cornell University Press, 2024). He is also editor of *New Anthropologies of Italy: Politics, History, and Culture* (Berghahn Books, 2024) and co-editor of *Beyond Description: Anthropologies of Explanation* (Cornell University Press, 2023) with Matei Candea.

Lotte Hoek is Professor of Cultural Anthropology at the University of Edinburgh. Her ethnographic explorations of the moving image are situated at the intersection of anthropology and film studies. She is the author of *Cut-Pieces: Celluloid Obscenity and Popular Cinema in Bangladesh* (Columbia University Press, 2014) and co-editor of *Forms of the Left in Postcolonial South*

Asia: Aesthetics, Networks and Connected Histories (Bloomsbury, 2021) with Sanjukta Sunderason. She is one of the editors of the journal *BioScope: South Asian Screen Studies.*

Caroline Humphrey is an anthropologist who has worked in Russia, Mongolia, China (Inner Mongolia), India, Nepal, and Ukraine. She has researched a wide range of themes, including the Soviet and post-Soviet economy and society; Buryat and Daur shamanism; trade and barter in Nepal; environment and the pastoral economy in Mongolia; the social life of Buddhism in Inner Mongolia; and urban transformations in post-Socialist cities (Buryatia, Uzbekistan, Ukraine). She has written on inequality and exclusion; theories of ritualization; the politics of memory; naming practices; ethics; and conceptions of freedom. Her recent publications include *A Monastery in Time: The Making of Mongolian Buddhism* (University of Chicago Press, 2013), *Trust and Mistrust in the Economies of the China–Russia Borderlands* (Amsterdam University Press, 2018), and *On the Edge: Life along the Russia-China Border* (Harvard University Press, 2021) with Franck Billé.

Webb Keane is George Herbert Mead Distinguished University Professor at the University of Michigan. His books include *Animals, Robots, Gods: Adventures in the Moral Imagination* (Penguin/Allen Lane, 2024), *Ethical Life: Its Natural and Social Histories* (Princeton University Press, 2016), *Christian Moderns: Freedom and Fetish in the Mission Encounter* (University of California Press, 2007), and *Signs of Recognition: Powers and Hazards of Representation in an Indonesian Society* (University of California Press, 1997).

Heonik Kwon is Senior Research Fellow of Social Anthropology at Trinity College, University of Cambridge, and a member of the Mega-Asia research group in the Seoul National University Asia Center. Author of prize-winning books on the intimate history of the Vietnam War, Asia's postcolonial Cold War, and the Korean War, his most recent book, *Spirit Power: Politics and Religion in Korea's American Century* (Fordham University Press, 2022), co-authored with Jun Hwan Park, deals with the place of religion and religious freedom in Cold War international politics.

Michael Lempert is Professor of Anthropology at the University of Michigan. He is author of *Discipline and Debate: The Language of Violence in a Tibetan Buddhist Monastery* (University of California Press, 2012; recipient of the 2013 Clifford Geertz Prize), co-author with Michael Silverstein of *Creatures of Politics: Media, Message, and the American Presidency* (Indiana University Press, 2012), and co-editor with E. Summerson Carr of *Scale: Discourse and Dimensions of Social Life* (University of California Press, 2016). His latest book, *From Small Talk to Microaggression: A History of Scale* (University of Chicago Press, 2024), traces how face-to-face interaction became a scaled object of knowledge in mid-twentieth-century America.

Natalie Morningstar is Lecturer in Social Anthropology at the University of Kent and Chandaria Teaching Associate in Human, Social and Political Sciences at Fitzwilliam College, Cambridge. Her work concerns the relationship between inequality, subjectivity, and political economy in the Republic of Ireland and Euro-America more broadly. She has published in the *Journal of the Royal Anthropological Institute*, *Focaal*, and *Social Anthropology*, among others, on topics such as critique, neo-liberalism, abortion, housing, and creative labour.

Sarah Pinto is Professor of Anthropology at Tufts University. Her work addresses cultures and histories of biomedicine in South Asia, and global transits of medical ideas with South Asia as hub. She is author of *Where There Is No Midwife: Birth and Loss in Rural India* (Berghahn Books, 2008), *Daughters of Parvati: Women and Madness in Contemporary India* (University of Pennsylvania Press, 2014), and *The Doctor and Mrs. A: Ethics and Counter-Ethics in an Indian Dream Analysis* (Women Unlimited, 2019/Fordham University Press, 2020).

Adam Reed is Reader in the Department of Social Anthropology at the University of St. Andrews. He has conducted research in Papua New Guinea and the United Kingdom and is the author of *Papua New Guinea's Last Place: Experiences of Constraint in a Postcolonial Prison* (Berghahn Books, 2003) and *Literature and Agency in English Fiction Reading: A Study of the Henry Williamson Society* (Berghahn Books, 2011). As well as continuing to do work with an English literary society, his most recent project centres on animal activism in Scotland.

Jack Sidnell is Professor in the Department of Anthropology at the University of Toronto. His research focuses on the intersection of language structure, social interaction, and reflexive reanalysis, especially in Vietnamese. He is the co-author of *The Concept of Action* (Cambridge University Press, 2017) and *Consequences of Language* (MIT Press, 2022), both with N.J. Enfield; the editor of *Conversation Analysis: Comparative Perspectives* (Cambridge University Press, 2009); and co-editor of *Conversational Repair and Human Understanding* (Cambridge University Press, 2013), *The Handbook of Conversation Analysis* (Blackwell, 2012), and *The Cambridge Handbook of Linguistic Anthropology* (Cambridge University Press, 2014).

Rupert Stasch is Professor of Social Anthropology at the University of Cambridge and previously taught at Reed College and University of California

San Diego. His book *Society of Others: Kinship and Mourning in a West Papuan Place* (University of California Press, 2009) and other publications draw on fieldwork conducted since 1995 with the Korowai people and extend the ideas of linguistic, semiotic, and symbolic anthropology to analysis of kinship, space, political transformation, and primitivist stereotypy. He is currently completing a book on interactions between Korowai and international tourists.

Fiona Wright is a social anthropologist and user-centred design researcher studying health and social care services in Scotland. She has worked as a Research Associate at the University of Cambridge and Research Fellow at the University of Edinburgh, and she is the author of the *The Israeli Radical Left* (University of Pennsylvania Press, 2018).

Index

Page numbers in italics denote figures. Footnotes are indicated by "n" followed by the note number.